W9-BCD-069

THE CENTURY PSYCHOLOGY SERIES

Richard M. Elliott, *Editor*

A HISTORY OF

EXPERIMENTAL PSYCHOLOGY

A HISTORY OF
EXPERIMENTAL
PSYCHOLOGY

EDWIN G. BORING

SECOND EDITION

PRENTICE-HALL, INC., Englewood Cliffs, New Jersey

PRENTICE-HALL INTERNATIONAL, INC., *London*
PRENTICE-HALL OF AUSTRALIA, PTY. LTD., *Sydney*
PRENTICE-HALL OF CANADA, LTD., *Toronto*
PRENTICE-HALL OF INDIA PRIVATE LIMITED, *New Delhi*
PRENTICE-HALL OF JAPAN, INC., *Tokyo*

TO

EDWARD BRADFORD TITCHENER

Editor's Introduction

The editor of this Series remarked in an introduction to the first edition of this book that Professor Boring would wish the merits of his work to be their own spokesmen. It is more difficult for him to be silent now. Even if psychologists are a crotchety lot, no audacious critic among them is going to rise and deny that Boring's history is a classic. And here it is again, in age having exactly achieved its majority, with even its early chapters largely rewritten and with treatment of the later period greatly expanded. It seems difficult to believe that anyone will again deem it necessary to undertake as meticulous and definitive a history of experimental psychology's early period as Boring here gives us. He has steeped himself in his subject as no one else ever will. The story is made One with great skill. Here are the men, their perspectives, their struggles to experiment in a sometimes refractory field, their triumphs, their littlenesses, and their legacies. Scientific psychology will advance, we know, and accept the ever widening challenge of the future. As its beginnings fade from memory, this book, and its notes, will be the one great quarry for reference on the early periods of our science.

The editor also recorded in an introduction to the first edition the gratification which he and the publishers felt that Professor Boring was permitting his history to become the initial volume of the Century Psychology Series. A bit of history may now be added: it was Boring who proposed to the publishers that the present editor work with them in launching the Series. Now, as this book becomes the fortieth volume of the Series, our thanks are due him three times over.

R. M. E.

Preface to the First Edition

That "psychology has a long past, but only a short history" was remarked by Ebbinghaus many years ago, but in general the histories of psychology have emphasized its long past at the expense of its short scientific history. It is now more than five years since I began to write this book, and there was at that time no historian who had written a book on the history of what was called in the '90's the 'new' psychology, or who had presented the experimental movement as anything other than the termination of the long development of philosophical thought about mind. The modern history of psychology cannot, however, be written merely by adding chapters to the older history. Strange as it may seem, the present changes the past; and, as the focus and range of psychology shift in the present, new parts of the past enter into its history and other parts drop out. Experimental psychology of to-day has its own history, even though that history is not all an account of experimentation. The systematic problems persistently enter into it, but they appear in a different way. Moreover, the degree to which they enter is itself a matter of history, which is independent of the will of the historian.

Of the purpose that has held me to this undertaking in the face of endless academic distractions, I need say only a word. The experimental psychologist, so it has always seemed to me, needs historical sophistication within his own sphere of expertness. Without such knowledge he sees the present in distorted perspective, he mistakes old facts and old views for new, and he remains unable to evaluate the significance of new movements and methods. In this matter I can hardly state my faith too strongly. A psychological sophistication that contains no component of historical orientation seems to me to be no sophistication at all.

When I began writing, I supposed that the history of experimental psychology could very well begin with Fechner's *Elemente* of 1860 and Wundt's *Beiträge* of 1862. In this sense experimental psychology is only seventy years old. However, the genetic account requires the explanation of the new movement in terms of its ancestry. Hence my picture shows the lines of descent debouching from Descartes, Leibnitz, and Locke on the philosophical side, and developing within

ix

the new experimental physiology of the early nineteenth century on the physiological side. It was of the union of these two movements that experimental psychology was born.

At the other temporal extreme, it is plain that there is as yet no sound historical perspective. I have thought it unsafe to say very much about psychology since 1910. Nevertheless, I have made exceptions in the case of *Gestalt* psychology and of behaviorism, both as yet undignified by the least trace of antiquity, because of the light that each casts backward upon the past. The genetic account is reversible, and history can be understood by its effects as well as by its causes.

In a word, then, my book deals with the psychology of a half-century from 1860 to 1910, with its preceding development and its consequences—a spindle-shaped history, as it were. Naturally the words "experimental psychology" must mean, in my title, what they meant to Wundt and what they meant to nearly all psychologists for fifty or sixty years—that is to say, the psychology of the generalized, human, normal, adult mind as revealed in the psychological laboratory. In making this choice I have had no doctrinaire's thesis to defend. Animal psychology is of the laboratory; the mental tests are in a way experimental; abnormal psychology may be experimental. The first two of these subjects I have brought into my exposition in so far as their development was interpenetrated with the growth of 'experimental psychology'; but I do not, of course, pretend to have written an adequate history of either movement.

Perhaps I should say also why there is so much biographical material in this book, why I have centered the exposition more upon the personalities of men than upon the genesis of the traditional chapters of psychology. My reason is that the history of experimental psychology seems to me to have been so intensely personal. Men have mattered much. Authority has again and again carried the day. What Johannes Müller or Wundt said was nearly always important, quite independently of the weight of experimental evidence for the view of either. Moreover, personalities have been reflected in schools, and the systematic traditions of the schools have colored the research. Then, too, with personalities playing such important rôles, it is inevitable that the psychologist should become interested in the psychology of history. Thus there is always the further question: if personalities lie, in part, back of psychology, what lies back of the personalities? I trust that I have been cautious in drawing such inferences; however, I have never been able to get this question out of my mind. . . .

It has been my good fortune to discover how very many persons were ready to give generously of their time and counsel when I sought aid concerning portions of the text. My gratitude to them all is much greater than these formal acknowledgments can express. It need scarcely be said, however, that the reader must not hold my friendly critics responsible for any portions of this book, for I have more than once insisted on having my own say in spite of advice. Professor H. S. Langfeld read the section on Stumpf and helped me greatly with it. Professor Kurt Koffka supplied some of the information about Stumpf's students. The section on G. E. Müller benefited from the unpublished paper of Dr. W. D. Turner, and some biographical obscurities were cleared up by letters from Professor Müller himself. Professor R. M. Ogden lent me his aid in the sections on Külpe, and the text shows the effect of some of his criticisms. He also transcribed some letters of Külpe's for me. Mr. David Shakow's unpublished biographical study of Ebbinghaus formed the starting-point for another section of the text. British experimental psychology on the formal academic side is obscure, and Professor William McDougall, Professor C. Spearman, Dr. C. S. Myers, and Mr. F. C. Bartlett have all supplied me with important information. Professor McDougall also read the entire chapter on British psychology; and I have made a number of additions to it at his advice. Dr. J. McK. Cattell has been kind enough to answer some of my questions about early American psychology. I owe a real debt, even though it be indeterminate, to my seminary at Clark University in 1921-1922 and to my seminary at Harvard in 1928. My wife has labored untiringly on the manuscript, the proofs, and the indices. Mr. K. W. Oberlin has read most of the galley proofs, and Mr. P. E. Huston all of the page proofs. Professor R. M. Elliott, the editor of this series, has in all the final stages of work stood by, ready with wise suggestions, and my publishers have shown all the coöperation that an author could ask. And there are still others, who might be added to this list, and who realize my gratitude though I make no formal acknowledgment.

The frontispiece is a reproduction of Dr. Felix Pfeifer's bronze plaque of Wundt. The plaque was made in 1905, the year of the golden jubilee of Wundt's doctorate. I am grateful to Dr. Pfeifer for permitting its reproduction, and to Professor K. M. Dallenbach for photographing the bronze at Cornell for me. . . .

In dedicating this book to Edward Bradford Titchener I am acknowledging my greatest intellectual debt. Whatever of merit in care, thoroughness, or perspective the book may have derives

originally from him. Especially was it due to his influence that I
gained the conviction that the gift of professional maturity comes
only to the psychologist who knows the history of his science. In
experimental psychology Titchener was the historian *par excellence*.
He should have written this book, and it is with great diffidence
that I offer a poor substitute.

E. G. B.

August 25, 1929
Cambridge, Massachusetts

Preface to the Second Edition

Can history be revised? Yes. As time goes on, there come to be second thoughts about the interpretation of it. There are also new discoveries. And, as the once recent past moves back into a more balanced perspective, its delineator must discard his preliminary sketches in order to preserve the now clearer view in more permanent colors. In addition, he has a newly recent past to sketch for the first time, a past which was only a future when he was first essaying description. There is much to revise in history as time goes on, but even more in *a* history which, like the present one, shows how psychology came to be what it is in its new present. Psychology has matured, not like a person who never picks up new ancestors as he grows older, but like a family which, when a scion marries, acquires suddenly all the ancestors of the new spouse.

Now let me be specific. What changes have I found I wish to make in my twenty-one-year-old book?

The old introductory chapter on the emergence of science I have scrapped, for I wanted to get more into the dynamics of history, to say something about why, as well as how, science emerged, to speak of the rôle of the *Zeitgeist* and of the great man in determining progress in science, and to show that these two views of the development and emergence of thought are not mutually exclusive but obverse and reverse of every historical process. I have tried to echo that thought throughout the book.

Chapters 2 to 7 are not greatly changed. The maverick chapter on hypnosis now justifies its existence as an approach to the new later chapter on dynamic psychology.

Chapters 9 to 13 are also not greatly altered. I have left Aristotle out of Chapter 9. It seemed better to pay "the greatest mind in the history of thought" the tribute of dignified silence than to give him a clap on the back with a couple of pages only.

Chapter 11 on the Scottish school, French empiricism and French materialism, all in the eighteenth century, is wholly new. Treating these two topics together is not entirely a *tour de force* for there was a current between the two countries, first from France to Scotland, and then later the other way. I have, moreover, now paid tribute to Cabanis, Charcot, Binet and Janet, though they are still peripheral to experimental psychology proper.

In Chapter 13 I have brought in Kant. German psychology and physiology do not quite make sense when he was slurred over, even if Wundt did have his master eye fixed on the British school.

The chapters on Fechner, Helmholtz and Wundt show no great changes. To Chapter 17 on Brentano, Stumpf and G. E. Müller, I have added Hering. Here I acknowledge Koffka's helpful criticism that Hering should have more attention in this book. The gamut of phenomenology and nativism runs: Goethe, Purkinje, Joh. Müller, Hering, Stumpf, the later Külpe, Wertheimer, Gestalt psychology.

Chapter 18 I have restructured, disentangling the early from the late Külpe, getting the relation to Mach and Avenarius and to positivism clearer.

The chapter on British psychology has now been filled out and up-dated. I have said a little more about McDougall. The long section on experimental psychology I have rewritten entirely, mostly from the historical articles of F. C. Bartlett and C. S. Myers.

The first of the two chapters on American psychology—Chapter 21 on the pioneers—is not much revised, though there are many new articles to cite. From there on to the end the book has been entirely rewritten, for the subject-matter of the remaining chapters was too new in 1929 to be written with assurance, or else the new material which this revision presents had not even happened yet. In Chapter 22 I take the view which I have long held—one which Woodworth seems to share with me—that all American psychology, except what centered about Titchener, is functional.

In 1929 Gestalt psychology had come but had not gone. Now it has accomplished its mission. I have tried in Chapter 23 to describe it as a whole.

Behaviorism seems to have been a movement in the *Zeitgeist*, not a simple revolution. Instead of giving it a chapter to itself, I have turned Chapter 24 to behavioristics, have picked up the threads of animal psychology and of objective psychology from the earlier chapters, and have then passed on through behaviorism proper to the newer positivism and what has sometimes been called operationism.

Chapter 25 on brain function is a paradigm of historical dynamics, a chapter in the social psychology of thought. It reviews this history from Flourens to Köhler, showing how thought develops, how slowly it changes, yet how inevitably it conforms eventually to discovery.

The chapter on dynamic psychology is, of course, brand new. The psychology of motivation has earned its right, to a great extent since 1929, to be considered part of experimental psychology. Like sensation and perception, learning and motivation must eventually have their separate volume, and I may indeed try my brain and hand at that piece of research and writing during the next few years.

In the retrospect at the end of the book I get the chance to re-assess psychology after twenty-one years, to reprove gently my self of 1929, and then to discuss this matter of the great man within the *Zeitgeist*.

I have tried to be brief, or at least to avoid prolixity. In Flourens' phrase: "J'ai voulu être court. Il y a un grand secret pour être court: c'est d'être clair." But this revision kept growing. I have omitted the old survey of experimental psychology by decades. Psychology now bulks too large to be thus prescribed in capsules.

Altogether the new edition is about one-third larger than the old, is one-half new writing and uses for its other half about two-thirds of the old edition. There must be a couple of thousand minor changes in what is reprinted. The old rule for the first edition and for my *Sensation and Perception in the History of Experimental Psychology* still holds: I speak with confidence up to twenty years ago (1930); I speak, but with less assurance, of the next decade; whatever I say for the most recent decade is based on gratuitous courage.

So much can happen as the years go by. In the twenty-one years since the first edition, nineteen of its more important characters have died: Stumpf, G. E. Müller, Schumann, von Ehrenfels, Mc-Dougall, C. S. Myers, Lloyd Morgan, Karl Pearson, J. M. Baldwin, Cattell, Jastrow, Thorndike, Franz, E. B. Holt, H. S. Jennings, Margaret Washburn, Pavlov, Wertheimer, Koffka. Outside the scope of the first edition but great losses to psychology are Freud and Janet.

Books have been coming out. Murphy's *Historical Introduction to Modern Psychology* had its first edition in 1929 and was revised in 1949. Woodworth's *Contemporary Schools of Psychology* of 1931 was revised in 1948. Fearing's *Reflex Action*, Heidbreder's *Seven Psychologies*, Flugel's *A Hundred Years of Psychology*, Zilboorg's *A History of Medical Psychology* and many other historically im-portant books appeared in this critical vigentennium. It was the need for more biographical information for the first edition of this book that led to the later publication of the three volumes of *Psychology in Autobiography*, a project that is about to be continued now that the then middle-aged are getting old enough to have pasts. Murchison's *Psychological Register* has also appeared since 1929, making unnecessary in this edition some of the selected bibliographies that I gave in the first. It would be a pleasant egoism to think that my book stimulated all this historical interest, but that would be wrong. Murphy published before I did, and undoubtedly the *Zeitgeist* has been getting in its work on all these authors and also on me. We writing psychologists are hard-working symptoms of what is going forward in the history of psychology.

The dedication of this book to E. B. Titchener is no less appropriate now than it was in 1929. What I said then, I still believe.

Criticism and bibliographical aid have been given me from time to time by Robert S. Harper, Herbert M. Jenkins, George A. Heise and James L. Morey, all of the Harvard Psychological Laboratories. I am grateful to them. My most specific debt in completing this revision is to Mollie D. Boring. Besides her typing and patient checking of facts and figures, she lent the project her critical skill, her never flagging enthusiasm and her inexhaustible sense of humor, and the book has profited immensely from her zeal. Audrey MacLeod has been my mainstay in reading the proofs. I have been fortunate in having both her patience and intelligence at my service in this task. Dr. Elliott, my always beneficent editor, has read the galley proofs and more than once, with humorous tolerance, diverted me from error.

Perhaps my greatest obligation is to my audience who are, of course, my motivators—the graduate students who read the first edition and who would, I felt, welcome this revision. If this faith in them proves to be but my happy delusion, nevertheless, like many wrong theories in science, it has served its purpose in motivating action. Now that my job is done, the publisher, whom I anthropomorphize as the friendly, helpful and wise Dana H. Ferrin, takes over. How pleasant it would be to think that he and Dr. Elliott have got in this manuscript, not all they wanted, but even all they, being realists, hoped for.

E. G. B.

January 11, 1950
Cambridge, Massachusetts

Contents

ORIGIN OF MODERN PSYCHOLOGY WITHIN PHILOSOPHY

THE FOUNDING OF EXPERIMENTAL PSYCHOLOGY

ESTABLISHMENT OF MODERN PSYCHOLOGY IN GERMANY

ESTABLISHMENT OF MODERN PSYCHOLOGY IN GREAT BRITAIN

ESTABLISHMENT OF MODERN PSYCHOLOGY IN AMERICA

ORIENTATION

CHAPTER I

The Rise of Modern Science

This book undertakes to tell how experimental psychology came to be what it is today. It deals with history, but it does not attempt to give all of the history of any topic because it selects that part of the past whose lineal descendants are today important. In the author's mind there is always—as indeed there would be in the mind of any psychologist studying history—the question as to *why* events transpired as they did, as well as to what the events were.

The progress of science is the work of creative minds. Every creative mind that contributes to scientific advance works, however, within two limitations. It is limited, first, by ignorance, for one discovery waits upon that other which opens the way to it. Discovery and its acceptance are, however, limited also by the habits of thought that pertain to the culture of any region and period, that is to say, by the *Zeitgeist:* an idea too strange or preposterous to be thought in one period of western civilization may be readily accepted as true only a century or two later. Slow change is the rule—at least for the basic ideas. On the other hand, the more superficial fashions as to what is important, what is worth doing and talking about, change much more rapidly, depending partly on discovery and partly on the social interaction of the wise men most concerned with the particular matter in hand—the cross-stimulation of leaders and their followers, of protagonists and their antagonists. A psychologist's history of psychology is, therefore, at least in aspiration, a dynamic or social psychology, trying to see not only what men did and what they did not do, but also why they did it or why, at the time, they could not do it.

This matter becomes clearer when we realize that there are two theories of history, the *personalistic* and the *naturalistic*. The personalistic theory, which is also the theory of common sense, says that astronomy forged ahead because Copernicus had the insight to see and the courage to say that the heliocentric view of the solar system is more plausible than a geocentric. The naturalistic theory, on the other hand, holds that it was almost inevitable that the helio-

3

centric view should be realized in the Age of Enlightenment, that it should then, as men's attitudes toward themselves shifted, come to seem plausible, and that Copernicus was, therefore, only the agent or perhaps the symptom of inexorable cultural change. Did Wundt found the new experimental psychology somewhere around 1860 or did the times compel the changes to which Wundt merely gave expression? Certainly Copernicus' and Wundt's opinions on these matters would not help us, for no one ever knows surely about his own motives or the sources of his insights, and the man of genius in his most brilliant flash of creative insight would not claim that his originality was uncaused—not in our modern culture would he claim it. As a matter of fact this dilemma is not real but a Kantian antinomy. Copernicus' and Wundt's thinkings are themselves both natural phenomena, and the course of history is no more nor less inexorable when it is interpreted as including the minute neural events which are the flashes of insight of those geniuses whose names mark the mileposts of science. Actually the naturalistic theory includes the personalistic. You get the personalistic view when you ignore the antecedants of the great man, and you get the naturalistic view back again when you ask what made the great man great. On either view there are Great Men, with nervous systems whose operations provide the opportunities for especially rapid scientific progress.

A truer dilemma arises when we ask about the rate of scientific progress. Does science run along on a plateau and then suddenly shoot ahead because of an important discovery, or does it move steadily, inevitably, onward, always by small increments? Is its course discrete and step-wise or is it gradual and continuous? Mature opinion favors many small steps as the general rule. Nearly all great discoveries have had their anticipations which the historian digs up afterward. Disproved theories hang on indefinitely, often for a century or more, until displaced by some positive substitute. Again and again it seems as if the crucial insight either does not come until the *Zeitgeist* has prepared for its reception, or, if it comes too soon for the *Zeitgeist*, then it does not register and is lost until it is unearthed later when the culture is ready to accept it.

Undoubtedly the smooth course of history on analysis would prove to be ultimately quantal, consisting of little bursts of progress, as this bit of discovery or that thrust of insight registers. It is when you consider larger units—the entire contribution of one man, the progress of a decade or a century—that you get the perception of large steps. Yet there have been moments when progress was rapid. An instance is Newton's conceiving of the principle of universal gravitation, a conception that certainly was formed quickly in 1666, although Voltaire's story that the idea came to Newton in an instant when he noticed the earth and an apple falling toward each other may exaggerate the suddenness of this basic insight. Be this as it may, the description of progress has necessarily to be made in terms of its differentials, those increments of change which are important enough and big enough to show whither knowledge is going.

THE EMERGENCE OF SCIENCE

How did science begin? There is an argument that science has no beginning in human history but is as old as perception, that it begins in the evolutionary scale with the capacity to generalize in perceiving an object. In observation both science and perception look to underlying generalities, seeing in the observed object the uniformities of nature.

Take what psychologists call *object constancy*. The retinal image of a seen object gets smaller as the object recedes although both the physical object itself and the perception of it remain constant in size. The uniformity of nature here is the rule that objects do not change size when they move or when their observers move. That is a scientific physical generalization. The human organism is, however, so constructed that its perception, in general, follows the same general rule: the organism sees the same object as the same size regardless of the distance between it and the object. So the scientific generality is 'understood' by the organism in the sense that its perception includes this generalization. The generalizing organism can be man, an ape, a chick or even a lower animal form, since some degree of objective generalization is present in all perception. Perhaps this analogy is too fanciful, since it makes the first scientist an organism no higher in the animal scale than a chicken or perhaps even a protozoan; nevertheless the similarity serves to warn us that we shall not find in human history an exact moment when science began.

Science in the modern sense of a social institution in which many men coöperate and one generation carries on the work of the preceding requires the existence of a written language, of books and eventually of libraries, all of which make communication free and allow the younger generation to consult the wisdom of the ancients long since dead. Egyptian priests could pass on the lore of the heavens to their successors, but dependence on oral communication alone is fatal to extensive progress, since memory traces change, deteriorate and presently are lost in death. Scientific progress needs written language and books.

When one takes the very longest view of the emergence of science, then indeed there are apparent huge steps—periods of rapid development and sudden change. The first 'mutation' came with the emergence of Greek civilization, the 'Greek miracle,' as it is often called; and the second came with the Renaissance and its shift of interest away from theological dogma to a concern with nature and eventually with the experimental method.

As contrasted with the systematized knowledge of the previous ages in Egypt, Mesopotamia and the Aegean, the Greek civilization of the third, fourth and fifth centuries B.C., seems indeed a miracle. These are the centuries of Plato (*ca.* 427-347 B.C.), Aristotle (384-322 B.C.) and Archimedes (*ca.* 287-212 B.C.). Aristotle, the greatest mind that ever lived, as some think, catalogued knowledge and increased it by his own wise pronouncements. Archimedes, as mathematician and physicist, actually anticipated the modern modes of scientific thinking in his way of dealing with general principles of nature. The total picture of this civilization, preserved to us and promoted by the use of an easily written language and the existence of books, shows a penetrating interest in knowledge and truth and an esthetic maturity in architecture and the arts that astonishes historians, astonishes them because, while they can describe the events, they cannot say why they occurred.

On the other hand, we must not forget that Greek civilization was meager as compared with our own. The Greeks were just as intelligent as we—there is no evidence that two millennia of evolution have improved man in the dimension in respect of which he excels the great apes. The educated Greek could live a full rich life—the richer because he was free to sample all knowledge and the cultivated arts and free of the modern pressure to adjust himself to more factual knowledge than he could possibly understand. He lived largely in the here and now. He had no history to learn and understand. Even Thucydides wrote history mostly within the span of his own memory. The ancient Greek had no important foreign languages to acquire, nor great foreign literatures to absorb and not much literature of his own. He felt no need to study other cultures. The Greek of the golden age lived in the best culture that had ever existed and that for him was surely enough. He did not need to travel to be educated, for there was no better place to go. Distances, moreover, seemed great. The gods could live on Olympus in northern Greece with no fear of inquisitive mortals' prying into their abode. There were no watches, no clocks. Discourse in Plato's Academy did not start at seven minutes past the hour. The economic system, which included slave labor, made it possible for the élite to give themselves fully to the advancement of a civilization to which the modern westerner owes an immeasurable debt. It was not, however, a civilization adapted to the emergence of experimental science. It favored intuition, insight and the intellectual processes, but not the extraction of secrets from nature by mechanical contrivance and experimental technique. That was not to come until almost two thousand years later.

In the Dark Ages (*ca.* 500-1200) and the Middle Ages (*ca.* 1200-1500), although science was advanced in the Byzantine culture of the east, the cultural life of western Europe was dominated by theological interest. When a man's thoughts passed beyond the immediate concern of his here and now, they were centered on the prospects of his soul and its chances of avoiding hell-fire. Thinking men were eager enough to know the truth, but the values of the times were such that they thought that the truth would be revealed to them in accordance with the divine will, and they looked for dogmas to guide them. Having accepted seven as a sacred number, it did not seem to them that God would place more than seven bodies in the immediate celestial universe—the Earth, the sun, the moon, Venus, Mars, Jupiter and Saturn—and Galileo's discovery of four moons for Jupiter appeared to them as sacrilegious. We are inclined to condemn the Middle Ages for their lack of science, their acceptance of unprovable dogma, their failure to advance what we call civilization yet men of intelligence equal to that of today's Nobel Prize winners held these dogmatically determined attitudes toward truth as vehemently as any scientist defends his modern version of reality. Both medievalism and modernism depend on many *a priori* values, and our interest in the medieval in this book lies only in the fact that it furnished the kind of thinking from which modern science had to emerge. This emergence changed basic values; it did not, of course, eliminate them.

Actually modern science did not make its appearance until the Renaissance and the accompanying revival of learning.

THE NEW LEARNING

What started the Renaissance off? We may be at a loss to explain the origin of the miracle of Greek civilization, but we can indeed say something of the dynamics of the revival of learning, of which one phase was the substitution of interest in evidentially established fact for theologically sanctioned dogma. It is usual to mention five events as 'causes' of the changed attitudes which made the new learning possible.

(1) The first of these is the invention of gunpowder and its use in warfare (15th century). That change helped to outmode the feudal system, to lay the basis for the democratization of society by weakening the bonds of personal fealty. The strengthening of national units at the expense of feudal estates broadened intellectual horizons and made learning easier.

(2) The invention of the printing press in 1440 suddenly made possible the mass production of books, multiplying many fold the effect that the invention of a written language had already had on civilization.

(3) The fall of Constantinople to the Turks in 1453 marked the end of the Byzantine Empire and the dissipation of its culture toward the west. The revival in Italy of interest in Greek civilization was furthered by the escape thither from Constantinople of Greek scholars.

(4) The discovery of America in 1492 was a phase of a period of geographical exploration and a search for convenient trade routes from western Europe to the far east. This event was due to no private whim of Columbus' but to the fact that the Middle Ages were passing and that concern with business and trade was beginning to surpass interest in the soul and theological dogma. Exploration was motived by the desire for wealth, and presently in the sixteenth century wealth was found, not only in trade with the Indies, but also in the silver and gold of Mexico and Peru. Besides the precious metals and the profits from trade, there was land—free land for the colonist who had the strength to take it and cultivate it. It is probable that no single factor has influenced more the character of the last four centuries in western Europe and America than the existence of 'free' land, even though it had first to be won from savages and then won again from nature to be called free.

Some historians have held that the democratic, practical spirit of America was due to its shifting westward frontier, beyond which there was always free land for every man with the wit and strength to become lord of his own acres. That may indeed be true, but there is also a much larger sense in which the free land of both the far west and the far east gave a special character to the four centuries which constitute modernity. In the Middle Ages power was derived from God—directly in the Church, or indirectly through the divine rights of kings, or, once established, by inheritance. as in the case of nobles. The powerful—kings, nobles, feudal lords and the Church—held the land, which thus became the symbol of power. In the new age the colonist could acquire land by hard work and the merchant could buy land. Gradually economic forces shifted the grounds for social status from hereditary or divine right to the possession of wealth in land or goods. This process of democratization played an enormously important rôle in the rise of science, because it both undermined the prestige of the givers of dogma and prepared the way for the promotion of science as soon as the commercial usefulness of science was demonstrated—and that was very soon.

(5) The fifth item of which so much has been made as a determiner of the new age of thought is the Copernican theory, published in 1543, the year of Copernicus' death. The geocentric theory of the celestial universe was also an anthropocentric theory: the universe was seen to revolve about man on the earth. The heliocentric theory made more sense scientifically, but it demoted man to an unimportant peripheral position on one of many planets. There are even those today who ascribe the present prevalence of psychoneurosis partly to man's loss of a sense of prestige and importance under the Copernican theory. Not only did the Copernican revolution rob man of his geocentric position in the universe; it also robbed him of his definite celestial site for heaven and depreciated the importance of his own soul as it multiplied the possibilities of many other souls on other planets.

As we have already noted, it is difficult in these matters of historical causation to tell cause from effect, reason from symptom. Many of the relationships are circular. The discovery of free lands, the gold and silver of the Incas and the riches of the Indies, helped to establish the spirit of the new age, but the spirit of the new age helped in turn to further exploration. The Copernican theory was both the effect of new modes of thinking and the cause of their promotion. Copernicus needed the changing interests of men of intellect to encourage him to press the simpler but heterodox view of the celestial bodies; yet he recognized that the Church would be against him and he hesitated, putting his theory forward as a speculation and not publishing it before his death. So the effect of change was to make more change easier, but progress was slow. We might, for instance, add the Reformation to our list of causes. Luther nailed his ninety-five theses to the church door in 1517, but his act was the result of growing general dissatisfaction with the Church as well as the cause of more dissatisfaction. Some historians list the emergence of science as a reason for the new age. It too was both an effect and a cause of the changing times. It was part of the new learning.

THE BEGINNINGS OF MODERN SCIENCE

The emergence of modern science is generally said to have occurred in the seventeenth century, because this century includes the remarkable work of Kepler, Galileo and Newton, as well as other important contributions to the new knowledge.

Copernicus (1473-1543) prepared the way. He put forward the heliocentric theory (1543) as an hypothesis without evidence or proof, but he argued clearly for its plausibility.

Kepler (1571-1630) is noted for having laid down the three laws of planetary motion in 1609-1619: (1) the planets have elliptical orbits, the sun is at one focus—a principle that takes the Copernican theory for granted; (2) the radius of a planet as it revolves around the sun sweeps out equal areas in equal times, a rule which means that the planet goes faster when, in its course along its elliptical orbit, it is nearer the sun; and (3) the square of the time of revolution of a planet about the sun is proportional to the cube of its average distance from the sun. These laws, all later verified, are beautiful examples of mathematical deduction in science. They are far beyond the kind of thinking that the Middle Ages produced or that the mystery-ridden Pythagoras could have managed. Archimedes' discovery of the hydrostatic principle that bodies lose in liquid a weight equal to the weight of the liquid displaced was a comparable kind of thinking, but it was rare in Grecian culture.

After Kepler there was the great Galileo (1564-1642), who discovered many principles of the dynamics of moving bodies—the law of falling bodies, the law of the pendulum, acceleration, inertia, the components of motion of a projectile. He heard about the invention of a telescope by a Dutchman in 1608, made one himself in 1609, trained it on Jupiter and discovered four of the moons. That made eleven, not seven, known bodies in the solar system, and Galileo ridiculed those who said that seven was a sacred number and that the Creator would not have made eleven celestial objects. Everybody knows how he held to the Copernican theory and was forced as an old man, almost blind, to recant, muttering a recantation of his recantation. That was in 1633. Many of his discoveries were not published until 1638, but they were generally known long before, partly through the extensive correspondence of Father Mersenne. Galileo died in 1642.

In that same year Newton (1642-1727) was born. He had one of the most brilliant minds of our civilization. As a young man of about twenty-five, in the years 1665 and 1666, his genius achieved the following insights. (1) He conceived and used the principles of the differential and integral calculus, although in this achievement he was anticipated by his teacher Isaac Barrow. Leibnitz made the same discovery independently. (2) Newton conceived the principle of universal gravitation and worked out the inverse-square law from one of Kepler's laws. Later he formulated the laws of motion, of which the third law (action and reaction are equal) was new, verified the inverse-square law in the case of the moon and the earth, and published his *Principia* in 1687. (3) Also in those early years he purchased a prism and, arranging experiments with it, demonstrated that white light is a mixture of lights for the different colors. He reported on this fact and the basic principles of color mixture to the Royal Society in 1672, to find them skeptical of so implausible an hypothesis as that white is a mixture of colors. In 1668 he constructed the first reflecting telescope. The rest of his life, which toward the end was filled with many honors, he spent in working out the consequences of these early insights and in making other discoveries in mathematics, mechanics and optics. He represents excellently the scientific ideal—at least the ideal for physical science—of the insight of genius, followed by mathematical deduction and experimental verification. The nature and manner of Newton's achievements make clear what was happening to science in the seventeenth century.

That the new science was in the air, that the concerns of the Middle Ages were receding, becomes certain when we consider all the outstanding events of this first rich century of the new age. Let us cite the items. (a) Back in 1593 Galileo had invented the thermometer. (b) In 1600 Gilbert published his treatise on magnetism in Latin, the first great scientific work to be published in England. (c) In 1609 came Kepler's laws and (d) Galileo's use of his new telescope to discover Jupiter's moons. (e) Harvey's discovery of the circulation of the blood is dated 1628, the first item of biological science which we cite for the new age. (f) Galileo's discoveries were finally published in 1638. (g) Then in 1643 Galileo's pupil, Torricelli, discovered and invented the barometer by inverting a tube filled with mercury and sealed at one end into a dish of mercury. He proved that the column was supported by the weight of the air by showing that the height of the column diminished when the tube was carried up a mountain. Thus he substituted a positive mechanical principle for the dogma: nature abhors a vacuum. No instance could show better the difference between medieval and modern scientific thinking. (h) Next was discovered "the spring of the air," the fact that gases expand to fill all free space, and out of that came von Guericke's invention of the air-pump in 1654 and his demonstration of atmospheric pressure with the Magdeburg hemispheres which could be pulled apart only with great difficulty when the air between them had been exhausted. (i) Robert Boyle's laws of gases followed in 1660. By this time there was so much going on in science that the men of science needed better means of communication than personal letters. (j) So the Royal Society was founded in 1660 for discussion and the publication of communications and (k) the Académie des Sciences in 1666. That was the time when Newton was having his brilliant new insights into celestial mechanics and optics. (l) Newton's first communication on white light as a mixture of colored lights was made to the Royal Society in 1672. (m) It was in 1674 that Leeuwenhoek used the microscope to discover microörganisms—bacteria and spermatozoa. (n) Then finally, after long hesitation because his earlier calculations for the moon did not check with theory, Newton published in 1687 his *Principia*.

One of the attributes of the science of the new age was its coöperative character. The Middle Ages were characterized by their authoritarianism, and their science by deference for the dicta of Aristotle. In the new age the ultimate arbiter was nature, to whom scientists put with increasing effectiveness their questions, believing in her uniformity and in the stability of her answers. Coöperation made sense in this attack upon nature's secrets, more sense than it could in a society which depended on revelation rather than discovery for its progress. But coöperation requires communication. Travel was difficult, letters were not so common, and journals were nonexistent. Nor was publication in books prompt. Often the most important contributions were imperfectly known by correspondence long before they were published, and often an important book appeared late in the life of its author or even posthumously.

The first remedy lay in correspondence and the second in societies of scientists. In Paris Father Mersenne, no mean scientist in his own right, undertook to correspond with many scientists—Descartes, Hobbes, Gassendi, Harvey, Galileo, Torricelli—and sometimes even to draw them into debate. Later the men of science who stayed in Paris formed the habit of meeting together, and out of that grew eventually the Académie des Sciences. In London it was Samuel Hartlib, a philanthropist interested in the new science, who about 1645 brought together the scientists for weekly discussion. Presently this group came to include Robert Boyle and Sir Christopher Wren, whom one historian has called the English Leonardo da Vinci of the seventeenth century. They planned a research university of science, in which philosophers would carry on research and give instruction in the various fields. The Royal Society grew out of their considerations.

The Royal Society was founded in 1660 and chartered in 1662. Charles II lent it his interest. The Académie des Sciences was founded in 1666 under the patronage of Louis XIV, "the great Louis." The Prussian Akademie der Wissenschaften at Berlin came a little later—in 1700. These academies performed the function that the learned and professional societies and the universities do nowadays: they brought scientists together for the exchange of information and for mutual stimulation. They also provided the first scientific journals by printing reports of their sessions and of communications received by them. The Royal Society began the *Philosophical Transactions* in 1665 and the Académie des Sciences its *Mémoires* in 1666. The publication of regular scientific journals independently of the societies did not occur until the end of the eighteenth century.

It is important for us to note that the ideal form of modern science was fixed by the physics of the seventeenth century. When it is argued in the twentieth century that psychology should strive to become scientific and that, to be scientific, it should become mathematical and deductive, the polemicists are seeking their sanctions in the history of physics which was first on the scene when science and philosophy were becoming separated in the age of Newton.

It has long been a question whether science uses a deductive or an inductive method. The Aristotelian method was deductive, reasoning from the general to the particular. Francis Bacon in his *Novum Organum* of 1620 sought to substitute induction. In the observation of many facts eventually the generalities may become apparent. Often we hear it said that a young science must collect facts and not expect soon to discover general laws. On the other hand, physics was quite young in the seventeenth century and we see it developing hand in hand with mathematics, which is essentially a deductive tool. Newton was held up in his theory of gravitation until he had devised the calculus. His inverse-square law of gravitation was deduced from one of Kepler's laws, and both Kepler's and Newton's laws needed observational verification after they were deduced.

Nowadays this procedure is called the *hypothetico-deductive method*: the scientist starts with an hypothesis, he deduces from it a consequence that can be observed, either directly in nature or in an experiment. If the predicted observation is verified, he has that fact and has also strengthened the hypothesis by this test of a deduction from it. Where does he get the hypothesis to begin with? From insight into relationships, from the results of other discoveries, from insufficiently supported intuition (a 'hunch'). Archimedes must have conceived the hydrostatic principle by insight into relationships. He then deduced the conclusion about King Hiero's crown. The story does not say that he then verified the hypothesis with experiments. It implies that the insight which sent him from his bath shouting "Eureka!" was too compelling for him to feel the need for verification. But Newton felt that need and held up publication of his theory of gravitation until he was able to make theory check with observation. Physics got its start in the new age by the brilliant insights of able intellects, by deduction and the appropriate use of mathematics to complete deductive processes which were too involved for simpler means. Two centuries later, psychology, with but partial success, was trying to fit itself to this same pattern.

The eighteenth century was not so productive as the seventeenth. The revolutionary changes of the century of Kepler, Galileo and Newton were followed by what was, relatively, a plateau. As one historian has put it, after Newton the world got not, as might have been expected, "a great burst of discoveries," but "a long period of slightly stunned assimilation." The new habits of thought were taking root. We must, however, leave the general history of science here and turn now to the history of biological science, from which scientific psychology eventually emerged.

THE BEGINNINGS OF PHYSIOLOGY

Biological science started as medical science which, with the Greeks and before them, was a mixture of anatomy, surgery and a knowledge of medicinal plants, supplemented by magic and other dogmatic principles. With occasional exceptions the law forbade the dissection of human bodies, so that advances in the correct knowledge of anatomy depended on the dissection of animals. Physiological knowledge was, of course, held back by ignorance of anatomy. Hippocrates (*ca.* 460-370 B.C.), the "Father of Medicine," showed what was then a rare objectivity toward medical fact and left eighty-seven greatly revered treatises for his successors to study; but, lacking resort to anatomical observation of the depths of the human body or the understanding of experimental method, he could not pass far beyond the limitation of the age in which he lived. Knowledge of superficial anatomy was supplied by the great artists, but the ban on dissection prevented the discovery of essentials.

Immediately after Hippocrates medical science advanced but little. Long afterward it was brought together by Galen (*ca.* 129-199 A.D.), who was an excellent practitioner, a good observer and in a limited way also an experimenter. Contrasted with his ancient predecessors, Galen was almost modern in some of his dicta. He localized the mind in the brain; Aristotle had had it in the heart. He distinguished between sensory and motor nerves, a distinction that was later lost and had to be recovered in the nineteenth century. By experiments with the transsection of the spinal cord he was able to localize some of its motor functions. All that sounds like good scientific progress, but along with it Galen also contributed a great deal of unevidenced systematized dogma, which doubtless caused him to be revered by the ancients, but which had to be overcome when science was ready to go along with the Renaissance. In medicine Galen thus came to play the authoritative rôle which Aristotle played for philosophy and other science. Thirteen hundred years later the leading medical men were still echoing Galen as the unimpeachable authority. For instance, Dubois Sylvius (1478-1555), Vesalius' teacher, more than a millennium later, was known as "a great Galenist."

In the sixteenth century the dissection of human bodies was being practiced, although with opposition from the Church. Both Leonardo da Vinci and Michelangelo studied the human body in this way. Andreas Vesalius (1514-1564), whose advent marked the triumph of observation over dogma in the medicine of the new age, began dissection as a boy and continued it after his training in Paris and his eventual establishment in Padua, where by 1537 he was lecturing to large audiences and demonstrating the anatomy of the human body to enthusiastic students. He published De fabrica corporis humani in 1543, a compendium remarkable for its objective freedom from Galenistic tradition and for its vivid and accurate wood-cuts. The modern tradition in anatomy stems from Vesalius, but it did not get under way until almost a century later, for Vesalius was ahead of his time. The Church disapproved of his lack of veneration for tradition and his work had to wait for the brilliant seventeenth century to pick it up and carry it along.

It was in that century of the new learning that Harvey did for physiology what Vesalius had done for anatomy. Harvey (1578-1657) was a pupil of Fabricus', who was a pupil of Fallopius', who was a pupil of Vesalius', nor was this connection with anatomy only formal. Fabricus knew about the valves in the veins and showed by experiments that they allowed the blood to flow toward the heart and not away from it. That discovery weakened Galen's assertion that the blood ebbs and flows back and forth in veins and, greatly diluted by the vital spirits, in the arteries. Fabricus was at Padua, whither Harvey went to complete his training. Back in England, Harvey continued his observations and experiments. What he did was to work out the exact connections of the cavities of the heart with each other and with the lungs, the arteries and the veins. The connections and the valves showed what way the blood must be flowing. As no good microscopic technique was yet available, Harvey could only infer the existence of the capillaries in the tissues and the passage of the blood from the arteries to the veins. His classic publication on this matter, *De motu cordis et sanguinis*, appeared in 1628.

There was no burst of good work in scientific physiology right after Harvey nor in fact in the eighteenth century. The perspective of the modern scientific age shows the seventeenth and nineteenth centuries as much more productive than the eighteenth. Leeuwenhoek (1632-1723), possessed of a microscope, could be the first to set eyes upon bacteria and spermatozoa (1674), but the great wave of activity in microscopic anatomy did not come until the improvement of the microscope in the nineteenth century. Neither the personalistic nor the naturalistic theory of science explains this contrast satisfactorily, although rationalizations after the fact are easy to find—easier than sure historical dynamics. In physics one can say that the eighteenth century had to assimilate the seventeenth before the nineteenth could go ahead. Another way to regard the matter is to note that the seventeenth century, when the new science was getting started, needed the big insights of genius which a very few men, like Galileo and Newton, could provide. Nineteenth century science was a chain reaction, with one discovery making another possible and one enthusiasm setting off another. Could such a social 'explosion' depend on a critical point not yet reached in the eighteenth century? Such speculations are useful as descriptions of what happened, but they 'explain' little.

Nevertheless, biology did have important names in the eighteenth century—Haller, Linnaeus, and finally Bichat.

Albrecht von Haller (1708-1777), a student of the great Boerhaave's, has been called the Father of Experimental Physiology by those who do not reserve this title for Johannes Müller of the nineteenth century. Haller brought together the accumulating knowledge in anatomy and physiology, contributed the results of many experiments of his own, and furnished the first modern handbook or systematic treatise in the field: *Elementa physiologiae corporis humani*, eight volumes which appeared in 1757-1766. Almost a century before him Glisson had shown that muscle is irritable, that muscular contraction is not mere swelling of the muscle caused by the flow of animal spirits into it but that the irritated muscle exerts contractile force without gaining in total size. Haller made much of this principle, calling the contractile force *vis insita* and arguing that it was unique in living tissue and not found elsewhere in nature. These were the days when the concept of animal spirits in the nerves was giving way to the notion of a *succus nerveus* (Borelli in 1680) or *vis nervosa* (Unzer in 1770). *Vis viva*, often applied to the activity of the nervous system, was also being used in the inorganic world as indicating what the nineteenth century came to call kinetic energy.

Carolus Linnaeus (Carl von Linné, 1707-1778) is the famous Swedish botanist who has the honor of being the founder of modern taxonomy in both botany and zoölogy. Linnaeus was a great observer and classifier. Psychologists know him because his classification of the sensible odors (1752) anticipates all the later systems, but his real significance to psychology lies in the fact that he made description and classification important. Thus he belongs in the tradition of induction that descends from Aristotle, reinforced by Francis Bacon; and that fact may explain in part why scientific biology lagged behind the science of the astronomer-physicists who in the seventeenth century had taken science over to mathematical deduction. It is possible to link Linnaeus with the phenomenology of good observers, like Goethe, Purkinje, Hering and the Gestalt psychologists, all of whom have stressed the importance of what we may call inductive insight, the observation of the good observer trained to see Baconian generalizations in his data.

The third important name for the eighteenth century—it comes at the very end and after the century's turn—is Bichat's (1771-1802), whose *Anatomie générale appliquée à la physiologie et à la médicine* was published in 1801, a year before its young author's death. M. F. X. Bichat is known for his description of the microscopic structure of tissues, his origination of the word *tissue* to describe living matter, his discovery of cells and his view that all tissues are constructed of cells. (Haller had thought that the anatomical element might be the fiber.) Bichat distinguished between the voluntary and involuntary bodily systems, suggested that the muscles themselves are sensitive, and localized the perceptive, memorial and intellectual functions in the brain, but the emotions in the viscera. He was limited in his observation because he had only the simple microscope to use. When the compound microscope became available about 1830, histological observation advanced rapidly.

In the early nineteenth century the great physiologists may be said to have been Charles Bell (1774-1842) in London, whom we shall meet in the next chapter because of his experimental work on sensory and motor nerves; François Magendie (1783-1855) in Paris, who also appears in the next chapter because he was in controversy with Bell about priority for the discovery of the separate functions of sensory and motor nerves; Johannes Müller (1801-1858) in Berlin, whom we encounter repeatedly in this book, who contributed to psychology the important doctrine of the specific energies of nerves, and who is Haller's rival for the title of Father of Experimental Physiology; and Claude Bernard (1813-1878), Magendie's pupil and the most famous of the four but the least important in the history of psychology, although his sage pronouncements on scientific principles and his late publication (mostly after 1860) have established him as the ready source of many apt quotations.

PHENOMENOLOGY IN GERMAN SCIENCE

At this point it will reward us to pause long enough to view the total scene, to see why psychology is a 'young science,' as we so often hear it called, and why scientific psychology began in Germany. In that undertaking we shall see also that taxonomic description fitted the German temperament better than the French and English, and that scientific 'phenomenology' also began in Germany. The term *phenomenology* came into psychology via Husserl in the early twentieth century and was adopted by the modern school of Gestalt psychology. It means the description of immediate experience, with as little scientific bias as possible. Some epistemologizing psychologists regard it, not as a *Wissenschaft* (science, 'ology') but as a *Vorwissenschaft* (discipline propaedeutic to science). If all science, the argument runs, deals with experience, then the description of experience must be ancillary to every science. We shall have more to say of this matter much later in this book (pp. 601-610). What we need to understand now is that phenomenology, by whatever name it be called, came early in the history of science. The phenomenological approach to science belongs with the descriptive, the classificatory and the inductive approaches; it contrasts with the mathematical and deductive attacks. It represents, moreover, an attitude that was suited to the painstaking and methodical Germans. Thus phenomenological description throve in Germany, providing a situation within accepted science where a new experimental psychology could take hold.

There are moderns who deplore the fact that experimental psychology did not begin with the topic of human motivation. They are sometimes found complaining about this item of history, but, though complaining about history may remove one's own frustration, it provides no new insights into the working of historical dynamics. There are good reasons why experimental psychology began as it did, and this section exhibits some of them.

The Renaissance started in Italy and worked its way northwest and north. In the seventeenth century, in the time of Galileo and Descartes, the new science, emphasizing mechanics and astronomy, was localized in Italy and France. England came into the picture as Italy began to fade out, but English science remained more nearly confined to the work of a few great men, of whom Newton was the foremost. In the eighteenth century France led all other nations, and the Académie des Sciences and Paris formed the scientific center of the world. This was the century of the great French *Encyclopédie*, compiled by Diderot and d'Alembert, assisted by Voltaire, Rousseau and many other famous Frenchmen. Voltaire undertook to introduce the French to British thought and science and was successful. German interest in science had begun with the foundation of the Berlin Akademie in 1700, and Frederick the Great for many years made Berlin a center for a freedom of thinking to which more than one French scientist, in trouble with the Church, escaped. So that was the order for the science of western Europe: Italy, France, England, Germany, with Italy dropping out, leaving French, English and German as the important scientific languages after Latin went out of style at the end of the eighteenth century.

The French and the English respected most the mathematical deductive style in science, the manner of Galileo and Newton. At that time biological science did not lend itself so readily to great generalizations, like the law of gravitation, generalizations from which facts could be deduced mathematically for empirical validation. Consequently it was left for the Germans, who have always had great faith that sufficient pains and care will yield progress, to take up biology and promote it. If Kant (*Critique of Pure Reason*, 1781), with meticulous care and without the help of the experimental method, could bring so evasive a subject as the human mind to heel, what was there to prevent Germany's having a scientific physiology and then, presently, a scientific psychology?

So we find in the Germany of the nineteenth century the beginning of a phenomenology, the careful collection of observational fact, that was sound, keen-sighted as to detail, conscientious and thorough, but not as a rule brilliant, and seldom concerned with large generalizations. The description of phenomenal experience is too basic readily to yield the large inductions.

In this tradition we may place the poet Goethe because he fancied that science was included within the broad repertoire of his brilliant competence and because he influenced science by his insistence on what may now be called phenomenological description. Goethe contributed to the theory of evolution by his principle of the metamorphosis of homologous parts in animals and plants. This is the doctrine that parts of different kinds of organisms correspond: a double flower has more petals but fewer stamens, as if stamens had been transformed into petals; a vertebrate has arms, forelegs, wings or fins, one homologous part being substituted for another. Goethe was a strong believer in expert observation and had great faith in his own expertness. Thus, bitterly and unreasonably attacking Newton's correct theory of color, he brought to bear upon the subject the two large volumes of observations and dicta about color, *Zur Farbenlehre*, which he published in 1810, showing what assiduity will do when backed by self-assurance, but not advancing science much except to stimulate other better scientists, like Purkinje.

Purkinje, a Czech physiologist of considerable importance, published two volumes of excellent visual phenomenology in 1824-1825, dedicating them to Goethe, who was by then one of the most reverenced persons in Germany. Purkinje was, indeed, an excellent phenomenologist and is known to psychologists today for the phenomenon which bears his name, the shift of the relative brightness of colors in night vision. That is the sort of basic fact which phenomenology can yield. It was seventy years before the observation could be definitely related to the anatomical fact that the retina has in it rods as well as cones and that the rods function only in reduced illumination.

Johannes Müller could hardly be called a phenomenologist, but his book on vision in 1826 contained an abundance of basic observation and it made a great impression. He demonstrated the German patience in description of fact by publishing the first general handbook of physiology (1833-1840) since Haller's. By then Germany was ready to take over from the French the business of cataloging facts and to do the job more thoroughly. Other German handbooks of physiology followed during the next one hundred years—Wagner's in 1842-1853, Hermann's in 1879-1882, Nagel's in 1905-1910. Müller's contribution shows how nineteenth-century experimental physiology was getting itself established. It was more inductive than deductive, more given to the fact-collecting which Francis Bacon recommended for science, the fact-collecting which Linnaeus favored and (if we note an outstanding instance in physical science) which Tycho Brahe (1546-

1601) did for astronomy, thus providing data for the use of Kepler and Newton later.

Now the important thing for us about all this early phenomenologizing by physiologists was that it tended to produce a certain amount of psychological fact. Purkinje and Müller got interested in the physiology of sensation and provided some of the phenomenological basis for the knowledge of vision. E. H. Weber (1834) a little later made his initial contributions in the tactual field. In this fashion, experimental psychology was getting under way as sense-physiology. Nor is it any wonder that experimental psychology began as phenomenology, as the taxonomy of consciousness. Nor that it began in Germany. The phenomenological tradition was in the air. Helmholtz, to be sure, was anything but a phenomenologist, for his modes of thought resembled Newton's, but his chief opponent, Ewald Hering, a physiologist by training and by university appointment, proved an effective successor to Purkinje, and, as phenomenologist, bears some of the honor and responsibility for the modern school of Gestalt psychology—as we shall see in due course (pp. 355 f.).

In brief, then, part of the story of how psychology came to join the family of sciences is that the Germans, with their faith in collecting data, welcomed biology to its seat in the circle of sciences, while the French and English hesitated because biology did not fit in with the scientific pattern already set by physics and celestial mechanics. Having accepted biology because they liked morphological description, it was inevitable that the Germans should eventually create the morphology of mind that both Wundt and Hering wanted. Nor does it make sense to say that, if the psychology of the earlier nineteenth century could have been left entirely in the hands of Helmholtzes, it would have resembled physics more. The development of psychology in 1860, when it was being 'founded,' as in 1900 when it was surging ahead, depended more on whither it could go by the course on which it was already launched than on the wills of the men who nursed it along. The *Zeitgeist* of 1860 to 1900 might hardly have moved fast enough to keep a dozen Helmholtzes busy. At any rate phenomenology comes first, even though it does not get far by itself.

NOTES

Histories of Science

The growing interest in the history of science and of thought makes good texts available. The basic reference work is G. Sarton, *Introduction to the History of Science*, I, 1927; II, 1931; III, 1947, which takes us from the early Greeks and Hebrews down through the fourteenth century. These volumes are for reference, not for continuous reading, but the introductory pages scattered through the various sections provide an excellent means of acquiring a perspective for a given period and topic.

One way to cover the entire field in about four thousand pages of reading would be to start with B. Russell, *A History of Western Philosophy*, 1945, which gives the history of thinking but not the history of discovery. Then one could follow with some standard text like W. T. Sedgwick and H. W. Tyler, *A Short History of Science*, 1921, at least for the ancient discoveries, supplementing it by some of the general discussions in Sarton's volumes. If one can manage a mass of undiluted fact without losing the use of his attention, then he may follow with A. Wolf, *A History of Science, Technology and Philosophy in the Sixteenth and Seventeenth Centuries*, 1935, and the companion volume *in the Eighteenth Century*, 1939, which give a great quantity of factual information clearly and present it adequately. After that he might go for the nineteenth century to J. T. Merz, *A History of European Thought in the Nineteenth Century*, I, 1896, II, 1903, volumes which give a good account of discovery as well as the evolution of thinking.

A simpler and wholly proper way to get up the history of modern science in a mere three hundred pages is to read the excellent account by H. T. Pledge, *Science since 1500: a Short History of Mathematics, Physics, Chemistry, Biology*, 1939, which is authoritative and recent, or the

older and more elementary W. Libby, *An Introduction to the History of Science*, 1917, which stresses the cultural and conceptual factors in science and was a very important book when published. J. B. Conant, *On Understanding Science*, 1947, discusses the dynamics of scientific progress by way of certain historical paradigms taken from the seventeenth and eighteenth centuries. Conant's book is well supplemented by I. B. Cohen, *Science, Servant of Man*, 1948, in which see also the excellent Bibliography and guide to further reading, 315-348.

The suggestion that historical determination is naturalistic rather than personalistic is not new. Count Leo Tolstoy saw the dilemma and wrote about it in his *War and Peace*, 1866 (see the second Epilogue, and also Tolstoy's Some Words about War and Peace, 1868, appended to some editions). His thesis was that war transcends the wills and decisions of the men who make the war, that they are but agents of greater natural forces. Many others have held this view, including Herbert Spencer. William James took, in a limited pragmatic way, the other side of the argument defending "the great-man theory of history" on the grounds that a belief in human decision as a proximal yet efficient cause is necessary since only omniscience can pass beyond relatively proximal causation and view the entire determining system. Certainly James preferred to think of people as making decisions at choice-points, decisions which determine the course of history. See William James, *Great Men and Their Environment*, originally printed in 1880, but now found in his *The Will to Believe*, 1899, 216-254. The anthropologist, A. L. Kroeber, has argued against social "dualism" (freedom and determinism, the individual and society) in The superorganic, *Amer. Anthropol.*, 1917, N.S. 19, 196-208. After him came W. F. Ogburn and D. Thomas, Are inventions inevitable?, *Pol.Sci.Quart.*, 1922, 37, 83-98, who list 148 simultaneous independent scientific discoveries as indicating that the *Zeitgeist* plays an important rôle in deciding when a discovery shall take place, that the times create a discoverer. The same case is argued by the fact that almost every important discovery in science turns out to have had anticipations; see E. G. Boring, The problem of originality in science, *Amer. J.Psychol.*, 1927, 39, 70-90; A. J. Ihde, The inevitability of scientific discovery, *Sci.Mo.*, 1948, 67, 427-429. The article by R. B. Warren, *op.cit.infra*, is also relevant here. At least two recent authors have sided with William James in emphasizing the importance of the contributions of great men—the leaders, the élite—to progress: Sidney Hook, *The Hero in History*, 1943; Eric Bentley, *The Cult of the Superman*, 1947.

The truth seems to be that thinking goes on within the culture, that the cultural forces are tremendously complex, that multiple causation is the rule, that a given decision often is a necessary, even if insufficient, cause of an historical event, but that the man who made the decision may not have been necessary. Someone else could have made the decision, perhaps under these conditions would have made it, thus becoming the means by which the *Zeitgeist* prevails. Thus decisions are important historical events, and, if one man does not make a decision which has been readied by the times, then another may. Similarly in science the crucial insights are the events that make the steps in progress. The great man has the crucial insight, becoming great because he had it. If he dies before he has the insight, then another may have it, since the times are ready for it, and greatness will go not to the first man who died too soon, but to this second who lived to show in his own wise choice for what the times were ready.

On the related question as to whether scientific progress is continuous, or discontinuous, gradual or sudden, see G. Sarton, *The History of*

Science and the New Humanism, 1937, 174-180.

On the psychology of scientific progress and the inhibitors of progress, including the inertia of accepted concepts, their failure to be accepted until they fit with the times, the way in which an old concept is accommodated to contradictory facts until it is finally ousted by a new conception, see Conant, *op. cit.,* 88-90, 98-109, *et passim.*

Emergence of Science

On the "miracle" of the emergence of Greek civilization, see Russell, *op. cit.,* 3-24; Sarton, *Introduction (op. cit.,* 1927), I, 3-37. The latter reference also gives a quick survey of Greek, Eastern and medieval science. See also C. E. K. Mees, *The Path of Science,* 1946, esp. 1-72, for another good survey.

It was the historian Turner who in 1893 explained the American character as a consequence of the existence of the westward-moving frontier, which he defined as "the higher edge of free land." See F. J. Turner, *The Frontier in American History,* 1920, which reprints the famous original paper of 1893 (pp. 1-38), and other later essays on related topics. The modern view relates the opening up of America and the Far East for colonization to the increase of the importance of wealth and trade, the consequent shift of status from the noble to the wealthy, the Renaissance, the revival of learning and the emergence of modern science, the Reformation and trend toward democratic institutions. See, for instance, the excellent discussion of the modern era, the last four centuries (perhaps 1550 to 1950, Copernicus to Einstein), by R. B. Warren, An attempt at perspective, *Proc. Amer. Philos. Soc.,* 1948, 92, 271-281. Warren suggests that this period, following the Middle Ages, might be called the age of materialism, as it gives place to a new 'modern age' which is beginning to find its pattern in the twentieth century.

On the Copernican revolution—the revolution in the position of man in the universe as well as the revolution of the earth around the sun—see the histories of science and thought cited above. Russell, *op. cit.*, 525-540, shows clearly how the new attitudes emerged with Copernicus, Kepler, Galileo and Newton.

For a readily accessible excerpt from Galileo's account of his researches on the pitch of tones, see W. Dennis, *Readings in the History of Psychology*, 1948, 17-24.

On Torricelli, the *horror vacui*, von Guericke, the spring of the air, Boyle and the gas laws, see esp. Conant, *op. cit.*, 29-64.

On the importance of the academies in the development of science, see M. Ornstein, *The Rôle of Scientific Societies in the Seventeenth Century*, 1928, an interesting and informative book with a bibliography of more than two hundred titles. See also the discussions in the histories of science,

esp. Libby, *op. cit.*, 99-113, on the beginning of the Royal Society.

Physiology and Phenomenology

See the histories of science, *opp. citt.*, on the scientific beginnings of anatomy and physiology; also, for the sixteenth, seventeenth and eighteenth centuries, Sir Michael Foster, *Lectures on the History of Physiology*, 1901; also E. Nordenskiöld, *History of Biology*, 1928.

On Goethe and the phenomenology of vision before Helmholtz, see E. G. Boring, *Sensation and Perception in the History of Experimental Psychology*, 1942, 112-119. On the relation of phenomenology and Gestalt psychology, see this book, pp. 355 f., 601-611.

For chapters on French, German and English science, see Merz, *op. cit.*, I, 89-301.

ORIGIN OF MODERN PSYCHOLOGY
WITHIN SCIENCE

CHAPTER 2

Psychophysiology in the First Half of the Nineteenth Century

We have said that experimental psychology was getting its start within experimental physiology during the first half of the nineteenth century. Now we must see what that statement means.

There were, if we note only what is obvious and important for psychology, between 1800 and 1850 nine important developments, all but two of which belong as much in the history of physiology as in the history of psychology. We may list them here and then go on to discuss four of them, leaving the other five to the separate chapters which follow.

(1) *Sensory and motor nerves.* Were they different? Galen had said they were, but they were usually thought to be passive conductors of the animal spirits. The notion of reflected (reflex) action implied that the animal spirits, passing in from the sense-organs along one nerve, were reflected out to muscles along others. In 1811 Sir Charles Bell published privately his discovery that the sensory fibers of a mixed nerve enter the spinal cord at a posterior (dorsal) nerve root, whereas the motor fibers of the same nerve leave the cord by an anterior (ventral) root. Magendie made the same discovery later in 1822, without knowing of Bell's work, and there was some controversy as to the scientific priority. The effect of this discovery was to separate nerve-physiology into the study of sensory and motor functions, of sensation and movement. We shall return to this matter later in the present chapter.

(2) *Specific nerve energies.* The next thing that happened was the division of the sensory fibers into kinds. Johannes Müller in 1826 argued for five kinds, one for each of the five senses, and he characterized the different kinds as having five different specific energies. The idea was not new with Müller. Charles Bell had already made the same argument in that privately printed paper of 1811. Thomas Young had suggested in 1801 that color vision could be accounted for

by three different kinds of visual fibers. John Locke's conception of secondary qualities (1690) implied that he thought that nerves are not mere passive conductors of the properties of the perceived objects, which is what Müller said he was chiefly arguing against. Müller made his 'doctrine' formal in 1838, and not so many years later Helmholtz hailed it as a principle as important for psychology as is the conservation of energy for physics. (That was another principle which Helmholtz had helped to get established—in the 1840s.) Later Helmholtz extended the doctrine of specific energies to account for different qualities within each sense—three energies for colors, a thousand or more for tonal pitches, and so on. This whole affair is discussed fully in Chapter 5.

(3) *Sensation*. There was a great deal of good work being done on the sense-organs and in the phenomenology of sensation in this period. Most of it was on vision. In the preceding chapter we noted the contributions of Goethe (1810) and Purkinje (1825). It was through his book on visual phenomena (1826) that Johannes Müller first became well known. That work in vision should precede work on the other senses was largely a consequence of the fact that, after mechanics, optics was the first special topic to establish itself within physics. The early interest in optics was due in part to the interest in astronomy and telescopes (Kepler recognized that the eye is an optical instrument) and the earlier interest in mathematics (there is a geometry of light; Euclid wrote an *Optics*). From the Egyptians to Kepler and Descartes there is a serial development of interests which runs: agriculture, the seasons, the celestial bodies, astronomy, telescopes, optics, the eye.

There was in this period some good experimentation upon hearing, Ohm's acoustic law, which asserts that the ear performs a Fourier analysis upon 'complex' sound waves, resolving them into harmonic components, was put forward in 1843. The outstanding and classical research, however, was E. H. Weber's on touch, which he published first in Latin in 1834 and then brought together in German with later results in 1848. That is the work on errors of localization and the cutaneous discrimination of paired stimulations. From these data he developed his doctrine of 'sensory circles,' a theory that anticipates the projection theory of space perception.

All this early work on sensation is considered separately in Chapter 6.

(4) *Phrenology*. Certainly Gall intended that phrenology should be psychophysiology when about 1800 he began his campaign to show that the various mental functions depend each specifically on its

proper region in the brain, that excess in one function results from an enlargement of the brain (and hence of the skull) in the corresponding region. Such a ready means for diagnosing personality by observation of people's crania made this specious doctrine immensely popular and excited many of the scientists of the day to combat it and to enquire further into the nature of the localization of brain functions. The history of phrenology and what the scientists thought about it is discussed in Chapter 3.

(5) *Localization of function in the brain.* The question of the bodily localization of such mental functions as sensation, intellect and emotion is very old, but in the nineteenth century, stimulated presently by the claims of phrenology, physiologists settled down to an acceptance of Galen's dictum that the brain is the organ of the mind and began to try to determine experimentally how much more specific the localization of functions in the brain could be. The most famous name early in the century is Flourens'. He opposed Gall and argued that there are specific functions which are narrowly localized in the brain and also general functions which depend upon larger portions of the brain. The view that mental functions are not too precisely localized persisted until after the middle of the century, when Broca reported in 1861 that he had found a specific center for speech, and Fritsch and Hitzig showed in 1870 that electrical stimulation of a series of spots in a given region of the cerebral cortex gave rise to the specific activation of different muscle groups. On these matters and what came after them, see Chapter 4.

(6) *Reflex action.* The notion that the movements of animals and some of the movements of men might be automatic and involuntary goes back to Descartes (d. 1650) and was fostered later by such French materialists as La Mettrie (1748) and Cabanis (1802). The word *reflex* in the modern physiological sense dates from 1736. The first important experimental results on reflex action were published by Robert Whytt in 1751. In the nineteenth century the important name is Marshall Hall's. In 1832 he insisted on the distinction between voluntary and involuntary action and thus started the controversy between the physiologist Pflüger and the philosopher-psychologist Lotze on whether reflexes from the spinal cord are conscious. Pflüger held that the cord reflexes are specifically useful, therefore show purpose, and, being purposeful, must be conscious. Lotze held that the brain is the organ of consciousness and that action which goes on only in the cord must therefore be unconscious. In those days—as indeed a full century afterward—men thought of consciousness as something that either exists or does not exist in a given event, not as a name

for a functional relation like discriminatory reaction. We shall come back to the history of reflex action later in this chapter.

(7) *Electrical nature of the nerve impulse.* The first wet battery was a frog's leg. Physics and physiology helped each other in learning about electricity. In the eighteenth century friction machines for generating static electricity were known, and Leyden jars for collecting charges. Franklin's experiment with the kite in the thunder storm was made in 1774. The nerve impulse, on the other hand, was thought to be animal spirits, or *succus nerveus*, or *vis viva*, or *vis nervosa*. Then in 1780 Galvani discovered that a frog's leg would twitch when the inside and outside of the muscle were connected in series with two different metals. By 1791 Galvani had constructed 'wet-cell batteries' out of frogs' legs. In 1800 Volta, with disks of two metals piled up with disks of brine-soaked cardboard in between, created the Voltaic pile which generated direct current. By 1811 a galvanometer had been constructed, and presently it was made more sensitive. Then in 1827 Ohm formulated his law of simple circuits and in 1831 Faraday discovered electromagnetic induction and thus the means for the faradic currents which experimental physiology uses for nerve stimulation. It was on such a foundation that du Bois-Reymond worked out his classical researches on animal electricity (1848-1849), studies which made use of the galvanometer to show that an electric impulse in a nerve is, as Bernstein later called it (1866), an electrical wave of negativity passing down the nerve. These early ideas led by the end of the century to the principle of refractoriness, and shortly thereafter to the all-or-none theory of conduction. We return to this matter later in the present chapter.

(8) *Velocity of the nerve impulse.* Men of science, down to and including Johannes Müller, had believed that the propagation of the nerve impulse is either instantaneous or very rapid indeed. Müller thought it must be comparable to the speed of light. That belief is consistent with the verdict of introspection which does not show that the perception of the movement of one's own muscles lags appreciably behind the conscious act of will to move the muscle. But Helmholtz in 1850 measured the speed of propagation in a frog's nerve and found it to be less than 50 meters per second, which is less than 100 miles per hour and hence less than one-eighth the velocity of sound. The incredulity with which his finding was at first greeted soon gave way to a conviction that some of the mysteries of the mind and of its physical agent, the nervous system, might be expected to yield to experimental control and measurement. This research of Helmholtz's is discussed again later in the present chapter.

(9) *The personal equation.* Meanwhile the astronomers had been discovering that human reaction time is both slow and variable. Having trouble in estimating to a fraction of a second the time of observation of the transit of a star, they began comparing themselves with each other and writing equations which specified the average lag of observation for one astronomer as compared with another—a *personal equation*, as they called it. That was in the 1820s. Later, when the development of the electromagnetic circuit made the construction of chronographs possible, they determined—in the 1850s —what they called the *absolute personal equation*, that is to say, the reaction time of the subject in making a movement as rapidly as he can after perceiving a signal. This discovery that mental processes take time and that the times can be measured had a great deal to do with the reaction-time researches and the 'mental chronometry' of the new psychology in the second half of the nineteenth century. Chapter 8 discusses the personal equation and the beginnings of this movement.

And that is our précis of the history of experimental psychology during this half century in so far as the events took place within physiology or in one case within physics and in another within astronomy. These men did not think of themselves as psychologists nor of their subject-matter as psychology. They were physiologists, physicists or astronomers. There were no scientists who styled themselves *psychologists* until well after 1860. All along there was, however, progress in the conventional history of psychology, the philosophers' attack on the problems of mind and of knowing, the British empiricists and associationists, Descartes and his tradition in France, Leibnitz, Kant and Herbart in Germany. We shall see eventually how natural science and mental philosophy came together in the middle of the nineteenth century to create what was later called the new psychology, experimental psychology or scientific psychology. First, however, we must examine these events, which, being the property of the physiologists of the earlier half of the nineteenth century, constituted the psychophysiological knowledge and the experimental psychology of that period.

SENSORY AND MOTOR NERVES: BELL AND MAGENDIE

Sir Charles Bell (1774-1842) was a brilliant physiologist, anatomist, surgeon and lecturer. Born in Edinburgh, he achieved fame in London and retired to Edinburgh at the age of sixty-two in order to gain more leisure for research. His prestige among scientists was great, at first in Great Britain only, but later also in France. He discovered the fact of the difference between sensory and motor nerves, anticipated Johannes Müller on the principle of specific nerve energies, established the muscle sense as a sense-department and described the reciprocal innervation of flexor and extensor muscles.

This fact of the anatomical and functional discreteness of sensory and motor nerves is known sometimes as Bell's law, but better as the Bell-Magendie law, for Magendie made the discovery independently though later and performed the more convincing experiment. This is the rule that the posterior (dorsal) roots of the spinal cord contain only sensory fibers and the anterior (ventral) roots only motor fibers. The two kinds of fibers may be combined in a single nerve; only in their connections with the cord are they always separate. Later Bell, extending his study to cranial nerves, showed that some nerves are entirely sensory, some entirely motor, and some mixed. He observed further that no motor fibers ever pass through a spinal ganglion. He suggested that this differentiation in the nerves indicates that separate sensory and motor tracts in the spinal cord and separate regions in the brain might be found.

There is little danger of overestimating the importance of these discoveries for the physiology of the nervous system. Thereafter the nerves were no longer to be regarded as transmitting promiscuously 'the powers of motion and sensation.' Bell established the fundamental dichotomy of sensory and motor functions and also what was called later 'the law of forward direction in the nervous system,' that is to say, the fact that conduction in a nerve normally occurs in only one direction. This law is basal to the conception of reflex action and the reflex arc. Even in his lifetime, Bell came to be ranked with Harvey. There is the story that Roux, the celebrated French physiologist, on the occasion of a visit from Bell, dismissed his class without a lecture, exclaiming: "C'est assez, messieurs, vous avez vu Charles Bell!"

Bell had come to his general conclusion about the spinal roots as early as 1807, working on his research until late at night and lecturing enthusiastically about his discoveries in the morning. He described sectioning the posterior nerve root without obtaining any convulsion of muscles, but obtaining violent muscular action when he touched the anterior root with his knife. He published his results in 1811 in a pamphlet of which only one hundred copies were printed for the information of his friends. Thus it came about that Magendie presently made similar experiments without knowing about Bell's. Magendie cut the posterior root, could get no movement by pricking or pressing the limb, and was about to conclude that the limb was paralyzed when the animal moved it spontaneously. Magendie concluded that the limb was not paralyzed but anesthetic. Then Magendie tried cutting the anterior root and found that he then had paralysis, for he could get no movement in it at all, whether the posterior root was cut or not, unless he stimulated the distal end of the anterior cut. Magendie's experiment was more thorough than Bell's and thus more convincing. History has settled the heated controversy that arose about priority of this discovery by naming the law of the spinal nerve roots for both men.

With the fundamental distinction among nerves so clearly before him, it is not surprising that Bell should have sought for further subdivisions among the nerves. He anticipated—in this pamphlet of 1811— Johannes Müller's definite formulation of the doctrine of specific nerve energies. He argued that the five senses are mediated respectively by five different kinds of nerves, and he added to the list in 1826 a sixth sense, the muscle sense. Bell also discussed what he called the "nervous circle," showing that sensation from muscle is necessary for good motor control. He also observed the fact of reciprocal innervation between extensor and flexor muscles, but missed the fact of inhibition by thinking that the reciprocal mechanism must lie at the periphery and not in the central nervous system.

François Magendie (1783-1855) was the foremost physiologist in France at the time that Bell was the leading physiologist in Great Britain. The two men contrasted in temperament Bell was an enthusiastic, dramatic investigator. Magendie was slow, cautious, conservative and contemplative, and it is possible that Bell's priority on this matter of the spinal nerve roots may have in part been due to his greater impetuosity as well as the fact that he was nine years older than Magendie. Magendie, the more deliberate, was ultimately the more convincing. Bell, socially responsive, published his results privately "for the observations of his friends," but Magendie published in a standard scientific journal. No wonder Magendie did not know about Bell's work. Magendie had been elected to the Académie des Sciences in 1819, just before his research on the nerve roots. He was appointed to the chair of anatomy in the Collège de France in 1831. He accomplished important research—on the blood, for instance— but he enters this book only because of his establishment of the distinction between sensory and motor nerves.

JOHANNES MÜLLER'S "HANDBUCH"

Johannes Müller bore somewhat the relation to Bell that Wundt later bore to Helmholtz. Bell was the brilliant investigator whose

success in research necessitated the reformulation of certain fundamental problems. Müller was also an investigator, but he is known
best for his systematic *Handbuch der Physiologie des Menschen*
(1833-1840), an exhaustive work of more than three quarters of a
million German words, depicting the physiology of the day and presenting a multitude of original observations and conjectures. He received his doctorate at Bonn in 1822, the year when Magendie
published his investigations on the spinal nerve roots. He remained at
Bonn as *Privatdozent* and professor until 1833, when he was called to
the chair of anatomy and physiology at Berlin. This was a post of
great distinction and served to mark Müller as the foremost authority
on physiology of his day, and his *Handbuch*, translated immediately
into English, as the primary systematic treatise. His subsequent influence has, therefore, been proportionately great. Helmholtz,
Brücke, du Bois-Reymond and Ludwig, all famous later, were among
his pupils. (On the way in which the four young brilliant physiologists agreed in 1845 to fight vitalism, see p. 708.)

The reader who has followed the very brief outline of the development of anatomy and physiology from Galen (*ca.* 175) to Vesalius
(*ca.* 1550) to Harvey (1616) to Haller (1752) to Bell (1811) must
not gain the impression that we have noted anything like the full expansion of knowledge. Especially during the preceding two and a
half centuries, a vast amount of patient investigation had been accomplished. If the reader will turn to Johannes Müller's *Handbuch*, he
will see that in the fourth decade of the nineteenth century there was
a great amount of physiological knowledge available, most of it
identical in its gross facts with the accepted physiology of today.
He will also gain some impression from the foot-notes of the large
amount of competent physiological investigation that was going on
in this first third of the century.

Müller's *Handbuch* was written on broad and exhaustive lines. It
is divided into eight books, the subject-matter of which gives some
notion of the breadth of physiological knowledge at that period. The
first book deals with the circulation of the blood and the lymph (288
pages). The second considers chemical matters of respiration,
nutrition, growth, reproduction, secretion, digestion, chylification,
and excretion (308 pages). The third is on the physiology of the
nerves (270 pages). Books iv, v, and vi constitute what might be
regarded as the experimental psychology of that period, and book iii
might be added to this group. The fourth book is on muscular movement in general and voice and speech in particular (248 pages),
adding to the third book's consideration of reflex action, a new con-

ception. The fifth book is devoted to the five senses and begins with the formulation of the famous doctrine of the specific energies of nerve substances (256 pages). The sixth book entitled "Of the Mind," deals with association, memory, imagination, thought, feeling, passion, the problem of mind and body, phantasms, action, temperament, and sleep—a truly psychological chapter (82 pages)! The last two books are on reproduction and development, embryonic and postnatal (179 pages).

Historically, the psychological portions of the *Handbuch* (books iv to vi) are the most important, but to Müller's treatment of sensation and sensory physiology we are to return later. Here we must mention particularly the matter of reflex action.

REFLEX ACTION

The gross phenomenon of reflex movement had long been known. Even Galen had described what we now call the pupillary reflex. The word *reflex* was first used by Astruc in 1736 and it meant simply "reflected" or "reflection," as in a mirror. Astruc thought of the animal spirits of sensation as reflected by the spinal cord or the brain through other nerves to produce movement. "As with light, angles of incidence and reflection are equal, so that a sensation produced by a concussion of the animal spirits against the fibrous columns [of the spinal cord] is reflected and causes motion in those nerve tubes which happen to be placed directly in the line of reflection."

In 1751 a Scot, Robert Whytt (1714-1766), published *An Essay on the Vital and Other Involuntary Motions of Animals*. He described experiments with frogs, showing that the spinal cord was both necessary and sufficient for the many automatic movements which occur in response to stimulation when the cord is severed from the brain. He showed also that reflected movement can occur when only a portion of the cord is available. He emphasized the distinction between voluntary movements which are the result of an act of will and involuntary ("spontaneous," "automatic") movements which occur instantaneously with "no time for the exercise of reason." Whytt believed that the production of movement by stimulation depends on a "sentient principle" in the nervous substance and that this principle is coextensive with mind. Thus he was arguing that reflex movement is involuntary, dependent upon the cord, independent of reason and will, yet dependent upon this sentient principle. Thus for Whytt the reflexes were almost, but not quite, unconscious.

That question as to whether involuntary movement is unconscious was to trouble psychophysiology for a long time. Influenced by Descartes and the theological necessity for keeping the immortal soul distinct from the mortal body, the usual view of the mind-body relationship, before psychophysical parallelism took over in the middle of the nineteenth century, was interactionistic. Body affects mind, and mind body. It was hard then to see how a sensation, having got into the mind, could create movement except under the sponsorship of the will. It was against this belief in the pervasiveness of the will in action that Whytt directed his monograph on involuntary movement, and he went more than half the way. He pointed out that habitual actions, like walking, occur without the continued exercise of the will or the knowledge of the actor, but he held on to his conception of a 'sentient principle' that was involved in sense-determined action, even when the action was effected by the spinal cord alone.

There were three other men who contributed to the knowledge and conception of reflex action during the eighteenth century. Albrecht von Haller (pp. 16 f.), publishing both before and after Whytt, described the action of muscle excised from the organism, with special attention to the long continued action of intestinal and heart muscle. These observations led Haller to substitute for Glisson's notion of irritability (pp. 16 f.) his own concept of the *vis insita*, a principle of action which, being local, is involuntary and unconscious. Then there was Unzer (1727-1799) who in 1771 discussed Haller's doctrine, reported the results of experiments upon the sectioning of the nerves and the cord in a frog, and emphasized again the distinction between voluntary and involuntary movement. In 1784 Prochaska (1749-1820) described more experiments on frogs with sectioned cords, and argued that this kind of action depends upon two factors, the *vis nervosa* and the *sensorium commune*. All nervous substance possesses *vis nervosa*, which does not, however, act alone. In reflected action the *vis nervosa* is activated through the *sensorium commune*, which exists in the brain, the medulla, and the spinal cord. The resulting action, Prochaska held, is automatic and not voluntary.

In the first half of the nineteenth century Marshall Hall and Johannes Müller were the chief contributors to the knowledge of reflex action. Hall reported his work in 1832, published it in 1833. Müller made his first report in the second *Abtheilung* of his *Handbuch* in 1834, acknowledging Hall's priority. Hall held that the reflexes depend only on the cord, never on the brain, and are always unconscious. Müller thought that some reflexes are mediated by the brain. Otherwise their views were alike.

Marshall Hall (1790-1857) was a Scot and a brilliant physician, working in London, where he contributed to the Royal Society the reports of many important physiological researches. He was studying circulation in the lungs and experimenting for this purpose with a decapitated newt, when he discovered that the brainless newt responded to stimulation of its skin. He then tried an experiment on a snake, dividing its spinal cord between the second and third vertebrae. "From the moment of the division of the spinal marrow it [the snake] lay perfectly tranquil and motionless, with the exception of occasional gaspings and slight movements of the head. It became evident that this state of quiescence would continue indefinitely were the animal secured from all external impressions. Being now stimulated, the body began to move with great activity, and continued to do so for a considerable time, each change of position or situation bringing some fresh part of the surface of the animal into contact with the table or other objects and renewing the application of stimulants. At length the animal became again quiescent; and being carefully protected from all external impressions it moved no more, but died in the precise position and form which it had last assumed."

On the basis of such experiments, Hall undertook to clarify the confusion about voluntary and involuntary, conscious and unconscious movement, that had been left over from the eighteenth century. He distinguished four kinds of bodily movement: (1) voluntary movement, dependent upon consciousness and the action of the cerebrum; (2) respiratory movement, involuntary and dependent upon the vital center in the medulla; (3) involuntary movement, dependent on muscular irritability under direct stimulation (Glisson's *irritability*, Haller's *vis insita*); and (4) reflex movement, dependent only upon the spinal cord, independent of the brain and consciousness. That doctrine made sense at the time. It distinguished the reflex from the other kinds of movement, stressing the fact that the reflected movements are consequent upon sensory stimulation, and thus preparing the way for the concept of the reflex arc which came later.

Marshall Hall was an enthusiastic person who both attracted followers and stirred up opposition. His report of his discoveries was vehemently attacked on the ground that he had found nothing new that Whytt and Prochaska had not already described. The dates on which he had borrowed Prochaska's monograph from the library of the Medical and Chirurgical Society were even brought out in evidence. (The facts: he read his first report when he was elected to the Royal Society in 1832, published it in 1833, read Prochaska in 1835, published a second report in 1837 without mention of Prochaska.) It is, indeed, not clear that Hall made any important new discoveries about reflex action. Whytt, Unzer and Prochaska had all shown that action in response to stimulation can be mediated by the cord when it is severed from the brain. On the other hand, Hall's experiments were striking, and a snake's long spinal cord is good material for sectioning. It is certain that Hall clarified thought on the matter of reflected, involuntary and unconscious movements, making the whole business seem important by the force of his personality. The controversy also helped to get attention for an important matter. Any promoter or advertiser knows that for getting attention denunciation is somewhat better than active support and, of course, ever so much better than being overlooked.

Marshall Hall's conclusion that the spinal reflexes are unconscious was attacked in 1853 by the German physiologist, Pflüger. Pflüger argued that consciousness is a function of all nervous action, that you can not distinguish between the action of the brain and the cord, and that spinal reflexes must therefore be regarded as conscious. He pointed out that these reflexes are purposive in the sense that they are specifically localized and useful to the organism. The frog's leg scratches the exact point where its skin has been irritated by the application of acid. Later in the same year Lotze, the philosopher who had so much to do with the founding of the new physiological psychology, reviewed Pflüger's monograph and supported the opposite view. He noted the evidence for consciousness' depending on the brain, human testimony as to the unconscious nature of many involuntary movements, and the fact that reflexes, while useful in ordinary situations, do not adapt themselves to changed situations. In 1853 the conditioning of reflexes was still half a century away in the future. Conscious action, Lotze held, is purposive because it adjusts the organism to novel events. It was natural for Pflüger, the physiologist, to appeal to the comparability of all nervous action, and quite as natural for Lotze, the philosopher. to rely on the evidence of introspection.

This problem is, of course, insoluble because the answer to it depends on the definition of consciousness. You can define consciousness so as to exclude spinal reflexes or to include them. There is a semantic legerdemain by which the reaction of iron filings to a magnet appears to be conscious. Lotze and Pflüger were, however, writing in a period when the dualism of mind and body was accepted as basic truth. They never would have been convinced that they were dealing with a 'pseudoproblem' that consisted only in a choice of definitions. In those days *die Seele* was mind and consciousness and will and soul, and the establishment of its physiological correlates was very important.

In the second half of the nineteenth century the new psychology got under way, and, although it was called *physiological psychology*, it was organized as the psychology of consciousness. Marshall Hall's conclusion that reflexes are unconscious was accepted. These unconscious reflexes were relegated to physiology, while the new psychology busied itself with voluntary action and especially with reaction times. It was convenient to believe for a few decades that the line between the conscious and the unconscious is clear and that the distinction between them can be used to delimit psychology (even "physiological psychology"!) from physiology. This differentiation broke down again in the twentieth century with Pavlov's discovery that unconscious movements can be learned (conditioned reflex), with Freud's discovery that most motives and some thinking are unconscious, and with the general rise of behavioristics as a protest against the 'mentalism' that Descartes' dualism had fixed upon the would-be new science.

THE ELECTRICAL NATURE OF THE NERVOUS IMPULSE

We have just noted how the knowledges of electrical currents and of the nervous impulse developed together, even though the nervous impulse is not an electric current. The seventeenth century furnished the means for generating static electricity and the eighteenth made it more available for use by the invention of the Leyden jar (1745). It was toward the end of this time that Galvani began his experiments on the stimulation of frogs' legs (nerve-muscle preparations) by electric discharges. By 1791 he had discovered that he could produce a kick in the leg by connecting the cut end with a part of the outside through two rods of different metals. His initial discovery was that a leg, with the nerve and a piece of the spinal cord attached, when hung from an iron trellis by a brass hook that passed through the piece of the cord, would twitch when discharges from an electric machine or a Leyden jar occurred in the vicinity or when lightning flashed in a thunder storm. Later he found that he could make the leg kick at any time by touching the nerve with a rod of one metal, the foot with a rod of another metal, and the two rods together. Here he actually had a wet battery furnishing the current to make the muscle twitch. A frog's leg, suspended by its nerve from a brass hook connected with the ground and with its foot touching a silver plate that was also grounded, would continue to kick indefinitely, because each kick broke the connection and allowed the leg to drop back to the plate to complete the circuit again. From these experiments Galvani concluded that animal tissues generate electricity and he wrote *De viribus electricitatis in motu musculari* in 1791.

That was the beginning of the belief in animal electricity. There was already established an interest in "animal magnetism." Mesmer, who had used iron magnets to cure patients of diseases in 1766 and thereafter, and who then found that he could effect the same cures without the iron magnets, concluded that it must be his own animal magnetism which was at work (p. 117). Galvani did not know that he had constructed the first electric battery, nor that the sort of continuous direct current which it generated would eventually be called, not animal electricity, but, after him, *galvanic current*. Electricity was still mysterious.

It was Volta who showed that this kind of electricity can be had without animal tissue. In 1800 he built what was later called a Voltaic pile—a pile of disks—silver, brine-moistened cardboard, zinc; silver, moist cardboard, zinc; silver, cardboard, zinc; and so on. The pile maintained a voltage between its topmost and bottommost disk. Volta thought that he had disproved the fact of animal electricity by constructing this inorganic battery, but Johannes Müller in 1834 still thought that the nerve impulse might be electrical, especially since its conduction is so rapid.

The discovery by Volta of means for producing galvanic currents led to the construction of a galvanometer for measuring the current and later to its refinement. Several physiologists presently became interested in the problems of animal electricity. In 1841 Matteucci presented to the Académie des Sciences a paper which showed that a galvanometer indicates a current flowing when it is connected from the surface of a muscle to a wound in the muscle, a current that was later called the *current of injury* and also the *current of rest*, since it flowed without observable muscular contraction. Johannes Müller showed this paper of Matteucci's to his brilliant pupil, du Bois-Reymond, who later succeeded Müller in the chair at Berlin. Du Bois' interest was caught at once. He published his first paper on *thierische Elektricität* in 1843, and his two volumes on the subject—soon to become the classic—in 1848-1849. He formulated what amounts to a theory of the polarization of animal tissues, for he suggested that muscle and nerve consist of electrically charged particles, with a positive charge on one face and a negative opposite. These particles, he argued, would orient themselves in the way the magnetized particles are supposed to make up a big magnet with a north pole at one end and a south at the other. His theory was wrong; yet du Bois advanced thought because he pointed toward the current concept of polarization.

It was these experiments of du Bois' that brought the nervous impulse out of the mystic realm of animal spirits and the pneumatics of the soul into the realm of materialistic science, suggesting to Helmholtz that the velocity of the impulse may not be instantaneous but finite and measurable. To that matter, so important for the establishment of a scientific psychology, we turn next.

THE VELOCITY AND CONDUCTION OF THE NERVOUS IMPULSE

It had been supposed that transmission of the nervous impulse was so rapid as to be practically unmeasurable. Johannes Müller in his *Handbuch* mentions three values that had been given. "Haller calculated that the nervous fluid moves with a velocity of 9,000 feet in a minute; Sauvages estimated the rate of its motion at 32,400, and another physiologist at 57,600 million feet in a second." It will be seen that Haller's estimate is 150 feet per second, which is close enough to the truth, since nerve velocity varies from 3 to 400 feet per second, depending on the diameter of the conducting fiber. The last figure cited by Müller is almost sixty times the velocity of light. This value had been arrived at by assuming that the rate of flow of animal spirits in the nervous tubes and of the blood in the arteries would be the same for vessels of the same size, and would vary inversely with the size of the vessel. Müller did not give credence to this logic, but he did accept the general belief that the rate of transmission is extremely rapid, perhaps of the order of the velocity of light. He wrote: "We shall probably never attain the power of measuring the velocity of nervous action; for we have not the opportunity of comparing its propagation through immense space, as we have in the case of light."

It was not many years, however, before his erstwhile pupil Helmholtz (pp. 297-315) measured the rate and found it to be much slower even than sound, in fact, only about ninety feet per second and less in a frog's motor nerve. He performed this experiment while he was professor of physiology at Königsberg, measuring the delay of the muscle twitch for different lengths of nerve on the myograph, which he had newly invented. To determine the time in sensory nerves—for, since the establishment of the Bell-Magendie law, it was not safe to assume that sensory nerves would have the same properties as motor nerves—he instituted reaction experiments, then already coming into use in astronomy for the determination of the personal equation (pp. 140-142). He stimulated a man upon the toe and upon the thigh, noting the difference in the reaction time. By this method he placed the rate of transmission for sensory impulses at between fifty and 100 meters per second. These times were measured more accurately later and corrected by du Bois-Reymond.

The importance for scientific psychology of the discovery that the transmission of the nervous impulse is not practically instantaneous, but relatively slow, is not to be underestimated. In the period under consideration, the mind had come to be largely identified with the brain, but the personality seemed rather to be a matter of the entire organism. Every one thought, as the average man thinks now, of his hand as of a piece with himself. To move his finger voluntarily was an act of mind in itself, not a later event caused by a previous act of mind. To separate the movement in time from the event of will that caused it was in a sense to separate the body from the mind, and almost from the personality or self. At any rate, Helmholtz's discovery was a step in the analysis of bodily motion that changed it from an instantaneous occurrence to a temporal series of events, and it thus contributed to the materialistic view of the psychophysical organism that was the essence of nineteenth century science. Johannes Müller's doctrine of the specific energy of nerves had served the purpose of a similar analysis on the sensory side. In Helmholtz's experiment lay the preparation for all the later work of experimental psychology on the chronometry of mental acts and reaction times. The most important effect of the experiment and all the research that followed upon it was, however, that it brought the soul to time, as it were, measured what had been ineffable, actually captured the essential agent of mind in the toils of natural science.

After Helmholtz, Bernstein was able in 1866 to describe the impulse as a *wave of negativity* passing along the nerve. He found that the surface of the nerve, as the impulse passes along it, becomes electrically negative to the surface ahead of the impulse and behind it. Since a region of injury in the nerve is also negative to the normal surface, the impulse was seen to be acting like an injury moving rapidly down the nerve. An injury is, however, simply the exposure of the inside of the nerve to an outside electrode, and Bernstein by 1871 was clear that the impulse consists in the spreading of the negative charge inside of the nerve to the positive outside. That view became in 1902, under Bernstein's *aegis* and with the help of the newly invented capillary electrometer, the membrane theory of nerve conduction, the theory which accounts for the wave of negativity as a wave of *electrical depolarization*. In these terms it became possible to measure not only the speed of the impulse but also its duration in passing.

Next the physiologists discovered *refractory phase*, the fact that immediately after the impulse has passed the nerve remains inexcitable for a brief period during which recovery of excitability is taking place. In 1874 Kronecker described the refractory period of heart muscle. In 1876 Marey supplied the name *refractory phase*. It was not, however, until 1899 that Gotch and Burch found that the same principle holds for nerve excitation. Then in 1912 Adrian and Lucas, with improved apparatus, were able to distinguish between the absolute refractory period, during which no stimulus is strong enough to excite the nerve, and the immediately subsequent relative refractory period, during which excitability increases and finally (after passing through a supernormal phase) returns to normal. They could even plot the curve of recovery. The whole process took about .03 seconds for frog's nerve.

At the same time the *all-or-none principle* was being discovered, the fact that a muscle or nerve fiber supplies the energy for the impulse and is completely discharged when excited at all. Bowditch showed in 1871 that this principle holds for heart muscle. Lucas showed in 1905 that it applies to skeletal muscle. He named it in 1909. Lucas and Adrian together are responsible for showing that the law applies to nerve. Lucas died suddenly in 1916 and Adrian published his lectures.

The *membrane theory* of nerve conduction was developed along with these discoveries of the nature of conduction. Ostwald had proposed the theory in 1890. Bernstein had amplified and established it in 1902. R. S. Lillie in 1909 began a series of experiments which supported it. The theory accounts for the facts of refractory phase and all-or-none transmission, and was well on toward acceptance among physiologists by 1920.

NERVE PHYSIOLOGY AS A PARADIGM OF SCIENTIFIC PROGRESS

We may pause here to note how these events illustrate the nature of scientific progress.

(1) Progress is continuous when viewed in large perspective, but intermittent and irregular when examined for small intervals of time. There were decades when nothing of great importance happened, yet a steady development from 1790 to 1920 nonetheless.

(2) Discovery depends upon previous discovery. The series, Galvani—Volta—du Bois-Reymond—Helmholtz—Bernstein—Lucas—Adrian—Lillie, labels a continuous development by noting eight successive prominent features of it. Lesser names would have to be introduced in a more precise account, as well as the names of persons

on the outside of the main trend, like Kronecker, Bowditch, Ostwald.

(3) Parallel lines of development touch and facilitate each other at times. Physics and physiology were thus related here. It was out of a frog's leg that Galvani chanced to construct the first electric battery, but later advance in the knowledge of nerve conduction waited on the availability of galvanic currents and of sensitive galvanometers. Du Bois could not have made his discoveries thirty years earlier for the means were not yet available. Similarly Bernstein had to wait thirty years (1871 to 1902) for the invention of the capillary electrometer to confirm his views on the nature of the nervous impulse.

There were like relations between physiology and psychology. Helmholtz' discovery that the nerve impulses take considerable time supported the other discovery that reaction takes time and that under some circumstances response to stimulation may be delayed in the nervous system. The preoccupation of the early experimental psychologists with consciousness tended to separate them from the physiologists for a time, so much so that there was a lag of approximately a decade before psychologists realized that the all-or-none theory of nerve-fiber conduction meant that they might no longer explain variation of sensory intensity as being due to degrees of excitation in the single sensory fiber.

(4) The fundamental concepts, which make up the particular *Zeitgeist* for a given topic, change under the pressure of new discovery, slowly and against resistance, yet inevitably when there are new concepts to supplant the old. The big event of the nineteenth century for psychology was the discovery of scientific men that the mind can be brought to time by the methods of natural science. The century began with the acceptance of Kant's dictum that psychology can not be experimental. Herbart in 1824 was saying that psychology can be *Wissenschaft* but not experimental. In 1850 Johannes Müller hesitated to accept Helmholtz' measurement of the rate of the nervous impulse, partly because he thought the soul is unitary and can not be divided. By the end of the century there were important psychologists, among them William James, who held that sensation, a conscious entity to be known by introspection, does not vary in degree but only in kind. ("Our feeling of pink is surely not a portion of our feeling of scarlet," said James.) Yet measurement and analysis were winning the day and nothing helped that advance more than the continuous reduction of the nervous system, the mind's agent, to measurement and finite control.

Viewed in the larger perspective, one can see Helmholtz' measurement of the velocity of the nervous impulse, an experiment which fits in naturally between du Bois' earlier and Bernstein's later work, as an event that would almost inevitably have occurred under some agency in the 1850s—or at least in the 1860s—if Helmholtz had not been there to have the simple insight that is so obvious in retrospect. All the same this discovery constitutes a point of anchorage in the history of psychology. The measurement was made in the middle of the century, exactly at 1850 as it happened, and just as psychology was getting ready to declare its immediate independence of both philosophy and physiology. It was also in 1850 that Fechner thought of the way for measuring sensation. His laborious experiments were mostly completed in the 1850s and his *Elemente der Psychophysik* came out in 1860. In the late 1850s the young Wundt, who had been only eighteen when Helmholtz performed this experiment, was lecturing on how the new experimental science of physiological psychology could be brought about. Helmholtz himself was busy with the experimental psychology of vision from 1852 on. Certainly the experiment on nerve-velocity could not have caused all this activity; rather it was part of the activity. Yet it was so dramatic that it did more than any other single bit of research to advertise the fact that mind is not ineffable but a proper subject for experimental control and observation by him who is wise enough to conceive the necessary means.

NOTES

Bell and Magendie

Sir Charles Bell's famous statement of his law of the spinal nerve roots is entitled *Idea of a New Anatomy of the Brain: Submitted for the Observations of His Friends*. It was a privately printed monograph of only 100 copies, issued in 1811. It is no wonder that Magendie did not know of this brochure. It has been reprinted first in *J. Anat. and Physiol.*, 1869, 3, 153-166, together with relevant letters and notes, 147-182; and again, with a German translation, as *Idee einer neuen Hirnanatomie*, 1911; and most recently in W. Dennis, *Readings in the History of Psychology*, 1948, 113-124.

There was also a third contender for priority in the matter of the discovery of this law—Alexander Walker, who published in 1809. This statement seems, however, rather a faulty plagiarism of Bell's lectures, and in it the

functions of the anterior and posterior roots are, by some strange mistake, reversed.

On this controversy, on Bell's contributions to physiological psychology, on the life of Bell, and for references on all these subjects, see the excellent account by L. Carmichael, Sir Charles Bell: a contribution to the history of physiological psychology, *Psychol. Rev.*, 1926, 33, 183-217. See also C. Eckhard, Geschichte der Leitungsverhältnisse in den Wurzeln der Rückenmarksnerven, *Beiträge Anat. Physiol. von C. Eckhard*, 1883, 10, 135-169.

Bell published a systematic text of dissection in 1798. In 1804 he contributed the sections on the nervous system to an *Anatomy of the Human Body* under the authorship of himself and his brother. His most important books from our point of view are the *Anatomy of Expression*, 1806, and *The Nervous System of the Human Body*,

1830, which sums up his researches from 1807 to 1829.

F. Magendie's first publication on the functions of spinal nerve roots is to be found in *J. physiol. expér. pathol.*, 1822, 2, 276-279, 366-371. See pp. 369 ff. for his comment on Bell's priority and his own independence. His most important book from our point of view is *Leçons sur les fonctions et les maladies du système nerveux*, 1839.

Johannes Müller

For the life and letters of Johannes Müller, see W. Haberling, *Johannes Müller: Das Leben des rheinischen Naturforschers*, 1924. For an appreciation of his influence in physiology, see T. L. W. Bischoff, *Ueber Johannes Müller und sein Verhältnis zum jetzigen Standpunkt der Physiologie*, 1858; R. Virchow, *Johannes Müller: eine Gedächtnisrede*, 1858; E. du Bois-Reymond, *Abh. berl. Akad. Wiss.*, 1859, 25-191. For Müller's important role in promoting the doctrine of the specific energies of nerves, see Chap. 5.

The *Handbuch der Physiologie des Menschen* appeared from 1833 to 1840. Müller worked continuously on it during his last years at Bonn and his first years at Berlin. The first *Abtheilung* of the first volume appeared in 1833, the second *Abtheilung* in 1834. The first edition of the first volume is rare. The first *Abtheilung* of this volume had reached a third revised edition in 1837, and the second in 1838, when the two were issued together with a single title bearing both dates. Meanwhile, the second volume was beginning to appear in three *Abtheilungen*: the first in 1837, the second in 1838, and the third, and thus also the entire second volume, in 1840. The immediate revisions, with the addition of much citation of new work, indicate how active research in experimental physiology had become. The need for such a book, and doubtless Müller's prestige, led to its immediate translation into English by W. Baly, the first volume in 1838 and the second in 1842. There was a second edition

of the translation of the first volume in 1840, and all editions contain notes, added by the translator, on very recent discoveries.

Reflex Action

On the history of reflex action, see F. Fearing, *Reflex Action: a Study in the History of Physiological Psychology*, 1930 (bibliography of 554 titles); J. F. Fulton, *Muscular Contraction and the Reflex Control of Movement*, 1926 (bibliography of 1066 titles), esp. 3-55. The older standard accounts are C. Eckhard, Geschichte der Entwicklung der Lehre von den Reflexerscheinungen, *Beiträge Anat. Physiol. von C. Eckhard*, 1881, 9, 20-192; G. S. Hall and C. F. Hodge, A sketch of the history of reflex action, *Amer. J. Psychol.*, 1890, 3, 71-86, 149-167, 343-363.

Robert Whytt's *An Essay on the Vital and Other Involuntary Motions of Animals*, 1751, 2 ed., 1763, was reprinted in *The Works of Robert Whytt*, 1768, 1-208. On his importance to psychology, see L. Carmichael, Robert Whytt: a contribution to the history of physiological psychology, *Psychol. Rev.*, 1927, 34, 287-304.

Albrecht von Haller's comments on involuntary movement and the *vis contractilis musculis insita* are to be found in his early *Prima lineae physiologiae*, 1747 and later eds., Eng. trans., 1764 and later eds., *passim*, and, of course, in his famous treatise, *Elementa physiologiae corporis humani*, 8 vols., 1757-1766, which discusses this matter in vol. IV, bk. xi, sect. 11, *passim*.

Unzer's and Prochaska's original papers are J. A. Unzer, *Erste Gründe einer Physiologie der eigentlichen thierischen Natur thierischer Körper*, 1771, and George Prochaska, *De functionibus systematis nervosi*, 1784 (see esp. chaps. 2, 4, 5, *passim*). Actually Prochaska's discussion had already appeared as Fasc. III of his *Adnotationem academicarum fasciculi tres*, 1780-1784. Both Unzer's and Prochaska's works were translated into English by T. Laycock in 1851, and Laycock's introduction constitutes a good discussion of their significance.

Marshall Hall reported his observations to the Committee on Science of the Zoological Society in 1832 and read his paper before the Royal Society in 1833: On the reflex function of the medulla oblongata and the medulla spinalis, *Philos. Trans.*, 1833, 123, 635-665. His later discussion consists in papers read in 1837 and published in 1837 as the second paper in Part I of *Memoires on the Nervous System*, under the title On the true spinal marrow and the excito-motory system of nerves. See Fearing, *op. cit.*, 128-135.

Eduard F. W. Pflüger's monograph is *Die sensorischen Funktionen des Rückenmarks der Wirbelthiere nebst einer neuen Lehre über die Leitungsgesetze der Reflexionen*, 1853. R. H. Lotze's judicious review and criticism of this monograph bears the same title and is to be found in *Göttingische gelehrte Anzeiger*, 1853, 3, 1737-1776. For Lotze's earlier comment on voluntary, involuntary and reflex movement, see his *Medicinische Psychologie*, 1852, bk. ii, chap. 3, sects. 24-25.

The English translation of Müller's *Handbuch* (1838-1842) uses the terms *reflex motion* and *reflected motion* interchangeably. The English noun *reflex*, in the sense of a reflection from a mirror, was used in the eighteenth century and occurs poetically in Tennyson in 1830, the time of Marshall Hall's writing. As an adjective applied to light, its usage is both earlier and later. *Reflected* and *reflection* have been more common. The same two nouns, *Reflex* and *Reflexion*, occur in German in the same sense, but *Reflexion* is more usual, and is the word that Müller used. It is perhaps fortunate that the more unusual term has been retained in both languages, since the original notion of reflection of the animal spirits by the spinal columns after the manner of light proved to be wrong, and the historical justification for the word is thus lost.

For Müller's discussion of reflex motion, see bk. iii, sect. iii, chap. 3 (1834); bk. iv, sect. ii, chap. 1 (1837). The author has not found the word *Reflexion* in the portion of the first volume published in 1833, but Müller asserts that he presented the essential notion there in his discussion of respiration; see foot-note at the beginning of the first reference, where he also yields priority to Hall.

Nervous Impulse

For a somewhat fuller resumé of this matter, see E. G. Boring, *Sensation and Perception in the History of Experimental Psychology*, 1942, 52-68, 91-93.

The story of Galvani and Volta has become a much discussed paradigm in the history of science because it illustrates accidental discovery (Galvani), progress gained through an initially wrong theory (animal electricity), later insight into fundamentals (two metals and an electrolyte) and the giving up of nonessentials (animal tissues) to achieve definite progress (Volta and the battery). See J. B. Conant, *On Understanding Science*, 1947, 65-73, 136-138, and the references to a dozen discussions of the topic given there, 132-134. The original reference to Luigi Galvani (1737-1798) is De viribus electricitatis in motu musculari, *Boniensi Scientiarum et Artium Instituto atque Academiae Commentarii* (part of the R. Accad. Sci. Inst. Bologna), 1791, 363-418. See Conant, *op. cit.*, 133, for comment on translations and the forthcoming complete English translation by H. L. Thomas and I. B. Cohen. The important letter of Alessandro Volta (1745-1827) on the Voltaic pile and the galvanic chain has been printed as On the electricity excited by the mere contact of conducting surfaces of different kinds, *Philos. Trans.*, 1800, 90, 403-431. Volta's writings were mostly in letters, collected and published in 1900 in two volumes; see Boring, *op. cit.*, 91.

The paper which Johannes Müller showed du Bois-Reymond in 1841 was by C. Matteucci, Note sur les phénomènes électriques des animaux, *C. R. Acad. Sci. Paris*, 1841, 13, 540 f. Emil du Bois-Reymond (1818-1896) began his work in electrophysiology with his Vorläufiger Abriss einer Untersuchung über sogenannten Froschstrom und über die elektromotorischen Fische, *Ann. Phys. Chem.*, 1843, 134, 1-30. His classical volumes are *Untersuchungen über thierische Elektricität*, I, 1848; II (1), 1849; II (2), 1860-1884. On du Bois' work, see J. F. Fulton, *Muscular Contraction and the Reflex Control of Movement*, 1926, 39-41.

Helmholtz sent his first note on the rate of transmission of the nervous impulse to du Bois to read before the Physikalische Gesellschaft in Berlin in order to establish priority for his discovery. See H. L. F. von Helmholtz, *Ber. könig. preuss. Akad. Wiss. Berlin*, 1850, 14 f. (cited erroneously by both König and Koenigsberger as *Berliner Monatsberichte*; the *Berichte* were published 1836-1855, and the *Monatsberichte* succeeded them in 1856). Du Bois immediately asked Humboldt to give the note publicity in Paris; see *Comptes rendus*, 1850, 30, 204-206; 1851, 33, 262-265. Helmholtz published at length in the summer: [*Müller's*] *Arch. Anat. Physiol.*, 1850, 276-364 (esp. 328-363); and again two years later, *ibid.*, 1852, 199-216. An Eng. trans. of the 1850 paper appears in Dennis, *op. cit.*, 197 f.

Haller had chanced upon an approximately correct value in 1762 by considering the rate of the movement of the tongue in pronouncing the letter *R*: Albrecht von Haller, *Elementa physiologiæ corporis humani*, 1762, IV, 373. His 9,000 *pedes in minuto* is equivalent to 45.4 meters per second, which is just about Helmholtz's higher value for the frog.

Joh. Müller's discussion of this matter occurs in the first volume of his *Handbuch*, bk. iii, sect. ii, introd., and, since a last edition of this volume is dated 1844, it has often been remarked that Müller's dictum that the rate was unmeasurable antedated its actual measurement by only six years.

The velocity of light is about 297,-500,000 meters per second; the velocity of sound is about 330 meters per second. Recent determinations give values for the velocity of the nervous impulse as high as 120 meters per second

for the largest nerve fibers and as low as 1 meter per second for the smallest. Thus the speed of light is from ten million to a billion times the speed of the nervous impulse.

Helmholtz's determinations for the frog's nerve were 0.0014 second for 60 mm. of nerve, and 0.0020 second for 50 mm. These figures give respectively 42.9 and 25.0 meters per second, values which lie within the true range as determined by modern methods.

Du Bois-Reymond, who was in intimate appreciative correspondence with Helmholtz, received Helmholtz's first two-page note. Müller, to whom du Bois tried to explain it, insisted on rejecting the conclusion, arguing that Helmholtz had not eliminated the time for the contraction of the muscle. Humboldt, du Bois wrote Helmholtz, "war ganz depaysiert," and at first refused to send the paper to Paris for publication there. Du Bois had first to edit it and then Humboldt, won over, had it published in the *Comptes rendus*, adding a further explanatory foot-note of his own. By summer Müller had also been won, and then Helmholtz published his longer paper, in which he included a measurement of the time of the muscular contraction and new determinations of the rate of transmission. His finding for the rate in sensory nerve came later.

The attitude of the times, which made the acceptance of this discovery difficult, is well set forth in a letter to Helmholtz from his father, a teacher of classics and philosophy in a *Gymnasium*. He wrote, in reply to Helmholtz's brief and enthusiastic account of his discovery: "As regards your work, the results at first appeared to me surprising, since I regard the idea and its bodily expression, not as successive, but as simultaneous, a single living act, that only becomes bodily and mental on reflection: and I should as little reconcile myself to your view, as I would admit a star that had disappeared in Abraham's time should still be visible."

On Helmholtz, see Chap. 15. On the measurement of the rate of the nervous impulse, see L. Koenigsberger,

Hermann von Helmholtz, 1902, I, 116 ff.; Eng. trans., 1906, I, 62 ff.; J. G. M'Kendrick, *Hermann Ludwig Ferdinand von Helmholtz*, 1899, chap. 6.

The text mentions briefly the contributions of H. P. Bowditch, H. Kronecker, E. J. Marey, W. Ostwald, F. Gotch and G. J. Burch, K. Lucas, R. S. Lillie and E. D. Adrian. Somewhat fuller comments and the original references are given in Boring, *op. cit.*, 92.

CHAPTER 3

Phrenology and the Mind-Body Problem

If in 1850 there could be resistance to the acceptance of Helmholtz's demonstration that nervous transmission is not practically instantaneous on the ground that the idea and its bodily expression are simultaneous, 'a single living act,' then it is clear that modern common sense, which identifies the mind with the brain, had not yet become the common view, and that even the localization of the mind at or within the brain was a matter of some doubt.

In phrenology, however, we find a movement, almost exactly contemporaneous with the developments considered in the preceding chapter, a movement which sought to establish the brain as the 'organ of mind,' and even particular parts of the brain as particular organs of separate mental faculties.

The more general of these two ideas was not entirely new. The idea was not favored by Aristotle, who referred the seat of life to the heart, and the Egyptians had localized thought in the heart but judgment in the head or kidneys. Pythagoras, however, thought of the brain as the seat of the mind and the intellect, and Plato held a similar view. It was the Pythagorean doctrine that prevailed. The Alexandrian anatomists held this belief, and they suggested an even more specific localization. Erasistratus referred sensation to the membranes of the brain, and movement to the brain substance itself. Herophilus regarded the brain ventricles as reservoirs of the vital forces, and Galen established this view by teaching that the animal spirits flow from the brain ventricles to the heart, and are thence distributed to the body by the arteries.

Even the belief in particular localization is quite old. Albertus Magnus (1193-1280) referred feeling to the anterior ventricle of the brain and, at times, memory to the posterior ventricle. Imagination was variously localized. Many views of like nature were expressed during the succeeding centuries. Willis (1621-1675), an anatomist just before Newton's day, placed memory and will in the convolutions of the brain, imagination in the corpus callosum, sense-perception in the corpus striatum, and certain emotions in the base of the cerebrum.

While the anatomist-physiologists were puzzling over the organ
of mind, the philosopher-psychologists were concerned with establishing the place of the seat of the soul. It is a familiar fact that Descartes (1596-1650) localized the soul in the entire body, but most
specifically in the pineal gland in the brain, where, he supposed, its
interaction with the body took place. He did not, however, by any
means identify the brain with the mind. He held to a complete
dualism between the two, and thought of the pineal gland merely as
the point at which the mind affects the flow of animal spirits, changing their course. The soul, being immaterial, does not occupy space,
but it needs a definite point of contact with the spatial brain. A
similar view without such specific localization was presented by Lotze
in his medical psychology of 1852.

All these guesses were, however, more matters of philosophical
view than of empirical proof. The effective impetus to the consideration of the brain as the organ of mind did not come until the
nineteenth century. Late in the eighteenth century there was, nevertheless, some specific preparation for it. It was then that Benjamin
Rush (1745-1813) in America, William Tuke (1732-1822) in England, and Philippe Pinel (1745-1826) in France independently began
their agitations for reform in the treatment of the insane. Up to this
time the insane had been outcasts, supposedly possessed of demons,
and had been scourged or cast into chains in dungeons. These re-
formers advocated the view that demoniacal possession is a disease,
and accomplished much in the way of liberation and sympathetic
treatment of those so afflicted. The work of change was slow and had
not even been extended from Paris to the French provinces at the time
of Pinel's death in 1826. Nevertheless, it was an important movement
of great influence that tended to fix the conception of mental disease
as against the notion of demoniacal possession for which the afflicted
person, at least in popular belief, shared the responsibility. To recognize the mind as subject to disease is a step in the direction of
realizing its dependence upon the body, the usual seat of disease. It is,
however, the prominence that the movement gained, rather than the
specificity of its bearing upon the problem of mind and body, that
makes mention of it important here.

PHRENOLOGY

It was out of this milieu that phrenology emerged at the hand of
Franz Joseph Gall (1758-1828). Gall was an anatomist who concerned himself primarily with the head and brain. As a schoolboy
he believed he had observed a relationship between some of the

mental characteristics of his schoolmates and the shapes of their heads, especially that those with prominent eyes had good memories. This idea he carried with him into adulthood and subjected to investigation. His first observations were made upon the classes of society which he found in jails and lunatic asylums, where the mental characteristics can be regarded as established because they have led their possessors to their present situations. For instance, the 'bump' on the head which phrenology takes as a sign of the faculty of acquisitiveness is the place which Gall thought was especially prominent in pickpockets. Later Gall extended his studies to his friends and to casts of the heads of persons whose mental traits were well known. A German by birth, he began lecturing on his new doctrine of physiognomy in Vienna, where in 1800 he was joined by Spurzheim as a pupil. The doctrine attracted a great deal of popular attention, which was not diminished by the fact that Gall in 1802 was ordered by the government, at the instance of the church, to discontinue his lectures. Spurzheim was now associated with Gall as a collaborator, and, after a lecture tour in Germany, they settled in Paris in 1807. They began to publish jointly, but in 1813 they agreed to separate. Gall remained in Paris to continue his lectures, writing and research, while Spurzheim fared forth to preach the new gospel in France and England, and finally in America.

The great first treatise on phrenology appeared under Gall's authorship, with Spurzheim's collaboration in the first two volumes, in 1810-1819. It is entitled: *Anatomie et physiologie du système nerveux en général, et du cerveau en particulier, avec observations sur la possibilité de reconnaître plusieurs dispositions intellectuelles et morales de l'homme et des animaux par la configuration de leurs têtes.* In 1822-1825 Gall published a new and much altered edition of this work under the title *Sur les fonctions du cerveau.*

The *Anatomie et physiologie du système nerveux* is a much more conservative and scientific work than many who now sniff at phrenology suppose. The first volume, published in 1810 with an atlas, deals with the *système nerveux en général* and is a very careful consideration of the more important nerves, the spinal cord, the cerebellum and the five senses. The last three volumes deal with the *physiologie du cerveau en particulier* and enter more properly into phrenology, although that term was not employed by Gall. Even some of Gall's physiological critics give him credit for his contributions to the anatomy of the nervous system. It is said that, when Gall and Spurzheim presented the monograph on their new science to the Institut de

France in 1808, Cuvier, then permanent secretary for physical science and chairman of the committee of review, was dissuaded by Napoleon from making a favorable report. For one thing Napoleon disliked recognition for the achievement of foreigners. Later, in 1821 and long after Waterloo, Gall was proposed for membership in the Académie des Sciences (the Institut's successor) but received only one favorable vote.

The modern character of phrenology was given it by Spurzheim (1776-1832), who adopted the term *phrenology* Gall's doctrine had been popularly referred to as his *Hirn- und Schädellehre*, and Gall spoke of physiognomy and craniology. Spurzheim was more of a propagandist than a scientist. He was influential, while with Gall, in dignifying phrenology by bringing it more into relation with the respectable traits of mankind than with those to be found in the inmates of jails and asylums. It was presumably he who first saw its more important relations to society, and Gall learned from him the importance of this extension. After his separation from Gall, Spurzheim worked out many details of the system, established a new and more complete topography of the skull together with a revised terminology for the faculties, wrote a series of books presenting his views and controverting the numerous and caustic derogators of phrenology, and finally died in Boston while advocating the doctrine in America.

It is plain that there are three fundamental propositions inherent in the phrenology of Gall and Spurzheim. In the first place, it is necessary for the doctrine to show that the conformation of the exterior of the skull corresponds to the conformation of its interior and of the brain. Gall held that it does, that the form of the brain is determined, at least, early in life, and that the skull is formed to conform to it. His view seems not to be correct as against small differences, for the thickness of the skull varies greatly and apparently adventitiously. In the second place, if the doctrine is to be allowed, it is necessary to believe that the mind can meaningfully and satisfactorily be analyzed into a number of faculties or functions, and to perform this analysis. Modern psychology has largely failed to establish any such units, but Gall had ready for use the faculties of the Scottish School (pp. 205-208). It was from the lists of Thomas Reid and Dugald Stewart that Gall obtained his analysis of the mind into thirty-seven powers and propensities. Finally, there is in this doctrine the central proposition that the faculties and powers of the mind are differently localized in the brain and that excess in any faculty is correlated with enlargement of a corresponding place in the brain. A protrusion of the brain (and of the skull if it conforms to the brain) would indicate an excess in the proper faculty. A recession in the brain would mean a lack of the faculty.

The work of the phrenologists has, in general, centered upon the central problem of correlation, and it must be admitted that, had the correlation been satisfactorily made out, we should have been in possession of a very important fact. If it were shown later that the outside of the skull did not conform to the brain, then we should have had to explain in some other way the relationship between the form of the skull and the nature of the mind. The established correlation itself would have been sufficient test of the adequacy of the mental analysis.

In the proof of this central theme, the modern anthropometrist is struck by the inadequacy of the method. Nowadays we should seek to avoid the danger of selection of cases to fit the theory by choosing in advance an 'unselected' group of persons, measuring all their 'bumps' accurately, estimating the degrees of all of their faculties in the accepted list without knowledge of their head measurements, and then determining the correlation between the two sets of data. Gall could have done this even without the modern mathematics of correlation or factor analysis, but physiology a century and more ago was still in the stage where personal observation and checks and safeguards depended more upon the rigor of the investigator than upon the recognized sanctions of science.

Gall's correlation as extended and modified by Spurzheim recognized thirty-seven "powers" of the mind which corresponded to an equal number of "organs" of the mind, the development of which might cause enlargements of the skull. The skull was therefore divided into thirty-seven contiguous patches, some large and some small, and the table of the corresponding faculties was drawn up. The mental analysis began with a dichotomy into affective powers and intellectual powers, and for each of these there was a two-fold subdivision. First there were the "propensities," affective powers, like "destructiveness," "amativeness," and "philoprogenitiveness." All these were grouped together at the lower part of the back of the head and at the sides above the ears. The other affective powers were the "sentiments," "cautiousness," "benevolence," "hope," which lay in a single region above the propensities on the back, sides and top of the head. The intellectual powers were all related to the forehead and consisted mostly of "perceptive" faculties like the perception of "size," "weight," "coloring," "time" and "tune." There were two

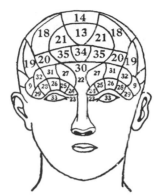

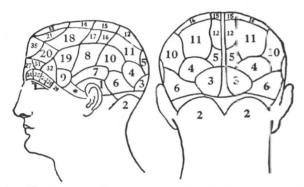

FIG. 1. THE "POWERS AND ORGANS OF THE MIND," ACCORDING TO SPURZHEIM, *Phrenology, or the Doctrine of Mental Phenomena, 1834.*

AFFECTIVE FACULTIES		INTELLECTUAL FACULTIES	
PROPENSITIES	SENTIMENTS	PERCEPTIVE	REFLECTIVE
? Desire to live	10 Cautiousness	22 Individuality	34 Comparison
* Alimentiveness	11 Approbativeness	23 Configuration	35 Causality
1 Destructiveness	12 Self-Esteem	24 Size	
2 Amativeness	13 Benevolence	25 Weight and	
3 Philoprogenitiveness	14 Reverence	Resistance	
4 Adhesiveness	15 Firmness	26 Coloring	
5 Inhibitiveness	16 Conscientiousness	27 Locality	
6 Combativeness	17 Hope	28 Order	
7 Secretiveness	18 Marvelousness	29 Calculation	
8 Acquisitiveness	19 Ideality	30 Eventuality	
9 Constructiveness	20 Mirthfulness	31 Time	
	21 Imitation	32 Tune	
		33 Language	

"reflective" intellectual powers, "comparison" and "causality," in the very center of the forehead.

It is impossible to evaluate the evidence for these relationships. The region for "adhesiveness" (a propensity), for example, was originally designated thus because it was prominent in a lady who had been introduced to Gall as a model of friendship and because it was said to be the region of contact when persons closely attached to each other put their heads together. (The region is just to the side of the middle of the back of the head!) However, the phrenologists claimed that these dubious initial findings were to be accepted because they were verified in all persons without exception. Thomas Brown, the philosopher, remarked that the theory would never gain acceptance because any one could test it simply by looking at heads; and Spurzheim rejoined that this was the very reason that it had gained acceptance.

The seriousness of the phrenologists' belief, as well as the dangers inherent in their interpretative method, can best be illustrated by a later phrenologist's phrenological biography of Gall. This writer closed his biography by a detailed examination of Gall's personality and cranium in respect of two dozen faculties. He began: "The organs of Amativeness, Philoprogenitiveness, Adhesiveness, Combativeness, and Destructiveness were all very well developed in Gall. His Secretiveness was also rather large, but he never made bad use of it. He was too conscious of his intellectual powers to obtain his ends by cunning or fraud." Our superficial acquaintance with Gall lets us see how the 'bump' of combativeness could be justified. Destructiveness also seems intelligible until we note that it was discovered because prominent "in the head of a student so fond of torturing animals that he became a surgeon," and "in the head of an apothecary who became an executioner." But the author of the biography himself found a need for explaining away secretiveness. Herein seems to lie the fundamental fallacy of this interpretative method: if a particular correlation obviously failed, it could be accounted for by other more dominant faculties that might be supposed to suppress it or to alter its direction.

Phrenology had a tremendous popular appeal. The most important and greatest puzzle which every man faces is himself, and, secondarily, other persons. Here seemed to be a key to the mystery, a key fashioned in the scientific laboratory and easy to use. It actually constituted a new intellectual gospel. Moreover, it was supported by men of prominence and intelligence other than Gall and Spurzheim. Perhaps the most important of these men was George Combe (1788-1858), a Scot who, after deriding phrenology, was converted by Spurzheim and took up the cause ardently from about 1817 until his death in 1858. He wrote and lectured much on phrenology, like Spurzheim visiting America to spread the doctrine. He was a strong candidate for the chair of logic at the University of Edinburgh, although he was rejected in favor of Sir William Hamilton. In America, as well as in England, the new 'science' spread. In America the Fowler brothers were chiefly instrumental in furthering the cause, and the Institute of Phrenology still existed in New York at least as late as 1912. At one time there were twenty-nine phrenological societies in Great Britain and several journals. The *Journal of Phrenology*, although passing through a series of changes of name and amalgamations, was born in Edinburgh in 1823 and died in Philadelphia only in 1911. Phrenology had flourished for a century!

It was never, however, generally accepted in science. In the days of Gall, when it was still scientifically possible if not plausible, it was opposed by Sir Charles Bell, Sir William Hamilton, Thomas Brown, and other men of equal prominence. It was also derided and ridiculed. Later, when knowledge of the physiology of the brain rendered it impossible, it still held its popular appeal, with scorn only from the scientifically informed. Quite early it came to occupy the position of psychic research to-day, looked at askance by most men of science because unproven, using unscientific methods and indulging in propaganda, and yet still not absolutely disproven.

The importance of phrenology for us lies in its effect upon the scientific thought of this period. While many expressed skepticism about the actuality of the correlations between faculties and prominences of the skull, there were also separate attacks upon the two other fundamental principles. The physiologists disbelieved the relationship between the exterior of the skull and the brain, and the philosophers objected to the analysis of mind into faculties with spatially distinct organs. Such a conception seemed to violate the principle of the unity of mind. Descartes assigned the pineal gland as the point of action between mind and body because every other organ in the brain was in duplicate, one on each side. What would Descartes have said to thirty-seven organs, every one of them in duplicate? In the nineteenth century, the notion of the unity of mind was still too strongly entrenched to abide the phrenological analysis. We have already seen that it was responsible for the resistance that Helmholtz encountered when he measured the rate of nervous transmission.

The theory of Gall and Spurzheim is, however, an instance of a theory which, while essentially wrong, was just enough right to further scientific thought. It was right in the first place in establishing the brain as the 'organ of mind,' a phrase which Gall used—or, if it was not right, at least by establishing that belief, it left science free for all the progress that resulted in physiological psychology. As long as the seat of the soul remained a matter for metaphysical speculation, to be affirmed or denied on other than empirical grounds, there was no scientific approach available for the study of the mind. But as soon as this metaphysical objection was overcome, not so much factually as in the acceptance of modes of thought, the physiology of the brain and the psychophysics of sensation were ready to be undertaken.

Another great impetus that phrenology gave to science was its suggestion of localization of function in the brain. Even though the phrenological correlations were not correct, still it was reasonable to suppose that different parts of the brain would have different physiological, and thus perhaps psychophysiological, functions. It was an important thing to have this belief established, but the account of the first attack upon the problem must be left for the next chapter.

In brief, phrenology was playing its ambiguous role as cause and symptom of the *Zeitgeist*, which was moving mind away from the concept of the unsubstantial Cartesian soul to the concept of the more material neural function. Phrenology was wrong only in detail and in respect of the enthusiasms of its supporters. How often the importance of a theory in scientific progress is other than what its proponents suppose or hope!

NOTES

René Descartes's discussion of the seat of the soul in the pineal gland occurs in his *Les passions de l'âme*, 1650, arts. xx-l. Most of these sections are translated in B. Rand, *Classical Psychologists*, 1912, 173-183. See also W. Dennis, *Readings in the History of Psychology*, 1948, 25-31.

It is important to note that the soul, being unextended and therefore not occupying space, was not thought of as confined within the pineal gland. It was associated with, but was not within, the body, and the pineal gland was the organ through which it affected the body, but not its container. Descartes's mechanics of the body was such as should have left him no difficulty in accepting Helmholtz's demonstration that the conduction of the nervous impulse takes an appreciable time; nevertheless, Descartes preserved the unity of the soul, which was really the underlying difficulty in the acceptance of those results. For

R. H. Lotze's view, see his *Medicinische Psychologie*, 1852, 115-122.

Pinel is known mostly for his work in the liberation of the insane, which was carried on after him by his pupil Esquirol. The English reform was an important, but not the principal, event in the life of Tuke. In America, a new country, tradition was less well established and the reform came much more easily than in France and England. Rush is primarily famous as a friend of Franklin, a signer of the Declaration of Independence, and a surgeon concerned with many humanitarian reforms. Both Tuke and Rush were Quakers. Rush wrote a book called *Diseases of the Mind* in 1812.

On the psychological antecedents of phrenology, see M. Bentley's article with that title, *Psychol. Monog.*, 1916, 21, no. 92, 102-115. He traces the primary thread of development from Locke through the French sensationists, and expresses a very proper appreciation of Gall's work. See also H. D. Spoerl, Faculties vs. traits: Gall's solution, *Character & Pers.*, 1936, 4, 216-231, who shows how Gall got his list of faculties from Reid and Stewart of the Scottish School.

Gall and Spurzheim

F. J. Gall began his lectures in Vienna in 1796. His doctrine came to be well known before his printed publication, largely by way of his, and later Spurzheim's, lectures, and also because some of his students published notes on his lectures.

The first publication of importance is the *mémoire* presented by Gall and G. Spurzheim as candidates for election to the Institut de France: *Recherches sur le système nerveux en général, et sur celui du cerveau en particulier*, 1809. The *mémoire* was presented on March 14, 1808, and a committee of five, including Pinel, with Cuvier as chairman, was appointed to examine the researches and the doctrine. Whether Napoleon actually interfered is not certain, although it is plain that he was opposed to the doctrine. Cuvier's long negative report of fifty-one pages is cautious and conservative, and shows that his committee realized that it was dealing with a difficult controversial matter. It concludes: "It is necessary again to repeat, if only for the instruction of the public, that the anatomical questions with which we have been occupied in this report do not have an immediate and necessary relation to the physiological doctrine put forth by M. Gall on the functions and the influence of the relative volume of the different parts of the brain, and that all that we have brought out concerning the structure of the encephalon would be equally true or false without there being the least thing to conclude from it for or against the doctrine which can only be judged by totally different means." In other words, Cuvier and his committee withdrew from a difficult position by judging that the essential thesis of Gall and Spurzheim was irrelevant to the field of the

mathematical and physical section of the Institut. For Cuvier's report, see *Mémoires de la classe des sciences mathématiques et physiques de l'Institut de France*, 1808, 109-160. On Napoleon and Gall, see Capen (cited below), I, 22-26.

(The *mémoire* was addressed to what we should now call the Académie des Sciences. The old Académie des Sciences had been suppressed by the Revolution in 793, and the Institut established by Napoleon in 1796. It was not until 1816 that the mathematical and physical division of the Institut came again to be known as the Académie des Sciences. Had the Académie des Sciences Morales et Politiques, suppressed by Napoleon in 1803 and reëstablished in 1833, been in existence in 1808, it could not very well have made Cuvier's report of no jurisdiction.)

We have seen that the four volumes of the *Anatomie et physiologie* appeared in 1810-819, and that Spurzheim collaborated on the first two. In 1825, Gall had completed the six volumes of *Sur les fonctions du cerveau et sur celles de chacune de ses parties*. This work reprints much of the *Anatomie et physiologie*, but omits the descriptive anatomy and includes a great deal of new material more directly relevant to 'physiognomical' doctrine. It was translated into English by W. Lewis in 1835. The editor, N. Capen, added a biography to the translation, I, 1-52. See also F. J. Möbius, *Franz Joseph Gall*, vol. VII of Möbius's *Ausgewählte Werke*, 1905; here there is also a biography, pp. 3-17.

Spurzheim, after he separated from Gall in 1813, published many books in English. They include *The Physiognomical System of Gall and Spurzheim*, 1815 (it was only in 1815 that T. Forster suggested the term *phrenology*); *Phrenology or the Doctrine of the Human Mind*, 1825; *The Anatomy of the Human Brain*, 1826; and *Outlines of Phrenology*, 1832. The introduction to the second work mentioned includes an historical account of phrenology and of Spurzheim's relation to Gall (3d Amer. ed., 1834, I, 9-12). The figure and its legend in the text are taken from this book.

Later Phrenology

Combe was even more prolific than Spurzheim. His first work is *Essays on Phrenology*, 1819. Other books on phrenology followed in 1824, 1825, 1827, 1839, and 1847. See also C. Gibbon, *Life of George Combe*, 1878.

O. S. Fowler (1809-1887) wrote very many books on phrenology and his brother, L. N. Fowler (1811-1896), a few. Together they founded the *American Phrenological Journal* in 1838, and they did more than any others to establish pnrenology in America. The British *Phrenological Journal* was published from 1823 to 1847. The American journal later took this name and combined with the British *Phrenological Magazine* in 1880. It ceased publication with the 124th volume in 1911.

As recently as 1938 there existed an Ohio State Phrenological Society which published a magazine, but in general it can be said that the popular appeal of phrenology has been drained off by the numerous unscientific societies which nowadays claim to provide more direct ways of understanding human nature and of helping people out of trouble.

CHAPTER 4

Physiology of the Brain: 1800-1870

In emphasizing the importance of Gall's work in localizing the mind within the brain, we must not be misled into believing that physiologists at the end of the eighteenth century were in doubt about the existence of an intimate connection between the mind and the brain. Bichat (1771-1802), for instance, had held that the brain is the center for intelligence, memory, perception, imagination and judgment, but that the emotions have their seat in the internal organs. Many other French physiologists of this period had similar views, and, because of their tendency to localize the emotions in the viscera, they can be regarded as the actual progenitors of the James-Lange theory of emotion. All in all, the point of view about the body and the mind was, at that time, not so very different from Descartes', whose influence is shown in this manner. Thus the mind is thought to be related to the whole body, not merely to the brain, yet to retain special points of contact which can be regarded as the seat of the mind or the seats of some of its functions. For these the brain is more likely to serve than are other organs. The necessity for this relationship is obvious. The human mind expresses itself in action; action depends upon the nerves; the nerves arise in the spinal cord and the brain. Were emotions known best by the actions to which they lead, rather than by the obvious disturbance of the viscera, Bichat and the others would doubtless have looked to the brain for *le siège des passions* also. As to whether such a gross anatomical analysis accounted for all of the mind, that was plainly not a problem for a physiologist then, any more than the physiologist to-day seeks to find an account of all the accepted facts of psychology.

Gall's extremely specific psychophysiology accomplished two things. In the first place, it forced the problem of the correlation of mind and brain to the fore because of the tremendous vogue of phrenology and because Gall was an anatomist of such scientific excellence that his movement could not be ignored by the scientists. In the second place, by going to extremes, Gall made a radical but less extreme view actually seem conservative. Without Gall, Flourens might never have conceived the problem of finding different functions for the cerebrum, the cerebellum, the medulla and the cord; and Flourens' position was much strengthened because he could appear as a conservative correcting the pseudo-science of Gall and Spurzheim. It is the familiar case where the truth is more nearly approximated because a traditional belief that deviates from the truth in one direction is offset by the dramatic and vigorous exaggeration that deviates in the other direction. No scientist consciously cultivates error; yet the truth—a scientific truth which may last for a century before some flaw in its formulation is discovered—is often the mean between an established misconception and an hyperbole which has been built up to overcome the inertia of tradition.

PIERRE FLOURENS

Flourens is the most important figure in the advance of the physiology of the brain away from both the too vague tradition of Descartes and the too specific doctrine of the phrenologists. First, however, we must mention Rolando, the anatomist after whom the central fissures of the cerebral hemispheres are named.

Luigi Rolando (1770-1831) was interested in the anatomy and pathology of the brain, but he also indulged in some physiological experimentation and speculation, which, published in 1809, led him to claim priority over Flourens in determining correctly the functions of the different parts of the brain—one says "correctly" because he, like most of the scientists, rejected Gall's localization as incorrect. In Rolando's view, the cerebral hemispheres are "the principal seat of the immediate cause of sleep, of dementia, of apoplexy, of melancholia and of mania." Such a statement is certainly equivalent to a localization of the higher mental functions in the cerebrum, although Flourens pointed out that it is not a statement that assigns perception and intelligence exclusively to the cerebral lobes. Rolando drew upon pathological observations and post-mortem examinations. He held further that activity of the cerebrum is due to the movement of its fibers, thus erroneously imputing movement to the fibers and making the white, rather than the gray, matter fundamental to psychophysiological functioning. Sensations, however, he localized in the medulla oblongata and not in the cerebrum. There was already anatomical evidence for this opinion, for all the sensory nerves of the head except the olfactory and the visual were thought to run to the medulla. (The sensory function of the trigeminal nerve, which is also motor, was not recognized; otherwise the belief was correct.) The medulla was already known to be essential to life, to contain the 'vital knot'; and it is to this vital knot that Rolando assigned also the principal center of sensibility. His chief argument was, however, directed to the cerebellum, which was, he thought, the organ for the preparation and secretion of nervous force. This conclusion came from his own experiments. Volta, as we have already observed (p. 30), had devised the Voltaic pile in 1800, thus rendering electric current available. Rolando used such a pile to stimulate the brain, and found that violent muscular contractions became more violent the nearer the electrodes approached the cerebellum through the brain substance. His experiments were crude and one does not know exactly where his stimulus was effective, but the gross fact that movement was more vigorous the nearer he came to the cerebellum was obvious enough and led him to characterize the cerebellum as the battery from which the nervous energy is derived.

Whereas Rolando was unconvincing in his experiments and vague and essentially incorrect in his theories, Pierre Flourens (1794-1867) was precise in his technique, clear and trenchant in his writing, and essentially right in his conclusions—at least he marks a definite step in both method and fact toward what is accepted as truth today. He early became a protégé of Cuvier's in Paris, where he lectured on the physiology of sensation and attracted much attention. His important researches on the brain were presented by Cuvier to the Académie des Sciences in 1822 and 1823, and, collected and printed together with an explanatory preface, they form his first important book in 1824. A few later papers were printed in another small book in 1825. In 1828 he was elected to the Académie on the occurrence of a vacancy, and in 1833 at Cuvier's dying request he was made *secrétaire perpétuel* in Cuvier's stead. He then held a professorship of comparative anatomy especially created for him at the museum of the Jardin du Roi. In 1840 he was elected to the Académie de France over Victor Hugo. In the interval, he published and also engaged to a small extent in politics. In 1842 he put out a revised edition of the papers of 1324-1825, and also his *Examen de la phrénologie*, in which he brought forward Descartes to confound Gall's doctrine and to establish the scientific physiology of the brain. In 1855 he was made professor of natural history in the Collége de France, and he died twelve years later.

In all things his touch was sure. As a writer he was both certain and forcible. In the preface to the *Examen* he says: "J'ai voulu être court. Il y a un grand secret pour être court: c'est d'être clair." And he was both brief and clear. He had the gift for annihilating an opponent, Rolando or Gall, in fair play and without bitterness.

His experiments were equally precise and simple. He operated cleanly and precisely without mutilating the tissues, and in the light of a few carefully formulated principles which rendered the results of his operations crucial. His problem was the determination of the functions of the different parts of the brain. He had two main principles. The first was that the experiments should bear "directly" upon the conclusion; that is to say, he would substitute the immediate observation of a correlation between a part of the brain and its function for the vague and indirect inferences that had previously been formed on the basis of pathological cases or by a more exclusively rationalistic process. His method was the method of extirpation of parts, and he is thus father of this extremely important method in the physiology of the brain. His emphasis upon "direct" observation amounts to an insistence upon carefully planned experiments as preferable to 'nature's experiments' that occur in accidental lesions and disease. It is the argument of the laboratory against the clinic. Flourens' second principle demands the isolation of the part whose function is to be determined. The satisfaction of this principle requires a clear notion in advance of the functional relationships that one seeks to study, and, on anatomical grounds, Flourens accepted as separate units for investigation the cerebral hemispheres, the cerebellum, the corpora quadrigemina, the medulla oblongata, the spinal cord, and the nerves —six units in all. Given this precise setting for the experiment, the method becomes one of operative technique. The given part must be removed cleanly, not merely mutilated, and without mutilation of the other parts. Flourens possessed this requisite skill; at any rate Cuvier and his contemporaries believed that he did.

We can best see Flourens' results and their great importance by a summary which notes the relation of his conclusions to the state of the problem in the twentieth century.

"The function of the *cerebral lobes* is willing, judging, remembering, seeing, hearing, in a word perceiving." The clean removal of the lobes at once abolishes voluntary action. The animal undisturbed may remain still until it dies of starvation; a bird will not fly unless thrown into the air. It also abolishes perception. With the lobes removed, the animal is blind and deaf; it does not respond to ordinary visual or auditory stimuli. Nevertheless it is sensitive to light, for the pupil still contracts to strong light. The modern phrase would be that the perception is abolished and that sensory discrimination remains. Presumably the same distinction must be made for the other senses, although it is not so easy to make the distinction in the tactual sphere. Perception occupies the superordinate relation to sensation or mere sensitivity that volition occupies to the immediate cause of movement.

Thus the cerebrum is the seat of perception, intelligence and the will.

"All the perceptions, all the volitions, occupy concurrently the same seat in these organs; the faculty ... of perceiving, or willing constitutes thus only one faculty essentially a unit." The physiology of the late nineteenth century challenged this statement in its determination of various cerebral centers. In the twentieth century the pendulum has swung first toward Flourens' view (Lashley's principle of equipotentiality) and then back toward a somewhat more precise localization of function.

"The function of the *cerebellum* is the coordination of the movements of locomotion." With the cerebellum removed, an animal may attempt to walk, but falls. It is sensitive and moves; it can perceive and will; but it cannot accomplish the complex coördinated movements of walking, flying, or maintaining position. This conclusion is still good doctrine.

The *medulla oblongata* is the organ of conservation. As such, it is the 'vital knot' and is essential to the life of the organism, including the nervous system itself, for if the nervous system be divided caudad to the medulla, the distal region dies and the proximal lives, and if it be divided cephalad to the medulla, still the distal region dies and the proximal lives. The medulla is thus the vital center of the nervous system. It orders the sensations before they are perceived; it brings together the volitions before they are executed in movement.

The *corpora quadrigemina* function for seeing; without them the animal is blind, though the cerebrum be intact. The function of the *spinal cord* is that of conduction; the function of the *nerves* is excitation.

"In the last analysis ... all these essentially diverse parts of the nervous system have all specific properties, proper functions, distinct effects; and, in spite of this marvellous diversity of properties, functions and effects, they nevertheless constitute of it a unique system." Thus the nervous system has a unity which comes about because in addition to the *action propre* of each part there is also an *action commune*, for the removal of any part reduces the energy of every other. "One point excited in the nervous system excites all the others; one point enervated enervates them all; there is a community of reaction, of alteration, of energy. Unity is the great principle that reigns; it is everywhere, it dominates everything. The nervous system thus forms but a unitary system." Such a statement anticipates by a century both Lashley's conception of equipotentiality and mass action, based on his own and Franz's studies of cerebral function, and the views of the Gestalt psychologists (Wertheimer, Köhler, Koffka) that the cerebrum acts as a whole and that its functions must be understood in terms of field theory.

Flourens' analysis of the brain into its essential unitary parts, although made on anatomical grounds, was justified by the results that the parts were actually differentiated in function. He felt that the analysis was still further substantiated by his discovery that a dose of opium produced the effect of the removal of the cerebral hemispheres and caused observable changes in the appearance of the hemispheres, that belladonna had the same relation to the corpora quadrigemina, and alcohol to the cerebellum.

In his notion that each part of the nervous system acts as a unit, that each represents essentially only a single function, Flourens was reinforced by his discovery that the parts "can lose a portion of their substance without losing the exercise of their functions" and that "they can reacquire it after having totally lost it." These facts of the recovery of function after its abolition by the extirpation of a part have constituted the outstanding problem of cerebral psychophysiology. It is in respect of them that the pendulum has swung back and forth between belief in exact localization and field theory, between *action propre* and *action commune*.

Obviously Flourens' formulation of his findings was couched against the functional atomism of phrenology. It was, however, primarily a justification of the experimental method, and as such it told against Gall for his lack of experimental control, against Rolando for ill-defined isolation of factors, especially in clinical material, and against the philosophers who reasoned about the nature and seat of the soul without arranging a crucial empirical test. He found both unity and diversification of function. The *action propre* of each of the six principal divisions of the nervous system was an analysis that looked in the direction of Gall; the *action commune* of all of these parts was the assertion of the unity for which the philosophers had contended. The position is less a compromise between two opposing views than it is the empirical intermediate to which Flourens' experiments led him.

It was in this way that the phrenologists and physiologists fixed in the first half of the nineteenth century the notion that the brain is the seat of the mind, and that the mental functions of the different structures of the brain form a fundamental physiological problem in the scientific study of this portion of the nervous system. Magendie, for example, although interested primarily in the nerves and believing that the problems of the mental functions belong to ideology and the problems of intelligence to metaphysics, nevertheless represented this general view. He argued that the seat of the sensations is neither in the cerebrum nor in the medulla, but in the spinal cord, a most natural argument for the joint discoverer of the sensory function of the posterior nerve roots of the cord, and in a sense a correct argument. He appealed for proof to the phenomena that we now call reflexes, phenomena that occur after the removal of the brain and cerebellum. This view, however, is really also Flourens' in so far as it was perception rather than sensibility that Flourens ascribed to the cerebrum and Magendie also admitted that the cerebrum perceives the sensations of the cord. He noted, moreover, that the cerebrum can reproduce these sensations and is thus the seat of memory, and he suggested further that there are different kinds of memory, memory for proper names, for substantives, for numbers, and so forth. Whether there are different organs for these different memories in the cerebrum he did not pretend to guess. He was an opponent of Gall and waited upon the ideologists for a better formulation of the problem. Magendie also suggested, because of the differences in the brains of animals at different levels in the scale of animal development, that the number of convolutions of the brain might be correlated with the degree of "perfection or imperfection of the intellectual faculties."

The principle that the brain is the organ of the mind was still further indicated to the scientists (for the public that accepted phrenology needed no further demonstration) by Desmoulins, a pupil of Magendie's, who in 1825 published a book which included his discovery that the brains of old people are lighter than the average for adults. He thus was able to attribute senility to atrophy of the brain. He failed, however, to gain acceptance for this view even among scientists, for his report on this matter had been indignantly rejected by the Académie des Sciences.

We have already seen that this whole matter is not without its ambiguities, that Pflüger could argue that the spinal cord is conscious because it mediates reflexes that have the characteristic of purposiveness, whereas Lotze could stick to the simpler view that consciousness is a correlate of the brain's action only (pp. 37-39, 46 f.).

HISTOLOGY OF THE NERVOUS SYSTEM

After the period of which we have been speaking, a new interest, coupled, as is nearly always the case, with a new method, developed in the physiological study of the brain. Indirectly, this interest came also to bear on the problem of localization of function, but it was not this problem that determined it. It was rather the improvement of the microscope about 1830 which led to a decade of illuminating histological research. It was Rolando who, in 1824, had first thought of cutting thin sections of the tissue of the brain, chemically hardened, for microscopic examination. A little later, Johannes Müller discovered that potassium bichromate formed an excellent material for preserving and hardening tissue. A section, of course, does not give the solid structure that is under consideration, and it was not until 1842 that Stilling perfected a method of cutting a continuous series of sections so that structures, like nerve fibers, could be traced beyond the plane of the section. Meanwhile in 1833, shortly after the Lister who improved the microscope had described cells, Remak found that the gray matter of the brain is cellular, and in the same year Ehrenberg described the fibers of the white matter. It was not until 1858 that Gerlach discovered that staining with carmine brings out the details of a microscopic preparation, thus again, by the discovery of a method, stimulating a profound interest in the minute structure of the tissues. Only now was it that the nerve-cells sprang, as it were, into sudden view.

In this same period, there was still another method of research that came into use. Nasse, in 1839, had found that a severed nerve trunk degenerates in its peripheral portion only. In 1852, Waller came to the conclusion that every nerve fiber is connected to a nerve cell, and that this 'secondary degeneration,' as it is called, occurs in the part of the nerve fiber distal to its cell. This fact led Waller to the formulation of a method for the tracing of nerve tracts: if a tract be severed, its course away from the center where its cells lie can be traced by following the degeneration, whatever the course of the fibers through the complicated structure of the brain and cord.

It is our purpose here simply to inquire into the state of the physiology of the nervous system at the beginning of the second half of the nineteenth century, the time at which 'physiological psychology' branched off from physiology on the one hand and philosophy on the other as an independent discipline. We should not, then, go further in this interesting development except to note that the much superior method of staining nervous tissue with nitrate of silver was not discovered by Golgi until 1873, nor was it until later that Golgi developed his theory of the nervous system as a network formed by the axon fibers and their collaterals. (To the dendrites he assigned only a trophic function.) The nature of the synapse, which showed the true function of the dendrites and the fact that each nerve cell and its fibers form an independent unit waited upon the research of Cajal; this discovery belongs to the year 1889. Cajal is thus the father of the neuron theory, so named by Waldeyer in 1891. At the period in which our present interest centers, it was supposed that the fibers merely formed a complicated network, anastomosing and dividing, and that the physiological account of mind was somehow to be gained from a further knowledge of this network.

At first glance this histological work seems to have but little bearing upon psychology; nevertheless, there is a very definite connection. Flourens left the brain a fairly simple organ. It consisted for him of a few gross parts, principally the cerebrum, the cerebellum, and the medulla; and each of these parts had its own peculiar functions. Within each part, however, Flourens thought that no differentiation of function was to be found. Perceiving, willing and judging, which had their common seat in the cerebrum, were after all simply different names for the single mental function of the cerebrum. To this extent Flourens upheld the philosophers in their insistence on the unity of mind. So it was that, with the cerebrum, for example, serving only a single function and any part of it being able to perform that function (as recovery from operative lesion indicated), there was no demand for a study of differentiation within the cerebrum or any other of the principal parts of the brain. The histological work changed all this. The brain was presently seen to be composed of an almost infinite number of separate cells, each bearing several processes, and some of these processes giving rise to long fibers, which pass in definite tracts through the brain and presumably connect the whole mass into a single complicated network. It was a great tangled skein of fibers bearing in its structure a very large number of cells like beads on threads, with the whole mass arranged in a definite way, the full usefulness of which was not yet understood.

We shall see later that the psychology of associationism was within philosophy the dominant psychology of this period, and that the scheme of mind for which the associationists stood is a mental arrangement that much resembles this physical arrangement of the brain. For the associationists, mind is composed of an infinitude of separate ideas, just as the brain is constituted of an infinitude of cells. But these ideas are bound together into more complex ideas or into higher mental processes by a huge number of associations, just as the nerve cells are connected by fibers. There are laws of association and laws of nervous connection, though neither was yet sufficiently well established to raise explicitly the question of the explanation of the one in terms of the other. The important point is that the new picture of the brain, arrived at unpsychologically by discoveries in histological technique, nevertheless bore a close resemblance to the new picture of the mind that associationism yielded. It was not that men were thinking explicitly of a cell for every idea, although the apparent infinitude of both made the correlation reasonable as to numbers, but rather that the new knowledge of the division of the brain into many tiny connected units implied that sometime further separation of localized mental functions, like the ideas, was to be sought.

THE SPEECH CENTER

The next definite step in the knowledge of the physiology of the brain was again immediately concerned with the localization of function. In 1861, the year after Fechner published the *Elemente der Psychophysik* and thus inaugurated an experimental method that is the exclusive property of a scientific psychology, Paul Broca (1824-1880) announced the localization of a center for speech at the base of the third frontal convolution of the left cerebral hemisphere. This date is, therefore, usually taken as marking the first scientific discovery of the localization of a mental function within a circumscribed region within one of the major divisions of the brain. Flourens' doctrine of the unity of the cerebrum had not before been successfully challenged. It must be admitted that Broca's 'discovery' has eventually come into question. Speech is too complicated a function to be localized in a single cerebral center. Nevertheless, Broca's finding at the time counted as a discovery, so important a one that its priority was disputed by two other claimants.

In 1825 J. B. Bouillaud had advanced the view on clinical evidence that the center for articulate speech lies in the anterior portion of the cerebral lobes. Bouillaud was a physician and an admirer of Gall. although not what one might call a phrenologist. He opposed Flourens' belief in the unity of the cerebrum and suggested the existence of separate motor, perceptual and intellectual organs in the brain. He also presented some evidence to the Académie des Sciences in 1827 for an experimental distinction between the anterior and posterior portions of the cerebrum, stating that the removal of the posterior portion does not abolish sensation. He did not, however, prevail, nor did Dax, who presented a similar view in 1836. Bouillaud continued to hold his views, while making valuable contributions to a knowledge of the treatment of diseases of the heart, and in 1865, four years after Broca's discovery and forty years after his own, presented an elaborate paper to the Académie de Médecine extolling Gall, equating phrenology to scientific psychology, and reaffirming his own priority over Broca. It seems to have been a case where Bouillaud had more or less chanced upon a conclusion that gained general acceptance later when Broca's more careful technique had convinced the scientific world of a fact which continued to be accepted for seventy years. Nor is it improbable that Bouillaud's championship of phrenology led the scientists to regard him less seriously than they otherwise would have done.

Broca's famous observation was in itself very simple. There had in 1831 been admitted at the Bicêtre, an insane hospital near Paris, a man whose sole defect seemed to be that he could not talk. He communicated intelligently by signs and was otherwise mentally normal. He remained at the Bicêtre for thirty years with this defect and on April 12, 1861, was put under the care of Broca, the surgeon, because of a gangrenous infection. Broca for five days subjected him to a careful examination, in which he satisfied himself that the musculature of the larynx and articulatory organs was not hindered in normal movements, that there was no other paralysis that could interfere with speech, and that the man was intelligent enough to speak. On April 17 the patient—fortunately, it must have seemed, for science—died; and within a day Broca had performed an autopsy, discovered a lesion in the third frontal convolution of the left cerebral hemisphere, and had presented the brain in alcohol to the Société d'Anthropologie.

There was nothing new about this method. For many years French surgeons, especially those connected with the École de la Salpêtrière (the Salpêtrière is a large government home and hospital for women that includes among its inmates many insane), had been doubting Flourens' doctrine of the unity of the nervous system and believing that they must find more specific localization of function within it. The mere fact that in mental disease disturbances of motor, of sensory, and of intellectual functions are not necessarily associated, kept them looking for a constant difference of brain lesion in the different cases. Some localizations had been seriously proposed, even though Bouillaud's had not met with approval. Broca's merit lay in his careful examination of a clean-cut case which chance threw into his hands and in the immediacy with which he seized upon the broader implications.

Citing now other cases in support of the crucial one, and showing for it that the defect did not lie in muscular movement, Broca concluded that he had to do with the loss of the memory for words, and that the left third frontal convolution contains a center for language. He also took the position that the convolutions of the brain furnish adequate topographical marks to use in connection with the problem of localization. The differences between the brains of animals, even between different mammals, had left the physiologists uncertain how to identify accurately a given point in the brain. Now it suddenly appeared that the convolutions may be significant as fixing the place of certain organs or centers, and it was even suggested that differences between the brains of different kinds of animals may mean some difference in their mental functions.

More important, however, than either of these conclusions was Broca's enunciation of what he regarded as the necessary consequence of his discovery, the general principle of localization of function. "Il y a, dans le cerveau, de grandes régions distinctes correspondantes aux grandes régions de l'esprit." Here is a most instructive situation for the student of science. Thirty years before, both more and less, Gall and Spurzheim had argued vehemently to a receptive public for localization of mental functions in the brain, and the scientific world had refused to believe, at first on general considerations and later on the specific experimental evidence of Flourens. Now we find the scientific world accepting localization as a great discovery and listening willingly to Broca's demolition of Flourens: "Du moment qu'il sera démontré sans réplique qu'une faculté intellectuelle réside dans un point déterminé des hémisphères, la doctrine de l'unité du centre nerveux intellectuel sera renversée, et il sera hautement probable, sinon tout à fait certain, que chaque circonvolution est affectée par des fonctions particulières." Is science fickle? No, there was a difference, a difference of method. Flourens and Broca, although they appear to be upon opposite sides of a great controversy, both belong in the straight course of scientific progress because they held to the experimental method, which Gall did not do, and did not seek to transcend their observations, as did Gall. Nowadays we accept neither Flourens' vague *actions communes* nor Broca's precise localization of so complicated a function as language. The pendulum swings back and forth—from exact localization with Gall, to communal action with Flourens, to specific localization with the men who came after Broca, to mass action with Lashley, to the conception of alternative connective tracts. We know more and more, even though we take back something that we once knew. And never are we at the end. "La science n'est pas; elle devient," said Flourens.

MOTOR AND SENSORY CENTERS

Broca's contention, based on his clinical evidence, was not long in receiving support of a different kind from experimental physiology. In 1870, Fritsch and Hitzig announced the experimental discovery of the localization of motor functions in the cerebral cortex. This result reveals a very interesting situation with respect to scientific opinion. For half a century preceding, practically all physiologists had accepted the dogma of the 'inexcitability of the cerebral cortex.' Operations upon the cerebrums of animals do not produce movements, and it was known that operations upon the brains of clearly conscious persons were accompanied by no sensory or other conscious phenomena. Mechanical and chemical stimulation of various sorts had been tried without results. Apparently the brain was both inexcitable and insensitive to any direct stimulation then known to physiologists. Magendie, Flourens, and many other more recent physiologists of note concurred in this view. It was the accepted dogma. It had not, however, been a universal finding. Haller had reported convulsive movements on forcing an instrument into the substance of the cerebral hemispheres. There had been other scattered reports of the direct stimulation of the brain. We ourselves have noted that Rolando stimulated electrically what he took to be the cerebellum. Fritsch and Hitzig offered an explanation of the growth of this dogma on two possible grounds. They found motor centers in only a limited region of the brain, and since, except in the conscious human subject, sensation could only be judged by movement, it seemed probable that the negative results meant merely that the chances were against the stimulation of the right region when there was not a systematic exploration of the entire surface of the cerebrum. They also discovered that hemorrhage reduced or even abolished excitability of the cortex, and that death also immediately abolished excitability. It is possible that some negative results were to be accounted for in this manner. That precautions against hemorrhage and death should not have been taken is very reasonable, when it is remembered that neither of these events interferes with the immediate excitability of the motor nerves. At any rate, Fritsch and Hitzig referred the discrepancy between dogma and experiment to technique; "the method," they remarked, "creates the results."

This famous joint experiment originated in Hitzig's observation that the electrical stimulation of the cortex of a man led to movement of the eyes. Hitzig verified this observation on a rabbit, and then, with the assistance of Fritsch, undertook a systematic study of electrical stimulation of the cerebral cortex of the dog. In a certain region of the anterior portion of the cerebral cortex they found that they could get movement uniformly. If the current was strong, the movements were convulsive and general. With weak current, however, they succeeded in finding different 'centers' for different groups of muscles—five in all in the first experiment: one for the neck, one for extension of the foreleg, one for flexion of the foreleg, one for the hind leg, and one for the face.

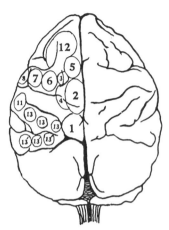
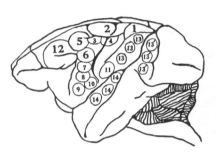

FIG. 2. LOCALIZATION OF MOTOR FUNCTION IN THE BRAIN OF THE MONKEY. After D. Ferrier, *Functions of the Brain*, 1876, 142.

1. Advance of opposite leg.
2. Movements of thigh, leg, and foot.
3. Movements of tail.
4. Retraction of opposite arm.
5. Apprehensile movements of opposite arm, hand, and fingers.
6. Flexion of forearm.
7. Retraction and elevation of angle of mouth.
8. Elevation of nose and upper lip.
9. Opening of mouth and protrusion of tongue.
10. Opening of mouth and retraction of tongue.
11. Retraction of opposite angle of mouth.
12. Opening of eyes, dilation of pupil, turning of head and eyes to opposite side.
13. Turning of eyes upward and to opposite side.
13.′ Turning of eyes downward and to opposite side.
14. Pricking of opposite ear, turning of head and eyes to opposite side, dilation of pupil.
15. Torsion of lip and nostril on same side.

A comparison of this figure with Fig. 1 (p. 55) shows not only the difference between the old and the new phrenology in the kind and range of faculties localized, but also how much less clear-cut a localization the experimental method yielded as against the uncontrolled empiricism of Gall and Spurzheim.

It was thus that the new and scientific 'phrenology' came into being. A tremendous amount of experimentation according to the new method was immediately begun. The findings of Fritsch and Hitzig were verified, and in a few years a very much more detailed map of the motor centers had been made out. The best known of the early workers were Ferrier in England, Nothnagel in Germany,

Carville and Duret in France. Figure 2 shows Ferrier's map of 1876 for the motor functions in the precentral part of the monkey's cerebral cortex. A little later, scattered through the last quarter of the century, came the researches of Goltz and Munk. Munk supported exact localization but Goltz stuck more closely to Flourens' position. There was a good deal of controversy, and nowadays we know why. Localization of a given function, exact at one moment of observation, may shift under altered bodily conditions, may be duplicated at another spot, may recover when lost, may occur as an artifact of too strong a stimulus.

No sooner were the motor centers thought to be established, than the search for sensory centers began. By the 1870s the effect of Johannes Müller's doctrine of specific nerve energies had been the establishment of a belief in the existence of five centers, one for each sense. The visual center was fixed first, and the centers for touch and hearing soon afterward.

There had long been evidence that the nerve fibers from the two retinas are projected upon the 'sensorium' of the brain. Galen (ca. 175 A.D.) explained the singleness of binocular vision by reference to the fact that some of the optic fibers cross at the chiasma and some do not. He thought that fibers from corresponding points on the two sides were actually joined. The conception of the horopter (Aguilonius, 1613) implied a paired correspondence between fibers from the two retinas. Newton (1717) was quite specific in his support of the notion that singleness of binocular vision is due to the coming together of fibers from corresponding points in the two eyes. David Hartley, influenced by Newton, supported a similar theory in 1749. W. H. Wollaston, a contemporary of Thomas Young's, told in 1824 how after excessive exertion he had twice lost sensitivity in one-half of his field of vision. There was good reason to believe that the semi-decussation of the optic nerves at the chiasma means that all the fibers from the left halves of both retinas (the fibers that serve for the right half of the visual field, since optical projection reverses the retinal image left and right) lead to some common locus ('center') in the left half of the brain, and conversely.

Ferrier first fixed the visual center in the occipital lobes. He found that a monkey, with an occipital lobe removed, was subject to abnormal eye-movements and acted as if blind in the eye opposite the side of the ablation. Munk (1881) showed that the removal of an occipital lobe does not entirely blind either eye, but produces hemianopia, the blindness for half of the field of vision in each eye. Goltz doubted these facts, but Munk was right.

By the end of the century, hearing had been localized in the temporal lobes, and somesthetic sensation in the post-central region, back of the motor area. The centers for taste and smell were uncertain.

In the twentieth century the tradition of Flourens and Goltz was continued by Franz (1902 *et seq.*) and Lashley (1917 *et seq.*), who showed how variable, how temporary and how inexact cortical localization of function may be. In 1929 Lashley summarized more than two decades of his and Franz's work by proposing the principles of equipotentiality and mass action. *Equipotentiality* means that one part of the cortex is as good as another in contributing to a certain function, like learning and 'intelligence.' *Mass action* means that all equipotential parts work together and that the loss of one diminishes efficiency in proportion to the magnitude of the loss, no matter where the loss occurs. The ability of rats, with different amounts of their cortices removed, to learn a maze accorded well with these two principles, but Lashley had no evidence that equipotentiality is not vicarious function, that the brain does not have alternative, if less efficient, ways of reacting when normal action is prevented. A dog, for instance, seems to have most of his functions duplicated in his two cerebral hemispheres, as if one hemisphere were provided as a spare for the other. For many functions there are, however, no substitutes. Lashley showed that pattern vision in the rat is abolished when the visual cortex is destroyed, although the rat may still discriminate brightness differences correctly. In man destruction of the visual cortex results in complete blindness for the part of the visual field which corresponds to the region destroyed. The human cortex functions for both pattern vision and brightness discrimination.

For the present status of the current researches on *action commune* and *action propre* in the cerebral cortex, the reader must refer to the texts on psychophysiology. Here we must content ourselves with a simple historical reflection.

Physiological psychologists still look for centers, find them, talk about them, yet never tell what a center is. In general, these men are connectionists, believing that the function of a nerve fiber is to transmit excitation from neuron to neuron, ultimately from a receptor in a sense-organ to an effector in a muscle or gland. On this view a center can be nothing more than a bottle-neck through which excitation essential for a given function must pass, a region so necessary that its destruction abolishes the function. That is good modern scientific sense. Thought about the centers easily gets mixed, however, with the century-old remnants of the Cartesian soul, the Sensorium, the little man inside the head who is the ultimate *I*. Is there not always some spot in the brain that is for a conscious function what the pineal gland was for Descartes' soul? Or, if that view is admittedly out of date, are there not special neurons in the brain whose excitation is always correlated with consciousness, whereas neurons at lower levels and in the spinal cord act without conscious accompaniment? The search for centers and for specific projection of peripheral excitation in the brain seems to reflect the older view that a conscious process ought to have in the brain, not a series of connections, but a localized seat. While this notion of a center as more of a seat than a bottle-neck is doubtless disappearing, its persistence after more than half a century of connectionistic neurology shows how slowly these basic conceptions die.

NOTES

The history of the physiology of the brain, with especial reference to localization of function, from Aristotle to Fritsch and Hitzig (1870) is given most excellently and completely by J. Soury, "Cerveau," in C. Richet's *Dictionnaire de physiologie*, II, 1897, 547-670. Soury has expanded this discussion in his two-volume work, *Système nerveux central*, 1899, 1863 pp. The reader who consults either of these sources will realize how very scanty indeed is the discussion of the text.

For Bichat, see X. Bichat, *Recherches physiologiques sur la vie et la mort*, 1799-1800 (An VIII), Eng. trans., 1827. For the French physiologists on the visceral seat of the passions as anticipating James and Lange, see E. B. Titchener, *Amer. J. Psychol.*, 1914, 25, 427-447.

For Rolando's experiments and theory, see L. Rolando, *Saggio sopra la vera struttura del cervello e sopra le funzioni del sistema nervoso*, 1809. The work is summarized in French by Coster, Expériences sur le système nerveux de l'homme et des animaux; publiées en Italie en 1809, et répétées en France en 1822, *Arch. gén. méd.*, 1823, 1, 359-418. If Flourens, whose memoirs were first reported in 1822, overlooked the Italian book, he at least made ample amends by reprinting Rolando's experiments in his own book, *q.v.*; P. Flourens, *Recherches expérimentales*, etc. (*vide infra*), 1824, 273-302.

Flourens

For a brief account of Flourens' work, see Soury, *op. cit.*, 1897. 616-619, or 1899, I, 518-522. Soury fully appreciates the lucidity of Flourens' mind. He remarks that, although the structure and the functions of the central nervous system are things infinitely complex and obscure, Flourens succeeded in realizing the complexity but not the obscurity.

The fundamental reference is M. J. P. Flourens, *Recherches expérimentales sur les propriétés et les fonctions du système nerveux dans les animaux vertébrés*, 1824, 331 pp. The additional memoirs were published as *Expériences sur le système nerveux*, 1825, 53 pp. The second edition of these two works bears the title of the first, and is dated 1842. Flourens observed in the preface that revision had been necessary, but the reader will find the essentials of the discussion unchanged. The work provides its own summaries; notably in the preface (1824, i-xxvi), at the close of the first three memoirs (1824, 121 f.), and in the chapter called "De l'unité du système nerveux" (1824, 236-241). Some excerpts in Eng. trans. have been published by Wayne Dennis, *Readings in the History of Psychology*, 1948, 129-139.

In an attempt to follow Flourens' rule for securing clarity by brevity, the text translates *sensation* and *sentir* as meaning "perception" when reference is to the cerebral hemispheres. The ambiguity of the French *sensation* is well known, and Flourens uses it in two senses, although his meaning is always clear in the larger context. The sensation that belongs to the medulla or the corpora quadrigemina is bare sensitivity as evidenced in a reflex, like the pupillary reflex. In one place he calls it *sentiment* for the medulla. The sensation of the cerebrum is the sensory experience that belongs to perception, contributes to judgment, and is bound up with the will. It is true that Flourens says that "les lobes cérébraux sont le siège exclusif des sensations, des perceptions et des volitions"; but then he also says "de vouloir, de juger, de se souvenir, de voir, d'entendre, en un mot de sentir"; and we must remember that all these are not separate but "une faculté essentiellement une." Cerebral sensation is plainly perception in the modern sense, and thus Joh. Müller, in summarizing Flourens, notes that in the cerebrum "die Empfindungen nicht bloss bewusst werden, sondern zu Anschauungen, Vorstellungen umgeshaffen." On the ambiguity of *sensation* and *sentiment* as applied to feeling, see E. B. Titchener, A note on *sensation* and *sentiment*, *Amer. J. Psychol.*, 1914, 25, 301-307.

It is quite clear that Flourens has given a positive meaning to the problem of the 'seat' of the faculties, a meaning that ought to have rendered obsolete such contentions as Bichat's, only a quarter of a century earlier, that the seat of the passions is in the viscera. On this point in Bichat, see Flourens, *De la vie et de l'intelligence*, 2d ed., 1858, 142-160, 251-261.

The key to Flourens on the doctrine of Gall is Flourens' *Examen de la phrénologie*, 1842. It puts the case of science against phrenology, and it also shows how seriously the phrenological vogue had to be taken by scientists. In the preface Flourens wrote: "The 17th century enthroned the philosophy of Descartes; the 18th that of Locke and Condillac; should the 19th enthrone that of Gall?...I cite Descartes often; I do more, I dedicate my book to him. I write against a bad philosophy, and I call back the good." Thus Flourens conjured up Descartes to depreciate Gall.

The text omits reference to much important work of Flourens that does not belong in the present context. The work of 1824 (first reported in 1822) describes experiments on the nerves which show that the primary division among nerves is between the sensory and motor functions. Thus Flourens verified the distinction made by Bell's law in the very year that Magendie was reporting this same law as an independent discovery. Flourens' experiments on the semicircular canals (1824, 1830) are, with Purkinje's work (1820, 1827), the pioneer studies on 'vestibular equilibration.'

Brain Physiology

The reader who wishes a picture of the physiology of the brain as it was known in the second quarter of the nineteenth century will do well to read Joh. Müller's account of it in *Handbuch der Physiologie des Menschen*, I, bk. iii, sect. v, chap. 3, or the English translation. He will note that Müller relied principally upon Flourens and the knowledge gained from pathology. For F. Magendie, see his *Précis élémentaire de physiologie*, 1816-1817, but esp. 2d ed., 1825, Eng. trans., 1826; and also his *Anatomie comparative du cerveau*, 1826. For Antoine Desmoulins (1796-1828), see his *Anatomie des systèmes nerveux des animaux vertébrés*, 1825, esp. II, 595-637. Magendie was Desmoulins's collaborator in the physiological portions of this book, although he is referred to in the third person.

While the discovery of secondary degeneration is due to O. Nasse, [*Müller's*] *Arch. Anat. Physiol.*, 1839, 405-419, it is more often associated with Waller and sometimes called Wallerian degeneration, because he employed it as a method of tracing nerve tracts. See A. Waller, *Philos. Trans.*, 1850, 423-429. Golgi's original paper of 1873 was in Italian, but his later book was translated into German: C. Golgi, *Untersuchungen über den fein-*

eren Bau des centralen und peripherischen Nervensystems, [1885], German trans., 1894. S. Ramon y Cajal wrote in Spanish and is available largely in secondary sources. The reference to the original description of the synapse is said to be *Riv. trimestr. micrograph.*, 1889, 1, 2 ff. The neuron theory was formulated by W. Waldeyer, *Ueber einige neuere Forschungen im Gebiete der Anatomie des Centralnervensystems*, 1891. For an excellent historical summary of the work of Golgi and Cajal, see J. Soury, Histoire des doctrines contemporaines de l'histologie du système nerveux central; théorie des neurones, *Arch. de neurol.*, 2me sér., 1897, 3; Golgi, 95-118; Cajal and the theory of neurons, 281-312.

On the general development of microscopy and cytology in this period, and the effect upon research of the improvement of the compound microscope in the 1830s, see E. Nordenskiöld, *History of Biology*, 1928, 389-405.

Speech Center

J. B. Bouillaud's original paper on the speech center is Recherches clinique à démontrer que la perte de la parole correspond à la lésion des lobules antérieurs du cerveau, et à confirmer l'opinion de M. Gall sur le siège de l'organe du langage articulé, *Arch. gén. méd.*, 1825, 8, 25-45. His later defense of localization was read before the Académie de Médecine in 1865. The other claimant for priority in this matter is M. Dax, who read a paper to the Congrès méridional at Montpellier in 1836, which was not published until 1865; *Gazette hebdomadaire méd. chir.*, 2me sér., 1865, 2, 259-262. For Broca's original paper, see C. Broca, *Bull. Soc. anat.*, 2me sér., 1861, 6, 330-357.

Localization

On the history of brain localization, see J. Soury, Cerveau, in C. Richet's *Dictionnaire de physiologie*, 1897, II, 898-952. There is an excellent elementary discussion as of its date in W. James, *Principles of Psychology*, 1890, I, 41-62. See also the historical paragraphs and references given by J. F. Fulton, *Physiology of the Nervous System*, 1938, 340, 347 f., 365, 375 f., 397 f.

For the early papers, see G. Fritsch and E. Hitzig, Ueber die elektrische Erregbarkeit des Grosshirns, [*Reichert und du Bois-Reymond's*] *Arch. Anat. Physiol.*, 1870, 300-332; D. Ferrier, *The Functions of the Brain*, 1876, 2nd ed., 1886, describing researches which began in 1873; H. Nothnagel, [*Virchow's*] *Arch. pathol. Anat. Physiol.*, 1873, 57, 184-214; 1873, 58, 420-436; 1874, 60, 128-142; 1875, 62, 201-214; C. Carville and H. Duret, *Arch. physiol.*, 2me sér., 1875, 2, 352-491; F. L. Goltz, *Ueber die Verrichtungen des Grosshirns*, 1881 (four papers, 1876-1881); H. Munk, *Ueber die Functionen der Grosshirnrinde*, 1890 (17 papers, 1877-1889).

For summaries of their own work as of 1912 and 1929 respectively, see S. I. Franz, New phrenology, *Science*, 1912, 35, 321-328; K. S. Lashley, *Brain Mechanisms and Intelligence*, 1929, esp. 23-26 86-89, 157-174. W. S. Hunter started to push the pendulum back away from *action commune* in his A consideration of Lashley's theory of equipotentiality of cerebral action, *J. general Psychol.*, 1930, 3, 455-468.

On the present status of the problem of brain localization, see C. T. Morgan, *Physiological Psychology*, 1943, 70-84, 330-353, *et passim*; J. F. Fulton, *Howell's Textbook of Physiology*, 15 ed., 1946, 178-547 *passim*.

CHAPTER 5

Specific Energies of Nerves

We have already seen how the establishment of the Bell-Magendie law of the sensory and motor functions of the spinal nerve roots served once and for all to separate these two functions within physiology, creating a primary dichotomy within the nervous system. The physiology of movement, as we have noted its development in the two preceding chapters, kept ahead of the physiology of sensation, largely because animals provide the convenient experimental material for the physiologist, and animal movement can be perceived by an experimenter whereas animal sensation can only be inferred. So some knowledge of reflex action came quite early. The study of nerve action from Galvani to du Bois-Reymond was possible because excitation of a motor nerve makes a muscle contract in an observable manner. Motor centers were mapped in the brain before sensory centers because the stimulation of certain cortical points made certain muscle groups move.

On the other hand, the problems of sensation were there for the physiologist to tackle. He had no mechanical recorder to hook onto the central end of a sensory nerve of an animal, but he did have 'immediate experience' available within himself. Goethe, Purkinje, Johannes Müller, E. H. Weber, and later Fechner, A. W. Volkmann and Helmholtz, all worked out the laws of their own experiences as they were consequent upon stimulation, and the last named five carefully controlled the stimulation. Newton long before had discovered the laws of color mixture in the same way. These physiologists were using what psychologists later called *Selbstbeobachtung* or *introspection*: they were reporting on their own immediate experiences under controlled conditions. In the next chapter we shall see how this kind of sense-physiology prospered in the first half of the nineteenth century, but first we must examine the basic principle of specific nerve energies.

BELL AND MÜLLER ON SPECIFIC NERVE ENERGIES

The doctrine of specific energies of nerves, as Johannes Müller named it, was the most important law in sense-physiology which these early decades produced. The law is associated especially with Müller's name because he had the most to say about it and insisted most emphatically upon it, and it is properly called the Müllerian theory when it is to be distinguished from the extension which Helmholtz gave it.

Careful study shows, however, that there is in this doctrine not one single principle that was new with Müller; everything of importance had already been stated by Sir Charles Bell, and there is no doubt that Bell himself thought as clearly in these matters as did Müller. For this reason, some persons have argued that Bell's name rather than Müller's should be attached to the doctrine. It seems probable, however, that, were this to be done, the critics would have little difficulty in showing that the essential facts were all known before Bell also; that, of the two most important principles, Aristotle implied one and the other has been explicitly a familiar doctrine in philosophy, at least since Descartes and Locke. In other words, we are dealing here simply with the continuity of thought that so frequently makes it impossible to date a discovery or to assign a theory to its originator. Certainly enough was known and already established in doctrine for the theory to have been formulated before the nineteenth century. Certainly Bell deserves credit for his insight in bringing various observations together and showing their meaning clearly. What Bell did not do was to organize this view as a distinct theory or to adopt a terminology that would serve to give it a name. Had he been less modest about his own achievement and in the degree of printed publicity which he gave it, we might have come to regard this theory as one of Bell's laws. Müller, because he comes later, deserves less credit for his insight; if this view was after all more or less the obvious fact to a thoughtful person in 1811 when Bell wrote of it, it must have been more nearly obvious in 1826 when Müller first wrote, and in 1838 when he gave it systematic position.

It seems quite clear, that, had it not been for Müller, many things that did happen would not have happened. Müller gave the theory explicit and precise formulation. It occupies almost 2 per cent of an entire volume of his *Handbuch*. He gave it, practically, a name. By including it in the *Handbuch*, he gave it also the weight of his own great personal authority and of the publicity of that important compendium. In short, though he may have originated nothing in it, he placed the seal of orthodoxy upon it. Had this not occurred, we might never have had Helmholtz's theory of hearing, now classical in itself. Conceivably we might not have had Helmholtz's or Hering's theories of vision. We should not have had the discovery of the sensory spots in the skin in the manner of its occurrence, for these researches were suggested explicitly by the theory. In time the doctrine became almost a dogma, and the fact that it does not quite make sense nowadays is due in part to the way in which the theory of sensory centers supplanted it and in part to the fact that the meaning of the word *energy* changed radically with the formulation of the theory of the conservation of energy. Müller meant *quality* by *energy*, and we still hold the belief that different neural systems excite different sense-qualities, even though we must now think of all neural impulses as alike in nature.

Johannes Müller formulated this doctrine of the specific energies of nerves under ten laws. To the modern reader who has not to combat the same current beliefs as Müller, these laws seem somewhat repetitious. We shall, at any rate, not quote them as they were given, for they can readily be found thus in other sources; rather we shall attempt to examine the principles contained in them, referring to the laws by number (I-X), and noting the empirical and historical background of each principle.

1. The central and fundamental principle of the doctrine is that we are directly aware, not of objects, but of our nerves themselves; that is to say, the nerves are intermediates between perceived objects and the mind and thus impose their own characteristics upon the mind.

Müller's dictum was: "Sensation consists in the sensorium's receiving through the medium of the nerves, and as the result of the action of an external cause, a knowledge of certain qualities or conditions, not of external bodies, but of the nerves of sense themselves" (V). "The immediate objects of the perception of our senses are merely particular states induced in the nerves, and felt as sensations either by the nerves themselves or by the sensorium" (VIII).

Bell's position was similar: "It is admitted that neither bodies nor the images of bodies enter the brain. It is indeed impossible to believe that colour can be conveyed along a nerve; or the vibration in which we suppose sound to consist can be retained in the brain: but we can conceive, and have reason to believe, that an impression is made upon the organs of the outward senses when we see, hear or taste." "The idea in the mind is the result of an action excited in the eye or brain, not of anything received, though caused by an impression from without. The operations of the mind are confined not by the limited nature of things created but by the limited number of our organs of sense."

Now there is nothing new in the idea that the nerves are intermediaries between the external world and the brain; that had been said by Herophilus and Erasistratus (*ca.* 250 B C.), and had been common doctrine since Galen (*ca.* 200 A.D.). That the nerves would thus impose their own nature upon the mind is a necessary consequence of the materialistic view of immediate causes, and of the brain as the organ of mind. Epistemologically, this principle in Müller has been characterized as "a fruit of the anthropocentric standpoint, as the newer philosophy from Descartes down to Kant and Fichte has developed it," and also as the mere "physiological counterpart of a Kantian category." It is more likely that Bell felt unconsciously the tradition of British empiricism.

It was essentially on this matter that Hartley wrote in his *Observations on Man* in 1749: "The white medullary Substance of the Brain is also the immediate Instrument, by which Ideas are presented to the Mind: or, in other words, whatever Changes are made in this Substance, corresponding Changes are made in our Ideas." "External Objects impressed upon the Senses occasion, first in the Nerves on which they are impressed, and then in the Brain, Vibrations of the small, and as one may say, infinitesimal, medullary Particles."

That the idea in the mind is the result "not of anything received" (Bell's phrase) from the external object by way of the nerves, that "the nerves of the senses are not mere conductors of the properties of bodies to our sensorium" (Müller's phrase), was apparent in Locke's doctrine of secondary qualities in 1690. Locke wrote: "To discover the nature of our *ideas* the better, and to discourse of them intelligibly, it will be convenient to distinguish them, as they are ideas or perceptions in our minds: and as they are modifications of matter in the bodies that cause such perceptions in us; that we may not think (as perhaps usually is done) that they are exactly the images and resemblances of something inherent in the subject; most of those in sensation being in mind no more the likeness of something existing without us than the names that stand for them are the likeness of our ideas, which yet upon hearing they are apt to excite in us." While the correspondence between the idea and the perceived body is close in the case of the primary qualities, it is not in the case of secondary qualities: "such qualities, which in truth are nothing in the objects themselves, but powers to produce various sensations in us by their primary qualities, *i.e.*, by the bulk, figure, texture, and motion of their insensible parts, as colours, sounds, tastes, &c., these I call *secondary* qualities." "If, then, external objects be not united to our minds when they produce ideas therein; and yet we perceive these *original* qualities in such of them as fall singly under our senses, it is evident that some motion must then be continued by our nerves, or animal spirits, by some parts of our bodies, to the brains or seat of sensation, there to produce in our minds the particular ideas we have of them."

2. No less important in the doctrine than this conception of the relation of the nerves to the mind is the principle of specificity. There are five kinds of nerves, and each imposes its specific quality upon the mind.

Müller's statement is: "Sensation consists in the sensorium's receiving ... a knowledge of certain qualities ... of the nerves of sense themselves; and these qualities of the nerves of sense are in all different, the nerve of each having its own peculiar quality or energy" (V). "The nerve of each sense seems to be capable of one determinate kind of sensation only, and not of those proper to the other organs of sense; hence one nerve of sense cannot take the place and perform the function of the nerve of another sense" (VI).

Similarly Bell: "The operations of the mind are confined ... by the limited number of our organs of sense." "If the retina were sensible to the matter of light only from possessing a finer sensibility than the nerve of touch, it would be a source of torment; whereas it is most beneficially provided that it shall not be sensible to pain, nor be capable of conveying any impression to the mind but those which operate according to its proper function producing light and colour." "The nerve of vision is as insensible to touch as the nerve of touch is to light."

Now this principle adds to the first only the notion that there are a few specific qualities or energies, which are immutable functions of the separate senses. There is little here that is not contained in Aristotle's original doctrine of the five senses. We may cite Aristotle directly: "In discussing any form of sense-perception we must begin with the sensible object ... By the 'peculiar object of sense' I mean a sense-quality which cannot be apprehended by a sense different from that to which it belongs, and concerning which that sense cannot be deceived, e.g., color is the peculiar object of vision, sound of hearing, flavor of taste. Touch, however, discriminates several sense-qualities. The other particular senses, on the contrary, distinguish only their peculiar objects, and the senses are not deceived in the fact that a quality is color and sound ... To the objects of sense, strictly regarded, belong such properties as are peculiarly and properly sense-qualities, and it is with these that the essential nature of each sense is naturally concerned." "It is necessary that if any sensation is lacking, some organ must also be lacking in us." This is the doctrine which had long been the common belief about senses. It is to be noted that it even asserts for touch a multiplicity of sense-qualities, an assertion that anticipated the nineteenth century discovery of several 'specific energies' within this sense-mode.

3. The third principle of the doctrine of specific energies deals with the nature of the empirical evidence for the first two principles. It asserts that the same stimulus affecting different nerves gives rise to the different qualities appropriate to the particular nerves, and, conversely, that different stimuli affecting the same nerve always give rise to the peculiar quality for that nerve.

Müller devoted three laws to this matter. "The same internal cause excites in the different senses different sensations—in each sense the sensations peculiar to it" (II). "The same external cause also gives rise to different sensations in each sense, according to the special endowments of its nerve" (III). "The peculiar sensations of each nerve of sense can be excited by several distinct causes internal and external" (IV). In support of these laws, Müller brought a very great deal of simple empirical evidence to bear. A blow on the head may be enough 'to give a person what will make his ears ring,' or 'what will make his eyes flash fire,' or 'what will make him feel.' "Pressure on the eye-ball gives rise to colors." An electrical stimulus can, according to the evidence which Müller accepted, become the cause of any one of the five sensations as it affects one nerve or another. Müller is especially complete in enumerating instances of this kind. Plainly then, among a multiplicity of causes the quality of sensation depends, not upon the nature of the cause, but upon the nature of the nerve which the cause affects. Otherwise there ought to be an electrical sense-quality.

If Bell was less replete with instances than Müller, still he was not less sure. "It is also very remarkable that an impression made on two different nerves of sense, though with the same instrument, will produce two distinct sensations; and the ideas resulting will only have relation to the organ affected." "In the operation of couching the cataract ... the pain is occasioned by piercing the outward coat, not by the affection of the expanded nerve of vision, ... but, ... when the needle pierces the eye, the patient has the sensation of a spark of fire before the eye." "When the eyeball is pressed on the side, we perceive various coloured light. Indeed the mere effect of a blow on the head might inform us that sensation depends on the exercise of the organ affected, not on the impression conveyed to the external organ; for by the vibration caused by the blow, the ears ring, and the eye flashes light, while there is neither light nor sound present." Even touch and taste, Bell thought, can be discriminated in mechanical stimulation of the tongue.

Now some of these illustrations come from what was then modern technique and some from common sense. To the former group belong Bell's instance of the operation upon the eye, all the experiments on stimulating the senses electrically (Volta, the inventor in 1800 of the Voltaic pile, described some of these), Magendie's observations that the retina, the optic nerve, and the olfactory nerve give no signs of pain on being pricked, and Tourtual's observation that, in extirpating the human eye, the section of the optic nerve gives rise to "the perception of a great light." In the antiquity of the notion, however, Müller himself believed. He suggested that even Plato possessed an imperfect idea that internal causes other than light could give rise to the sensations of light and color. He cited Aristotle on dreams to the same end, and noted that Spinoza observed that the colors seen after gazing at the sun occur in the absence of light. Another historian goes further and cites Aristotle as knowing that light sensations may follow upon mechanical stimulation.

The contribution of Bell and Müller to theory really lies in this point. There was evidence long before them of the independent variability of stimulus and sense-quality, but it was scattered, meager and casual. They brought the new evidence together; they found more of it; and some of it partook of the nature of experimentation.

4. When we take up the doctrine in this order, the fourth point seems trivial. It consists merely in Müller's emphasis upon the equivalence of internal and external stimuli. It seemed important to Müller because the localization of the mind in the brain had only recently become unquestionable doctrine, and, unless the mind were limited to some restricted portion of the body, any internal condition could be thought of as acting directly upon the mind and not by way of the nerves.

Müller thus devoted his first law to this point. "External agencies can give rise to no kind of sensation which can not also be produced by internal causes, exciting changes in the condition of our nerves." For this reason he separated the second and third laws, quoted above, so that he might deal separately with the internal and external causes. Bell did not raise this point because he was taking it for granted that only the brain is the organ of the mind: "all ideas originate in the brain: the operation of producing them is the remote effect of an agitation or impression on the extremities of the nerves of sense."

The entire history of the notion of the brain as the seat of the mind is the necessary preparation for this view. When this matter is settled, the point becomes redundant, although Müller avoided an appearance of redundancy by dealing with the question first.

5. To say that the mind is directly aware only of the state of the nerves is to raise at once the problem of how it becomes aware of external objects, the fundamental problem of knowledge. Müller's answer to this question lay first in the relation of the nerves to external objects. The nerves, like all other objects, have definite relations to external objects. Unless an external agent possess certain properties, it affects a particular nerve not at all or only exceptionally. Plainly, the eye ordinarily perceives light, but not pressure. Exceptionally it may perceive pressure, but then it perceives it as color. And so with the other senses.

Müller's manner of expressing this point was as follows. "Inasmuch as the nerves of the senses are material bodies, and therefore participate in the properties of matter generally occupying space, being susceptible of vibratory motion, and capable of being changed chemically as well as by the action of heat and electricity, they make known to the sensorium, by virtue of the changes thus produced in them by external causes, not merely their own condition, but also the properties and changes of condition of external bodies. The information thus obtained by the senses concerning external nature, varies in each sense, having a relation to the qualities or energies of the nerve" (VIII). Müller also spoke of the "specific irritability" of the organs of sense, borrowing this phrase from Glisson's concept of the irritability of muscle (1677), a concept which Haller had later made familiar.

Bell met the problem almost as explicitly. Of the ideas, which "originate in the brain," he said: "Directly they are consequences of a change or operation in the proper organ of the sense which constitutes a part of the brain ... It is provided, that the extremities of the nerves of the senses shall be susceptible each of certain qualities in matter; and betwixt the impression of the outward sense, as it may be called, and the exercise of the internal organ, there is established a connection by which the ideas excited have a permanent correspondence with the qualities of bodies which surround us."

We must note that this view of the correct perception of objects depends on this concept of *specific irritability* or, as Sherrington named it in 1906, *adequate stimulation*. It is plain that the eye most readily and naturally perceives light; the ear, sound; the skin, pressures; and so on. A pressure is not actually an 'inadequate,' but a less adequate, stimulus to vision. Sounds may be felt, but less readily than pressures. In other words, because there is a predominant and more adequate relation of the stimulus to the nerve, we come predominantly to perceive objects truly by way of the nerves. When an 'inadequate' stimulus is effective, illusion results.

Thus Müller's doctrine shifted the old problem of the perception of objects, the basic problem of idealistic philosophy, from explanation by representation of the object in kind (cf. Locke's primary qualities, pp. 174 f.) to explanation in terms of specific functional relationships between terms (object and its perception) which do not necessarily resemble each other. So the doctrine anticipates, not only Sherrington's adequate stimulus, but also the isomorphism of Gestalt psychology (p. 615).

6. There remains the question of the locus of the specific principle, whether it lies in the nerve or at one or the other termination. Müller had no certain answer to this question. "It is not known," he said, "whether the essential cause of the peculiar 'energy' of each nerve of sense is seated in the nerve itself, or in the parts of the brain or spinal cord with which it is connected; but it is certain that the central portions of the nerves included in the encephalon are susceptible of their peculiar sensations, independently of the more peripheral portion of the nervous cords which form the means of communication with the external organs of sense" (VII). Bell noted of the general theory that "there is here no proof of the sensation being in the brain more than in the external organ of sense. But when the nerve stump is touched the pain is as if in the amputated extremity." We have already quoted Bell's assertion that "all ideas originate in the brain"; that "directly they are consequences of a change or operation in the proper organ of the sense which constitutes a part of the brain."

This addendum to the doctrine is important, for it tended to localize the specificity in the brain. The stimulation of the proximal ends of severed nerves shows that the specificity is not in the sense-organ or in the peripheral portion of the nerve. If it is not in the peripheral portion, there is a certain presumption against its being in the central portion, and thus by a process of elimination it would have to be in the central termination. This view plays at once into the hands of those who would find localization of function in the brain. A belief in sensory centers for the five senses is only a step further. Such a belief was not for the moment a popular view, not because it was new, but because it was too familiar in phrenology. With the 'new phrenology' that followed Fritsch and Hitzig (1870), science was ready to accept a belief in such centers and to find evidence, some of it rigorously experimental, for localizing them. Müller's seventh law, in a way, then, foreshadowed the accepted gospel of the late nineteenth century.

7. We need finally but to mention briefly that Müller in his last law discussed the selective power of the mind over against the specific energies. This point is an entirely gratuitous addition, which goes to show the degree of completeness which Müller sought in his compendium. The mind "has a direct influence" upon sensations, "imparting to them intensity"; that is to say, we can attend to parts of the visual field to the exclusion of others or to parts of the tactual field, or we can make the same discrimination with respect to time in the case of hearing. Moreover, the mind "also has the power of giving to one sense a predominant activity." Of course selection, attention or determination has remained a persistent problem in psychology. It is interesting to see that Müller, a physiologist, was unable to avoid the problem; but then, Müller perhaps ought also to be considered as an early nineteenth century experimental psychologist, for one of the eight major sections of the *Handbuch* is entitled "Of the Mind," and deals, not with sensation and movement, which are treated elsewhere, but with what have since been called the 'higher mental processes.'

As is always the case with a broad doctrine presented in elaborate detail, Müller's theory led to criticism, which came in this instance from Lotze, E. H. Weber, and others. It was possible, in particular, to criticise the factual evidence marshaled in support of the doctrine. Some facts were not easily verifiable, and remained doubtful as to their exact nature. Especially is it not always clear that the effect of the stimulus is as simple as the name of the stimulus implies. For instance, Weber wondered whether the electrical excitation of sound might not be due to the electric stimulation of the muscles of the middle ear, which might thus act upon the drum-skin and produce at least the mechanical equivalent of sound at that point. In spite of the argument from the effectiveness in certain cases of inappropriate stimuli, it became obvious that most inappropriate stimuli are completely inadequate. It is plain that light is never the stimulus to hearing, taste or smell (though it may be to warmth); that heat or cold never gives rise to sight, sound, or odor; that the stimuli for taste and smell are quite ineffective in producing sights or sounds. If they were, illusion might be so common that the perception of reality would be seriously hampered.

Such criticism does not alter the central doctrine which rather depends upon these facts. It did serve, however, to show the naïveté of the distinction between appropriate and inappropriate stimuli. If a metallic rod gives rise to pressure on the nerve of touch and to taste on the nerve of taste, still there is no reason to believe that this distinction occurs for any other reason than that the rod is sapid as well as heavy; no one is surprised because a lump of sugar on the skin arouses pressure. If sounds are sometimes felt, it is simply because they consist of vibrations, and as such are mechanical as well as acoustic stimuli. In other words, the entire argument from 'inadequate' stimuli simply reflects the then popular conception that somehow or other the nerves conducted to the brain, not exactly properties of the object, but rather incorporeal copies of the object. In spite of the philosophical sophistication of the times, this was the view that both Bell and Müller explicitly opposed, and as against that point of view, it is important to see that very different objects produce the same effect by the same nerve, and the same object very different effects by different nerves, provided the nerves are affected at all. Certainly the criticism cleared the air of a misleading epistemology, although it left the theory unscathed. It became plain that the doctrine was essentially nothing more than the fact that a given nerve, however affected, if affected at all, gives rise to a sense-quality that depends only on the specific character of the nerve. The matter of adequate stimuli thus became another problem, and here it was clear that the relationships were to be understood by reference not to the common-sense classes of objects, but rather to the physical nature of the stimuli and their effects. The physiologist was brought back to Locke's doctrine of secondary qualities, dependent upon the "powers" of the object, "which in truth are nothing in the objects themselves."

Lotze and other of Müller's critics argued that sensory nerves must be all alike and not possessed of different kinds of 'energy.' That, as it turned out, was a correct criticism of Müller's preference for thinking of qualitative specificity as resident in the nerves rather than in the respective sites of their central terminations. Müller had not gone far enough. He had substituted specific energies for the older *vires nervosae* and had explained perception by the fixed functional relations of the specific irritabilities of the sense-organs. We know now that qualitative difference lies not in the nerve excitations themselves but in their different central effects. The nervous system works not by differences in the nature of transmission but by the different functional effects of one neuron upon a next.

SPECIFIC FIBER ENERGIES

While this criticism was going on, the so-called extension of the Müllerian theory had already begun. The extension consists merely in applying the principle of the dependence of qualitative difference upon specific nerves to differences of quality within a single modality of sense. This development is usually attributed to Helmholtz, who made such effective use of it in his theory of hearing; but once again we find that the man who gave his name to the theory was not the very first to propose it. Priority seems to belong to Natanson, who made this suggestion in 1844, only six years after Müller had formally promulgated the complete, systematized doctrine in his *Handbuch*. Volkmann followed him immediately with a similar view. If Müller's theory is a doctrine of specific *nerve* energies, then Helmholtz's extension of the doctrine is a theory of specific *fiber* energies.

Natanson laid down the fundamental principle that every organ of the nervous system has but a single function. It follows that there must be as many organs as functions—that is to say, as sensory qualities. This proposition led Natanson to posit separate nerves for temperature, for touch and for the perception of resistance; for sweet, sour and bitter; for the simple smells (which he could not of course at that time name); and for the fundamental colors, red, yellow and blue. In other words, he divided up four of the five senses into what he regarded as simple sensations. No such analysis was available for the tones, and Helmholtz's boldness in supposing several thousand specific auditory energies was too great a complication for him to dare.

There was, however, nothing so bold in Helmholtz's theory of vision, which he published in 1852 and included in the second volume of his *Handbuch der physiologischen Optik* (1860). Here he stated the theory concisely, giving credit for it to Thomas Young. "The eye is provided with three distinct sets of nervous fibers. Stimulation of the first excites the sensation of red, stimulation of the second the sensation of green, and stimulation of the third the sensation of violet." It is quite clear that Helmholtz knew that he was extending Müller's theory to account for qualities within the single sense. That he did not argue for this finer specificity at length is probably due to the fact that he did not regard the extended theory as new, for he was attributing it to Thomas Young.

Actually Thomas Young, with this theory of specificity for different color qualities, was anticipating both Bell and Müller on their more general theory of specificity of the different senses. Young first presented his idea in a paper which he read in 1801 and published in 1802. "Each sensitive point of the retina," he observed, must contain "a limited number of particles" that vibrate in resonance with the frequencies of "the three principal colours, red, yellow, and blue." These particles excite the nerve, and it is possible that "each sensitive filament of the nerve may consist of three portions, one for each principal colour." Young even specified that the magnitudes of the "undulations" for red, yellow and blue would be proportional to the numbers 8, 7 and 6. Later in 1802 he correctly changed these numbers to 7, 6 and 5. If Charles Bell in 1811 had had his attention called to what Thomas Young had said ten years before, it is to be doubted that he would have been greatly surprised. Bell thought that nerve-specificity was fairly obvious and might have been readily willing to extend the principle to fiber-specificity. Johannes Müller, on the other hand, would hardly have been prepared in 1826 to have gone so far. His marshalling of arguments to support nerve-specificity shows that the thought of fiber-specificity for qualitative distinctions was far from his mind.

Helmholtz's resonance theory of hearing first appeared in 1863. In it he made explicit and conscious use of Müller's doctrine. Continuous homogeneous sounds can be analyzed into harmonic components. Resonators make such an analysis, and we also seem to be able to make it introspectively. The thing to look for in the ear is, therefore, a set of resonators, each of which will give rise separately to a tonal sensation. Helmholtz looked and found (for the first edition of *Die Lehre von den Tonempfindungen*) the arches of Corti. Later he thought that transverse fibers of the basilar membrane were better, but the argument remained the same. There had been estimated to be about 4,500 outer arch fibers. If every one of these arches resonates best to a different frequency, is tonal hearing explained? Yes, if we but take "a step similar to that taken in a wider field by Johannes Müller," for each arch fiber excites a different nerve fiber, and the separate tonal sensations as well as the harmonic analysis of complex clangs by the ear are accounted for. Of course, this step means 4,500 specific auditory energies (and some later research doubled this number), but it was the logical, almost irresistible step to take, and Helmholtz did not hesitate to take it.

We may merely indicate here the later developments of the theory. For a considerable period it was the only theory available for the physiological explanation of qualitative difference. Blix and Goldscheider, independent discoverers in 1883-84 of the separate sensory 'spots' in the skin for warmth, cold and pressure, were consciously seeking separate endings because they seemed to be required by this theory. The analysis of taste into sweets, sours, salts and bitters came to be taken as indicating four specific gustatory energies. Hering's theory of vision assumed six visual energies—a further modification, since a pair of nerve fibers would have to be excited by the two antagonistic processes of a single visual substance: assimilation of one substance would give rise to green by exciting the appropriate fibers; dissimilation of the same substance would give red by exciting the other fiber; and so for the other two pairs.

One important effect of this acceptance of the specific energies was the support that it ultimately gave to the theory of cerebral localization. We have seen that Müller was led to conclude that the seat of the specific differences must lie in the brain or the central portion of the nerves. Helmholtz, who in 1863 created the analogy of the nervous system to a telegraph system, argued that the nerves were all alike and indifferent conductors of excitation, and that the specificity must therefore lie in the brain. Du Bois-Reymond, whose work on the electrical nature of nervous conduction gave him a right to speak, held also to this view, and even went so far as to say that, were it possible to cross-connect the auditory and optic nerves, we ought to see sounds with our ears and hear light with our eyes.

There was opposition, of course. Lotze had argued for a locus of specificity in the peripheral sense-organs, and Hering held a similar view. Munk was the first to point out the relation of the doctrine of Müller and Helmholtz to the 'new phrenology' of cerebral localization. The Müllerian doctrine meant that five separate sensory centers ought to be found in the brain, and these, with more or less uncertainty, were later indicated. The Helmholtzian view fitted in with the network theory of Golgi: within each sensory center, there may be a cell or group of cells for every sensory quality. While this extreme view has not been openly championed, it is logically the ultimate consequence of Müller's doctrine, and has therefore come rather subtly to be taken for granted in many discussions which turn on the physiology of qualitative difference.

We should note in passing that this outcome of the evolution of the doctrine of specific energies has hardly made for clarity of thinking. In vision and touch, at least, there has developed a certain contradiction between the perceptual theories of spatial and qualitative difference. The modern projection theory of space perception requires that the retinal image be projected, point for point, upon the visual area of the cortex. The psychophysiology of color requires that there be not less than three sets of fibers, one for each component of the visual system of qualities. How would such two systems be related in the unitary perception of a single colored picture? There is, as yet, no satisfactory answer to that question.

NOTES

An excellent history and examination of the theory of specific energies of nerves is R. Weinmann, *Die Lehre von den Sinnesenergien*, 1895. Other sources are A. Goldscheider, *Die Lehre von den specifischen Energien der Sinnesorgane*, 1881; M. Dessoir, *Arch. Anat. Physiol.*, 1892, 196-232; W. Nagel, *Handbuch der Physiologie des Menschen*, 1905, III, 1-15. The only complete reference in English is not very satisfactory: A. J. McKeag, *The Sensation of Pain and the Theory of Specific Sense Energies*, 1902; but there are scattered accounts in textbooks, and E. B. Holt's partially philosophical discussion in *The New Realism*, 1912, 314-330, is especially enlightening.

For a briefer discussion of specific nerve energies, its extension to specific fiber energies, its relation to cerebral localization of function and cortical projection, and finally the modern end-products of these theories in the isomorphism of Gestalt psychology, see E. G. Boring, *Sensation and Perception in the History of Experimental Psychology*, 1942, 68-90, 93-96. See also chap. 25 of this book, pp. 664-691.

Bell and Müller

For Johannes Müller's doctrine, see his *Handbuch der Physiologie*, II, bk. v, the introductory section, in any edition or the English translation. This portion of the *Handbuch* first appeared in 1838. The first eight of the ten laws and most of the discussion of them are reprinted in English in B. Rand, *Classical Psychologists*, 1912, 530-544. Müller originally advanced the theory in *Zur vergleichenden Physiologie des Gesichtssinnes*, 1826, 44-55. See also his *Ueber die phantastischen Gesichtserscheinungen*, 1826, 6-9.

Charles Bell's similar discussion

which forms the basis for the claim of priority for him, is the privately printed monograph of 100 copies distributed personally to his friends, the monograph which we have already discussed in connection with the law of the spinal nerve roots: *Idea of a New Anatomy of the Brain*, 1811. The reprint, *J. Anat. Physiol.*, 1869, 3, 154-157, gives his view. It has also been reprinted in the original English, with a German translation, by E. Ebstein, *Charles Bell: Idee einer neuen Hirnanatomie*, 1911; and by W. Dennis, *Readings in the History of Psychology*, 1948, 113-124. Carmichael (cited below) again reprints nearly all the significant passages.

L. Carmichael, *Psychol. Rev.*, 1926, 33, 188-217, esp. 198-203, is Bell's champion for his priority over Müller. Dessoir, *op. cit.*, 202, gives Bell credit; Weinmann, *op. cit.*, 20, does not. An historian must necessarily speak of "the Müllerian doctrine" because, in spite of Bell's priority, it was Müller's formulation of the theory that was known and that exerted its great influence. Bell's views and discoveries, unformulated in a 'doctrine' and incompletely explicated, would not have had the same influence upon the history of psychology. It would have been Müller's theory, even had he got it from Bell, that was so effective.

On Müller, see also G. Murphy, *Historical Introduction to Modern Psychology*, 2 ed., 1949, 92-97, and reprinted excerpts in B. Rand, *Classical Psychologists*, 1912, 530-544, and Dennis, *op. cit.*, 157-168.

The quotations from the philosophers are from Aristotle's *Treatise on the Principle of Life* (Hammond's trans., 1902), bk. ii, chap. 6; bk. iii, chap. 1; John Locke's *Essay Concerning Human Understanding*, 1690, bk. ii, chaps. 8, 9; and David Hartley's

Observations on Man, 1749, pt. i, chap. 1, sect. i. They will all be found in context in Rand, *op. cit.*, 59-62, 242-249, 315-320. In this connection see also Weinmann, *op. cit.*, 11-21, 76-94; and, especially for the relation to Locke's secondary qualities, Holt, *op. cit.*, 313-321.

For R. H. Lotze's criticism, see his *Medicinische Psychologie*, 1852, 182-197, and other references cited by Weinmann, 39-42, *q.v.* For E. H. Weber on the same matter, see his *Der Tastsinn und das Gemeingefühl*, in R. Wagner's *Handwörterbuch der Physiologie*, 1846, III, ii, 505-511 (pp. 37-46 of the 1905 separate reprint).

Fiber Energies

The extension of the theory dates from Natanson, *Arch. physiol. Heilkunde*, 1844, 3, 515-535; and A. W. Volkmann, Wagner's *Handwörterbuch* (*op. cit.*), 1844, II, 521-526.

For H. L. F. v. Helmholtz's discussion of color theory and, therefore, of specific fiber-energies, see his Ueber die Theorie der zusammengesetzen Farben, *Ann. Phys. Chem.*, 1852, 163, 45-66, esp. 47-49 (reprinted in his *Wissenschaftliche Abhandlungen*, 1883, II, 1-23, esp. 6f.); *Handbuch der physiologischen Optik*, sect. 20, in the 1 ed., 1860, reprinted in the 3 ed., 1911, and the Eng. trans., 1924; see also the discussion in 2 ed., 1896.

For Thomas Young's theory of color and his simple suggestion of fiber-specificity, see his On the theory of light and colours (read Nov. 12, 1801), *Philos. Trans.*, 1802, 92, 20 f.; *Miscellaneous Works*, I, 146 f.; An account of some cases of the production of colours not hitherto described (read July 1, 1802), *Philos. Trans.*, 1802, 92, 395; *Miscellaneous Works*, I, 176 f.; also *Lectures* (delivered 1802-1803), 1807, I, 440; II, 617.

On the last three paragraphs of the chapter, see Weinmann, *op. cit.*, 31-35, 63-68. Holt, *op. cit.*, 321-330, gave an argument for the dependence of qualitative difference upon frequency of excitation rather than difference of fiber.

Specificity and Localization

It is in the *Tonempfindungen*, *loc. cit.*, that Helmholtz gave the 'telegraph theory' of the nervous system. Here he argued that there are no specific differences between nerves or the natures of their conductions, that the nerves are like telegraph wires which passively conduct electricity. The specificity must therefore lie in the terminations, just as is the case with the various instruments that can be attached to the end of an electric wire. It is interesting to note that Helmholtz is here arguing for a view of the nerves as passive conductors in the interests of a theory of the specificity of nerve terminations. Müller argued against a belief in the nerves as passive conductors in practically the same interests, but in order to combat an older theory that had been safely disposed of later.

The reader must not assume from the text that this idea of the specificity lying in the brain was new with Helmholtz. We have seen that Müller definitely left the issue open, although some writers have supposed that his constant use of the term *nerves* was meant to exclude their terminations in the brain. The title of Weber's discussion, cited above, is *Endigung der Sinnesnerven in besonderen Organen des Gehirns*. Even Bell, who later derided the phrenology of Gall and Spurzheim, had this view in 1811. He wrote then: "The idea or perception is according to the part of the brain to which the nerve is attached" (*op. cit.*, 154). "The operations of the mind are seated in the great mass of the cerebrum, while the parts of the brain to which the nerves of sense tend, strictly form the seat of sensation, being the internal organs of sense" (*op. cit.*, 157).

CHAPTER 6

Physiological Psychology of Sensation:
1800-1850

While the doctrine of the specific energies of nerves was destined to play a dominant rôle in the formulation of the psychophysiological problems of sensation, it was rather the result of a general scientific interest in sensation than the cause. The first half of the nineteenth century saw great progress in the knowledge of the laws of sensation, a progress that was the natural result of growing concern with the physiology of the nervous system, and, in particular, of the division of the peripheral nervous system, by the formulation of the Bell-Magendie law, into motor and sensory nerves. Much of this research into sensation was concerned with the physics of the sense-organs. Nearly all of it lies in a continuous line of development to the modern experimental psychology of sensation, and for this reason its careful examination cannot be undertaken here where we are seeking merely to obtain a broad picture of the development of experimental psychological physiology up to the middle of the last century. The details of the separate discoveries and their organization by the German systematists belong in the particular histories of the five senses.

It is obvious, after the event, that the more psychological part of this work made use of an informal method of introspection; that is to say, it made use of the sensory experiences of human beings, usually the experience of the experimenter himself. As long as such an uncritical method of introspection was able to produce results that were readily verifiable by any other scientist, there was no need to refine the procedure or even to give it a name, nor was there any need to bring up the solipsistic issue raised by modern behavioristics and to say that the data were not the observer's experiences, but only his reports of them. The modern scientist avoids epistemological issues when he can. Newton could find that blue and yellow lights when mixed look white; Tartini could observe that two simultaneous tones of different pitch may seem to be accompanied by a third tone of lower pitch; Weber could note that two points on the skin, when close enough together, feel like one; all these observations could be made without critical discussion of the nature of the experience that is a factor in them.

At first this interest in the dependence of experience upon its physiological conditions was but incidental, the physiological attack upon the problem of sensation consisted in bringing together anatomical and physical knowledge, for both physics and anatomy were well advanced with respect to light and the eye, and to sound and the ear. Thus it was in vision and hearing that sensory physiology was first extended. It would seem as if a similar appeal might have been made to mechanics in extending the knowledge of the sense of touch, for mechanics was as well advanced as were optics and acoustics; but here there was no detailed anatomy into which physical knowledge could fit. Anatomy had shown the eye to be an optical instrument and the ear an acoustic machine, but of the skin it had no detailed structural picture to present. The other two senses, smell and taste, remained even more obscure, and most of what little we know of them even now was not forthcoming until the end of the century.

The development of sensory physiology was also aided by the increasing necessity for the publication of scientific handbooks. Scientific information was increasing so rapidly that it was becoming more and more important to bring all the material available at a given date together in compendia. It has often been said that science progresses unevenly, that the frontier of knowledge is ragged, that unknown territory always lies between the outposts, and that the conditions for advance are more or less fortuitous. While such a statement is correct, it is also true that the organization of systematic compendia exhibits baldly the existing lacunæ and directs attention upon them. It may require a stroke of genius, or at least a happy thought, before the gap can be filled in; nevertheless we should not minimize the importance of systematization in bringing scattered facts together and exhibiting both the unexplored regions and the known territory which impinges upon them.

Of systematic physiological texts, which, being systematic, had to treat of sensation, there were many. In 1803 Charles Bell published the third volume of *The Anatomy of the Human Body* (a joint work with his brother). This volume is devoted to the nervous system and the organs of sense and is an excellent compendium of the knowledge of sensation at that date. Here Bell found ten times as much to say about sight and hearing as about the other three senses. In general, however, it is the Germans who have excelled in the organization of compendia. Beside works dealing with a single sense, there were several early in the century devoted to sensation in general: Steinbuch in 1811, Purkinje in 1819-1825, and Tourtual in 1827. We have already seen the tremendous importance that is to be attached to the publication of Johannes Müller's *Handbuch der Physiologie des Menschen* (1833-1840). More than 15 per cent of these volumes is devoted to sensation, and a third as much to "the mind." The *Handbuch* treats most fully of vision and hearing; there was still but little to be said of the other three senses. It was followed, however, almost immediately by Wagner's *Handwörterbuch der Physiologie* (1842-1853), which contains E. H. Weber's famous section on *Der Tastsinn und das Gemeingefühl*, thus largely eliminating one deficiency. This practice continued to the end of the century. Hermann's *Handbuch der Physiologie* (1879-1880) devoted an entire volume of more than a thousand pages to sensation; its sections are written by Hering, Hensen, Vintschgau, and other well-known physiologists of that period. Schäfer's *Text-Book of Physiology* (1900) was a still more recent example of similar character, but the coming of age of experimental psychology and its especial activity in the field of sensation has tended in the present century to remove the treatment of these problems from the physiological texts.

VISION

Vision was the best known of the five senses. For this the publication of Newton's *Opticks* (1704) a century earlier is doubtless responsible. Not only did this book and the subsequent work of the physicists render a fairly complete knowledge of the laws of refraction and of optical instruments available for application to the problem of the eye, but it is also true that the *Opticks*, especially in respect of color, contributed some incidental psychological information.

In the eighteenth century there was not much discovery in the psychophysiology of vision. In 1759 William Porterfield published his two-volume *A Treatise on the Eye, the Manner and Phaenomena of Vision*, 885 pages which became for fifty years the standard handbook in that field. It was presently complemented by Joseph Priestley's *The History and Present State of Discoveries Relating to Vision, Light and Colours*, 812 pages published in 1772. Plateau in his bibliography of vision in 1878 was able to cite only about sixty references for the eighteenth century against more than seven hundred for the first three-quarters of the nineteenth.

Thomas Young enters the picture at the change of centuries. His early paper on accommodation of the single eye for distance was published in 1793 and his later and more important paper in 1801. His contributions to color theory—the essential conception of what was later called the Young-Helmholtz trichromatic theory and the related notion that different color qualities are aroused by the actions of different kinds of nerve fibers—these insights, brilliant because they came early with little help from the *Zeitgeist*, are dated from 1801 to 1807.

Then there was the brilliant and versatile poet, Goethe, one of the most revered and influential persons in the intellectual life of Germany in the late eighteenth and early nineteenth centuries. Goethe was embittered against Newton because his attack on Newton's color theory (1791-1792) had not met with scientific acceptance. The tensions engendered by this frustration finally in 1810 produced the 1411 pages of Goethe's *Zur Farbenlehre*, filled with generalizations, speculations, anecdotes and dicta, which might have taken a lesser man half a lifetime to compile. Nowadays no one recalls this episode in Goethe's life except as an example of how personal pride distorts the use of evidence and how frustration induces scientific activity, but no one said that sort of thing about the great Goethe then, although Helmholtz did only forty years later. Instead Goethe stimulated research on color.

He stimulated Purkinje, whose volumes on vision in 1819 and 1825 have been cited above. The second volume is dedicated to Goethe, and indeed it can be said that Goethe and Purkinje promoted and helped to establish the phenomenological tradition in psychology, the descriptive approach which was carried forward later by Hering and the Gestalt psychologists. (See pp. 18-21.) Goethe also interested his friend Schopenhauer in color, and Schopenhauer's color theory was published in 1816.

After Purkinje there was Johannes Müller who published in 1826 both *Zur vergleichende Physiologie des Gesichtssinnes* and *Ueber die phantastischen Gesichtserscheinungen*. These books, as we have seen, contained in them the beginning of his doctrine of the specific energies of nerves. The first is much broader than a mere comparative physiology, for it deals also with the problems of external reference, the unity of the two fields in binocular vision, convergence and accommodation, and even Goethe's color theory. The second, a much smaller book, is concerned with more purely psychological problems.

Treviranus' work on the visual organ, published two years later, gave very complete tables of the dimensions and other optical constants of the eyes of a great variety of animals, and treated mathematically the optical system that is the eye. We saw that even

Flourens (1824) in his gross anatomy of the brain had to distinguish between what we may call sensation and perception. This distinction was elaborated by Heermann for vision in 1835 in his *Die Bildung der Gesichtsvorstellungen aus Gesichtsempfindungen*. In 1836, A. W. Volkmann wrote *Neue Beiträge zur Physiologie des Gesichtssinnes*, a book that Müller frequently referred to in his section on vision in the *Handbuch* two years later. This Volkmann (who is not the Volkmann who wrote the *Lehrbuch der Psychologie* in 1856) contributed the section on vision in Wagner's *Handwörterbuch der Physiologie* in 1846. Another important work by Burow on the physiology and physics of the human eye appeared in 1841. It dealt with eye-movement and the problems of convergence and accommodation. Most of the experimental observations appeared, of course, in separate monographs. These books are the milestones that mark the progress of the physiology of sight.

In this period, almost every account of vision concerns itself primarily with the physics of the stimulus, the anatomy of the eye, and consequently the relation between these two subjects—that is to say, with the eye as an optical instrument. Bell's account is typical, but the emphasis had shifted only a little thirty-five years later with Johannes Müller. Of the stimulus, beside the general fact that it is normally light, we are told of colors produced by refraction, by reflection, by transmission and by interference. All the essential structures of the human eye were known except the variability of the curvature of the lens. The comparative anatomy of the eye was studied for its own sake, but also because it seemed as if a knowledge of simple vision in subvertebrate forms would lead to a recognition of the more important elements in vertebrate vision.

Starting with physics and the stimulus, the progress of knowledge was from without in. Thus a knowledge of the eye as an optical system, which results in the formation of an image on the retina, was the all-important problem. Bell (1803) treated it in detail. Treviranus (1828) was primarily concerned with it. Müller (1838) made it the primary problem, dealing with refraction by the lens and other media, the achromatic character of the system, and the defects of the system in myopia and presbyopia and their correction by lenses. In Wagner's *Handwörterbuch*, beside Volkmann's section on sight (1846), there is a section by Listing on dioptrics (1853), which contains the principle of the reduced eye and Listing's law of the relation of the image to the curvature of the retina and to torsion of eyes in movement. The problem by this time had been extended to binocular vision and eye-movement. Such was the setting upon which Helmholtz's classical analysis of physiological optics (1866) supervened. Wundt (1862) and Hering (1868) dealt with the same problem. It was at first the fundamental problem of vision.

The facts were fundamental, partly because the doctrine of the specific energies of nerves raised the question of the mechanism of perception. If we put the matter at the philosophically unsophisticated level of Johannes Müller, we shall only be presenting the problem as the physiologists of his day saw it. The common view was that perception consisted in the transmission, in some way or other, by the nerves to the brain of properties emanating from perceived objects. Müller argued that we perceive directly not the properties of objects, but the properties of the nerves themselves. How, then, did we come to know about objects correctly? Because the state of the nerves corresponds to the state of objects in ways that can be formulated under certain definite laws. Now this means that we perceive by sight, not an object nor even the light from it, but the state of the optic nerve and of the retina which is but the extension of the optic nerve. Aside from color, the most obvious thing about visual perception is that it yields correct information about space, size, shape and position. This fact comes about because the eye as an optical instrument projects an image of the perceived object upon the retina, an image that is as correct a copy of the object as a bidimensional picture could be. It seemed to Müller and other physiologists, therefore, that, by showing how the image on the retina resembles the object, one comes near to explaining perception. If the excitation on the nerve is a pattern, and the sensorium perceives directly the state of the optic nerve, no wonder then that it perceives a pattern; and, if this pattern is the optical image of an object, no wonder that it perceives it correctly.

Müller was also, of course, quite clear that the retina would thus at times misrepresent external space. All the arguments for specific energies that are dependent on 'inadequate' stimulation of the retina show that illusion is possible, that the sensorium is not always correctly informed. The size of the visual field is simply the size of the retina, for it is the retina that the sensorium perceives directly. Absolute size is thus dependent upon the size of the retinal image— that is to say, upon the visual angle and not upon the size of the object. The perception of direction depends upon the point of the retina stimulated, both relatively and absolutely. The image on the retina is inverted, but Müller saw no problem as to why we do not see things upside down. It was plain to him that there is no meaning to 'up' except the sensation that results from the excitation of the bottom of the retina, and that only a man with a knowledge of physiological optics would ever, in directly perceiving his retina, know that this sensation actually came from the bottom of the retina. There is here in Müller the hint that one learns 'up' from 'down' by experience. In general, Müller remains good doctrine today, although we know that perceived size is neither entirely relative nor entirely proportional to visual angle.

It is plain that, for Müller, the theory of vision is merely the theory of the excitation of the retina by the optical image. In these terms he compared vision in mammals with vision in lower forms and deduced the functions of the lens and iris, citing Magendie's experiment in which images projected by an actual eye were seen on an artificial screen. He fixed upon the retinal cone as the essential organ and noted that acuity must depend on the density of the cones, being less in the periphery than in the center of the retina. He even raised the problem of the spatial limen. Two cones in the fovea subtend an angle of about 40″ of arc and Müller cited Volkmann and Weber as agreeing that two points separated by this angle are but just discriminable. Treviranus' threshold of acuity was too fine for the size of the cones.

The retina further imposes its nature on external reality by being blind at the point of entrance of the optic nerve. A knowledge of the *blind spot* existed, however, more than a century before the time under discussion. Mariotte discovered it and described it in 1668 and in 1682-1683. It must have been fairly common knowledge, for Charles II (died 1685) is said to have used it in jest with his courtiers to show them how they would look when their heads were off.

There was also in this half-century some knowledge of the laws of color. The first two laws of *color mixture* had been laid down by Newton (1704), and involve, of course, a knowledge of complementaries. The physiologists knew these facts, and the third law was formulated by Grassmann in 1853. Color mixing by means of rotating disks was first accomplished by van Musschenbroek in 1760; the law of such mixture was worked out by Plateau in 1853, and the method was perfected by Maxwell in 1857. The colored disks are often called Maxwell's disks.

Herschel's measurement of the spectrum (1800) was known to Bell, who noted that the spectral colors are not equally bright and that maximal brightness occurs in the yellow-greens. Later Fraunhofer (1815), using a simple and none too easy method of heterochromatic photometry, determined the relative brightness of the spectrum at the positions of eight widely separated Fraunhofer lines, the first plotting of a *luminosity curve*. Vierordt made similar determinations in 1869, but these curves lacked significance, because there was at that time no way of determining the absolute energies of the lights, a deficiency eventually remedied by Langley's invention of the bolometer in 1883.

In 1825 Purkinje described what happens to colors as illumination changes from dark to daylight at dawn (or the opposite at twilight), and psychologists have since recognized this excellent bit of phenomenological description by naming the phenomenon after its discoverer. There were many verifications of Purkinje's observations up to Aubert's in 1865 as well as later.

The persistence of sensation after the cessation of the stimulus was known to Newton, who described the circle of light seen on whirling a luminous body (1704), and there were several mentions of the phenomenon before Newton in the seventeenth century, including Robert Boyle's (1663). Buffon (1743) coined the phrase *accidental colors* to cover all instances of positive and negative afterimages, the flight of colors and similar chromatic events that happen in the absence of a stimulus. Benjamin Franklin (1765) showed how the afterimage may be positive on the dark field of the closed eyes and negative on a field of white paper when the eyes are open. This demonstration, which came to be called "the Franklin experiment," was much discussed by scientific men. In 1786 R. W. Darwin, Charles' father, gave a full account of "ocular spectra," being the first to use the term *spectrum* for an afterimage. A spectrum (spectre) is an appearance (apparition). Newton used the word for the ghostly band of colors seen in the dark when a beam of white light is dispersed by a prism. The chief facts about afterimages were already at hand at the start of the nineteenth century.

The phenomena of dark and light *adaptation* were not well understood until Aubert took them in hand in 1865, to be followed by Hering in 1872. On the other hand, knowledge about simultaneous contrast goes back to Leonardo's rules for painters (*ante* 1519). There was a great deal of interest in colored shadows, without any realization that shadows, lacking contours and object-character, are especially subject to chromatic induction. Hering used shadows effectively for color contrast, but the proper explanation belongs to the twentieth century.

The knowledge of the blind spot stimulated interest in *peripheral vision*. Thomas Young (1801) determined the limits of visibility for the field of vision and described the decrease in acuity at the periphery. The phenomenologist, Purkinje (1825), verified Young, and described how the color of a stimulus, which passes from the center of the retina to its periphery, may first change in hue and then later inevitably becomes gray. Szokalsky (1842) first suggested that the retina is divided into different zones of color sensitivity, and Aubert (1865) accomplished the first thorough experimental measurement of the zonal changes.

Cases of defective color vision were described in 1684 and 1777, but the nature of this deficiency was not understood until 1794, when Dalton, the Quaker chemist, described his own defect, which came later to be called *Daltonism*. Both Thomas Young and Goethe discussed this kind of *color blindness*, and Seebeck in 1837 concluded that there were two types—as indeed there are. In 1845 Herschel suggested that Daltonism is "dichromic," being limited to the yellows and blues with the reds and greens missing. In the latter half of the nineteenth century color blindness assumed great theoretical importance because the exact nature of the deficiency was crucial in a decision among rival theories of color—especially as between Helmholtz and Hering.

Before Helmholtz and Hering the only important *color theories* were those of Thomas Young (1807), Goethe (1810) and Schopenhauer (1816). The German writers of handbooks mentioned Goethe's most frequently, of course. Müller, however, criticized it. It remained for Helmholtz (1852 *et seq.*) to give Young's theory its full importance in Germany. Hering did not promulgate his theory until 1874. After that there were for a while plenty of other theories, of which Ladd-Franklin's (1892) came perhaps to be the best known.

Binocular vision furnished one of the most obvious conundrums in this field. Touch something with both hands and there seem ordinarily to be two touches, unless one is thinking only about the object touched. Look at something with both eyes and nearly always there is only one 'look,' whether one thinks about the object or about the eyes that are seeing it. How does two-eyed vision get single? There were three theories. The astronomer, Kepler (1611), had said that singleness of vision is due to projection of the seeing to the object seen, the object theory, which works in touch where a pencil feels like a single pencil when held between two fingers. Porta, a physicist, had already suggested (1593) that the two retinal images alternate in perception, first one and then the other, as occurs in what is now known as retinal rivalry. Gall, the anatomist-phrenologist, also held this view. The correct view was, however, anatomical. Half of the fibers from each retina cross at the optic chiasma and half do not. That fact suggests that the projections of the two retinas on the brain by the nerve fibers are superimposed, and that singleness of vision results when one brain pattern coincides point-for-point with the other. As early as the second century Galen conceived this kind of function for the chiasma, and Newton explicated the view in 1717. In the nineteenth century Müller is found accepting it and elaborating it.

The discovery and definition of the *horopter* by Aguilonius in 1613 supported the view that the two retinas are composed of corresponding points. The horopter is the locus of all points seen as single in binocular vision, *i.e.*, the locus of all points whose images fall on corresponding points of the two retinas. In the horizontal plane, it is a circle which passes through the fixation point and the two centers of the eyes. Vieth showed that in 1818 and Müller expounded it so successfully in 1826 that the horopter came to be "Müller's circle."

The discovery of the horopter led, of course, to the realization that vision is not single for parts of the visual field that do not lie on the horopter. There was in the seventeenth and eighteenth centuries much discussion of why this kind of doubleness is not ordinarily seen, whether because of alternation of vision or of object projection. It was Wheatstone who, in 1833, discovered that the *retinal disparity* which is due to *binocular parallax* is synthesized by the nervous system into a perception of solidity. He proved his point by the invention of the *stereoscope*, and published about it first in 1838, thereby just missing its inclusion in Müller's *Handbuch*. Sir David Brewster invented his stereoscope a little later (1843), and Oliver Wendell Holmes designed the hand stereoscope (1863), which graced so many Victorian parlors. Holmes suggested that the corporeality of photographic scenes viewed stereoscopically would make foreign travel less necessary!

The fact that the eyes *converge* differently in fixating objects at different distances must have been known to anyone who ever studied vision. Aguilonius (1613), Descartes (1637) and Berkeley (1709) described the geometry of the phenomenon, and the two latter assumed that a conscious clue to the distance would be provided by the degree of convergence. These facts were taken for granted in the nineteenth century.

There was, however, little early agreement on how the eye accommodates itself to focus at different distances. Kepler (1604) had shown that the 'crystalline' is not the sentient substance in the eye but a lens which forms an image on the sentient retina. The theories that grew up during the seventeenth and eighteenth centuries were that *accommodation* is due solely to change in size of the pupil, that it is due to elongation of the eyeball under tension from the external muscles, or to change of curvature of the cornea under action of these muscles, or to the movement of the lens back and forth within the eyeball, or, finally, to the change of shape of the lens. The last view is the correct one. It was supported by Descartes (1637), John Hunter (1794), Thomas Young (1801), Purkinje (1825) and Helmholtz (1866)—an array of very distinguished proponents. The chief evidence lay in the observation of the change in the distances between the images of a flame reflected from the cornea and the anterior and posterior surfaces of the lens when near-and-far fixation is altered. These images were first observed by Purkinje (1825) and later by Sanson (1838) and Cramer (1851). The images have been named for Sanson, who was not their discoverer, and the theory for Helmholtz, who was not its originator.

In all this discussion in the early nineteenth century, the physiologists touched upon psychological matters more or less according to their temperaments. Even Bell, who consciously sought to avoid vague speculation, was occasionally driven back upon 'attention' for an explanation. Müller, of course, was as near to being an experimental psychologist as any one could be then, and he frequently sought explanations in terms of the 'mind.' He discussed attention to visual phenomena as against those of the other senses, and the attentive selection of one object within the visual field. The spatial reference of objects to the external world was for him, as we have seen, a matter of 'judgment,' not at all a matter of vision itself. So, he said, perceived form depends not only on sensation, but also on association; and the perception of distance, not on sensation, but on reasoning. In retinal rivalry, attention favors the persistence of one image over the other. While such statements seem vague, we must remember that each one is in a way the formulation of a psychological problem. Later we shall understand better how physiological psychology sprang into a separate existence, if we have seen first how physiology was unable to avoid raising its problems for it.

HEARING

After sight, the sense-physiologists were most interested in hearing. The physics of acoustics was well advanced by 1800, and the anatomy of the external and middle ears, as well as the grosser structure of the inner ear, was fairly well understood. Nevertheless, on the whole, much less was known of hearing than of vision, and thus less was written. Bell found about half as much to say about hearing as about sight; Steinbuch about a quarter as much; Müller about three quarters as much. Harless wrote the section on hearing in

Wagner's *Handwörterbuch* in 1853. Most of the observations upon which these books drew occurred in monographs and articles, and not in separate books. We shall get an excellent picture of the period if we follow, in the main, Johannes Müller.

The texts all emphasized physical acoustics: the conduction of sound in solids, liquids and gases, the physics of sonorous bodies like strings and columns of air, reflection and interference of waves, resonance and the rate of propagation. Müller performed numerous experiments on the conduction of sound from one medium to another, in order to analyze the acoustic properties of the ear. The anatomy of the ear was brought into relation with acoustics. Both Bell and Müller discussed at length the comparative anatomy of the ear and the nature of hearing in different animal forms. The outer ear was obviously for the collection and concentration of the sound against the tympanic membrane, which would thus vibrate with the sound. Both Bell and Müller showed that the chain of small bones in the middle ear would conduct the sound to the oval window. Bell realized correctly the function of the round window—to move out and in as the oval window moves in and out. Without the round window the oval window could not move at all. Müller supposed that the conduction of sound in the middle ear occurred in the way that sound vibrations are transmitted through any solid, and not by the movement of the bones as a system of levers. The stapes could not move, he thought, because it presses against the incompressible liquid of the inner ear. Unlike Bell, he did not know that the structure of the inner ear is such as to allow the round window to relieve pressure exerted at the oval window, so that mass movement can occur. To the tensor tympani Müller assigned its correct function: the maintenance and adjustment of tension on the tympanic membrane. He showed by experiments that low and high tones require different tensions for the best transmission through a membrane, and he concluded that the tensor tympani acts reflexly in such adjustments. He believed that he could contract this muscle in himself voluntarily. He confessed complete ignorance of the function of the other muscle of the middle ear, the stapedius. The function of the Eustachian tube puzzled him especially. He outlined nine theories of its use and favored the correct theory that the tube is designed to equalize air pressure between the atmosphere and the middle ear. Hearing, he showed by experiment, is diminished when the pressure is unequal.

In his theory of the inner ear Müller swung wide of the truth. The eighth nerve, which is called the auditory nerve because it leads to the ear, is distributed to both the cochlea and the semi-circular canals, and Müller naturally believed that both the cochlea and the canals were organs of hearing. He noted that neither (presumably because they are closed tubes filled with liquid) had very good acoustic properties. He assumed that sound has two routes through the middle ear; that it passes from the tympanic membrane by way of the bones to the oval window and by way of the air to the round window. Presumably the former route, he thought, is more effective upon the canals, and the latter upon the cochlea. Indeed, it seemed that the former route must be more effective, for Müller showed by experiments that sound is transmitted from solids (the bones) to liquids more readily than from gases (the air) to liquids. The round window is probably, so he believed, merely a less effective auxiliary and is not essential to hearing, for frogs do not have it. Still it must operate in man, for a person can hear, through one or both windows, when the bones of the middle ear are lost. If this mechanism is poor acoustically, the defect is partially compensated by the disposition of the auditory nerve, which is spread out upon the spiral lamina so as to gain extended contact with the acoustic undulations. In this way Müller got the sound to the auditory nerve, just as in dealing with vision his primary object was to get the light by way of an optical system to the optic nerve; and, as we have seen, this is really the main problem of the author of the theory of the specific energies of nerves. Applied to hearing, its solution seems more naïve, because Müller knew less of the nature of the auditory endings than of the structure of the retina. Knowledge of the eye preceded knowledge of the ear.

Of the nature of the auditory stimulus there was little for Müller to say except what is implied in the physics of sound. He noted in addition that sounds may be heard by conduction through the bones of the skull, but he was not sure whether these vibrations acted directly or by affecting the tympanic membrane.

On the problem of tone and successive noise, Müller referred to Savart's experiments (1831). In these experiments a note was produced by a card in contact with the teeth of a revolving wheel. One tooth gives a single sound that is not a note. Several may give a rattle. At the correct rate, however, several give a note, and a note may be got from only two teeth.

Müller also cited Savart on the limits of hearing. The upper limit he took as 24,000 cycles per sec. or more; the lower as 16 cycles and less. There were other determinations by Biot (1814) and Despretz (1845).

There were no systematic determinations of the differential limen at this time, nor before 1888 in Wundt's laboratory. Delezenne

(1827) showed that this threshold is less than 1/120 of an octave and Seebeck (1846) found various values, all less than .5 cycles.

The question of analysis of compound wave-forms, the question that largely determined Helmholtz's theory of hearing, was not to be satisfactorily dealt with by Müller. He noted that wave-length must determine pitch, that amplitude must determine intensity, and that two tones of the same wave-length would reinforce each other and give a more intense sound. That we hear both tones when they are of different wave-lengths must be due, he thought, to the fact that the ear appreciates the maxima of each and thus hears both. In this discussion he represented the frequencies by series of dots rather than wave-forms, and he remarked that the perception of one tone in the presence of another is a more difficult perception than that of one tone alone. Bell, although extremely vague, is thought to have come nearer the truth, as Helmholtz saw it, by guessing that the ear must be something like a musical instrument with strings of different lengths.

The solution of this problem had been available since 1822, when Fourier showed that any irregular periodic wave-form can be resolved in a sum of sine components. The necessary insight came in 1843 when G. S. Ohm applied this principle to hearing, noting that the ear hears for an irregular or 'complex' wave-form the Fourier sine components. This is *Ohm's acoustic law*. It became later, of course, the basis for Helmholtz's resonance theory of hearing, for analysis by resonance gives the same result as Fourier's analysis. Müller wrote without this knowledge.

Beats offered no problem to Müller. They seem to be explained physically by interference. The facts of difference tones, then known as the sounds of Tartini, Müller presented without explanation. Tartini had described these tones in 1714. Romieu argued in 1751 that a difference tone is due to beats, being a pitch that arises from the beat frequency. Vieth gave the name *combination tones* to these phenomena in 1805. Hällström in 1832 extended Romieu's theory to difference tones of higher orders—difference tones between the generators and the first difference tone, difference tones between difference tones, and so on. That was all before Ohm's law was known. In 1856 Helmholtz published his classical study of combination tones, reporting the discovery of summation tones and verifying the facts of higher orders of difference tones.

There was little known about the localization of sound at this time E. H. Weber (1846) had shown that discrimination between hearing with the left and the right ears is immediate and accurate, but there was little progress in this field until the 1870s.

Such, then, was the picture of the psychophysiology of hearing in the first half of the last century. It was Helmholtz (1863) who was to extend and revise it, a service which he also performed for vision.

TOUCH

While the psychophysiology of sight and hearing was developing, there seemed to be very little to do or to say about touch. Bell and Müller dismissed it with but a few pages. It was sometimes classed with taste and smell as a 'simple sense.' It is indeed simple in that the physical stimulus would seem to act directly upon the nerve endings in the skin and other tissues. The theories of sight and hearing had been concerned mostly with getting stimulation to the nerve—that is to say, with the projection of the optical image on the retina and the conduction of sound to the auditory endings in the inner ear. The tactual stimuli—pressures, temperatures, movements and the rest —act immediately on the nerves in the skin without any obvious transmitting mechanism.

It remained for Ernst Heinrich Weber (1795-1878), professor of anatomy and later of physiology at Leipzig (1818 *et seq.*), to bring the facts and problems of touch into due prominence. Most of these facts were Weber's own experimental finding. In 1834 he published some experiments on touch in a Latin monograph: *De tactu: annotationes anatomicæ et physiologicæ*. The important work, however, that is now regarded as one of the classics in the psychology of sensation, was his *Der Tastsinn und das Gemeingefühl* (1846), which constituted the section on touch in Wagner's *Handwörterbuch*. Let us see what Weber knew about touch.

In the first place, it was necessary for him to limit his problems. *Touch* was a vague term. Seemingly all of the skin and much of the insides of the body were supplied with sensory fibers leading to the dorsal roots of the spinal cord. Sensitivity was quite general, and *Gemeingefühl* was a term practically synonymous with *touch*. Weber, however, distinguished clearly between touch and the *Gemeingefühl* (common sensibility). Touch belongs to the skin. Common sensibility is possessed by the skin and internal organs in common; and it includes all pain.

The sense of touch (*Tastsinn*) provides us with three classes of sensation: pressure sensations (*Druckempfindungen*), temperature sensations (*Temperaturempfindungen*) and sensations of locality (*Ortempfindungen*). Although Weber often spoke of a pressure 'sense,' a temperature 'sense' or a local 'sense,' it is quite clear that he was using the term loosely, and that these 'senses' were for him all parts of the sense of touch. Pressure and temperature he thought of as two kinds of touch sensation; locality, the *Ortsinn*, appeared to be secondary and to depend upon the other sensations for its arousal, although separate from them. Warmth and cold Weber regarded as positive and negative sensations of temperature, like light and dark in vision. In support of this last relationship he mentioned a pathological case where warmth and cold could not be distinguished. The relation of temperature to pressure within the *Tastsinn* is shown, he argued, by the fact that cold bodies appear heavier than warm bodies of equal weight. Weber's experiment with the *Thaler* is fairly well known. He found that one of these coins, when removed from cold water to the forehead of a subject, felt heavier than two of the same coins superposed and warmed in warm water before being put on the forehead. He noted also the relation of cold and warmth in the facts of successive contrast (facts that were described by John Locke).

To understand Weber's view of the *Ortsinn*, we must realize that the sense of locality is not an essential part of other sensations. Ordinarily it seems as if locality and pressure, for example, were inseparably connected, as, when one finger is touched and then another, we think we have two different sensations. We shall know better, Weber observed, if we touch one finger with another: then both fingers are stimulated equally, each by the other, and we feel only one sensation. Sensation itself varies, Weber held, only in quality and degree; its spatial characteristics depend on the activity of the mind and the relationship of sensations.

Nevertheless, to assign the *Ortsinn* in part to the 'mind' did not mean to Weber that it could not be investigated. It is against this problem that Weber brought his famous 'compass test' to bear, the experiment that has since become the measurement of the limen of dual impression. Weber found that the threshold for the perception of two points varied greatly in different parts of the body; for example, the upper arm gave a threshold thirty times as great as the volar surface of the little finger. These differences led him to conclude that they must depend on the distribution of the nerve fibers and that spatial discrimination is most accurate where the fibers are most dense. If one regards the cutaneous zone in which any given nerve fiber would be affected as a circle, then it is clear that the skin can be divided up into a very large number of sensory circles. In the compass experiment, two points applied within the same sensory circle would give rise to the stimulation of but one fiber, and thus to the perception of a single point; two points on adjacent circles, however, would stimulate adjacent fibers and give the per-- ception of a line; and the perception of two separated points would occur only when the sensory circles stimulated were separated from each other. Such was Weber's view of the *Ortsinn*. The rôle of the mind in all this is to interpret spatially the pattern of excitation.

Weber was not able to deal so specifically with the *Gemeingefühl* as with touch. He noted that common sensibility is distributed all over the body; that it supplements touch in the skin; and that the other organs of sense—the eyes, the ears, the nose and the tongue— also possess it. It is finest in the skin and the muscles. Pain is its most marked characteristic and is elicited by the stimuli appropriate to touch. Both pressure and pull upon the skin may give rise to pain as well as pressure. Similarly, both heat and cold may arouse pain. Weber worked out the thermal thresholds for pain very carefully. There are, moreover, many other sensory items that belong in the *Gemeingefühl*, like shudder and tickle, but there is little to be said of them.

Weber recognized the sensitivity of muscles and placed their sensations in the *Gemeingefühl*, because they are internal, because fatigue seems qualitatively akin to pain, and because some muscular contractions (*e.g.*, that of the uterus) are very painful. It would seem that Weber did not know about Charles Bell's discussion of the "muscle sense," or the sixth sense, as it came later to be called. The sensitivity of muscles had been known since Aristotle. Bell simply described the functions of the sense and named it. His important paper was published in 1826, although the germ of distinction is to be found in the paper of 1811 which announces the law of the spinal roots. Neither Müller nor Weber mentioned Bell in his discussion of muscular sensibility, nor some of the others who had discussed muscular sensation—Steinbuch (1811), Bichat (1812), Thomas Brown (1820).

Weber's knowledge of the sensitivity of the skin is the result of a great many experiments which he performed himself and reported in *Der Tastsinn und das Gemeingefühl*. From his own determinations he knew that the degree of perceived weight varies for the same weight with different parts of the skin; that the capacity for discrimination between weights and between temperatures varies with the region of the skin, much as does the *Ortsinn;* that a difference of about half a degree centigrade could readily be perceived, and that discrimination is very much better when the stimulus is large. He also was ready to assert that the intensity of a thermal sensation is greater, for the same temperature, if the stimulus is larger, and he concluded that there must consequently be summation at the brain, which is greatest in the case of adjacent fibers.

The most notable of these experiments on the measurement of sensitivity were, however, those that form the basis of Weber's law, as Fechner afterwards named it. Weber had reported these results in *De tactu* in 1834; now he enlarged upon them a little. He formulated no specific law. He simply made it clear that the smallest perceptible difference between two weights can be stated as a ratio between the weights, a ratio that is independent of the magnitudes of the weights. He extended his original experiments on weights to the visual discrimination of the lengths of lines and the auditory discrimination of the pitches of tones. His findings for the ratios that represent the least perceptible differences were: weights, 1/40; lines, 1/50 or even 1/100; tones, about half of a musical comma, or 1/160. Weber believed that he had here established an important general principle, but he could not have realized that these simple experiments would lead eventually to the whole structure of psychophysics.

Of the actual physiology of touch Weber knew little. He thought that the papillæ of the skin and the hair-bulbs must be the organs. He believed that touch is confined to the skin, for he tried in vain to elicit pressure, warmth and cold from the internal organs and from the deep tissues exposed in wounds. The *Gemeingfühl* he described as pretty generally distributed over the body, although the tendons, cartilage, and bones are insensitive. The nerves of touch and of common sensibility run to the cord; do they then pass to the brain? Weber brought out a great deal of evidence to show that they must terminate in the brain.

Weber was less inclined than Müller to run into psychological vagueness; nevertheless, having got the tactual excitations to the brain, he could not but note that they would then come under the influence of the mind. One function of the mind is of course perception (*Vorstellung*). Weber described perception as consisting in bringing sensations under the categories of space, time and number. In general, however, he tended to avoid metaphysical problems. In demonstrating the influence of the mind upon sensation, he preferred to cite the experiments of Bessel on the personal equation.

TASTE AND SMELL

At the beginning of the nineteenth century, as little was known about taste and smell as about touch, and exact knowledge of these senses had changed very little by the middle of the century. Such progress as was to be made was reserved for the very end, the 1880s and 1890s. There was, to be sure, one very thorough treatise on smell written early in the century: it is a book of over 700 pages by Cloquet entitled *Osphrésiologie,* published about 1821. Half of it, after the French fashion, was devoted to the pathology of olfaction. All later works used it as a foundation. There was no similar work on taste.

Bell (1803) knew that the papillæ of the tongue are the organs of taste and that, where there are no papillæ, there is no taste. Horn (1825) showed that different papillæ are differently sensitive. Here was a hint of difference of function, but as yet there was no adequate classification of taste. Nausea was thought of as a taste quality.

In smell there was Linnæus' classification of odors into seven groups, as well as Haller's three-fold distinction between sweet, foul and indifferent odors; but there was no fine structure that could be correlated with the classes. The olfactory organ showed no mechanism that could give a clue.

The normal stimulus to taste was seen to be a substance in solution. Müller held that gases could also be tasted and that mechanical stimulation might elicit tastes. For smell, the normal stimulus seemed to be either a gas or a substance finely divided in the air. Müller believed that the mucous membrane must be moist for stimulation to occur.

NOTES

The reader must bear in mind that this section gives the picture of the physiology of sensation only in its broad outlines. A more detailed picture for the period can be had by reading successively the sections on sensation in Bell (1803), Müller's *Handbuch,* and Wagner's *Handwörterbuch.* In general, see the pages of E. G. Boring, *Sensation and Perception in the History of Experimental Psychology,* 1942, where all these matters are discussed in much greater detail.

Plainly such a sketch as this cannot be fully documented, but nearly all the references are to be found in Boring, *op. cit.* We may recapitulate here the more important works:

Vision

I. Newton, *Opticks,* 1704. C. Bell, *Anatomy of the Human Body,* 1803,

III, 224-372; the entire work is in four volumes by both John and Charles Bell. Thomas Young, *A Course of Lectures on Natural Philosophy and the Mechanical Arts,* 2 vols., 1807, his first book, but his more important memoirs of 1801-1802 are reprinted in the first two volumes of the *Miscellaneous Works of the Late Thomas Young,* 3 vols., 1855. J. W. Goethe, *Zur Farbenlehre,* 2 vols., 1810. A. Schopenhauer, *Ueber das Sehen und die Farben,* 1816; 2 ed., 1854. J. G. Steinbuch, *Beytrag zur Physiologie der Sinne,* 1811, 140-270. J. E. Purkinje, *Beobachtungen und Versuche zur Physiologie der Sinne,* 2 vols., 1819-1825; the subtitles are *Beiträge,* and *Neue Beiträge, zur Kenntnis des Sehens in subjectiver Hinsicht.* Joh. Müller, *Zur vergleichenden Physiologie des Gesichtssinnes des Menschen und der Tiere nebst einem Versuch über die Bewegungen der Augen und* über den menschlichen Blick, 1826, 462 pp.; *Ueber die phantastischen Gesichtserscheinungen*, 1826, 177 pp. C. T. Tourtual, *Die Sinne des Menschen*, 1827. G. R. Treviranus, *Beiträge zur Anatomie und Physiologie der Sinneswerkzeuge des Menschen und der Thiere*, 1828; the first *Heft* deals solely with the eye, and apparently no other *Hefte* were published. Heermann, *Die Bildung der Gesichtsvorstellungen aus Gesichtsempfindungen*, 1835. A. W. Volkmann, *Neue Beiträge zur Physiologie des Gesichtssinnes*, 1836. Müller, *Handbuch der Physiologie des Menschen*, 1838, II, bk. v, sect. i (pp. 1088-1214 in the Eng. trans.). C. A. Burow, *Beiträge zur Physiologie und Physik des menschlichen Auges*, 1841. V. Szokalsky, *Ueber die Empfindungen der Farben in physiologischer und pathologischer Hinsicht*, 1842. A. W. Volkmann, R. Wagner's *Handwörterbuch der Physiologie*, 1846, III, i, 264-351. J. B. Listing, *ibid.*, 1853, IV, 451-504. H. L. F. v. Helmholtz, *Handbuch der physiologischen Optik*, 3 vols., 1856-1866, Eng. trans., 1924-1925. H. Aubert, *Physiologie der Netzhaut*, 1865. E. Hering, *Zur Lehre vom Lichtsinne*, 1878. *Cf.* Boring, *op. cit.*, 97-311. W. Dennis, *Readings in the History of Psychology*, 1948, has made available some classical pages in this field: Newton on color, pp. 44-54; Thos. Young on accommodation, pp. 96-101, and on color, p. 112; Dalton on color blindness, pp. 102-111.

On Purkinje, see E. Thomsen, Ueber Johannes Evangelista Purkinje, *Skand. Arch. Physiol.*, 1918, 37, 1-116.

Hearing

Bell, *op. cit.*, 373-453. Steinbuch, *op. cit.*, 270-300. Müller, *Handbuch, op. cit.*, bk. v, sect. ii (pp. 1215-1311 in the trans.). C. Harless, Wagner's *Handwörterbuch, op. cit.*, 1853, IV, 311-450. E. H. Weber was interested in hearing when he was first at Leipzig. He wrote a comparative anatomy of the ear, *De aure et auditu hominis et animalum*, 1820; and a physics of sound in 1825. *Cf.* Boring, *op. cit.*, 312-436.

On the early history of hearing before the nineteenth century, see G. V. Békésy and W. A. Rosenblith, The early history of hearing—observations and theories, *J. acoust. Soc. Amer.*, 1948, 20, 727-748

Touch

In the same works: Bell, 472-480; Steinbuch, 53-140; Müller, bk. v, sect. v (1324-1332 in the trans.); and E. H. Weber, *De tactu: annotationes anatomicæ et physiologicæ*, 1834; *Der Tastsinn und das Gemeingefühl*, Wagner's *Handwörterbuch*, 1846, III, ii, 481-588. This last article has been reprinted separately in 1851 and later. *Cf.* Boring, *op. cit.*, 463-573. See also the excerpts from Weber in 1834 and 1846, Dennis, *of. cit.*, 155 f., 194-196.

Smell

Bell, 454-457. Steinbuch, 303-307. H. Cloquet, *Osphrésiologie, ou traité des odeurs, du sens et des organes de l'olfaction;* the second revised and enlarged edition is dated 1821, and there is a German translation in 1824. Müller, bk. v, sect. iii (1312-1318 in the trans.). F. Bidder, Wagner's *Handwörterbuch*, 1844 II, 916-926. *Cf.* Boring, *op. cit.*, 438-449.

Taste

Bell, 458-471. Steinbuch, 300-303. Müller, bk. v, sect. iv (trans., 1318-1323). Bidder, Wagner's *Handwörterbuch*, 1846, III, i, 1-11. *Cf.* Boring, *op. cit.*, 449-462.

CHAPTER 7

Hypnotism

While all the main threads of experimental psychology lie wholly within physiology during the first half of the nineteenth century, there were during this period two discoveries important for psychology that came from other fields. One, which we shall consider later, is the discovery of the personal equation by the astronomers. The other is hypnotism, the early study of which constitutes practically the beginning of the experimental psychology of motivation.

Hypnosis is doubtless a very old mental phenomenon, not so old as perception, but as old as social relations and sleep-walking and religious ecstasy. It seems to have been induced intentionally in some savage ceremonials. It was not, however, such phenomena that first led to its scientific consideration.

Magnetism used to be regarded as a mysterious natural force, and Paracelsus (1493-1541), the physician and mystic, had designated magnets as bodies which, like the stars, especially influence the human body by means of a subtle emanation that pervades space. Van Helmont (1577-1644) inaugurated the doctrine of animal magnetism by teaching that a magnetic fluid radiates from all men and may be guided by their wills to influence the minds and bodies of others. In the century and a half following him, there arose numerous men in Europe who appeared to effect mysterious cures of the sick by the laying-on of hands or even without contact. Greatrakes (1629-1683), an Irishman, is one of the best known, and his remarkable cures in England of many in the crowds that flocked to him attracted both public and scientific attention. Still, aside from the theory of animal magnetism, which was certainly not an illuminating theory, these phenomena remained inexplicable and lay outside of science.

MESMERISM

The matter came to a head with Friedrich Anton Mesmer (1734-1815), who discovered how to produce these phenomena and lent them his name, for the process of inducing them came to be called *mesmerism.* Mesmer was a physician in Vienna who at first held a belief similar to van Helmont's. His early views grew out of his attempt to explain the supposed effect of the stars upon human beings, the fundamental principle of astrology. There must be, he thought, some effective principle that permeates the universe, a principle that is probably to be identified with electricity or magnetism. This belief led him to experiment with the effect of magnets upon persons, and, in stroking their bodies with magnets or in making passes with magnets over their bodies, he discovered that he could often induce what we now call hypnosis. These facts and this view he presented to the world in a work published in 1766. As a physician, he adopted the magnetic method for healing certain diseases. Mesmer himself said in 1779 that he had never thought that the metal magnets were essential to his cures, but merely that animal magnetism, the magnetism of iron and planetary influence are similar and perhaps of the same nature. At any rate in 1776 he abandoned the use of metal magnets, speaking only thereafter of *animal magnetism*, as van Helmont and others had before him. He effected the cure of a psychoneurotic patient in 1774 with the use of metal magnets, and other cures shortly thereafter with only his own person as a source of magnetism.

In 1775, before he had many cures to his credit, Mesmer sent a letter on the subject of animal magnetism to the various scientific academies. The letter was ignored by all but one, which replied unfavorably. In Vienna his doctrine aroused enemies, and principally on this account Mesmer removed to Paris in 1778.

In Paris he constructed his famous *baquet*. It seems to have been an oak chest, containing chemicals and fitted with many appendages of iron. It was supposed to have been magnetized by Mesmer and to be capable of transmitting the magnetism to the subjects who sat in a circle about it, with their hands joined or connected by cords. (This circle appears to be the ancestor of the circle of spiritualistic sitters of the present day.) The room which contained the *baquet* was dimly lighted and hung with mirrors; strains of soft music sounded through it at intervals; Mesmer appeared, sometimes in magician's dress, and passed about the circle of sitters, touching one, making passes over another and fixing a third with a glance. The effects were emotional and various; many cures occurred; and hypnosis undoubtedly played an important rôle in these results. Often, when he fixed a sitter with his eye and said to him, "Dormez!" the man seemed to go at once to sleep. In Paris, public interest in the affair became very great. Scientific commissions were appointed to examine the phenomena but reported negatively (1784); that is to say, while not denying the effects produced, they found in 'animal magnetism' no similarity to magnetism as it was known in minerals. After all, such a report was not so very different from Mesmer's own view.

What happened next is a comment on the power of words in human affairs. Mesmer had discarded magnets as irrelevant to the phenomena, but he kept the phrase *animal magnetism*, thinking that there must be some similarity between the new power and magnetism. The investigators found no such relationship and therefore declared against 'animal magnetism' in the sense that it was not magnetism. Since the phenomena could hardly be produced by collusion of the subjects with Mesmer, it seemed plain that there must be some force which, if it were not magnetism, must be something else. This 'something else' came to be supposed to be a secret of Mesmer's, for how could he produce these effects without knowing how he did it? The French government is said to have offered him 20,000 francs to disclose the secret and Mesmer to have refused—refused, of course, to tell what he never knew, for he had no secret to disclose. He knew only that he obtained certain results in a certain way, and he believed that the results were due to a magnetic power within himself, but there was nothing to say beyond what every investigator of his methods knew. He was, however, from the first opposed by the medical profession and the scientists, and when he "refused" to reveal his "secret," he gradually fell into disrepute, and finally, denounced as an impostor, withdrew from Paris to Switzerland, where he died in 1815.

It is interesting to see just what factors were at work in this rapid rise and decline of mesmerism, especially because the little drama was reënacted more than once afterward. The affair was a conflict between radicalism and conservatism in science and in the medical art. Mesmer was seeking something new, just as his scientific contemporaries were engaged in discovery; but the new thing that he found was very new in that it appeared, as Mesmer incorrectly formulated the principle, to break with accepted scientific tradition and medical practice. Had he been content to work quietly on the nature of animal magnetism, there would have been no conflict. The discovery, however, seemed to have in it immediate practical possibilities, and Mesmer's temperament led him to utilize these powers to the full without further effort to understand their nature. This course led to publicity and thus to increased opportunity for therapeutic aid. Few men can resist the pressure of popular acclaim, and it may be that Mesmer yielded to the public's love of mystery in much of the hocus-pocus that surrounded the *baquet*. On the other hand, he may have discovered that it was an important condition in inducing the 'magnetic' effects.

Now science felt that it had disposed of magic long before Mesmer, and the similarity of Mesmer's methods to the procedure of the magician and charlatan provoked its opposition. Had Mesmer known the secret of his own success, he might in part have met the opposition, but that secret presupposes a state of psychological knowledge that did not then exist and is only imperfectly revealed to us a century and a half later. In any case, however, he would have had to contend with scientific conservatism. New discoveries make headway in science but slowly, even though discovery is the business of science. This is, so it seems to the author, essentially as it should be. Scientific progress is most sure when it is the resultant of a force operating for change and the opposing inertia of criticism. The views of both Mesmer and Gall were too broadly drawn to command acceptance, and both men were read out of the body scientific; yet neither man was wholly wrong. We reject today mesmerism and phrenology, but we accept hypnosis and, with certain limitations, localization of cerebral function. The historical perspective shows, however, that the conservative scientists were simply fulfilling their critical function in 1784 and 1808.

ELLIOTSON AND MESMERISM

There were many individuals in the first third of the nineteenth century who practised mesmerism, as the new power was now called, but there was no such general interest as had been excited by Mesmer, nor did the practice then come again to an issue with the scientists. A little later, however, on a less public scale, the drama of Mesmer was reënacted in England. The occasion for controversy was John Elliotson (1791-1868).

In 1837, Elliotson was professor of the practice of medicine at University College, London, and senior physician at the University College Hospital. For twenty years Elliotson had been a pioneer in medical science, distrustful of the old, but believing profoundly in the possibilities of the new. First as physician at St. Thomas' Hospital he gained consent to give clinical lectures. Later he was appointed to University College and was largely instrumental in the establishment of the hospital in connection with the college. He was a man of great imagination, fertile in new ideas. In the traditions of the past he saw mainly a force that prevents progress. But he was not a visionary, for many of his ideas were sound. The establishment of University College Hospital was one of these ideas. He saw what is accepted as obvious today, the fact that a medical school needs a hospital attached to it for demonstration and research. He was vigorously opposed in this venture by his conservative colleagues, but he won his fight. He was the first man in England to adopt the use of the stethoscope, which had been invented on the Continent. This practice his colleagues condemned, ridiculed or ignored. They spoke about his "hocus-pocus," and one is said to have remarked of the stethoscope, "Oh, it's just the thing for Elliotson to rave about!" Elliotson also introduced several novel practices in the use of drugs, practices which after the first resistance of the medical profession have become established. Altogether it is plain that he was a radical in temperament, although an effective radical from the point of view of medical progress. It is not surprising that, being met with contempt and ridicule, he should have replied in kind. He did not hesitate to point out some of the absurdities of conventional medical practice of his day, and he thus hindered the progress that he sought to promote by obscuring it behind the barrier of personal prejudice which controversy and recrimination erect.

It was, then, in 1837 that Elliotson's imagination was aroused by a demonstration of mesmerism by Dupotet. He had seen a demonstration in 1829, but the possibilities of the phenomenon seem not to have occurred to him before. He immediately began mesmerizing patients in the hospital, with important results in the treatment of certain nervous cases. Mesmerism was, however, then in the depths of scientific disrepute. His colleagues refused to witness his demonstrations, annoying him in many petty ways. The dean urged him to desist on the ground that the reputation of the medical school was of more importance than scientific research and medical progress, but Elliotson indignantly refused. In 1837 the council of University College passed a resolution forbidding "the practice of mesmerism or animal magnetism within the Hospital." Elliotson immediately resigned from both the college and the hospital, which he had been instrumental in founding, and never entered either institution again. He complained that the council had acted without discussion of the matter with him and without witnessing any of his mesmeric demonstrations.

As so often happens, this crisis fixed Elliotson's determination to study and to utilize mesmerism still further and thus also fixed the opposition of the medical profession toward him. Elliotson was, however, not to be left alone. Braid's interest in mesmerism dates from 1841, and Esdaile's, in India, from 1842. In England in 1842, W. S.

Ward amputated a leg with the patient under mesmeric trance and reported the case to the Royal Medical and Chirurgical Society. The evidence indicated that the patient had felt no pain during the operation. The society, however, refused to believe. Marshall Hall, the pioneer in the study of reflex action, urged that the patient must have been an impostor, and the note of the paper's having been read was stricken from the minutes of the Society. It was further urged that the method, if correct, was immoral, since pain is "a wise provision of nature, and patients ought to suffer pain while their surgeons are operating." Eight years later, Marshall Hall informed the society that the patient had confessed to an imposition but that the source of his information was indirect and confidential. The patient, however, then signed a declaration that the operation had been painless.

In 1843 Elliotson began, under his own editorship, the *Zoist*, which described itself as "a journal of cerebral physiology and mesmerism, and their applications to human welfare," and which served as a place where new biological and even sociological ideas could be reported and discussed, free from the inhibitions of conservative tradition. There are several instances about this time of the refusal of scientific journals or proceedings to publish accounts of mesmeric phenomena. The *Zoist* continued until 1856, when its mission was considered to have been accomplished.

In 1846 it became Elliotson's turn to deliver the Harveian Oration. He accepted in spite of bitter opposition and reviewed the history of scientific opposition to great medical discoveries, not omitting Harvey's discovery of the circulation of the blood. In founding the oration, Harvey had specified that the orator should present his own work "with an exhortation to others to imitate, and an exhortation to study and search out the secrets of nature by way of experiment." Elliotson did not fail at the close of the oration to exhort his audience to the experimental study of mesmerism.

In 1849 a mesmeric infirmary was opened in London, and soon similar clinics were established in other cities of Great Britain. At Exeter, the surgeon claimed at one time that he had mesmerized 1,200 patients and performed 200 painless operations. All this activity the medical journals ignored, but the *Zoist* served as a medium for those who were interested in the work.

Elliotson, like Mesmer, had originally been interested primarily in the therapeutic value of mesmerism, but interest had meanwhile been shifting toward its possibilities as an anesthetic agent. As a matter of fact, with so little understood of hysterical diseases, one might expect that the anesthetic use of mesmerism, more than its therapeutic use, would be the one to lead the medical world to accept mesmerism. The medical profession was earnestly desirous of alleviating the pain of surgical operation, in spite of the remark about Ward's case which we noted above. What happened was that a more reliable, comprehensible and 'respectable' anesthetic came to hand at exactly the same time. While the anesthetic effect of certain drugs seems always to have been known (*e.g.*, Homer mentions the effects of nepenthe), the regular surgical usage of modern times dates only from the employment of ether in 1846.

In 1844 an American dentist, Wells, had one of his own teeth extracted painlessly while he was under the influence of nitrous oxide. The failure of a public demonstration in Boston prevented him from continuing his plan for painless extraction, but another American dentist, Morton, using ether vapor, put the practice into effect in Boston in 1846. News of these results reached England a few months later; ether anesthesia was tested at once, and it rapidly became the general practice in surgical operations. The use of chloroform began in 1847. The dramatic appearance of ether, chloroform and nitrous oxide on the medical stage in the middle 1840s must have forestalled the acceptance of mesmerism as an anesthetic agent. The reason we do not use hypnosis nowadays for anesthesia is that the drugs are more reliable.

Another historical accident of these times that affected the status of mesmerism was the sudden rise of spiritualism. For some time clairvoyance had been regarded as a possibility, although looked at askance by scientists. Elliotson, however, had sought to connect clairvoyance with mesmerism, a natural mistake for his radical temperament. In 1848 spiritualism was born in the mysterious rappings that began in the home of the Fox sisters in Hydesville, New York. These phenomena developed sensationally in Rochester, where the Fox sisters went to live, and the hypothesis that they represented communication from the world of the dead transmitted through the "medium" of certain persons was formed. The word *medium* was attached to the person possessing this power, and sittings for the purpose of eliciting these phenomena were found often to produce new mediums. The development was rapid. By 1852 the interest spread to England, and in 1853, in the form of a craze for table-tipping, all over the Continent. Elliotson himself rejected spiritualism, while believing, although less surely, in clairvoyance. Nevertheless there was a striking similarity between some of the phenomena of spiritualism and those of clairvoyance, and especially between the nature of the spiritualistic sitting and the séances of

Mesmer about the *baquet*. Because of this similarity, the revived mesmerism suffered still more in repute.

ESDAILE AND ANESTHESIA

While all this was going on in England, James Esdaile (1808-1859) was advocating and practising mesmerism in India. Here the British government proved more open-minded than the medical profession. Esdaile had read of Elliotson's work, and in 1845 it occurred to him to try mesmerism upon a patient who was suffering great pain. To his surprise he was successful in inducing the mesmeric state and in rendering his patient entirely without pain. He began, then, to practise mesmerism for anesthetic purposes. A letter to the Medical Board describing his work remained unanswered, but a later report to the government, after he had more than 100 cases to describe, led to the appointment of a committee of investigation. The report of the committee was cautious but favorable to further research, and the government accordingly in 1846 established a small mesmeric hospital in Calcutta where Esdaile might continue his work. After almost a year, the official visitors of the hospital were convinced of the effectiveness of mesmerism as an anesthetic and of its partial effectiveness in reducing operative shock. Three hundred native citizens of Calcutta signed a petition for its continuance. Nevertheless, the government closed the hospital. In 1848 a new mesmeric hospital, dependent upon private resources, was opened, and Esdaile was placed in charge. In six months, however, the government transferred Esdaile to another hospital for the express purpose of effecting a combination of mesmerism with the common practice of medicine. Here he remained at work until he left India on account of the climate in 1851. He settled in Scotland and continued his active interest in mesmerism, corresponding with Elliotson, until his death in 1859. Elliotson, seventeen years his senior, lived until 1868.

Had not the Indian government supported Esdaile's work, he would have had as difficult a time as Elliotson. The Indian medical journals attacked him and suggested that his success was due to the fact that the natives liked to be operated upon and were trying to please Esdaile. Esdaile, before he left India, had performed about 300 major operations and innumerable minor ones, all of them in mesmeric trance and seemingly painless. Natives came to him when they avoided operation by others. Esdaile could attempt certain operations that other surgeons feared to undertake. It seems that Esdaile reduced mortality in the operation for scrotal tumors from about 50 per cent to about 5 per cent. The mesmerized patients lay relaxed and quiet during operation. Detailed descriptions and statistics were available. It was quite unreasonable to suppose that these natives were merely indulging a fancy for pleasing Esdaile.

Neither in India nor in Great Britain could Esdaile get the medical journals to print accounts of his work. For a time, the only available descriptions lay buried in reports of the Indian government. In 1846 and again in 1852, however, he published a separate book, describing his work in India. Sir James Simpson, the first to discover and apply the anesthetic properties of chloroform, had urged Esdaile before the later report to publish, but Esdaile could not get his paper accepted.

Esdaile's predominant interest in the anesthetic aspect of mesmerism led him to prefer mesmerism to the new-found agents, ether and chloroform. In this matter he may have been prejudiced by his own habits, but it was also apparent that ether and chloroform left deleterious after-effects and, if not expertly administered, might be fatal. From both these evils mesmerism seemed free. When the Congress of the United States in 1853 sought to bestow an award of ten thousand dollars on the discoverer of the anesthetic powers of ether and described ether as the first anesthetic, Esdaile, without claiming the award, sent a letter of protest on the ground that mesmerism was prior. As a matter of fact, the priority was not very great. The important events were these. Ward in England amputated a leg under mesmeric trance in 1842. Wells in America had a tooth painlessly extracted under nitrous oxide in 1844. Esdaile in India began and accomplished many operations with mesmeric analgesia in 1845. Morton in America extracted teeth under ether anesthesia in 1846, and the practice spread to England in the same year. Simpson introduced chloroform as an anesthetic in 1847.

BRAID AND HYPNOTISM

We must now turn our attention to James Braid (*ca.* 1795-1860), famous as "the discoverer of hypnotism," and much better known than Elliotson or Esdaile. Unlike them, Braid never broke with the medical profession, and he thus provides us with an opportunity for gaining insight into the causes of conservative opposition to mesmerism.

In the first place, we must note that Braid was never regarded as a mesmerist either by himself or by the mesmerists. He described the mesmeric trance as a "nervous sleep" and invented for the underlying doctrine the term *neurypnology* (a contraction of *neurohypnology*). In general, the prefix of the term came to be dropped, a change which led to the words *hypnotic, hypnotize* and *hypnotism*.

Braid was a hypnotist; Elliotson was a mesmerist. The importance of words in the discussion and comprehension of men is very great indeed. We have just seen that Mesmer's failure to drop the word *magnetism* when he found that magnets had nothing to do with his phenomena obscured the real importance of his discovery, probably in his own mind as well as in the minds of others. Conversely, the introduction of the new word *hypnotism* tended to set off Braid's theory from every other that went by the name of 'mesmerism.'

There is, however, something more than words to be considered. The very fact that Braid chose a new word means something about him. Let us compare him with Elliotson. Elliotson was undoubtedly the more brilliant of the two; he was a discoverer of several important medicinal facts and a leader among his colleagues (when he could persuade his colleagues to be led), but also an extremist in his enthusiasms. Braid was a sound medical practitioner of Manchester; he was unusually, but not remarkably, skillful as a surgeon; he is known only for his work in hypnotism; and he was not an extremist. The most impulsive and dramatic act of his life, so far as our knowledge of him goes, was when, only five weeks after a public mesmeric demonstration by Lafontaine on the stage at Manchester, he himself sought the stage to refute Lafontaine and to present his own theory and demonstrations that had been elaborated in that brief interval. In the issue thus raised, both circumstances and his temperament made him a champion of the middle ground. On the one side, the medical profession looked askance; on the other, the mesmerists disowned him. Nevertheless, he kept on, experimenting and writing, seeking always to give scientific meaning to his findings and thus narrowing the gulf between himself and medicine. As the personal separation between Braid and medical men became less, his breach with the mesmerists became greater. Elliotson in general ignored him, but on two occasions the *Zoist* made its contempt for Braid quite clear. On the other hand, in phenomena and even in theory it is plain that Braid belonged in interests with the mesmerists. It would appear, then, that the breach between medicine and mesmerism was after all more a matter of personalities than of science. If Elliotson, when unjustly rebuffed, could have adjusted himself to the situation, changed his obnoxious terminology and gone on quietly with research while cultivating the good-will of his colleagues, the story of mesmerism might have been different. On the other hand, it was fortunate for science that Braid's first impulse in connection with mesmerism was his desire to refute Lafontaine, for thus the breach with the mesmerists started at the very beginning, and this breach helped to preserve his scientific reputation. We can trace some of these motives as we tell the story of Braid.

In 1841, Lafontaine gave a series of public exhibitions of mesmerism in Manchester. This was three years after Elliotson's resignation from University College, two years before the *Zoist* began publication and four years before Esdaile undertook to induce mesmeric trance in India. There was much public interest in these exhibitions; the subject has always created interest, and in this case the *Manchester Guardian* had printed very unfavorable comments in advance. The first meeting was small, but the audience rapidly grew to huge proportions. Braid was present at the second meeting and is said to have been "loud in his denunciation of the whole affair." Other medical men joined with him; but the sympathies of the audience were with Lafontaine. It was easy to charge fraud, because the mesmerist operated principally upon two subjects whom he brought with him. At the next exhibition, however, Braid became suddenly convinced that there was something more than collusion beneath the phenomena. According to his own statement, he came to this conclusion because he observed the inability of one of the subjects to open his eyes. He is said by another physician present on the stage to have tested the subject by forcing a pin under one of her nails without eliciting any evidence of pain. The "leading ophthalmist" of Manchester, who was also on the stage, likewise changed his opinion when he noted, on forcing the subject's eyes open, that the pupils were contracted to two small points. Plainly, Braid was in a dilemma. He had publicly committed himself against Lafontaine and mesmerism, and now he had evidence which he would have accepted in the clinic as showing that the phenomena were 'real.'

It is here that he showed the scientific balance of mind that ultimately led to the discovery of the essential truth hidden in mesmerism. He might have withdrawn, reiterating his denunciation, and then have kept his counsel, but he was too open-minded. He might have become a complete convert to mesmerism as Combe had to phrenology under similar circumstances, but he was too conservative. What he did do was to observe the next exhibition carefully, and then go home to plan experiments and to elaborate a theory that would bring these facts into relation with scientific physiology.

The mesmerists' theory, so far as it can be called a theory, was that the cause of the phenomena resided in the person of the mesmerist; it was animal magnetism. This view was too vague and mysterious to satisfy Braid; he was sure that there must be some more immediate physiological cause residing in the person of the subject. To his surprise, he found that he could induce an artificial sleep in the members of his family and in his friends by having them stare fixedly at some bright object above the line of vision. He thus came to the conclusion that the mesmeric phenomena were merely the evidences of a sleep "caused by paralyzing the levator muscles of the eyelids through their continued action during the protracted fixed stare." In his enthusiasm for this discovery, he sought the stage only a few weeks after Lafontaine had left it, mesmerized many persons before large and intensely interested audiences and expounded his physiological theory. He presented phenomena similar to Lafontaine's, but he was not branded as a mesmerist because his theory fitted in with conservative physiological belief, and because he presented it as an attack upon mesmerism. It is also probable that the new theory could be more readily tolerated since it did not magnify the theorist as a man possessed of peculiar power over his fellowman. Modesty begets sympathy, and an egotistical theory, even if right, would be bound to meet with resistance. It was for this reason that Elliotson failed.

Braid and his biographers have regarded this formulation of a theory as the "discovery" of hypnotism. Braid at least showed all the enthusiasm of a discoverer, developing his theory by experiment and writing. He immediately met with opposition from the medical men, from the mesmerists and even from laymen. His first book is a brochure entitled: "Satanic Agency and Mesmerism Reviewed, in a Letter to the Rev. H. McNeile, A.M., of Liverpool, in Reply to a Sermon Preached by Him at St. Jude's Church, Liverpool, on Sunday, April 10th, 1842." In 1843 he published his fundamental work, *Neurypnology, or, the Rationale of Nervous Sleep; Considered in Relation with Animal Magnetism,* and the term *hypnotism* and its derivatives date from this year. Half a dozen other books and many articles in journals followed in the next decade. Later, as opposition waned, his publication also decreased; and he died suddenly in 1860. Just before his death he had the satisfaction of having his work taken up by Azam in France, and of learning that Broca had presented a paper on the subject to the Académie des Sciences, a paper which seems to have met with a favorable reception and which resulted in the appointment of a committee of investigation.

Braid's earlier views of hypnotism emphasized the importance of sensory fixation. His method of inducing hypnosis by having the subject stare fixedly at some object naturally stressed this notion. It is, however, but a step in thought from visual fixation to the fixation of attention, and from the very beginning, when he used the word *monoideism* to describe the hypnotic state, Braid had this broader and more psychological view in mind. Later he came to recognize more clearly the importance of the factor of suggestion in inducing the phenomena, and his emphasis shifted even more from the physiological to the psychological aspect of the state. He was also, it is interesting to note, quite clear about the division of consciousness in so far as he found that memories would persist from one hypnotic state to another, although unavailable to the subject when awake. Though, as the champion of the middle ground, he had to defend himself on both sides, he was nevertheless not a propagandist, but a man primarily interested in the nature of the phenomena; and it is thus that we get with Braid a great step forward from vague theory and personal controversy to an analytical description of empirical fact. The scientific knowledge of hypnosis begins with Braid.

Viewed in its entirety, the history of hypnosis consists of three short periods of intense interest, separated by long periods in which there was little general interest, but in which the thread was maintained continuously by a certain amount of practice along the lines of the immediately preceding development. In the 1780s Mesmer flourished in Paris, but he was soon discredited, and for a half-century mesmerism became the property of a few honest disciples and many charlatans. In the 1840s came the revival of mesmerism within medicine and the new theory of hypnotism. In the 1850s there was a decline in interest, for the therapeutic value of hypnotism was not clearly established; as an anesthetic it was of less general application than ether or chloroform, and as a controversial subject it was dead as soon as the nature of the phenomena had been indicated by Braid. This time the period of quiescence was but little more than two decades, for the next revival belongs to the 1880s.

It is the period of Braid that is of particular importance to us here. In it we see how physiological thought of the middle nineteenth century took up with the problem of mesmerism, a problem essentially psychological in so far as it was not merely occult. It cannot be argued that the development of hypnosis contributed immediately and directly to the beginning of physiological psychology; rather is this development a symptom of the thought of the times out of which physiological psychology emerged. Later, it is true, the method and facts of hypnosis were ready for assimilation by psychology, especially in France, and for further elaboration within psychology.

LATER HYPNOTISM

With the later history of hypnosis we are not concerned at present, for the reason that what might have developed into an experimental or physiological psychology of motivation in the 1860s was in fact relegated to the field of abnormal psychology as not quite 'scientific,' a topic still somewhat mysterious and not wholly freed from the taint of magic. People like to wonder if the course of history could have been different from what it was. The next chapter shows how the astronomers, disturbed by finding that personal equations had to be introduced into their observations, discovered reaction times, and, bequeathing both their new facts and methods to the psychologists, did almost as much as anyone else (before Ebbinghaus' work in 1885 on memory) to make the new experimental psychology something more than the study of sensation and perception. Would it have been possible, these people ask, for the medical men to have left their unwelcome discovery of hypnosis on psychology's door-step in the 1860s and so to have got a scientific dynamic psychology of motivation under way then without science's having to wait on Charcot and Freud and Janet and Morton Prince until dynamic psychology could in the 1920s become something more than ab-normal psychology?

Presumably, if you are going to start supposing the occurrence of one event contrary to fact, there is nothing to prevent you from sup-posing many more. It is the author's opinion, however, that the times were not right in the 1860s for a viable scientific psychology of motivation. The topics of sensation, perception and memory had already had a century and a half of thinking done on them, partly within physiology and partly within philosophy. That human re-action should take up time was indeed a new thought (p. 42) and it is remarkable that Helmholtz's discovery in 1850 should have borne fruit so rapidly, but in that field the conception of neural conduction had also had long preparation and was now consistent with the tele-graph and the use of electric circuits. Before they could get on with motivation as a topic of research, the experimental psychologists had to get accustomed to simple connectionistic ways of thinking. Only then were they ready to superimpose the dynamic conceptions of attitude, set, Einstellung, determining tendency, wish (Freud) and suggestion (hypnosis). Such at least is the author's view, a complacent one which is consistent with what happened and somewhat more plausible than a protest against the willfulness of history.

After the Académie des Sciences, under the stimulation of Azam and Broca, had considered hypnotism in 1860 and Braid had died in the same year, little of importance occurred until 1878. 'Durand de Gros' had in 1860 coined the word Braidism as a substitute for hypnotism, because the emphasis in describing the state had shifted from sleep to suggestion. Liébeault, who began the study of hypnotism in 1860, settled in 1864 at Nancy, where for twenty years he practised hypnotism as a therapeutic agent. Braid's work meanwhile sank into obscurity in England, whereas it had never become well known on the Continent. In 1875, Richet in France called attention to the phenomena of hypnosis and attested to their genuineness. In 1878, Charcot began his demonstrations of hypnosis, and his particular view of hypnosis came to be an important doctrine of the school of the Salpêtrière, of which he was the leader. Almost simultaneously, interest in hypnosis sprang up in Germany. Heidenhain's work belongs to these years, and in 1881-1882 Preyer translated Braid's works into German. It was in 1882 that Liébeault converted Bernheim to the new art. Liébeault had cured a case of sciatica that had resisted Bernheim's treatment. Bernheim's subsequent work created the Nancy school of hypnosis. Thus it came about that Braid's work, after being lost sight of, was again revived. Interest was again quickened by controversy, but this time the controversy did not turn upon the 'genuineness' of hypnosis. Hypnosis was accepted as a fact, and the dispute was concerned with its nature. The theory of the Nancy school, which differed but little from Braid's later views, held that the phenomena were to be understood in terms of suggestion and were thus entirely normal phenomena. The school of the Salpêtrière believed that the phenomena were essentially hysterical in nature and thus symptoms of abnormality. The verdict of time has favored the Nancy school, but the controversy was fortunate, for it dismissed forever the suspicion that hypnosis was not a proper subject for scientific inquiry. (See pp. 696-699.)

NOTES

There are several excellent accounts of the facts of hypnosis: A. Binet and C. Féré, *Le magnétisme animal*, 1887, Eng. trans., 1888; A. Moll, *Der Hypnotismus*, 1889 and four subsequent editions with Eng. trans. of all; J. M. Bramwell, *Hypnotism, Its History, Practice, and Theory*, 1903. All of these accounts treat of the history of hypnosis. Binet and Féré, chaps. 1-3, are most complete on its origins; Moll, chap. 1, is extremely detailed and lacks on this account perspective; Bramwell, pp. 3-39, deals mostly with Elliotson, Esdaile and Braid. On Braid, see below.

The account in the text sacrifices detail to perspective, but the reader should realize that the total literature on hypnosis is very extensive. Dessoir's bibliography in 1888-1890 noted 1,182 titles by 774 authors: M. Dessoir, *Bibliographie der modernen Hypnotismus*, 1888, with a *Nachtrag* in 1890. B. Rand, in J. M. Baldwin's *Dictionary of Philosophy and Psychology*, 1905, III, ii, 1059-1067, gives a bibliography of 411 titles. See also the bibliography in Bramwell, 440-464.

Three more recent accounts of hypnosis are as follows: P. Janet, *Les médications psychologiques: études* historiques, psychologiques et cliniques sur les méthodes de la psychothérapie, 1919, I, chaps. 4-8, Eng. trans., 1925, an excellent history, a judicious review and an interesting account, 217 pp. in all; C. L. Hull, *Hypnosis and Suggestibility: an Experimental Approach*, 1933, the classic experimental work on the topic; and A. Jenness, Hypnotism, in J. McV. Hunt's *Personality and Behavior Disorders*, 1944, I, chap. 15, the current summary with a bibliography of about 120 titles. See also the discussion by G. Zilboorg, *A History of Medical Psychology*, 1941, 342-369.

Mesmer

F. A. Mesmer's early work, before his discovery of the irrelevancy of magnets, is *De planetarum influxu*, 1766. His own account of the beginnings of that doctrine of animal magnetism that came to be called mesmerism is his *Mémoire sur la découverte du magnétisme animal*, 1779, Germ. trans., 1781, Eng. trans., 1948. The Eng. trans. has the title *Mesmerism* and an introductory historical sketch by G. Frankau, who says that the government did not offer Mesmer 20,000 francs for his "secret," but that Marie Antoinette offered him 20,000 francs as an inducement not to leave Paris. There are many legends about Mesmer and not all of them are confirmed. There are also several later books by Mesmer; the last is a general account, *Mesmerismus*, 1814, published long after he had been driven from Paris and but a year before his death. W. Dennis, *Readings in the History of Psychology*, 1948, 93-95, reprints two pages of Mesmer's comments on animal magnetism in 1779.

Elliotson

On John Elliotson, see Bramwell, *op. cit.*, 4-14. Practically all of his writings on mesmerism were perforce in the *Zoist*, since the medical journals refused them. There was published in London and Philadelphia a pamphlet by him, describing among other things Ward's amputation under mesmeric anesthesia: *Numerous Cases of Surgical Operations without Pain in the Mesmeric State; with remarks upon the opposition of many members of the Royal Medical and Chirurgical Society and others to the reception of the inestimable blessings of mesmerism*, 1843. Elliotson's *Harveian Oration* was also published in London in 1846 with an English translation of the Latin.

Esdaile

On James Esdaile, see Bramwell, *op. cit.*, 14-21. Some of his publications are now rare; see the list in Bramwell, 456. His *Mesmerism in India, and Its Practical Application in Surgery and Medicine*, 1846 (second printing, 1847), is not rare and gives a good account of his work. The separate publication of 1852, which was originally solicited by Simpson for a journal and then rejected on the advice of his editorial colleagues, is *The Introduction of Mesmerism, as an Anæsthetic and Curative Agent, into the Hospitals of India*.

Anesthesia

On the discovery of anesthesia in America, see C. A. H. Smith, *Scientific Monthly*, 1927, 24, 64-70. Wells and Morton had been associated in early dental practice, although not directly in this discovery. Wells's public failure to demonstrate nitrous oxide as an anesthetic in Boston in 1845, owing to his lack of skill in administering the gas, led to his being ridiculed, to his retirement from practice, and thus indirectly to his suicide. Morton, though a dentist, administered ether for a surgical operation at the Massachusetts General Hospital in Boston in 1846. He was successful, but strange to say he met with violent opposition from the newspapers and the public. One of the clergy argued that he was interfering with the Divine will in abolishing pain (the same argument that had been raised against Ward's amputation of a leg under hypnosis), and others, including many of the medical profession, heaped abuse upon him. The case is very similar to Elliotson's, except that the more open-minded surgeons immediately adopted the new method. In a few years, the greatness of the discovery was so well recognized that a dispute arose between Morton and Jackson, his one-time patron and adviser, as to priority, a dispute that prevented the United States Congress from making the award that Esdaile claimed belonged to hypnosis.

Braid

On James Braid, see the reprint of his *Neurypnology* (1843) in 1899, with editorial additions by A. E. Waite. This book contains a biographical account of Braid by Waite, pp. 1-66. Braid tells the story of the inception of the idea of hypnosis, in connection with Lafontaine's exhibitions, in chap. 1. (See also another account of Lafontaine's Manchester meeting in Bramwell, 465-467.) Waite adds a bibliography of thirty-four titles for Braid, pp. 364-375. Bramwell, 460-464, gives forty-nine titles of books and articles by Braid and twenty-seven contemporaneous titles about him. The translation of Braid into German by W. Preyer is *Der Hypnotismus; ausgewählte Schriften*, 1882. The French translation was by J. Simon, *Neurypnologie*, 1883. When the historians state that Braid discovered hypnotism in 1843 and that the discovery was lost sight of for forty years, they have in mind this revival about 1880, and that the translations of his work into German and French occurred forty and forty-one years, respectively, after its publication. Dennis, *op. cit.*, 178-193, reprints a discussion by Braid in 1846 of his own and Baron von Reichenbach's early researches on magnetism and hypnotism.

Braid, as we have seen, coined the word *hypnotism* and all its common variants. He did not use the word hypnosis, which appeared later in the 1880s. Cf. A. Lehmann's lectures of 1889, *Die Hypnose*, 1890. The word was used medically of narcotic sleep in the 1870s.

The term *Braidism*, analogous to *mesmerism*, was invented by J. P. Philips, writing under the *nom de plume* 'Durand de Gros': *Cours théoretique et practique de Braidisme, ou hypnotisme nerveux considéré dans ses rapports avec la psychologie, la physiologie, et la pathologie*, 1860.

Later Hypnotism

A. A. Liébeault's first work was *Du sommeil et des états analogues, considérés surtout au point de vue de l'action de la morale sur le physique*, 1866. He published other books on hypnosis in 1883 and later, but he was in general more of a practitioner than writer. He had, nevertheless, the scientist's enthusiasm for the new method, for in Nancy he would give hypnotic treatment to the poor gratis, though he charged for medical treatment.

The revival of hypnosis begins with Charles Richet's favorable pronouncement in his article, Du somnambulisme provoqué, *J. anat. physiol.*, 1875, 11, 348-378. J. M. Charcot's first accounts of his demonstrations are in the *Gazette des hôpitaux civils et militaires*, 1878, 51, 1074 f., 1097, 1121; and *Compt. rend. soc. biol.*, sér. 6, 1878, 5, 119, 230, but the School of the Salpêtrière is to be known through his later writing; see his *Œuvres complètes*, 1890, IX, 213-480, where twenty-seven papers on hypnotism and metallotherapy have been reprinted. Hippolyte Bernheim's first book after his conversion by Liébeault is *De la suggestion dans l'état hypnotique et dans l'état de veille*, 1884; and there are numerous later books.

The revival in Germany seems to have begun with R. Heidenhain's *Der sogenannte thierische Magnetismus*, 1880, which appears to have run through four editions in the same year. W. Preyer published *Die Katapledie und der thierische Hypnotismus* in 1878, and *Die Entdeckung des Hypnotismus* in 1881. He was the German exponent of Braid.

The result of all this new interest in hypnosis is shown by the establishment of the *Revue de l'hypnotisme* in

France in 1887 and of the *Zeitschrift für Hypnotismus* in Germany in 1892. In England a great deal about hypnosis appeared in the *Proceedings* of the Society for Psychical Research, which was founded in 1892.

CHAPTER 8

The Personal Equation

While the physiologists were concerning themselves with problems of nerve conduction, localization of function in the brain
and sensation, and the medical men were combating hypnosis as an
anesthetic and curative agent, the astronomers were taking serious
account of a physiological or psychological source of error in their
observations, a personal difference between individual astronomers in
their observation of the times of stellar events. Although Maskelyne,
the astronomer royal at the Greenwich Observatory, observed and
recorded such a difference in 1795, the real discoverer of the personal
difference was Bessel, the astronomer at Königsberg, who saw the
significance of the event at Greenwich and investigated the matter
during the 1820s. His positive results led some astronomers in the next
decade to measure the *personal equation*, as it came to be called, and
to correct for it. In the 1840s, this practice became frequent and the
astronomers sought for ways to eliminate the error. The perfection of
the chronograph in the next decade, and other methods for 'doing
away with the observer' were developed. While these methods succeeded, it is nevertheless true that there was more about the personal
equation written in astronomical journals in the 1860s than in any
other decade, and interest was maintained up to about 1890.

The astronomers thought of the error as physiological, but it is
obviously the sort of physiological problem that, along with sensation, was destined to become the property of the new physiological
psychology.

MASKELYNE AND BESSEL

At Greenwich in 1796 Maskelyne, as every psychologist knows,
dismissed Kinnebrook, his assistant, because Kinnebrook observed the
times of stellar transits almost a second later than he did. Maskelyne
was convinced that all through 1794 there had been no discrepancy
between the two of them. Then in August, 1795, Kinnebrook was
found to be recording times about a half-second later than Maskelyne.
His attention was called to the "error," and it would seem that he

must have striven to correct it. Nevertheless, it increased during the succeeding months until, in January, 1796, it had become about eight tenths of a second. Then Maskelyne dismissed him. The error was serious, for upon such observations depended the calibration of the clock, and upon the clock depended all other observations of place and time.

The accepted manner of observing stellar transits at that time was the "eye and ear" method of Bradley. The field of the telescope was divided by parallel cross-wires in the reticle. The observational problem consisted in noting, to one tenth of a second, the time at which a given star crossed a given wire. The observer looked at the clock, noted the time to a second, began counting seconds with the heard beats of the clock, watched the star cross the field of the telescope, noted and "fixed in mind" its position at the beat of the clock just before it came to the critical wire, noted its position at the next beat after it had crossed the wire, estimated the place of the wire between the two positions in tenths of the total distance between the positions, and added these tenths of a second to the time in seconds that he had counted for the beat before the wire was reached. It is obviously a complex judgment. Not only does it involve a co-ordination between the eye and the ear, but it requires a spatial judgment dependent upon a fixed position (the wire), an actual but instantaneous position of a moving object, and a remembered position no longer actual. Nevertheless, "the excellent method of Bradley" was accepted and regarded as accurate to one or at least two tenths of a second. In the face of this belief, Kinnebrook's error of eight tenths of a second was a gross error and justified Maskelyne's conclusion that he had fallen "into some irregular and confused method of his own" and his consequent dismissal.

Had it not been for Bessel (1784-1846), this event, recorded in the pages of *Astronomical Observations at Greenwich*, might have passed into oblivion. In 1816 von Lindenau mentioned the incident in a history of Greenwich Observatory which he published in the *Zeitschrift für Astronomie*, and Bessel noticed it. Bessel was the astronomer at Königsberg, where in 1813 a new observatory had been erected under his supervision. He was a man of unusual intellect, a pioneer in the more exact measurements of modern astronomy and an investigator with a special interest in instrumental errors of measurement. A great mind is least bound by tradition and least impressed by prestige, and it was natural, in view of his special interest, that the incident of Maskelyne and Kinnebrook should suggest to Bessel the possibility of a personal error of observation which the accepted method of Bradley did not guard against. It seemed to him that Kinnebrook, when informed of his "error," must have tried to correct it and that his failure to succeed might mean that the error was involuntary. Moreover, it is probable that Bessel had been thinking about errors of observation, for Gauss, at the Göttingen observatory, had discussed the theory of them in 1809. At any rate, Bessel sent to England for a copy of Maskelyne's complete observations and, after studying them, determined to see whether this personal difference, which seemed incredibly large in view of the supposed accuracy of the method, could be found amongst observers more experienced than Kinnebrook.

His first attempt in 1819, while he was visiting Encke and von Lindenau, was thwarted by cloudy weather, but a year later he found an opportunity to compare himself with Walbeck at Königsberg. They selected ten stars; each observed the transit of five one night and the transit of the other five the next night, and so on, for five nights. Bessel was found always to observe earlier than Walbeck. The average difference was 1.041 secs., with but little variability about the average. If Kinnebrook's error of 0.8 sec. was 'incredible,' this difference was even more so, though Bessel recorded: "We ended the observations with the conviction that it would be impossible for either to observe differently, even by only a single tenth of a second."

It was fortunate that the difference was so large, for it stimulated Bessel to further work, and, when published in 1822, it attracted immediate attention. As a matter of fact, this difference is so large that it has been questioned. How was it possible for there to be a deviation of more than a second in estimating fractional intervals between clock-beats a second apart? Some have suggested that Bessel and Walbeck counted their beats in different ways. The clock beats as its hand moves from one second to the next, and one person might assign the beat to the second from which the hand had moved and another to the second toward which the hand was moving. Others have pointed out that, although this difference is almost the largest on record, it is simply the limiting case of personal differences that vary from zero up to a second. This latter view is supported by the belief that so keen an observer as Bessel would hardly have missed so gross an artifact as a difference in methods of counting. Whichever way it was, an artifact or a true difference, it was fortunate, for it led Bessel to continue the investigation.

In 1823 Bessel had an opportunity to observe with Argelander. This time Bessel had Argelander observe seven stars while he himself determined by observation the clock-corrections. From these data the right ascensions of the stars were computed and compared with similar observations and computations for the same stars in 1821, when Bessel had both observed the stars and made the clock-corrections. The personal difference between the two astronomers is represented by the equation $A-B = 1.223$ sec. From the first, Bessel presented the differences in this manner, with the result that a difference between two observers came to be referred to as a "personal equation."

Bessel next conceived the notion of determining the personal equation indirectly by means of a third observer. He was especially anxious to compare himself with Struve of Dorpat who, like himself, was more practised in the observation of transits than were Walbeck and Argelander. No opportunity for a direct comparison with Struve immediately presented itself, but Walbeck compared himself with Struve on passing through Dorpat in 1821, and Argelander compared himself with Struve on a similar visit in 1823. The first four equations given below were therefore known, and it became possible to eliminate both Walbeck and Argelander algebraically and to find without direct observation the relation of Bessel to Struve; thus:

By direct comparison:	$W-B = 1.041$ sec. (1820)	$A-B = 1.223$ sec. (1823)
By direct comparison:	$W-S = .242$ sec. (1821)	$A-S = .202$ sec. (1823)
Hence, by subtraction:	$S-B = .799$ sec.	$S-B = 1.021$ sec.

The difference between the two values of $S-B$ suggests that there is variability in the personal equation. Ultimately, Bessel established the fact of variability. In 1825, a visit of Knorre to Dorpat and then to Königsberg gave another indirect value for $S-B$. Only in 1834 did Bessel and Struve find an opportunity to compare themselves directly, but certain joint observations made in 1814, before Bessel had ever heard of Kinnebrook's dismissal, furnished data for another direct comparison. In all, then, there were finally available five determinations of $S-B$, three indirect and two direct, ranging from 1814 to 1834. The values in seconds are:

Direct (1814)	Indirect (1821)	Indirect (1823)	Indirect (1825)	Direct (1834)
0.044 sec.	0.799 sec.	1.021 secs.	0.891 sec.	0.770 sec.

Thus Bessel may be said to have discovered not only the personal equation, but also its variability. He found a gross error, and he showed that one could not reliably 'calibrate the observer' in order to correct for it.

Bessel's interest did not stop here. He found for himself that his error was less with a clock beating half-seconds, and again for himself that the rate of motion of a star did not affect the error. The latter point was not, however, verified later. He was also concerned to discuss the nature of observation by the 'eye and ear' method, but to this point we shall return later.

Obviously the first result of Bessel's discovery was to lead the astronomers to determine personal equations and to correct for them. There was no reason to believe that the variability of the personal equation was so great as to render correction entirely useless. In the four values for S – B determined after the discovery of this individual difference (1821-1834), all show that Bessel always observed in advance of Struve by an amount varying between 0.770 and 1.021 sec. No correction can apparently then be accurate to one tenth of a second, but presumably correction in this case would reduce error from about a second to about one fourth of a second.

ASTRONOMICAL USE OF THE PERSONAL EQUATION

About 1830, Robinson, the director of the Armagh Observatory in Ireland, determined the probable errors of observations of the sun's limbs and, publishing his report much later, described these values as personal equations. In 1833, two astronomers, Wolfers and Nehus, at the Göttingen observatory in Germany, where Gauss was director, determined their relative personal equation and corrected their observations for it. In 1837, Gerling, the director of the observatory at Marburg, planned to investigate, with the coöperation of Gauss at Göttingen and Nicolai at Mannheim, the differences in longitude of the three observatories, which form a triangle with mountains near one visible at the other two. The method involved the observation of heliograph signals flashed in daytime and flashes of gunpowder at night. Before computing the results, Gerling visited the two other observatories and determined his personal equations with the other observers for flashes of light and for stellar transits. Beside the three principal astronomers, Gauss's assistant and Gerling's assistant also observed; thus there were five observers in all, and the equations between Gerling and the other four made it possible to reduce all the results to Gerling's times.

In 1838, Airy, the astronomer royal at Greenwich, began the practice of recording personal differences in the observation of transits, computed as Maskelyne had done from the calibration of the clock. This practice was continued until 1853, and the annual variations in the differences for Main-Rogerson and for Main-Henry became available for fourteen and thirteen successive years respectively. There were at least three other determinations of personal equations for the purpose of correction in the early 1840s: that by Quetelet, in comparing the longitudes of Brussels and Greenwich; that by Struve, in comparing the longitudes of Pulkova and Altona; and that by Goujon, in determining the diameter of the sun. Had the personal equation been as little variable as other errors of observation, undoubtedly the practice of determining it and correcting for it would thus have grown up. Its repeated determination, however, served principally to exhibit its variability, and astronomers turned their attention to its control and elimination.

Various alternative methods of dealing with the personal equation or of determining it were suggested quite early. Gerling, in the work just mentioned, had sought to determine it by observations of transits, using a spring pendulum instead of a star. This method had in it the possibility of determining the true time as well as the observed time, but the problem was not faced until the chronograph was perfected later. In 1843 Arago sought to avoid the difficulty which seemed to be caused by the divided attention required in the 'eye and ear' method. He had one observer at the telescope make a sharp stroke when the star appeared to cross the wire, and another observer estimate the temporal position of the sound of this stroke between the two beats of the clock. The first observer had thus to attend only to a visual stimulus, the second only to an auditory one. Under these conditions, the personal difference practically disappeared; nevertheless, the method did not come into use. Arago even went further by eliminating the second observer. He constructed a device in which the observer at the telescope could pull a trigger at the instant of transit and thus cause the pointer of the chronometer to make a mark upon the dial so that the fraction of a second could be read off later. In 1849 Faye described a photographic method, especially applicable to the sun (where there is abundance of light): instantaneous photographs are made of the field, including the cross-wires, at times determined electrically, thus 'excluding the observer' entirely. In 1852 a binocular eyepiece was developed at Greenwich such that two observers could observe the transit of the same star simultaneously. This method ruled out the calibration of the clock as a factor, because, even if the clock had been wrong, a personal difference in the estimation of tenths of a second when two observers were listening to the same beats would be immediately obvious. Just at this time, however, a satisfactory chronograph became available and distracted attention from these new methods.

Repsold had constructed a chronograph at the Hamburg observatory in 1828, but the speed of movement was not constant, and Repsold died two years later, before the instrument was perfected. There was, therefore, no satisfactory device of this sort until one was developed by workers in the United States Coast Survey about 1850. The superintendent of the Survey, Bache, was the leading spirit in this work, but the credit is due jointly to six men who worked in cooperation.

The chronographic method was adopted at Greenwich in 1854. The chronograph was simply the forerunner of the modern kymograph, a drum on which a pointer traces a long spiral line. An electromagnet, connected with a second-clock, causes the pointer to draw a jag in the line every second. At the instant of transit the observer taps a key, which causes another pointer, tracing a line on the drum parallel to the first line, to make a jag. By comparison of the two lines the astronomer can note the time of transit and measure it to a fractional part of a second. The observer's task is as simple as in Arago's device where he pulled a trigger to make the hand of the chronometer mark on the dial between the divisions for the seconds. In the first two years of the use of the chronograph, the Greenwich observatory discovered that the instrument reduced the personal equation to less than one tenth of a second, the goal of precision that the astronomers had originally been seeking.

The chronograph, however, made easy the measurement of the absolute personal equation. Heretofore, astronomers had had to be content with the measurement of relative personal differences for pairs of observers, but it was not possible for them to say how much any one of them deviated from the truth. With the development of electrical devices that were, as compared with the times under consideration, practically instantaneous in operation, it became possible to arrange an artificial star or point of light that would move across the telescopic field and would record automatically on the chronograph the instant when it was bisected by the crucial cross-wire. The astronomer might observe the transit of this artificial star by any method he wished. He could use the 'eye and ear' method, or he could tap a key at the instant of transit in order to make a mark on the chronograph. At last it was possible to write a personal equation for one astronomer without regard to any other astronomer and to attempt to reduce all observations to their 'true' values instead of to a system of times based upon one man.

This new method seems first to have been suggested by Prazmowski in 1854, although not actually used by him. In 1858 Mitchel reported similar experiments (begun in 1856) which showed the amount of the absolute personal equation as varying between one tenth and two tenths of a second. Beside determining the "absolute personality of the eye," as he called it, he also investigated the absolute "personality of the ear" and the absolute "personality of touch" by using auditory and tactual instead of visual stimuli. In the same year (1858) Hartmann published results obtained by a similar method, results which are notable in that they indicate a partial reduction of the variability, that still persisted, to but one of its psychological conditions.

We must also note that, even before the chronograph had been generally adopted as an astronomical instrument, F. Kaiser of Leyden had begun to measure the absolute personal equation by means of another device. He had the usual standard clock and in addition another clock which beat at a slightly different rate from the standard clock. The artificial star, moved by clockwork, caused the auxiliary pendulum to be released automatically at the instant of transit, and an assistant then counted the beats of one pendulum until the beats of the two pendulums coincided. Since it is known how much the faster pendulum overtakes the slower in a single swing, it is easy to compute, when the number of swings required for the two to reach coincidence is known, at just what fraction of a second the one pendulum was released after the other had beat. In Kaiser's experiment, this computation gave the true time of transit, as compared with the time observed by the 'eye and ear' method. The experiments were made from 1851 to 1859 and published four years later.

During the 1860s, the decade when work on the personal equation reached its culmination, there were many measurements of the absolute equation by means of artificial transits and the chronograph or the chronoscope. The Hipp chronoscope, an instrument which measures time-intervals in thousandths of a second and which was familiar to all nineteenth-century psychologists, was used in 1862 by Hirsch (assisted by Plantamour) for this purpose. Interest had now, however, definitely centered on the variability of the personal equation. It is true that the new methods had reduced the indeterminate variability to an amount which, had the methods been in use, would have caused neither Kinnebrook's dismissal from the Greenwich observatory nor Bessel's astonishment at the inaccuracy of observation nevertheless, refinement is never at an end in scientific measurement and the astronomers still wanted to discover the causes of the variability and thus either to eliminate it or to take account of it.

A great deal of the investigation resulting from this interest in both the 1860s and the 1870s took the form of measuring the dependence of the size of the personal equation upon various astronomical conditions. It was found that the personal equation varies from the sun or moon to the stars, from the first limb of the sun or moon to the second, with the magnitude of a star, with the direction of motion of a star, with the rate of a star and with still other less fundamental changes.

The discovery of so many astronomical conditions of variation suggested that there might be even more and rendered hopeless the attempt to take them all into account by allowing for them. It was becoming quite plain that what was needed was not an astronomical, but a psychological, analysis of the variants. If the personal equation is different for the sun and the stars and even for different magnitudes of stars, presumably it depends upon the brightness of the visual sensation. If it varies for different rates of motion of the star, one wants to know how the time-element enters into the observation itself. Bessel, we have seen, recognized how importantly personal variability entered into these differences, and thus really set the problem as a psychological problem. Thus astronomy begot two descendants in the new experimental psychology—the complication experiment and the reaction experiment. To them we now turn.

THE COMPLICATION EXPERIMENT

It was Herbart in 1816 who established the term *complication* as meaning a mental complex which includes processes from more than one sense department. Under this definition the 'eye and ear' method of the astronomers was a complication, and Wundt applied Herbart's term to the psychological experiment which he based on the astronomers' discovery and discussed first in 1863.

There was from the very first a certain amount of interest in the psychophysiological explanation of the personal difference. Bessel himself discussed the problem in 1822: "If it is assumed that impressions on the eye and the ear can not be compared with each other in an instant, and that two observers use different times for carrying over the one impression upon the other, a difference originates; and there is a still greater difference if one goes over from seeing to hearing, and the other from hearing to seeing. That different kinds of observation are able to alter this difference need not seem strange, if one assumes as probable that an impression on one of two senses alone will be perceived either quite or nearly in the same instant that it happens, and that only the entrance of a second impression produces a disturbance which varies according to the differing nature of the latter."

Here lies the germ of the theory of *prior entry*, which came later to be good psychological doctrine. If the time of a given event is observed later by some persons than by others, then there is a delay in the later observations to be accounted for; but since the different observations must be fundamentally similar in their mechanisms, it thus seems probable that there is actually a delay in both cases and that the delay is simply greater in the one than in the other. The problem is one of the cause and locus of the delay. Most men who thought at all about this problem in 1822 believed that the transmission of the nervous impulse was practically instantaneous, but the most casual introspection shows that the processes of the mind consume time. Hence Bessel placed the locus of time in the mind; it occurred, he thought, in "the carrying over of one impression upon the other."

The astronomer Nicolai, however, in 1830 suggested that the delay might occur in the nerves, or at least in the reflex times for the eye and the ear. He wrote of the personal difference "In my opinion it can scarcely have its bases in any other causes than that a difference exists in different individuals for mental reflexes from external impressions of the eye and of the ear. Thus one comes to believe that in one individual the mental reflex from the eye, for example, occurs earlier than the mental reflex from the ear, or, otherwise expressed, that in a united activity directed upon the same object, the object of both senses is in such an individual seen earlier than it is heard; and that in another individual both reflexes either differ in lesser degree or occur at the same time or even in the opposite order (*i.e.*, the reflex from the eye is later than the reflex from the ear) In this manner the reported phenomenon is explained quite completely and univocally. Thence there would follow the important result already discussed that the opposing interaction between two organs of consciousness is not quite instantaneous."

Nicolai may not have meant that the delay was in the nerve, since he spoke of "mental reflexes," but Johannes Müller certainly so understood him. Müller, as we have noted elsewhere (p. 41), believed that the conduction of nervous action is practically instantaneous. He, therefore, after quoting Nicolai in 1834, pointed out that the delay might be occasioned by the time required for the sensorium to take cognizance of impressions. He wrote: "It is well known that the sensorium does not readily perceive with equal distinctness two different impressions; and that. when several impressions are made on the nerves at the same time, the sensorium takes cognizance of but one only, or perceives them in succession. When, therefore, both hearing and sight are directed simultaneously to one object, this will necessarily be first heard and then seen. The interval of time, however, between the two perceptions by the sensorium may be greater in some individuals than in others: some persons may receive and be conscious of many impressions at the same moment, for which others require a considerable interval." Thus Müller very nearly stated the principle of prior entry as a condition of attention, for, although he did not mention attention, he appealed actually to the limited range of attention in his explanation.

In 1850, Müller's belief in the instantaneousness of nerve action was overthrown by Helmholtz's measurement of the velocity of the nervous impulse, but his view nevertheless persisted as the basis of Wundt's psychology of the complication. Helmholtz's discovery, coming as it did in the very year of the perfection of the chronograph, paved the way for a single explanation of the absolute personal equation, which depends upon nothing more than reaction time. If nervous conduction is slower even than sound, then reaction times have a simple physiological meaning and no vague process of the mind needs to be invoked.

The subsequent investigations of the astronomers brought out many new facts concerning the personal equation and suggested three different types of explanation.

In the first place, there was the peripheral explanation in terms of the retina. C. Wolf, who published in 1864 an elaborate study of absolute personal equations with artificial transits, sought experimentally to demonstrate that an important factor in the personal equation may be the persistence of the visual image upon the retina. His view never gained acceptance, and it is too involved to be described here. Newcomb (1867) and Gill (1878) accepted the fact that the personal equation varies with the magnitude of the star and, although their views differ in detail, were in accord in believing that a star of large magnitude, approaching a crossline, would appear to coincide with the line earlier, since the periphery of its image would approach the line sooner than the periphery of a star of lesser magnitude.

Then there was the afferent explanation, which took account of possible differences in times of conduction of the auditory and visual impression. However, Nicolai's theory of individual differences for the times of the two senses never gained ground, in spite of Helmholtz's demonstration that the rate of nervous action is measurable and relatively slow. Investigation of such a view should have been favored by the invention of the chronograph, the chronoscope, and the method of measuring reaction times, but the issue was confused by the fact that the astronomers with the new method still remained interested in personal equations more than in reaction times. Wolf, for instance, used the 'eye and ear' method for observing artificial transits, where the true time was known, in preference to the reaction method.

Indirectly, however, Wolf contributed to the problem of explanation by showing that the personal equation depends upon the rate of movement of the star, thus contradicting Bessel's negative conclusion with respect to rate. This finding tells against Nicolai. If the error of observation is greater when the star is moving rapidly, then it is plain that the essential cause of the delay must be sought in the retina, as Wolf believed, or in the brain. The error would seem to be due to some constant observational lag which allows for a greater displacement of the more rapidly moving star. If it were simply a matter of different rates of nervous conduction for sight and hearing, then the speed of the star's transit ought to make no difference. The theory based on rate of conduction presupposes that the observational stimulus is an instant taken out of a continuous series and thus independent of change within the series.

Finally, there was the central mode of explanation. It was favored by the inadequacy of the other two modes and also by Hartmann's experiments in 1858 which showed 'expectation' to be a very important determinant of the personal equation. Bessel had discovered that the equation is greater for sudden phenomena, like occultations and emergences, than for definitely anticipated events like transits. In the observation of a transit by the 'eye and ear' method, there are two rhythmical series, the successive beats of the clock and the successive coincidences of the star with the cross-wires of the reticle. Hartmann, using artificial transits of a point of light shining through a rotating disk, allowed the disk to continue in rotation so that successive transits occurred at equal intervals. He used the 'eye and ear' method, and he discovered that the absolute personal equation became, on the average, very small indeed, and that the single times of observation were sometimes positive and sometimes negative, i.e., the observer seemed sometimes to note the coincidence before it occurred. The inference is that in these experiments the observer was responding to his expectation of the event as established by the preceding rhythmical series and might have made the observation even if the event had somehow been forestalled immediately before the moment of its occurrence. Later, the psychologists discovered this same fact for simple reaction times: with a warning signal at a fixed short period before the stimulus, some reaction times are negative and the average is very small. The reaction is to the estimated interval and not to the stimulus.

The importance of all this astronomical work for experimental psychology becomes evident when it is recalled that the most active period of experimentation upon the personal equation belongs to the 1860s and 1870s, the period of the birth of physiological psychology. It was already plain that at bottom the problem is psychological, that expectation, preparation and attention are factors in the explanation.

The explanation also raises questions of the time-relation of ideas and impressions, and it was this problem that first interested Wundt. In 1861, he constructed a simple pendulum that swung across a scale and caused a spring to give a click at a given point in its excursion. He described these experiments in 1863 in his lectures on the human and animal mind. In the first edition of his famous *Physiologische Psychologie* (1874), he devoted an entire chapter, entitled Course and Association of Ideas, to these matters and described a new pendulum which is still known in many laboratories as "Wundt's complication clock." It was even later, however, that the complication experiment and the reaction experiment came to be clearly differentiated, though the results of each were referable to attentional predisposition or attitudinal.

The point of the complication experiment did not immediately become clear. The first experiments by a psychologist were performed in St. Petersburg by von Tchisch in 1885. He used Wundt's complication clock, with a pointer sweeping over a scale and a bell sounding at a predetermined point. The observer noted where the pointer appeared to be on the scale when he heard the bell. Von Tchisch found many conditions that altered the apparent point of coincidence of sight with sound and was especially troubled by the fact of apparent negative displacement, *e.g.*, the bell appeared to sound when the pointer was at "4," when actually it was known that the bell did not sound until the pointer had got to "5." Von Tchisch seems actually to have believed in the miracle that you can hear the bell before it sounds, a contention which James ridiculed when he discussed the problem in his new *Principles of Psychology* in 1890. The matter finally got clear with the experimental work of Geiger's (1902) and the neat demonstration of H. C. Stevens' (1904).

What actually happens in the phenomenon of *prior entry* is that attentive predisposition favors earlier clear perception. If you are expecting the bell, listening for it, then the sound comes into consciousness more quickly than does the visual appearance of the pointer, and conversely. Suppose the bell actually sounds when the pointer is at 5, and that, when you are listening for the bell, sound comes in twice as rapidly as sight. The bell rings when the pointer is at 5, but everything takes time. When the pointer has got to 6 you hear the bell; but, when the pointer has got to 6 you are seeing the pointer back at 4, for it takes twice as long for the sight to come in as the sound. So you report hearing the bell at 4, although actually it rang at 5, an apparent negative displacement of one unit. On the other hand, if you put your expectation on the pointer instead of the bell and reverse the times for the two, then the pointer will have got to 7 when you hear the bell, but, when the pointer is at 7, you see it back at 6. That is a positive displacement of one unit, for now you see the bell ring at 6, although actually it rang at 5. Later Dunlap (1910) tried to explain this phenomenon of prior entry by reference to eye movements, but Stone (1926) showed that the relationship holds also for sound and touch.

This experiment shows how much the thinking about mind and the nervous system had changed from 1850 to 1900. In 1850 Helmholtz was demonstrating against incredulity that the nerve impulse takes time to travel, is even slower than sound. Half a century later psychologists were ready to accept the principle that the latent times for perception vary so greatly that attentive predisposition may cause an incoming impulse to mill around in the brain waiting for the attention to be ready to receive it.

It is also of great interest to note that this experiment, like the related experiments on reaction times, shows that perception depends upon predisposition—on attitude, as we should call it nowadays, when dynamic psychology emphasizes this fact.

THE REACTION EXPERIMENT

The measurement of the absolute personal equation by the astronomers was actually the observation of a reaction time. The determination of the times of various mental processes by the reaction method and the subtractive procedure was one of the outstanding psychological activities of the new psychology and of Wundt's laboratory in the 1880s, but Wundt did not originate this technique, although later he pushed it to its limits until Külpe, his junior colleague, showed how the procedure involved a basic error. Still the late nineteenth century is properly known as the period of *mental chronometry*.

The investigator who took over the reaction experiment from the astronomers was F. C. Donders, a Dutch physiologist, already well known for his work on vision. In the *simple reaction*, as it came to be called, a subject reacts to a given predetermined stimulus by a given predetermined movement. In 1868 it occurred to Donders that he might complicate this simple reaction by adding to it other mental processes. Then, if the reaction time was lengthened, the increase would be a measure of the time used up by whatever it was he had added.

Donders began with the measurement of the time for choice. Instead of having his subjects react to stimulus *A* always with a movement *a*, he added other stimuli each with a different prescribed reaction: for stimulus *A*, movement *a;* for *B*, *b;* for *C*, *c;* and so on. Since the times were increased by this change, he computed the time for pure *Choice* by subtracting the simple reaction time from these longer times.

Next it occurred to Donders that these Choice times must really include both Discrimination and Choice; so he undertook to measure discrimination by using at random a large number of stimuli, *A, B, C, D*, but allowing only the reaction *a* for the stimulus *A*. Thus the subjects had to discriminate the stimulus *A* from all the others before reacting. Later Wundt said that this was really a choice between reacting and not reacting, but no matter. By subtracting, Donders could now get times for Choice, Discrimination and Reaction. That is the *subtractive procedure.* In general the reaction times increase with such complications but they are not very constant, and they were ultimately given up because of this inconstancy.

In 1888 in Wundt's laboratory, Ludwig Lange discovered the difference between what were called the sensorial and muscular reactions. With attention on the stimulus (sensorial reaction) the times are longer than with attention on the reacting movement (muscular reaction). Wundt thought, not very accurately, that the difference is about 0.1 sec., and that the introspective difference is that the stimulus is apperceived in the sensorial reaction and only perceived in the muscular reaction. Thus he concluded by the subtractive procedure that the time of apperception is about 0.1 sec.

Wundt's compounding of reactions can be understood if we bring together in a table seven of his reaction times. The phrase at the left of this table is the name of the compound reaction which is measured directly. The phrase at the right is the name of the psychological process whose time is the difference between the corresponding compound reaction time and the time of the next preceding reaction in the table. The parenthesis at the right shows which item must be subtracted from which in order to get the time of the process. For simplicity, Wundt's discrimination and choice reactions are omitted.

1. Reflex	Inherited sensory-motor reaction	REFLEX (1)
2. Automatic action	Learned automatic action	VOLUNTARY IMPULSE (2-1)
3. Simple muscular reaction	One stimulus, one movement, with attention on movement	PERCEPTION (3-2)
4. Simple sensorial reaction	One stimulus, one movement, with attention on stimulus	APPERCEPTION (4-3)
5. Cognition reaction	Many stimuli, each clearly perceived, one movement	COGNITION (5-4)
6. Association reaction	Many stimuli, reaction with association	ASSOCIATION (6-5)
7. Judgment reaction	Many stimuli, associations followed by judgments	JUDGMENT (7-6)

As a matter of fact the subtractive procedure never worked well. The times were too unreliable, and the differences between them were more so. It was, however, Külpe who in 1893 argued successfully that these total processes are not compounded of elements with separate part-times, that judgment is not reflex + impulse + perception + apperception + cognition + association + judgment itself. The change in the task and in the attitude which induces action alters the whole process instead of merely adding an additional part. Lange's sensorial and muscular simple reactions differ in constitution, not by the mere addition of an apperceptive component. Thus Külpe was able to show the basic significance of Lange's experiment, viz., that the predisposition (attitude) alters the ensuing perceptual and reactive process. This early conclusion was supported later by Watt (1904) and Ach (1905), both working in Külpe's laboratory at Würzburg (pp. 403-406), and is one of the many ways in which Külpe helped psychology to move away from Wundt's elementism toward the holism of the opposite camp, which stretches from William James on down to the Gestalt psychologists.

It was in this way that the discovery of the personal equation by the astronomers and their later success in measuring absolute personal equations led into both the complication experiment and the reaction experiment of the new scientific psychology. Although the early excitement about the significance of both these experiments turned out not to be fully justified, from present perspective they can both be seen as early examples of the effect of predisposing attitude on perception and reaction, primitive events in the experimental dynamic psychology of motivation. (See pp. 715 f.)

NOTES

There are at least three good accounts of the history of the personal equation, all excellent as of their respective dates. They are: C. A. F. Peters, *Astronomische Nachrichten*, 1859, 49, 2-30, esp. 16-24; or, with slight modifications, his *Ueber die Bestimmung des Langenunterschiedes zwischen Altona und Schwerin*, 1861; R. Radau, [*Carl's*] *Repertorium für physikalische Technik*, 1866, 1, 202-218, 306-321, and, less importantly, 1867, 2, 1-9; 1868, 4, 147-156; or the corresponding French account, *Le moniteur scientifique du Dr. Quesneville*, 1865, 7, 977-985, 1025-1032; 1866, 8, 97-102, 155-161, 207-217; 1867, 9, 416-420; and finally E. C. Sanford, *Amer. J. Psychol.*, 1888-89, 2, 3-38, 271-298, 403-430. Sanford gives a bibliography of 108 titles. An account of the physiology and psychology of the personal equation, with less emphasis upon its history, is S. Exner, *Arch. ges. Physiol.*, 1873, 7, 601-660; 1875, 11, 403-432; or, in condensed form, Hermann's *Handbuch der Physiologie*, 1879, II, ii, 255-277.

Maskelyne and Bessel

N. Maskelyne's original account of Kinnebrook's persistent "error" and his subsequent dismissal is found in *Astronomical Observations at Greenwich*, 1799 (the portion for 1795), 3, 319, and esp. 339 f.

For Bessel's discovery, see F. W. Bessel, *Astronomische Beobachtungen in Königsberg*, 1823 (for the year 1822), 8, iii-viii; 1826 (1825), 11, iv; 1836 (1832), 18, iii; *Abhandlungen*, 1876, III, 300-304. That Bessel should see the significance of Maskelyne's note about Kinnebrook appears less surprising when we recall that this was a period of great interest in observational and instrumental errors and in the mathematical theory of errors. Laplace was the pioneer in the theory of errors, but the contributions of Gauss were so striking that the normal law of error is sometimes (incorrectly, it would seem, because of both de Moivre's and Laplace's priority) called the 'Gaussian law.' Gauss was director at Göttingen, and we have seen in the text the intellectual rapport that existed between the different German directors. C. F. Gauss's mathematical theory of errors was put forth in his *Theoria motus corporum cœlestium*, 1809. For his application of the fundamental principles to astronomical and geodetic observation, see his *Abhandlungen zur Methode der kleinsten Quadrate*, 1887, 54-91 (1826), 92-117 (1809), 129-138 (1816), 139-144 (1822). In other words, the determination and control of errors of observation was a much discussed matter. We even have the personal equation for Gauss and Gerling.

Astronomical Use

For T. R. Robinson's early determinations of personal equations with the sun's limbs, see his report almost thirty years later, *Places of 5,345 Stars Observed at the Armagh Observatory (First Armagh Catalogue of Stars)*, 1859, x f. For the equation of Wolfers and Nehus in 1833 at Altona, see Peters, later the director at Altona, *op. cit.*, 1859, 18. For C. L. Gerling's experiment, see *Astron. Nachrichten*, 1838, 15, 250-278, esp. 259 f. Airy had the transit observations recorded at Greenwich by observers from 1838 on, and computed by the method of least squares the average personal equation between Main and Rogerson and between Main and Henry for the years 1846-1853. Peters computed them for 1841-1845. See Peters, *op. cit.*, 19 f. For the other instances of the use of the personal equation in the early 1840s, see R. Sheepshanks and A. Quetelet, *Sur la différence des longitudes des observatoires de Greenwich et de Bruxelles*, esp. 4-13, in *Nouveaux Mémoires de l'Académie Royale des Sciences et Belles-lettres de Bruxelles*, 1843, 16, no. 1; O. W. Struve, *Détermination de la longitude entre Pulkova et Altona,* 1843; J. J. E. Goujon, *Comptes rendus,* 1849 (observations, 1835-1848), 28, 220-223.

The astronomers wished to 'exclude' the ever-variable observer from the observations. Of course, such a desire is a paradox; there can be no observation without an observer. Most of the plans, however, meant the reduction of the observation to visual space with observation made at leisure: this is what the physical scientist always attempts—to translate the observation automatically into the visual reading of a scale. Such readings are the most acute and the least variable of all sensory discriminations. Arago's method is to be found in *Comptes rendus,* 1853, 36, 276-284. Faye's photographic methods are in *Comptes rendus,* 1849, 28, 241-244; 1858, 46, 705-710; 1860, 50, 965-967. There were also other methods not mentioned in the text. One was to illumine the cross-wires rhythmically and to adjust the time and rate of the illuminations so that the star crossed the successive wires at successive flashes. The time of transit could be computed from the adjustment of the flashes. Another method was to move the telescope by clockwork with the star and at the same rate, and to adjust the setting of the telescope so that the star remained bisected by the critical cross-wire. The time of transit was then computed by observing the adjusted setting of the telescope. These methods do not actually eliminate the observer, but allow him to make a spatial reading visually at leisure, thus leaving the observer in while securing maximal accuracy.

Chronograph and Chronoscope

For a general description of the chronograph and the chronoscope and their use in the reaction experiment, see W. Wundt, *Grundzüge der physiologischen Psychologie,* 1911, III, 359-388; E. B. Titchener, *Experimental Psychology,* 1905, II, i, 142-167; ii, 326-356. The development of a satisfactory chronograph by Bache and his colleagues in the United States Coast Survey is described by B. Peirce, *Proc.* *Amer. Acad. Arts and Sci.,* 1859, 4, 197-199.

As a practical instrument, the chronoscope antedated the chronograph. Wheatstone constructed a chronoscope in 1840 and used it for measuring the velocity of cannon-balls. Mathias Hipp, a watchmaker and mechanic, conceived the idea of a chronoscope in 1842 and, after having seen Wheatstone's model, constructed one in the following year. Improvements in both Wheatstone's and Hipp's chronoscopes were made during the decade, and in 1849 Oelschläger described experiments upon the times of falling bodies measured with a new form of the Hipp chronoscope. All this happened before the perfection of the chronograph, but the chronoscope does not seem to have been taken up by astronomers until Hirsch's experiment, in 1862. On the early history of the chronoscope, see B. Edgell and W. L. Symes, *Brit. J. Psychol.,* 1906, 2, 58-62, 86-88, and references there given.

Later Development in Astronomy

The first suggestion for the determination of absolute personal equations is said to have been made by Prazmowski in *Cosmos,* 1854, 4, 545 (cf. the relevant paragraph by Le Verrier in *Comptes rendus,* 1854, 38, 748 f.). O. M. Mitchel's experiment is reported briefly in *Roy. Astron. Soc., Monthly Notices,* 1858, 18, 261-264, and *J. Franklin Inst.,* 1858, 66, 349-352. J. Hartmann's study is in [*Grunert's*] *Arch. Math. Physik,* 1858, 31, 1-26, and (slightly abbreviated) *Astron. Nachrichten,* 1865, 65, 129-144.

For F. Kaiser's method of the double vernier pendulum, see *Verslagen en mededeelingen der koninklyke Akademie van wetenschappen, Amsterdam, afdeeling natuurkunde,* 1863, 15, 173-220; 1868, 2de Reeks, Deel 2, 216-236. The first article is in Dutch, but the second is in German. Kaiser notes that he is utilizing the principle of the nonius or vernier, and Sanford's vernier chronoscope, employing the observation of visual instead of auditory coincidence of the two pendulums, was patterned after it; cf. E. C. Sanford, *Amer. J. Psychol.*, 1890, 3, 174-181; 1898, 9, 191-197.

The reference to A. Hirsch's first use of the Hipp chronoscope for the observation of artificial transits is *Bull. Soc. Sci. nat. Neuchâtel*, 1863, 6, 365-372.

For a complete discussion of the dependence of the personal equation upon numerous astronomical variables, see Sanford, *Amer. J. Psychol.*, 1889, 2, 271-298.

Complication Experiment

Bessel's discussion of the carrying-over of one impression upon the other occurs in his first publication on the personal equation, *op. cit.*, 1822, p. vii. Nicolai's theory and account of the personal equation is reported by Treviranus in *Isis von Oken*, 1830, 23, 678-682. Joh. Müller's discussion of the problem occurs in his *Handbuch der Physiologie des Menschen*, bk. iii, sect. iii, introd. (any edition or the Eng. trans.).

The later experiments mentioned are: J. Hartmann, *op. cit.* and C. Wolf, *Annales de l'Observatoire Impérial de Paris, Mémoires*, 1866, 8, 153-208. For the later discussion of stellar magnitude and the personal equation, see S. Newcomb, *Astron. and Meteorol. Observations, U. S. Naval Observatory*, 1867, append. 3, 27, and D. Gill, *Roy. Astron. Soc., Monthly Notices*, 1878, 39, 98.

W. Wundt's early discussion of the matter and his mention of his complication pendulum of 1861 is to be found in his *Vorlesungen über die Menschen- und Thierseele*, 1863, I, lect. 23, which is amplified in the second edition, 1892, lect. 28 (also Eng. trans.). In this connection it is interesting to note that Wundt in 1861 made an address at Speyer in which he argued for individual differences in the order in which sight and hearing enter into these observations: cf. E. B. Titchener, *Amer. J. Psychol.*, 1923, 34, 311. For the more formal incorporation of these data into systematic physiological psychology, see

Wundt, *Grundzüge der physiologischen Psychologie*, 1874, chap. 19, esp, pp. 727-780; cf. the corresponding section in later editions, *e.g.*, 1911, III, 44-79, 357-451. W. James has an excellent and clear summary and criticism of the Wundtian view: *Principles of Psychology*, 1890, I, 409-416, 427-432. See also the discussion by E. B. Titchener, *Lectures on the Elementary Psychology of Feeling and Attention*, 1908, 242-259, 371-375.

The chief experimental references on the complication experiment and prior entry, the ones cited in the text (with Angell and Pierce's added), are: W. von Tchisch, Ueber die Zeitverhältnisse der Apperception einfacher und zusammengesetzter Vorstellungen, untersucht mit Hülfe der Complicationsmethode, *Philos. Stud.*, 1885, 2, 603-634; J. R. Angell and A. H. Pierce, Experimental research upon the phenomena of attention, *Amer. J. Psychol.*, 1892, 4, 528-541; M. Geiger, Neue Complicationsversuche, *Philos. Stud.*, 1902, 18, 347-436; H. C. Stevens, A simple complication pendulum for qualitative work, *Amer. J. Psychol.*, 1904, 15, 581; K. Dunlap, The complication experiment and related phenomena, *Psychol. Rev.*, 1910, 17, 157-191; S. A. Stone, Prior entry in the auditory-tactual complication, *Amer. J. Psychol.*, 1926, 37, 284-291.

Reaction Experiment

On the invention of compound reactions and the subtractive procedure, see F. C. Donders, Die Schnelligkeit psychischer Processe, *Arch. Anat. Physiol.*, 1862, 657-681, which includes Donders' analysis of the reaction process into twelve hypothetical successive physiological events.

At that time Wundt, as we have seen, was more interested in the complication experiment. The implications about the significance of compounding in the first edition of his *Physiologische Psychologie* (1874, *loc. cit. supra*) are not too clear, but they are quite explicit in the second edition, 1880, II, 219-260, esp. 247-260. By 1911, under the influence of Külpe and the times, he had somewhat modified his position, but see, nevertheless, his 6 ed., 1911, III, 388-451, esp. 424-451.

The classical experiment, which might almost be said to begin the experimental psychology of motivation, is Ludwig Lange's on the two types of reaction: L. Lange, Neue Experimente über den Vorgang der einfachen Reaction auf Sinneseindrücke, *Philos. Stud.*, 1888, 4, 479-510. That, however, occurred late in the period of the study of compound reactions. For the chief product of Wundt's laboratory in this field and period, see the papers by E. Tischer, M. Trautscholdt, M. Friedrich, J. McK. Cattell, G. Martius and E. B. Titchener in Wundt's *Philos. Stud.*, 1883-1892, vols. 1-8. For Külpe's first development of Lange's lead, see O. Külpe, *Grundriss der Psychologie*, 1893, 421-437; Eng. trans., 1895, 408-422. but the *coup de grâce* for compounding of reactions came later in Külpe's Würzburg school.

In general, on the compound reactions, see J. Jastrow, *Time-Relations of Mental Phenomena*, 1890: and, less directly, E. B. Titchener, *Experimental Psychology*, 1905, II, i, 185-195; ii, 356-392.

ORIGIN OF MODERN PSYCHOLOGY
WITHIN PHILOSOPHY

CHAPTER 9

Beginnings of Modern Psychology: Descartes, Leibnitz and Locke

By this time it is clear to the reader that problems of scientific psychology grew up within science and forced themselves in the natural course of development upon scientific attention. Still *psychology*, as a subject-matter with that name, before the middle of the nineteenth century was a formal division not of science, but of philosophy. In the very beginning, with the Greeks, there was, of course, no such clear distinction. Aristotle, for example, did not need to distinguish between the rationalistic and empirical methods. It was later, as we have seen, that the two diverged and still later (*ca.* Locke, 1690) that philosophy became predominantly psychological, thus making psychology philosophical and not scientific. All these differences, however, are ultimately artificial and appear only at the veneer of knowledge. They are essentially matters of human convenience in the formalization of knowledge at a particular time. Fundamentally knowledge is one.

That such an essential unity may force a formal synthesis is exactly what the history of psychology in the nineteenth century demonstrates. Here was empirical science, on the one hand, rapidly developing, proving fertile in its research, perpetually facing new and difficult problems. The advance of the physiology of the nervous system in particular kept raising, and sometimes solved, psychological problems: the problems of sensation and the sensory nerves and organs, of the brain and its functions, of the 'mental organs.' Other formal divisions of science contributed to psychology incidentally: physics, the perceptual laws of color and of sound; medicine, the phenomena of hypnosis; astronomy, the facts and partial explanation of the 'personal equation.' The men who made these discoveries did not call themselves psychologists. On the other hand, here at this time there was also a psychology, an essentially rationalistic psychology, which was the property of the philosophers. Because of the continuity of the name, it seems to us to have been older than the 'mental knowledge' of the scientists. That the new 'scientific psychology' was nothing other than a fusion of these two psychologies could be easily discerned in the early nineteenth century—the philosophers' psychology and the sensory psychology of the physiologists, plus brain physiology, reflexology, phrenology, hypnosis and the personal equation, all of which came from other regions of science.

If we place the beginning of 'scientific psychology' at 1860, we are merely choosing a convenient year, the date of Fechner's *Elemente der Psychophysik*. There are no such abrupt occurrences in the history of scientific thought. Lotze tried to write a 'medical psychology' in 1852, but nevertheless remained largely the metaphysician throughout. Johannes Müller had essayed a chapter "On the Mind" in 1840, yet scarcely excelled the layman-philosopher in result. Nevertheless, the fusion of the two psychologies had been impending ever since Hartley (1749) or perhaps Descartes (1650). For all this, however, in the middle of the nineteenth century with Fechner and especially with Wundt there was a formal, conscious recognition of the essential identity of the two psychologies, and, since the philosophic member had been called "psychology" and the scientific member "physiology," the birth of "physiological psychology" was a natural consequence and of the utmost importance in the history of psychology.

In this history of experimental psychology, we must, therefore, go back into philosophical psychology in order to see what it was that, married to physiology, gave birth to physiological, experimental psychology. Yet we need not stress this pre-scientific psychology so much as we have stressed the 'pre-psychological science,' partly because the early philosophical psychology is already better known and partly because our dominant interest in experimental psychology throws the greater weight upon the scientific antecedents. We do not need, however, to go back to Descartes.

We may even dare almost to ignore Aristotle (384-322 B.C.), the greatest mind in the history of thought, as he has been said to be, the encyclopedic genius whose dicta and doctrines dominated the thinking of all wise men in western culture for many centuries before the emergence of modern science about 1600. The Church accepted Aristotle. His word became the final appeal in those ages when men were primarily concerned with saving their immortal souls and were perpetually seeking authority through revelation in order that they might discover the truth. Later, with the Renaissance, the problems of living became more important than the problems of eternity and scientific method replaced authority as the avenue to truth. Yet Aristotle's wisdom was not obliterated even then. Again and again it still prevails today in some value-judgment or else as the historical antecedent of some current mode of thought.

It was Aristotle who declared that the soul is unitary, thus influencing Descartes, making it difficult for Helmholtz to prove that the nervous impulse takes time for its transmission, supporting the holistic argument in the contest between elements and wholes which continued from William James to Gestalt psychology. It was Aristotle who declared that the soul is free, thus taking sides against a wholly deterministic psychology and in general supporting the philosophers against the scientists who wished to tie the soul to the uniformities of nature. It was Aristotle who reinforced the basic dichotomy between form and matter which characterizes all materialistic thinking. Aristotle said that the mind is a *tabula rasa*, a blank tablet as yet unwritten on by experience, thus supporting the school of empiricism, which began with Hobbes and Locke. Aristotle laid down the basic principles of memory—similarity, contrast and contiguity—which have not yet ceased to dominate theoretical thinking about learning. Aristotle said that there are five senses, one of them (touch) being more complex than the others, and that basic distinction is still with us, no matter how much the five may have to be subdivided. There have in the history of psychology been many nominations of a sixth sense, but none of a seventh, for no one ever accepted a sixth as good gospel. And then Aristotle said that the seat of the soul is in the heart, but in that he said something that seems nonsense to the modern. Galen's view that the brain is the organ of mind long prevailed against Aristotle, and nowadays of course we have enough evidence to know what we mean when we assert the mind is in the brain or that it is not.

The shift within philosophy from Aristotelian dogma came along in the seventeenth century with the emergence of science, in the century of Kepler, Galileo and Newton. It began with Descartes' revolt against "the ancients" and his revision of the conception of the human mind as partly free and rational and partly mechanically automatic. Descartes is the father of dualistic thinking in psychology and also of the physiological psychology of the reflex. It continued with English empiricism, which began with Hobbes and was put most certainly on its way by John Locke, who originated the important doctrine of association of ideas which was later to become the chief basis for the new psychology of Wundt and the other experimental psychologists of the latter nineteenth century. And then there was Leibnitz, an opponent of Locke's, who maintained the conception of mind as active process and who thus stands as an ancestor to all those who later opposed Wundt's elements, like Brentano. Descartes gave modern psychology the dualism of mind and body, but he thought of the two as separate and interacting. Leibnitz furnished modern psychology with parallelism as a suitable form of dualism, the form that seemed satisfactory after the acceptance of the theory of the conservation of energy in the 1840s. This chapter is principally concerned with the contributions of these three men—Descartes, Leibnitz and Locke.

RENÉ DESCARTES

René Descartes (1596-1650) marks the actual beginning of modern psychology when the historical divisions are drawn broadly as ancient, medieval and modern. Descartes was primarily a philosopher, but also a scientist, a physiologist and the father of physiological psychology and reflexology. Besides, he was no mean mathematician, for he invented analytic geometry, thus rendering geometry an invaluable tool for scientific work.

The life of Descartes was that of a gentleman-intellectual. He was possessed of a modest competence and saved from dilettantism by his genius, his unquenchable curiosity and thirst for knowledge, his craving for evidence and proof, combined with his utter indifference to the dicta of dogmatic authority. He liked to think, and from schooldays on, beginning with the sympathetic understanding of a schoolmaster, he spent his mornings in bed thinking. His famous "Cogito, ergo sum" must have had a personal meaning to him. To think was to be. Nevertheless this matutinal cogitative existence was interrupted during his youth again and again, at times by the demands of his boisterous pleasure-loving friends, and at times by his enlistment in one or another of the armies of mercenaries which kings and princes used in those days in their quests for more power and wealth.

There were several crucial times in Descartes' life, and at each of them he rejected the more gentlemanly life and turned toward philosophy. The first occasion was when the master let him lie abed at school to think. The next came while he was at war, in winter quarters on the banks of the Danube, on November 10, 1619. On that night he had a dream that put into his mind the principle of the analytic geometry, the way for making geometry algebraic. He carried that precious insight around in his head for sixteen years and through several battles before he published it and made it safe for posterity. The dream, nevertheless, marked Descartes' certain conversion toward philosophy. His next crisis was in 1629, after his philosophy was becoming formed and had impressed the Cardinal de Bérulle, who persuaded him that he ought to publish. That was a further acceptance of responsibility and marks the beginning of Descartes' escape from social demands. He retired to Holland and lived during the next twenty years in thirteen different towns and twenty-four different houses, always keeping his address unknown to the increasing number of persons who recognized his genius, but remaining in scientific correspondence with other philosophers through Father Mersenne, one of the few whom he kept informed of his whereabouts.

In 1634 Descartes prepared *Le monde* for publication, meaning it to be a New Year's present to Father Mersenne. It was essentially a philosopher's wise improvement on Genesis. It took, for instance, the Copernican theory for granted. Then came the news of what the Inquisition had done to Galileo, and Descartes desisted, knowing that his work was more heretical than Galileo's. He was a devout Catholic, and this 'conversion' was not cowardice but an intellectual crisis. He resolved to find the right way to justify both the Pope and Copernicus, an ambition never wholly fulfilled.

In 1637 Descartes published the *Discours de la méthode*, which included the analytic geometry. Two of his philosophical works appeared in 1641 and 1644, but the other important works came out posthumously, after Descartes' death in Sweden in 1650. The responsibility for that tragedy lies definitely at the feet of the rugged and selfish Queen Christina, who asked Descartes to come to Stockholm to teach her philosophy. Descartes wished not to surrender his seclusion and freedom but he had a great respect for royal prerogative, and, when Christina presently honored him by sending a warship to fetch him, he yielded and went to teach her, a not very apt pupil, philosophy, three times a week, at five o'clock in the morning in her cold library during an unusually rigorous Swedish winter. Illustrating his own belief that natural law applies to man, he died, before the winter was over, of pneumonia.

Descartes' *Passions de l'âme*, written for Christina in 1649, was published in 1650. This work contains his philosophical psychology, much of what he has to say about the nature of the soul and some of his physiological psychology. His *Traité de l'homme* came out in 1662. It has in it more of the physiological psychology and thus the discussion of automatisms. *Le monde*, withheld from publication thirty years earlier, appeared at last in 1664. These books had in them many other of Descartes' incidental scientific contributions

For instance, there is Descartes' demonstration that Kepler was right in believing that the crystalline body in the eye is a lens which forms an image on the retina. Descartes took the eye of a bull, scraped off the sclerotic coat at the back of it, fitted it into a hole bored in his shutter and showed that an inverted image of the external scene was formed on the back of the eyeball.

Descartes is responsible for directing French psychological thought toward materialism, as appears later in the work of La Mettrie and Cabanis (pp. 211-216). Nevertheless, as in the case of Galileo, the Pope and *Le monde,* he never compromised his religious faith. He believed in a free insubstantial soul and a mechanically operated body, and he resolved the possible incompatibility of these two entities by his *dualism.* Matter and the body are *extended substance,* the soul is *unextended substance.* Descartes held that these two kinds of substance interact with each other in the human organism, body affecting mind and mind body. Thus he becomes also the father of the mind-body theory of *interactionism.*

To the working of the body Descartes was anxious to apply the principles of physics. That thought must have been in the air, for in some of the public gardens there were mechanical figures of persons who would appear or disappear when some mechanism was activated. Descartes, with these analogies in mind, held that the body is a *machine.* That statement must be true of the human body when it is considered without its soul. Animals, having no souls, are automata. This mechanical view is, as a matter of logic, not open to argument, for it follows necessarily from the definition of the body as all that pertains to the inanimate. Thus it freed Descartes to proceed with his physics of physiology. In a sense it was actually supported by theology, which taught that animals have no souls. If they have no souls they are by definition automata, and even vivisection on them becomes permissible. (Much confusion has resulted from the fact that both *soul* and *mind* are *l'âme* in French and *Seele* in German. It is much easier in English to keep psychology separate from theology.)

Of the body, that extended substance to which the laws of the inanimate are applicable, Descartes had considerable knowledge. Harvey had just discovered the circulation of the blood in 1628. Descartes knew the gross facts of circulation and of digestion correctly. He knew that muscles operate in opposing pairs. He knew that the nerves are necessary for sensation and for movement, but he thought of the nerves, according to the belief of the times, as hollow tubes conducting the animal spirits indifferently in either direction. Thus he was led to a 'pathway' theory of the peripheral nervous system that is not unlike the modern theory of the reflex arc. It is also an anticipation of the projection theory. Descartes could write:

> It is to be observed that the machine of our bodies is so constructed that all the changes which occur in the motion of the spirits may cause them to open certain pores of the brain rather than others, and reciprocally, that when any one of these pores is opened in the least degree more or less than is usual by the action of the nerves which serve the senses, this changes somewhat the motion of the spirits, and causes them to be conducted into the muscles which serve to move the body in the way in which it is commonly moved on occasion of such action; so that all the movements which we make without our will contributing thereto ... depend only on the conformation of our limbs and the course which the spirits, excited by the heat of the heart, naturally follow in the brain, in the nerves, and in the muscles, in the same way that the movement of a watch is produced by the force solely of its mainspring and the form of its wheels.

This, then, is the body. What is the nature of the soul?

The unextended soul, which is "all that is in us and which we can not conceive in any manner possible to pertain to a body," perceives and wills. It thus interacts with the body. Perceptions and passions are primarily dependent upon the body, but the soul knows them. Most actions originate with the will, but not all, for there are some that the will cannot bring about directly. Descartes mentioned the pupillary reflex and speech. In the latter, the will acts indirectly, for we can will to say the words, and thus the muscles move correctly; but we cannot directly will to move these muscles thus and thus, so that the words are formed. In general, there is less to say about the soul than about the body. In so far as the soul is free, there is nothing to say, for freedom is without laws and cannot be generalized under them. The important thing then is to inquire the manner in which the soul interacts with the body, but first we must note Descartes' view of introspection.

The persistent problem of introspection is the question as to whether in a perception, for example, the perception itself is also a knowledge of itself, or whether we have to 'perceive' the perception to know that we have it, thus presumably establishing an indefinite regress. Such a regress has been objected to on several grounds, and yet the opposite view, viz., that to perceive is to know that one perceives, raises the question as to why a true knowledge of one's own mind is difficult to come at. If the mind is there, one ought also to have a true and irrefutable knowledge of it. Descartes took the position that the knowledge of mind is immediate but that we have nevertheless to learn about it because the ancients, for whom Descartes had little patience, have misled us.

Everyone, feeling the passions in himself, stands in no need whatever of borrowing any observation elsewhere to discover their nature, nevertheless, what the ancients have taught on this subject is of such slight intent, and for the most part so untrustworthy, that I can not have any hope of reaching the truth, except by abandoning the paths which they have followed.

Others, we shall see (Mach, pp. 394 f.), have made the same decision, though they have explained the dilemma differently.

The interaction between the soul and the body, Descartes thought, occurs at the pineal gland, the "conarium," which is the only part of the brain which is single, that is to say, the only part that is not duplicated in the two halves. Descartes was convinced that the soul, being unitary (Aristotle), could not affect the body at two separate points, and, since the brain seems to be the organ to which sensation proceeds and where motion originates, he selected the only unduplicated part of the brain as the point of interaction.

Descartes' mechanistic bias is evident in his whole discussion of the manner in which the mutual action between soul and body takes place. His thought is entirely spatial and has to do with the direction and loci of the animal spirits. The conarium, by inclining to this side or that, directs the spirits here or there in this or that particular recollection or imagination or movement. Similarly in perception the spirits come from different directions. Descartes, for instance, felt it necessary for the visual nerves to be redistributed in order to compensate for the inverted retinal image. The top of the world, it would seem, is the top of the brain for the soul that can see it only through the pineal body!

The reader must not, however, get the impression that Descartes thought of the soul as shut up within the conarium. This belief is a very common misapprehension. The 'gland' is simply the point of interaction, and not the seat of the soul in any more complete sense. The body is extended; the soul is not extended; but the extended, when acted upon by the non-extended, requires some definite point of action, which is the conarium. However, "the soul is united to all parts of the body conjointly." The entire body is its seat, so long as the body remains intact. It is true that when a member is cut off, the soul is not divided, because, since it is unitary, only as much of the body as remains a unit is its seat. When the unity of a body is lost in death, the body is no longer a seat of the soul. One might think, of course, that the soul, being united to the entire body, might act directly on any part or be acted upon by any part. Such a view was, however, untenable for Descartes, because the body would then become an unaccountable mechanism instead of a perfect machine.

It is also important to note that Descartes believed in the existence of *innate ideas*, ideas which are not derivable from experience but which come to the mind with such certainty and inevitability that their acceptance is assured. Of such ideas those of God and of self are the most obvious. The geometrical axioms also belong in this class, as do the conceptions of space, time and motion. This view was destined to pass on down through psychology via the Scottish philosophers, Kant and finally the nativists (Hering, Stumpf and the Gestalt psychologists). It was sharpened by the opposition of the English empiricists (Locke, Berkeley and Hume), the English associationists (the Mills and Bain) and finally the modern empiricists (Lotze, Helmholtz, Wundt and his followers).

With this general summary we must leave Descartes. It is enough if the reader realizes Descartes' more fundamental systematic conceptions which still influence or even dominate psychology: the mechanistic approach, the dualism of mind and body, their interaction, the brain as the important locus for the mind, the localization of the mind nevertheless in the entire body, and yet the specific localizations within the brain, the innate ideas which led on into the doctrine of nativism.

GOTTFRIED WILHELM LEIBNITZ

German psychology is sometimes said to have begun with Gottfried Wilhelm Leibnitz (1646-1716), and indeed, if we are to speak of national tendencies in psychology at all, it could hardly have begun sooner, for the period of Leibnitz's life is the period of the emergence of German culture. For this reason, the principal contemporary intellectual life lay west of the Rhine: Malebranche and the Cartesian tradition in Paris, Spinoza (d. 1677) in Holland, Newton and Locke in England. Leibnitz was one of the great mathematicians of his day, although he was surpassed by Newton. Both he and Newton independently discovered the calculus as a general method, invented a system of notation for it and used it in the solution of problems. (It is customary now to give Newton the credit for the method and Leibnitz for the system of notation, and Isaac Barrow anticipated them both.) The publication of Locke's *Essay* in 1690 stimulated Leibnitz to a reply, the *Nouveaux essais*, which he never printed because Locke's death occurred at the time of its intended publication (1704). The *Essais* were first published half a century after Leibnitz's death. Throughout his life Leibnitz was engaged in political writing. He traveled on the Continent, sometimes for political purposes, and exerted a great intellectual influence, although the final recognition of his greatness was posthumous. The growth of his philosophy formed a persistent background to his other numerous activities, and it is with a part of his philosophy that we are here concerned.

Leibnitz is less important for experimental psychology than Descartes or Locke; than Descartes, because Descartes really stands at the beginning of modern psychology and many of its concepts, and even anticipates physiological psychology; than Locke, because Locke initiated English empiricism and thus associationism, from which, on the philosophical side, physiological psychology directly sprang. Nevertheless, Leibnitz had a psychological view of the world and thus heads a tradition of activity-psychology, which has persisted mostly in Germany and Austria, but also in England. Brentano's school of act psychology, which can also count Aristotle among its direct ancestors, borrowed less from physiology and became less involved in experiment than has the other half of modern psychology. It therefore interests us less than does the tradition which Wundt represents. Nevertheless, the whole psychological family is so intimately connected that it is impossible to ignore one branch and yet understand the other in anything like its entirety.

Let us see if we can in a few words comprehend Leibnitz's view of nature, his monadology, and its relation to modern psychology.

Activity lies at the very base of the system:

> Substance is being, is capable of action. It is simple or compound. Simple substance is that which has no parts. Compound substance is a collection of simple substances or monads. *Monas* is a Greek word which signifies unity, or that which is one.

The *monad* is the element of all being and partakes of its nature, and being is activity. If we ask further concerning the nature of the monad or activity, we can only be told that it is most like *perception*. *Activity* and *consciousness* are thus two words for the same thing and lie at the bottom of nature.

The monad is *indestructible, uncreatable* and *immutable*, but it is not static. It undergoes a continuous process of *development* in accordance with its own laws but loses in developmental change neither its identity nor its unity. We see in the calculus a similar situation. A function is a unity with its own internal laws that characterize it. To understand it we may break it up into atomic differentials, but this is an artificial analysis. In reality there are no differentials, and the true function is revealed only as the infinitesimal differentials reach their limit, zero, and disappear.

Immutable, uncreatable, indestructible monads can have no effect upon one another, for what could they do but change, create or destroy each other? Thus it appears that the world is an infinite *pluralism* of independent monads. Thus, too, there are no causes. A cause would either imply mutual effects between monads (and there are none) or else such an analysis of the monad as to render its internal development a causal chain (but the monad is unitary and has no parts). Cause as anything more than coincidence is sheer illusion. A monad is like a watch, perfectly constructed, wound up and set going forever. It will continue without an external agent according to the laws of its own nature. Two such watches will be found always to agree, and yet neither is the cause of the other. Thus harmony in nature comes about without effective causation because harmony preëxists in the laws of the monads.

It is the same way with *compound substance*. In compounding, there is no creative synthesis nor any synthesis at all. The apparent synthesis is simply the synchronous arrival of many monads at a given point in their development.

This development is in a way a process of *clarification*. If the very essence of being is something like perception, its development would naturally be a clarification. Substance thus shows *degrees of consciousness*. The supposedly unconscious is really only relatively unconscious and has the possibility of becoming conscious (*cf.* the potentiality of matter and the actuality of mind in Aristotle, whence comes this doctrine). The lower degrees are for Leibnitz *petites perceptions;* the conscious actualization of these is *apperception*. The sound of the breakers on the beach is apperception; it is summed, however, of the *petites perceptions* of all the falling drops of water, no one of which is conscious alone.

In this miniature sketch of Leibnitz's monadology we see the beginnings of many big things.

In the first place, there is the *psychological view* of the universe. It is not idealism, for consciousness does not explain or create matter. Consciousness is matter, and matter consciousness.

In the second place, there is the insistence on *activity* as essential to substance. This is the view of all modern act psychologies: Brentano's, James', Stumpf's, Külpe's (in the later days) and McDougall's. It is argued that the most obvious thing about mind is its activity, that mental activity is so immediately patent to all psychological observation that not only can it not be denied, but it must also necessarily be the starting point for all psychologizing. Leibnitz, moreover, left the scientific psychologist not even the appeal to a static physics; all substance for him is active.

Hardly separate from the notion of activity is the principle of *unity*. A persistently, actively evolving mind is continuous and therefore unitary. Unity as a mental attribute we have met in Descartes. It also, like activity, has seemed obvious as applying to the mind, and the appeal to the unity of mind has persisted. The most recent instance of this view has been in *Gestalt* psychology, where analysis is deplored and unitariness of mind repeatedly exhibited.

Leibnitz also gave us a doctrine of degrees of consciousness and thus also of the *unconscious*. The *petite perception* of the monad is unconscious. The sound of the single falling drop of water may be regarded as an unconscious perception. This continuum passes through perception to apperception. There are many echoes of this view. The negative sensations of Fechner were *petites perceptions*. There is the apperception of Herbart and Wundt. There is the whole doctrine of the unconscious, recently become so important and often related to apperception and the degrees of consciousness.

Finally it must be observed that Leibnitz helped establish *psychophysical parallelism*, the theory which in the relating of mind and body has been the usual alternative to the interactionism of Descartes. (Earlier Spinoza had helped to formulate this view.) The relation between Leibnitz's monads is one of parallelism; the two self-contained perpetual watches agree, not because of any causal interrelation, but because their laws are parallel. The case of the soul and the body is simply a special case. The two are not causally related; they follow parallel courses, and the resultant correlations appear as if one caused the other.

In all this we are to remember that Leibnitz's philosophy was a great and influential philosophy. It is not enough to note mere anticipations of later thought. We have here the actual beginnings of later theories in the sense that the development of thought was continuous and the lines of influence are clear.

JOHN LOCKE

We must now turn our attention from the Continent to England, where empiricism and associationism were beginning. It is this tradition more than any other which has influenced modern psychology. It had a great effect upon German act psychology, upon systematic British psychology, and upon James in America, but it is most peculiarly the philosophical parent of experimental psychology. It is hard to see how physiology alone could have given rise to anything more than a sense-physiology or a reflexology. The English tradition was the necessary complement for experimental psychology. By furnishing at first the problems of psychology, it defined psychology as something broader than that which the physiological methods were ready to attack alone. At times it has held back experimentation by providing a speculative content for the chapters of psychology that could not yet be founded upon experimental data, but in the same way it stimulated effort to extend laboratory technique to the 'higher mental processes.' It is the English tradition that made perception the primary problem in psychology and that indicated the fundamental line of attack. Thus Wundt (1862) began his psychology with an experimental study of perception, and Helmholtz (1866) founded his psychology of perception upon empiricism. It was the English tradition that made association the key to the 'higher' processes. Thus Ebbinghaus (1885) could see how to extend the scope of experimental psychology to association and memory. It was the English tradition, now embodied in physiological psychology, that insisted upon a psychological problem of the 'still higher' mental processes. Thus Külpe became dissatisfied with the 'sensationism' of Wundt and developed the systematic experimental introspection of the Würzburg school (1901-1909; pp. 401-410). Very important for psychology in general and for experimental psychology in particular is this English tradition.

Chronologically Thomas Hobbes (1588-1679), a contemporary of Descartes, a political philosopher, and the author of *Leviathan*, begins the English school. Hobbes sought, like Locke after him, to refer the content of the mind to sense-experience and thus to do away with the innate ideas, which Descartes espoused. Hobbes also outlined the doctrine of association as dependent upon the "coherence" of past ideas. This theory, however, was vague and incomplete in Hobbes. His primary importance is for political philosophy, and it is only because of his priority that it is necessary to mention him here. Chronologically be begins the new school, but Locke heads it spiritually. Locke did not, it seems, obtain his inspiration from Hobbes. We may rest content, then, with the mere mention of Hobbes and pass on to Locke.

On the surface, the life of John Locke (1632-1704), not unlike the life of Leibnitz, seems to be a political life, for politics in those days offered a practical medium for philosophical thought. Locke, however, did not attain fame as a philosopher until the publication of his *Essay* in 1690, when he was fifty-seven years old. Only in the fourteen years remaining to him did he live the life of a great philosopher, but it is not accurate to say that he matured late. His fundamental beliefs in liberty and tolerance, which guided his thought until his death, were formed early, as were also his habits of philosophical and scientific thought and discussion. The *Essay* was begun in 1671. After experimenting with life as a tutor at Oxford and as a physician, he had in 1666 formed a friendship with the great man who was shortly to become the Earl of Shaftesbury. They were drawn together by common ideas upon the matter of political freedom and tolerance, and Shaftesbury took Locke as his private secretary. Locke lived with Shaftesbury until the latter's political eclipse in 1675. It was during this period that he was accustomed to have meetings with his intimates in which questions of science and theology were debated. On one such occasion, the group "found itself quickly at a stand by the difficulties that arose" in their discussion of morality and religion, and it occurred to Locke that what was needed first was a criticism of human understanding itself. He thought then that he could write the criticism itself on one sheet of paper, but the undertaking grew in the intervals that Locke returned to it until it resulted twenty years later in the famous *Essay*.

This sort of work had to be sporadic. With Shaftesbury's fall in 1675, Locke went for a few years to France, where he was able to engage in philosophy and to meet many of the thinkers of the day. He returned to London in 1679 upon Shaftesbury's restoration, but three years later his patron was arrested, tried and acquitted, and went to Holland where he died within a few months. Locke, under suspicion, followed him to Holland for another period of thought and writing. Here the *Essay* was completed. Then Locke returned to England with William and Mary in 1690, and the *Essay Concerning Human Understanding* was published a few months later.

It had been a turbulent setting for the contemplative life, but now he became rapidly famous as a philosopher, refused important political commissions and for the most part lived quietly, in ill health, with friends near London until his death in 1704. By 1700 his *Essay* had gone into its fourth edition, and to this edition Locke added a chapter on the "Association of Ideas." French and Latin translations followed shortly. English empiricism was fairly begun.

For Locke ideas are the units of mind. An idea is "the object of thinking." Ideas are such things as are "expressed by the words, whiteness, hardness, sweetness, thinking, motion, man, elephant, army, drunkenness, and others." In short, they are logical concepts. Some modern psychologists would call them 'meanings.' They are, as it were, items of knowledge. If we can divide what we know consciously at any given time into components, we find that we have ideas. It is this meaning of *idea* that we have in the phrase *association of ideas*. The Lockian conception approximates present-day common sense: the man in the street believes that his 'head is full of ideas,' and that these ideas are 'what one thinks about,' e.g., whiteness or elephants.

This view, we are about to see, persisted through the English school, at least as far as James Mill (1829), and its correctness is a matter of controversy even today. Introspective psychology (Titchener; pp. 417-419) failed to find such ideas immediately obvious in consciousness, and sought to explain the common belief of men that they have just such ideas by calling them 'meanings,' which do not exist in the mind, but are immediately implied by mind. Nevertheless, the Lockian notion has persisted. The strict introspectionists were accused of blindness to all conscious contents but sensations and images. Ward in 1918 began his psychology by defining the presentation as the equivalent of Locke's idea. The Würzburg school admitted such ideas as "imageless thoughts." Some act psychologists seem to have had an equivalent in their 'acts' or 'functions.' The experimental phenomenologists of the modern *Gestalt* school deal with these ideas as phenomena. Even Titchener would seem to have thought that the psychologist can, if he wishes, do something with 'meanings.' It is plain, then, that the Lockian idea had strength, although in arriving at maturity it has continuously changed its appearance.

It is also important to note that Locke's idea is an *element*. The mind is capable of *analysis* into ideas. The full significance of this fact will become more apparent as we deal with the compounding and association of ideas. We may note, however, that the elementary status of the idea has led to an entirely different controversy from the one mentioned in the preceding paragraph. Wertheimer could in 1921 object to analysis and elements, while welcoming the Lockian material into consciousness; whereas Titchener could cultivate analysis into elements while rejecting the Lockian stuff.

Locke's interest in philosophy had come about by his reading of Descartes while he was a student at Oxford. He was destined, however, to become an opponent of Cartesian psychology. It was

Descartes' doctrine of innate ideas to which Locke objected and to which his empiricism was opposed. Ideas, Locke thought, are not inborn; they come from *experience*.

> Let us suppose the mind to be, as we say, white paper, void of all characters, without any ideas; How comes it to be furnished? Whence comes it by that vast store, which the busy and boundless fancy of man has painted on it with an almost endless variety? Whence has it all the materials of reason and knowledge? To this I I answer, in one word, From *experience*. In that all our knowledge is founded, and from that it ultimately derives itself.

Neither the conception nor the figure is new. Aristotle, as we have seen, had the notion of the mind as a *tabula rasa*, but it was only incidental to him. Locke makes the principle the central dominating point of his whole psychology. English *empiricism* is the result.

It was out of this view that the dilemma of idealism and realism arose. Locke himself wrote:

> Since the mind, in all its thoughts and reasonings, has no other immediate object but its own ideas, which it alone does or can contemplate, it is evident that our knowledge is only conversant about them.

He illustrated the problem with his famous experiment of the three basins of water: one hand is placed in cold water, the other in warm; then both are placed together in water of a neutral temperature and the one feels it as warm and the other as cold. Error and illusion always furnish the crucial situations for the discussion of this problem. But Locke was not an idealist. He believed in the reality of the neutral water, even though it was known in that instance only falsely as both warm and cold. He distinguished between adequate and inadequate, between true and false ideas. It is possible to transcend illusion by reflection.

We come thus to his doctrine of ideas. There are, he said, two sources of ideas: *sensation* and *reflection*. Sensation is the obvious source: by the senses, sensible qualities are conveyed into the mind from external bodies and there produce perceptions. There remains, however, the question as to how the mind obtains knowledge of its own operations. The answer to this persistent problem lies in the existence of reflection, which "might properly enough be called internal sense," and which is thus a second source of ideas—of ideas about ideas and the manner of their occurrence. This is the doctrine of the *inner sense*, subsequently important in act psychology. It is not that Locke believed that being aware of an idea is different from the mere having of an idea; in this point he held with Descartes. But Locke added the act, the 'operations of the mind,' as a second object of immediate knowledge. The dichotomy resembles closely some modern dichotomies (Witasek, Messer, Külpe, pp. 447-453), where act or function, on the one hand, and content, on the other, are the two materials of which mind is constituted.

Ideas may be simple or complex, and either kind may be ideas of sensation or of reflection. The simple ideas are unanalyzable, but the complex ideas may be resolved into simple ideas. The compounding of complex ideas out of simple ideas is one of the operations of the mind which reflection reveals. This notion of mental combination and analysis is very important, for it is the beginning of the 'mental chemistry' which characterizes associationism, which (in the guise of *Vorstellungen* as *Verbindungen*) is the core of the Wundtian tradition and which is at the bottom of all the controversy about analysis and elements later.

Locke was not very clear about the nature of these *compounds*. He thought there were three kinds: modes, like "triangle," "gratitude," "murder"; substances, like "a sheep," or collectively "sheep"; and relations, which arise from comparing one simple idea with another. We shall see later how this principle was developed almost to an absurdity in the duplex and complex ideas of James Mill, who held that the idea of a house is a compound of all the ideas of every item that enters into the construction of a house, and who asked then how complex the idea "called Everything" must be. Locke similarly mentioned "the universe" as an example of a complex idea.

The chapter "Of the Association of Ideas" was added by Locke, as we have noted, to the fourth edition of the *Essay*. It is supposed first to have been written for the Latin translation: "De idearum consociatione." It adds little to the doctrine except to give prominence in the English title to the word *association*, by which the theory was later to be known. In the text of this chapter, as elsewhere, Locke spoke mostly of connections or combinations of ideas; he used the word *association* and the word *associate* only once each.

Locke's doctrine of *association* is, then, his doctrine of the combination of ideas. It is plain that he is thinking of both simultaneous and successive association. Simultaneous association, however, was for him simply the complex idea, very much as it was for Wundt. The important thing thus is to see that he thought of successive combinations as essentially the same sort of thing. In his chapter on association he stressed the importance of custom as establishing these connections and thus anticipates the law of frequency which emerged very slowly within associationism.

For psychology, perhaps one of the most important of Locke's special theories is his doctrine of primary and secondary qualities, as they apply to simple ideas of sense. There are in the doctrine three kinds of qualities or powers.

1. The *primary qualities* are those that inhere in bodies and are singly perceived by the senses. They form the main avenue of contact between the mind and the external world. These qualities are

> such as are utterly inseparable from the body, in what estate soever it be; and such as, in all the alterations and changes it suffers, all the force can be used upon it, it constantly keeps; and such as sense constantly finds in every particle of matter, though less than to make itself singly perceived by our senses; *e.g.*, take a grain of wheat, divide it into two parts, each part has still solidity, extension, figure, mobility; divide it again, and it retains still the same qualities: and so divide it on till the parts become insensible, they must retain still each of them those qualities.... These I call *original* or *primary* qualities of body, which I think we may observe to produce simple ideas in us, viz., solidity, figure, motion or rest, and number.

2. The *secondary qualities* of an object are powers that the object possesses for producing ideas which do not exist within the objects in the form in which they are perceived. They are

> such qualities, which in truth are nothing in the objects themselves, but powers to produce various sensations in us by their primary qualities, *i.e.*, by the bulk, figure, texture, and motion of their insensible parts, as colours, sounds, tastes, *etc*.

3. For the sake of completeness, Locke adds a third category: *powers*. Objects have powers to affect other objects beside the organs of sense, which are also objects. "The sun has a power to make wax white, and fire, to make lead fluid." These powers, however, have by definition nothing to do with the production of ideas.

Actually all of the qualities are powers of objects to affect the nerves (about which Locke has very little to say) and thus to produce ideas. The essential difference between the primary and the secondary qualities is that, in the first case, the ideas are like the properties of the objects that produce them, and thus the properties may be said to be perceived 'directly as such'; whereas in the second case, the ideas do not resemble the properties of the object at all, but are produced indirectly by the action of other powers (properties). There is a certain confusion of thought because the qualities reside in the object. They are not subjective. It is ideas that are the subjective data produced by objective qualities. The secondary qualities, although they are not ideas but only produce ideas as do the primary qualities, are "in truth nothing in the objects themselves but powers."

The doctrine can be stated more clearly if we partly surrender the Lockian terms. All objects, let us say, have properties which have power to affect other objects. When they do not arouse ideas of sense, they are called by Locke simply "powers." When they affect the nerves of sense and thus arouse simple ideas of sense, they are called "qualities." When these resultant ideas are like the original properties of the object, so that the properties of the object are directly perceived in them, the qualities are "primary." When, however, the resultant ideas do not directly represent properties of the object nor resemble them, but are aroused indirectly, then the qualities are "secondary." Thus extent is a primary quality, because it can give rise directly to the idea of visual extension, which is like the extension of the stimulus; but vibration-frequency is a secondary quality when it arouses a pitch, because it does not resemble the pitch which it arouses, nor is the aroused pitch at all a frequency.

While Locke's use of the term *quality* is in one way the exact opposite of the modern usage (for nowadays quality is an attribute of the subjective sensation and not of the stimulus-object), nevertheless it foreshadows the modern use. Color, sound, smell and taste are qualities for us and were secondary qualities for Locke. So, too, our other attributes of sensation were primary qualities for Locke.

A more important thing about this doctrine is that it raises implicitly the question of the whole mechanism of relation between the stimulus and the resultant sensation (or idea). The secondary qualities have to be introduced because there is not exact correspondence between the two. The mind does not mirror the external world; it knows about it for the most part indirectly. It was this problem of the difference between the properties of objects and the characteristics of sensations that the doctrine of the specific energies of nerves sought in part to meet, and we have seen in discussing that doctrine how Locke can be said to have anticipated one of its principles.

There is also a relation between Locke's doctrine and modern Gestalt psychology's doctrine of isomorphism, which holds that the attributes of the perception must correspond in order (though not in form) with the attributes of the underlying cerebral events—extension with extension, time with time, though perhaps not sensory quality with neural qualitative difference. This last instance would more likely resemble Locke's secondary qualities.

We have finished our brief survey of Locke's psychology. We have not been complete. There are many other interesting items, like Locke's recognition of the range of consciousness or attention, when he shows that we cannot distinguish the difference between a 1,000-sided figure and a 999-sided one, although we can distinguish such a difference when the numbers are small. We have, however, said enough for our purposes in pointing out in Locke the nature of the idea, the empirical principle of knowledge, the rôle of reflection, the compounding of complex ideas and their analysis into simple ones, the origin of the phrase *association of ideas*, and the theory of primary and secondary qualities. In the next chapter we shall see how English empiricism and associationism in the eighteenth century developed from this beginning.

NOTES

In connection with this chapter, the reader may wish again to refer to chap. 1 on the rise of science and its emergence from philosophy. Descartes and Hobbes were contemporaries of Francis Bacon; Leibnitz and Locke, of Newton.

For the history of systematic psychology prior to Descartes, a history with which this book does not deal, see especially G. S. Brett, *History of Psychology*, 1912, I; 1921, II, also M. Dessoir, *Outlines of the History of Psychology*, 1912 (Eng. trans. from German), 1-88; portions of O. Klemm, *History of Psychology*, 1914 (Eng. trans. from German); and W. B. Pillsbury, *History of Psychology*, 1929. Brett is the most complete. These four books (including vol. III of Brett) are the available general histories of psychology from ancient times to the present, and the reader may supplement the present text by references to them. They all, however, present psychology more as an outgrowth and branch of philosophy than as an experimental science, and it is for this reason that the present work was originally undertaken. B. Rand, *Classical Psychologists*, 1912, gives in English psychologically important excerpts from representative great psychologists from the Greeks to the present day. There is also now W. Dennis, *Readings in the History of Psychology*, 1948, which gives more recent and hence more scientific excerpts, all but two of them since 1600. Rand reprints 43 contributions, whose average date is 1319 A.D. Dennis reprints 61 contributions, whose average date is 1779. The student who is unfamiliar with the original sources will find these books useful in connection with the present chapter and the succeeding chapters. There is also G. Villa, *Contemporary Psychology*, 1903 (Eng. trans. from Italian), which begins with Descartes but is less satisfactory than the other texts mentioned. H. C. Warren, *History of the Association Psychology*, 1921, is an excellent text for English empiricism and associationism, and is thus generally relevant to this chapter and the next.

In these chapters, the author is dealing with philosopher-psychologists only as they furnish the background for experimental psychology or incidentally enter into it. He makes, therefore, no attempt to treat the great names completely in the text or in these bibliographical notes. For complete accounts, the reader must consult the histories of philosophy and other special texts. In general, B. Rand's bibliography in J. M. Baldwin's *Dictionary of Philosophy and Psychology*, 1905, III, may be relied upon for a list of the complete works of a given author and the secondary sources, biographies, commentaries, translations and criticisms, up to the date of its publication.

Aristotle

Aristotle's most important psychological work is *De Anima;* next in importance are *De Sensu et Sensili*, which contains much of the doctrine of sensation, and *De Memoria et Reminiscentia*, where occur the laws of memory and 'association.' The two latter are parts of the *Parva naturalia*, and both it and the *De Anima* have been translated into English by W. A. Hammond, *Aristotle's Psychology*, 1902. Another excellent English account of Aristotle's psychology is given by Grote in the appendix to A. Bain, *Senses and Intellect*, 3 ed., 1872, 611-667. Aristotle's writings were very numerous, and the literature upon them is very great indeed. See, *e.g.*, Rand in Baldwin's *Dictionary*, III, 75-99; G. Sarton, *Introduction to the History of Science*, 1927, I, 127-136.

Descartes

Descartes' chief psychological works have been cited in the text with their initial dates of publication. There are many editions, collections, selections and translations. This is not the place to attempt a bibliography, but for the older items see Rand in Baldwin's *Dictionary* (*op. cit.*), III, 173-180. Excerpts from *Les passions de l'âme* (overlapping but not identical throughout) have been reprinted by Rand, *Classical Psychologists* (*op. cit.*), 168-190, and W. Dennis, *op. cit.*, 25-31. The biographical accounts are also too numerous to list (see Rand in Baldwin's *Dictionary*, *loc. cit.*), but special mention may be made of the

vivid account by E. Bell, *Men of Mathematics*, 1937, 35-55.

On Descartes, the psychologist, as viewed by philosophers, see Brett, *op. cit.*, II, 196-217; Dessoir, *op. cit.*, 89-96; Klemm, *op. cit.*, *passim*. See also incidental references in E. G. Boring, *Sensation and Perception in the History of Experimental Psychology*, 1942 (use index). The account of Descartes as a physiological psychologist and the ancestor of reflexology is given by F. Fearing, *Reflex Action*, 1930, 18-28.

Leibnitz

G. W. Leibnitz's philosophy is mostly in scattered writings and in letters. It is best to consult compilations of his works. His *Œuvres philosophiques* (containing his French writings and translations of the Latin), edited by R. E. Raspe, 1765, contain the first printing of the *Nouveaux essais sur l'entendement humain*, which Leibnitz never published because Locke, to whose *Essay* they were a reply, died (1704) at the time they were completed. These *Essais* are the chief psychological work of Leibnitz. They are given in Eng. trans. by A. G. Langley, as *New Essays Concerning Human Understanding*, 1896.

Our text, however, has concerned itself with the more fundamental and therefore more influential portion of the philosophy. For the explication of it, the reader should consult the *Système nouveau de la nature et de la communication des substances*, 1795-1796; *La monadologie*, 1714; *Principes de la nature et de la grâce*, 1714. All of these, as well as some extracts from the *Essais*, are given in Eng. trans. with notes by G. M. Duncan, *Philosophical Works of Leibnitz*, 1890 (1 ed., rearranged and somewhat revised, 1908). Rand, *Classical Psychologists*, 208-228, reprints some of Duncan's translations.

For a general bibliography and biographies of Leibnitz, see Rand, Baldwin's *Dictionary*, III, 330-338. On Leibnitz as mathematician, see E. Bell, *op. cit.*, 117-130. For secondary discussion of Leibnitz in the history of psychology, see Brett, *op. cit.*, II, 301-308; Dessoir, *op. cit.*, 126-132; Klemm, *op. cit.*, scattered *references* (see index) and on the unconscious, 172-177; L. Binswanger, *Einführung in die Probleme der allgemeine Psychologie*, 1922, esp. 187-193 (but see index).

It is not true to say that psychophysical parallelism was first held by Leibnitz; Spinoza held a parallelistic view before him. *Cf.* J. M. Baldwin, *History of Psychology*, 1913, I, 131-156, esp. 142-146.

Leibnitz (posthumous IQ $= ca.$ 185) was one of three most brilliant persons among the three hundred geniuses whose intelligences Cox appraised posthumously: C. M. Cox, *Early Mental Traits of Three Hundred Geniuses*, 1926, 705. Cox also assessed Hobbes and Locke as superior and Descartes as brilliant. It seems probable, however, that the posthumous effect of an adult on human thought corresponds not too closely to the posthumous evidence of his intellectual precocity.

Hobbes

Thomas Hobbes' important psychological works are *Humaine Nature: or the Fundamental Elements of Policie*, 1650, and *Leviathan, or the Matter, Form and Power of a Commonwealth, Ecclesiastical and Civil*, 1651. See Rand, *Classical Psychologists*, 147-167, and Dennis, *op. cit.*, 32-41, for excerpts. See also Brett, *op. cit.*, II, 219-222; Warren, *op. cit.*, 33-36; G. Murphy, *Historical Introduction to Modern Psychology*, 2 ed., 1949, 21-27; and the histories of philosophy.

Locke

John Locke's *Essay Concerning Human Understanding* (1690; 4th ed., 1700) has been reprinted in many editions, with and without notes, separately and in his *Works*. The edition by A. C. Fraser (1894), with many notes and biographical and critical introductions, is very useful. The literature is large; see Rand, Baldwin's *Dictionary*, III, 341-347. The reader who is following the present text with the histories of psychology should see Rand, *Classical Psychologists*, 232-255, and Dennis, *op. cit.*, 55-68 (both excerpts from the *Essay*); Brett, *op. cit.*, II, 257-264; Klemm, *op. cit.* (see index); Warren, *op. cit.*, 36-40. On the relation of primary and secondary qualities to the doctrine of specific nerve energies and the doctrine of isomorphism, see Boring, *op. cit.*, 68-96.

CHAPTER 10

British Empiricism: Berkeley, Hume and Hartley

From Locke, British psychology passed to Berkeley, Hume and Hartley, and then, in the nineteenth century and after an interval when the Scottish school was dominant, to the Mills and Bain.

GEORGE BERKELEY

Locke's immediate successor in British philosophy was George Berkeley (1685-1753), later the Bishop of Cloyne. In one important respect the intellectual biographies of the two men are in striking contrast. Locke published his important contribution which marks him as a great philosopher when he was fifty-seven, after a varied life of political and intellectual activity. Berkeley published his two important contributions in successive years when he was about twenty-five. At this time, he had never been out of Ireland to associate with thinkers on the Continent or even in England; his intellectual background was that of a student and junior fellow at Trinity College, Dublin.

Berkeley put out the *New Theory of Vision* in 1709 and the *Principles of Human Knowledge* in 1710. Actually, we know very little of the intellectual history that led up to these two remarkable books. Berkeley was born of an English family in Ireland. He was a precocious youth. He was matriculated at Trinity College, Dublin, less than two weeks after his fifteenth birthday (1700). During the next decade he was to become a philosopher of the first order. He received his bachelor's degree in 1704, the year of Locke's death, and his master's degree in 1707, when he was almost immediately made a junior fellow. In 1705 he joined enthusiastically with college friends in the formation of a philosophical society for the discussion of "the new philosophy of Boyle, Newton, and Locke." He kept in these days a *Common-Place Book*, a diary of philosophical queries, memoranda and propositions, in which the trend of his thought is evident. Before he was twenty years old, he was referring in this book to a "new Principle," which he seemed already to believe would be the key to unlock the mystery of nature. As the principle develops, we presently discover it to be the beginning of the very doctrine for which Berkeley is now famous, 'subjective idealism.' The *New Theory of Vision* was founded upon the new principle, but vision was an inadequate medium for the convincing presentation of a principle so fundamental. It was possible to argue that what was true of one sense might not be true of another. Perhaps Berkeley feared to give so radical a view its full importance all at once. Be this as it may, he took the bull by the horns in the following year, and the *Principles of Human Knowledge* presents his whole philosophy.

The remainder of Berkeley's life is much less interesting to us because it comes after this formative period and the publication of these books. From 1713 to 1728 he spent much time in England, as well as Ireland, and visited France and Italy. This period is marked by Berkeley's prosecution of his great project for founding a university in Bernuda for the Indians and the colonists. In this matter he was motivated by his educational ideas, by a conviction that the future of civilization lay in the West, and perhaps also by his personal desire for the academic-philosophic life, a desire that may have been temporarily enhanced by the numerous unexpected delays he experienced in obtaining a charter and grant for the university while at the court of George I. The charter was given and the grant finally approved by George II; Berkeley, newly married, sailed not to Bermuda but to Newport, Rhode Island, where he remained for three years hoping that his plans would be furthered; but the grant was never paid. He then returned to London for a few years, and in 1734 was made Bishop of Cloyne in County Cork in Ireland. Here he remained for eighteen years, again actively engaging in philosophical speculation and writing at a time when Hume and Hartley were writing and publishing their important works. The retired bishopric of Cloyne was not, however, the academic-philosophic seat for which Berkeley longed. In 1752 he moved to Oxford and took up private residence close to New College, but in the following year he died.

We shall now turn our attention to three important and interrelated contributions of Berkeley's to psychology: his "new Principle," his theory of visual space-perception, and what we may call for want of a better name his theory of 'meaning.' That these three contributions are not separable one from another will shortly be obvious.

1. Berkeley in his philosophy was historically naïve. He knew Descartes and Locke thoroughly and the *Common-Place Book* of his college days abounds in explicit references to Locke's *Essay*. He was probably not influenced by Malebranche, although certain similarities between the philosophies of the two men have led some critics to infer a direct relationship. Of Leibnitz and Spinoza, and of the "ancients," as Descartes called them, he knew little. His contemporary interest deviated in the direction of the science of Newton and Boyle, but, unlike Descartes and Leibnitz, he entirely lacked the scientific temperament. However, he shared with Descartes, who emphatically rejected the older philosophy, a freedom from the constraints of tradition. Actually what he set out to do was to improve upon Locke. If Locke's greatness had been temporary, Berkeley's might have been too; but, as it is, his "new Principle" has the distinction of being toward the universe an extreme point of view which is the most obvious and immediate consequence of Locke's position: it is the left wing of empiricism.

This principle consisted essentially in the denial of matter as such and in the *affirmation of mind as the immediate reality*. Locke had denied the innate ideas of Descartes but had not transcended the dualism. There were still two worlds, the one knowing about the other through experience. Berkeley simply cut the knot, as a young man in his early twenties without the force of accepted tradition upon him can so often do. The ideas themselves are the one thing of which we are sure. *Esse* is *percipi*. Perception is the reality (as indeed Leibnitz had said). The problem is not as to how the mind is related to matter (Descartes) nor as to how matter generates mind (Locke), but rather as to how mind generates matter. It was a bold, clean stroke, and the logical next step after Locke. It failed of becoming accepted truth largely because it was a suicidal step for philosophy to take, for it leads to solipsism, the belief that there is only one mind, in which other minds exist as ideas, and it thus abolishes the social nature of science and philosophy as collective thought. The position is not capable of disproof; it is merely a *reductio ad absurdum*, which may be rejected along with other things that seem absurd where reasoning is law.

The solution of many problems of *visual perception*, Berkeley found, is aided by this view. Take, for instance, the question of the size of the moon and its distance from the earth. It is said to be just so big and such a distance from the earth, but it is plain that these measures cannot apply to the visible moon, "which is only a round luminous plane, of about thirty visible points in diameter." This description would not apply if the observer could be moved from the earth to a point near the moon, but the simple fact here would be that the moon had changed, if indeed one still called the changed object the moon. In the same way we could remove the problem of the familiar illusion of the size of the moon and in fact all illusions, for perception is not illusion when *esse* is *percipi;* it is the constancy of objects that is the illusion and that requires explanation.

Thus we can pass at once to the problems of visual perception where Berkeley anticipated modern fact, but in passing we must note that the "new Principle," because of its generality, went a long way toward settling a psychological approach upon philosophy. The relation of *esse* to *percipi* is still with us, a fact which explains in both historical and rational terms why philosophy is so much interested in psychology.

It is also desirable at this point to note that Aristotle, Locke, and Berkeley tended to fix upon psychology one of its primary principles of classification. Aristotle established the primary division of the senses into five. Locke emphasized the sensory nature of ideas. Berkeley, insisting upon the primacy of ideas, was obliged in the first place to separate ideas by sense-departments. Thus vision and touch, as systematic classes, are prior, for example, to form. There are no abstract forms. "The extensions, figures, and motions perceived by sight are specifically distinct from the ideas of touch, called by the same names; nor is there any such thing as one idea, or kind of idea, common to both senses." In Locke's famous hypothetical case of the man born blind and suddenly receiving his sight, the seen sphere would not look round because it was already known by touch to be round. In some such way, 'quality,' which marks off the senses from one another, has come quite generally to be considered the primary sensory attribute and classificatory principle, even though it has never been the only principle, and though space quite early demanded independent consideration.

2. In the *New Theory of Vision* Berkeley began by separating distance from areal space and dealing with *distance.* "Distance of itself, and immediately, can not be seen. For distance being a line directed endwise to the eye, it projects only one point in the fund of the eye—which point remains invariably the same, whether the distance be longer or shorter." Thus most persons, he thought, agree that the perception of distance "is rather an act of judgment grounded on experience." Here he mentioned the equivalents of many of the 'secondary criteria' listed today: interposition, aerial

perspective, relative size. He knew about light and shade from Locke's discussion of the sphere which is perceived as a sphere and not as a disk, though he did not mention it here. Linear perspective as a criterion is only with difficulty separated from interposition and relative size. Relative movement is the only remaining criterion of those usually given today. We see, then, in 1709 the third visual dimension separated from areal dimensions of the retina and made secondary, as a psychological problem, to them; and we find listed most of the secondary criteria of distance.

Berkeley also was able to indicate the nature of the primary criteria of distance. He listed three. First, there is the distance between the pupils, which is altered by turning the eyes when an object approaches or recedes—what is now called 'convergence.' Then there is the blurring that occurs when the object is too close to the eye. This criterion, in spite of controversy about it nearly two centuries later, is probably not valid, for objects blur beyond, as well as nearer than, the focus of the eye. Finally Berkeley noted the "straining of the eye," by which, when objects are brought too near, "we may nevertheless prevent, at least for some time, the appearance's growing more confused"—accommodation, in other words. We must not deceive ourselves about the extent of Berkeley's knowledge. He understood but vaguely the mechanism of the perception of distance. He was essentially correct in two of his three primary criteria, but he was a long way off from a knowledge of the physiology of convergence or the theory of the horopter and corresponding points, and he knew nothing of Helmholtz's theory of the physiology of accommodation.

More important than the recognition of the mechanism of perception was the idealistic (introspective) slant that Berkeley gave it. Descartes had recognized convergence: the eyes, he noted, feel out distances as if the lines of vision were two staffs attached to them. Such a view, however, leads to a geometry of binocular vision; the perception of distance becomes the perception of angles. Berkeley avoided even mentioning angles, except to expostulate against their introduction into the discussion. He talked about distance between the pupils and thus of the positions of the eyes on turning. What he meant is that distance, in this instance, is an awareness of the positions of the eyes and is—as every one knows at once from experience—not an awareness of angles. So, too, the straining of the eyes when an object approaches is sensory. Blurring, if we consider it at all, is also sensory. What he did, then, was to make the perception of distance, even though it is mediate, a matter of sensation or idea.

This is essentially the introspectionist's context theory of the visual perception of distance. Presently we shall see how this context theory, which is representative of modern associationism, was in general anticipated by Berkeley.

Having disposed of distance, Berkeley turned to *magnitude*. One might suppose that, with a true image upon the retina, magnitude would be directly perceived. Extension for Locke was a primary quality. Berkeley's position, however, admitted of no such belief as Locke's, which was both the common belief of his time and that of a century later before the law of the specific energies of nerves. Magnitude, by which Berkeley meant objective size, is no more directly perceived than distance. In the first place, magnitude depends upon distance: far objects are small and near objects large. If we perceive magnitude at all, it is by taking distance into account, and the perception of distance itself is a secondary matter of judgment. Secondly, perceived magnitude does not accord with the geometry of space: there is a *minimum visibile* and a *minimum tangibile*, both of which are finite quantities and not the infinitesimal points which are the minima of geometry. This argument, of course, shows the psychological principle of the limen entering in to distinguish mind from matter. Thus Berkeley rescued even the idea of size from an objective world.

3. We have been speaking entirely of perception. The reader must not suppose that Berkeley's denial of the primacy of matter obliterated the problem of perception, for it merely inverted it. We have to ask, not how the mind apprehends matter, but rather how it dispenses it. In the empiricism of Locke, matter generates mind. In the empiricism of Berkeley, mind generates matter. We must substitute for a theory of knowledge about objects a psychological description of objects; and it is plain that these objective ideas are formed through experience and that Berkeley was thus no less an empiricist than Locke.

To the author it seems that Berkeley's *theory of objects* is a direct anticipation of Titchener's context theory of meaning and that both theories imply association without mentioning it—Berkeley because he wrote too long before the theory, Titchener because he wrote so long after it. Be this as it may, it is plain that Berkeley undertook the solution of the problem of meaning and that he solved it in terms of the relation or connection between ideas, as did all the associationists after him—James Mill (pp. 225 f.), Wundt (pp. 329 f.) and Titchener (pp. 417 f.). We can do no better than to quote the text of the *New Theory of Vision*.

It is evident that, when the mind perceives any idea, not immediately and of itself, it must be by means of some other idea. Thus, for instance, the passions which are in the mind of another are of themselves to me invisible. I may nevertheless perceive them by sight, though not immediately, yet by means of the colours they produce in the countenance. We often see shame or fear in the looks of a man, by perceiving the changes of his countenance to red or pale.

Moreover it is evident that no idea which is not itself perceived can be to me the means of perceiving any other idea. If I do not perceive the redness or paleness of a man's face themselves, it is impossible I should perceive them by the passions which are in his mind.

Elsewhere he wrote:

Sitting in my study I hear a coach drive along the street; I look through the casement and see it; I walk out and enter it. Thus, common speech would incline one to think I heard, saw, and touched the same thing, to wit, the coach. It is nevertheless certain the ideas intromitted by each sense are widely different and distinct from each other; but, having been observed constantly to go together, they are spoken of as one and the same thing.

The last sentence contains the theory of association in principle, if not explicitly in words. So also, as we have already implied, Berkeley appealed to "an habitual or customary connexion" between ideas in his explanation of the perception of distance.

Not that there is any natural or necessary connexion between the sensation we perceive by a turn of the eyes and the greater or lesser distance. But—because the mind has, by constant experience, found the different sensations corresponding to the different dispositions of the eyes to be attended each with a different degree of distance in the object—there has grown an habitual or customary connexion between those two sorts of ideas; so that the mind no sooner perceives the sensation arising from the different turn it gives the eyes, in order to bring the pupils nearer or farther asunder, but it withal perceives the different idea of distance which was wont to be connected with that sensation. Just as, upon hearing a certain sound, the idea is immediately suggested to the understanding which custom has united with it.

Similarly Berkeley discussed the meanings that come to be attached to words in the process of their becoming language, and how in the perception of objects the secondary (associated) idea is often taken note of to the exclusion of the primary idea which gives rise to it. This view is not very different from the more modern one that objective meaning is given by the addition of a context to a core, or the simpler one that it takes at least two sensations to make a meaning.

DAVID HUME

David Hume (1711-1776) was Berkeley's philosophical successor. Biographically there is a superficial similarity between the two men, for both were somewhat precocious, both were given to mature philosophical thought and writings in youth, both developed their philosophies in relative isolation without the social stimulus of intimacy with other great men, and both published their most important books while still in their twenties—Berkeley at twenty-five, Hume at twenty-eight. However, except for this precocious seriousness, there is little psychological similarity between the two. Hume was a young man much concerned with his own personality, extremely ambitious, but at the same time a perfectionist, dissatisfied with poor work in himself. A restless, nervous personality he was, subject, it would seem, to an internal conflict, for he was persistently driven on by an urge for production and greatness, and constantly held back by his own standards of accomplishment. He completed "a college education in Scotland," at about fifteen (the usual age for its completion, he himself said), and presumably went to the university at Edinburgh, although he never graduated. He tried to study law, but he could not shift his interest from philosophical to legal matters. He tried business, but it was less "suitable" than the law, and the venture lasted only a few months. He was the second son in the Hume family at Ninewells, not far from Edinburgh, a secondary estate in an old family. He had thus a meager competence, and, when he was twenty-three, after the failure of the law and of business to provide a satisfactory means of support, he undertook to make his slender income support him in seclusion in France, while he continued with the studies that had long been his compelling interest. It is impossible to say how far his philosophy had developed at this time, but at any rate it took shape rapidly during three years in France. He returned home when he was twenty-six with a manuscript almost completed, and two years later, in 1739, the first two volumes of what he called *A Treatise on Human Nature* were published. The third volume appeared the following year.

The *Treatise*, while lacking a finished style or even a clearly defined subject-matter, is generally regarded as showing the vigor of a young man and as Hume's most important work. It sold well, although not so well but that its ambitious author was greatly disappointed in its reception. He began almost immediately the writing of *Philosophical Essays* which should make his points more succinctly and clearly, and these resulted in the publication of the smaller *Enquiry Concerning the Human Understanding* in 1748. Hume advised his public to read the latter work as shorter and simpler, and thus "really much more complete"; but he seems to have been influenced in this judgment by his disappointment that the *Treatise* had not brought him greater fame.

The last thirty years of Hume's life concern us less than the brief period that led up to the *Treatise*. During them, fame and, in its wake, wealth came to him. He lived as a writer, although he engaged in numerous other occupations incidentally. He was companion to an insane but wealthy marquis under very trying circumstances; he was judge-advocate in a minor military expedition against the coast of France; he was secretary to a general on a Continental diplomatic mission; he was a librarian; he entered actively into politics. All these activities he undertook between 1745 and 1763. Twice he sought a university chair of moral philosophy (or "pneumatic philosophy," the equivalent of psychology) but failed, for his orthodoxy was insufficient for such a post. Later his writing turned toward politics and his fame consequently increased. In 1753 he began his *History of England*, which was completed in its entirety in 1761 and which was an unusual financial success, in part perhaps because he allowed his account to reflect a Tory bias. In 1763, he went to Paris with a secretarial connection in the British embassy and was there received with great acclaim at the court and among the European scholars who gathered in Paris. No man could ask for greater contemporaneous recognition, and Hume was happy in Paris. although he always underrated his success. After three years he returned home, became an under-secretary in London for two years and finally in 1769 settled in Edinburgh for the last seven years of his life. His greatest claim to immortality, however, lies in the work of his secluded youth. His keen ambition, ingrafted upon a sensitive, self-depreciatory personality, led him always to impose high standards of excellence upon himself, but it led him also to court fame, society and its approval, and it is probable that these latter ends distracted him from greater philosophical accomplishment.

Nevertheless, he was a great philosopher—the last great British philosopher, in the opinion of those who think that Kant was his intellectual successor. Our interest, however, centers less in his philosophy than in certain of his contributions to psychology. In general, it is to be noted, he preserved the tradition that philosophy is at bottom psychological; he re-emphasized Locke's notion of the compounding of simple ideas into complex; and he developed and made more explicit the notion of association. His most important direct contribution to modern psychology is, however, his clear distinction between impressions and ideas. When psychology was to seek much later for systematic classifications through which to view its complex material, it was to find fewer distinctions than it required for adequacy, and nothing, except the Aristotelian division of the five senses, proved more useful than this distinction between sensation and perception (impression), on the one hand, and image and idea, on the other. We shall also have to consider Hume's doctrine of causation, not because that problem is necessarily psychological, but partly because Hume made it psychological, and partly because his solution throws light on the perplexing problem of psychological causation as many psychologists deal with it today.

Hume made the distinction between *impressions* and *ideas* fundamental. He sought to "restore the word, idea, to its original sense, from which Mr. Locke had perverted it," when he used it to include sensation. An idea is obviously the experience we have in the absence of its object; it was used by Hume in the sense of the words *idea* and *image* today. Over against it may be set *impression*, a word that carries the modern meaning of *sensation* and *perception*. Hume himself did not like the word, since it seemed to indicate the manner of the production of perceptions in the soul, but he knew of no other suitable name "either in English or any other language." Both impressions and ideas are then simply the respective experiences themselves; they are not defined physiologically, or by reference to external object present or absent; they are recognizably distinct kinds of experience both of which Locke included under the term *idea*.

What is, then, the difference between them? The important difference seemed to Hume to lie in their *vivacity*. The impressions are more vigorous, lively, violent than the ideas; the ideas are relatively weak and faint.

Those perceptions, which enter with most force and violence, we may name impressions; and under this name I comprehend all our sensations, passions and emotions, as they make their first appearance in the soul. By ideas I mean the faint images of these in thinking and reasoning; such as, for instance, are all the perceptions excited by the present discourse, excepting only those which arise from the sight and touch, and excepting the immediate pleasure or uneasiness it may occasion. Everyone of himself will readily perceive the difference betwixt feeling and thinking.

The systematic usefulness of this distinction has tended to escape criticism because of the readiness with which every one perceives "the difference betwixt feeling and thinking"; nevertheless, there is a difficulty. Perhaps ideas are generally fainter than impressions; but are they always so? May not the faintest impression be weaker than the strongest idea? Is the idea of thunder never more vigorous than the impression of the barely perceptible tick of a watch? Some psychologists adopted Hume's criterion in addition to Külpe's valid physiological distinction of peripheral and central excitation; but the criterion was later dismissed experimentally by showing that it was easy to compare images and sensations in intensity, and that images can be more intense than sensations, although perhaps not as intense as the strongest sensations.

We are not to suppose, however, that this difficulty escaped Hume's keen mind. He noted that ideas in dreams, in madness, in violent emotions, may approach impressions in degree; that impressions are sometimes "so faint and low, that we cannot distinguish them from our ideas." Nevertheless "in their common degree" they are easily distinguished. Yet Hume failed us in our desire for a universal definition. He never told why the faintest impression is still an impression and not an idea, nor why the strongest idea, in a dream for example, is not an impression. Had he been physiologically minded, like Descartes or Hartley, he might have solved the problem as Külpe did; but he was not.

The fact that Hume must have believed in a difference in 'quality' between impressions and ideas is favored by his view that ideas are *faint copies* of impressions. Both ideas and impressions, he thought, may be *simple* or *complex*. A simple idea always resembles some simple impression, although a complex idea, since it may be constituted of simple ideas in some novel manner, need not resemble any impression. Thus it falls out that there is a one-to-one correspondence between simple ideas and simple impressions, in exactly the same manner as we picture the relationship nowadays between images and sensations. But how can an idea resemble a sensation and yet not be identical with it? It would resemble it without identity if it were of the same quality and different intensity, but intensity, we have seen, is not always an adequate criterion. By a "faint copy" Hume must have meant that there was some difference other than faintness, the difference that exists without respect to vivacity between a copy and the original. It is unlikely that so rigorous a thinker as Hume would have failed to preserve some ground of distinction.

Hume regarded the impressions as *causing* their corresponding ideas. We shall understand this matter better when we have seen presently what Hume meant by a cause. Here we may record that he noted four facts as establishing the causal relation: (1) simple ideas resemble their simple impressions; (2) the two have concurred at some time; (3) the impression was initially prior to its idea; and (4) ideas never occur when their corresponding impressions can not occur (*e.g.*, visual ideas in the congenitally blind). The last three facts satisfy Hume's conditions for establishing causation; the first seems to be unnecessary. We must not miss the historical importance of the enunciation of this relationship. The dependence of images upon prior sensations is taken so much for granted today, that we are likely to forget that the conception needed clearly to be introduced into empiricism and that, in the face of the Cartesian innate ideas, it was not obvious.

Here we may pause briefly to note some incidental systematic matters in Hume's psychology. He used the word *perception* loosely to include both impressions and ideas. Impressions may be either *sensations* or *reflections*. A reflection is an impression that is aroused by an idea. Thus a sensation of pain may be copied by the mind as an idea of pain which, recurring, may arouse a reflection of aversion, which in turn may be copied as an idea of aversion, and so on. It is plain that the reflection must play a rôle in the passions. It was three years earlier (1736) that Astruc first applied the word *reflexion* to what we now call reflex movement or action, but some time before the word came to be used in this new sense.

We have already seen that Hume espoused Locke's notion of *complex ideas*, thus tending to establish some kind of 'mental chemistry' as the psychological method. These complex ideas may be of *relations*, of *modes* or of *substances*. Hume named seven ideas of relation, but it seems rather that among them resemblance, quantity, quality and perhaps contrariety are primary, and that identity, space and time, and cause and effect, although listed with the others, really reduce to them. Hume's modes are our present-day modalities: colors, sounds, tastes, and so on. Substances or objects are ideas that have names and are referred to as things but are really explained associatively as complexes. Here Hume followed Berkeley in an associative theory of meaning.

Association with Hume came more nearly into its own as the fundamental law of connection among ideas, although Hume, like Locke, did not emphasize the word. It is also true that association now took on something of the character of an act of associating and was not merely a description of the constitution of a complex.

As all simple ideas may be separated by the imagination, and may be united again in what form it pleases, nothing would be more unaccountable than the operations of that faculty, were it not guided by some universal principles, which render it, in some measure, uniform with itself in all times and places. Were ideas entirely loose and unconnected, chance alone would join them; and 'tis impossible that the same simple ideas should fall regularly into complex ones (as they commonly do) without some bond of union among them, some associating quality, by which one idea naturally introduces another.

Hume thought of association as an *attraction* or force among ideas whereby they unite or cohere. He was thus anticipating not so much a 'mental chemistry' as a mental mechanics. He noted that the connections are not necessary nor inseparable but merely such as commonly prevail; thus he spoke of the attraction as a "gentle force." In this thought he anticipated the later notion that associations are *tendencies* in that they do not always occur and must therefore be dealt with statistically. He laid down three *laws* of association: resemblance, contiguity in time or place, and cause and effect. Later, however, he virtually reduced cause and effect to contiguity, so perhaps there were but two left.

We may turn now to Hume's famous doctrine of *cause and effect*. This relationship is puzzling because causes seem to *act* to produce their effects, and the action is ordinarily entirely unobservable. Hume's analysis led him to define it by reference to three conditions.

1. In the first place, a cause and its effect are always *contiguous* in both space and time: there cannot be causal action at a distance, nor after the lapse of an interval of time. This notion of the spatial and temporal immediacy of cause and effect explains in a large measure the popular belief that a cause somehow or other 'does something to' its effect.

2. In the second place, a cause is always *prior* to its effect. This is an obvious simple principle which serves to differentiate the two. It is perhaps a little more obvious than it has any logical right to be, for common sense anthropomorphizes the situation and thinks of an irreversible action which can proceed only forward in time, whereas neither term is logically prior to the other and the relation is symmetrical. Nevertheless, there must be some way of naming the two terms, even though the definition makes a 'final cause' a verbal paradox.

3. Finally, there must be between a cause and its effect a *necessary connection*. Hume's giving to this condition a status correlative to the other two is a tribute to the fact that contiguity alone does not

seem to yield sufficient immediacy or intimacy. However, Hume, after insisting upon it, proceeded to annihilate it. He asked how we can observe necessity and replied that necessity is an illusion that exists in the mind and not in objects. We have, then, rather to ask how the idea of necessity arises, and he found that necessity is an impression of reflection, which is "that propensity, which custom produces to pass from an object to the idea of its usual attendant." "Necessity is nothing but that determination of thought to pass from causes to effects and from effects to causes, according to their experienc'd union." In other words, it is contiguity after all; nevertheless it is a little bit more. Contiguity is a 'gentle force'; necessity is stronger. Contiguity becomes necessity when there is a "constant conjunction of two objects." Things may be associated by contiguity when they occur together. They are associated by cause and effect when they always occur together. Having been indissoluble in experience, they are conceived by the mind as necessarily connected.

This view of cause and effect as correlation has been extremely important for psychologists. Many physical laws are causal, and psychology, struggling consciously to be a science and taking physics as the model, has often sought laws of mental causation. Physics, however, had become quantitative before psychology had asserted its scientific independence of philosophy, and there came, in the middle of the nineteenth century when causation was confused with the conservation of energy, to be added to Hume's notion the additional condition that a cause and its effect must be equivalent in energy. This was a condition that psychology could not satisfy: there was no common mental energy to which all psychological phenomena could be reduced. Those who believed that cause and effect ought to imply quantitative equivalence said that psychology could not be causal, but others reverted to an approximation of Hume's view. Ernst Mach and Karl Pearson, for instance, looked upon cause in the entire psychophysical domain as a correlation of events in time. If their view differed from Hume's at all, it was mostly in the fact that they could not ask for contiguity in space as well as time, since mental events are not localized.

So much for Hume's psychology. It had influence because it fitted into the development of empiricism and associationism and because his thoughts were carefully reasoned and were the pronouncements of a keen intellect and a famous man. Still more influential, however, was Hume's idealism or, as it is generally called, his *skepticism*. Hume carried well on toward its extreme logical conclusion the thought that was implicit in Locke's empiricism and Berkeley's idealism, the notion that the mind can know directly only its own processes and that the world of real objects can not be finally certified as anything more tangible than the ideas which constitute man's belief in it. Thus Hume was led to doubt the existence of God, of the personal ego and of the external world. The power of his logic was convincing, but philosophers were not ready to accept such a *reductio ad absurdum*, even though its alternative remained obscure. They rose to combat Hume. The first of importance was the Scottish philosopher, Thomas Reid, whose answer to Hume we shall consider in the next chapter. The greatest of all was Kant who, roused by reading Hume, embarked on his constructive compromise between mind and matter, the astute compromise that formed the background of German philosophy of the nineteenth century. Kant belongs to the next chapter but one.

Although Hume went further than Locke and Berkeley toward the subjectivistic ultimate, even he did not go all the way, for that would have landed him in solipsism. The very fact that Hume regarded impressions as the causes of ideas is put forward as an inconsistency in Hume's position, since Hume seems to regard these prior impressions as more objective than their consequent ideas. As so often happens, Hume meant different things to different persons. Reid and Kant reacted negatively to one aspect of his philosophy, his subjectivism and skepticism, whereas Mach and Pearson reacted positively to a quite different aspect, his positivism as it appears in his doctrine of cause and effect.

More recently Hume has become a useful contrasting background for the display of Gestalt psychology. Hume's reduction of the universe to impressions, ideas and events, and his view of causation as merely a contiguous sequence of terms is everything that field theory and Gestalt psychology are not.

DAVID HARTLEY

David Hartley (1705-1757) is an important figure, but not, like Hume, a great man. He is important because he was the founder of associationism. He was not the originator; that was Aristotle or Hobbes or Locke, as one pleases. The principle had been used effectively and greatly developed by Berkeley and Hume. Hartley merely established it as a doctrine. He took Locke's little-used title for a chapter, "the association of ideas," made it the name of a fundamental law, reiterated it, wrote a psychology around it, and thus created a formal doctrine with a definite name, so that a school could repeat the phrase after him for a century and thus implicitly constitute him its founder. It is apt to be thus with 'founding.' When the central ideas are all born, some promoter takes them in hand, organizes them, adding whatever else seems to him essential, publishes and advertises them, insists upon them, and in short 'founds' a school. Hartley was less of a 'promoter' than some present-day founders of psychological schools or other men of his own times, for he was not temperamentally a propagandist. Nevertheless, as we pass from Hume to him, it is important to see that origination and founding may be very different matters. Whoever discovered 'association,' there is not the least doubt that Hartley prepared it for its *ism.*

There could scarcely be a greater contrast of personality than that between Hartley and Hume. From the restless, versatile, ambitious, energetic Hume, always dissatisfied, generous but also a little quarrelsome, we turn to a calm, persistent, self-complacent man, assured, benevolent and tolerant. Hume's life could hardly be reduced to a paragraph; Hartley's could. We can do no better than quote a part of the description of Hartley by his son, making allowances for the fact that it is a son who writes, but realizing that the account at least fits the superficial facts.

> The philosophical character of Dr. Hartley is delineated in his works. The features of his private and personal character were of the same complexion. It may with peculiar propriety be said of him, that the mind was the man. His thoughts were not immersed in worldly pursuits or contentions, and therefore his life was not eventful or turbulent, but placid and undisturbed by passion or violent ambition. . . . His imagination was fertile and correct, his language and expression fluent and forcible. His natural temper was gay, cheerful, and sociable. He was addicted to no vice in any part of his life, neither to pride, nor to sensuality, nor intemperance, nor ostentation, nor envy, nor to any sordid self-interest: but his heart was replete with every contrary virtue. . . . His countenance was open, ingenuous and animated. He was peculiarly neat in his person and attire. He was an early riser and punctual in the employments of the day; methodical in the order and disposition of his library, papers and writings, as the companions of his thoughts, but without any pendantry, either in these habits, or in any other part of his character. . . . He never conversed with a fellow creature without feeling a wish to do him good . . .

This is human perfection, and yet perfection seems to be but average in greatness. It is not merely that the ordinary man reacts against assured, tolerant, benevolent poise in self-defense (for one

could still love Hume after two centuries, but scarcely Hartley).
It is more that the driving force that leads to greatness runs to extremes of good and bad, or of truth and error. Some error is the
price of much truth, some smallness of much greatness.

Hartley was the son of a minister and was prepared for the
church, but he was prevented from taking orders because of conscientious scruples against signing the required Thirty-nine Articles,
in particular the one dealing with eternal punishment. This heterodoxy is the most dramatic thing in Hartley's life, but the reader will
note that an insurmountable objection to the doctrine of eternal
punishment is but the price of the tolerance and benevolence of the
man. Unable to enter the church, Hartley studied for the medical
profession and continued to practise throughout his life, a kindly
physician of scholarly habits, who dispensed his philosophy for
mental ills along with his other drugs. He knew his Latin and wrote
in Latin on the association of ideas in 1746. He knew science in
general, as one still could in those days. He extended his admiration
especially to Locke and to Newton, and his psychology was a result
of a fusion of Locke's theory of the association of ideas and Newton's theory of vibrations. His friends for the most part were within
the clergy. His one great book is the *Observations on Man*. It was
published in 1749. Six years later he died.

Hartley got the notion of his vibrational, associational psychology
from reading Newton and Locke. It was natural for a physician to
attempt to apply Newton's conceptions to the nervous system. He
was thus in a sense a physiological psychologist, the first important
one in England. The general application of the theory of association
was suggested to him by a publication of the Reverend John Gay's
(*ca.* 1731), but some idea of the final result is said to have been in
Hartley's mind even earlier—that is to say, in his early twenties,
perhaps while he was still at Cambridge. At any rate, his book was
definitely begun about 1731 and completed about 1747, although
it was not published until 1749. Thus it is plain that Hartley wrote
relatively independently of Hume. Hume's *Treatise*, not widely read
at first, was published in 1739-1740, and his *Essays*, brought together
as the *Inquiry*, a year after the completion of Hartley's *Observations* (though a year before its publication). Hartley's Latin essay
appeared in 1746. It is plain that the *Observations* represent a philosophical avocation, secondary to Hartley's busy life as a physician,
and completed as leisure permitted during a long period of about
eighteen years.

Hartley was a *dualist* in his psychology. He was anxious to make it clear that he did not hold to a materialistic conception of the free and immortal soul. Although his laws of ideas in the mind and of vibrations in the body are very like, he insisted that they are parallel and not the same. Thus Hartley is for all practical purposes a psychophysical parallelist, although he does not represent the direct tradition from Leibnitz to Bain in this view. He is the first clear dualist of mind and matter after Descartes, and like Descartes he had particularly before him the problem of mind and body. Both Hartley and Descartes were brought to this problem by an interest in physiology, and thus they were both primitive physiological psychologists.

On the physiological side, Hartley had first to indicate the parts of the body that have to do with mind, that are 'the seat of' the mind. He was quite explicit: the brain, the spinal cord and the nerves have to do with sensation and motion; ideas, however, depend upon the brain alone. Within the nervous system he embraced Newton's notion of *vibratory action*, instead of the currently accepted theory of the flow of animal spirits in tubes. There occur (he thought) in nervous substance "vibrations of the small, and as one may say, infinitesimal, medullary particles." These are exceedingly small, longitudinal vibrations of the particles; "that the nerves themselves should vibrate like musical strings, is highly absurd." Within the nerves these small vibrations give rise to sensation or motion; but within the brain there may be even smaller vibrations, "diminutive vibrations, which may also be called Vibratiuncles, and Miniatures, and which are the physiological counterpart of ideas." The small, but larger, vibrations in the nerves arouse these miniatures in the brain, and the vibratiuncles thus correspond directly to the vibrations. Hartley's thought resembles Hume's transferred to the physiological sphere. Hume said that ideas were faint copies of impressions. Hartley said that the vibrations for ideas are miniatures of the vibrations for sensations. Hume said that the ideas resembled the impressions in a one-to-one correspondence. Hartley said the vibratiuncles resemble their respective vibrations in "kind, place, and line of direction" (and he seems also to have meant *rate*), differing only "in being more feeble." Thus Hartley really accepted Hume's fundamental view.

Hartley's argument for the dependence of sensations upon vibrations in the nerves was drawn primarily from the facts of the *persistence of sensation* after the removal of stimulus, facts already advanced by Newton. Hartley mentioned the persistence of vision in whirling a burning coal and in the mixture of colors on their quick succession (both illustrations of Newton's), the positive afterimage, the persistence of colors when the eyeball is pressed, the persistence of the experience of heat after the removal of the hot object, and the fact that tones, although consisting of separate pulses, are nevertheless heard as smooth. What sort of a mechanism would make it the general rule that sensation would not disappear instantaneously upon the removal of its object? Vibrations, Hartley urged; vibrations, though they are effects from a cause, also involve some self-perpetuation, for it takes a little while for them to die out.

When we have finished on this simple level with the body, there is little left to say about the mind, for the parallelism is so close that the one implies the other.

> Sensations, by being often repeated, leave certain Vestiges, Types, or Images, of themselves, which may be called, Simple Ideas of Sensations.

This statement is against Hume's doctrine. In it the word *image* appears, but it is not stressed in the text.

After the object of sensation has been removed, the sensation and its vibrations persist briefly but become fainter the while. Thus a sensation may be as weak as an idea. Moreover, by repetition and in the other ways, an idea and its vibratiuncles may become strong, as strong as a sensation (*e.g.*, in dreams). Thus we see that for Hartley, as for Hume, the separation of ideas and sensations with regard to their relative intensities is only a matter of common occurrence and admits of exceptions. The fundamental distinction for Hartley is not that the vibrations for ideas are always smaller than those for sensations, but that they lie always in the brain and are aroused on their first occurrence by vibrations from the nerves.

We are now ready to consider the laws of *association*. There must really be two laws, one for the mind and one for the body; and Hartley gave both in different places. Here again we must note, however, that the parallelism is so close that the one seems only a repetition of the other with a change of phrase.

> Any sensations A, B, C, *etc.*, by being associated with one another a sufficient Number of Times, get such a Power over corresponding Ideas, a, b, c, *etc.*, that any one of the Sensations A, when impressed alone, shall be able to excite in the Mind, b, c, *etc.* the Ideas of the rest.

The parallel law is identical in wording, except that the word *Vibration* is substituted for *Sensation*, and *Miniature Vibration* for *Idea*.

It is apparent, first, that Hartley in his laws of association appealed fundamentally to contiguity as a principle, although he did not name it thus. There was no law of resemblance (*cf.* Hume) to interfere with the simplicity. Hartley was thus directly in accord with the modern view of association.

Association, Hartley thought, may occur among sensations, ideas or motions, or among all of them. The addition of 'motion' to the list is the logical outcome of his physiology, but the point gains interest for us because of the modern behavioral conception of association as conditioned reflex.

Beside mere contiguity, a further condition of association for Hartley is *repetition*. The sensations, ideas, motions, vibrations or vibratiuncles must be associated with one another "a sufficient number of times." With Ebbinghaus' invention of experimental methods for measuring memory (1885), repetition was seen to be the all-important condition. The infinite variety of chance contiguities in the psychological life render a single concurrence scientifically negligible. Necessarily, then, the thought of repetition as an important condition has always been present in the discussion of association, but it had never been given its proper emphasis. Even in Hartley the notion was only just emerging.

There are many other ways in which Hartley anticipated modern doctrine. He noted the validity of both *simultaneous* ("synchronous") and *successive* association, thus making association adequate for the explanation both of trains of thought and of the fusion of simple ideas within a complex—Wundt's view, approximately. In successive association, he argued that associations might occur between *remote* members and argued further that, the more remote the members, the weaker must be the associations, a conclusion reached experimentally by Ebbinghaus. He thought that associations in successive trains must always be *forward* and never backward.

On the physiological side, it is interesting to see that Hartley, even more than Descartes, thought naturally of some sort of *brain localization*. He spoke of "the primary seat" of a given vibration in the medullary substance, and he drew several conclusions from the manner in which separate vibrations, under certain conditions, must be spatially related in the brain. We have seen elsewhere how the question of brain localization was vehemently argued back and forth by the physiologists of the nineteenth century. When one reads the arguments against phrenology and its localizations in the early part of that century, one is apt to conclude that brain localization had never had a respectable position as a tenet of intellectual

men. It is then that one does well to go back fifty years to Hartley—
or even a hundred and fifty, to Descartes.

We have to note finally that association for Hartley, because it
can be simultaneous as well as successive, becomes clearly the basis
of mental *compounding*, and that we are thus carried one step
further toward the 'mental chemistry' of the Wundtian school.

> Upon the whole, it may appear to the reader, that simple ideas of
> sensation must run into clusters and combinations, by associations;
> and that each of these will, at last, coalesce into one complex idea,
> by the approach and commixture of the several compounding parts.
> It appears also from observation, that many intellectual ideas, such
> as those that belong to the heads of beauty, honour, moral qualities,
> *etc.*, are, in fact, thus composed of parts, which, by degrees, coalesce
> into one complex idea.

These quotations contain the key for associationism as a systematic principle. They also reveal Hartley's total program.

In the continuation of this program he first applied association
to a variety of psychological matters much simpler than morality.
He pointed out that the relation of perceived visual distance to
visual size, which Berkeley discussed, is a matter of association.
Pleasure and pain, he observed further, are habitually related to
sensations by association, and thus emotions are nothing more than
aggregates of sensations, pleasures and pains, or their ideas. Words—
and here Hartley is again building on Berkeley in the matter of
meanings which we already examined—acquired their meanings
by way of their associated ideas. Recollection is a use of association;
memory is accurate association; even imagination proceeds by association, as in dreams, though inaccurately and not in the original
form. There can be no doubt that Hartley is right in assuming that
Locke's principle of association is capable of being made into the
fundamental psychological law—as eventually it was by the Wundtians.

Hartley's further extension of the universal principle to the problems of "the moral qualities" need not concern us. It was these
matters presumably that interested Hartley most, but history is a
poor respecter of wishes. As it worked out, the important contributions of this kindly, scholarly, assured physician were something
other than what he valued most himself.

NOTES

Like the last chapter, the present one deals with philosopher-psychologists as they form the pertinent background of modern psychology in general and experimental psychology in particular. If the reader wishes a thorough knowledge of these men, he must go to their texts and to the numerous commentaries and criticisms that are in existence. There are many methods of approach. We may content ourselves with again mentioning B. Rand's bibliography in J. M. Baldwin's *Dictionary of Philosophy and Psychology*, 1905, III.

He who reads merely for psychology can follow the text with the histories of psychology: G. S. Brett, *History of Psychology*, 1921, II; O. Klemm, *History of Psychology*, Eng. trans., 1914; M. Dessoir, *Outlines of the History of Psychology*, Eng. trans., 1912; W. B. Pillsbury, *History of Psychology*, 1929; H. C. Warren, *History of the Association Psychology*, 1920. The last is the most useful for the present chapter.

A taste of the originals can be had in the reprinted psychological excerpts in B. Rand, *Classical Psychologists*, 1912, and W. Dennis, *Readings in the History of Psychology*, 1948. After reading the excerpts in these books for each author, the reader will find that the present text takes on new significance.

Berkeley

The two important works of George Berkeley are *An Essay towards a New Theory of Vision*, 1709, and *A Treatise Concerning the Principles of Human Knowledge*, 1710. There are various edited reprints. *The Works of George Berkeley*, edited by A. C. Fraser, may be especially mentioned; also C. P. Krauth's edition of the *Principles*. See Rand, Baldwin's *Dictionary*, III, 120-122; and for excerpts from the *New Theory of Vision*, see Rand, *Classical Psychologists*, 256-278.

For Berkeley, in the history of psychology, see Warren, *op. cit.*, 40-42; Brett, *op. cit.*, II, 264-270; Klemm, *op. cit.* (see index).

For Berkeley's biography and an account of his philosophy, see A. C. Fraser, *Life and Letters of George Berkeley*, 1871. See also J. S. Mill, *Three Essays on Religion*, 1874, 261-302. It is possible that the sharp contrast between Berkeley's "academico-philosophic" life (Swift's phrase) at Dublin and the busy political worldly-meticulous life of the project for an American university is to be partly explained by Berkeley's unexpectedly coming into a small fortune in 1723. When Esther Vanhomrigh, immortalized as "Vanessa" by Swift, discovered that her passion for Swift was insufficiently requited, she changed her will, making Berkeley and another her beneficiaries instead of Swift, and presently died, as the biographers put it, of a broken heart. Berkeley, it seems, had met her only once at a dinner in London with Swift; but Berkeley was in Dublin as Dean of Dromore, Swift was in Dublin as a voluntary political exile, and "Vanessa" was living near Dublin to be near Swift. This completely unexpected acquisition of wealth may have changed Berkeley from the unpopular, eccentric student-philosopher of Trinity College days to a promoter; certainly as a joint executor of "Vanessa's" will he had no end of other business detail to attend to at this time.

It was Berkeley who wrote: "Westward the course of empire takes its way"; and his belief in the decay of European civilization may have been enhanced by his experiences with the politics of the courts of Anne and the first two Georges. It is doubtful whether he had any very practicable ideas for the Bermudian university, and the congregation at Newport, Rhode Island, which received him unannounced (the pastor stopped his sermon to go to the wharf), can hardly have been more surprised by Berkeley than was Berkeley ultimately by his three years' visit to America. Berkeley,

California, was named for him and has since become the seat of a great university. Berkeley, the city, in 1860 occupied a position in the westward course of empire similar to that of Bermuda in 1728.

Berkeley's theory of the visual perception of size as dependent upon the visual perception of distance was anticipated by Nicolas de Malebranche, *Recherche de la vérité*, 1764, I, chap. 9 (various reprints and Eng. trans.). See N. Smith, Malebranche's theory of the perception of distance and magnitude, *Brit. J. Psychol.*, 1905, 1, 191-204.

The passages quoted in the text in connection with Berkeley's (context) theory of perception are from the *New Theory of Vision*, pars. 9, 10, 16-18, 45-47. The interested reader will do well to read these sections and the related text, and also pars. 50 and 51, which sum up the matter excellently. Cf. here E. B. Titchener, *Text-Book of Psychology*, 1910, 367-371; *Beginner's Psychology*, 1915, 26-30. Then compare again the latter with Berkeley, par. 46.

Hume

The full title of David Hume's chief work is *A Treatise on Human Nature being an Attempt to Introduce the Experimental Method of Reasoning into Moral Subjects* (1739-1740), but it was not an early experimental psychology. There are numerous editions. One with notes and a long expository introduction is edited by T. H. Green and T. H. Grose, 1878. For excerpts, see Rand, *Classical Psychologists*, 279-312. There are also several editions of *An Enquiry Concerning the Human Understanding*, 1748, which came out of the *Philosophical Essays*, published in the 1740s. In general, see Rand in Baldwin's *Dictionary*, III, 271-277. See also Brett, *op. cit.*, II, 270-278; Warren, *op. cit.*, 43-47.

There are several biographical accounts, including his own *Life*. A full account is J. H. Burton, *Life and Correspondence of David Hume*, 1846, 2 vols., upon which the text is based. See also T. H. Huxley, *Hume*, 1879; James Orr, *David Hume*, 1903, esp. 14-84.

Hume's philosophy is skeptical, and he also criticized the church. For both reasons, for they are only remotely the same, he was not a strong candidate for a chair of moral philosophy.

Hume's success grew, as success so often does, out of his attempt to compensate for felt inferiority. He was sensitive, self-critical, ambitious and in need of approval. If you mix those ingredients with genius you get success and fame. Hume's quarrel with Rousseau, then almost insane, for whom he found a refuge in England, and who then turned upon him with ill-grounded suspicions, illustrates both his generous nature and his emotional reaction to an affront.

When Hume is said to have attained wealth, the statement means that in his later years the income from his writings was about £1,000 per annum, a sum which meant much more then than now.

T. H. Green (*op. cit.*, 3) notes that the proper succession is from Hume (and Leibnitz) to Kant. It was Hume's *Treatise* that woke Kant from his "dogmatic slumber." In psychology, however, Hume's more immediate relationship seems to be to English empiricism and associationism; but we must not forget that he was a much greater man than these contributions alone imply.

The experiment that established the intensity of images as a fact and as comparable to the intensity of sensations, with the possibility that a given image may be more intense than a given sensation, is one by A. deV. Schaub, *Amer. J. Psychol.*, 1911, 22, 346-368. See 347-349 for a brief resumé of Hume and modern psychologists on this point. The experiment might seem unnecessary were it not for the fact that competent psychologists held the other view.

The question of a textural or qualitative difference between images and sensations is difficult. E. B. Titchener (*Text-Book of Psychology*, 1910, 198 f.) was not able, at the time he was writing, to conclude whether there is a textural difference or not. The difficulty is, of course, that we never experience merely a simple impression or a simple idea (in Hume's terms); all experience is always a matter of complex impressions and ideas, and even Hume never held that a complex idea resembles a complex impression or is a 'faint copy' of it.

The (disputed) experimental basis for the assertion that ideas of imagination are more vivid than ideas of memory is reported by C. W. Perky. *Amer. J. Psychol.*, 1910, 21, 422-452. Titchener believed her.

On Humian causality in modern science, see K. Pearson, *Grammar of Science*, 1892, chap. 4 on "Cause and Effect," and also in the later editions (1900, 1911); E. Mach, *Principien der Wärmlehre*, 1896, 430-437, the chapter on "Causalität und Erklärung," and also in the later editions (1900, 1919); *Analyse der Empfindungen*, 2 ed., 1900, and later eds., chap. 5, on causality and teleology; also Eng. trans. of the 2 ed. or later. In general, Pearson (1892) borrowed from Mach (*Analyse*, 1 ed., 1886), but in this discussion Pearson seems to have the priority. At any rate, it all goes back to Hume.

Hartley

David Hartley's book is *Observations on Man, His Frame, His Duty, and His Expectations*, 1749. The second English ed., 1791, contains the Eng. trans. of H. A. Pistorius's notes and additions to the German trans., and also a brief biography by his son (III, i-xv). Other biographical accounts are mostly drawn from this one: *e.g.*, that of G. S. Bower, *Hartley and James Mill*, 1881, 1-7, which is also inaccurate in some details.

It is not entirely irrelevant to Hartley's character to note that he studied Mrs. Stephens' remedy for the stone, becoming convinced of its efficacy, that he then persuaded Parliament to award her the large prize offered for the discovery of a cure, and that it was this remedy, consisting largely of soap, which he consumed in large quantities in an ineffectual attempt to cure himself. Dosed with this remedy, he died of the stone.

In the histories of psychology, see Brett, *op. cit.*, II, 278-286; Warren, *op. cit.*, 50-64; Th. Ribot, *English Psychology* (trans. from German, 1870), 35-43. For excerpts, see Rand, *Classical Psychologists*, 313-330, and W. Dennis, *op. cit.*, 81-92. For writings of Hartley and concerning him, see Rand in Baldwin's *Dictionary*, III, 234 f.

If Hartley is the founder of associationism, then the date is 1746 and not 1749, for the theory is contained in his *Conjecturæ quædam de motu, sensus et idearum generatione*, 1746. See Bower, *op. cit.*, 5; Rand, *Psychol. Rev.*, 1923, 30, 306-311.

On Gay's earlier use of association as a fundamental principle, see Hartley's preface to the *Observations;* also Rand, *Classical Psychologists*, 313; Early development of Hartley's doctrine of association, *Psychol. Rev.*, 1923, 30, 306-320, esp. 311-313.

For Hartley's place in the history of physiological psychology, see F. Fearing, *Reflex Action*, 1930, 83-86.

CHAPTER 11

Scottish and French Psychologies of the Eighteenth Century

With Hartley in 1749 British empiricism had developed into British associationism. Associationism was to reach its culmination with James Mill in 1829, as we shall see in the next chapter. After James Mill its extreme tenets about mental compounding were to be tempered by John Stuart Mill and others, until Wundt in the 1870s took the principle over in a more sophisticated kind of mental chemistry as one of the basic—in a sense the one basic—law of his new psychology. From Hartley to James Mill was, however, seventy years. What happened to psychology in the meantime?

There were lesser English associationists, men who wrote books which maintained the tradition and which were important at the time: Abraham Tucker (1705-1774) who published *Light of Nature Pursued* in 1768; Joseph Priestley (1733-1804), the chemist who discovered oxygen, who was also a student of Hartley, and who in 1775 published an abridged edition of Hartley's *Observations on Man* with three essays of his own appended; Archibald Alison (1757-1839) with his *Essays on the Nature and Principles of Taste* in 1790; and Erasmus Darwin (1731-1802), the poet-naturalist, the grandfather of Charles Darwin and Francis Galton, in his *Zoonomia* of 1794.

Meanwhile in Scotland *faculty psychology* was to approach *associationism* under the ministration of what is called the Scottish School. There we have Thomas Reid (1710-1796), the Presbyterian philosopher, who analyzed the mind into faculties and first raised in acute form the problem of how sensations, which exist in and of themselves, become transformed into perceptions which indicate real objects. Reid's successor was Dugald Stewart (1753-1828), who came to have more influence than Reid in both Great Britain and France. After Stewart there was Thomas Brown (1778-1820), who carried on the Scottish tradition and brought it over to associationism. It was Brown who made it clear that the principle of association, which he called "suggestion," can be used to explain the distinction between perception and sensation. On this view sensations are elementary and perceptions are both complex and meaningful, gaining their meaningfulness from their complexity. That view James Mill could use and did. It was essentially what Wundt took from associationism fifty years later to make this new system adequate as a psychology. Thus James Mill will be found to depend on the Scottish tradition as well as the English.

In France there were two movements under way at this time. One was clearly *empiricistic* and grew out of the importance which the philosophy of John Locke had acquired in France. In this connection the names of Condillac and Bonnet are most important. Condillac (1715-1780) is remembered for his intellectual empiricism and his figure of the statue which, endowed with but a single sense, nevertheless could with experience become possessed of all the chief intellectual faculties. Bonnet (1720-1793) accepted Condillac's empiricism, supplementing it with a limited amount of physiological hypothesis. These men, referring back to Descartes and Malebranche, impressed by Locke, too early to know the Scottish philosophers, did a great deal to establish an empiricism as common-sense psychology in nineteenth-century France.

The other French trend was *materialism.* Here the outstanding names are La Mettrie, who was Hartley's contemporary, and Cabanis, who made his most important contribution just after the turn of the century. La Mettrie (1709-1751) is one of the early objectivists, writing at a time when the conflict between materialism and spiritualism was acute. Cabanis (1757-1808) supported the same tradition at a time when it was less unpopular. Both men were extending to man Descartes' notion that animals are automata, and they are thus important antecedents to modern behavioristics.

In this chapter we consider the contributions of these last named seven men. Arranged in order of the dates of their principal contributions they are: La Mettrie (1748), Condillac (1754), Bonnet (1760), Reid (1764), Stewart (1792), Cabanis (1802) and Thomas Brown (1820).

In Germany this was the period of Kant (1724-1804) who rose to the height of his influence while alive in the decade after his publication of the *Critique of Pure Reason* in 1781. Kant's greatest influence was, however, posthumous, for he set his mark on German thought of the entire nineteenth century. We shall speak briefly of his relation to modern psychology in the next chapter but one.

THE SCOTTISH SCHOOL

Thomas Reid (1710-1796) was descended from a line of Presbyterian ministers. His father had the living at Strachan in Kincardineshire for fifty years. He himself graduated from Aberdeen at the age of sixteen, remained there as a librarian for ten years, then accepted the living at Newmachan near Aberdeen, until in 1752 he was appointed Professor of Philosophy in King's College, Aberdeen, after having established his reputation by publishing in 1748 an *Essay on Quantity, Occasioned by Reading a Treatise in Which Simple and Compound Ratios Are Applied to Virtue and Merit*. Reid took the position that virtue and merit will not submit to mathematical treatment.

It was the skepticism of Hume that aroused Reid to philosophic action, just as it aroused Kant twenty years later. Reid, admitting the soundness of Hume's logic, attacked his premises. It is not true, Reid insisted, that the mind knows only its own processes and can at best only dubiously infer the existence of real objects and other minds. All human experience tells against the validity of this premise. "Common sense," which is "the consent of ages and nations, of the learned and unlearned," the verdict of "the structure and grammar of all languages," gives the lie to Hume's postulate. Certainly that was good doctrine for a Presbyterian philosopher. Reid said that he would countenance no view that degrades the dignity of man, and, as we shall see in a moment, he thought that the means by which a sensation comes correctly to indicate its external object is solely the will of God. With refutation of Hume as his intent, he published his *Inquiry into the Human Mind on the Principles of Common Sense* in 1764 and was called the same year to Glasgow as Professor of Moral Philosophy, the chair that Adam Smith had just vacated.

Reid retired from Glasgow in 1781 and died in 1796. As an old man he published *Essays on the Intellectual Powers of Man* (1785) and *Essays on the Active Powers of the Human Mind* (1788). It is these books more than the *Inquiry* that have caused Reid to be classified as a faculty psychologist. You can get from them his list of twenty-four active powers of the mind (such as self-preservation, hunger, instinct of imitation, desire for power, self-esteem, gratitude, pity, duty, imagination) and the half dozen intellectual powers (like perception, judgment, memory, conception, moral taste). It was from Reid, and his disciple Stewart, that Gall originally obtained the list of twenty-seven powers of the mind which he sought, in establishing phrenology, to localize twenty-seven regions of the brain (pp.

53 f.) Gall was then in Paris, and this is only one of several ways in which Scottish philosophy influenced French psychology in the eighteenth and early nineteenth century.

It is plain that Reid's chief problem lay in the fact of perception of objects. Locke, Berkeley and Hume had established the validity of sense-qualities, but Hume had cast doubt on the existence of real objects. To Reid Hume's doubt contradicted the wisdom of the ages as found embodied in the nature of language. All mankind could not be wrong, he argued. The philosopher must, he thought, accept perception along with sensation, but the two must be distinguished.

On this matter, Reid argued, language itself is ambiguous. For instance, the smell of a rose *as sensation* is in the mind, but *as perception* it is out in the rose itself. If the rose is to be perceived as well as sensed, both the conception of it and also the instantaneous conviction of its objective existence must be added to the sensation. How does that expansion of sensation into perception come about? Not by reason, Reid averred, for the "greatest part of men," as well as infants and children, can perceive though wholly "destitute of reason." The explanation must lie in the will of the Creator: it is God in his wisdom who adds to sensation the necessary *pluses* to turn sensation into man's wisdom about the external world.

Though Reid may seem to us to have substituted his own scientific agnosticism for Hume's subjectivistic skepticism, at least he clarified and formalized the problem of objective reference by establishing the distinction between the words *sensation* and *perception*. He was not himself an associationist, but presently from 1820 to 1910 Thomas Brown, James Mill, John Stuart Mill, Wundt and Titchener were all to pick up Berkeley's principles of 1709 and to argue that patterns of sensations have objective reference (or other meanings) simply *because* they are associatively complex. That is the basic thesis of mental chemistry, of associationism.

Dugald Stewart (1753-1828), the son of Matthew Stewart, who was Professor of Mathematics at Edinburgh for twenty years, was himself Professor of Moral Philosophy at Edinburgh for thirty-five years (1785-1820). He was Reid's chief disciple, interpreter, expositor and popularizer, bearing to Reid somewhat the relation of G. F. Stout to James Ward a century later—except for the fact that Reid was more comprehensible to the laity than Ward and that Stewart spent a lifetime at this adjutant's job, whereas Stout's excursion from logic into psychology was brief. Stewart published the first volume of his *Elements of the Philosophy of the Human Mind* in 1792, the second in 1814 (shortly before the sixth edition of the first volume), and the third in 1827. There were many editions and the first collected works appeared in 1829, the year after Stewart's death.

Dugald Stewart added to Reid's philosophy nothing that is important for us. He lectured at Edinburgh in the days when the popularization of culture was being regarded by the Scots as important, lectured to classrooms filled with lay listeners, business men, lawyers and other professional persons seeking to broaden their minds. It was easy for him to popularize Reid's doctrine of faculties. Men have always accepted readily such contentions as that imitation is explained by referring it to an instinct of imitation, or a good memory depends on having a good faculty of memory. Such naming is word magic, but it is in part what Stewart gave the intellectual public of Edinburgh. It is also what Gall in Paris and Gall's successors picked up from both Reid and Stewart for their new phrenology.

Thomas Brown (1778-1820) grew up in Edinburgh. At the age of twenty he published a competent criticism of Erasmus Darwin's *Zoonomia*. He studied for and took an M.D. degree. When twenty-six years old he ventured, in support of Sir John Leslie's appointment at the University, to defend against orthodox opinion Hume's doctrine of cause and effect. Brown soon became a disciple of Dugald Stewart, albeit a critical disciple. Stewart, twenty-five years his senior, liked Brown and encouraged him. Later, in 1810, when Stewart's health was beginning to fail, Stewart got Brown appointed as his coadjutant. For ten years they seem both to have used the title Professor of Moral Philosophy, but Brown did all the work. Brown was a brilliant and prodigious worker. He got up nearly all of the lectures in his course in his first two years, the lectures that were later published in what was practically their original form. As this partnership continued, Stewart's enthusiasm cooled when Brown proved ready, as it appeared, to compromise with associationism. After ten years of this partnership Brown died, in 1820, and Stewart was obliged to retire from the chair. Brown's lectures were published posthumously, immediately after his death, as *Lectures on the Philosophy of the Human Mind* (1820).

By this time, the Scottish dislike of Hume's skepticism, born of Scottish religious orthodoxy, was becoming transformed into a general dislike of associationism, an objection to its being analytical and atomistic and to its seeming to contradict the orthodox conception of the unity of the soul. On this issue Brown compromised. He needed some principle like association to account for the way in which mind proceeds about its business. So he called the principle *suggestion*, which smacked less of artificial compounding and sounded more like the familiar process by which thought leads on to thought.

For the solution of the problem of objective reference in perception—Reid's basic problem—Brown appealed to muscular sensation. While Charles Bell has been said to have 'founded' the muscle sense in 1826, it is true that sensitivity of muscles and the organs of bodily movement had long been recognized and but recently emphasized by Steinbuch in 1811 and Bichat in 1812. Brown argued that it is the felt resistance of muscular exertion which gives us the belief in real external objects. The smell of Reid's rose is at first pure sensation, but, as soon as we have found that there is something there that it requires muscular effort to move, then the sensed rose begins to suggest resistance. By such suggestion it is turned into the perception of a real object. There is so little distinction between Berkeley's use of association to create the belief in external objects and Brown's use of suggestion for the same purpose, that it is no wonder Dugald Stewart's enthusiasm for Thomas Brown cooled; but this loss to Scottish orthodoxy turned out to be psychology's gain. Brown's philosophy in this way came to reinforce associationistic empiricism; and Brown to the modern reader, it must be said, seems to belong more with Berkeley, Lotze and Wundt than with Reid and Stewart.

Not only does Brown's theory of perception, like Berkeley's, sound much like an early form of Titchener's context theory of perception (pp. 415 ff.), though without Titchener's caveat that familiar perceptions have no conscious context, but Brown's theory of space perception, with its appeal to muscular sensation as the stuff that gives the perception unity and significance, is a direct antecedent of Lotze's and Wundt's empiristic theories of space (pp. 266 ff.).

We must also note that Brown, while avoiding the term *association*, advanced the doctrine of association. He was the first person to consider in detail the secondary laws of association. Both before and immediately after him the associationists—Berkeley, Hume, James Mill, John Stuart Mill—dealt almost exclusively with the general laws of association but not with particular ones. They said what sorts of relationships lead to associatedness, but not why one particular idea is aroused instead of another when either might be. Brown appealed to such differentiae as the relative duration of the original sensations, their relative liveliness, their relative frequency, their relative recency, the reinforcement of one by many other ideas, as well as differences in the habits and natures of individuals.

From Brown the line of associationism passes directly to James

Mill, but we must reserve the Mills for the next chapter and move over to the Continent to note what effect Locke and Hume were having on French eighteenth-century psychology. Reid's influence in France was pretty much reserved for the nineteenth century.

FRENCH EMPIRICISM

The intellectual relations between France and Great Britain were ancient and many. The French culture was, however, older and the French tended to look down on both the Scots and the English. Away back before there were any Scottish universities—St. Andrews, the first in Scotland, was founded in 1411—the young Scot used to go to France for his advanced education, because the journey by sea was safer than the land journey to Oxford, because he would be treated more civilly by the Parisians than by the Oxonians, and because geography did not matter in university education when Latin was the common academic tongue. Scotland continued to be an importer of culture from France, not an exporter, until the nineteenth century when Reid's faculty psychology became one of the media of French reaction against the materialistic philosophy which was so strong in the eighteenth century.

Before that time, however, the French had come to accept Locke's empiricism. At the end of the seventeenth century the French were thinking that the English were boors. They had murdered their King and had supported a revolution. Revolution for the French was still far away. It was the satirical Voltaire, briefly exiled by an offended government and in England (1726-1729), who returned to France to attack the established French modes by his brilliant promotion of English culture. The French then began to take account of English thought, and it was in this atmosphere that the Abbé de Condillac discovered John Locke.

Étienne Bonnot de Condillac (1715-1780) was a French ecclesiastic and intellectual, a friend of Diderot and later of Rousseau. He undertook—ultimately with great success—to introduce the philosophy of Locke to France, and he thus stands in the history of French philosophy for sensationism and empiricism. He stood out against Descartes' innate ideas, against Malebranche's faculties, against Leibnitz's monads. He wrote with brevity, clarity and tolerance a rigorously logical exposition in the best French literary vein and his reward was the great influence that his name carried in French thinking for fifty years.

His first publication of importance, *Essai sur l'origine des connoissances humaines* (1746), was mostly a presentation of Locke's views, coupled with the assurance that Locke was right in saying that ideas arise from sensation, but with less certainty that they arise from sensation's twin, reflection. Locke had made reflection the means by which the mind is aware of its own processes and thus the equal in experience to sensation. Condillac's *Traité des Systèmes* (1749) is his attack on Descartes and the other older philosophers and his defense of Locke against them. His most important work is his *Traité des sensations* (1754) in which he used the famous figure of the sentient statue to show how analytical empiricism works out.

Actually Condillac did away with Locke's reflections as well as with Descartes' innate ideas. He decided that neither were necessary. The whole mental life, he held, can be derived in experience from sensation alone. Imagine a statue, he argued, endowed with but a single sense. Let us suppose that sense to be smell, which is perhaps the simplest of the five senses. The statue smells a rose, or rather the statue is, for the time being, a rose, since there is nothing else to its existence than this odor. Thus it may be said to be attending to the odor and we see how attention comes into mental life. The first odor goes and another comes. Then the first returns and the statue knows that what was can come again. That is memory. When what was recurs with what is, the statue may be said to be comparing. One odor is pleasant, another unpleasant. Thus in the inherent values of the odors the statue learns of desire and aversion. In similar fashion judgment, discernment, imagination and all sorts of abstract notions were represented by Condillac as possible of development in experience with only a single sense as the medium. Later the addition of other senses would still further enhance the statue's capacities. Such was Condillac's empiricism.

This cold analytical procedure appealed to the French of the eighteenth century. It was not inconsistent with the Abbé de Condillac's religious views, and it complemented satisfactorily the materialism then also popular, the materialism which La Mettrie was offering psychology, as we shall see presently. Condillac's sensational empiricism finally failed because, so its modern critics believe, it was too simple. In the first place, it may be said that it is never possible to reduce the mind to sensory experience alone. The mind must contribute its own categories to constitute the subjective whole: Descartes' innate ideas, Locke's reflections, Kant's categories and intuitions, something. In endowing the statue with a sense, Condillac was giving it unwittingly a whole set of properties. In the second place, we may note here that simple analysis of this sort has never worked. The nineteenth-century French felt that it was too cold;

by then they wanted statues with more warmth, like live people. In the twentieth century we say that psychology cannot ignore the whole man and that analysis without synthesis fails.

Almost at once Condillac's views received much support and some criticism and modification from the Swiss naturalist and philosopher, *Charles Bonnet* (1720-1793). Bonnet is perhaps best known for his study of the behavior of insects and other lower animal forms and he published a *Traité d'insectologie* in 1745. For us his important book is his *Essai analytique sur les facultés de l'âme*, which appeared in 1760, six years after Condillac's treatise.

Bonnet, for the most part, repeated Condillac, using again the parable of the sentient statue. The differences between Condillac and Bonnet were two.

Condillac had avoided physiology. The biologically minded Bonnet introduced it. His statue had nerves and you hear a great deal about the nervous fluid and the agitation of the nervous fibers, discussion which resembles Hartley's speculation about vibrations and diminutive vibrations. It has even been said that Bonnet is one of those who anticipated the doctrine of specific nerve energies because he wrote: "Every sense is probably limited to different specific fibers." He also remarked: "The Intelligence which could have read the brain of Homer would have seen in it the *Iliad* represented by the varied play of a million fibers."

Bonnet's other deviation from Condillac lay in Bonnet's ascription of activity to the soul. Condillac had tried to get along with a mere *tabula rasa* for a soul, letting sensations write upon it as they came, one after the other. Bonnet was perhaps the first admirer of Condillac's to note this defect in his system.

There is no doubt that the existence of this French empiricism strengthened the hands of the English associationists of the nineteenth century—the Mills, Bain and Spencer. The tradition of Locke thus came back to England from both Scotland and France.

FRENCH MATERIALISM

While Scotland was reacting against Hume's skepticism and moving toward religious orthodoxy, France was shifting toward materialism away from Descartes' preservation of the soul as the unextended substance of his dualism. Animals, he said, are automata like the moving statues in the royal gardens which appear or disappear when the visitor provides the stimulus by stepping on a concealed plate; but man is automatic only in his bodily constitution. His body interacts with his soul, affecting it or being controlled by it

Descartes, profoundly religious, was set to protect the integrity of the soul; yet his conception of the mechanics of animals was symptomatic of the new learning and in itself provided a basis for the movement away from spiritualism toward materialism.

It was, however, and quite inevitably, the progress of science that, as it came in with the new learning, favored materialistic philosophy. Science of necessity tends toward mechanism and so away from animism, for science seeks a clarification of the understanding of the universe by finding unity in it. Science is thus naturally monistic, not dualistic, and its logic and techniques are adapted to defining mechanisms for the body but not animisms for the soul.

Thus you found Descartes before 1650 thinking of the muscles as contracting because the animal spirits inflate them, and of the animal spirits as "a very quick wind," "a very active and pure fire," as if they resembled the unextended substance of the soul in being nearly incorporeal. In 1669 Huygens referred to the animal spirits as a *vis viva*, a term also applied to what physics later called *kinetic energy*. In 1677 Glisson had demonstrated muscular irritability and the fact that a contracting muscle does not swell up and occupy more space. In 1680 Borelli was calling the animal spirits the *succus nerveus*, a more material term. By 1708 Hermann Boerhaave (1668-1738), the famous Dutch physiologist of Leyden, was seeking some still more substantial mechanism for explaining animal motion. Boerhaave influenced La Mettrie, as we shall see in a moment. All this thought and work was leading naturally up to Robert Whytt's pioneer studies of reflex action in 1751. At the same time Albrecht von Haller (1708-1777), the Swiss, was preparing physiology for its introduction to the world as a separate and important science in the eight volumes of his *Elementa physiologiae corporis humani* (1757-1766). It was in this atmosphere of change and under the direct influence of Boerhaave and Haller, that La Mettrie turned materialist in the 1740s.

Julien Offray de La Mettrie (1709-1751) as a youth studied theology, becoming a Jansenist, a member of a sect within the Roman Church which followed St. Augustine and which believed in predestination. Thus, even as a theologian, he was becoming a determinist. When a friend presently advised him that he could gain a better living as a physician than as a priest, he turned to the study of natural philosophy and medicine, and at the age of fifteen received his doctor's degree and began to practice as a physician in Rheims. When he was twenty-three he went to Leyden to study with the great Boerhaave. In 1734, at the end of his first year in Leyden, he published a translation of Boerhaave's *Aphrodisiacus*, adding to it a treatise by himself on venereal disease. This youthful presumption excited the jealousy and consequent anger of the medical profession, who protested. La Mettrie countered with another original treatise, this time on vertigo (1736). Criticism of him thus became still more violent, and presently he was forced to retreat into publishing only translations.

In 1742 La Mettrie returned to Paris and obtained there a commission as physician of the guards under the Duc de Gramont, whom he accompanied to war. The Duke was killed in the siege of Freiburg and La Mettrie fell very ill with a fever. It was during this fever and his realization that his mental powers were diminished along with his physical powers that the conviction came to him with the force of a conversion that thought is after all nothing but the result of the mechanical action of the brain and the nervous system. He never lost this compelling faith. He was a man of strong impulses, prone to act against convention. Being unable to distinguish between thought and the soul, his new belief meant to him that the soul is as mortal as the brain and that man is but a machine—as much so as Descartes believed the animals to be. La Mettrie took a couple of years to mature this thought and then published *L'histoire naturelle de l'âme* in 1745, putting forward a mechanistic conception of the soul and a materialistic philosophy of life. Had *l'âme* not meant both *soul* and *mind*, he might have defended himself by this distinction; yet La Mettrie was not built for compromise. There was an outcry against him and his materialism, and he was forced to retire again to Leyden the next year. There, in 1748, he published his more mature book on the same theme, *L'homme machine*, the volume which gives him a place in the history of behavioristics. There was, however, criticism of La Mettrie in Holland as well as in France. In February 1748—it is not clear whether *L'homme machine* had already appeared—Frederick the Great, on more occasions than one the champion of freedom of thought, rescued La Mettrie with appointment as Court Reader in Berlin.

In these later years La Mettrie developed his doctrine of hedonism. the conception that pleasure is the end of life and that all motivation is selfish. He wrote various treatises, *L'art de jouir ou l'école de volupté* and *Vénus métaphysique*, which appeared in 1751 and are to be found in La Mettrie's *Oeuvres philosophiques*, which he dedicated to Haller. He died at the end of 1751 when only forty-one years old— from indiscreet eating according to one biographer but not according to Frederick the Great, who wrote a eulogy for La Mettrie.

La Mettrie was not a mature and seasoned philosopher. He accepted the consequences of a conviction with adolescent assurance and went through to the logical consequences of his assumptions, stimulated by opposition and criticism to greater positiveness. The *obiter dicta* of *L'homme machine* do not concern us. La Mettrie is important because, taking an extreme position, he became a signpost for a trend—the trend toward materialism away from spiritualism, the trend toward the mechanistic and physiological interpretation of the mind. In this way he was both effect and cause, both representing and promoting the *Zeitgeist* of scientific materialism. He fitted in with the empiricism that Condillac was getting from Locke, for Condillac's educable statue was possessed of but little more soul than La Mettrie's machine man. The difference was that Condillac left the soul out of his psychological considerations, whereas La Mettrie insisted on enslaving it to mechanical law. His vigorous insistence thus makes him the first thorough-going 'objective psychologist' whom we have had occasion to consider in this book.

La Mettrie's urging the French of the middle eighteenth century on toward materialism, mechanism and hedonism shows that trend clearly enough. We can afford merely to mention *Claude Adrien Helvétius* (1715-1771) who became famous for ideas similar to La Mettrie's which he published in *De l'esprit* in 1758. Helvétius wrote mediocre poetry and poor mathematics but pretty good philosophy. As farmer-general of the state he had a good income which he resigned as soon as he felt that he had enough money to enable him to retire to live the life of a philosopher. His social ideals were so high and his generosity so great that it seems odd that his *De l'esprit* should have caused such an outcry against him as a materialist. He followed Condillac in favoring sensationism, viewing the dynamics of man hedonistically, but without La Mettrie's atheistic fervor. Helvétius is usually placed in the history of utilitarianism, and we might regard him as an early dynamic psychologist. His book was, however, condemned, publicly burned by the hangman and consequently, as happens when censorship is exercised, widely read throughout France. Thus his significance in the history of psychology is similar to La Mettrie's.

In a sense the French psychology of the eighteenth century culminated in the contribution of *Pierre Jean George Cabanis* (1757-1808), who is sometimes called the founder of physiological psychology by those who do not give this title to Descartes. As a youth Cabanis, inattentive to formal schooling and unsuccessful at it, was sent by his father to Paris and told to look after himself. He seems to have done pretty well, for, in the midst of a discursive adolescent life, he acquired an excellent acquaintance with the writings of many important authors—Homer, Cicero, Augustine, Locke, Descartes, Goethe and the Gray who wrote the *Elegy*. He was prepared later to become a philosopher, but actually at the age of twenty-one he decided to settle down to the study of medicine, adding Hippocrates and Galen to his reading and presently beginning to lecture on the history and practice of medicine.

That went on until the Revolution. Then it was Cabanis who in 1789 brought the news of the fall of the Bastille to the Council and Mirabeau. Mirabeau liked Cabanis then and took him first as his personal physician and presently as his intimate friend. It was two years later that Mirabeau died in Cabanis' arms. Thus it happened Cabanis fitted himself into the Revolution, becoming a member of the legislative Committee of Five Hundred and presently being appointed professor of hygiene at Paris in 1795 and professor of legal medicine and the history of medicine in 1799. His important ideas began to form when he was asked in 1795 to determine whether the victims of the guillotine were conscious after beheading. He concluded that they are not, that consciousness is the highest level of mental organization and is dependent on the functioning of the brain, which may be regarded as the organ of consciousness, just as the stomach is an organ of digestion or the liver an organ for filtering the bile. If a man's body twitches after his execution, the movement, separated from the brain, is unconscious and at the level of instinct. Cabanis collected his papers on these matters in his most important work. *Rapports du physique et du moral de l'homme*, which was published in 1802. When Napoleon came to power, Cabanis found himself out of favor. He died in 1808.

Cabanis accepted La Mettrie's mechanism, which held that the brain is the organ of thought, without accepting his materialism in religious matters. He rejected Descartes' notion that the soul is independent of the body, even though the two interact. There was still in the early nineteenth century a belief in "incorporeal mental states" which had no dependence on the body. Ecstasy was thought to be one, but Cabanis was against this thesis. In general, he accepted Locke and Condillac, but he added to Condillac's simple analysis the unifying principle of developmental levels. He distinguished between unconscious instincts, semiconscious states, and the wholly conscious states which depend on the action of the brain. He also noted developmental levels in the mind of the individual as he grows up. He used more clinical observation to support his theses than had theorists like La Mettrie. He emphasized especially the importance of the bodily sensations, regarding them as essential in the development of experience. Condillac's statue, he thought, could hardly have begun its mental life with smell alone. It needed awareness of its own body in order to get a start on unifying the experience that was to come to it.

Descartes. Condillac. La Mettrie. Cabanis. There we have the setting for French psychology of the nineteenth century and the early twentieth. It was a physiological psychology—not in the formal systematic sense that Wundt meant when he gave that name to the new experimental psychology, but in the practical sense of its being founded on physiologists' facts and being medically informed. The German psychology was physiological in name, the French in fact. Thus the name of Charcot, the great clinical psychologist of the latter half of the nineteenth century, stands out above all others of this period. Later, Ribot was to write on abnormal psychology and Binet to study the development of intelligence. As science progressed and speculation without factual basis became unacceptable, the French settled down to a clinical psychology. They are said to be 'a practical people.'

NOTES

On the lesser English associationists—Tucker, Priestley, Alison and Erasmus Darwin—see H. C. Warren, *A History of Association Psychology,* 1921, 60-69.

Scottish School

In general, see James McCosh, *The Scottish Philosophy,* 1875, a book by an enthusiastic Scot, Princeton's president and a dissenter from the associational analysis of the mind, who discusses happily the views of fifty philosophers in this school.

Thomas Reid's three chief works are cited in the text. In general, see his *Works,* which reprints all these volumes. The 1 ed. of the *Works* is dated 1804, and it and later eds. begin with Dugald Stewart's Life and writings of Reid, *ca.* 35 pp. In addition the 1846 and later eds. contain a couple of hundred pages of Preface, notes and supplementary dissertations, by Sir Wm. Hamilton, who provides a very sophisticated level of criticism. There are many eds. of all the books, and

many criticisms and some more biography, all of which are cited by B. Rand, in J. M. Baldwin's *Dictionary of Philosophy and Psychology,* 1905, III, 435 f. For excerpts from the *Intellectual Powers of Man*, the sensation-perception problem, see B. Rand, *Classical Psychologists,* 1912, 361-373. See also G. S. Brett, *History of Psychology,* 1921, III, 14-16.

The three volumes of Dugald Stewart's chief work are cited in the text. In general see his *Works,* 7 vols., 1829, or better his *Collected Works,* 10 vols. plus a Supplement, 1854-60, edited by Sir Wm. Hamilton. Vol. 10, 1858, 243-324, is a Life of D. Stewart, by John Veitch.

On the relation of Reid's and Stewart's powers of the mind to Gall's list of faculties for phrenology, see H. D. Spoerl, Faculties vs. traits: Gall's solution, *Character & Pers.,* 1936, 4, 216-231.

Thomas Brown's chief work is his *Lectures on the Philosophy of the Human Mind,* 1820, 4 vols.; 20 ed.,

1860. The best life is D. Welsh, *Accounts of the Life and Writings of Thomas Brown*, 1825, which is also reprinted in vol. I of the 8 ed. of the *Lectures*, 1834, and later eds. Rand, *Classical Psychologists*, 374-394, reprints three excerpts from the *Lectures* on muscular sensations, space perception and simple relative suggestion. W. Dennis, *Readings in the History of Psychology*, 1948, 125-128, reprints Brown on the secondary laws of learning. For Brown's other writings and for a score of articles or chapters about him, see Rand in Baldwin's *Dictionary* (*op. cit.*), III, 131 f.

On Brown see also H. C. Warren, *A History of Association Psychology*, 1921, 70-80; G. Murphy, *Historical Introduction to Modern Psychology*, 2 ed., 1949, 59-63.

On the place of the Scottish School in the history of the concept of perception, see E. G. Boring, *Sensation and Perception in the History of Experimental Psychology*, 1942, 13-19.

French Empiricism

E. B. de Condillac's three important psychological books are cited in the text. His *Traité des sensations*, 1754, has an Eng trans., 1930. See his *Œuvres complètes*, 23 vols. in the 1798 ed., and so on up to the 16 vols. of the 1821-22 ed. Excerpts are in B. Rand, *Classical Psychologists*, 1912, 340-360. See also Rand in J. M. Baldwin's *Dictionary of Philosophy and Psychology*, 1905, III, 156 f., for the list of his works and their editions and a score of articles about him. The most important book about him from the point of view of the text is L. Dewaule, *Condillac et la psychologie anglaise contemporaine*, 1892. See also G. S. Brett, *History of Psychology*, 1921, II, 290-295; H. C. Warren, *History of Association Psychology*, 1921, 181-186; G. Murphy, *Historical Introduction to Modern Psychology*, 2 ed., 1949, 36-38. Brett, p. 291, notes that the parable of the sentient statue which learns was probably not original with Condillac.

Charles Bonnet's *Essai analytique sur*

les facultés de l'âme, 1760, is reprinted in his *Œuvres d'histoire naturelle et de philosophie*, 18 vols., 1779-1788. For excerpts, see Rand, *Classical Psychologists*, 331-340. For bibliography, see Rand in Baldwin's *Dictionary*, 128 f. For life and works. see A. Lemoine, *Charles Bonnet de Genève, philosophe et naturaliste*, 1850; M. Offner, *Die psychologie Charles Bonnets*, 1893; E. Claparède, *La psychologie animale de Charles Bonnet*, 1909 (life, 11-25); G. Bonnet, *Charles Bonnet (1720-1793)*, 1929. See also Brett, *op. cit.*, II, 297-300; Warren, *op. cit.*, 186-189.

Since this book slights the history of French psychology which is more important in the abnormal than in the experimental field, we do well to mention here a few names which the text omits.

The background for Condillac's and Bonnet's contributions was Cartesian philosophy—the philosophy of Descartes, Malebranche, Spinoza and lesser men. One of the lesser men was Marin Cureau de La Chambre (1594-1669), who wrote his *Système de l'âme* in 1664. La Chambre was actually two years older than Descartes, though he published his important volume long after Descartes' death. In it he had a conception of "l'union et liaison des images" which has caused him to be regarded as an anticipator of Locke in respect of associationism. A much more important anticipator of Condillac is Nicolas Malebranche (1638-1715), a Cartesian and a contemporary of Locke's, who published his *Recherche de la vérité* in 1674, long before Locke's *Essay*. Malebranche also had what is regarded as a doctrine of association. He met Berkeley—indeed his death is said to have been hastened by the choler brought on in a metaphysical argument with Berkeley.

The next section considers the materialism of La Mettrie and Cabanis. Helvétius belongs there with La Mettrie, although he was also influenced by Condillac, as were all French psychologists of the latter eighteenth century. At the start of the nineteenth century, besides Cabanis, there was Maine de Biran.

François Pierre Gonthier Maine de Biran (1766-1824), a contemporary of Dugald Stewart's, Thomas Brown's and Cabanis', was a French noble who, being imprisoned for a year by the Revolution, spent his time in studying Locke and Condillac. He published *Essai sur les fondements de la psychologie* in 1812. He made the criticism of Condillac that Bonnet had made, that the mere sequence of sensations is not enough to generate mind, that there must in addition to sensory experience be some contribution by the mind itself. Biran thought that the contribution might be described as the developmental capacity of the mind.

In general, on the French psychology of this period, see M. Dessoir, *Outlines of the History of Psychology*, trans. 1912, 221-230; Warren, *op. cit.*, 181-200.

French Materialism

J. O. de La Mettrie's *L'homme machine*, 1748, had a 2 ed. and an Eng. trans. of it in 1750. The 1912 Eng. trans. contains the Eulogy of La Mettrie by Frederick the Great. For La Mettrie's bibliography and articles about him, see Rand in Baldwin's *Dictionary* (*op. cit.*), 327 f. See also Brett, *op. cit.*, II, 358 f.; J. P. Damiron, *Mémoires pour servir a l'histoire de la philosophie au XVIIIe siècle*, 1858, I, 1-92 (pp. 1-14 are a Life of La Mettrie); and, for his place in the history of physiological psychology, F. Fearing, *Reflex Action*, 1930, 88 f. He is, of course, one of the first mechanists.

P. J. G. Cabanis' *Rapports du physique et du moral de l'homme*, 1802, had a 2 ed. in 1805, a "new" ed. of 3 vols. with a short Life in 1824, an 8 ed. with a long Life (pp. vii-lxviii) by L. Piesse in 1844. For six articles about Cabanis, for his other publications and his *Oeuvres* (in which the *Rapports* are called *Traité*), see Rand in Baldwin's *Dictionary* (*op. cit.*), 137 f. See also Brett, *op. cit.*, 375-382; G. Murphy, *Historical Introduction to Modern Psychology*, 2 ed., 1949, 38 f.

CHAPTER 12

British Associationism: the Mills and Bain

The nineteenth century saw the culmination of associationism in James Mill and its modification from a mental mechanics to a mental chemistry by John Stuart Mill. It saw associationism made over by Bain into the system that was to become the substructure for the new physiological psychology, and it saw the new theory of evolution first brought to bear upon psychology by another associationist, Herbert Spencer. It also saw Wundt use association as the basic principle in his new system of psychology, the system that he built both to guide and to justify the new experimental psychology—but that belongs in a later chapter.

JAMES MILL

In James Mill (1773-1836), associationism as a principle of mechanical compounding reached its climax. He may be said to stand for a 'mental compounding,' just as his son, John Stuart Mill, represents 'mental chemistry.' The two Mills and Bain brought philosophical psychology to the point where scientific psychology could take it over.

Like his English predecessors whom we have studied in the last two chapters but one, James Mill was not a professional philosopher or psychologist. He was primarily interested in history and the theory of government, but he published in 1829 an important book, the *Analysis of the Phenomena of the Human Mind*, which, although second in importance to his history of British India, played a highly significant rôle in the history of psychology.

James Mill was a Scot by birth, and at about eighteen years of age came under the favorable notice of Sir John Stuart, whose wife arranged that Mill should receive a benefaction that enabled him to go to the University of Edinburgh. At this time Mill was 'destined for the church,' as the phrase was, and he prepared himself in theology, philosophy and the classics, improving his insufficient income by tutoring. In philosophy he sat under the inspiring lecturer Dugald Stewart. He was licensed as a preacher in 1798, but he was not successful for the excellent reason that the congregations that he addressed could not understand what he was saying. Faced with failure and being forced to live in penurious circumstances, he finally gave up tutoring and sporadic preaching, and in 1802 went up to London in company with Sir John Stuart, then a member of Parliament.

In London he began a seventeen-year period in which writing and journalistic work were his sole source of revenue. He married in 1805 a young woman whose face was her fortune—an investment, so some biographers think, that was less happy than would have been an interest in philosophy and government. John Stuart Mill, namesake of James Mill's friend and patron, was born in 1806, and three brothers and five sisters followed him. James Mill's income was precarious and he had to use it to assist his father and sister as well as to support this large family. His natural disposition to be stern, uncompromising and at times petulant was not softened by these circumstances, nor by his wife's disappointment in the outcome of her marriage. However, he exhibited withal an amazing vigor. Several volumes of the *History of India*, incited in its writing by his pecuniary need, he composed at one end of a table, while John Stuart Mill went to school to his father at the other, learning among other things Greek and, in the absence of dictionaries, interrupting his father for the meaning of every new word! Such circumstances must have called for an unyielding nature.

James Mill's editorial connections were numerous, as were also the magazines to which he constantly contributed. The *Edinburgh Review* is the best known; his contributions to the *Westminster Review* are of a later date. His ten articles on government for the *Encyclopædia Britannica* were so important that they were later reprinted together. The *History of India*, begun in 1806, was finally published in 1817, and produced a change in his fortunes. It was an immediate success, and in 1819 he received, largely on its account, an appointment to the East India Company—a commercial post then not dissimilar to a government diplomatic position. He began at £800, but at the time of his death seventeen years later his annual stipend had increased to £2,000, a large salary for an academic man in those days.

Unlike the *History of India*, the *Analysis of the Human Mind* was not a response to financial need. It was the work of six summer vacations. Mill began it in 1822, and it was finally published in 1829. In it we have to do, therefore, with the single psychological work of an important man of unusual intellectual vigor, who published it at the age of fifty-six and who died seven years later (1836).

Of the twenty-five chapters that the two volumes of this work contain, only the first three need concern us seriously. James Mill followed Hartley (and Hume with a change of words) in making *sensations* and *ideas* the fundamental classes of elements, and the first two chapters deal respectively with these elements. The third chapter is all-important, for it is on the association of ideas. The remaining twenty-two chapters deal with consciousness, conception, imagination, classification, abstraction, memory, belief, ratiocination, evidence, reflection, pleasure, pain, will, intention and kindred topics. The list is worth giving because it shows how the scope of psychology was becoming fixed in convention, and some such convention we still have with us. For a long time after the establishment of experimental physiological psychology, systematic psychologists would lay down premises that more or less committed them to a sensationistic psychology; and yet, when these same men came to write their systematic works, they were never content to write as if psychology were nothing more than what their premises had yielded; they always responded to conventional pressure by an effort to deal in some fashion with some of these 'higher mental faculties.' It seemed that almost everybody knew what psychology was about, though no one knew what it was. Such a state of affairs can be explained only historically, and the list of James Mill's chapters serves to make the point, although it could have been made equally well in connection with any of his predecessors or with his successor, Bain.

We have seen in the preceding chapter that the distinction between sensation and perception had been coming, at the time of James Mill, to be more and more clearly made. Sensation was held to be primary and perception to be derived from it. In systematic classification one must, it was argued, begin with sensation, and hence psychology was thrown back to Aristotle's division of the senses into five for its fundamental principle of classification. Berkeley, for example, could argue that form is not a sensation and that the visual and tactual perceptions of a sphere have, since they belong to different senses, nothing in common. There is no sensation of sphericity. This point is clear in Berkeley, who made the differences of sensible qualities primary, and in Hume, who held that differences of sensory mode are elemental. As we have already noted, such a view was the natural outcome of empiricism.

In a 'mental chemistry,' however, it is important to know the number of elements; and, in accounting for complex phenomena, the more elements there are the better. Aristotle himself had hedged on the question of touch; it was for him a single sense, but nevertheless more complex than the others. Consequently we had during the nineteenth century a search for more mental elements and, in particular, a search for more sense-departments; and the new senses that have been 'discovered' have always come out of Aristotle's complex sense of touch, which, as we already know, at one time during this century had its complexity covered by the broad term *Gemeingefühl*.

James Mill's chapter on *sensation* shows this tendency when it was first becoming explicit. He subscribed to eight senses: Aristotle's five including touch, muscular sensations (which Thomas Brown and Charles Bell had also just added to the list as a sixth sense), sensations of disorganization in any part of the body (which, including itching and tickling, resembled E. H. Weber's later *Gemeingefühl*), and sensations in the alimentary canal (which we now know make up the larger part of the sensations of internal origin). What Mill said about these senses does not matter. It is enough to see that he felt the empiricist's need for making sensation primary and the associationist's need for finding as many different elements as possible to enter into association. When psychology gave up the primacy of objects, denying that there are simple sensations of a *man* or of a *chair*, it had before it the positive task of making a very few elements account for all of the tremendous complexity of mental life.

For James Mill sensations were one of the "primary states of consciousness"; *ideas* were the other. Here he followed Hartley and Hume, although he did not, like Hume, place himself in the difficult position of maintaining that ideas are weaker than sensations. An idea for him was simply a copy of a sensation, though ordinarily distinguishable from it. The two are enough alike, he thought, sometimes to be confused. They differ, in spite of resemblance, in fundamental nature—in the fact that an idea never occurs unless its sensation has previously occurred and in the further fact that the law of association applies to ideas but not to sensations. The word *image* had not yet come into a technical meaning, but Mill used it as he used *copy*.

> After I have seen the sun, and by shutting my eyes see him no longer, I can still think of him. I still have a feeling, the consequence of the sensation, which, though I can distinguish it from the sensation, is yet more like the sensation than anything else can be; so like, that I call it a copy, an image, of the sensation, sometimes a representation or trace of the sensation.

James Mill's chapter on the *association of ideas* is classic because it represents at its culmination both the full power of associationism and its defects. One might read the chapter today either to understand how comprehensive and fundamental this principle of association can be or, on the other hand, to exhibit the impossibilities to which this very universality leads.

Mill began by pointing out that the nature of consciousness itself is associative.

> Thought follows thought; idea follows idea, incessantly. If our senses are awake, we are continually receiving sensations, . . . but not sensations alone. After sensations, ideas are perpetually excited of sensations formerly received; after those ideas, other ideas; and during the whole of our lives, a series of those two states of consciousness, called sensations, and ideas, is constantly going on. I see a horse: that is a sensation. Immediately I think of his master: that is an idea. The idea of his master makes me think of his office; he is a minister of state: that is another idea. The idea of a minister of state makes me think of public affairs; and I am led into a train of political ideas; when I am summoned to dinner. This is a new sensation. . . .

And thus the process continues throughout all waking life. This picture agrees essentially with the popular notion of association today. We have only to note in criticism that Mill, when he actually came to the discussion of association, illustrated his points by the use of objects rather than by the use of sensible qualities. *Seeing the horse* was, for Mill, a sensation; *thinking of his master* was an idea. It is this reversion to Lockian terms that opens the way for Mill to progress to his comprehensive theory of compounding, as we shall see presently.

The law of association does not (we are again following Mill) operate upon sensations. In a manner of speaking sensations are associated, but only because the nature of objects is such that certain sensations concur or habitually concur. They are found 'in association,' but the law is the law of objects as the producers of sensations, and this relationship is not at all what is meant by *association*. These concurrences are, however, very important, especially those that are often repeated. They may be, of course, either synchronous or successive, and the successive, Mill thought, are more frequent than the synchronous.

Out of these concurrences of sensations, concurrences depending upon the laws of objects, the law of the association of ideas arises.

> Our ideas spring up, or exist, in the order in which the sensations existed, of which they are the copies. This is the general law of the "Association of Ideas": by which term, let it be remembered, nothing is here meant to be expressed, but the order of occurrence.

Association is, therefore, not a power, nor a force, nor a cause; it is simply a matter of concurrence or contiguity. Sensory contiguities are copied in ideational contiguities.

Mill expressly denied the validity of two of Hume's three laws of association. Cause and effect Hume himself had reduced to priority and frequency—that is to say, to contiguity. Resemblance, Mill thought, is not effective except when the similar terms have been often together—as indeed they so often are. Contiguity is thus the only principle beneath the law.

Next we learn that the association of ideas, following of course the objective relationships of which they are counterparts, may be either *synchronous* or *successive*. The perceptions of objects are built up of synchronous associations: the sight and sound of a violin; the color, hardness, shape, size and weight of a stone; a more complex group in the case of an animal or a man. The successive associations are, however, more numerous (so Mill believed), and their nature is best seen in the habitual sequence of words in thought. For example, in the Lord's Prayer, *Our* suggests *Father; Father* suggests *which,* and so on.

With James Mill, as with Thomas Brown, we reach a clear rec-ognition of the conditions of association. Associations, Mill noted, may vary in strength, and there are three *criteria of strength*. One is 'permanence': the more permanent associations must be stronger. Another is 'certainty,' which plainly meant for him correctness and probably also meant the subjective assurance with which the associa-tion comes. The third is 'facility,' which may be equated to spon-taneity or lack of effort in the formation of the association, and perhaps also to the readiness or speed of association. (One thinks at once of the later use of reaction times as a measure of associative strength.) These three factors are the observational criteria; but what causes the differences? Mill put forward frequency and vividness as the two *conditions of association,* and in so doing he anticipated what, in some quarters, is good modern doctrine. When impressional and associative tendencies have been distinguished, the differentiation has been by reference to frequency and vividness. *Vividness,* of course, is a vague term, and Mill expressly stated that he did not mean by it *intensity*. For illustration, he cited indissoluble associations induced by emotional situations. Eighty years later he might have turned to attention for an explanation, though it is not clear nowadays that the one word is any less vague than the other.

James Mill might argue that successive associations are more frequent than synchronous associations; nevertheless, the latter are equally important in a purely associational psychology like his. Thought, regarded in this way, seems to be made up of so much of each kind that it is hard to give either a predominance over the other. The subsumptive power of synchronous association is, however, very greatly increased by Mill's introduction of what amounts to a principle of fusion. Mill did not call it 'fusion' or even recognize the inclusion of something new; but he was nevertheless quite explicit in his discussion of the property that synchronous associations have of combining or blending to form an apparently simple whole.

He first cited examples from sensation. The seven spectral colors rapidly rotated on a color-wheel appear to give one uniform color, white. "The several sensations cease to be distinguishable; they run, as it were together, and a new sensation, compounded of all seven, but apparently a simple one, is the result." This is not a case of association, for the colors are sensations; but, he argued, just the same thing may happen with ideas, or with sensations and ideas. At a simple level we find the phenomenon in the ideational equivalents of the touch blends. For example, the idea of weight appears simple, but actually it involves both the idea of resistance (in turn including muscular ideas and ideas which constitute the will) and the idea of direction (involving at least the ideas of extension, place and motion). Mill remarked that it is a "good metaphysician" who can trace the composition of the idea of weight, and indeed we now begin to see that his method may be as much metaphysical as psychological. In the same way, Mill taught that objects gain their objectivity by synchronous association: in the idea of a tree or a horse or a man there are a very great many simple ideas united by association, and—here is the crucial point—so intimately united that the object appears unitary. Words, too, get their meanings by association, and yet, because of the intimacy of the associative union, appear to be almost simple ideas.

It is plain that this discussion has landed us in an *associative theory of meaning*, very similar to the modern context theory (Titchener, pp. 415 ff.), if not identical with it. We met it first in Berkeley (p. 184). It has kept turning up since. Now we find it in even clearer form in James Mill. There is no need to enter into the whole matter again; we should note only two specific additions that James Mill made. The one is that he appealed to attention in order to explain the familiar experiential fact that conscious meanings seem to be immediately and not associatively given. Mill thought that in an association the attention may be absorbed entirely by the consequent term of the association, so that the antecedent term is instantly forgotten.

In such a case, the association would not appear to be an association. The other important new point is the statement that organic sensations are the most frequent antecedent terms that are thus forgotten. Thus James Mill recognized both the dilemma of the adequate observation of meaning and also the fact that organic sensations exhibit this difficulty in extreme degree.

Even so far it may have been possible for the reader to follow James Mill without vigorous dissent. It soon appears, however, that in admitting fusion in synchronous association, Mill has admitted to systematic psychology a rational principle capable of devouring observational fact. If we can discover several components, associatively combined, in the apparently, but not actually, simple idea of a stone, why not go on? Mill did go on. We need not trace his entire progress but may content ourselves with quoting the last paragraphs of the chapter on association of ideas, paragraphs which show where he came out.

> Brick is one complex idea, mortar is another complex idea; these ideas, with ideas of position and quantity, compose my idea of a wall. My idea of a plank is a complex idea, my idea of a rafter is a complex idea, my idea of a nail is a complex idea.
> These, united with the same ideas of position and quantity, compose my duplex idea of a floor. In the same manner my complex ideas of glass, wood, and others, compose my duplex idea of a window; and these duplex ideas, united together, compose my idea of a house, which is made up of various duplex ideas. How many complex, or duplex ideas, are all united in the idea of furniture? How many more in the idea of merchandise? How many more in the idea called Every Thing?

In this *reductio ad absurdum* we see the persistent danger of philosophical psychology, unchecked by scientific control. A rational principle is captured by the empirical method and may then be turned loose to carry us even to the brink of absurdity. There is no logical reason to suppose that the idea of *everything* might not be an association of every idea of a thing, but there is not the least observational ground for maintaining, even with maximal telescoping, that a consciousness can contain a literally unlimited number of ideas at once. What meaning can one give to the conception that ideas coexist when indistinguishable? As a matter of fact, James Mill actually made no such assertion; he merely left us with a question. In the same manner we may leave him and turn to the somewhat more satisfactory envisagement of the same problem by his son, John Stuart Mill.

JOHN STUART MILL

John Stuart Mill (1806-1873) was an abler man than his father and had a much greater effect on the history of thought. This influence came, however, by way of his philosophy and his logic and bore on psychology for the most part indirectly because psychology, still philosophically minded, could not fail to take account of the psychologically minded philosopher, Mill. It was, for instance, Mill's treatment of the psychological problem of the syllogism that Helmholtz had in mind when he discussed perception in the *Optik* in 1866. Yet Mill never wrote a psychology like that of his English predecessors. His psychology is to be found in his *Logic* (1843), his *Examination of Sir William Hamilton's Philosophy* (1865) and in the notes of his edition of his father's *Analysis of the Human Mind* (1869). Thus his work lasts after the formal date when experimental psychology is said to have been 'founded' (1860). He belongs at this point in our history because of the way in which he modified his father's doctrines of association, mental composition and perception.

We have already seen something of John Stuart Mill's relation to his father, and his educational precocity is a matter of common knowledge. Mill, the son, never went to school except to his father. His entire youthful education was personally accomplished by careful, painstaking and exacting paternal instruction. What he learned was further impressed by his becoming presently the tutor of his younger sisters and brothers. He began the study of Greek at the age of three. Before he was eight he had read Æsop's *Fables*, the *Anabasis*, all of Herodotus, some of Plato and many other of the standard Greek texts. He had also read more of English history than most well-educated young men two or three times his age. At eight he began Latin, geometry and algebra, and by the time he was twelve he had read more Latin than is usual in the education of youth. He kept on with his Greek and his history and read in proof his father's *History of India*, which was published when the son was eleven. In the next two years his interest centered upon scholastic logic. He then went to France for a year, returned to England and to the study of psychology, and finally, when just seventeen, entered the employ of the East India House, in whose service his father then was. His education was stern and uncompromising. He had no boyhood friends, no child's play and very little youthful reading. He did not realize that his education was unusual for his age, for he had no one with whom to compare himself, and his father always kept before him the degree to which he fell short of the possible ideal.

Mill remained with the East India Company thirty-five years, until the government, against his protest, took over its functions in 1858. Like his father he was successful in what was essentially governmental diplomatic work, and he obtained in this way a first-hand experience with politics that rendered him more than a merely academic writer on political subjects. His early writing was in journals and newspapers. The effect of his relation to his father was marked. He admired and feared his father and hesitated to differ with him openly, and his first book, the *Logic*, did not appear until seven years after his father's death (1836). There were several years of depression when Mill, brought up in an austere personal life to scorn all emotion, began to doubt the value of his political and social activities. The entire relation of this father to this son is an interesting psychological study.

John Stuart Mill's reading of Whewell's *History of the Inductive Sciences* stimulated his interest in logic and resulted in 1843 in the publication of the *Logic*, still a very important book for those concerned with the logic of science. After this, his interest and writing shifted to political economy. He married in 1851, when he was about forty-five years old, and during the seven years of married life before his wife's death he was greatly stimulated and aided by her in his political thought and productivity. After her death and the dissolution of India House (1858), he spent most of his time, except for three years in Parliament, writing at Avignon, where she died. The decade of the sixties was the period of his life in which his psychological interest came most to the fore. The *Examination of Sir William Hamilton's Philosophy* appeared in 1865. The new edition of James Mill's *Analysis* with notes by John Stuart Mill, Bain and others was published in 1869. Most of his other writings were still, however, on political economy. He died, while still active and not quite yet sixty-seven years old, in 1873, the year before Wundt published the first edition of the *Physiologische Psychologie*.

John Stuart Mill accepted from his predecessors *sensation* (or impression) and *idea* as his systematic elements. He differed from his father in his reversion to Hume's belief that ideas are distinguishable from sensations in that they are weaker. Hume's view has proven untenable, but Mill had so little to say of sensation that the matter is unimportant.

In laying down the *laws of association*, also, Mill went back from his father's view to Hume's in adding 'similarity' to 'contiguity' as a principle of association. In 1843 he was, like his father, quite clear in showing that contiguity as an effective principle depends upon the frequency of concurrences, and in 1865 he named 'frequency' as a separate law. It is interesting to see that the importance of frequency, implicit even in Berkeley, was thus becoming recognized, even though, with contiguity having become a mental rather than an objective togetherness, it is almost impossible completely to separate contiguity and frequency: what we have in association is frequency of contiguities. In 1843 Mill named "intensity" as a third law of association, thus harking back to James Mill's vividness as a condition of association. In 1865, he omitted this law but created a new one which he called "inseparability." Inseparability, however, is simply the limiting case of frequency: when the contiguity admits of no exception and the frequency is great, the association becomes indissoluble. It is plain, then, that these laws of 1865 do not represent laws that operate in complete independence but different aspects of the single principle of association, aspects which Mill wished to emphasize for systematic use later on. The formal statement is that Mill held to three laws in 1843: *similarity, contiguity* and *intensity,* with frequency subsumed under the second; that in 1865 he stated as laws four principles of association: *similarity, contiguity, frequency* and *inseparability,* omitting *intensity.* The crystallizing mind of James Mill, having separated these items, would have kept them rigidly distinct. The more subtle mind of his son separated them for expository purposes and proceeded to build upon the central truth underlying the entire structure.

The really important thing, then, with John Stuart Mill is what he did with association after he had got it. James Mill had built up mental composition, a theory of indefinitely complex mental mixtures, with the elements lost but nevertheless within the mixture. We left James Mill raising the question of the degree of the complexity of the idea of Every Thing. John Stuart Mill saw the impossibility of this *reductio ad absurdum,* and for mental coalition he substituted mental chemistry.

In the first place, we must note that John Stuart Mill admitted his father's notion of associative coalescence. Ideas may coalesce by forming so rapid an association that some of the ideas are not attended to and thus tend to drop out or even actually to disappear; or at the very least, being unattended to, to be immediately forgotten (*cf.* Berkeley, p. 184). Thus total perceptions or ideas may be telescoped or short-circuited, a doctrine of the decay of mental formations that was not unfamiliar sixty years later (*cf.* Titchener, pp. 415 f.).

This notion of fusion leads, however, at once into the chemical view. If an idea may actually disappear or even be diminished in

effectiveness, the associative whole is not merely a sum of its elemental parts; we have in it something new, just as water is more
than hydrogen plus oxygen, and is also not all of hydrogen nor all
of oxygen. Nor can the laws of the whole be predicted from the
laws of the parts; they must be determined for themselves by experiment. The "compound" is not then a mere mixture with elements adhering to each other in it; it is a generated product of
combination, and thus the chemical analogy is fruitful. Here Mill
in the *Logic* of 1843 is worth quoting.

> It is obvious that the complex laws of thought and feeling not only
> may, but must, be generated from these simple laws [of association].
> And it is to be remarked, that the case is not always one of Composi-
> tion of Causes: the effect of concurring causes is not always pre-
> cisely the sum of the effects of those causes when separate, not even
> always an effect of the same kind with them.... The laws of the
> phenomena of the mind are sometimes analogous to mechanical, but
> sometimes also to chemical laws. When many impressions or ideas
> are operating in the mind together, there sometimes takes place a
> process of a similar kind to chemical combination. When impres-
> sions have been so often experienced in conjunction, that each of
> them calls up readily and instantaneously the ideas of the whole
> group, those ideas sometimes melt and coalesce into one another, and
> appear not several ideas but one; in the same manner as when the
> seven prismatic colors are presented to the eye in rapid succession,
> the sensation produced is that of white. But in this last case it is cor-
> rect to say that the seven colors when they rapidly follow one an-
> other *generate* white, but not that they actually *are* white; so it
> appears to me that the Complex Idea, formed by the blending to-
> gether of several simpler ones, should, when it really appears simple,
> (that is when the separate elements are not consciously distinguish-
> able in it) be said to *result from*, or be *generated by*, the simple ideas,
> not to *consist of* them.... These are cases of mental chemistry: in
> which it is possible to say that the simple ideas generate, rather than
> that they compose, the complex ones.

The reader must grasp here the evolutionary idea if he is to understand the difference between the two Mills. He may be accustomed
to think that ideally, if we knew *all* about hydrogen and oxygen, we
should know all about water. He must realize that such a view is a
matter of faith, for we never know about any element that *all* which
we think ideally would enable us to predict the laws of the compound. We have always to study the compound directly, independently of its known or supposed elemental composition. Since we
cannot prove the faith, Mill takes us to what we can prove: observational fact. If we dare not reason from the simple to the complex, we

must go directly to both in experience and experiment. On this point Mill was quite explicit, for he added two cautions to the foregoing discussion of mental chemistry. The first is that we must go to experience to discover how any particular complex idea has been generated; it is not enough to reason that it may have been generated in such and such fashion. The second is that, even when we know the generative process, we cannot deduce the laws of the resultant: those laws must be found in every case from direct experiment.

Thus Mill, though not a scientist, thought clearly in the logic of science: and thus he rescued the doctrine of association and mental combination from the rationalism of his philosophical father and turned it over to experimentalism.

There remains for our consideration only John Stuart Mill's theory of *perception*, or perhaps we should say his psychological theory of matter. After all, the problem of perception as distinguished from sensation is originally the problem of the belief in objects or matter as lying behind experience. It was only because associationism sought to solve this problem by way of association that introspectional psychologists ever came to regard perception as a complex or an integration.

This problem takes us from the *Logic* to Mill's later work, the *Examination of Sir William Hamilton's Philosophy*. Here Mill undertook to face "the question of the reality of matter" by the formulation of a "psychological theory of the belief in an external world." He posited at the outset the notion that the mind is capable of expectation and that therefore, "after having had actual sensations, we are capable of forming the conception of Possible sensations," which we *might* feel though we are not at the moment feeling them. Now the thing that seems most definitely to distinguish matter from sensation, Mill thought, is the fact that sensations are fugitive and transitory, whereas matter is fixed and permanent. How, in view of this great difference, can Berkeley have been right in making matter sensory? Mill held that Berkeley was essentially right; that the sensations are not permanent like matter, but that the possibilities of sensation can be permanent; and that, when we perceive matter, we are actually conceiving of permanent possibilities of sensations which are not present. Matter is nothing other than these "Permanent Possibilities of Sensations"; nor its perception anything other than a belief in them.

I see a piece of white paper on the table. I go into another room. If the phænomenon always followed me, or if, when it did not follow me, I believed it to disappear *è rerum natura*, I should not be-

lieve it to be an external object. I should consider it as a phantom—
a mere affection of my senses: I should not believe that there had
been any Body there. But, though I have ceased to see it, I am persuaded that the paper is still there. I no longer have the sensations
which it gave me; but I believe that when I again place myself in the
circumstances in which I had those sensations, that is, when I go
again into the room, I shall again have them; and further that there
has been no intervening moment at which this would not have been
the case. Owing to this property of my mind, my conception of the
world at any given instant consists, in only a small proportion, of
present sensations. Of these I may at the time have none at all, and
they are in any case a most insignificant portion of the whole which
I apprehend. The conception I form of the world existing at any
moment, comprises, along with the sensations I am feeling, a count-
less variety of possibilities of sensation: namely, the whole of those
which past observation tells me that I could, under any supposable
circumstances, experience at this moment, together with an indefinite and illimitable multitude of others which I do not know that I
could, yet it is possible that I might, experience in circumstances not
known to me. These various possibilities are the important thing to
me in the world. My present sensations are generally of little importance, and moreover are fugitive: the possibilities, on the contrary,
are permanent, which is the character that mainly distinguishes our
idea of Substance or Matter from our notion of sensation.

While John Stuart Mill is not here following his own caution,
given twenty-two years earlier, that we must stick to experience
and experiment, his view is nevertheless historically important for
two reasons.

In the first place, by linking it with the doctrine of association, he
gave a psychological theory of the object that is essentially like
Berkeley's or James Mill's. Association guarantees certain possibilities and joins them together in groups. The object comes into
experiential being because, given one sensation, all the others
forming the group which constitute the object, are, under the
associative law of inseparability, permanent possibilities of sensation.
It is not quite so nearly the context theory of meaning as those we
found in Berkeley and James Mill; but it is very near this theory.
It is not new, but it came in 1865 from the pen of a very influential
man, when experimental psychology could already be said to have
been born.

In the second place, we must note that this theory of the object
as the permanent possibilities of sensation anticipates a modern view
of perception. The crux of Mill's theory is that one may be conscious of the possibility of a sensation without being conscious of
the sensation (or its idea). One may 'have' in mind the possibility

without the sensation. In just the same way it has been argued that one may 'have' in consciousness a meaning without its representative content. The Würzburg school called such meanings 'imageless thoughts.' (Ach (1905, pp. 404 ff.) of this school developed the concept of the 'determining tendency'—a tendency, because it is not necessarily realized in conscious content. Titchener in the context theory (1909) showed that the conscious content which is the context may drop off in a familiar perception and the meaning be 'carried by the determining tendency' for that contextual content (pp. 415 f.). When one asks what such unconscious contexts actually are, one can only answer that they are potential contextual contents. The skilled musician playing in the key of F, 'knows unconsciously' that B is to be flat and not natural when he perceives a symbol that in itself might have either meaning. He has the meaning, but not the content. In such a case one can define the actual meaning in behavioral terms or as potential content. A potential content is, however, nothing else than a possibility of sensation or image. A similar relationship, so the author believes, can be demonstrated between Mill's notion of possibility, Ach's determining tendency, and Titchener's context theory. This is not, however, the place to go into all these matters; we must content ourselves with this bare indication of Mill's modernity.

ALEXANDER BAIN

Bain (1818-1903) comes nearer to being a psychologist through and through than any person we have yet studied. Let us call the roll. Descartes, philosopher and physiologist; Leibnitz and Locke, philosophers and men of political affairs; Berkeley, philosopher, bishop and educationalist; Hume, philosopher, historian and politician; Hartley, learned physician; James Mill, historian and diplomatist; John Stuart Mill, philosopher, logician and political economist; Charles Bell, Flourens, Johannes Müller, E. H. Weber, physiologists all. There was as yet no formal place in the world for a psychologist nor did Bain find such a place. The only post that he occupied for any great length of time was a chair of logic at Aberdeen, but he held this appointment *faute de mieux*.

Bain was a poor boy. His father was an Aberdeen weaver with five children and an income that he maintained only by working longer hours as the pay for piece-work persistently decreased. After a scanty schooling, Bain learned to work at the loom, earning money to pay for his board at home and to increase his education in an irregular fashion. He was precocious, but, having no easy access to books, was unable to utilize his intellectual ability to the full. Scientific and mathematical books, when he could borrow them, he soon assimilated. He was once allowed to examine the first volume of Newton's *Principia* for a half-hour, but it was several years before he succeeded in effecting its loan from a less cautious owner. By the time he was seventeen, he had mastered, largely by his own initiative, geometry, algebra, analytical and spherical trigonometry, and fluxions (the Newtonian equivalent of the Leibnitzian calculus); he had studied astronomy and had read considerable natural philosophy; he had become interested in metaphysics and had read Hume's *Treatise;* and he had begun Latin by way of a copy of the *Principia* and an English translation. No wonder that a minister of the church, on becoming acquainted with him, at once urged him to go to Marischal College, then separate from the university at Aberdeen.

At college this self-made student did excellently with poor instruction and was graduated after four years when he was twenty-two, dividing highest honors with another student. His interest and knowledge in natural philosophy had been increased, but the course in moral philosophy, the principal work of the last year, attracted his interest most, although pedagogically and inspirationally this course was about as poorly given as a college course could well be. When its professor, a year later, became an invalid, Bain was employed as a substitute to read the professor's notes and thus conduct the class. He added at times a very little of his own interpretation, only as much as he dared, and even thus he came under suspicion, a suspicion founded originally on the fact that he had never become a communicant of the church.

For the twenty years after his graduation, from 1840 to 1860, Bain remained an involuntary free-lance in London and Scotland. He applied several times for Scottish university chairs, but, though he had strong support, he was always, except once, finally defeated by academic politics and his taint of liberalism. Once he was appointed professor of mathematics and natural science at Glasgow, but the chair was ill-paid, the work was arduous and unsuited to Bain's increasing interest in psychology, and Bain resigned after a year. In London he had formed a friendship with John Stuart Mill, twelve years his senior, and with the intellectual circle in which Mill moved. He wrote for magazines, mostly on subjects that we should now call psychology and the philosophy of science. One gets some notion of the completeness of his psychological interest when one learns that in his article on toys in the *Westminster Review* of 1842 he developed his associative law of similarity. He helped Mill in the final revision of the *Logic* in that same year and published a laudatory review of it immediately after its publication in 1843.

Meanwhile he was preparing for his great effort, a large systematic psychology. He began actual composition about 1851, and the work, for convenience of publication, was finally divided into two volumes. *The Senses and the Intellect* appeared in 1855, and *The Emotions and the Will*, after a delay by the publisher because the first volume had not at first sold well, in 1859. Bain was then forty-one years old. The two volumes are really one work and represent Bain's most important contributions to thought. They were successful, and Bain spent much time during the later half of his life in revising them. Revised editions of the first volume appeared in 1864, 1868, and 1894; of the second, in 1865, 1875, and 1899; that is to say, Bain's remained the standard British psychological text for almost a half-century, until Stout's replaced it.

In 1860 Marischal College was combined with the University of Aberdeen, which had previously consisted only of King's College, and a new chair of logic (and English) was created. For this chair Bain applied, and, after opposition to which he was now accustomed, he received the appointment. He held the post for twenty years, finally resigning on account of his health. His local success is indicated by the fact that he was then thrice (although still against opposition) elected rector of the university.

In neither English nor logic was Bain especially proficient, and he set about remedying the defect by writing textbooks. From 1863 to 1874 he published three manuals of grammar and rhetoric. In 1870 he published his *Logic*, based in part upon John Stuart Mill's but also containing much original exposition.

Although for a decade Bain was thus diverted from his primary interest by the exigencies of his appointment, the diversion was only partial. Having already twice revised *The Senses and the Intellect* and once *The Emotions and the Will*, in 1868 he published for instructional purposes an abridgment of these two large volumes, as *Mental and Moral Science*.

Moreover, in the next year there appeared the edition of James Mill's *Analysis* to which Bain and others added copious notes.

In 1872 Bain published his *Mind and Body*. Back in the 1840s he had written on the conservation of energy and the mechanical equivalent of heat. Now he was seeking to resolve the inconsistency between the facts of natural and those of moral philosophy, posing the question: Is the open system of the will compatible with the closed system of energy? Bain's answer, presupposed in his psychological books, was what we now call psychophysical parallelism, although that phrase is not Bain's. This book is important in view of the extensive discussion of the problem of mind and body that flourished in the 1880s and even more in the 1890s.

It was in 1876 that Bain founded *Mind*, the first psychological journal in any country, although it had a more philosophical cast than its younger cousins. It was early to start a journal of experimental psychology anywhere and especially early in Great Britain which was slow to adopt the new science. Bain made his brilliant pupil, Croom Robertson, then professor of the philosophy of mind and logic at University College, London, the editor of *Mind*, and supported the journal financially until Robertson's early death in 1892.

Bain's last years were spent in retirement at Aberdeen. In spite of ill health he lived to be eighty-five, dying in 1903, which was also the year of the death of his contemporary, Herbert Spencer. His importance is partly due to his longevity. He had written his psychology before Fechner, Helmholtz or Wundt, and he lived through, actively revising his works, the entire period of the formation and establishment of the new psychology.

Actually he was not a great man, in the sense that Descartes or Locke or Hume or Johannes Müller or Helmholtz or even Wundt was great. There was never any school or great theory that derived from him. He represented the culmination of associationism and the beginning of its absorption into physiological psychology. He is important mostly as a cardinal point in the historical orientation of psychology. His careful, scholarly work is a worthy monument to mark the turning point of psychology from empirical associationism to physiological experimentalism.

We cannot, of course, undertake to abstract these systematic psychological treatises of Bain's. We must content ourselves with noting his position on four important matters: psychophysical parallelism, physiological psychology, the doctrine of association and the doctrine of the will.

1. Bain has been said to have originated the theory of psychophysical parallelism, but such a statement is not true. Bain gave the view concrete form in a distinctly psychological setting. Parallelism in its most general form goes back, as we have seen, to Leibnitz, who conceived of harmony in a pluralistic universe as pre-established in the parallel courses of the monads. Parallelism of mind and body was for him simply a special case. His contemporary, Malebranche, also

held a view of psychophysical parallelism; so did Hartley. The reason that we do not ordinarily cite Hartley in this connection is that Hartley was not interested in developing the view for its own sake. As a physician, he accepted materialism as applying to the body; to save the soul from materialism, he was forced into a dualism, and parallel accounts of mind and body were the easiest way out. For him Cartesian interaction would have been suspected of materializing the soul. So too Fechner, in his crusade against materialism, appealed to parallelism in 1851.

Bain did not at first make a direct issue of the matter. His psychology of 1855-1859 simply took this point of view for granted. There are, he thought, two sides to every psychological question, the "physical side" and the "mental side"; and he frequently discussed a particular topic successively under these two heads. Later, as the psychological problems raised by the doctrine of the conservation of energy became more acute, he developed in *Mind and Body* the view of the "physical side" as a closed causal system with cause and effect quantitatively equivalent in terms of energy, and of the "mental side" paralleling it without quantitative equivalence. Bain himself regarded the view as hardly more than a metaphysical makeshift. He was not clear himself as to whether he was dealing with two aspects of one substance or two different substances. Of his facing of this problem he wrote later:

> It was necessary to classify the various alternative suppositions as to One or Two Substances, and to maintain the essential phenomenal distinctness of the psychical and the physical, while upholding the indissoluble union of the two. The expounders of the doctrine of the Trinity had formulated the mode of expressing the mystical union that we find in the Athanasian creed, as 'not confounding the persons nor dividing the substance,'—a not inapt rendering of the union of mind and body.

2. It is a necessary consequence of this parallelistic view that Bain should have written a physiological psychology, and in realizing this intention Bain adopted the form which later, after Wundt had put his seal upon it, was to become the standard pattern for textbooks of psychology. Physiological psychology, we now know, was not at all new with Bain. Descartes was a physiological psychologist, but we may follow Descartes' own practice and dismiss him as an "ancient." Hartley wrote a physiological psychology, but his physiology was the speculative physiology of Newton and not the result of scientific discovery. In the nineteenth century, however, scientific physiology developed rapidly and physiological psychology within

it—a matter which we have already considered in detail in earlier chapters. It was pretty obvious whither psychology was tending. In 1852 Lotze wrote his *Medicinische Psychologie* with the subtitle *Physiologie der Seele*. We shall see in the next chapter that there is surprisingly little physiology and surprisingly much metaphysics in this soul physiology; nevertheless, the occurrence of the title at this date is significant. It is almost certain that Bain did not know this book of Lotze's; he never spoke German, and it is doubtful if he read it. It is also probable that he did not know Johannes Müller's psychological physiology. He rarely mentioned German sources. He had had, however, a postgraduate course in anatomy; he knew Dr. W. B. Carpenter personally and used his *Human Physiology* and later Longet's *Physiology*, in working up his material on the senses. (This was long before Carpenter had published his *Mental Physiology*.) What Bain did was to devote nearly all of his introduction to a long chapter on the nervous system, then to plunge into movement, sense and instinct, whence he passed to the higher functions. As we have noted, as far as possible he would discuss both the physical and the mental aspects of every topic. Much of the introduction on the nervous system was not coordinated with the later psychology, but in this matter his books differ little from many later texts.

The physiological approach led Bain to emphasize the senses. His discussion was full and his classification conventional. To Aristotle's five senses he added only the rubric "organic." This last class, however, he recognized as very important, especially because it includes the muscular sensations that are involved in his theory of action.

Movement also, as a physiological datum, came into Bain's psychology in its own right—not merely as a muscular sensation. As we have seen, the knowledge of reflex action as unconscious movement had greatly advanced within the preceding century. Thus Bain, like Hartley but with more reason, could consider *movement* as a psychological term, one that could properly become involved in associations.

3. Bain's discussion of the intellect was nothing more than his discussion of association. He held to two fundamental laws: *contiguity* and *similarity*.

As we should now expect, Bain held the law of contiguity to be a matter of the recurrence of previous concurrences of actions or sensations: they "tend to grow together, or cohere, in such a way that, when one of them is afterwards presented to the mind, the others are apt to be brought up in idea." Thus this law seemed to

Bain primarily to explain retentiveness. It depends, he noted, upon
the *repetition* of contiguities and also upon *attention.* It depends
further upon the general retentiveness of the individual, for there
are *individual differences* in the "aptitude for acquirement." These
principles were still to be regarded as basic fifty years later—at the
turn of the century.

The law of similarity Bain, like John Stuart Mill, brought back
into psychology after its banishment by James Mill. Bain's particular
systematic purpose in this matter was to provide a psychological
account of "constructive association," a phrase which he used for
invention and mental creation in general. If contiguity explains only
retention, *i.e.*, the recurrence of past occurrences, how can there be
constructive imagination as well as memory? Bain thought that a
principle of "agreement" needed to be added in order to account for
what is novel in thought. Most of Bain's illustrations of the associative operation of similarity are susceptible of reduction to
contiguous partial identities, but there is no need for us to criticize
Bain on this point, for his second law was never taken over by the
new psychology as was his first.

It is important to mention that Bain discussed "compound association" at length. He thought of a realized association as a result of all
the associative factors operating. "Associations that are individually
too weak to operate the revival of a past idea, may succeed by acting
together." This doctrine he developed through the various higher
degrees of complication.

4. An intellectualistic psychology like associationism had not
tended to raise the problem of the *will.* For several reasons, however,
Bain had to face the problem. The growth of science had made
materialism a general issue. The gradual establishment of the doctrine
of the conservation of energy seemed to turn the physical world into
a closed causal system. The doctrine of association was operating
similarly in the mental world. One doctrine was materialistic and the
other mechanistic; both tended to supersede the will, and in both
Bain was personally interested. No wonder he could not avoid the
problem.

Bain pointed out, in the first place, that the nervous system is
capable of *spontaneous action.* Action is spontaneous, he thought,
when it occurs independently of any external stimulation as in *reflex*
and *instinctive* action. All action, however, involves actual movement and thus gives rise to muscular sensations or sensations of innervation (a theory which Bain later came to hold, and discarded
still later). Thus in movement, or even in intended movement,

there is a definite sensory experience, which is the experience of effort and the experiential aspect of the will. Entering into association, the experience of effort may become an essential accompaniment of any part of the actional situation, even though there is no movement or intended movement; and thus the will may ultimately seem to pervade the mental life.

In this fashion Bain explained away that argument for freedom which is based upon the experience of volition. His use of the phrase *spontaneous action* seems to imply that freedom is somehow nevertheless left in, but actually it is not, nor could it be in such a system. Spontaneous action was free only of association; it was determined by the constitution of the nervous system. Probably Bain, who had met with such bitter defeats at the hands of religious orthodoxy, was willing to preserve a little ambiguity in the word *spontaneous*, a word which Darwin complained he could not understand in this connection.

In brief, then, we see that Bain anticipated much of later psychology, just as he represented the culmination of the old. In regard to each of the four points which we have considered, he stands exactly at a corner in the development of psychology, with philosophical psychology stretching out behind, and experimental physiological psychology lying ahead in a new direction. The psychologist of the twentieth century can read much of Bain with hearty approval; perhaps John Locke could have done the same.

EVOLUTIONARY ASSOCIATIONISM

After Bain, associationism may be said to have been carried further in the direct line of Spencer and Lewes, but this stage of the development we can dismiss briefly for the reason that the events occurred after the 'founding' of physiological psychology and thus could not form a preparation for it nor actually affect it greatly. There are some indirect effects of Spencer's psychology, it is true, and these we shall have an opportunity to note presently.

Herbert Spencer (1820-1903) wrote the first edition of his *Principles of Psychology* in 1855. He had thus published a complete psychology when Bain had published only the first volume of his. Nevertheless, Spencer in psychology comes after Bain. This first psychology of Spencer's never exercised great influence; it was simply another associational psychology, although by a very great man. Spencer's real influence upon psychology dates from the two volumes of the second edition published in 1870 and 1872. Here we find what has been called *evolutionary* association-

ism. It is true that Spencer claimed to have anticipated the evolutionary view in the first edition, and it is also true that he did
more specifically anticipate Darwin (1859) by a year or so; but
the completed psychological view must be studied in this second
edition.

From the ideas of Locke to the sensations and ideas of Bain
had been a long course of development. For Locke an idea might
be *an elephant* or *drunkenness*, but for Bain sensations were no
longer objects or meanings and the ideas were counterparts of
sensations. Conscious data of the latter sort Spencer called *feelings*, and he distinguished both between centrally initiated feelings
(emotions) and peripherally initiated feelings (the organic and
the external sensations), and between primary feelings (sensations
and emotions proper) and secondary feelings (fainter ideational
revivals of the primary). He felt, however, the inadequacy of the
concept of analyzed experience, as history had developed it, and
added, therefore, a new class of elements, *relations between feelings*.
There may be, he thought, relations of coexistence, of sequence and
of difference, occurring as data. In this way Spencer regained a
little of what had been lost to the mind since Locke.

There are, however, two points of particular interest about
these relations. The first is that, taking these relations as given in
consciousness, Spencer reduced the task of association. Some things
that would have been associations for his predecessors became
simple elementary relations for Spencer. In this way the account
of the mind was simplified and seemed a more precise picture of
the relatively simple mind which James Mill, for instance, had bur-
dened with an impossible number of associated simple ideas. The
other point is that a relation between feelings, given as a conscious
element, is but little different from a feeling of relation. We thus
see in Spencer the origin of James' feelings of relation and of many
other later attempts to add an imageless element to the inventory
of consciousness.

Spencer's belief about *association* was that it held together both
feelings and relations. The fundamental principle operating in it
is, he thought, *similarity*, for association is between terms of the
same kind. On the other hand, since associations are built up in
experience, it is plain that Spencer could not abandon contiguity
entirely. That he did not is plain when we see that he noted both
vividness and repetition as conditions of association and even went
further in anticipating one of Ebbinghaus' laws when he observed
that successive repetitions exhibit a diminishing effect.

Association in Spencer's hands was used further to accomplish what compounding was not already given in the relations at the start. He did not seek literally in this way to generate objects psychologically, because he thought that objects as such do not belong to the psychological world; but he undertook the corresponding task of distinguishing between subjective and objective mental states. For this differentiation he gave a list of differences that bears considerable resemblance to some later introspectionists' accounts of the difference between idea and perception.

The really important novelty in Spencer's psychology is, however, his *evolutionary* doctrine, which amounts to his making the associative law of frequency operate phylogenetically. Association, when often repeated, entails an hereditary tendency which in successive generations becomes cumulative: such was Spencer's view of the inheritance of acquired associations and the formation of instincts. Racially, the doctrine runs, instincts are formed in this way out of reflex actions, which are at the bottom of psychic life. Volitions are formed in another way. Cognition and memory evolve from instinct. There is an evolutionary hierarchy, with simpler states giving rise to more complex.

Of the indirect influences of this evolutionary associationism upon subsequent psychology four should be mentioned. One we have already noted, viz., that Spencer, feeling the limitations of the ultimate elementism of associationism, sought to extend the list. Associationism led naturally to sensationism and the effort to transcend it went on for a long time both within and without introspectional psychology.

Another influence was directed toward animal psychology. The crucial point in this development is the publication of Darwin's *Origin of Species* in 1859, but both Darwin and Spencer immediately extended the principle to include mind—Spencer in the way we have just seen and Darwin primarily in his *Expression of the Emotions in Man and Animals* (1872). In the past it had been easy to deny animals souls and therefore minds (Descartes), but the doctrine of evolution changed all this and an animal psychology became necessary. It began by way of the anecdotal method and presently became experimental (Thorndike, 1898, unless one presses certain earlier experiments on behavior).

A much more subtle influence lies in the relation of the theory of evolution to American psychology. The outlines of this relationship are only just beginning to become clear. America in the late nineteenth century was still a new country with its western frontier only having just recently reached the Pacific Ocean. It still had the pioneers' spirit, the readiness to accept change, the lack of veneration for the old, the belief that usefulness is the chief good. In a new country with free land it is the fittest who survive, those strong enough to wrest a living from nature. Of course Darwin's theory was destined for enthusiastic reception in such an atmosphere. And the result of this theory was that American psychology went functional, assessing mind and mental activity in terms of use and survival value. William James was the first to see psychology in this way. John Dewey supported him. Together they brought functional gospel into philosophy as pragmatism. Ladd was another early functionalist. Stanley Hall and Mark Baldwin were the evolutionists in American psychology. Cattell, who put himself back of mental testing, was more effective than any of these last three although he accepted no label and organized no self-conscious school. To these matters we return in later chapters. Here we note only that America was predisposed for both evolutionism and functionalism and, in the act of taking over the new scientific psychology from Germany, reshaped it effectively, radically and only half consciously into a psychology of use.

With all this in mind we can see meaning in what otherwise would seem a paradox, that James could in 1876 offer the first course on physiological psychology in America and also use as a text Spencer's *Principles of Psychology*. Spencer was useful, James wrote C. S. Peirce, because " 'He left a Spencer's name to other times, linked with one virtue and a thousand crimes.' The one virtue," James continued, "is his belief in the universality of evolution—the 1000 crimes are his 5000 pages of absolute incompetence to work it out in detail."

Finally, we must note that evolutionary psychology played into the hands of nativism and against geneticism. It is almost paradoxical that such should have been the case. Locke's empiricism led to associationism, and the genetic view of perception, for example, was the natural result. In fact, this view was as often called empiristic as genetic. Nativism, the opponent theory, seemed to go back through Kant to the innate ideas of Descartes', the very view that Locke brought empiricism to combat. Spencer's theory was essentially a resolution of the two views, although, because of the failure of science generally to accept the doctrine of the inheritance of acquired characters, his synthesis lacks the importance that it would otherwise have. Spencer simply substituted phylogenetic origin for ontogenetic origin in many cases. What is empiristically derived in the race may nevertheless be native in the individual, he might have said.

The other important author of evolutionary psychology at this time was *George Henry Lewes* (1817-1878). His influence, however, has not been nearly so great as Herbert Spencer's, and we can afford to pass him by. In dealing with Spencer, we have already gone far beyond the middle of the nineteenth century, and our main purpose here has been to show the preparation in philosophical psychology for the new experimental psychology that we habitually think of as beginning about 1860. Now we must return to Kant, Herbart and Lotze in the corresponding period in Germany.

NOTES

See the general remarks at the beginning of the notes in Chap. 10 (p. 200).

James Mill

The *Analysis of the Phenomena of the Human Mind*, 1829, was reprinted in 1869 with many added notes by Bain, Findlater and Grote, and a subsequent general editing and annotation by John Stuart Mill. This is the edition ordinarily available. For excerpts, see B. Rand, *Classical Psychologists*, 1912, 462-482; or W. Dennis, *Readings in the History of Psychology*, 1948, 140-154.

For James Mill's life, see A. Bain, *James Mill*, 1882; G. S. Bower, *Hartley and James Mill*, 1881, 8-23; and references in John Stuart Mill, *Autobiography*, 1873, esp. 2-61.

On his psychology, see Th. Ribot, *English Psychology*, Eng. trans., 1874, 44-77; H. C. Warren, *History of the Association Psychology*, 1921, 81-94; G. S. Brett, *History of Psychology*, 1921, III, 29-35; G. Murphy, *Historical Introduction to Modern Psychology*, 2 ed., 1949, 102-104.

The attempt to psychologize philosophy by reference to the lives of its authors must be made only with great caution; nevertheless, to the present writer, there appears to be a consistency between, on the one hand, the hard, inflexible persistence of James Mill, which brought him against great odds from penury to comfort, and, on the other hand, his clear, direct style and his courage in pressing a few simple principles to their ultimate psychological limits.

John Stuart Mill

For the psychology of the younger Mill, see his *System of Logic, Ratiocinative and Inductive*, 1843, esp. bk. vi, chap. 4 on the laws of the mind and mental chemistry; *Examination of Sir William Hamilton's Philosophy*, 1865, esp. chap. 11 on the psychological theory of the belief in an external world; and notes in James Mill, *Analysis of the Phenomena of the Human Mind*, 1869.

Mill's writings were extensive, and there is also a large critical literature upon his work. See Rand in Baldwin's *Dictionary of Philosophy and Psychology*, III, 372-376. The best biographical account is obtained by reading J. S. Mill's *Autobiography*, 1873, and then A. Bain, *John Stuart Mill*, 1882, which supplements it. In general brilliance J. S. Mill far surpassed the other men mentioned in this chapter. Because of his remarkable youth, Cox gives him the highest childhood 'intelligence' of any of the geniuses whom she studied (IQ = 190), and even as against the biographical record of young manhood she rates him as high as Berkeley. See C. M. Cox, *Early*

Mental Traits of Three Hundred Geniuses, 1926. See also W. L. Courtney, *Life of John Stuart Mill*, 1889.

In the histories of psychology, see Ribot, *op. cit.*, 78-123; Warren, *op. cit.*, 95-103; Brett, *op. cit.*, III, 206-211; Dennis, *op. cit.*, 169-177.

Alexander Bain

The two volumes of Bain's psychology are *The Senses and the Intellect*, 1855, and *The Emotions and the Will*, 1859. The text gives the dates of the three revisions of each. For excerpts on association, see Rand, *Classical Psychologists*, 483-504. The briefer textbook is *Mental and Moral Science: a Compendium of Psychology and Ethics*, 1868. In 1872, the mental and moral sciences were separated into two books, but the American edition of *Mental Science* is dated 1868.

For Bain on parallelism, see his *Mind and Body*, 1872. This book has been reprinted without change under many subsequent dates and has also been translated into French, German and Spanish. See also Bain's chapter on *The Correlation of Mental and Nervous Forces*, printed as an appendix to Balfour Stewart, *Conservation of Energy*, 1874. For a brief account of the history of psychophysical parallelism, see under *Parallelismus* in R. Eisler, *Wörterbuch der philosophischen Begriffe*, 1910, II, 975-983. For an indication of the degree of interest excited in this problem, see the bibliography on mind and body by Rand, in Baldwin's *Dictionary*, III, 1091-1099.

For Bain's life, see his *Autobiography*, 1904, with a supplementary chapter by W. L. Davidson, who also adds a complete bibliography of Bain's writings. We have referred above to Bain's biographies of James Mill and of John Stuart Mill. These books show their author's biographical interest immediately after his retirement from the Aberdeen chair, and the latter book also bears upon his own life.

In the histories of psychology, see Ribot, *op. cit.*, 194-254; Warren, *op. cit.*, 104-115; Brett, *op. cit.*, III, 206-212; Murphy, *op. cit.*, 104-108.

Dr. W. B. Carpenter, mentioned in the text, was long an acquaintance of Bain's and was the originator of the phrase *unconscious cerebration* in his *Mental Physiology*, 1881.

Evolutionary Associationism

The important second edition of Herbert Spencer's *Principles of Psychology*, 1870-1872, is really simply the fourth and fifth volumes of the ten-volume *System of Synthetic Philosophy*, 1860-1897. The *Psychology* was several times revised; there was a fifth edition in 1890. For excerpts, see Rand, *Classical Psychologists*, 505-529. See, in general, Ribot, *op. cit.*, 124-193; Warren, *op. cit.*, 118-137; Brett, *op. cit.*, III, 213-219. The literature on Herbert Spencer—expository, critical and biographical—is very large.

On evolutionism in British and American psychology—mental evolution, mental inheritance, functional psychology and its later derivatives, animal psychology, behaviorism and behavioristics, mental testing, psychotherapy—see the later chapters of this book esp. pp. 550-583, 641-659. See also Murphy, *op. cit.*, 108-126.

For the text's quotation from James, see R. B. Perry, *The Thought and Character of William James*, 1935, I, 475; for James' relation to Spencer, 474-493.

George Henry Lewes' psychology is to be found in the five volumes of his *Problems of Life and Mind*, 1873-1879 (divided into three series; the two volumes of the third series were published posthumously). In general, see Ribot, *op. cit.*, 255-314; Warren, *op. cit.*, 137-153.

CHAPTER 13

German Psychology before 1850: Kant, Herbart and Lotze

So much for British empiricism and associationism, which formed the chief philosophical preparation for the new scientific psychology. Both Helmholtz and Wundt, as we shall see, relied primarily upon the British tradition. It is not to be expected, however, that the German psychologists would remain indifferent to the German philosophical tradition. It was after all in the country of Leibnitz that the new psychology came into being. The German philosophers who had the most influence in these matters were Kant, Herbart and Lotze. Only in a much lesser degree was Christian Wolff influential. He systematized and popularized Leibnitz, and thus helped to create the atmosphere under which Kant grew up and which subsequently Kant undertook to change.

Let us date these men by relating them to the British line of descent. Leibnitz (1646-1716) was Locke's contemporary, as we have already seen. Christian Wolff (1679-1754) was Berkeley's. Kant (1724-1804) was the contemporary of the Scottish School, younger than Reid, older than Dugald Stewart, much later than Hartley, much earlier than Thomas Brown and James Mill. Herbart (1776-1841) was the contemporary with James Mill, publishing his important psychological work a few years before James Mill published his. Lotze (1817-1881) was Bain's contemporary, and John Stuart Mill's.

IMMANUEL KANT

Immanuel Kant was born in the university city of Königsberg, in East Prussia, in 1724, and he never travelled more than forty miles from his birthplace in the entire eighty years of his life. He matriculated at the University in 1740, at the age of sixteen, spent six years in studying science, mathematics and philosophy, interrupted his study to gain a competence from private tutoring in 1747 and was finally enabled by the support of a friend to return to study in 1755. He received his doctor's degree that same year at Königsberg at the age of thirty-one and was immediately habilitated as a *Dozent*, a status which he held for fifteen years—for he twice failed of promotion at Königsberg and seems never to have thought of trying elsewhere. At this time he had become a disciple of Leibnitz and his interpreter, Christian Wolff. It was not until 1770 that he obtained the chair of logic and metaphysics at Königsberg, and by then he had come under the influence of British empiricism and Hume's skepticism. Hume, he said, woke him from his "dogmatic slumbers," and he undertook to find a rigorous *via media* between the pietism, in which he had matured and which his interest in Swedenborg reinforced, and the subjective skepticism toward which Hume directed his thought. The result was, of course, that remarkably influential book, the *Critique of Pure Reason (Kritik der reinen Vernunft)* which appeared first in 1781, and with revision in 1787.

With this book Kant became famous. Students flocked to his classes. Young philosophers came on pilgrimages to Königsberg. Kant, who never married, had to keep changing the restaurant where at one o'clock he ate his only heavy meal, because the public came there to see the great man eat. Fame did not, however, disturb Kant or dissipate his intellectual endeavor. His *Critique of Practical Reason* appeared in 1788, his *Critique of Judgment* in 1790. He had a decade of effective work and great prestige.

Then in 1792 his prestige suddenly interfered with his effectiveness. The German government was the agent Kant's publication on moral rationalism, although a compromise with Hume, did not square with Lutheran doctrine. The first part of his book, *Die Religion innerhalb der Grenzen der blossen Vernunft*, appeared in Berlin, but the second part was stopped by the Government. Kant was told of the displeasure of Frederick William II, but completed publication in Königsberg. His lecturing on religion was interdicted. He was, in consequence, greatly depressed and resigned his chair in 1797 when he was seventy-three years old. He died in 1804.

The effect of Kant upon psychology, ultimately upon the new experimental psychology, was twofold. (1) He favored *subjectivism*, keeping alive the faith in the importance of those mental phenomena which can not be reduced to brain or body processes. (2) And he gave support to *nativism* in theories of space because he subjectified space and time into *a priori* intuitions, removing them from the objective external world.

The reason that Locke's empiricism led on to Hume's skepticism lay in subjectivism. Locke had said: "Since the mind, in all its thoughts and reasonings, hath no other immediate object but its own ideas, which it alone does or can contemplate, it is evident that our knowledge is only conversant about them." Yet Locke never accepted the full force of his own conclusion, for his very doctrine of secondary qualities, in asserting that some sense-qualities do not correspond in kind with the properties of the objects which produce them, also asserts that the objects themselves are in knowledge, that in some way the mind can be "conversant about them." Berkeley went further, undertaking to show how it is that we can generate knowledge of matter out of the mind's awareness. Hume's skepticism was more extreme because he subjectified the concept of cause and effect, holding that repeatedly observed succession creates the idea of causation, and because he also questioned the separate existence of the ego. He thus abolished the reason for a belief in an external world as a necessary cause for the experience of a unitary perceiving being. Even Hume was not, however, consistent, for his notion that ideas are but faint copies of impressions implies that the impressions cause the ideas and are themselves more immediately related to some sort of an external world. Extreme subjectivism of this sort seems always to lead eventually to absurdities.

Kant sought a compromise, a compromise between the demands of religion and this subjectivistic skepticism. He undertook to place the contributions of the mind in their proper sphere over against the things-in-themselves, those 'outside' objects which the mind can never know directly. Locke had said: "Nihil est in intellectu quod non fuerit in sensu." Leibnitz had added: "Nisi intellectus ipse." Now Kant, giving over Leibnitz's pre-established harmony of monads, sought to determine the nature of this intellect that is prior to experience.

One comes to understand the nature of the intellect by examining the nature of its contributions. First there are, Kant asserted, the *categories* of the understanding, such attributes as unity, totality, reality, existence, necessity, reciprocity and cause-and-effect—there were twelve of them altogether—which are furnished by the mind as categories in respect of which the data of experience are disposed. They come from within, not from without. In addition to the categories there are space and time, which are *a priori Anschauungen*, presentations, modes of appearance. The word *Anschauung* is always translated *intuition*, but the German word is better because it implies that spatial arrangement of objects is given in perception. Things-in-themselves are not *in themselves* related in space. They are put into spatial relation by intuition because such perceptual order is a psychological necessity.

Similarly events are dated in time. In a manner of speaking space is a more objective intuition than time, Kant thought, because it relates objects to one another, whereas time is more subjective because it relates events to the perceiver. The 'real' world lacks both space and time, which are given only in understanding it.

Kant emphasized the contribution of the mind by discussing the *antinomies*. They are certain contradictory pairs of propositions, which are mutually incompatible and which yet equally seem true and necessary. For them it is not conceivable that either proposition is wrong and yet both can not be right. Three of the antinomies are these: (1) space and time must be limited and yet they must also be infinite; (2) every substance must be resolvable into parts and yet some substances must be ultimate and unresolvable into parts; (3) freedom of action must occur along with caused action, and yet all action is surely caused. These contradictions disappear when they are regarded as pertaining to intuitions, as modes of apprehension of experience. Space exists only in respect of what is perceived in it and perception is never actually infinite.

It is not in the present book that we shall come to any satisfactory understanding of Kant's difficult reaffirmation of the relation between the subjective and objective worlds. We must content ourselves with obtaining an insight into his effect upon psychology.

Kant in founding German idealism was re-establishing Cartesian *dualism* for psychology, a dualism threatened by British empiricism. It was natural after Kant for Herbart and Fechner and Wundt to take mind for granted as something other than neural action. The new experimental psychology, beginning at this time, was almost bound to systematize itself as a science of consciousness. In France, England, Russia and America it was easier for psychology to turn objective than in Germany, which remained true to consciousness— to phenomenal experience, as the Gestalt psychologists call it.

The other Kantian influence was *nativism*. In this respect Johannes Müller followed Kant in his theory of space perception. He was not very explicit, but then, as Lotze remarked, a nativistic theory is hardly a theory since it merely asserts that spatiality is given and does not show how it was generated. Helmholtz, when he first defended the empirical view of space perception, felt it necessary to begin by attacking Kant; but Hering, as we shall see, followed Kant and warred with Helmholtz. So today Gestalt psychology, true to the Kant-Müller-Hering-Mach-Stumpf line of descent, is nativistic in that it relies on the given properties of the psychological field to explain the events within the field.

Kant's immediate successors in Germany were Fichte (1762-1814), Hegel (1770-1831) and Schelling (1775-1854). They were his successors in thought as well as in time, but, important as they are in the history of philosophy, they do not belong in this book. They were contemporaries of one another and also of Herbart (1776-1841), who thus, in returning to empiricism, placed himself in opposition to the tradition of his day. In fact, in German thought, Herbart's psychology derives more directly from Leibnitz than from any of the intervening philosophers. It is also more nearly compatible with the British development than is Kantianism.

JOHANN FRIEDRICH HERBART

Johann Friedrich Herbart (1776-1841) was a philosopher and is best known as the 'father' of scientific pedagogy, which he founded upon psychology. His psychology is therefore of primary concern when Herbart is considered as an educational theorist, but it also in its own right occupies an important place in the history of psychology. Herbart's two psychological texts are his most important books, and, in spite of his denial of the possibility of psychological experiment, his work had a definite influence upon the later experimental psychology. It is, moreover, interesting to note that the dependence of scientific education upon psychology, a dependence which Herbart was the first to emphasize, has remained a tenet of educational theory until the present day, although opinion as to the exact manner in which psychology can be applied to education has varied greatly at different times. Within the present century, not only has psychology affected education, but the demand of education upon psychology has had a notable effect upon the latter.

Herbart, owing to an accident in infancy, was a delicate child. He did not go to school until he was twelve but was educated by his mother, a woman of unusual ability. He was somewhat precocious; his interest in logic is said to have begun during this early period. Altogether, his childhood has some resemblance to John Stuart Mill's. At twelve he began attendance upon the *Gymnasium* in Oldenburg, his native city, and he continued there for six years. Kant had made a profound impression upon him at sixteen. At eighteen he went to Jena to study philosophy under Fichte, at a time when Kant at Königsberg was at the full height of his reputation. His own philosophy was, however, in process of formation, and he could not entirely accept Fichte's teaching. After three years he left Jena to become the private tutor of the sons of the governor of Interlaken. It was this chance event that shifted his interest from philosophy to education and led to his first constructive thinking upon educational problems. Thus, after two years of tutoring and when he was still only twenty-three, he spent three years in Bremen in study and cogitation. Before leaving Switzerland he had visited Pestalozzi, the famous Swiss educational reformer. From Bremen he went for seven years (1802-1809) to Göttingen, where he first presented himself for the doctor's degree, and after receiving it, became a *Dozent* in the university. In coming up for his degree he formally opposed the doctrine of Kant, and in the years following he continued with the maturing of his own philosophy and his theory of education. He published in both fields during these years.

The promise of achievement in Herbart was confirmed when in 1809, at the age of thirty-three, he was called to Kant's chair in Königsberg. Kant had died in 1804. Herbart stayed at Königsberg for twenty-four years, and these years form the important period of his life. He devoted them to the completion of his system of psychology and to the working-out of practical pedagogical problems. In 1816 he published his *Lehrbuch zur Psychologie* and in 1824-1825 his *Psychologie als Wissenschaft*. He also wrote a *Metaphysik* (1828-1829), for psychology and metaphysics were not, in Herbart's view, distinct subject-matters. Meanwhile his reputation increased, his class-room was crowded, and his fame spread throughout Germany.

In 1833, disturbed by Prussian antagonism to new educational experiments, he was glad to return to Göttingen as professor of philosophy, a chair now famous, for he was succeeded in it by Lotze, who in turn gave place to G. E. Müller. This appointment Herbart held until his death, eight years later, in 1841.

We need now to consider the manner in which Herbart prepared the way for experimental physiological psychology. It may seem strange to say that he anticipated this movement at all, for he expressly denied the applicability of experiment to psychological problems, and he disbelieved in the relevance of physiology. Nevertheless, he had so positive an effect that there have been those who have dated the beginning of modern German psychology from him. What did Herbart think psychology should be?

1. The title of his second work practically gives the answer to this question: *Psychologie als Wissenschaft, neu gegründet auf Erfahrung, Metaphysik und Mathematik.* Psychology is a science and it is grounded upon experience, metaphysics and mathematics.

Psychology is *science*. This as an explicit contention is something new, although we must remember that *Wissenschaft* includes but is not limited to experimental science. Herbart did not think that psychology could be experimental, though he did go on to claim for it the mathematical method, which is a fundamental tool of experimental science—the new science of Galileo and Newton. Herbart was against the use both of experiments and of physiology in psychology, but he was for the separate recognition of psychology as an important *Wissenschaft*. In that argument he was not excluding philosophy from psychology. On the contrary he was including metaphysics as being quite as basic to psychology as are experience and mathematics. It was much later that psychologists began to write "antimetaphysical" chapters—as Mach did in 1886. What Herbart gave to psychology was status. He took it out of both philosophy and physiology and sent it forth with a mission of its own.

Psychology is *empirical*, for it is grounded upon experience. This is not to say that it is experimental, for experiment is a method. Observation, not experiment, is the method of psychology, which thus grows out of experience. It is obviously an attribute of science to be empirical; science could hardly fail to be founded upon experience. This definite appeal of Herbart's to observation had, however, the effect of separating him explicitly from the *a priori* psychology of Kant and of uniting him potentially with the empiristic psychology of England, the school which provided the most immediate philosophical ground for the new psychology.

Psychology is *metaphysical*. This is, of course, an Herbartian tenet that was not handed on to the new psychology. It was natural enough, however, for Herbart to take this view, for he was a philosopher writing in the age when all philosophy had acquired a psychological cast. It seems that he believed that the metaphysical nature of psychology is one of the things that differentiate psychology from physical science. Psychology is metaphysical; physics is experimental. There is no doubt that it was this view, thoroughly exemplified in Herbart's psychological writings, that was largely responsible for the repudiation of Herbart by later scientific psychologists, like Wundt, who really owed much to him. For the same reason, the new psychology in Germany is said to have begun with Wundt and not with Herbart—nor with Lotze, who was equally metaphysical in his method.

Psychology is *mathematical*. This is another distinction between psychology and physics. Physics uses both of the scientific methods: calculation and experiment. Psychology can use only the former. We shall see later just what was the nature of Herbart's metaphysical calculation, divorced from experiment. This use of mathematics Herbart fully exhibited in the *Psychologie als Wissenschaft*, and that fact means that Fechner's mental measurement was not a new idea in so far as it was measurement. Fechner's originality lies in his combination of Herbart's use of mathematics with Weber's use of experiment. There is, moreover, much else in Fechner that is of Herbartian origin, like the concept of the limen—which might almost be said to have made psychophysics possible.

Is psychology *analytical*? Here we must pause. Herbart declared that it is not. The mind is unitary and can not be divided into parts. This is the familiar objection to analysis that we have encountered from Descartes to the present day. Herbart firmly took his stand against analysis and thus seemed to separate himself widely from British empiricists. We may ask, however, whether science is not essentially analytical. Herbart answered this question in the negative. The experimental method is necessarily analytical, but science is not; and psychology is an unexperimental science. In fact, it is because of the unity of the soul that psychology can not be experimental. Nevertheless, it is not clear, in spite of formal statement to the contrary, that Herbart avoided the analytical method. Even unexperimental mathematical science would seem to be analytical.

At any rate, Herbart's psychology is *mechanical*, with a statics and a dynamics of the soul. Herbartian ideas (Locke's sense, *Vorstellungen*) interact and vary in strength as the result of the interaction. One idea, a, may arrest another idea, b, and the law of their relation is expressed in an equation where the terms are a and b. As quantities, a and b represent the strengths of the ideas. There is nothing of elementism in saying that the ideas have degree or magnitude, but there is all of analytical elementism in separating one idea from another so that the two can interact. Kant had said that psychology can be neither experimental nor mathematical, because either method requires the existence of two independent variables, and ideas can vary only in time. Herbart seems to have followed Kant in respect of experiment, but in the interests of the use of mathematics he pointed out that ideas have two variables, time and intensity. Actually, as Herbart's statics show, ideas have a third dimension, quality, which individualizes each idea and makes a different from b. Herbart thus of necessity met the analytical conditions for mathematical treatment by analyzing mind into separate ideas which vary independently in intensity. This analysis gave him the statics of the soul. The addition of time as a variable gave him the dynamics.

It is not fair to blame Herbart for this confusion. In denying analysis, he was fighting the division of the mind into separate faculties. He was rejecting a kind of analysis to which psychology has never returned. Nevertheless, Herbart worked with ideational elements, elements which were so much more rigidly defined and so much less fluid than the elements of the associationists that they could even be fitted into mathematical formulae. Titchener has remarked that mental analysis is one of the things that Fechner got from Herbart, and he is right in spite of Herbart's repudiation of elementism.

We have seen what Herbart said psychology is. We have now to ask what, for him, it is *not*. The notion that it is not analytical we have refused to accept. What else is it not?

Psychology is not *experimental*. This contention of Kant's Herbart accepted. There is simply no obvious way, he thought, of experimenting upon the mind; and he thus expressed the view of the modern Cartesian who is puzzled as to what it can be that an experimental psychologist does. We know now that both Kant and Herbart were wrong, that there is a sufficient number of independent mental variables to render experimentation possible. To have asked Herbart, however, to see this fact and act upon it would have been simply to ask him to do what Fechner and Wundt did later. We must not be surprised that Herbart missed a point of logic and failed fully to anticipate the future.

Psychology is not *descriptive*. Its business is not a mere description of the mind but the working-out of its mathematical laws. In this point Herbart was reflecting the spirit of science, and there are many today who feel that a mere description of phenomena, without the formulation of laws and the usual accompaniment of quantification, is futile.

Psychology is not *physiological*, or at least not primarily so. Herbart was not interested in physiology, and he did not see that it could provide an approach to the problem of the mind. Since he was also not interested in experiment, he was not drawn into a consideration of the physiological technique for controlling the variables with which he dealt. It is no coincidence that physiological and experimental psychology began together; the one method requires the other.

Herbart did, however, recognize the relation between mind and body, and he laid down these three principles of connection. Bodily conditions may hinder the arousal of an idea (*e.g.*, in sleep): this is repression (*Druck*). They may facilitate the arousal of an idea (*e.g.*, in intoxication or passion): this is reinforcement (*Resonanz*). When the feelings or, through practice, the ideas cause movement (*e.g.*, in emotion or simple action), there is cooperation between soul and body. But all this discussion constituted for Herbart simply a special chapter of a psychology which is not physiological in fundamental nature or method.

2. Let us now consider the nature of Herbart's systematic unit, the idea or *Vorstellung*. (We may use the word *idea* in Locke's sense, remembering that the German word includes both perceptions and ideas as the modern English usage goes.) Here we shall discover why it is said that Herbart is the next step beyond Leibnitz.

We have already seen that these ideas are, according to Herbart, distinguishable from one another in respect of *quality*, and that every idea is invariable in quality. There is no shading-off of one idea into another; the differences are discrete. Every idea may, however, vary in *intensity* or force (*Kraft*), an attribute which is equivalent to clearness.

This force, which expresses itself in the clearness of the ideas, may be understood as a tendency of the ideas toward *self-preservation*. Each idea makes an effort to conserve itself as it enters into relation with others: the ideas are *active*, especially when there is opposition among them. Herbart thought of this tendency as the fundamental principle of mental mechanics, much as gravitation is the fundamental principle of physical mechanics. "Every movement of the ideas is confined between two fixed points: their state of complete inhibition, their state of complete liberty"; and there is a "natural and constant effort of all the ideas to revert to their state of complete liberty (absence of inhibition)." Thus Herbart is seen to be a dynamic psychologist, fitting into a line of succession from Leibnitz to Freud.

The basis of the opposition between the Herbartian ideas lies in their qualities: *a* and *b* may be opposed to each other, *a* and *c* may not. The effect of opposition upon their intensities is mutual, if *a* and *b* are simultaneous and opposed, each diminishes the other. The "metaphysical reason why opposed ideas resist one another is the unity of the soul of which they are the self-preservations." "If they did not on account of their opposition inhibit one another, all ideas would compose but one act of the soul; and in so far as they are not divided into many by any kind of inhibitions whatever, they really constitute but one act." In other words, those ideas that can together constitute a single mental act do not resist each other; however, in general, when one considers the multiplicity of ideas, inhibitions resulting from mutual opposition are seen to be the rule of consciousness. Actually, Herbart was giving a mechanical explanation of the fundamental fact of the limited range of consciousness.

The next point—and it is of primary importance—is that Herbart believed that no idea is completely destroyed by inhibition. Under opposition, it merely "yields" as much as is necessary, loses in intensity or clearness and passes from a *state of reality* to a *state of tendency*. Thus the suppressed ideas exist, but only as tendencies. We must accept this statement as it is made. To say that something, no longer real, exists as a tendency is not necessarily a paradox, though superficially it may appear that what exists is real and that a tendency can not do the one without being the other. Today we still have with us the problem of the nature of the 'unconscious.' Literally, the 'unconscious' is unconscious consciousness, but the apparent paradoxical nature of this phrase does not exclude us from facing the many problems of mental tendencies or potentialities.

It was out of this mechanics that Herbart derived his notion of the threshold or *limen of consciousness*. "By the limen of consciousness," he wrote, "I mean those limits that an idea seems to overleap in passing from a state of complete inhibition to a state of real idea." Now we see why the strength of an idea is equivalent to its clearness, for the strong ideas in preserving themselves are above the limen and are therefore conscious; and the inherently weak ideas or those that have been weakened by inhibition may lie below the limen and be unconscious. Strength gives clarity.

It is plain that the composition of consciousness at any moment is the resultant of the mechanical interplay of many ideas. Of all those ideas below the limen, only those that fit in with the unity of consciousness find so little resistance that they can rise above. Thus we have the appearance of the conscious ideas 'selecting' from among those that are unconscious the ones that are consonant with themselves. There is, however, no free selection; everything depends upon the mechanics of resultants. It is in connection with this picture of the mind that the word *apperception* appears in Herbart's exposition. As with Leibnitz, any idea that rises into consciousness is apperceived, but Herbart meant more by the word, for no idea rises except to take its place in the unitary whole of the ideas already conscious. The apperceiving of an idea is therefore not only the making of it conscious, but also its assimilation to a totality of conscious ideas, which Herbart called the "apperceiving mass." Herbart is perhaps more famous for his doctrine of apperception than for anything else. The phrase *apperceptive mass* appeared in common speech for many years. Yet Herbart made less of apperception in psychology than might be supposed. This view of his became important because it is a psychological picture of the process of education and Herbart is famous, as indeed he would have wished to be, for his educational theory.

The details of this portion of Herbart's psychology derive, of course, directly from Leibnitz. *Apperception* was Leibnitz's word. The notion of activity in ideas was Leibnitz's, although the picture of their mechanical interaction is the exact antithesis of his doctrine of pre-established harmony between completely independent monads. Leibnitz's *petites perceptions* have become with Herbart inhibited ideas. Both men use the same conceptions of degrees of perception and of the striving of ideas for self-realization. Herbart's limen of consciousness is only a step beyond Leibnitz. There are thus plenty of grounds for saying that Leibnitz, and not Kant, was Herbart's tutor.

We may also at this point look ahead. Leibnitz foreshadowed the entire doctrine of the unconscious, but Herbart actually began it. Wundt was to appeal first to unconscious inference in order to explain perception, and then to apperception. Fechner was to take from Herbart the notion of the measurement of the magnitude of conscious data, the notion of analysis, and, most important of all, the notion of the limen. Moreover, this Herbartian concept of the limen was to lead Fechner to his notion of degrees of intensity below the limen, his "negative sensations." The conception of active ideas striving for realization was to effect act psychology slightly and abnormal psychology greatly. Freud's early description of the unconscious might almost have come directly from Herbart, although it did not. There was still a use for some of Herbart's psychology fifty and even a hundred years afterward; moreover, if Herbart is established as an ancestor of dynamic psychology, then his genes may still be reproducing themselves a century from now.

3. It is quite true that Herbart's picture of apperception and the constitution of consciousness in general makes it appear that the principal mental thing that is going on all the while is inhibition. The activity of combination is mostly negative; the apper-

ceiving mass of ideas selects new constituents by suppressing all but a few, which come up into consciousness of their own force, when not opposed. Nevertheless Herbart had something to say about the union of ideas when there is little or no conflict. There are three cases.

When there is no opposition between the ideas and they belong to the same "continuities" (modalities), they unite and we have *fusion*. The example is red and blue uniting to give violet. When there is no opposition and the ideas belong to different continuities, as with a sound and a color, they may still form a unity, and such a unity Herbart called a *complication*. It is this use of the words *fusion* and *complication* that was taken over by Wundt and those who followed his lead. Thus the problem of the personal equation, which we studied in an earlier chapter, leads in psychology to the complication experiment, because it involves the union of impressions from the eye and the ear. (See pp. 142-147.)

Inhibition also leads to laws of union when the inhibition is incomplete. Two ideas of equal strength completely inhibit each other—at least Herbart thought that he had proved this to be a fact; but two ideas of unequal strength can never inhibit each other, and thus both remain, contributing their resultant to consciousness. (The mathematics of this case we shall examine in a moment.) Three or more unequal ideas may also yield a conscious resultant or may result in the complete inhibition of one, as the case may be. Herbart deals with these cases mathematically, but it will not profit us to follow him.

4. We have spoken repeatedly of Herbart's mathematical method, and yet the reader can scarcely be expected to say how, without experimental quantitative observation, it is possible to apply mathematics to psychology. There is no way to describe Herbart's procedure except by illustration. Let us therefore take the case of two simultaneous ideas of unequal intensity, a case which leads to one of Herbart's fundamental laws of the statics of the soul—that a strong idea can not inhibit a weak when there are only two in competition.

Let there be then, Herbart said, two simultaneous opposing ideas, a and b; and let a be greater than b. Each will have an inhibitory effect on the other, so that each is diminished in force.

Herbart said further that the decrement in b will bear the same ratio to the total strength of b that a, which causes the decrement in b, bears to the total force of a and b together, *i.e.*, $a + b$. Then Herbart immediately wrote a proportionality, but the argument may be clearer to the reader if we pause to call this decrement d.

Thus the foregoing statement becomes:

$$a + b : a : : b : d;$$

but this is an equation, and

$$d = \frac{ab}{a + b}.$$

Hence the proportionality that Herbart wrote without this step:

$$a + b : a : : b : \frac{ab}{a + b}.$$

Since it is hardly likely that the reader will regard the formation of this proportionality as obviously correct, we may translate Herbart into a somewhat simpler statement. If d is the decrement of b, then the ratio $\frac{d}{b}$ will be the proportional amount or fraction of itself by which b is diminished by a. This effect of a on b is, however, also dependent upon the relation of a to the total force of consciousness, $a + b$, for the larger a is with respect to b, the more effect does it have on b relative to b, $i.e.$, the proportional amount that b is reduced is the proportion that a holds to the total force of consciousness. Thus:

$$\frac{d}{b} = \frac{a}{a + b}, \text{ and } d = \frac{ab}{a - b}.$$

If the reader is not now convinced, he is mistrusting Herbart's metaphysical rationalism, upon which these statements are founded, and not his mathematics, which merely proceeds from it. Let us go on.

After b is diminished by d, the residual strength of b is

$$b - d = b - \frac{ab}{a + b} = \frac{b^2}{a + b}.$$

But $\frac{b^2}{a + b} = 0$, only when $b = 0$ or $a = \infty$. Neither of these conditions can be true, for $b \neq 0$ by the hypothesis that b is a conscious idea; and $a \neq \infty$ because no idea can be of infinite strength. Hence it follows that

$$b - d = \frac{b^2}{a + b} \neq 0.$$

This is to say that, in the case we are discussing, the residual strength of b, after inhibition by a, can never be zero: a can not completely inhibit b when there are only these two ideas interacting.

If the stronger idea can not completely inhibit the weaker, one would hardly expect that the weaker could completely inhibit the stronger. We may, however, proceed exactly and apply the same process to show that b diminishes a by an amount $\dfrac{ab}{a+b}$ to a value $\dfrac{a^2}{a+b}$. Thus we find not only that a can not be completely inhibited by b but also that, in their interaction, action and reaction are equal, for each is reduced by the other in the same amount, $\dfrac{ab}{a+b}$.

The final result is the general law: Of two simultaneous ideas of unequal strength, neither can suppress the other below the limen. The range of consciousness, Herbart might have said, is greater than two ideas.

Herbart went on to show that, when three ideas interact, one may be completely inhibited; and thence he passed to other derivations in his mental statics and thence to his mental dynamics. There is no need to follow him further, for we have seen, at an elementary level, the nature of his method.

What is the matter with it? The mathematics is sound; we all believe that consciousness is capable of supporting at least two ideas simultaneously; and yet this law and the others with it have never made a place for themselves in psychology. The trouble must be that the premises, though rationally plausible, are not convincing. The original statement that the relative inhibition of b would be in the proportion of a to the total strength of a and b is too simple, or at least too little grounded upon experience, to seem probable. Herbart, if he could not use experiment, at least needed some substitute for it. He exhibited the not uncommon case in science in which inadequate data are treated with elaborate mathematics, the precision of which creates the illusion that the original data are as exact as the method of treatment. It is often that the person who works well with mathematics lacks the gift of criticism against experimental results or even against his assumed postulates.

5. History has criticized Herbart for us. His belief in a scientific psychology founded upon experience has persisted. His mathematical method proved vital only when united to experiment, and thus to physiology, both of which he rejected. His view of the relation of consciousness to unconsciousness is still of use, although

with many modifications. His metaphysical foundation for psychology, however, has not survived. It is not that psychology is not founded upon metaphysics; psychologists involve themselves in metaphysics more often than they realize. What the history of psychology has shown is that there is an incompatibility between the empirical and the metaphysical bases of psychology. Herbart's metaphysics led him to substitute *a priori* generalizations for inductions based upon observation. Such a procedure might have attained some truth had he been willing afterward to appeal to experimental verification, but he was not willing. Herbart's *Psychologie als Wissenschaft* was thus only part of what a scientific psychology required.

Herbart represents, therefore, a transition from the pure speculation of Kant and Fichte and Hegel to the antimetaphysical experimentalism of Fechner and Wundt and Helmholtz. Hence it is natural that Herbart's school, the group of men who are called Herbartians, should contain the name of no experimentalist. Drobisch, the logician at Leipzig, was a prominent Herbartian. It was he who helped to bring Wundt, instead of Horwicz, to Leipzig in 1874, but he was not a psychologist. Waitz, Lazarus and Steinthal were all Herbartians, but with ethnographic interests. W. F. Volkmann, Ritter von Volkmar, is perhaps the Herbartian who had the most direct influence upon modern psychology, for he wrote in 1856 a *Lehrbuch der Psychologie* which remained the only up-to-date textbook of psychology in German until Wundt published the *Physiologische Psychologie* in 1874. In general, Herbart's effect upon experimental psychology was not through the Herbartians at all. What happened was that his work directly influenced Fechner and Wundt, both in respect of what they borrowed from it and also in respect of what they positively rejected.

HERMANN LOTZE

Lotze is less important in the history of psychology than Herbart. Herbart, for all his metaphysics, stands for the reaction in psychology away from the philosophy of Fichte, Hegel and Schelling toward a scientific psychology. Lotze remained more nearly in the direct tradition of these three post-Kantian philosophers. We can see the differences in the genetic course of the interests of the two men. Herbart, although he published his *Metaphysik* only a few years before his death, nevertheless tended to move from philosophy toward psychology. Lotze moved in the opposite direction. Frequently, though not always, it is a man's later work that determines his place in the history of thought—perhaps because his later work has upon it a stamp of maturity.

Lotze's chief gift to posterity was, therefore, his metaphysics. He enters, however, into the history of psychology for three other reasons. (1) In the first place, there is the fact that he published a "medical psychology, or physiology of the soul" in 1852, the first book claiming to be a physiological psychology, just as Herbart's was the first claiming to be a scientific psychology. (2) Then there is his theory of space, the foundation of the later empiristic theories based on local signs. In that he was against the Kantian tradition, picking up the thread from Thomas Brown. Helmholtz's and Wund's empiricist theories derive most directly fom Lotze. (3) And finally there is the fact that Lotze, in Herbart's chair at Göttingen after 1844, a philosopher with this interest in the new physiological (medical) psychology, was, like William James in America, the pioneer of the new psychology. Stumpf and G. E. Müller were his students. Brentano, throughout the vicissitudes of his early professional life, was Lotze's protégé. Even after Lotze's productivity had turned into metaphysics, he continued to lecture on psychology and to exert a strong personal influence upon psychologists in Germany and Austria. That was natural enough when all the German psychologists held chairs of philosophy.

Rudolph Hermann Lotze (1817-1881) was the son of an army physician and was born at Bautzen in 1817, the year after the publication of Herbart's *Lehrbuch*. When Lotze was still an infant, however, his father's regiment moved to Zittau, and there Lotze spent his youth. He went first to the *Stadtschule* and then at the age of eleven to the *Gymnasium*, which he attended for six years before he was ready to enter the university. His father died when he was twelve. The *Gymnasium* at Zittau was an excellent school and had several famous graduates. Not very much seems to be known about this period of Lotze's life; during it his interest in philosophy began and his especial interest lay in poetry.

At the age of seventeen (1834) Lotze went to the university at Leipzig and matriculated under the faculty of medicine. In thus selecting a profession he was following in his father's steps, but by temperament he was more disposed toward the arts and philosophy than toward science and medical practice. The result was a varied education. At Leipzig he began the writing of poems, of which he published a volume in 1840, his first publication after his dissertation. He was also drawn into philosophy, where he came under the inspiration of Christian Weisse, an Hegelian. On the scientific side he was thrown with E. H. Weber, A. W. Volkmann and Fechner.

Weber, twenty-two years older than Lotze, had been professor of anatomy at Leipzig since 1818. He had just (1834) published his *Annotationes anatomicae et physiologiae*, which includes the section *De tactu*, the classical and pioneer report of experimental researches on touch, later (1846) expanded into the better known *Der Tastsinn und das Gemeingefühl* in Wagner's *Handwörterbuch*. A. W. Volkmann had then just been promoted from *Dozent* to *ausserordentlicher Professor* of zootomy at Leipzig, a post which he held for three years before he went to Dorpat. He was writing his *Physiologie des Gesichtssinnes* (1836), which Johannes Müller so frequently cited in portions of his *Handbuch*, also then in preparation. In this same year (1834) Fechner, with a reputation based upon his research on the galvanic battery, had been appointed professor of physics, a post which he held until he resigned on account of ill health five years later. This was before Fechner's philosophical or psychophysical interests had occupied his attention, but nevertheless it was the same Fechner, and he must have given his science the cast that would attract a young, philosophically minded medical student. Weber, Volkmann and Fechner were all within six years of each other in age and were all in their thirties, young men for their positions but twice the age of Lotze, who went to Leipzig at seventeen. He was a silent listener in Fechner's circle and corresponded with him and with Frau Fechner after he had left Leipzig a decade later (*cf.* p. 277). When he wrote his *Medicinische Psychologie*, he dedicated it to Volkmann and included in it a pre-Fechnerian discussion of Weber's law.

Lotze remained four years at Leipzig and then took his degree in medicine. He was still half a philosopher: his dissertation was on "the future biology according to philosophical principles." He spent, however, one year in the practice of medicine at Zittau, the home of his childhood, before it became plain to him that he was destined for an academic life. In 1839 he returned to Leipzig and was habilitated as *Dozent* in both the faculty of medicine and the faculty of philosophy, an unusual attainment. The poems of his student days were published in 1840, and he then began a period in which medical and philosophical publication were of about equal frequency. In 1841 his *Metaphysik* appeared, and also a critique of the theory of space of Weisse, his philosophical master. The next year there was his *Allgemeine Pathologie und*

Therapie als mechanische Naturwissenschaften, by which he is said to have "lept into fame." There was even a second edition of this book six years later. In 1843 his *Logik* was published. Meanwhile Fechner had resigned but was still living in Leipzig. Volkmann had gone to Dorpat and thence to Halle.

In 1844, when still only twenty-seven, Lotze accepted the offer of Herbart's chair at Göttingen, where he remained for thirtyseven years, almost until his death, being succeeded by G. E. Müller. For a while after his change to Göttingen, his interests seemed more physiological than philosophical. He wrote three chapters for Wagner's *Handwörterbuch der Physiologie: Leben und Lebenskraft* (1843), *Instinkt* (1844), and *Seele und Seelenleben* (1846). In 1851 he published his *Allgemeine Physiologie des körperlichen Lebens,* and then in 1852 his famous *Medicinische Psychologie,* followed in the next year by *Physiologische Untersuchungen,* which completed his important psychological writing. After this, Lotze turned almost entirely to philosophy. His most important work was the three volumes that constituted the *Mikrokosmus,* which appeared from 1856 to 1864. His *System der Philosophie* in two volumes was published in 1874 and 1879. In 1881 he was persuaded by Zeller and Helmholtz, both his enthusiastic supporters, to accept the chair at Berlin, but he died of pneumonia three months after the change.

Lotze was a quiet, methodical man, with the sensitiveness of the esthete and the industry of the scientist. He was a meticulous and uninspiring lecturer, and he never had large classes. He was too much of a humanist to be a mechanist, and he spent his life in synthetizing these opposing views of the world. He came to no dogmatic conclusion and he founded no school, but his rare sympathy created for him, especially through his writings, a wide sphere of influence. His lectures, given ex tempore from carefully prepared notes, led to the posthumous publication of the dictata of his various courses, including psychology, which was the only subject upon which he lectured every year for the entire thirtyseven years at Göttingen. Opposed to pure materialism, he naturally influenced in psychology the antimechanical systems and thus came less into contact with experimental psychology.

It is not strange that such a man should influence markedly his pupils and others who came within his circle of friends. Thus we make particular mention, because they are famous psychologists, of Brentano, Stumpf and G. E. Müller. Brentano, after being *Dozent* at Würzburg in 1866-1872, was promoted to a professorship. He was a priest and was appointed as a priest. In 1869 he had written the leading memoir in refutation of the dogma of the infallibility of the Pope, and, when this dogma, after violent controversy, was accepted by the Catholic Church, he felt it necessary to resign his priesthood and thus his professorship, after he had held it but a year. This was a situation that would naturally appeal to Lotze, who used his influence successfully to have Brentano appointed as a layman to the chair of philosophy at Vienna. Stumpf was a student of Lotze's in 1867-1868, received his doctorate at Göttingen in 1869 and was *Dozent* there from 1870 to 1873 when he went to Würzburg in Brentano's place. G. E. Müller, after studying at Berlin and Leipzig, went to Göttingen at about this time and received his doctorate there in 1873. He returned in 1876 and became *Dozent* for four years, writing *Zur Grundlegung der Psychophysik* (1878). The year 1880-1881 he spent at Czernowitz, but in 1881 he returned to Göttingen to succeed Lotze, who, as we have seen, went to Berlin a few months before his death. Brentano mentions Lotze in the preface of his *Psychologie* (1874); Stumpf dedicated the *Raumvorstellung* (1873) and Müller dedicated the *Psychophysik* (1878) to Lotze.

In this personal way Lotze exerted some influence upon experimental psychology, although it was not great. Primarily, however, it was Lotze's *Medicinische Psychologie oder Physiologie der Seele* in 1852 that leads to his inclusion in this history.

The title of this book of Lotze's reflects his dual interest in physiology and philosophy at the time of its writing. The content reveals further that Lotze was at heart a metaphysician. Just as his medical dissertation was founded upon "philosophical principles," so was his *Psychologie* a metaphysician's psychology. For this reason, the book as a whole never had great influence in a psychology that repudiated metaphysics. Herbart was overtly and thoroughly metaphysical, but it was not his metaphysical psychology that he contributed to experimental psychology; it was his empiricism, his mathematics, his analysis, his notion of activity and his concept of the limen that were taken out of his psychology and built into a new structure. Lotze's psychology yielded fewer useful elements of this sort, little more, in fact, than the basal conception of a physiological psychology and the specific view of psychological space. Let us glance at its contents.

The first book of the *Medicinische Psychologie* is entitled "The General Fundamental Concepts of Physiological Psychology" (this phrase, *physiological psychology*, is explicitly used), with chapters on the existence of the soul, the psychophysical mechanism, and the essence and destiny of the soul. Physiology is brought into the second chapter in connection with the problems of mind and body, phrenology, and the seat of the soul, but the entire cast of the book, as these subject-matters would lead one to expect, is not physiological.

The second book has the title, "The Elements and the Physiological Mechanism of the Mental Life." The first chapter on sensation has little that is novel after Johannes Müller and Weber, though it is interesting to find, as we have already noted, a discussion of the proportions between stimulus and sensation eight years before Fechner immortalized Weber's law (1860), although one year after Fechner's first discussion of this phase of the mind-body problem (1851). The second chapter on feeling, and the third on movement and instinct, also contain little that is factually new or theoretically important. Lotze included Weber's *Gemeingefühle* under feeling. The final chapter is on space-perception and included the famous doctrine of local signs to which we shall return presently.

The third and last book reflects Lotze's interest in therapy and pathology, and thus makes the book more nearly a medical than a physiological psychology. It bears the title, "Development of the Mental Life in Health and Disease," and the chapters are on states of consciousness, the developmental conditions of the mental life and the disturbance of the mental life. Of these chapters, the first discusses consciousness and unconsciousness, attention and the course of ideas; the second, animal minds and instincts, and innate individual capacities (*Anlagen*); and the last, psychopathology.

If Herbart marked the transition from metaphysical to physiological psychology, Lotze marked a further stage of the same course of change. Herbart was full of argument, with few facts and no physiology. Lotze was full of physiological fact and was thus the more scientific of the two. Nevertheless, Herbart influenced factual scientific psychology the more, paradoxical as it may seem, because with a negligible factual basis he contributed methods and conceptions; whereas Lotze, with many facts, failed to add much to the theoretical structure. If Lotze's facts had been new—but they were not. On the scientific side, Lotze was writing a textbook and not an opus.

His *theory of space-perception* was, however, an important and influential contribution. Lotze began it by asserting that the mind is capable of the notion of space and that it is compelled by this notion to arrange sensory content spatially, even though that content has nothing in itself inherently spatial. This view contains two important points.

In the first place, we must note that Lotze believed that perceived space is derived from conscious data that are themselves non-spatial. He accused others of begging the question in their theories of space-perception. He complained that the view still persisted that somehow small copies of objects enter in the mind in modified form and, being disposed in respect of space, are thus immediately perceived spatially. Even Johannes Müller, who fought this view in his theory of the specific energies of nerves, did not wholly avoid its error, for he held that there is a spatial projection of objective images upon the nervous substance and that the mind, in perceiving the state of the nerves rather than the object, directly perceives the spatial relations of this image. Such a view, Lotze thought, is not a theory of space, for it puts space in at the start and comes out with it at the end. A true theory of space is an account that goes behind space and shows how it is derived from what is non-spatial. This conclusion of Lotze's, we may object, hardly seems in itself to be a justification for his assumption that primary data of space are non-spatial. It was legitimate for him to say that the older beliefs begged the question and were therefore not theories at all; but such a conclusion did not prove that there must be a theory of space. Perhaps none was needed. It is probable, however, that Lotze was arguing from empiristic intuition, that he felt sure that the raw data of experience have intensity and quality only, and that spatiality must therefore somehow be derived from these more primary other data.

In the second place, we must observe that even Lotze was not ready to try to conjure space out of something not at all spatial: the mind, he said, has an inherent capacity for arranging its content spatially. How else would it ever come to read space into what is not in itself spatial? It is quite obvious that some principle of this sort was needed, but it is also obvious that its admission robs of some of its cogency the argument that the older views begged the question. Lotze, like the others found that he must put space into the mind before he was able to create it there. Nevertheless, Lotze may be said to have avoided begging the question, because, though he derived the perception of space in part from a capacity for spatial perception, space and the capacity for perceiving it are two different things, and Lotze did not fail to give us an account of the manner in which the one gives rise to the other. By his own criterion he had a theory.

The problem of nativism and empiricism in theories of space was not raised until a decade later, when Helmholtz attacked nativism. Nevertheless we can ask to which class Lotze's view belongs. His emphasis upon the innate capacity of the mind for spatial perception seems to place him with the nativists, until one realizes that the main force of his theory was to show that the perception of space is generated in experience from non-spatial materials. There is no doubt, therefore, that he belongs with the empiricists in this issue.

Now, the primary data of experience Lotze believed to be qualitative and intensive, and his theory held that it is from its intensive aspect that space evolves. Let us consider the space of touch first and of vision later.

Every tactual sensation (we are following Lotze) has its *local sign*, which is not a new attribute but a specific aggregation of intensities. A touch upon the skin has a diffuse effect because of the yielding and elasticity of the tissues, and it thus sets up a pattern of intensities. This pattern is different in every part of the skin that can be touched because of the differences in the tissues: some parts are hard and others soft, under some there are veins or tendons, and the pattern, depending on all these factors, varies in different places with the conformation of the body. It is exactly this intensitive pattern that *is* the local sign: it is local in its dependence of bodily locality and it is local in its mental function as a sign; and yet, being only a sign of position, it is not in itself spatial but only a pattern of intensities.

A very telling argument that was brought against this view of Lotze's lay in an appeal to bodily symmetry. The two halves of the body are alike in conformation: why do we not then, it was asked, confuse the right hand with the left? The fact is, of course, that the two hands are distinguished more readily than are very many more adjacent parts of the body which are more different in structure. Lotze replied to this objection by saying that the body is not perfectly symmetrical and that no two hands are ever exactly alike—an answer that leaves us still dissatisfied.

The local signs thus give us different experiences for different localities, but they do not give us space, which is a continuous manifold. How does a consciousness of space arise? It comes, in Lotze's theory, by way of experience and *movement*. When, in movement of the body, a stimulus changes its region of stimulation, the local signs change, and successive local signs are the signs of adjacent localities. If we are equipped with a large number of local signs and we know which signs are adjacent, we can solve out, as it were, a kind of solid space. There is no reason why we should do this, except that the mind tends to arrange all content spatially. Lotze believed that the mind, possessed of this tendency and having put all the local signs into relation by movement, creates a psychological space out of them. Wundt and other empiricists held a similar view later, but Lotze was the originator of it.

With vision the case is less clear than with touch, because a photic stimulus does not mechanically create an intensive pattern. Here, however, Lotze appealed to the innate mechanism by which we tend to fixate whatever comes into attention. The fixation of an object that lies originally in the periphery of the visual field requires a movement of the eyes and, moreover, a different movement for every point of the periphery. Experientially these movements are intensive patterns and thus furnish the visual local signs. The theory, of course, fails to show how the eyes 'know' where to move in the first instance, but presumably Lotze felt that this matter could be dismissed to physiology and thus left out of account in psychology. At any rate, such movement is instinctive and thus is all ready to play its rôle in experience as soon as experience begins.

However, the problem of vision is not yet entirely solved. We can still tell where an object is without moving the eyes. How can we if it is movement that creates the local sign? To this objection Lotze replied that we can experience a tendency to movement without the movement's taking place. It thus appears that the visual local sign is really only a tendency to movement, although its spatial meaning has been derived through actual movement in the past. If this argument seems forced, nevertheless we have to remember that it reflects a real difficulty. Again and again introspection yields experience that is like the experience of movement when there is no movement observable. Quite generally against this dilemma psychologists have taken refuge in 'tendencies to movement,' 'incipient movements,' 'covert movements' or 'implicit movements.'

Finally, we must note that Lotze so far recognized the fact that perceptions degenerate as to hold that the local signs might in the course of experience become actually unconscious. In the case of vision not only do we no longer need, after sufficient experience, to have actual movement, but we may even have nothing experiential at all. This addition of unconscious local signs detracts from the beautiful simplicity of Lotze's theory, but the fact is obvious so far as ordinary introspection can reach. Lotze was never one to avoid such facts when he realized their existence.

In brief, then, Lotze's theory of space is this. Every visual or tactual stimulus sets up, or tends to set up, an experiential intensitive pattern that is specific for the point stimulated. By movement these local signs can be related spatially and brought to mean locality in a single total system of space; and, because the mind tends to arrange its contents in space, it takes advantage of these local signs to create both space and locality for all the particular sensations. Physical locality is, of course, the starting point, and it yields intensive patterns which have in themselves nothing of space, except that they depend upon space. The mind, by way of movement, gets back the space which was lost in the purely intensive patterns. There is, however, no *petitio principii* here. That we should start with physical locality and end with mental localization is not to beg the question, but simply to treat of perception, which in its essence is the awareness of objects as they really are.

NOTES

Kant

Kant is much more than a man and a system of ideas; he is actually a subject, a field. Let the reader consult B. Rand's bibliography in J. M. Baldwin, *Dictionary of Philosophy and Psychology*, 1905, III, 286-320, for what had been said about Kant at that date. Besides the many editions of Kant's collected works and 81 separate works, for many of which there are successive *verbesserte Auflagen*, Rand gives a list of 15 biographical books and articles about Kant, and well over 1400 critical articles about his philosophy.

On Kant's life, see J. H. W. Stuckenberg, *The Life of Immanuel Kant*, 1882; or, in German, A. Hoffmann, *Immanuel Kant*, 1902, who brings together the contributions of three early authors; or some of the other references that Rand gives.

For brief elementary accounts of Kant's philosophy, see J. Royce, *The Spirit of Modern Philosophy*, 1892, 101-134; A. K. Rogers, *Student's History of Philosophy*, 3 ed., 1932, 376-400, or an earlier ed.; G. S. Brett, *History of Psychology*, 1921, II, 337-350 (not much related to the present text); B. Russell, *A History of Western Philosophy*, 1945, 701-718 (closely related to the present text). For re-

printed important passages from Kant, see B. Rand, *Modern Classical Philosophers*, 1908, 376-485.

Herbart

There are two editions of J. F. Herbart's collected writings. The more familiar is G. Hartenstein's. Herbart's *Lehrbuch zur Psychologie*, 1816, 2 ed., 1834, has been translated into English by M. K. Smith, 1891. B. Rand, *Classical Psychologists*, 1912, 395-415, reprints excerpts from this translation. The *Psychologie als Wissenschaft*, 1824-1825, has not been translated. Herbart also published *Psychologische Untersuchungen* in 1839-1840, shortly before his death. For his other writings, see Rand in Baldwin's *Dictionary* (*op. cit.*), III, 253-257.

On Herbart's psychology, see, in the histories of psychology: Th. Ribot, *German Psychology of To-Day*, trans. from French, 1886, 24-48; M. Dessoir, *Outlines of the History of Psychology*, trans. from German, 1912, 210-221; O. Klemm, *History of Psychology*, trans. from German, 1914, esp. 103-111; J. M. Baldwin, *History of Psychology*, 1913, II, 76-82; G. S. Brett, *History of Psychology*, 1921, III, 76-82; G. Murphy, *Historical Introduction to Modern Psychology*, 2 ed.

1949, 49-54. See also O. Flügel, *Herbarts Lehren und Leben*, 1912; John Adams, *Herbartian Psychology Applied to Education*, 1897; and W. T. Harris' preface to Smith's translation of the *Lehrbuch* (*op. cit.*), v-xix.

For Herbart's life, see Flügel, *op. cit.*; A. M. Williams, *Johann Friedrich Herbart*, 1911, 8-22. The biographical charts in the front of B. C. Mulliner's translation of Herbart's *Application of Psychology to the Science of Education*, 1898, are more useful than the text.

For W. Wundt's comments on the Kantian and Herbartian psychologies, see his *Grundzüge der physiologischen Psychologie*, any of the six editions, the end of the very first section. The discussion differs in the last three editions.

The exposition of Herbart's psychology involves at every point the *Vorstellung*, a word that cannot be properly translated into English. Smith has translated it "concept"; Baldwin in translating Ribot has used "representation." Both words fail to carry the meaning. Another translation of letters and lectures (not cited here) has used "presentation," which is literally correct, but this English word has never gained the general connotation of *Vorstellung*. To keep the German word is awkward. The text has therefore kept to the word "idea," although this translation is only correct when *idea* means what Locke meant by it, *i.e.*, both perception and idea.

Another word that gives difficulty is Herbart's *Hemmung*. Smith translates it by "resistance," "arrest," and "suppression"; Baldwin by "arrest." It has seemed better to the present author to give *Hemmung* its modern connotation and in general to say "inhibition."

For Herbart's derivation of the law that two unequal ideas cannot inhibit each other, see *Psychologie als Wissenschaft*, sect. 44. This mathematically derived law is the one most usually cited (*cf.* the commentaries mentioned above); but Ribot, *op. cit.*, 35, introduces a gross error in one of the equations.

In the text we have not mentioned Herbart's connection with associationism. Herbart can not be called an associationist, for the meaning of that word has become too specific. Nevertheless, although his theoretical basis differs utterly from that of the English school, his treatment of the facts is almost (as James pointed out) identical. *Cf.* also Herbart's discussion of the then recent history of psychology (Descartes, Leibnitz, Wolff and Locke), *Psychologie als Wissenschaft*, sects. 17-22.

On the Herbartian school, see esp. Ribot, *op. cit.*, 49-67.

On Herbart's relation to physiological experimental psychology and also for an excellent account of his psychology, see Th. Ziehen, *Das Verhältnis der Herbartschen Psychologie zur physiologischexperimentellen Psychologie*, 1900, printed in Schiller and Ziehen, *Sammlung Abhandl. Gebiete päd. Psychol. Physiol.*, III, Heft 5. Much less satisfactory is F. Willers' dissertation, *Die psychologische Denkweise Herbarts im Verhältnis zu der modernen physiologischen Psychologie*, 1913.

Lotze

Beside R. H. Lotze's *Medicinische Psychologie*, 1852, there is his *Grundzüge der Psychologie*, 1881, which is the immediately posthumous publication of the summaries of his lectures on psychology in the winter of 1880-1881, summaries which Lotze dictated at the end of each lecture. There are two English translations of these notes under the title *Outlines of Psychology*, one by G. T. Ladd in 1886 (excerpts on theory of local signs in Rand, *Classical Psychologists*, 545-556) and the other by C. L. Herrick in 1885. To the German *Grundzüge* is appended a bibliography of Lotze's writings by E. Rhenisch. For bibliography, see also Rand in Baldwin's *Dictionary*, III, 347-350.

On Lotze's psychology, see especially Ribot, *op. cit.*, 68-95. For biographical accounts and discussion of his work in general, see Rhenisch, *Rev. philos.*, 1881, 12, 321-336; R. Falckenberg,

Hermann Lotze (for he dropped his first name in later years), 1901; G. S. Hall, *Founders of Modern Psychology,* 1912, 65-121; M. Wentscher, *Hermann Lotze,* 1913, and, more briefly, *Fechner und Lotze,* 1925, 73-201. Less important are T. M. Lindsay, *Mind,* 1876, 1, 363-382; and L. Baerwald, *Die Entwicklung der Lotzeschen Psychologie,* 1905 (dissertation).

In the histories of psychology, beside Ribot, *loc. cit.,* see Baldwin, *op. cit.,* II, 82-86; Brett, *op. cit.,* 139-151; Murphy, *op. cit.,* 145-148.

On E. H. Weber and A. W. Volkmann, see pp. 100-102, 110-112; on Fechner, see pp. 275-296.

The history of the Göttingen chair is this: Herbart, 1833-1841, eight years; Lotze, 1844-1881, thirty-seven years; G. E. Müller, 1881-1921, forty years, for it was about 1921 that Müller ceased to lecture and Ach went to Göttingen.

Falckenberg, *op. cit.,* 193-203, gives indexes of letters of Lotze's, including correspondence with the Fechners and with Stumpf.

Lotze's philosophy was an *Ideal-Realismus.* He was a mediator between opponent views, between idealism and realism, between spiritualism and materialism. He thus, as we shall see in the next chapter, had much in common with Fechner.

His position on the problem of mind and body has not been discussed in the text because it enters into the history of thought more as a phase of his philosophy than as an influence upon experimental psychology. It is enough to say that he was antimaterialistic in his psychology in spite of his physiological interests. See Hall, *loc. cit.;* Wentscher, *Fechner und Lotze* (*op. cit.*), and more especially Th. Simon, *Leib und Seele bei Fechner und Lotze,* 1894, and A. Lichtenstein, *Lotze und Wundt,* 1900 (dissertation), 50-80.

For support of the author's view that Lotze's psychology was more metaphysical than scientific, see Ribot, *op. cit.,* 69-75; E. B. Titchener, *Experimental Psychology,* II, pt. ii, pp. cxi f., clix. The writers of the histories of psychology testify to the same fact by their scant mention of Lotze's name. We have said in the text that Lotze made his psychology physiological by giving the physiological facts, but bare facts did not interest Lotze greatly. He distinguished between *cognitio rei,* an intuitive knowledge of the essential nature of things, and *cognitio circa rem,* a knowledge of the more obvious external relations of things. The former is the metaphysician's truth, the latter is the scientist's fact, and it is plain, in this sense of the words, that Lotze preferred truth to fact, that he felt that scientific knowledge *about* things was but superficial in failing to penetrate to their true essence. See Lotze, *Medicinische Psychologie,* 3-65, esp. 55 ff.; Ribot, *loc. cit.*

THE FOUNDING OF EXPERIMENTAL
PSYCHOLOGY

CHAPTER 14

Gustav Theodor Fechner

W e come at last to the formal beginning of experimental psychology, and we start with Fechner: not with Wundt, thirty-one
years Fechner's junior, who published his first important but youthful psychological study two years after Fechner's epoch-making
work; not with Helmholtz, twenty years younger, who was
primarily a physiologist and a physicist but whose great genius extended to include psychology; but with Fechner, who was not a
great philosopher nor at all a physiologist, but who performed with
scientific rigor those first experiments which laid the foundation for
the new psychology and still lie at the basis of its methodology.*
There had been, as we have seen, a psychological physiology:
Johannes Müller, E. H. Weber. There had been, as we have also
seen, the development of the philosophical belief in a scientific or a
physiological psychology: Herbart, Lotze; Hartley, Bain. Nothing
is new at its birth. The embryo had been maturing and had already
assumed, in all great essentials, its later form. With Fechner it was
born, quite as old, and also quite as young, as a baby.

THE DEVELOPMENT OF FECHNER'S IDEAS

Gustav Theodor Fechner (1801-1887) was a versatile man. He
first acquired modest fame as professor of physics at Leipzig, but
in later life he was a physicist only as the spirit of the *Naturforscher*
penetrated all his work. In intention and ambition he was a philosopher, especially in his last forty years of life, but he was never
famous, or even successful, in this fundamental effort that is, nevertheless, the key to his other activities. He was a humanist, a satirist, a
poet in his incidental writings and an estheticist during one decade
of activity. He is famous, however, for his psychophysics, and this
fame was rather forced upon him. He did not wish his name to go
down to posterity as a psychophysicist. He did not, like Wundt,
seek to found experimental psychology. He might have been content
to let experimental psychology as an independent science remain in

the womb of time, could he but have established his spiritualistic *Tagesansicht* as a substitute for the current materialistic *Nachtansicht* of the universe. The world, however, chose for him; it seized upon the psychophysical experiments, which Fechner meant merely as contributory to his philosophy, and made them into an experimental psychology. A very interesting life to us, who are inquiring how psychologists are made!

Fechner was born in 1801 in the parsonage of a little village in southeastern Germany, near the border between Saxony and Silesia. His father had succeeded his grandfather as village pastor. His father was a man of independence of thought and of receptivity to new ideas. He shocked the villagers by having a lightning-rod placed upon the church tower, in the days when this precaution was regarded as a lack of faith in God's care of his own, and by preaching—as he urged that Jesus must also have done—without a wig. One can thus see in the father an anticipation of Fechner's own genius for bringing the brute facts of scientific materialism to the support of a higher spiritualism, but there can have been little, if any, direct influence of this sort, for the father died when Fechner was only five years old. Fechner, with his brother and mother, spent the next nine years with his uncle, also a preacher. Then he went for a short time to a *Gymnasium* and then for a half year to a medical and surgical academy. At the age of sixteen he was matriculated in medicine at the university in Leipzig, and at Leipzig he remained for the rest of his long life—for seventy years in all.

We are so accustomed to associating Fechner's name with the date 1860, the year of the publication of the *Elemente der Psychophysik*, and with the later years when he lived in Leipzig while Wundt's laboratory was being got under way, that we are apt to forget how old he was and how long ago he was beginning his academic life. In 1817, when Fechner went to Leipzig, Lotze was not even born. Herbart had just published his *Lehrbuch*, but his *Psychologie als Wissenschaft* was still seven years away in the future. In England, James Mill had barely completed the *History of India* and presumably had not even thought of writing a psychology. John Stuart Mill was eleven years old; Bain was not born. Phrenology had only just passed its first climax, and Gall was still writing on the functions of the brain. Flourens had not yet begun his researches on the brain. Bell, but not Magendie, had discovered the Bell-Magendie law. It was really, as the history of psychology goes, a very long time ago that Fechner went as a student to Leipzig.

It happened that E. H. Weber, the Weber after whom Fechner

named "Weber's Law," went to Leipzig in the same year as *Dozent* in the faculty of medicine and was made in the following year *ausserordentlicher Professor* of comparative anatomy. After five years of study, Fechner took his degree in medicine, in 1822. Already, however, the humanistic side of the man was beginning to show itself. His first publication (1821), *Beweiss, dass der Mond aus Jodine bestehe*, was a satire on the current use of iodine as a panacea. The next year he wrote a satirical panegyric on modern medicine and natural history. Both these papers appeared under the *nom de plume* 'Dr. Mises,' and 'Dr. Mises' was reincarnated in ironical bursts altogether fourteen times from 1821 to 1876. Meanwhile Fechner's association with A. W. Volkmann had begun. Volkmann came to Leipzig as a student in medicine in 1821 and remained, later as *Dozent* and professor, for sixteen years.

After he had taken his degree, Fechner's interest shifted from biological science to physics and mathematics, and he settled down in Leipzig, at first without official appointment, for study in these fields. His means were slender, and he undertook to supplement them by the translation into German of certain French handbooks of physics and chemistry. This work must have been very laborious, for by 1830 he had translated more than a dozen volumes and nearly 9,000 pages; but it was work that brought him into prominence as a physicist. He was also appointed in 1824 to give lectures in physics at the university, and in addition he undertook physical research of his own. It was a very productive period. By 1830 he had published, including the translations, over forty articles in physical science. At this time the properties of electric currents were just beginning to become known. Ohm in 1826 had laid down the famous law that bears his name, the law that states the relation between current, resistance and electromotive force in a circuit. Fechner was drawn into the resulting problem, and in 1831 he published a paper of great importance on quantitative measurements of direct currents (*Massbestimmungen über die galvanische Kette*), a paper which made his reputation as a physicist.

The young Fechner in his thirties was a member of a delightful intellectual group in the university community at Leipzig. Volkmann, until he went to Dorpat in 1837, was also a member of this group, and it was Volkmann's sister whom Fechner married in 1833. The year after his marriage, the year in which, as we have already seen, Lotze came to Leipzig as a student, Fechner was appointed professor of physics. It must have seemed that his career was already determined. He was professor of physics at only thirty-three, with a program of work ahead of him and settled in a congenial social setting at one of the most important universities. We shall see presently how far wrong the obvious prediction would have been. Fechner for the time being kept on with his physical research, throughout the still very fertile decade of his thirties. 'Dr. Mises,' the humanistic Fechner, appeared as an author more than half a dozen times. Toward the end of this period there is, in Fechner's research, the first indication of a quasi-psychological interest: two papers on complementary colors and subjective colors in 1838, and the famous paper on subjective after-images in 1840. In general, however, Fechner was a promising younger physicist with the broad intellectual interests of the *deutscher Gelehrter*.

Fechner, however, had overworked. He had developed, as James diagnosed the disease, a 'habit-neurosis.' He had also injured his eyes in the research on after-images by gazing at the sun through colored glasses. He was prostrated, and resigned, in 1839, his chair of physics. He suffered great pain and for three years cut himself off from every one. This event seemed like a sudden and incomprehensible ending to a career so vividly begun. Then Fechner unexpectedly began to recover, and, since his malady was so little understood, his recovery appeared miraculous. This period is spoken of as the 'crisis' in Fechner's life, and it had a profound effect upon his thought and after-life.

The primary result was a deepening of Fechner's religious consciousness and his interest in the problem of the soul. Thus Fechner, quite naturally for a man with such an intense intellectual life, turned to philosophy, bringing with him a vivification of the humanistic coloring that always had been one of his attributes. His forties were, of course, a sterile decade as regards writing. 'Dr. Mises' published a book of poems in 1841 and several other papers later. The first book that showed Fechner's new tendency was *Nanna oder das Seelenleben der Pflanzen*, published in 1848. (Nanna was the Norse goddess of flowers.) For Fechner, in the materialistic age of science, to argue for the mental life of plants, even before Darwin had made the mental life of animals a crucial issue, was for him to court scientific unpopularity, but Fechner now felt himself possessed of a philosophic mission and he could not keep silence. He was troubled by materialism, as his *Büchlein vom Leben nach dem Tode* in 1836 had shown. His philosophical solution of the spiritual problem lay in his affirmation of the identity of mind and matter and in his assurance that the entire universe can be regarded as readily from the point of view of its consciousness, a view that he later called the *Tagesansicht*, as it can be viewed as inert matter, the *Nachtansicht*. Yet the demonstration of the consciousness of plants was but a step in a program.

Three years later (1851) a more important work of Fechner's appeared: *Zend-Avesta, oder über die Dinge des Himmels und des Jenseits*. Oddly enough this book contains Fechner's program of psychophysics and thus bears an ancestral relation to experimental psychology. We shall return to this matter in a moment. Fechner's general intent was that the book should be a new gospel. The title means practically "a revelation of the word." Consciousness, Fechner argued, is in all and through all. The earth, "our mother," is a being like ourselves but very much more perfect than ourselves. The soul does not die, nor can it be exorcised by the priests of materialism when all being is conscious. Fechner's argument was not rational; he was intensely persuasive and developed his theme by way of plausible analogies, which, but for their seriousness, resemble somewhat the method of Dr. Mises' satire, *Vergleichende Anatomie der Engel* (1825), where Fechner argued that the angels, as the most perfect beings, must be spherical, since the sphere is the most perfect form. Now, however, Fechner was in dead earnest. He said later in *Ueber die Seelenfrage* (1861) that he had then called four times to a sleeping public which had not yet been aroused from its bed. "I now," he went on, "say a fifth time, '*Steh' auf!*' and, if I live, I shall yet call a sixth and a seventh time, '*Steh' auf!*' and always it will be but the same '*Steh' auf!*'"

We need not go further into Fechner's philosophy. He did call, or at least so Titchener thought, a sixth and a seventh time, and these seven books with their dates show the persistence and the extent of Fechner's belief in his own gospel. They are: *Das Büchlein vom Leben nach dem Tode*, 1836; *Nanna*, 1848; *Zend-Avesta*, 1851; *Professor Schleiden und der Mond*, 1856; *Ueber die Seelenfrage*, 1861; *Die drei Motive und Gründe des Glaubens*, 1863; *Die Tagesansicht gegenüber der Nachtansicht*, 1879. As it happened, the public never "sprang out of bed," not even at the seventh call, as Fechner had predicted it would. His philosophy received some attention; many of these books of his have been reprinted in recent years; but Fechner's fame is as a psychophysicist and not as a philosopher with a mission.

His psychophysics, the sole reason for Fechner's inclusion in this book, was a by-product of his philosophy. We return to it.

It was one thing to philosophize about mind and matter as two alternative ways of regarding everything in the universe, and another thing to give the idea such concrete empirical form that it might carry weight with the materialistic intellectualism of the times or even be satisfactory to Fechner, the one-time physicist. This new philosophy, so Fechner thought, needed a solid scientific foundation. It was, as he tells us, on the morning of October 22, 1850, while he was lying in bed thinking about this problem, that the general outlines of the solution suggested themselves to him. He saw that the thing to be done was to make "the relative increase of bodily energy the measure of the increase of the corresponding mental intensity," and he had in mind just enough of the facts of this relationship to think that an arithmetic series of mental intensities might correspond to a geometric series of physical energies, that a given absolute increase of intensity might depend upon the ratio of the increase of bodily force to the total force. Fechner said that the idea was not suggested by a knowledge of Weber's results. This statement may seem strange, for Weber was in Leipzig and had published the *Tastsinn und Gemeingefühl* in 1846, and it was important enough to be separately reprinted in 1851. We must remember, however, that Weber himself had not pointed out the general significance of his law and may have seen its most general meaning only vaguely. He had hinted at generality in his manner of talking about ratios as if they were increments of stimulus, and in extending his finding for touch to visual extents and to tones. He had formulated no specific law. It was Fechner who realized later that his own principle was essentially what Weber's results showed, and it was Fechner who gave the empirical relationship mathematical form and called it "Weber's Law." In recent times there has been a tendency to correct Fechner's generosity, and to give the name *Fechner's Law* to what Fechner called "Weber's Law," reserving the latter term for Weber's simple statement that the just noticeable difference in a stimulus bears a constant ratio to the stimulus. (See formulas 1 and 6 *infra*. pp. 287, 289.)

The immediate result of Fechner's idea was the formulation of the program of what he later called psychophysics. This program, as we have already observed, was worked out in the *Zend-Avesta* of 1851. There was still, however, the program to carry out, and Fechner set about it. The methods of measurement were developed, the three psychophysical methods which are still fundamental to much psychological research. The mathematical form both of the methods and of the exposition of the general problem of measurement was established. The classical experiments on lifted weights, on visual brightnesses and on tactual and visual distances were performed.

Fechner the philosopher proved to have lost none of the experimental care of Fechner the physicist. His friend and brother-in-law, A. W. Volkmann, then at Halle, helped with many of the experiments. Other data, notably the classification of the stars by magnitude, were brought forth to support the central thesis. For seven years Fechner published nothing of all this. Then in 1858 and 1859 two short anticipatory papers appeared, and then in 1860, full grown, the *Elemente der Psychophysik*, a text of the "exact science of the functional relations or relations of dependency between body and mind."

It would not be fair to say that the book burst upon a sleeping world. Fechner was not popular. *Nanna*, *Zend-Avesta* and similar writings had caused the scientists to look askance at him, and he was never accepted as a philosopher. No one suspected at the time what importance the book would come to have. There was no furor; nevertheless the work was scholarly and well grounded on both the experimental and mathematical sides, and, in spite of philosophical prejudice, it commanded attention in the most important quarter of all, namely, with the other scientists who were concerned with related problems. Even before the book itself appeared, the paper of 1858 had attracted the attention of Helmholtz and of Mach. Helmholtz proposed a modification of Fechner's fundamental formula in 1859. Mach began in 1860 tests of Weber's law in the time-sense and published in 1865. Wundt, in his first psychological publications in 1862 and again in 1863, called attention to the importance of Fechner's work. A. W. Volkmann published psychophysical papers in 1864. Aubert challenged Weber's law in 1865. Delbœuf, who later did so much for the development of psychophysics, began his experiments on brightness in 1865, inspired by Fechner. Vierordt similarly undertook in 1868 his study of the time-sense in the light of the *Elemente*. Bernstein, who had just divided with Volkmann the chair of anatomy and physiology at Halle, published in 1868 his irradiation theory, a theory that is based remotely on Herbart's law of the limen, but directly on Fechner's discussion. The *Elemente* did not take the world by the ears, but it got just the kind of attention that was necessary to give it a basic position in the new psychology.

Fechner, however, had now accomplished his purpose. He had laid the scientific foundation for his philosophy and was ready to turn to other matters, keeping always in mind the central philosophical theme. Moreover, he had reached his sixties, the age when men begin to be dominated more by their interests and less by their careers. The next topic, then, that caught the attention of this versatile man was esthetics, and, just as he had spent ten years on psychophysics, so now he spent a decade (1865-1876) on esthetics, a decade that was terminated when Fechner was seventy-five years old.

If Fechner 'founded' psychophysics, he also 'founded' experimental esthetics. His first paper in this new field was on the golden section and appeared in 1865. A dozen more papers came out from 1866 to 1872, and most of these had to do with the problem of the two Holbein Madonnas. Both Dresden and Darmstadt possessed Madonnas, very similar although different in detail, and both were reputed to have been painted by Holbein. There was much controversy about them, and Fechner plunged into it. There were several mooted points. The Darmstadt Madonna showed the Christ-child. The Dresden Madonna showed instead a sick child and might have been a votive picture, painted at the request of a family with the image of a child who had died. There was the general question of the significance of the pictures, and there was also the question of authenticity. Which was Holbein's and which was not? Experts disagreed. Fechner, maintaining the judicial attitude, was inclined to believe that they might both be authentic, that if Holbein had sought to portray two similar but different ideas he would have painted two similar but different pictures. And finally, of course, there was the question as to which was the more beautiful. These two latter questions were related in human judgment, for almost every one would be likely to believe that the authentic Madonna must be the more beautiful. Some of these questions Fechner sought to have answered 'experimentally' by a public opinion poll on the auspicious occasion when the two Madonnas were exhibited together. He placed an album by the pictures and asked visitors to record their judgments; but the experiment was a failure. Out of over 11,000 visitors, only 113 recorded their opinions, and most of these answers had to be rejected because they did not follow the instructions or were made by art critics or others who knew about the pictures and had formed judgments. Nevertheless the idea had merit and has been looked upon as the beginning of the use of the method of impression in the experimental study of feeling and esthetics.

In 1876 Fechner published the *Vorschule der Aesthetik*, a work that closed his active interest in that subject and laid the foundation for experimental esthetics. It goes into the various problems, methods and principles with a thoroughness that rivals the psychophysics, but is too far afield for detailed consideration in this book.

There is little doubt that Fechner would never have returned either to psychophysics or to esthetics, after the publication of his major book in each subject-matter, had the world let him be. The psychophysics, however, had immediately stimulated both research and criticism and, while Fechner was working on esthetics, was becoming important in the new psychology. In 1874, the year of the publication of Wundt's *Grundzüge der physiologischen Psychologie*, Fechner had been aroused to a brief criticism of Delbœuf's *Étude psychophysique* (1873). The next year Wundt came to Leipzig. The following year Fechner finished with esthetics and turned again to psychophysics, publishing in 1877 *In Sachen der Psychophysik*, a book which adds but little to the doctrine of the *Elemente*. Fechner was getting to be an old man, and his philosophical mission was still in his mind. In 1879, the year of Wundt's founding of the Leipzig psychological laboratory, Fechner issued *Die Tagesansicht gegenüber der Nachtansicht*, his seventh and last call to the somnolent world. He was then seventy-eight years old. Finally, in 1882, he published the *Revision der Hauptpunkte der Psychophysik*, a very important book, in which he took account of his critics and sought to meet the unexpected demand of experimental psychology upon him. In the following years there were half a dozen psychophysical articles by him, but actually his work was done. He died in 1887 at the age of eighty-six in Leipzig, where for seventy years he had lived the quiet life of the learned man, faring forth, while keeping his house, on these many and varied great adventures of the mind.

This then was Fechner. He was for seven years a physiologist (1817-1824); for fifteen a physicist (1824-1839); for a dozen years an invalid (1839 to about 1851); for fourteen years a psychophysicist (1851-1865); for eleven years an experimental estheticist (1865-1876); for at least two score years throughout this period, recurrently and persistently, a philosopher (1836-1879); and finally, during his last eleven years, an old man whose attention had been brought back by public acclaim and criticism to psychophysics (1876-1887) —all told three score years and ten of varied intellectual interest and endeavor. If he founded experimental psychology, he did it incidentally and involuntarily, and yet it is hard to see how the new psychology could have advanced as it did without an *Elemente der Psychophysik* in 1860. It is to this book, therefore, that we must now turn our attention.

PSYCHOPHYSICS

When Fechner began work on what was eventually to become the *Elemente der Psychophysik*, he had—beside his philosophical problem, his experience in physical research and his habits of careful experimentation—Herbart's psychology as a background. From Herbart he obtained the conception that psychology should be science, the general idea of mental measurement, the related notion of the application of mathematics to the study of the mind, the concept of the limen (which Herbart got from Leibnitz), the idea of mental analysis by way of the facts of the limen, and probably also a sensationistic cast to all of his work, a cast which resembles Herbart's intellectualism. When Fechner wrote the *Zend-Avesta*, Lotze had not published his psychology. There was really no psychology at all except the very influential psychology of Herbart and the psychological physiology of Johannes Müller and E. H. Weber. Fechner was, however, too much of an experimentalist to accept Herbart's metaphysical approach or to admit the validity of his denial of the psychological experiment. Instead he set himself to correct Herbart by an experimental measurement of mind. All this, we must not forget, was done in the interests of his philosophical attack upon materialism.

There is also to be mentioned Fechner's mathematical background. It will be recalled that Fechner had turned in part to the study of mathematics after he had obtained his doctor's degree. Fechner himself acknowledges debts to "Bernoulli (Laplace, Poisson), Euler (Herbart, Drobisch), Steinheil (Pogson)." He was thinking, however, more of the mathematical and experimental demonstration of Weber's Law. Steinheil had shown that stellar magnitudes follow this law; Euler, that tonal pitch follows it. It is plain, however, that Fechner placed the name of Daniel Bernoulli (1700-1782) first with reason. Bernoulli's interest in the theory of probabilities as applied to games of chance had led to the discussion of *fortune morale* and *fortune physique*, mental and physical values which he believed (1738) to be related to each other in such a way that a change in the amount of the 'mental fortune' varies with the ratio that the change in the physical fortune has to the total fortune of its possessor. (Thus in gambling with even stakes, one stands to lose more than one gains, for a given loss after the event bears a larger ratio to the reduced total fortune than would the same physical gain to an increased total fortune—a conclusion with a moral!) In this way *fortune morale* and *fortune physique* became mental and

physical quantities, mathematically related, quantities that correspond exactly, both in kind and in relationship, to mind and body in
general and to sensation and bodily energy in particular, the terms
that Fechner sought to relate, in the interests of his philosophy, by
way of Weber's law.

On the purely mathematical side, Fechner is less clear as to his
background, but it is plain that Bernoulli, Laplace and Poisson were
important. Nowadays we are apt to think especially of Fechner's use
of the normal law of error as representing his mathematical interest.
Fechner's method of constant stimuli makes use of this law, and the
method has assumed importance because it is closely related to the
biological and psychological statistical methods that also make use
of normal distributions. The method of constant stimuli was, however, only one of Fechner's three fundamental methods.

Nevertheless, it is interesting to answer the question that arises
about Fechner's use of the normal law. The principles were all contained in the earlier mathematicians' work on the theory of probabilities, work of which Bernoulli's is representative. Laplace,
whom Fechner specially mentioned, developed the general law.
Gauss gave it its more usual form, and the law ordinarily bears his
name. Fechner refers to Gauss in his use of it, but Gauss seems to
have been less important than Laplace. There is nothing new in
making this practical application of the theory of probabilities. Since
1662 there had been attempts to apply it to the expectation of life,
to the evaluation of human testimony and human innocence, to
birth-rates and sex-ratios, to astronomical observations, to the facts
of marriages, smallpox and inoculation, to weather forecasts, to
annuities, to elections, and finally (Laplace and Gauss) to errors of
scientific observation in general. It was in 1835 that Quetelet first
thought of using the law of error to describe the distribution of
human traits, as if nature, in aiming at an ideal average man, *l'homme
moyen*, missed the mark and thus created deviations on either side
of the average. It was Quetelet who gave Francis Galton the idea
of the mathematical treatment of the inheritance of genius (1869),
but Fechner had nothing of this sort in mind. The older tradition,
however, he must have known, at least in part. and it is from it that
he took for the method of constant stimuli the normal law of error,
now so important to psychologists. It was easier to assume then than
it is now that the normal law, as indeed its name implies, is a law of
nature which applies whenever variability is uncontrolled.

Beside this general background and knowledge, Fechner brought
to the problem of psychophysics several very definite things. First,

there was the fact of the limen, made familiar by Herbart but also obvious enough in other ways, as, for example, in the invisibility of the stars in daylight. Second, there was Weber's law, a factual principle which, if not verified, could still be expected to persist in modified form. Third, there was the experimental method, which was equally fundamental and which derived from Fechner's own temperament in defiance of Herbart. Fourth, there was Fechner's clear conception of the nature of psychophysics as "an exact science of the functional relations or the relations of dependency between body and mind." This conception was the *raison d'être* for the entire undertaking. Finally, there was Fechner's very wise conclusion that he could not attempt the entire program of psychophysics and that he would therefore limit himself, not only to sensation, but further to the intensity of sensation, so that a final proof of his view in one field might, because of its finality, have the weight to lead later to extensions into other fields.

We must pause here to note that Fechner's view of the relation of *mind and body* was not that of psychophysical parallelism, but what has been called the *identity hypothesis* and also *panpsychism*. The writing of an equation between the mind and the body in terms of Weber's law seemed to him virtually a demonstration both of their identity and of their fundamental psychic character. Nevertheless, Fechner's psychophysics has played an important part in the history of psychophysical parallelism for the reason that mind and body, sensation and stimulus, have to be regarded as separate entities in order that each can be measured and the relation between the two determined. Fechner's psychology therefore, like so much of the psychology that came after him, seems at first to be dualistic. It is true that he began with a dualism, but we must remember that he thought he had shown that the dualism is not real and is made to disappear by the writing of the true equation between the two terms.

It is so easy nowadays to think that the Weber-Fechner law represents the functional relation between the measured magnitude of stimulus and the measured magnitude of sensation, that it is hard to realize what difficulty the problem presented to Fechner. It seemed plain to him, however, that sensation, a mental magnitude, could not be measured directly and that his problem was therefore to get at its measure indirectly. He began by turning to *sensitivity*.

Sensation, Fechner argued, we cannot measure; all we can observe is that a sensation is present or absent, or that one sensation is greater than, equal to, or less than another sensation. Of the absolute magnitude of a sensation we know nothing directly. Fortunately, however, we can measure stimuli, and thus we can measure the stimulus values necessary to give rise to a particular sensation or to a difference between two sensations; that is to say, we can measure threshold values of the stimulus. When we do this we are also measuring sensitivity, which is the inverse of the threshold value. Fechner distinguished between absolute and differential sensitivity, which correspond respectively to the absolute and differential limens. He recognized the importance of variability in this subject-matter and the necessity of dealing with averages, extreme values, the laws of averages and the laws of variability about the averages—in short, the necessity of using statistical methods.

Since Fechner believed that the stimulus, and hence sensitivity, can be measured directly but that sensation can not, he knew that he must measure sensation itself indirectly, and he hoped to do it by way of its differential increments. In determining the differential limen we have two sensations that are just noticeably different, and we may take the just noticeable difference (the jnd) as the unit of sensation, counting up jnd to determine the magnitude of a sensation. There was a long argument later as to whether every liminal increment of sensation (δS) equals every other one, but Fechner assumed that δS = the jnd, and that the sensed differences, being all just noticeably different, are equal and therefore constitute a proper unit.

One does not in practice count up units for large magnitudes. One works mathematically on the general case for the general function which can, perhaps, later be applied in measurement. Fechner went to work in the following manner. In expounding him we shall use the familiar English abbreviations instead of Fechner's symbols: S for the magnitude of the sensation and R for the magnitude of the stimulus (*Reiz*).

Weber's experimental finding may be expressed:

$$\frac{\delta R}{R} = \text{constant, for the jnd.} \quad \textit{Weber's Law} \quad (1)$$

This fact ought to be called "Weber's law," since it is what Weber found. Fechner, however, used the phrase for his final result.

He assumed that, if (1) holds for the jnd, it must also hold for any small increment of S, δS, and that he could thus express the functional relation between S and R by writing:

$$\delta S = c \, \frac{\delta R}{R} \qquad \textit{Fundamental formula} \ (2)$$

where $c =$ a constant of proportionality. This was Fechner's *Fundamentalformel*, and we must note that the introduction of δS into the equation is the mathematical equivalent of Fechner's conclusion that all δS's are equal and can be treated as units. One has only to integrate to accomplish the mathematical counterpart of counting up units to perform a measurement. If we can write the fundamental formula, we can certainly measure sensation. Fechner, therefore, integrated the equation, arriving at the result

$$S = c \, \log_e R + C \qquad\qquad (3)$$

where $C =$ the constant of integration and $e =$ the base of natural logarithms. In formula (3) we really have the desired result, since it gives the magnitudes of S for any magnitude of R, when the two constants are known. Fechner had thus demonstrated the fundamental point of his philosophy. Nevertheless this formula was unsatisfactory because of the unknown constants, and Fechner undertook to eliminate C by reference to other known facts. He let $r =$ the threshold value of the stimulus, R, a value at which S, by definition, $= 0$. Thus:

When $R = r, \quad S = 0$

Substituting these values of S and R in (3), we get:

$$0 = c \, \log_e r + C$$
$$C = -c \, \log_e r$$

Now we can substitute for C in (3):

$$\begin{aligned} S &= c \, \log_e R - c \, \log_e r \\ &= c(\log_e R - \log_e r) \\ &= c \, \log_e \frac{R}{r} \qquad\qquad (4) \end{aligned}$$

We can shift to common logarithms from natural logarithms by an appropriate change of the constant from c to, let us say, k:

$$S = k \log \frac{R}{r} \qquad \textit{Measurement formula} \ (5)$$

This is the formula for measurement, Fechner's *Massformel*. The scale of S is the number of jnd that the sensation is above zero, its value at the limen. Beyond this point Fechner went one more step. He suggested that we might measure R by its relation to its liminal value; that is to say, we might take r as the unit of R. If r be the unit of R, then:

$$S = k \log R. \qquad \textit{Fechner's Law} \ (6)$$

This last formula, (6), Fechner called "Weber's Law." It is only as we view the matter now that we see that formula (1) is really Weber's law and that formula (6) should be called Fechner's law. We must remember that $S = k \log R$ is true only when the unit of R is the liminal value of the stimulus and in so far as it is valid to integrate S and to assume that $S = 0$ at the limen. Furthermore, the entire conclusion depends on the validity of Weber's finding, formula (1), a generalization that further experimentation has verified only approximately in some cases, but not exactly nor for the entire range of stimuli.

About this claim of Fechner's that he had measured sensation vigorous controversy raged for forty years or more; and two of the fundamental objections are of sufficient interest to deserve brief mention here.

One argument was that Fechner had assumed the *equality of all jnd* without sufficient warrant and that he had thus in a sense begged the question, since there is no meaning to the statement that one δS equals another unless S is measurable. There is certainly some force to this criticism, but it can be met in two ways.

It was actually met in part by Delbœuf's notion of the sense-distance and the experiments on supraliminal sense-distances. Delbœuf pointed out that we can judge the size of the interval between two sensations immediately and directly. For example, we can say of three sensations, A, B and C, whether the distance AB is greater than, equal to or less than the distance BC. Thus we perform a mental measurement immediately, and the question is not begged. Now suppose $AB = BC$ psychologically, and suppose that we find that the stimulus for B is the geometric mean of the stimuli for A and C. Then we have shown that the *Fundamentalformel* holds for a large S like AB, and, if the same law holds for large distances judged equal and for jnd, we may assume that jnd must also be equal. As a matter of fact, Weber's law has not been shown to hold generally nor exactly. It depends on what arbitrary scale of stimulus units is being used and it is apt to be wrong for the low values of any convenient measure of stimulus intensity. Modern findings show that the assumption of equality for intensive jnd is often inconsistent with the direct judgmental comparison of supraliminal intensive differences. There is evidence, for instance, that jnd for the pitch of tones are equal in this sense, but that jnd for the loudness of tones are not.

The other way to meet the objection that all jnd are not equal is to say frankly that the equality of units must be an assumption. Certainly one jnd is equivalent to another in that

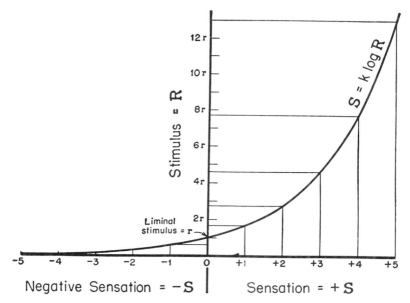

FIG. 3. FECHNER's LAW: $S = k \log R$. The positions of the equally spaced vertical ordinates represent an arithmetic series of S; their successive heights the corresponding geometric series of R. Thus the curve shows how a logarithmic function represents a correlation between an arithmetic and a geometric series. It also shows why the function requires the theoretical existence of negative sensations, for, when $S = 0$, $R = a$ finite value, r, the limen; and S passes through an infinite number of negative values when R varies between r and 0. In this diagram R is plotted with r as the unit and k is arbitrarily chosen as 4.5 for common logarithms.

both are jnd. The issue can be met thus on purely logical grounds, though this solution leaves open still the question of the exact sense in which jnd as such are equal. So it must be with all units, and even Delbœuf's sense-distances are not more satisfactory in this regard. The obvious fact is, nevertheless, that the Fechner Law states a relationship between two entities that are not identical. S must be something, and it is not R. Something other than the stimulus has been measured.

The other important criticism of Fechner has been called the *quantity objection*. It was argued that it is patent to introspection that sensations do not have magnitude. "Our feeling of pink," said James, "is surely not a portion of our feeling of scarlet; nor does the light of an electric arc seem to contain that of a tallow candle within itself." "This sensation of 'gray,'" Külpe remarked, "is not two or three of that other sensation of gray." Must not Fechner have tricked us when he proved by his figures something that we all can see is not true? The criticism is not valid, yet Fechner himself was to blame for this turn that criticism took. As we have seen, Fechner had said that stimuli can be measured directly and that sensations can not, that sensations must be measured indirectly by reference to the stimulus and by way of sensitivity. No wonder the critics accused Fechner of measuring the stimulus and calling it sensation. No wonder they argued that his own statement that sensation can not be measured directly is equivalent to saying that it can not be measured at all.

Actually the 'quantity objection' was met by being ignored. The experimentalists went on measuring sensation while the objectors complained, or at least they went on measuring whatever Fechner's S is. There are, however, two remarks that can be made about this matter. (1) Sensation can indeed be measured as directly as is the stimulus. You can compare directly in judgment two sensory differences. You can say that the difference AB is greater than, or less than or equal to the difference BC, when A, B and C are serial intensities or qualities or extents or durations. Such judgments boil down to the crucial judgment of *equal* or *not-different*. Such a comparison is quite as direct for the sensation as it is for the stimulus. Similarly, to compare weights you use a balance and form the judgment *equal* when the scalepans are *not-different* in height. Or for length you note on a tape the mark that is *not-different* in position from the end of the measured object. (2) Contrariwise, we may say that the stimulus is just as unitary and simple as the sensation. A meter is not made up of 100 parts which are called centimeters, or of a thousand parts which are called millimeters, or of 39.37 parts which are called inches. A meter in itself is just as unitary as a scarlet. The magnitude of neither implies complexity but simply a relationship to other objects that is got by the conventional methods of measurement.

We must now turn to certain matters that are connected with Fechner's name: Inner psychophysics, the limen of consciousness, negative sensations and the psychophysical methods.

Fechner distingushed *inner psychophysics* from outer psychophysics. Outer psychophysics, he said, deals with the relation between mind and stimulus, and it is in outer psychophysics that the actual experiments are to be placed. Inner psychophysics, however, is the relation between mind and the excitation most immediate to it and thus deals most immediately with the relationship in which Fechner was primarily interested. $S = k \log R$ is a relationship in outer psychophysics. Between R and S, excitation, E, is interposed. Just where is the locus of this logarithmic relationship, between R and E or between E and S? It is possible that S is simply proportional to E and that the true law is $E = k \log R$, a statement which means that Weber's law does not solve the problem of mind and body as Fechner hoped it would. Fechner, however, maintained that E is probably proportional to R and that Weber's law is the fundamental law of inner psychophysics, $S = k \log E$.

This view Fechner supported with five arguments. (1) In the first place, he said in the *Elemente*, it would be inconceivable that a logarithmic relation should exist between R and E. Such a statement is hardly an argument, and Fechner took it back in the *Revision*. (2) Then he observed that the magnitude of S does not change when sensitivity is reduced, whereas it should if $S = kE$ and E is involved in the change of sensitivity. (3) Further he noted that Weber's law holds for tonal pitch, and that it would be impossible for the vibrations of E to have other than a proportional relation to the vibrations of R. (Of course he was in error in supposing that nervous excitation is vibratory.) (4) Next he pointed out that a subliminal S probably has an E, that the invisible stars in daytime probably give rise to excitation which is below the limen of consciousness. Such a fact could be true only if $S = k \log E$. (5) Finally, he appealed to the distinction between sleep and waking, and between inattention and attention, as indicating the existence of a limen of consciousness rather than a limen of excitation. This last argument is the most cogent. Certainly the mere fact of the selectivity of attention seems to mean that there are many excitations, all prepotent for consciousness, of which only a few become conscious. However, Fechner's entire argument would not be taken very seriously at the present time. It is important for us merely to see why Fechner, working in outer psychophysics, thought he was solving the problem, all-important to him, of inner psychophysics.

From this discussion we see how important the fact of the *limen of consciousness* was to Fechner. What Fechner called Weber's Law is based upon the limen, for, if $S = k \log R$, then, when $S =$

0, R is some finite quantity, a liminal value. Herbart's limen of consciousness is thus simply a corollary of this law. In fact, Fechner was further consistent with Herbart in relating the limen to attention: when consciousness is already occupied with other sensations, a new sensation can not enter until it overcomes the "mixture limen."

The psychology that depends upon this law also requires the existence of *negative sensations*. Figure 3 shows graphically the logarithmic curve that gives the relationship of S to R for "Weber's Law." The function requires that R = r, the limen, when S = 0, and thus it gives negative sensations for subliminal values of R, for theoretically when R = 0, S is negative and infinite. Fechner believed that "the representation of unconscious psychical values by negative magnitude is a fundamental point for psychophysics," and by way of this mathematical logic he came to hold a doctrine of the unconscious not unlike that of his predecessors, Leibnitz and Herbart.

Fechner's claim to greatness within psychology does not, however, derive from these psychological conceptions of his, nor even from the formulation of his famous law. The great thing that he accomplished was a new kind of measurement. The critics may debate the question as to what it was that he measured; the fact stands that he conceived, developed and established new *methods of measurement*, and that, whatever interpretation may later be made of their products, these methods are essentially the first methods of mental measurement and thus the beginning of quantitative experimental psychology. Moreover, the methods have stood the test of time. They have proven applicable to all sorts of psychological problems and situations that Fechner never dreamed of, and they are all still used with only minor modifications in the greater part of quantitative work in the psychological laboratory today.

There were three fundamental methods: (1) the *method of just noticeable differences*, later called the *method of limits*; (2) the *method of right and wrong cases*, later called the *method of constant stimuli* or simply the *constant method*; and (3) the *method of average error*, later called the *method of adjustment* and the *method of reproduction*. Each of these methods is both an experimental procedure and a mathematical treatment. Each has special forms. The constant method has been much further developed by G. E. Müller and F. M. Urban. More recently the method of adjustment has shown certain advantages over the others. Changes and development, however, add to Fechner's distinction as the inventor. There are few other men who have done anything of equal importance for scientific psychology.

The storm of criticism that Fechner's work evoked was in general a compliment, but there were also those psychologists who were unable to see anything of value in psychophysics. But three years after Fechner's death, James wrote: "Fechner's book was the starting point of a new department of literature, which it would perhaps be impossible to match for the qualities of thoroughness and subtlety, but of which, in the humble opinion of the present writer, the proper psychological outcome is just *nothing*." Elsewhere he gave his picture of Fechner and his psychophysics:

> The Fechnerian *Maasformel* and the conception of it as the ultimate 'psychophysic law' will remain an 'idol of the den,' if ever there was one. Fechner himself indeed was a German *Gelehrter* of the ideal type, at once simple and shrewd, a mystic and an experimentalist, homely and daring, and as loyal to facts as to his theories. But it would be terrible if even such a dear old man as this could saddle our Science forever with his patient whimsies, and, in a world so full of more nutritious objects of attention, compel all future students to plough through the difficulties, not only of his own works, but of the still drier ones written in his refutation. Those who desire this dreadful literature can find it; it has a 'disciplinary value;' but I will not even enumerate it in a foot-note. The only amusing part of it is that Fechner's critics should always feel bound, after smiting his theories hip and thigh and leaving not a stick of them standing, to wind up by saying that nevertheless to him belongs the *imperishable glory*, of first formulating them and thereby turning psychology into an *exact science*,'
>
> > " 'And everybody praised the duke
> > Who this great fight did win.'
> > 'But what good came of it at last?'
> > Quoth little Peterkin.
> > 'Why, that I cannot tell,' said he,
> > 'But 'twas a famous victory!' "

It is plain to the reader that the present author does not agree with James. Of course, it is true that, without Fechner or a substitute which the times would almost inevitably have raised up, there might still have been an experimental psychology. There would still have been Wundt—and Helmholtz. There would, however, have been little of the breath of science in the experimental body, for we hardly recognize a subject as scientific if measurement is not one of its tools. Fechner, because of what he did and the time at which he did it, set experimental quantitative psychology off upon the course which it has followed. One may call him the 'founder' of experimental psychology, or one may assign that title to Wundt. It does not matter. Fechner had a fertile idea which grew and brought forth fruit abundantly.

NOTES

The more important of Fechner's writings are mentioned in the text. The *Elemente der Psychophysik* was reprinted without change in 1889. To the end of the first volume of this edition Wundt has added a bibliography, originally compiled by R. Müller, of 175 of Fechner's publications. This bibliography has been reprinted by Kuntze, *op. cit. infra*. See also the bibliography of Fechner and about him, B. Rand, in Baldwin's *Dictionary of Philosophy and Psychology*, 1905, III, 199 f.

On Fechner's life, see J. E. Kuntze, *Gustav Theodor Fechner*, 1892; K. Lasswitz, *Gustav Theodor Fechner*, 1896, *et seq.*; G. S. Hall, *Founders of Modern Psychology*, 1912, 123-177; O. Külpe, Zu Gustav Theodor Fechner's Gedächtnis, *Vtljhrschr. wiss. Philos.*, 1901, 25, 191-217; and very briefly Wundt and Titchener, *opp. citt. infra*.

On Fechner's work and thought, see Kuntze, Lasswitz and Hall, *opp. citt.*; Th. Ribot, *German Psychology of To-Day*, trans. 1886, 134-187; W. Wundt, *Gustav Theodor Fechner*, 1901; E. B. Titchener, *Experimental Psychology*, 1905, II, pt. ii, pp. xx-cxvi. For a resumé of his philosophy, see W. James, *A Pluralistic Universe*, 1909, 133-177; and the very brief discussion in O. Külpe, *Die Philosophie der Gegenwart in Deutschland*, 1905, 72-78 (or earlier editions); but for James' evaluation of Fechner and psychophysics, see his *Principles of Psychology*, 1890, I, 533-549. On Fechner's philosophy, see also R. B. Perry, *Philosophy of the Recent Past*, 1927, 81-86. See also O. Klemm, *History of Psychology*, trans. 1914, 242-257; G. S. Brett, *History of Psychology*, 1921, III, 127-239: G. Murphy, *Historical Introduction to Modern Psychology*, 2 ed., 1949, 82-94.

The question of the equality of the jnd units led to a tremendous controversy. It is not possible here to indicate the nature of it or to give the more important references. The entire matter is discussed very thoroughly and references are given in Titchener, *op. cit.*, pp. lxviii-lxxxix. For what happens to the general problem of measurement when the ground is shifted from the jnd to supraliminal sense-distances, see Titchener, *op. cit.*, II, i, pp. xxi-xxvii; ii, pp. cxvi-cxliv. Titchener's sense-distance is Delbœuf's *contraste sensible*, so Delbœuf receives credit for origination and Titchener for useful development. G. E. Müller used instead the concept of *Kohärenzgrad*.

On the 'quantity objection,' the controversy that it represents and the ways of meeting it, see Titchener, *op. cit.*, II, ii, pp. xlviii-lxvii; E. G. Boring, The stimulus-error, *Amer. J. Psychol.*, 1921, 32, 449-471, esp. 451-460. Both passages give many references. The quotations of the text are from James, *Principles of Psychology*, I, 546; Külpe, *Outlines of Psychology*, 45.

The principal references to Fechner's *Elemente* itself (reprint of 1889) are: derivation of Weber's law, the *Fundamentalformel* and the *Massformel*, II, 9-29; the three fundamental methods, I, 69-133, esp. 71-76; inner psychophysics, II, 377-547 in general, but 428-437 for Weber's law, limen of consciousness, II, 437-464; negative sensations, II, 39-46.

Ten of Fechner's pages about the *Fundamentalformel* and the *Massformel* are reprinted in Eng. trans. in B. Rand, *Classical Psychologists*, 1912, 562-572, and W. Dennis, *Readings in the History of Psychology*, 1948, 106-213.

On the history of psychophysics and of sensory measurement in general up to 1940, see E. G. Boring, *Sensation and Perception in the History of Experimental Psychology*, 1942, 34-45, 50-52, and the many references there cited for the dreary literature which James so much deplored.

CHAPTER 15

Hermann von Helmholtz

H ermann Ludwig Ferdinand von Helmholtz (1821-1894) was a very great scientist, one of the greatest of the nineteenth century. By interest and temperament he was a physicist, though circumstances led him at first into physiological research. If we must classify him at all in accordance with the formal divisions of science, we must say that psychology ranks only third among his scientific contributions; nevertheless Helmholtz, with Fechner and Wundt, is first in importance in the establishment of experimental psychology. He was a man of wide interests, tremendous energy, and great technical and mechanical skill. He was always fundamentally the physicist in method and point of view in physiology and psychology as well as in physics. His contact with Johannes Müller had something to do with his interest in psychology, but it was not all. No man of such versatile genius and vigorous attack could have been working in physiological research in Germany in the 1850s and 1860s, when the problems of physiological psychology were so obvious, and have avoided contact with them. In physiological optics and physiological acoustics Helmholtz's genius found ready utilization. In the general problems of science he was forced to consider psychology. The times claimed his attention for psychology, though it is also true that Helmholtz helped to determine the times. It was the times that set the problems, but it was Helmholtz's genius that saw the problems and advanced their solution. Unlike Wundt, Helmholtz held no brief for the formal establishment of psychology as an independent science; nevertheless the weight of his work and the effect of his prestige were such as to make him, with Wundt and Fechner, a 'founder' of the new science.

To the reader of this book Helmholtz's name is not new. We have already seen how he measured the rate of the nervous impulse after Müller had deemed the determination impossible (pp. 41-43). We have examined Helmholtz's extension of Müller's doctrine of the specific energies of nerves (pp. 91-95) We have pictured the knowledge of the physiological psychology of sensation in the first half of the nineteenth century up to the time when Helmholtz's researches added so much to the knowledge of sight and hearing. We have now to say something about Helmholtz as a scientific personality and to indicate the range and nature of his direct contributions to psychology.

Helmholtz was born in Potsdam, near Berlin, in 1821. His father, after a military experience, had become a teacher of philology and philosophy in a *Gymnasium*. His mother, Caroline Penne, was the daughter of an army officer and a descendant of William Penn. Helmholtz was a weak child with a very ordinary education. He did not do very well in his school studies, but his apparent mediocrity seems to have been due to his independence of thought rather than to any lack of ability. He had at home for play a large set of wooden blocks, and with these he learned many geometrical principles for himself before he encountered them at school. He read what scientific books his father's library afforded, and sometimes at school neglected the tiresome Cicero or Virgil to work out optical problems secretly beneath his desk, where his teacher could not see what he was doing. He had no gift for languages. His father tried to interest him in poetry and even to train him in writing poetry, but without much success. Neither the home environment nor the school curriculum was adapted to bring out the precocious mathematical and scientific capacity of the youth. At home he was present at many philosophical discussions between his father and his father's friends, discussions that centered for the most part about Kant and Fichte. It may be that Helmholtz's later reaction toward scientific empiricism and away from Kant's intuitionism began then.

At the age of seventeen, Helmholtz was quite clear in his own mind that he wanted to be a physicist. In fact, these interests were already well begun. There seemed, however, to be no prospect of a livelihood in pure science for this youth whose future was still so obscure. His father had been in the army. It was arranged, therefore, for him to enter a medico-chirurgical institute in Berlin where tuition was free for youths of promise who would undertake to train themselves to be surgeons in the Prussian army.

From 1838 to 1842 Helmholtz studied at this institute, and for the next seven years, that is to say until he was twenty-eight years old, he was an army surgeon in Berlin. His passion for science was not, however, suppressed by these circumstances. He contrived to lead the academic life while still nominally a surgeon. Although he was never a student at the University of Berlin, he managed to become attached to its academic circle. He became acquainted with

Magnus, professor of physics, whom he was later in 1871 to succeed, and with Johannes Müller, professor of physiology. It was his natural bent for physics that took him to Magnus, and his training in medicine that threw him into physiology with the great Müller. Müller was then reaching the height of his influence: his *Handbuch* had been appearing from 1833 to 1838. Helmholtz's closest friendships were formed among Müller's students. There was Brücke, later professor of physiology at Vienna, and Virchow, later professor of pathology at Berlin, and Ludwig, later professor of physiology at Leipzig, and, most important of all, du Bois-Reymond, who succeeded Müller as professor of physiology at Berlin. The friendship with du Bois-Reymond was always close; we have already seen how he aided Helmholtz in the exposition and publication of his results on the measurement of the rate of the nervous impulse.

In 1842 Helmholtz published his first paper, his medical dissertation. In it he showed that the nerve cells of ganglia are individually connected with separate nerve fibers that lead from them, a discovery that foreshadows the neuron theory. The compound microscope had been invented in the preceding decade, and this was the period in which many histological discoveries were being made. Helmholtz, however, had but a poor instrument with which to work. This paper is the beginning of the long series of his scientific publications; more than two hundred articles and books had appeared under his authorship by the time of his death fifty-two years later.

In 1847, while still a surgeon in the army, at the age of twenty-six (Newton was twenty-four when he had his three great scientific insights, pp. 10 f.), Helmholtz read before the *Physikalische Gesellschaft* in Berlin his famous paper on the conservation of energy (*Ueber die Erhaltung der Kraft*). Nobody ever 'discovered' the law of the conservation of energy. The idea had been developing since Newton. Joule a few years earlier had demonstrated the fact that heat has a mechanical equivalent. Helmholtz brought together much of the previous work and gave the theory mathematical formulation. He was still being the physicist within physiology, for one of his motives was to show that this principle works within the bodily machine, that the living organism is no exception to the laws of physics. The paper aroused vigorous discussion. Magnus declined to express an opinion, but many of the older physicists discounted the novelty of the view and thus the importance of the formulation. The younger physicists, on the contrary, seized upon the paper with avidity as marking a crucial advance in man's knowledge of the universe. Both groups were, of course, right. The idea was not new; ever since Descartes there had been those who thought of the body as a machine. Nevertheless, the theory needed formulation, clarification and emphasis. (See p. 708 for the way in which Helmholtz, du Bois, Brücke and Ludwig formed a pact to fight vitalism.)

By this time it was clear that the young man, who had entered the army as a surgeon in order to make a living, properly belonged in academic spheres. In 1849, at the age of twenty-eight, Helmholtz was called to Königsberg as professor of physiology and general pathology, and he remained in this position for seven years. His first scientific contribution of importance while at Königsberg was the measurement of the rate of conduction of the nervous impulse. We have already considered the significance of this research and seen the opposition it had to overcome before acceptance (pp. 41 f.). It was at Königsberg, Kant's university, that Helmholtz's interest in problems of sensation began to take shape and that his thought first directed itself to the scientific empiricism which he was later to oppose to Kant's intuitionism. He turned first to physiological optics. He invented the ophthalmoscope in 1851 and later the ophthalmometer. The ophthalmoscope was regarded as a wonderful instrument, for it enabled the investigator to look directly into the eye and seemingly to bring the interior of the 'bodily machine' under direct observation. It was also in this period that Helmholtz took up with Thomas Young's theory of color vision, although he can not be said to have adopted it until about 1860. The result of all this work was the undertaking of the writing of the *Handbuch der physiologischen Optik*, of which the first volume appeared in 1856. This volume shows how Helmholtz was working as a physicist within sense-physiology. His perceptual theory came later.

Meanwhile Helmholtz's fame was growing. In 1854 he paid his first of many visits to England. His contact with English thought was much closer than was usual in Germany, and in certain limited respects Helmholtz belongs more in the British than in the German tradition.

In 1856 Helmholtz went to Bonn for two years as professor of physiology. Here his interest in sensation extended to include physiological acoustics.

In 1858 he was called as professor of physiology to Heidelberg, where he remained until 1871. The years at Heidelberg include the culmination of his genius in the investigation of the physical physiology of sensation. The second volume of the *Optik* appeared in 1860. Then, as if this classic work were not in itself enough for one man, he published the entire *Tonempfindungen*, including his resonance theory of hearing, in 1863. He completed the last volume of the *Optik* in 1866, and the complete work appeared in the following year. Within sixteen years, between the ages of thirty and forty-six, Helmholtz conceived, constructed and published the works that are still classics for the experimental psychology of sight and hearing.

Magnus died in 1870, and in 1871 Helmholtz was called to Berlin as professor of physics, thus at last realizing in a distinguished appointment the desire of his youth. He had succeeded in being a physiologist as a surgeon, and a physicist as a physiologist. Now his natural genius was formally recognized. He was fifty years old, and remained at Berlin until his death twenty-three years later.

In 1887 he was made the first director of the new Physical-technisches Institut at Charlottenburg. In 1893 he visited America and the World's Fair at Chicago. During the return voyage to England, he was injured by a fall down the stairway of his ship. He died, partly as the result of these injuries, in 1894.

At Berlin Helmholtz occupied himself with the development of the theory of the conservation of energy, with problems of hydrodynamics, electrodynamics and physical optics. It was his pupil Hertz who contributed to the physical foundation of wireless telegraphy and the radio. Nevertheless Helmholtz maintained his interests in psychology and popular epistemology throughout his life. He revised the *Optik* once and the *Tonempfindungen* three times. He published *Die Thatsachen in der Wahrnehmung* in 1878. Earlier he had defended psychological empiricism against psychological nativism by a series of papers on the geometrical axioms. His point in this matter was that the axioms are not innate ideas but are arrived at through individual experience.

Helmholtz was a dramatic lecturer. At Berlin he developed impressive lecture-demonstrations. On four occasions he published collections of popular scientific lectures which present many of his general views.

Now we may survey briefly the contributions to psychology of this physicist, who was also one of the great pioneers in establishing the new experimental psychology.

SENSE-PHYSIOLOGY

Helmholtz's greatest contribution to the experimental psychology of sensation is the *Optik*. We have just seen that this very important work appeared in three parts in 1856, 1860 and 1866, and that it was then issued as a whole in 1867. It remains today a gospel in this field. Helmholtz undertook a revision of the work in his later years, and the second edition was published posthumously in 1896, with a huge bibliography of 7,833 titles appended by Arthur König, the editor. When a third edition was proposed a decade later, the editors after careful consideration came to the conclusion that, while the content of the first edition had stood the test of time in a most remarkable fashion, the additions and alterations in the second edition had not fared so well. It may have been that the older Helmholtz, physicist, had been less immersed in this subject-matter than the younger Helmholtz, physiologist-psychologist. It may have been that the editors in their appendices wanted to say their own says about more recent changes in the field. At any rate they reprinted the first edition with extensive additional sections by themselves in 1909-1911. Still later, at the American celebration of the centennial of Helmholtz's birth, an English translation of the third, and therefore the first, edition was decided upon, a translation which appeared with a few further additions in 1924-1925. After sixty years and more this treatise was still considered a fundamental text in psychophysiological optics, for it was translated and published for use and not merely as an historical record.

It is not possible to indicate here the broad range of the content of this handbook. The three volumes have been characterized respectively as physical, physiological and psychological in their treatment of vision, but the psychologist would be more likely to define their subject-matters as physiological, sensory and perceptual, with the physical attack running throughout. The beginner in psychology knows, of course, most often about Helmholtz's theory of vision, the 'Young-Helmholtz' theory, yet this is but a small portion of the half million words that make up the *Optik*, as the seasoned investigator who uses the *Optik* as a *Handbuch* knows. In the last volume we find Helmholtz's more general psychology, the doctrines of empiricism and unconscious inference which we shall presently consider.

The *Tonempfindungen* of 1863, while a less extensive work than the *Optik*, occupies a similar scientific place. It is the classic text on the psychology of tone. Helmholtz revised it in 1865 and again in 1870 and 1877, and in 1875 the first English translation, extensively supplemented with notes by Ellis, appeared. Students of both psychology and music still use the book, which is better known than the *Optik* in Great Britain and America because of its early translation.

The first of the three parts of the *Tonempfindungen* is the most important for psychologists. It contains Helmholtz's account of auditory stimuli and of Ohm's law of auditory analysis, his discussion of the anatomy of the ear, the attendant resonance theory of hearing (now so definitely associated with Helmholtz's name), and the report of Helmholtz's researches on combination tones and on the nature of vowel qualities. The other two parts of the book deal with harmony and other musical matters.

The historical importance of the publication of these two books in the 1860s can hardly be exaggerated. Fifty years before, physiologists had much to say about vision and hearing, the historic senses which Newton discussed, and little about the other senses. Then E. H. Weber wrote the first thoroughgoing psycho-physiology of the cutaneous and other bodily senses (1834, 1846). Now Helmholtz, like Newton in having the physicist's point of view but writing when the meaning of psychology was becoming a little more obvious, was placing vision and hearing again in the van among the senses about which enough was known to permit the writing of scientific texts. Fechner showed that psychology could employ the scientific method of measurement. Helmholtz showed what could be done in research and in the accumulation of facts in the two leading sense-departments. The movement toward a psychological science was already under way. With a method of measurement available, with an exhibit of what could actually be done if the experimenter would but get to work, and with the general notion already explicit, it only remained for Wundt to seize the opportunity, to cry the slogan, and psychology as 'an independent science' would be 'founded.' And that is exactly what Wundt did, after Helmholtz and Fechner had prepared the way.

Helmholtz did not, of course, 'found' experimental psychology, for he thought of psychology as essentially physiological, and of physiology as essentially physical. Had the question been raised, he would have opposed 'mentalism,' just as he did oppose vitalism. Psychology was for him an exact science, dependent upon the use of mathematics, as Herbart had tried to show, and upon experiment, which Herbart denied. Johannes Müller exerted a great influence upon Helmholtz's thought in psychological matters, and here we should note the importance that Helmholtz ascribed to the doctrine of the specific energies of nerves. Helmholtz once likened Müller's formulation of this theory to Newton's formulation of the law of gravitation, so great and general a value did he attach to it. After all, quality then seemed to be the fundamental dimension of experience, and to say that difference of quality meant difference of place, and perhaps of structure, in the nervous system was to enunciate a great generalization. Unfortunately history has not entirely realized Helmholtz's anticipations.

Helmholtz's extension of the theory of specific energies to the different qualities within the single sense-department—his theory of 'specific fiber energies'—is extremely important as influencing later thought. He seems to have made the extension unconsciously, as a matter of course, or else to have assumed that Thomas Young originated it, long before Müller or even Bell. It was, however, Müller's doctrine, thus conceived, that gave Helmholtz's theories of vision and of hearing their fundamental form. About both these theories controversy still waxes and wanes. Nevertheless, even should they both be abandoned, we should find that much of our knowledge of the psychology of vision and hearing had originated in research inspired, positively or negatively, by Helmholtz's theories or their consequences.

EMPIRICISM

Helmholtz was not a systematic psychologist, but his work in vision brought him to the problem of visual perception and thus of perception in general. In many ways, perception has been the central problem of systematic psychology, and it thus comes about that Helmholtz occupies an important position in the history of systematic psychological thought. That Helmholtz was primarily an experimentalist simply goes to show that systematization and experimentation can not be separated in the history of psychology, or, for that matter, in the history of science.

Helmholtz stood for psychological empiricism. He belongs thus systematically more with British thought than with German, in the tradition of John Locke down to the Mills, rather than in the tradition of Leibnitz, Kant, and Fichte. German philosophical psychology had stressed intuitionism—that is to say, the doctrine of innate ideas, of *a priori* judgments, of native categories of the understanding. British psychology was built about empiricism, the doctrine of the genesis of the mind through individual experience.

Helmholtz took his stand with the latter group against the reigning German philosophy of Kant and Fichte. Later within psychology the opposition became that between geneticism and nativism in perception, with Lotze, Helmholtz and Wundt representing geneticism, with Müller, Hering and Stumpf representing nativism.

Kant had laid down the twelve categories of the understanding, the forms of mind which condition judgments, and had shown that judgments may be *a priori* (given in the understanding) or else *a posteriori* (dependent upon experience). (See pp. 246-249.) Examples of *a priori* judgments were supposed to be the geometrical axioms and such physical axioms as causality, the indestructibility of matter, and the nature of time and space, including the three-dimensionality of space. Fichte had centered his philosophy about the notion that time and space are *a priori* intuitions. It was this doctrine that Helmholtz undertook to combat. He had already formulated the empiristic view in 1855 while he was still at Königsberg, Kant's university, and somewhat after the appearance of Lotze's genetic theory of space in 1852. He defended it vigorously in the introduction to the third volume of the *Optik* (1866). His papers on the geometrical axioms came later (1866-1894). *Die Thatsachen in der Wahrnehmung* (1878) presents the view. We may turn to Helmholtz's own account of his grounds for the empiristic theory.

The *empiristic theory* seeks to demonstrate that at least no other forces are necessary for their origin beyond the known faculties of our minds, even though these forces themselves may remain entirely unexplained. As it is in general a useful rule for scientific investigation to make no new hypotheses so long as the known facts appear to be sufficient for explanation, I have thought it necessary to prefer the empiristic view in its essentials. The *nativistic* theory gives even less explanation of the origin of our perceptual images, for it simply plunges into the midst of the matter by assuming that certain perceptual images of space would be produced directly by an inborn mechanism provided certain nerve fibers were stimulated. In the earlier forms of this theory some sort of self-observation of the retina was presupposed, for we are assumed to have an inborn knowledge of the form of this membrane and of the position of the separate nerve endings in it. In the recent form of this view, especially as developed by E. HERING, there is an ideated subjective visual space wherein the sensations of the separate nerve fibers are supposed to be registered according to certain innate laws. Thus in this theory, not only is KANT's assertion adopted, that the general perception of space is an original form of our ideation, but there are laid down as innate certain special space perceptions.

Helmholtz did not believe that the nativistic theory could be disproved. He held rather, as Lotze had, that it was no theory at all, for it says nothing about space except that space is not generated in experience and must therefore, *faute de mieux*, be native. In general he believed that the nativistic view was unnecessary and gratuitous, that the development of perceptions in experience is to a certain extent demonstrable, and that there is no need of hypothesizing in addition another ground of perception unless positive evidence can be adduced for it.

Since Kant and Fichte had used the *geometrical axioms* as examples of *a priori* intuitions, Helmholtz undertook to show that they too are the products of experience. In all he published seven papers on this matter in 1866, 1870, 1876, 1877 and 1894. The fundamental ground of all geometrical proof lies, he argued, in the demonstration of the congruence of figures, and this demonstration can be achieved only by the superposition of the one figure upon another. Superposition, however, involves movement (and presumably also the fact that objects do not change in size or form when moved), and these facts of movement are known only by experience. The telling part of Helmholtz's discussion was, however, his pictures of non-Euclidean space.

He raised the question as to what geometry would be developed by beings who lived in another kind of space than ours. There might, for example, be "sphere-dwellers," who lived entirely in a spherical surface; for them the axiom of parallels would not hold, for any two straight lines, if sufficiently produced, would intersect in two points. Beings who lived in an egg-shaped surface would find that circles of equal radii at different places would have different circumferences. Dwellers in a pseudosphere or in other non-Euclidean spaces would have still different axioms and different geometries. So too we can conceive, though not imagine, hyper-spaces of four or more dimensions—space, for example, where there are forms that bear the same relation to the sphere as the sphere does to the circle.

So effectively were these pictures drawn that in certain limited circles they became the vogue of the times. Zöllner, the astronomer at Leipzig, came out with the theory that space must be curved and finite (a theory that has a modern ring), or else, he said, since time is infinite, all matter would already have been volatilized. This theory is interesting, but thereafter Zöllner was drawn into a consideration of the performances of the great American medium, Slade. Zöllner —and in part he had the support of Weber and Fechner—suggested that many of Slade's phenomena were accomplished by the use of a fourth dimension; in a fourth dimension objects could be taken out of a closed box as readily as, in three dimensions, they can be lifted out of a square. As has always been the case when psychic research is in question, the result was a violently emotional and personal controversy. Helmholtz was criticized as having laid the ground for a mystical view and thus for a great scientific scandal. One of Helmholtz's accusers was even dismissed from Berlin on account of the nature of his accusations. Helmholtz had done his task so well that the argument for empiricism was now used as an argument for the reality of a kind of space that had never been experienced.

Before we leave this topic, it will be interesting to contrast Helmholtz with Johannes Müller in respect of it. Müller, as we have seen, had a great influence upon Helmholtz, and Helmholtz acknowledged his greatness and especially the importance of the theory of the *specific energies of nerves*. Yet Müller was a nativist. His doctrine of specific energies has been called a naïve Kantian physiology. Space, he thought, is native to the mind, which can thus perceive spatially the image upon the retina. Helmholtz, while acknowledging the theory of specific energies as a very great discovery, took the opposite view about space. He followed and extended Lotze's treatment. He admitted for the different nerve fibers the equivalent of non-spatial local signs and then proceeded to show that it could be only by experience that these characteristics come to generate the space which is known in adult experience. We are observing one of those curious turns in scientific thought: Helmholtz accepted Müller's theory and used it in the interests of an opposite view. The change came about with the general development of thought. In the 1830s it seemed sufficient to get the stimulus-object as an image on the retina near enough to the brain, the seat of the mind, for the mind directly to perceive it. In the 1860s science was not satisfied with the attribution of vague powers to the mind; it wanted a more positive account of how the mind perceives.

In this connection Helmholtz also took up the facts of the singleness of perception in binocular vision. He accepted the doctrine of corresponding retinal points for the two retinas, a doctrine consonant with the theory of specific nerve energies. Yet the theory of corresponding points works only for the horopter: from all other places a point should appear double. Helmholtz refused to accept Hering's sensations of retinal disparity; they were to him another nativistic mystery. He argued that certain double images come through experience to be perceived as single, a genetic process in which uncon-

scious inference plays a rôle. To the place of "unconscious inference" in Helmholtz's psychology we shall turn in a moment. It is a
topic which has not yet lost its importance.

We ought to observe that Helmholtz admitted the existence of
instincts, briefly, as a mystery which he was not prepared to explain.
He felt bound to admit that some animals possess at birth a great deal
of specific knowledge which they can not have acquired by way of
individual experience. This point is a concession to the enemy, and
Helmholtz did not develop it. He was conversant with Darwin's and
Lamarck's views and sympathetic with them. Spencer had not yet
shown that nativism may become a positive theory when made over
into a phylogeneticism.

UNCONSCIOUS INFERENCE

The doctrine of unconscious inference (*unbewusster Schluss*) is
historically a very important part of Helmholtz's theory of perception and thus of his systematic psychology. The doctrine is really a
corollary of the empiristic position. It is most familiar to the psychologist in connection with Helmholtz's theory of color contrast.
Red and verdigris are complementaries: they contrast. A gray stimulus appears on a red ground. It contrasts with the red and by unconscious inference we see it as the opposite, that is to say, greenish.
The theory has never commanded general acceptance, and stated
baldly in this way it seems to violate those excellent principles which
Helmholtz urged against nativism; it would seem to be simply a
verbal cloak for scientific ignorance. A much better illustration, although one which Helmholtz did not argue so explicitly, is found in
connection with stereoscopic vision. A geometer, given all the data
of retinal disparity and binocular parallax, could figure out the depths
of distant objects, but the perceiving subject makes that calculation
instantly by 'unconscious inference.'

Helmholtz was arguing, in the first place, that perception may
contain many experiential data that are not immediately represented
in the stimulus, a view which ought to have the support of every
psychologist who has ever studied an illusion. He was arguing, in the
second place, that these aspects of the perception that do not immediately represent the stimulus are, in a sense, additions which accrue
to the perception in accordance with its development in past experience. He decided to call these unconsciously determined phenomena
inferences, in an attempt to characterize their nature in a single word,
and even then he sought both to affirm and to deny their inferential
nature by the use of a paradoxical phrase: *unconscious inference.*

In spite of misgivings about the term, we must take this doctrine of the great empiricist seriously.

Helmholtz adopted this theory while he was at Königsberg, for it is an essential phase of his empiricism. He expounded its essentials in a lecture that was published in 1855. He used it in the second volume of the *Optik* in 1860. In the third volume in 1866 he gave the full exposition which we follow here. He revised it somewhat in *Die Thatsachen in der Wahrnehmung* of 1878. In the meantime, however, the doctrine had received additional support, in its espousal by Wundt in the *Beiträge zur Theorie der Sinneswahrnehmung*, in the years 1858 to 1862, while Wundt was in Helmholtz's laboratory at Heidelberg. There is no doubt, however, that the theory belongs more to Helmholtz; Wundt admitted that. Helmholtz was the senior, had the theory first and kept it; Wundt was the younger, took up the view later and presently abandoned it. Nevertheless, there may have been mutual interaction: Helmholtz's thorough discussion of 1866 is four years after Wundt's in the *Beiträge*.

We begin our account by quoting from the *Optik* one of Helmholtz's general statements about unconscious inference.

> The psychic activities, by which we arrive at the judgment that a certain object of a certain character exists before us at a certain place, are generally not conscious activities but unconscious ones. In their results they are equivalent to an *inference*, in so far as we achieve, by way of the observed effect upon our senses, the idea of the cause of this effect, even though in fact it is invariably only the nervous excitations, the effects, that we can perceive directly, and never the external objects. Nevertheless, they thus appear to be differentiated from an inference, in the ordinary sense of this word, in that an inference is an act of conscious thinking. There are, for example, actual conscious inferences of this sort when an astronomer computes the positions of the stars in space, their distances from the earth, etc., from the perspective images he has had of them at different times and at different points in the earth's orbit. The astronomer bases his conclusions upon a conscious knowledge of the laws of optics. In the ordinary acts of seeing such a knowledge of optics is lacking; still it may be permissible to designate the psychic acts of ordinary perception as *unconscious inferences*, as this name distinguishes them sufficiently from the ordinary, so-called conscious inferences. While the similarity of the psychic activities in the two cases has been doubted and will perhaps always be doubted, still no doubt can remain of the similarity of the results of such unconscious inferences and of the conscious inferences.

Helmholtz had three positive statements to make about these unconscious inferences.

1. *Unconscious inferences are normally irresistible.* In the typical case, they appear to be irresistible, but Helmholtz's account is so full of instances of the way in which they can be modified that it seems better to qualify his general statement slightly. He means, of course, that experiences like contrast colors and the singleness of binocular vision come, under given conditions, immediately and universally and you can not modify them—at least not readily or ordinarily—by taking thought. They are "irresistible." Helmholtz said, because, since they are unconscious, you can not correct them by conscious reasoning. The exact degree of irresistibility which he had in mind will appear more plainly in our consideration of the next point. It is enough to note here that irresistibility is Helmholtz's ground for considering unconscious inferences as facts of sufficient precision for inclusion under scientific law.

2. *Unconscious inferences are formed by experience.* Thus the doctrine of unconscious inference becomes the tool of empiricism. These inferences, Helmholtz thought, are at first conscious (unless the instincts be an exception) and develop by *association* and *repetition* into unconscious inferences. In this way Helmholtz comes directly into accord with English associationism, where association is always the servant, and often the only servant, of empiricism. Nevertheless, this view should present no difficulty to any modern psychologist. It is the commonplace of introspective psychology that a conscious state, by repetition and under the law of habit, is telescoped and reduced until the given process is largely or entirely unconscious, as far as introspection can reveal, and as against what at first seemed to be the logically necessary essentials. Helmholtz's view is merely the principle of conscious decay under habituation.

It is now plain just what Helmholtz meant when he called the unconscious inferences "irresistible." He meant that well-established associations are virtually inevitable, but that, being associations, they may occur with all degrees of inevitability, and that, being learned, they may also be unlearned. A word gives rise to its meaning 'inevitably,' we should say, except for the fact that the meaning can be changed or, under certain conditions, prevented from occurring. Delayed perceptions also throw light on this matter. The stereoscopic perception of the form of a crystal from an outline stereogram may not give the perception of a solid crystal at once, yet the perception of a solid object becomes irresistible as soon as the 'idea' of the crystal is realized. The perception of any strange sensory pattern, originally unintelligible, is similar; now it is one thing, now another, until some perception finally remains fixed as embodying the 'true' meaning. In a sense each false completion of the perception is at the moment 'irresistible,' if we remember what this word means.

Helmholtz made an especial appeal to optical *illusions* as supporting the empiristic argument. Many of the optical illusions are practically compulsory. On the other hand, as we now know more definitely than did Helmholtz, many of them can be reduced, or even abolished, by the assumption of the 'analytic attitude' toward them. Helmholtz said that we can learn to correct them, and on this ground he laid down a general principle, distinguishing *sensation* as prior to unconscious inference from *perception* which is dependent on unconscious inference:

> Nothing in our sense-perceptions can be recognized as sensation which can be overcome in the perceptual image and converted into its opposite by factors that are demonstrably due to experience.

That which is alterable in experience must have come about by way of experience. In a strict sense, then, it is only sensations that are 'irresistible.' The perceptual additions are introduced by no conscious process and are therefore normally immediate. The real test that they are perceptual, and not sensory, is that they can be 'resisted' by indirect means.

3. *Unconscious inferences are, in their results, like conscious inferences from analogy and are thus inductive.* Helmholtz began his discussion with this point, which explains the name *unconscious inference;* but it is obviously the least important and the most disputable. Helmholtz referred to J. S. Mill's discussion of the circularity of the syllogism, concluding with Mill that we have here to do with analogical induction, that unconscious inference, like conscious inference, can by analogy actually lead to a conclusion about a novel case. All men are mortal; Caius is a man; therefore Caius is mortal. The difficulty here is that you must already know about Caius if you already know about all men, because Caius is a man. The analogical induction is: since all men in my experience have been mortal, and since Caius, a new experience, turns out to be a man, I infer that he too is mortal. This is the sort of generalization that the brain makes quickly and automatically in perception, so Helmholtz called it *unconscious inference,* knowing fully that he was being paradoxical, that inference is habitually understood to be conscious.

PERCEPTION

Helmholtz's fundamental theory of perception is very simple. The bare sensory pattern, as directly dependent upon the stimulus-object, he called a *Perzeption*. A pure *Perzeption* is, however, comparatively rare; it is nearly always supplemented and modified by an imaginal increment, dependent upon memory and induced by unconscious inference, which makes it over into what may be called an *Anschauung*, which is also literally the *Wahrnehmung*, since it is by *Anschauungen* that objects are correctly perceived and truly identified (*wahr* = 'true'). If the sense-impressions are entirely lacking and we have only the imaginal equivalent of the *Anschauung*, then the experience may be called a *Vorstellung*, a use of this German word more nearly like the English *idea* than is usually the case. *Perzeptionen* are rare. *Vorstellungen* lie outside the universe of discourse. The key to perception lies in the *Anschauungen*, which involve both sensation and imagery, both stimulation and unconscious. inference. This view of perception is really the historical link between the problem of perceptual complexity in English associationism and the same problem in the German tradition which Wundt began.

Helmholtz also, like Mill and all those before him since Locke, undertook to say something of the nature of the *object*. To say how experience becomes differentiated into objects is to attack the problem of perception in what is historically the older and alternative way. The object, according to Helmholtz, is nothing more than an aggregate of sensations, an aggregate which has been formed in experience because the sensations habitually occur together, and which is not analyzed into its sensory constituents except by a special act of attention. This is the empiristic theory of the object, now familiar to us. Helmholtz, however, went further to say that the object is built up in experience by a sort of "mental experimentation"; we discover by trial and error which sensations can be changed by the will and attribute to the object those that can not.

Thus the *properties of objects* are merely their effects upon our senses, the relations of the objects to the organs of sense. This is the view to which we were led by Locke's doctrine of secondary qualities and by that portion of Johannes Müller's doctrine of the specific energies of nerves which anticipates the modern distinction between adequate and inadequate stimulation.

The *permanence of objects*, in Helmholtz's discussion, results from the mental experimentation. The objects can not be changed by the will except to be made to disappear. When they disappear, they can be brought back by the will, simply by bringing them again into relation to the sense-organs. We turn the head and the object goes; we turn it back and the object comes again. It must have been there

all along. Helmholtz in all these matters was influenced by John
Stuart Mill, and we seem to have in his theory of objective permanence only an incomplete discussion that is consonant with Mill's
view that objectivity depends upon the conception of the permanent
possibilities of sensation. (See pp. 231 f.)

SCIENTIFIC OBSERVATION

The consideration of the laws of perception led Helmholtz to an
interesting discussion of the nature and limitations of scientific observation, a discussion that is relevant to all psychological observation, especially the introspective observation of 1880-1910 and the
phenomenological observation of 1910-1940. He noted that we have
in scientific observation ordinarily to deal with *Anschauungen* and
not *Perzeptionen;* that is to say, the observation depends upon the
past experience of the observer, his unconscious inferences and the
resulting modification of the sensory core. For this reason two
different observations of a stimulus-situation may both be 'correct'
in so far as they are accurate records of the experience. There may
be a personal equation in any observation, and Helmholtz even went
so far as to say that most of the observations in the *Physiologische
Optik,* being his own, may be subject to this personal error. He had
written, as it were, a book about himself. Only the way in which
these observations have stood the test of repetition now shows that
Helmholtz was being overcautious for the sake of making a point,
that his facts of physiological optics were based more upon *Perzeptionen* and less upon *Anschauungen* than he may have supposed. To
this conclusion there is a moral of which Helmholtz was fully aware.
There is the influence of a 'laboratory atmosphere' upon observational results, which means that investigators are likely to observe
what they are trained to observe, and there is also the contrary fact
that good observers have to be trained.

How, then, are psychological observers to be trained? Helmholtz
noted that attention is normally to objects and not to sensations, and
that the correction of the objective *Anschauungen* is very difficult.
Some observers, like Purkinje, were, he thought, peculiarly gifted in
observing sensations and in abstracting from the imaginal supplements which unconscious inference adds. More often, however, the
attention has to be especially directed toward the phenomenon before the observation can be made. The right direction of attention
may happen by chance; it may be indicated by previous observation
or by a theoretical implication; it may require special conditions.
Helmholtz gave numerous instances. He mentioned, seemingly as

cases of specially directed attention, Purkinje's remarkable observational power, the perception of double images in binocular vision and the perception of the luminous dust of the eyes, which is always present in all people but is generally first noted by persons with eye-trouble who attribute it to the trouble. He showed the necessity for auxiliary aids by citing Mariotte and the discovery of the blind-spot, the existence of which can be shown only experimentally; the perception of harmonics and some combination tones in clangs and dyads, tones which can only be perceived when attention is directed specifically toward them in advance; and the appearance of a landscape when viewed from between the legs, a case where the colors come out vividly instead of being toned down by the unconscious modifications of habitual perception.

This question of training good laboratory observers produced one of the violent controversies of the 1890s. The American functionalists argued then that the Wundtians trained their subjects to give the kinds of reaction times that the Leipzig theory required. The Wundtians said that they practised their subjects without prejudice and that the theory was founded on the discovery that practised subjects always gave a particular result.

All in all it turns out that Helmholtz, the physiologist turned physicist, had a great deal of importance to say about the new scientific psychology.

NOTES

For Helmholtz and the measurement of the rate of the nervous impulse, see pp. 41 f. For Helmholtz and the doctrine of the specific energies of nerves, see pp. 91-95. For the physiological psychology of the nineteenth century up to Helmholtz's epoch-making attack upon the problems of sight and hearing, see pp. 96-114.

The best biography of Helmholtz is L. Koenigsberger, *Hermann von Helmholtz*, 3 vols., 1902-1903, and Eng. trans. J. G. McKendrick, *Hermann Ludwig Ferdinand von Helmholtz*, 1899, is briefer but excellent. There is also G. S. Hall, *Founders of Modern Psychology*, 1912, 247-308; and J. Reiner, *Hermann von Helmholtz* [1905].

Helmholtz's two handbooks are: *Handbuch der physiologischen Optik* (1856-1866), 1867; 2 ed. (1885-1894), 1896; 3 ed., 1 ed. with additions by A. Gullstrand, J. von Kries and W. Nagel, 1909-1911; French trans. of 1 ed., 1867; Eng. trans. of 3 ed. with further additions, 1924-1925; *Die Lehre von den Tonempfindungen als physiologischer Grundlage für die Theorie der Musik*, 1863; later editions, 1865, 1870, 1877; Eng. trans. with additions by A. J. Ellis, 1875, 1885, *et seq.*

Especially relevant to this chapter is *Die Thatsachen in der Wahrnehmung*, 1878 (more usually 1879), an address in Berlin in 1878, reprinted in *Vorträge und Reden*, 1884, II, 217-271.

Helmholtz's writings are very extensive. Many of his more popular writings have been reprinted as *Populäre wissenschaftliche Vorträge* (Eng. trans., 1881), 1865-1871, 1876, and *Vorträge und Reden*, 1884. Many of the technical and less accessible papers are reprinted in the three volumes of his *Wissenschaftliche Abhandlungen*, 1882-1883, 1895. The last and posthumous volume contains A. König's bibliography of 217 titles, pp. 607-636, which is also published separately.

Beside the discussions of Helmholtz's psychology in the biographies, see V. Heyfelder, *Ueber den Begriff der Erfahrung bei Helmholtz*, 1897; F. Conrat, *Helmholtz' Verhältnis zur Psychologie*, 1903, and *Hermann von Helmholtz' psychologische Anschauungen*, 1904; P. Hertz and M. Schlick, *Hermann v. Helmholtz' Schriften zur Erkenntnistheorie*, 1921, which again reprints *Die Thatsachen in der Wahrnehmung*. For brief comment, see G. Murphy, *Historical Introduction to Modern Psychology*, 2 ed., 1949, 137-143.

Helmholtz's medical thesis and first publication on the relation of nerve cells and nerve fibers of ganglia is *De fabrica systematis nervosi evertebratorum*, 1842, reprinted in *Wissenschl. Abhandl.*, II, 663-679.

Helmholtz's famous paper on the conservation of energy, *Ueber die Erhaltung der Kraft*, 1847, was only the sixth publication that he had ever made. It is reprinted in *Wissenschl. Abhandl.*, I, 12-75.

Helmholtz must be regarded as extending the theory of specific nerve energies to individual nerve fibers in 1852 when he first discussed the probable correctness of Thomas Young's theory of color. This early paper is *Ueber die Theorie der zusammengesetzen Farben* (reprinted in *Wissenschl. Abhandl.*, II, 3-23), and in it Helmholtz gave his color theory, discussed Müller's doctrine as if it applied to the separate visual qualities and attributed the entire view to Thomas Young (1802).

The section of the text on Helmholtz's empiricism and the following sections draw primarily upon the general introductory section to the third volume of the *Optik*, "Von den Wahrnehmungen im allgemeinen" (1866). *Die Thatsachen in der Wahrnehmung* is really more epistemological than psychological. For popular accounts of Helmholtz and the geometrical axioms, see Hall, *op. cit.*, 256-269; McKendrick, *op. cit.*, 250-267. Helmholtz did not, of course, think up non-Euclidean geometry by himself. That goes back to N. I. Lobachevski (1835) and G. F. B. Riemann (1354). It was his suggesting that these geometries would seem real if experience were consistent with them that created the excitement which created all the discussion and excitement.

For Helmholtz's espousal of empiricism while he was still at Königsberg, see his *Ueber das Sehen des Menschen*, 1855, reprinted in *Vorträge und Reden*, 1884, I, 365-396. In general on nativism and empiricism, see E. G. Boring, *Sensation and Perception in the History of Experimental Psychology*, 1942, 28-34, 49 f.

The doctrine of unconscious inference is implicit in the paper just cited, but it was not so named. Neither does the term occur in the discussion of visual contrast of 1860. Here the phrase is "illusion of judgment": see the *Optik*, II, sect. 24, the very end of the discussion. Wundt really used the phrase first in 1858 (*Beiträge zur Theorie der Sinneswahrnehmung*, p. 65) and stressed it in 1862 (*ibid.*, 422-451). For Wundt's relation to Helmholtz, see W. Wundt, *Erlebtes und Erkanntes*, 1920, 155-169. Hall on this point is inaccurate.

'Unconscious inference' is the best translation of *unbewusster Schluss*. The English *Optik* says "unconscious conclusion." Baldwin in translating Ribot says "unconscious reasoning." Others have used *inference*, which seems to the author best as denoting the inductive nature of a process. (Here and elsewhere the author has departed at will from the Eng. trans. of the *Optik*, usually in the interests of a more literal translation.)

For brief excerpts in Eng. trans. of Helmholtz on color theory, see B. Rand, *Classical Psychologists*, 1912, 582-596, or W. Dennis, *Readings in the History of Psychology*, 1948, 199-205; for Helmholtz on perception, Dennis, *op. cit.*, 214-230.

CHAPTER 16

Wilhelm Wundt

Wundt is the senior psychologist in the history of psychology. He is the first man who without reservation is properly called a psychologist. Before him there had been psychology enough, but no psychologists. Johannes Müller was a physiologist. John Stuart Mill was a logician and economist. Lotze was a metaphysician. Helmholtz was a physiologist and physicist. Bain was really a psychologist, but formally a logician. Fechner, whom psychology claims, was first a physicist and then by his own major intent a philosopher. Wundt held a chair of philosophy, as the German psychologists did, and wrote voluminously on philosophy; but in his own eyes as in the eyes of the world he was, first and foremost, a psychologist. When we call him the 'founder' of experimental psychology, we mean both that he promoted the idea of psychology as an independent science and that he is the senior among 'psychologists.'

Wilhelm Wundt was born in Baden in 1832 in Neckarau, a suburb of Mannheim. His father was a Lutheran pastor. He led the life of an only child, although he had three brothers and sisters; two of them, however, died so early that Wilhelm did not remember them; one brother, eight years older, had left home for school when Wilhelm was very young. Wilhelm and his parents moved to Heidensheim, a village in central Baden, when the boy was about six. After two years in the *Volkschule*, his education was undertaken by a vicar, Friedrich Müller, presumably Wundt's father's assistant, who shared his room with his pupil. This vicar soon came to command the affection and admiration of the young boy to a degree which his parents had never done, and, when the vicar shortly was called to the neighboring village of Münzesheim, Wilhelm was so disconsolate that his parents allowed him to go to live with the vicar and thus continue his private education. The young Wundt seems to have had no boyish friends and no habits of play. Except on Sundays, he spent his time in vicar Müller's house working on the tasks that the vicar had left, indulging often in flights of fancy and longing always for the vicar's return from his parish duties.

When the boy was thirteen, he entered the *Gymnasium* at Bruschal, a school in which the Catholic influence predominated. Partly for this latter reason his parents decided to send him elsewhere, and he went the next year to the *Gymnasium* at Heidelberg. Here he made friends, developed a habit of intensive reading and in general entered upon the life of learning in which he was to become so distinguished. He was ready for the university when he was nineteen.

Certainly this was a sober childhood and a serious youth, unrelieved by fun and jollity, which prepared the young Wundt for the endless writing of the ponderous tomes which eventually did so much to give him his place in history. He never learned to play. He had no friends in childhood and only intellectual companions in adolescence. He failed to find parental love and affection, substituting for the more happy relationship this deep attachment for his vicar-mentor. One can see the future man being formed—the humorless, indefatigable, aggressive Wundt. Yet we must not forget that he had also tremendous ability, enough to account for his enormous encyclopedic erudition. It was, however, this motivational pattern which made him presently the psychologist most to be reckoned with, a pattern which we see already well formed before Wundt had even arrived at his university training.

In 1851 Wundt went to Tübingen. His parents chose it for him from among the smaller universities in or near Baden: Heidelberg, Freiburg and Tübingen. However, he remained but a year, for the next autumn he went to Heidelberg for three and a half years. It was at Tübingen that he made the decision to become a physiologist. His father had died, and his mother's means were small. Wundt had some doubts as to whether he was suited to be a physician, but the medical training offered an indeterminate compromise between preparing to become a doctor, a profession which would earn him a livelihood, and studying the sciences, a task more congenial to Wundt's scholarly temperament. So Wundt, like Lotze and Helmholtz before him, went into medicine because of the necessity for earning a living. It is thus, in a sense, because young men have to be self-supporting and because the medical faculties of the German universities gave a truly academic training, which could nevertheless be made profitable later in the practice of a physician, that modern psychology began as physiological psychology.

Wundt's first year at Heidelberg was devoted to the study of anatomy, physiology, physics, chemistry and some practical medicine. Out of this came his first publication on the sodium chloride content of urine (1853). In his second year he was more definitely introduced to the practice of medicine, and his interest in the physiological work of Johannes Müller at Berlin and of Ludwig at Leipzig increased. In his third year he became an assistant in a medical clinic in Heidelberg and also published a paper on the effect of the section of the vagus on respiration (1855). By this time he had received a thorough practical training in the medical art, a training from which he had not failed to absorb the purely scientific content. Moreover, he had made a start in research.

Whatever had been his doubts four years before, it was now quite clear to him that he was not directed toward the medical profession. In the spring of 1856, he went for the second semester to Berlin, to Johannes Müller's institute of physiology, two years before Müller's death, to study physiology under the man who was then the world's greatest physiologist—the 'father of experimental physiology,' as he has since been called, by a title similar to Wundt's in experimental psychology. Wundt said that he found "the character of German science at Berlin purer in its depth and in its many-sidedness than in the universities of southern Germany." The training at Heidelberg had been too practical for his academic temperament. At Berlin he met not only the best science of his day but also the greatest minds. Besides Müller in physiology and Magnus in physics, he seems to have seen most of du Bois-Reymond, who was then engaged in trying to settle a controversy concerning muscular contractions, one that had arisen between Eduard F. Weber (the youngest of the three Leipzig Weber brothers, of whom Ernst Heinrich was the oldest) and A. W. Volkmann in Halle (Fechner's friend). If anything remained to determine Wundt for the academic life, this stimulating experience at Berlin was decisive.

Wundt returned to Heidelberg, still in 1856, took his doctorate in medicine and was then habilitated as *Dozent* in physiology, an appointment that he held from 1857 to 1864. He was already beginning to show signs of his future productivity. He published three purely physiological papers in 1856-1857, and then, in 1858, his first book, *Lehre von den Muskelbewegungen*. His earlier interest in pathological anatomy had already passed; his interest in physiology was paramount; but his bent toward psychology had begun. In 1858 he published the first section of the *Beiträge zur Theorie der Sinneswahrnehmung*, the section on touch, which draws largely upon E. H. Weber, Johannes Müller and Lotze. Wundt already was conceiving of perception as something psychologically more than the physiologist's sensation. The last paragraph of this section contains a brief discussion of unconscious inference (*unbewusster Schluss*: the phrase is used) as the mechanism of perception; and this paragraph must have been written, perhaps published, before Helmholtz came to Heidelberg.

It was in the fall of 1858—altogether an important year for Wundt —that Helmholtz came from Bonn to the physiological institute. Helmholtz's arrival coincided with a curricular change that required all persons coming up for the state examination in medicine in Baden to have had a semester's laboratory course in physiology, and Wundt was appointed assistant to drill the sudden inroad of students in the standard experiments on muscle twitches and conduction of the nervous impulse. Wundt stood this dreary routine for a while, without being convinced of its value for potential doctors, and then after several years resigned to resume his docentship. He did not, as one text has it, resign because he knew too little mathematics to satisfy Helmholtz; of this statement Wundt himself remarks that Helmholtz needed no assistance with his mathematics. Altogether there seems to have been respect and mutual admiration between Helmholtz, eleven years the senior, and Wundt, the junior, but no great personal intimacy. Perhaps, as Titchener has observed, their temperaments were too different. Nevertheless, the fact remains that they were both at Heidelberg in the same laboratory for thirteen years until Helmholtz went to Berlin in 1871.

It was in these seventeen years at Heidelberg (1857-1874) that Wundt changed from a physiologist to a psychologist—the first psychologist, we have said. He was *Dozent* in physiology or assistant in the physiological practicum until 1864; then he was made *ausserordentlicher Professor*. In 1871, when Helmholtz went to Berlin, Wundt was his natural successor, but he was not appointed. The chair fell to Kühne, and Wundt stayed on until 1874, when he was appointed to the chair of inductive philosophy at Zürich, a title that signalized his shift of interest. At first at Heidelberg he lectured in alternate semesters on experimental physiology and medical physics, lectures that resulted later in two books, which he began when he resigned the assistantship. These books are the *Lehrbuch der Physiologie des Menschen* (1864, with new editions in 1868 and 1873) and the *Handbuch der medicinischen Physik* (1867).

It is worth noting that Wundt's emphasis on medical physics means, for all that Johannes Müller had done, that it was still necessary to keep saying that physiology is a science in the sense of physical science. It is quite reasonable, then, that Wundt should also have felt the need for stressing the fact that psychology too, as physiological psychology, is a science. Even today psychologists

have not ceased to be self-conscious about the scientific nature of
psychology. In 1858-1859 Wundt began to formalize his epistemological notions by offering lectures on an introduction to the
study of the natural sciences. The next year he lectured on anthropology, defined as the natural history of man. He introduced other
physiological topics as replacements for the old lectures.

Meanwhile he was working on the *Beiträge zur Theorie der Sinneswahrnehmung*. The first section of 1858 was followed by two
more in the following year, one more in 1861 and the last two sections in 1862. The entire book, with its introduction that Titchener
says outlined the program of Wundt's life, was also published in
1862. The correspondence of this program with subsequent events
can not, however, mean that Wundt clearly foresaw, even by intention, his future. How could he? He was still a *Dozent* in physiology
with physiological projects under way; there were in the world no
experimental psychologists to show that the world could provide a
place for the working-out of such a program. Nevertheless Wundt
had an idea, and its value was to be attested by the later use that he
was able to make of it.

We must pause a moment over the *Beiträge*. Here we have a book
that has some claim to being the beginning of experimental psychology, partly because it is in content experimental psychology,
partly because it presents a formal plea for experimental psychology,
called by that name, and partly because, for all its shortcomings, it is
Wundt's first book in experimental psychology.

It was not, of course, the very first book in experimental psychology nor the greatest of its date. Fechner's *Elemente* had appeared two years before the completed *Beiträge*, although two
years after its first portion. Fechner, thirty-one years older than
Wundt, had begun work while Wundt was yet a student in physiology. The experimental contents of the *Beiträge* were new, but
they were hardly so psychologically original as Weber's work on
touch had been. No, the actual experimental content of the book is
of primary psychological importance only because it shows Wundt,
while still immersed in physiology, beginning to think and work in
experimental psychology and, moreover, in the crucial field of perception.

The book, however, made a claim for experimental psychology.
Wundt spoke of an *experimentelle Psychologie*. He was not as specific as he was later. He argued merely that "all psychology begins
with introspection [*Selbstbeobachtung*]," and that there are two
Hilfsmittel: experiment and *Geschichte*, the natural history of man-

kind. One works, he said, inductively by these means. Thus Titchener was able to say that Wundt throughout his life carried on the three phases of the psychological program of the *Beiträge*: experimental psychology, social psychology (*Geschichte*) and a scientific metaphysics (referring here to Wundt's discussion of induction). The prognostic significance of this tripartite scheme need not concern us; it is important to see that Wundt took the method of experiment, even though he did not think it the only psychological method, so seriously that he spoke readily of experimental psychology. Elsewhere Wundt has told us more of his own thinking. It was about 1858 that Herbart's *Psychologie als Wissenschaft* especially engaged him in the days when he was first beginning to lecture on the general principles of natural science. It was then that he came to the conclusion that psychology must be *Wissenschaft*, but that, *als Wissenschaft*, it must be dependent upon experiment as Herbart had said it is not. For many years Wundt had to fight the Herbartian tradition, but nevertheless it was Herbart that gave to him, as well as to Fechner, the notion of a scientific psychology, though to Fechner and Wundt *scientific* meant *experimental*. These matters were not clear to Wundt when he published the first part of the *Beiträge* in 1858, but, when he came to add the general introduction to the entire book in 1862, he had had the benefit of much thought and lecturing and of Fechner's *Elemente* and could speak easily of an "experimental psychology."

In the years of the *Beiträge*, Wundt's other interests in psychology were rapidly expanding. In 1861 we find him speaking before the astronomical section of the *Naturforscherversammlung* in Speyer on the psychophysiological explanation of the personal equation. In 1862 he offered at Heidelberg a course of lectures on "psychology from the standpoint of natural science," and in the following year he published them as the *Vorlesungen über die Menschen- und Thierseele*, a book that was important enough to have a revised edition almost thirty years later, an English translation of the revision, and then repeated reprintings until after Wundt's death. It has been described as the naïve psychology of the physiologist, but actually, whatever its structure, it contained an indication of many problems that were to make up the body of experimental psychology for many years. The personal equation was there and with it the reaction experiment; the perceptual problems of the *Beiträge* were treated more popularly; the psychophysical methods, only three years old, were summarized; and many other more systematic matters, all foretastes of Wundt's later expository method, were included. The Heidelberg course continued under its first title every year until 1867; then the title changed to "Physiological Psychology": perhaps physiological psychology as a formal subject-matter with this name can be said to have begun in 1867. The later 1860s were, however, as we have said, taken up with physiological work and publication, the work upon which Wundt embarked when he gave up the assistantship in the physiological practicum for doctors preparing for the state examinations. The psychological work was indirectly all a preparation for the great *Physiologische Psychologie* of 1873-1874, but it is doubtful that Wundt was actually working at the book in the 1860s. His capacity for intense work and immense production was too great to have made so long a period of preparation necessary.

Wundt thought and wrote at an unusually effective rate all his life. It has been said humorously that Cattell's presentation of an American typewriter to Wundt in 1883 may have had something to do with the remarkable volume of Wundt's published writings. Nothing could be farther from the truth. In 1857 he had only just become *Dozent* in physiology. Six years later he had performed experiments and written the *Beiträge* with its systematic introduction; he had worked up lectures in psychology and had published them in a second book; he had got hold of various fundamental ideas, like the notions of experimental psychology and of historical psychology, and the fact that the experiments on the personal equation opened the way to the psychology of the temporal course and association of ideas. All this was in psychology only. Meanwhile he was publishing on physiological subjects; he was lecturing on microscopic anatomy with demonstrations, on medical physics, on the physiology of generation and development, on anthropology, and so forth, with the topics constantly changing; and he was engaged in the uninteresting mass instruction of the doctors in the practicum. In default of an adequate biography, one can study his bibliography and list of lectures for these years, and then one begins to realize the measure of Wundt's capacity.

Wundt's lectures on physiological psychology, begun in 1867, were to become a book, the most important book in the history of modern psychology, his *Grundzüge der physiologischen Psychologie*. The first half was published in 1873 and the second in 1874, both while Wundt was still at Heidelberg. This book was, on the one hand, the concrete result of Wundt's intellectual development at Heidelberg and the symbol of his metamorphosis from physiologist to psychologist, and, on the other hand, it was the beginning of the new 'independent' science. It was a systematic handbook in both senses of the word; it was built about a system of psychology, and it attempted systematically to cover the range of psychological fact. It was much more sophisticated than the two earlier books on psychology. The doctrine of unconscious inference was gone; the notion of apperception had appeared, although it did not reach its full vigor until later editions. It is easy for the critical reader to stress the changes in the successive six editions of the *Physiologische Psychologie* (1873-1911); however, the great changes, like those in the doctrines of apperception and of feeling, and the broad expansion of the text, are significant only when one realizes that the essential structure of the system was predetermined in 1874 and held to ever after. Wundt did not write another, more mature system of psychology: he modified, improved and expanded the original. It was called a "physiological psychology," and it was his great argument for an experimental psychology.

Wundt stayed at Zürich only a year (1874-1875). In 1875 he accepted the call to Leipzig to a chair of philosophy. This change is significant. It brought Wundt formally into the field where psychology was supposed to belong, and it brought him there from physiology. Thus began that paradoxical situation, which still obtains, whereby experimental laboratories grew up as adjuncts to German chairs of philosophy. It was not the Herbartians at Leipzig who called Wundt in preference to his competitor, Horwicz, but Zöllner, who arranged to have a chair divided and to get Wundt as one of two where there was but one before. It is doubtful, however, if any of them fully realized how much of an experimentalist they were getting. They may have thought of Wundt as a misfit scientist converted to philosophy—and indeed there was some truth about the conversion to philosophy. They did, nevertheless, also get an experimentalist in Wundt. With the system published, Wundt in his new chair was able to start out directly upon its extension, by way both of its internal logic and of external experiment.

The experimental work was not long in appearing. When Wundt came to Leipzig in 1875 he was given space for experimental demonstrations in connection with his lectures. In 1879, four years after he had come, Wundt founded, as almost every psychologist knows, the very first formal psychological laboratory in the world. The first published research from it was Max Friedrich's on apperception time in compound reactions. Of course, as we have so often remarked in other connections, nothing that is called 'first' is ever literally first; there always turn out to have been 'anticipations.' William James also had a room formally set apart for psychological experimentation at Harvard University in 1875, and Stumpf is said to have had an acoustic 'laboratory' of tuning-forks in a cigar-box still earlier. Such laboratories, however, were not 'founded'; they simply occurred and existed. Besides, the phrase for a psychological laboratory in German is *Psychologisches Institut*, and institutes are recognized administrative units, though laboratories may be merely places for work. This first *Psychologisches Institut* at Leipzig was a primitive affair of a few rooms, soon increased to eleven, in an old building since torn down. It gave way to much better quarters in 1897, but it was in this first building that experimental psychology actually got its *de jure* independence. There, more than in any other place, were trained the men who furnish the important names in the subsequent history of experimental psychology, not only Germans, like Kraepelin, Lehmann, Külpe and Meumann, but also the majority of the first generation of experimentalists in America, men like Stanley Hall, Cattell, Scripture, Frank Angell, Titchener, Witmer, Warren, Stratton and Judd. Hall's contact was slight. Cattell was Wundt's first assistant, self-appointed with genuine American intrepidity. Wundt relates that Cattell simply came to him and said: "Herr Professor, you need an assistant, and I will be your assistant!" In this connection we may remark that Cattell must be one of the few students who brought to Wundt, accustomed to assign problems arbitrarily to students, his own problem, the problem of individual differences, and who succeeded in working upon it, for all that Wundt called it *"ganz amerikanisch"*—as indeed the problem has turned out to be.

The list of Wundt's fifteen assistants from 1885 to 1909 is J. McK. Cattell, L. Lange, O. Külpe, A. Kirschmann, E. Meumann, F. Kiesow, P. Mentz, E. Mosch, R. Müller, W. Möbius, W. Wirth, E. Dürr, F. Krüger, O. Klemm and P. Salow. That series includes at least ten famous names in the history of experimental psychology.

The productivity of the new laboratory required a medium of publication. Thus in 1881 Wundt founded the *Philosophische Studien* essentially as the organ of the laboratory and of the new experimental psychology. Although the British *Mind*, which Bain founded in 1876, was actually the first psychological journal, the 'new psychology' did not immediately flourish in England, and this journal never became permanently its organ. The *Philosophische Studien*, then, was the first effective organ for experimental psychology, and the output of Wundt's laboratory was its main source of nutriment. Nowadays the title sounds strange, but we must remember not only that Wundt was professor of philosophy, but also that Wundt believed that philosophy should be psychological and that he was then well started upon the philosophical decade of his life, a decade in which his important books were a logic, an ethics and a system of philosophy. After all, the philosophers who called Wundt to Leipzig were not paid in such bad coin.

The 1880s formed Wundt's philosophical decade. In 1880–1883 he published the two large volumes of his *Logik*, a book that contains many of his views on psychology and psychological method. In 1886 there appeared his *Ethik*. In 1889 he issued the *System der Philosophie*, a book that Titchener describes as a complete program of a scientific philosophy, the outcome (so Titchener thought) of the plan for a scientific metaphysics outlined in the *Beiträge* twenty-seven years earlier. These three books together contain about 2,500 pages of text and might well occupy a scholar for ten years. They did not, however, exhaust Wundt's energy. In 1880 he also published the second edition of the *Physiologische Psychologie*, much revised and enlarged into two volumes. In 1887 the third edition appeared. Beside minor articles, he was writing at length in the *Studien*. And all the while he was directing the work of this new, successful and highly productive venture, the Leipzig laboratory. There are few men who can accomplish so much at so effective a level in so brief a time.

For the remainder of Wundt's life psychology was a going concern, spreading out in Germany and America. In 1890 Wundt had got experimental psychology permanently established in the world of science. He had christened the new psychology "physiological psychology." He had made the argument for a scientific psychology and had begun experimental psychology. He had founded the first laboratory or institute of psychology and had proved that it could be productive. The researches were increasing and the facts were piling up. Wundt had begun a journal of theoretical and experimental psychology and had maintained it. Other laboratories, patterned upon Leipzig and founded by men trained at Leipzig, were beginning to be established in Germany and America. But the character of the new psychology in Germany was already determined by Wundt. To some extent he had also predetermined

American psychology, at least as far as the laboratories were concerned, although America, except for Titchener, was destined to
have a psychology more or less its own from the very start.

In 1889 Wundt received the honor of being made rector of
the university at Leipzig. The measure of his work is, however,
to be found in his writings. Every major enterprise that he had
begun he continued with revised editions. The fourth edition of
the *Physiologische Psychologie* appeared in 1893; the fifth, expanded into three volumes, contained the radical change necessitated by the adoption of the tri-dimensional theory of feeling and
came out in 1902-1903; the sixth, much like the fifth, was issued
in 1908-1911. The new theory of feeling first appeared in the
Grundriss der Psychologie in 1896 and stimulated a very great
deal of experimental work in its support and refutation. By 1911
this popular book had passed into the tenth revised edition, followed by five more unaltered reprintings. The *Vorlesungen der
Menschen- und Thierseele* of 1863 Wundt revised in 1892, and
then twice more, publishing the last revision in 1919. He wrote
a little *Einführung in die Psychologie* in 1911. All this mass of
publication was psychological in the strict sense of the word, but
Wundt also continued to revise and publish his philosophical texts.
There were three revised editions of the *Ethik* between 1892 and
1912; three of the *Logik*, which expanded into three large volumes,
between 1893 and 1921 (for the last was published posthumously);
three of the *System der Philosophie* between 1897 and 1919.

Still we have not told the entire story. The 1890s were a period
of activity in which he rounded out his system of psychology and
altered it almost completely to accord with his changed views upon
feeling. The new century, however, brought him the leisure to
return to the unfulfilled task, outlined in the *Beiträge* of 1862—the
writing of the *Völkerpsychologie*, the natural history of man, which
alone, Wundt thought, could give the scientific answer to the
problems of the higher mental processes. The first volume of this
work appeared in 1900, was later revised and finally became two
volumes in a second revision. The second volume was published
in 1905-1906 and became two volumes on revision. Then, from
1914 to 1920, six more volumes appeared, making ten in all. When
the reader has comprehended the magnitude of this work, he
should then consult Wundt's bibliography in order to see how actively he was engaged in the writing of articles besides his work
on the books. Without a break, the enormous productivity and
fertility of 1857-1862 was continued for sixty-three years, until

Wundt's death in 1920. Even his death seems to have accorded with his systematic habits. All the revisions had been completed. The *Völkerpsychologie* was at last finished. He wrote his life's psychological reminiscences in 1920, and died shortly thereafter, on August 31 at the age of eighty-eight.

At first the new psychology seemed to center in Wundt and Leipzig. Later, of course, psychology passed beyond Wundt. There were other experimental schools and controversy within Germany and in America. In the last two editions of the *Physiologische Psychologie*, Wundt stressed his system of psychology more and abandoned the attempt to make the work a complete handbook of psychological knowledge. The *Philosophische Studien* ceased in 1903, except for a *Festschrift* in Wundt's honor, and Wundt sought to use the other journals, especially the *Archiv für die gesamte Psychologie* which replaced the *Philosophische Studien*. He had been too long independent, however, to work through the medium of others, and he soon began the *Psychologische Studien* as the organ of the Leipzig school.

Wundt was an encyclopedist and a systematist. He had an almost unrivaled capacity for bringing together a tremendous array of facts into a systematic structure. The parts of such a structure tend to become theses, so that systematic writing of this sort takes on the nature of the demonstration of a proof. Thus Wundt was also an effective polemicist. In all this work his method resembles more the method of the philosopher than that of the scientist. At bottom his temperament seems to have been philosophical. It is not that he wrote philosophically and also on philosophy because he had come to hold a chair of philosophy instead of physiology; he was appointed as a philosopher because, even when a physiologist, his bent had been philosophical toward the theory of science.

Was Wundt an experimentalist as well as a philosopher? This question is a very difficult one to answer. It is clear that Wundt came by a rational philosopher's method to his convictions about experimental psychology, that he founded a laboratory, began an experimental journal, conducted experimental research, and always held his theories in the light of all the available experimental fact and subject to revision on the basis of new experimentation, and that he did all this, not because he was by nature an experimentalist, but as the result of a philosophical conviction. He was an experimentalist; but his experimentalism was the byproduct of his philosophical views. Wundt never held that the experimental method is adequate to the whole of psychology: the higher processes, he thought, must be got at by the study of the history of human nature, his *Völkerpsychologie*. Thus he could come at and formulate and promulgate an elaborate theory of feeling, one that vitally affected his entire system, all before there was much experimentation to support or refute it. Thus also in his psychology conceptual matters like the doctrines of analysis and apperception could seem to others to be his important contributions. With less vitality, he might have held the belief in the experimental method for psychology without ever putting it into practice; but Wundt was Wundt: he could found a laboratory, direct a mass of experimental research and issue a new experimental journal, all in the decade when his primary concern lay in the writing of three huge encyclopedic books on logic, ethics and scientific metaphysics.

WUNDT'S SYSTEM

It is hard to say how much of Wundt's system of psychology is essentially part of the history of experimental psychology. At first glance the *Physiologische Psychologie* gives the impression of being experimental through and through. In so far as it is a handbook, it is an experimental handbook; but the system is not the handbook, though both lie within the same covers and on the same pages. The appeal of Wundt's argument is constantly to experiment, and the uncertain points within the argument constantly led to the setting of problems within the Leipzig laboratory. However, all these matters are details within the system and not of the system itself. The general truth is that the system in its broad outlines is of the order of a classificatory scheme, incapable of experimental proof or disproof. Even such a basic principle as the tenet that "feeling is the mark of the reaction of apperception upon sensory content" is not so formulated that its truth or falsity can be demonstrated by experiment. Nevertheless the divorce is not complete. Wundt, by his definition of psychology, made introspection for the time being the primary method of the psychological laboratory. His tridimensional theory of feeling stimulated a great mass of experimentation and was perhaps disproved by the experiments—at least it failed to be proved when it should have been. In general, we might say that the relation of experiment to many of Wundt's important systematic conceptions is less the relation of proof to conclusion than that of illustration to principle. The principles stand as plausible and in accord with personal experience; the experiments illustrate them more precisely. The same experiments might fit another system.

For purposes of exposition, we may distinguish roughly four periods in the development of Wundt's system of psychology, and it will be useful for us to keep these periods in mind, because in part they represent the changing influence of Wundt's psychology upon experiment and because in part they are indicative of the psychology of the times.

1. The 1860s, as we have already seen, were the *presystematic*, formative period in Wundt's psychological thinking. Both the theory of perception and the distinction between feeling and sensation were then founded upon the doctrine of unconscious inference.

2. With the writing of the *Physiologische Psychologie*, the primary principle of Wundt's system became clear, and we find the doctrine of *psychological compounding* explicit. Unconscious inference had gone, although we find now that "cognitive signs" enter into the theory of perception as marking off the objective from the subjective. In general it appears that mind is to be described in terms of formal elements, like sensation, which have attributes of their own and which are connected by association—the fundamental psychological principle borrowed from England, and, as far as history has progressed, necessary as the synthetic principle in an analytic system of consciousness. Apperception appeared, but it was not yet very important. Feeling was but an attribute of sensation. All this holds essentially for the first three editions of the *Physiologische Psychologie* (1874-1887) and thus overlaps the founding of the laboratory and of the *Philosophische Studien*.

The elementism involved in psychological compounding by association has had a very great effect upon psychological work, even though, as we shall see later, Wundt seems not to have meant it in quite so mechanical a sense as his critics have thought. Until phenomenological observation eventually came into fashion in the laboratory, practically all introspection was analytical; and introspective analysis meant the resolution of experience into compounds of sensations or other elements like them. It is true that Külpe's school of imageless thought was opposed to the sensory nature of certain conscious data; nevertheless it was motivated by the effort to find new elements for thought. Even the modern movement of *Gestalt* psychology, with its great experimental vitality, might be said paradoxically to owe something to Wundt's elementism, for it is the opposition of this movement to Wundt's

analysis and compounding that gave it its effective urge for productivity.

3. In the *Grundriss* of 1896 Wundt promulgated the *tridimensional
theory of feeling*. This is the view that feelings vary not only with
respect to the dimension of *pleasantness-unpleasantness*, but also,
simultaneously and independently, in respect of two other dimensions, *strain-relaxation* and *excitement-calm*. The systematic importance of the theory was tremendous. At one bold stroke, it
added to the elements already available for compounding at least
as many again. First, feeling had been but an attribute of sensation;
then there had been just the various intensities of pleasantness and
unpleasantness; now, within the dimensions of pleasantness-unpleasantness, strain-relaxation, and excitement-calm, there were not
only as many new simple feelings as there had been elements
before, but, with the possibility of feelings compounding and compounding again into total feelings, there were very many more.
The change seems in part to be an admission that sensationism
and associationism were alone inadequate for a satisfactory picture
of the mind. Moreover, the sanction for this multiplicity of feelings
was empirical but not experimental—if we may use the word *empirical* to designate the method by which the psychologizing philosopher consults his own experience and the casual experience of
others without rigorous experimental control. Such an origin left
Wundt free to employ the newly created feelings for many purposes where the older, more limited concepts were inadequate. It
is true that Wundt did not, like Külpe later, seek to make these
new elements into thought processes; nevertheless it is impossible to resist the impression that these feelings, responsible to
nothing but the will of their master, prevented many problems
from coming clearly to the fore, like the problem of meaning,
which Wundt had in part in earlier days met by the hypothesizing
of cognitive signs.

Although this multitude of feelings began life as a partially
irresponsible invention, Wundt could not rest without an experimental foundation for them. If experiment did not lead to the feelings, at least the feelings led to experiment—as was so often the case
with Wundt. Wundt himself, in Lehmann's published curves of
pulse and breathing, sought and thought he found bodily correlates
for each of the six terms of the tridimensional system. Then there
followed a period of great experimental activity. There was,
especially in Germany, much testing of these correlations. There
was some work in America also. In Germany, where Wundt now

held in psychology the position of authority that Johannes Müller
had once held in physiology, the general tendency of experimenters
may be said to have favored the theory, even when their experimental results showed contradictions or gave out equivocal support.
In America, Titchener pressed the method of impression into service
and sought, first by his own experiments and then by way of papers
from his laboratory at Cornell, to refute the doctrine by showing an
identity between the two new paired dimensions and the orthodox
dimension of pleasantness-unpleasantness. This is not the place to
enter into the history of the experimental work upon feeling that
Wundt aroused; it is enough for us to see that the state of psychology at the end of the last century and the beginning of the
present was such that a purely systematic venture of this sort could
excite endless work in the psychological laboratories of the two
countries that led the way in the new science.

4. The final period in the life of Wundt's system dates approximately from the beginning of the present century. The fifth edition
of the *Physiologische Psychologie* (1902-1903) presents the full
argument for the new theory of feeling, and it also marks the
increased importance of *apperception* as a systematic concept. Feeling and apperception are not unrelated, for feeling is the experiential symptom of apperception. "Feeling is the mark of the
reaction of apperception upon sensory content." The trouble with
apperception had been that it was an activity and did not lend itself
readily to the observational method that Wundt's experimentalism
demanded. The new theory of feeling provided a way out of the
difficulty, a way that was not possible with the older parsimonious
theory of pleasantness-unpleasantness. As we have already seen, these
twenty years of the twentieth century spanned Wundt's writings
of the ten volumes of the *Völkerpsychologie*, a work that was undertaken in part because Wundt thought it provided the proper approach to the 'higher mental processes.' It is possible that, if Wundt
had been younger, we should have had a seventh edition of the
Physiologische Psychologie with the results of this labor carefully
integrated with the rest of the system.

SYSTEMATIC FUNDAMENTALS

Wundt held that psychology is *Erfahrungswissenschaft*, the
science of experience. It is not metaphysics and must develop itself
without recourse to metaphysics. Herbart had ordained psychology
a science, but one founded on experience, metaphysics and mathematics and not upon experiment. To this conception Fechner not

only admitted experiment but made it fundamental. Wundt ruled out the metaphysics, which Fechner, with his dominant philosophical interest, had not avoided and which Lotze in his 'physiology of the soul' had cultivated. German psychology had always been metaphysical. Wundt, almost a philosopher, began the antimetaphysical tradition which still persists.

Thus Wundt argued that psychology is not the science of 'inner experience,' because the distinction between inner and outer experience is not valid; feeling is 'inner' in that it is consciously subjective, and perception is 'outer' in that it refers to objects, but psychology deals with both alike. Nor is there, Wundt thought, an 'inner sense.' The data of experience are merely themselves; a perception does not have to be perceived in order to be a perception; it has only to occur. There is, he admitted, a distinction between physics and psychology, but this difference lies in the point of view with which experience is regarded and is thus not within experience.

The valid differentiæ of psychology come then in marking it off from physics. Psychology deals, not with inner experience, but with *immediate experience*, and its data are *anschaulich*, a word that in this context may be translated as 'phenomenal,' although it actually goes further in indicating the palpable nature of the stuff of experience. Physics takes experience mediately and its data are conceptual. In fact, it is because its data are conceptual that its method is mediate, for its elements are inferred and are not given immediately as phenomena in experience. The permanence of matter is conceptual, for no experience in itself is permanent.

The subject-matter and the method of psychology cannot be discussed separately. If the subject-matter is immediate experience, it is plain that the method is immediate experiencing. For want of a better name, we may call the method *Selbstbeobachtung*, without intending anything about the self, or introspection without implying anything about a mental eye that turns about and looks into the mind. These words are names only; they signify nothing more than that having an experience is the same as observing it. We shall see in due course how Avenarius and Mach led Külpe and Titchener later to modify this concept slightly. The important fact for us is that Wundt, when he said in the *Beiträge* in 1862 that *Selbstbeobachtung* is the method of psychology, laid down the law that psychology is introspective, a law which, in spite of 'objective psychologies,' withstood serious attack until behaviorism came into vogue in America (*ca.* 1913).

Physics may be conceptual; nevertheless it represents a very real world. Mind and matter, or mind and body, can not, however—so Wundt thought—be compared. They are totally different universes. Thus Wundt was a dualist, and, as a dualist, he was a psychophysical parallelist. The theory of interaction he rejected because natural science is organized into a closed system of causality which can not affect the mind or be affected by it. One may get, it is true, the appearance of interaction, as in the case of sensation where nervous stimulation seems to give rise to sensory experience, but the instance is only one of appearance. It is the case where identical conditions give rise to both physical and psychical processes, which are thus concurrent but neither identical nor causally related to each other. Moreover, sensation is an exceptional case. Psychophysical parallelism is not universal nor a general metaphysical principle. It holds only in those cases where it has been demonstrated to apply, where we actually find concurrence. In this manner Wundt, for all that he founded 'physiological psychology' and wrote chapters on the nervous system, really went far toward dismissing the body from psychology. It is only in the latter half of his intellectual life that other psychologists began to insist upon bringing the body back into psychology, and on counting its behavior as a proper datum.

Finally we must note that Wundt outlined the problem of psychology as (1) the *analysis* of conscious processes into *elements*, (2) the determination of the manner of *connection* of these elements, and (3) the determination of their laws of connection. Physics abstracts properties; psychology isolates part-contents, which still maintain their phenomenal actuality. The goal of psychology is the analysis of mind into simple qualities and the determination of the form of their ordered multiplicity. The method, Wundt thought, is adequate to the problem except in the case of the higher processes, where analysis fails and we are reduced to the comparative observation of social phenomena, as when we use the study of language as the key to the psychology of thought.

Unfortunately, *multiplicity* is an equivocal word. As we have seen, Wundt fixed the notion of elementism upon psychology. On the other hand, it must be said that Wundt was no more interested in analysis than in synthesis, in elements than in manifolds. Which is the conscious reality, the element or the manifold? Wundt seemed to say that the manifold is the phenomenal reality, but that the element is also real and not an artifact of the method. There is an ambiguity here. When we come in a moment to Wundt's theory of actuality, we shall find it hard to believe that he ever meant the element as anything more than an analytical abstraction posited in the interests of description. Nevertheless it is quite clear that he thought of the elements as being experienced as such, and in fact his conception of introspection almost demands such a view. If introspection is the mere having of experience immediately, then it cannot be an inferential process of abstraction, and the elements must stand up under attention immediately in the given. It is only fair to Wundt to remark here that the conceptual nature of elements was not so clearly seen in the nineteenth century as in the twentieth. In chemistry atoms are very real things, and, being real, seem also to be actually phenomenal.

MENTAL PROCESS

The obvious objection to psychological elementism is the fact that phenomenal experience is a constant flux. It is not even a kaleidoscopic change of parts, for there are no separate parts. It is, as James made clear, like the flow of a stream that can not properly be thought of as a grouping of elements. Wundt sought to emphasize this fact by naming the element a "mental process." The force of this term is that it persistently asserts that experience is *active* in the sense of changing process, although not in the sense of an activity that requires an agent.

This view leads over into Wundt's *theory of actuality*. Primarily this theory is nothing more than that the mind, as actual, is immediately phenomenal and is thus not substantial. But essentially the mind is active, and we thus find the original and the modern meaning of the word *actual* combined in its application to the mind. Man has, we might say, a 'real, live mind.'

The term *mental process* might have been expected to secure psychology against the introduction of substantial states of mind, but the word has not always kept its meaning. In the hands of introspectional psychologists, such mental processes as sensations, images and simple feelings were often treated as static bits of consciousness and thus given over to a false elementism for which Wundt is held responsible and against which the new movements of both *Gestalt* psychology and behaviorism have reacted. Of course Wundt was partly responsible, for to hold that an element is a process is to present a difficult and somewhat ambiguous concept.

Wundt developed his notion of mental content by a statement of oppositions. Mind is actual; it is therefore not substantial. It is activity and not passive being. It is process and not object. Hence it proceeds by way of lawful development and not by way of fixations. These statements summarize his theory of mental actuality.

MENTAL LAW

Wundt's fundamental principle of law was that of *psychic causality*. Under this principle he meant to include all laws of the interdependence of conscious data. It is a principle which holds in the purely phenomenal realm and should not be confused with psychophysical causality, which involves the dependence of mind upon body.

It has been argued that cause and effect are physical concepts that can not apply to mind. Wundt's answer to this argument was that psychic causality is different from physical causality, but that the word *cause* is applicable to mental events if we understand what it means in that sphere. In the first place, physical causality is a conception that is bound up with the nature of interdependent substances; there is (as we have just seen) no mental substance for mind is 'actual.' We must therefore dismiss the notion that psychic causality deals with the interrelation of separate substantial permanent mental things. In the second place, we find that physical causality was then understood in terms of the quantitative equivalence of cause and effect in terms of energy; the two are not only correlated events in which the cause is prior to the effect, but they are so related that the cause can be translated into the effect by reducing the relation to the transfer of a determinable amount of energy. This is a common nineteenth-century view of causality, though wrong. There is no mental energy, nor any other all-pervading concept to which everything psychic can be reduced. Therefore we must understand that there is no equivalence intended when we speak of psychic causality. Psychic causality is simply the principle of growth or development of the mind, where lawful change is the natural process of an active mind. The reader who refers here to Hume's discussion of causality will see that Wundt's doctrine is consistent with it, and that in physics the principle of quantitative equivalence has been grafted on to the general notion of cause as the doctrine of the conservation of energy developed. Wundt held not only that the phenomenal mind is always in change but that the changes are lawful. Psychic causality as a principle is merely an assertion that the course and pattern of the constantly flowing, conscious stream depend upon definite laws of sequence, that 'this' regularly follows 'that,' even though 'this' and 'that' are themselves processes and not fixed substantial things.

Under the general law of psychic causality may be subsumed all the other laws. One of the most important of these is the law of *psychic resultants* or the principle of *creative synthesis*. In this principle we have Wundt's 'mental chemistry.' It is not strikingly different from John Stuart Mill's. The important change in the doctrine of synthesis came between James Mill and John Stuart Mill. James Mill asserted that very many ideas can be knit together by association into a complex idea, and that the nature of the complex resultant is to be understood by the fact that all of the components are still actually present in it. John Stuart Mill, however, used the chemical analogy, pointing out that the combination of elements gives rise to resultants that have properties which were not properties of the elements. This view is creative synthesis, which may be thought of as lawfully and causally determined. When the objection is raised to Wundt's associationism as being a 'mental chemistry,' the objector is more often thinking of the strict atomic-molecular mental chemistry of James Mill than of the more reasonable 'mental chemistry' of John Stuart Mill and Wundt. Such an argument is always confusing, for it was John Stuart Mill who used the term *mental chemistry* in opposition to the very doctrine that is now often intended by the phrase.

Then there is Wundt's law of *psychic relations:* a psychic content acquires significance from the other contents with which it stands in relation. Such a view includes plainly the associationistic theory of meaning and of the object, a theory which we have already examined in detail (pp. 184-186, 225 f.; also pp. 415 f.).

Wundt's thought, however, can be illustrated at a much more concrete and specific level, for he uses the principle in accounting for the facts of the Weber-Fechner Law. Fechner had said that this law is psychophysical, that it expresses a measured relationship between mental and bodily process. Others had held that it is purely physiological, a relationship between some peripheral and some more central nervous process. Wundt declared that it is purely psychological. Sensation, nervous excitation, and stimulus are all proportional in respect of their intensities, but a judgment of the amount of difference between two sensations is proportional to the magnitudes of the sensations. Such a statement is identical with the statement that the judged difference is directly proportional to the logarithm of the sensory magnitudes judged. Thus it is plain that a law of psychic relations would be operating. The significance of the difference between sensations depends on the relation of their absolute magnitudes. Wundt's psychological law of relativity grew out of this argument.

There was also for Wundt a law of psychic contrast, which seems to be a special case of the law of psychic relations. Opposites mutually reinforce each other. Wundt based the law on the facts of affective contrast where opposition within the pairs of feelings is most obvious.

Association for Wundt was one of the most important cases of the operation of the law of psychic resultants. It is natural, since he drew so much upon English psychology, that he should develop it at length. Association is a fundamental principle of connection and in its primitive form it is simultaneous, although it readily becomes successive. It occurs passively, for active association is apperception. Wundt distinguished several cases of association.

1. First, there is *fusion*, which may be the intensitive fusions of tones or feelings, or the extensive fusions of sight or touch. A fusion, he held, always involves a blending of the elements with a consequent loss of independence among them, a dominance of one element over the others, which thus play a contributory rôle, but a recoverability of independence of any element by apperceptive isolation. The typical instances are the tonal clang and its analysis into harmonics, visual localization analyzable into the visual content and the kinesthetic localizing content, and the complex feeling.

2. Secondly, there is *assimilation*, by similarity or by contrast. Here the examples are the optical illusions. When the phenomenal extension of a line is increased by the addition of a geometrical extension, assimilation by similarity is taking place; when the extension is diminished by an extended motive, the assimilation is by contrast. A very great many illusions come under this class because the dichotomy 'similar-contrasting' is exhaustive wherever the effect of the added motive is of the same nature as the motive.

3. Finally, there are the *complications* where the association is between different sense-departments. The term, as we have seen, comes from Herbart (p. 258). Its importance is partly derived from the cultivation of the 'complication experiment,' the classical psychological experiment which grew out of the astronomer's discovery of the personal equation in the 'eye and ear' method of observation (pp. 142 ff.). Nevertheless, the complication, once defined, comes for Wundt to include almost all complex perceptions: the visual perception of a body as hard or cold, the addition of a visual image of an orchestral instrument to its sound, most mechanisms of localization and most linguistic associations between ideas, like the sounds of the words that stand for them, or the look of the words.

4. Beside these immediate perceptual associations, there is the whole class of memorial associations, a class which became more

important after Ebbinghaus had invented the experimental method of working upon association and memory (1885).

APPERCEPTION

Wundt's doctrine of apperception has been the occasion for a great deal of discussion in psychological writing and also for some criticism of Wundt, but it seems that Wundt attached rather less importance to it than did some of his followers and critics. We may, therefore, content ourselves with the bare mention of the three aspects of Wundt's doctrine: apperception as phenomenon, as cognition and as activity.

1. Wundt's faith required that he should deal only in those systematic terms which can be clearly established as occurring in phenomenal experience. Thus apperception, although neither an element nor a complex of elements, must have its *phenomenal* side. Now it is certainly a phenomenal statement to say that there are two degrees of consciousness, that all processes within the range of consciousness lie, as we may put it, within the field of consciousness (*Blickfeld*), but that of these processes few are brought within the focus of consciousness (*Blickpunkt*). These processes within the *Blickpunkt* are apperceived. That comes from the definition of *apperception*. The range of the *Blickpunkt* is the range of attention, which is always less than the total range of consciousness and thus measures apperception. In this way the phenomena of apperception came under experimentation. The range of the *Blickpunkt* had been determined under various conditions to be about six items or groups —so Wundt believed. The discovery that the so-called 'muscular reaction time' was generally about one tenth of a second less than the sensorial reaction time was taken to mean that the latter involved the time of apperception of the sensory impression, whereas the former did not, and that apperception thus required about one tenth of a second. (See pp. 148 f.) Experimental findings of this sort naturally seemed to confirm the scientific status of apperception.

There is also, in Wundt's doctrine, the phenomenal relation of apperception to feeling. Association is passive, but apperception is active, Wundt asserted. Is this activity of apperception given in immediate experience? In a sense Wundt thought that it is, for apperception is ordinarily accompanied by a feeling of activity, which is what marks it off phenomenally as active.

After Wundt had developed the tridimensional theory of feeling, the relation between feeling and apperception became important. The feelings come about, Wundt believed, as apperception operates;

feeling is normally the mark of the reaction of apperception upon sensory content. On this view, feeling is the sign of apperception and thus its phenomenal representative. This phase of the theory is, however, less important because of the failure of Wundt's extended tridimensional theory of feeling to establish itself experimentally.

2. Wundt further distinguished apperception from association by saying that apperception occurs in logical connections between mental contents, whereas associative connections are not logical. Thus apperceptions may be analytic or synthetic. Judgment is analytic apperception, for it isolates a content. The synthetic apperceptions may be of various degrees of intimacy, from the bare *agglutination* up through the typical *apperceptive synthesis* all the way to the *concept*.

It is plain that apperception was held by Wundt to have a *cognitive* function. Is this function exhibited on the phenomenal level? Wundt doubtless thought it is. His primary contribution to psychology had been to exclude the logically conceptual. He had abandoned the unconscious inference. Followers of Wundt (like Titchener, who continued the course laid down by Wundt further than Wundt ever went) never accepted the concept as phenomenal. Külpe rejected it at first and then admitted it. The important things to note are that Wundt did not go all of the way upon the path that leads away from knowledge toward phenomenal experience, and that this cognitive function of apperception was never sufficiently defined by experimental settings to gain a clear scientific meaning.

3. Finally we remark that Wundt held that apperception is *active*. This is a view consonant with his theory of actuality; apperception is a constant current in the stream of consciousness. Moreover, as long as apperception means flux and change, there is nothing in it inconsistent with Wundt's system. Difficulty arises only when activity is taken as implying an active agent. Wundt would of course have denied the imputation of an external free active apperception, as he was bound by his systematic position to do. He is surely protected by his own caveats. But did he let the concept in surreptitiously? Perhaps. Even the zealot can not get more than just so far ahead of his *Zeitgeist*.

THE WORK OF THE LEIPZIG LABORATORY

Wundt's laboratory did more than set the fashion for the new psychology; it defined experimental psychology for the time being, because the work of this first laboratory was really the practical demonstration that there could be an experimental psychology and was thus an example of what an experimental psychology would be like in fact. It is important, therefore, for us to examine into the nature of the work of the Leipzig institute in its earlier years in order to see what effective methods and experimental subject-matters formed the foundation of the new scientific psychology.

Practically all the work from the Leipzig laboratory was published in the *Philosophische Studien* (1881-1903) and there is not very much in this journal that did not come either directly from Leipzig, or from Wundt's students so soon after leaving Leipzig that they still represented the intentions of Wundt. If we omit theoretical papers, many of which Wundt wrote himself, and the propædeutic experimental work on apparatus and method, especially the psychophysical methods, we have left about a hundred experimental researches that characterize the laboratory's first twenty years.

About a third of these researches represent problems on topics that would ordinarily be labeled 'sensation,' and more than half of the total deal with matters of sensation and perception. Such papers were always in the majority, and the relative proportion of them became greater as the period advanced and the total output increased. When Wundt is called a 'sensationist,' we must mean not only his systematic pronouncements but also the dominant character of the experimental work which he determined. A sixth of his laboratory's output dealt with the problem of action, the reaction experiment and the mental chronometry that came out of the 'subtractive procedure' as applied to reaction times. This work was, next to sensation and perception, the most important topic of the period 1881-1895 and was at its height in the middle quinquennium of these three. As the interest in the reaction experiment began to wane, research on attention and on feeling got under way. These two topics received their maximal emphasis in the 1890s, and each represents about a tenth of the work of these twenty-odd years. Scattered all the way through this total period there were occasional studies of association, which increased in number after Ebbinghaus had experimentalized the problem of memory in 1885. Wundt and Leipzig were, however, never important in the development of the psychology of learning; Wundt went his own way, and his laboratory with him, and outside discoveries did not greatly deflect his course.

Within the field of *sensation and perception*, most of the work was on *vision*. There had been more to say, or at least more was known, about vision than about any other sense, all the historical way from Newton to Helmholtz. To the classical knowledge

Wundt added his new conviction about experimental psychology, his genius in formulating significant problems and Fechner's new method of measurement. There were half a dozen papers on the psychophysics of light and the excitation of the retina (1884-1902). There were three papers on the psychophysics of color (1891-1898). Kirschmann and Hellpach investigated peripheral vision (1889-1900). Kirschmann made his classical studies on visual contrast (1890) and on color-blindness (1892). There were also studies of the Purkinje phenomenon and of negative after-images. In the field of visual perception there were the well-known half-dozen studies by Titchener, Kirschmann and Arrer on binocular vision (1892-1901). Beside two unimportant studies of the perception of form, there was Martius' work on apparent visual size (1889) and Thiéry's study of optical illusions (1895). Marbe and Dürr worked on seen movement with Külpe at Würzburg (1898-1899). Altogether these visual studies represent about a quarter of the total work of the Wundtian school during its first two decades.

In the field of *auditory sensation,* Tischer, Lorenz, Merkel, Luft and Frank Angell published psychophysical papers (1883-1891). Scripture and Krueger investigated beats and combination tones (1892-1901); and less well-known authors, the fusion and analysis of clangs. Lorenz's paper on tonal interval was famous because of the controversy it involved (1890).

Touch, ever since E. H. Weber's *Tastsinn und Gemeingefühl,* has been for psychologists the third most important sense. Kiesow, Stratton and Bader published research from Leipzig on tactual sensation (1895-1902). The perceptual problems of tactual localization and the two-point limen found their place in the *Studien,* although some of these, like Washburn's, were not worked out at Leipzig (1895-1902).

Kiesow's classical studies of *taste* (1894-1898) were begun at Leipzig, but the problem of smell was not attacked directly.

There should also be mentioned here the classical work on the *time-sense,* the perception or estimation of temporal intervals, by Kollert, Estel and Meumann (1881-1896). Here, as in the preceding instances, the range of dates shows how a problem seldom completely disappeared but would be reinvestigated later in the light of criticism and the advance of knowledge.

Next to sensation and perception, the topics connected with the *reaction experiment* made the greatest claim upon the attention of the Leipzig laboratory. This work seemed for a while to be the great discovery of the 'new' psychology, because it appeared to give rise

to a chronometry of the mind. We have discussed compound reactions and the subtractive procedure already (pp. 147-149). To
get a 'sensorial' reaction by adding apperception to the other processes already in the 'muscular' reaction, and then to find by sub
tracting the 'muscular' reaction time from the 'sensorial' that
apperception takes about a tenth of a second—that must have been
an exciting discovery when it was made, even though it was destined
to be discredited later. By proper compounding and subtraction you
could measure, it seemed, the times for cognition, discrimination,
will and association. The possibilities appeared to be unlimited.
What an answer to Herbart, who said that mind could not be experimented upon! Unfortunately the promise of the method was not
realized, for the constancy of the measured times was not great,
and later introspection showed that in a more complicated reaction
the entire conscious pattern is changed and that the alteration is not
merely the insertion of another link in a chain.

It is, however, no disgrace to the Wundtian laboratory that it
investigated this method completely, for the result might have been
different. There were important papers on the times of different
mental processes by Friedrich, Merkel, Cattell, L. Lange, Martius,
Titchener and Kraepelin (1881-1894). Lange's classical paper, showing that the difference between the sensorial reaction and the muscular reaction (and therefore the explanation of the old problem of
the absolute personal equation) is to be laid at the door of the predisposing attention (1888), did much to stimulate the movement
and also to direct interest from reaction to attention. Fifty years
later it was recognized as a pioneer research in the experimental
dynamic psychology of attitude. Naturally there was work upon
the variation of reaction time in different sense-departments and
with different sensory intensities.

In the field of *attention*, there were researches on the complication experiment, the range of attention and the fluctuation of attention, all classical topics which appeared to represent the surrender
of vague mental functions to the rigor of experimentation. The complication experiment was the oldest; as we have seen, the name came
from Herbart and the experiment from the astronomers' troubles
with the relative personal equation. The facts of attentional accommodation and of prior entry were the results of the work accomplished by von Tchisch, Pflaum and Geiger (1885-1902). Dietze's
study of the range of auditory attention (1884) is important because
it was at the basis of Wundt's conception of attention as bidimensional, as embracing not only simultaneous but also **successive**

events. Later Eckener, Pace, Meumann and Marbe described the fluctuation of weak stimuli (1892-1896), results that were interpreted by Wundt as meaning that attention fluctuates.

The experimental study of *feeling* at Leipzig was entirely the work of the 1890s, the decade in which Wundt developed his new tridimensional theory which the laboratory was called upon to support. On the introspective side, the most important research was Cohn's development of Fechner's method of impression as the method of paired comparisons (1894). Later there were half a dozen researches on the method of expression, relating changes of pulse, breathing, muscular strength and so on, to correlated feelings (1895-1903). Most of these papers sought to support Wundt's new theory and are now seen, with the theory, to have failed.

While there was almost as much work done at Leipzig on *association* as on feeling or on attention, the results were less significant. None of the Leipzig studies of association is 'classical' in the sense that it fixed another form of investigation for some time to come or represented the first work on an important section of the psychological subject-matter. Trautscholdt's study of the statistics of association (1882) is perhaps best known because there have been so many later classifications of association and because it was cited by Wundt in the succeeding four editions of the *Physiologische Psychologie*. The other studies on tonal memory, recognition, practice, mediate association and the course of association (1886-1901) made little impression as compared with the effective research upon memory by Ebbinghaus and G. E. Müller that belongs to the same period.

It is fashionable nowadays for psychologists to complain about the narrowness of the Wundtian psychology and even at times to regret their heritage. Almost all the new schools have been founded as a protest against some one or other characteristic of Wundt's psychology, but we may welcome the schools without condoning the complaint. At any one time a science is simply what its researches yield, and the researches are nothing more than those problems for which effective methods have been found and for which the times are ready. Each step in scientific progress depends on a previous one, and the process is not much hurried by wishing. Progress does, it is true, depend also on insight and it is fair to note that it was Ebbinghaus and not Wundt who had the flash of genius about how to investigate learning. So too with the other great problems of emotion, thought, will, intelligence and personality, which were to be successfully attacked sometime and for which the Wundtian laboratory was not yet ready. We need not, however, despise our heritage because, with its help, we have in time advanced far beyond it.

For all this, there is some evidence that the historical weight of the Wundtian psychology has, because of its priority, been more influential than the mere mass of its discovered facts would require. For many years the chapters of any ordinary textbook of psychology were very largely the same as the fields of research reported in the *Philosophische Studien*. Ultimately the composition of the psychological text tended to change, and it might have changed more rapidly had not the 'founder of experimental psychology' made the line between orthodoxy and heterodoxy so pronounced.

NOTES

For Wundt's life, see E. B. Titchener, Wilhelm Wundt, *Amer. J. Psychol*, 1921, 32, 161-178, 575-580; W. Wundt, *Erlebtes und Erkanntes*, 1920. Except for the first two pages, Titchener writes of Wundt's intellectual development as a carrying-out of the program laid down in his *Beiträge* of 1862. Wundt himself gives psychological reminiscences, dealing more with the psychology of his life than with the objective fact; nevertheless, by careful reading, much of his biography up to the end of the century can be pieced together. Perhaps the accounts are not so incomplete as they seem: Wundt's life was quiet and uneventful as against the affairs of the world—the life of a *Gelehrter* where all the noteworthy occurrences are mental. There is also G. S. Hall's account in *Founders of Modern Psychology*, 1912, 311-458; it is clear that this biography is inaccurate in some details, and Wundt himself has condemned it as "von Anfang bis zu Ende erfunden" (*Erlebtes und Erkanntes*, 155). Some very vivid and anecdotal reminiscences of Wundt by seventeen of his American students are given in *Psychol. Rev.*, 1921, 28, 153-188.

The importance of Wundt's discussion of the personal equation with the astronomers in 1861 at Speyer has not

been worked out. See Titchener, *Amer. J. Psychol.*, 1923, 34, 311. Titchener here refers to the two-line note on p. xxi of Wundt's *Beiträge (op. cit., infra)* as highly significant, but the relationship is not obvious. Titchener does not mention the fact that Wundt himself noted the importance of the event in the preface of the first edition of the *Physiologische Psychologie*, 1874, p. v.

For Wundt's own statement as to why he called a predominantly experimental journal of psychology *Philosophische Studien*, see that journal, 1883, 1, 615-617.

Wundt's writings were much too extensive to list all the more important ones here. There is a complete bibliography by his daughter, Eleonore Wundt, *Wilhelm Wundts Werk*, 1927, published as No. 28 of the "Forschungsinstitut für Psychologie," in *Abhandl. sächs. staatl. Forschungsinstitut*. This bibliography includes even obscure minor articles and contains over 500 titles. It gives also the titles of Wundt's lecture courses in every semester from 1857 to his last lecture in 1917. More accessible but less complete is the bibliography by Titchener *et al.*, *Amer. J. Psychol.*, 1908, 19, 541-556, with seven supplementary lists in *ibid.*, vols. 20-25 incl. and 33.

The important psychological **and**

philosophical books (not physiological), mentioned in the text, are in their various editions as follows:

Beiträge zur Theorie der Sinneswahrnehmung (1858-1862), 1862.

Vorlesungen über die Menschen- und Thierseele, 1863; 2 to 6 eds., all revised but the fifth, and the second greatly revised, 1892, 1897, 1906, 1911, 1919. Eng. trans. of second edition by J. E. Creighton and E. B. Titchener, 1894.

Grundzüge der physiologischen Psychologie (1873-1874), 1874; 2 ed., 1880; 3 ed., 1887; 4 ed., 1893; 5 ed., 1902-1903; 6 ed., 1908-1911. Every new edition was revised and expanded. The first was a single volume; the second, third, and fourth were two volumes; the fifth and sixth were three volumes.

Logik, 1880-1883; revised editions in 1893-1895, 1906-1908, 1919-1921.

Ethik, 1886; revised editions in 1892, 1903, 1912.

System der Philosophie, 1889; revised editions in 1897, 1907, 1919.

Grundriss der Psychologie, 1896; revised editions in 1897, 1898, 1901, 1902, 1904, 1905, 1907, 1909, 1911, and five unaltered editions later. Eng. trans. of first edition by C. H. Judd, 1896; also for some of the revisions.

Völkerpsychologie; vol. I, 1900, revised, 1904, revised and expanded into vols. I and II, 1911 and 1912 respectively; vol. II, 1905-1906, revised and expanded into vols. III and IV, 1908 and 1910 respectively; vols. V to X, 1914, 1915, 1917, 1917, 1918, 1920, respectively.

Einleitung in die Philosophie, 1901; eight subsequent impressions up to 1922.

Einführung in die Psychologie, 1911; three later impressions up to 1918. There is an Eng. trans. by R. Pintner, 1912.

Wundt's penchant for writing can be statisticized, though one must not lose one's sense of humor in so doing. His daughter's bibliography cites 491 items, where an 'item' is taken as any writing, from one of less than a single page up to the entire 2,353 pages of the last edition of the *Physiologische Psychologie*. If we exclude mere reprinted editions, but include all the pages of every revised edition, the adding-machine shows that Wundt in these 491 items wrote about 53,735 pages in the sixty-eight years between 1853 and 1920 inclusive. In spite of all the many one-page items, Wundt's average adventure into print was about 110 pages long, with over seven such adventures in the average year. If there are 24,836 days in sixty-eight years, then Wundt wrote or revised at the average rate of 2.2 pages a day from 1853 to 1920, which comes to about one word every two minutes, day and night, for the entire sixty-eight years.

A very great deal has been written about Wundt's systematic views, psychological and philosophical. Any large library is likely to contain a dozen or more German dissertations about him. The most useful books are E. König, *W. Wundt, seine Philosophie und Psychologie*, 1901, and R. Eisler, *W. Wundts Philosophie und Psychologie*, 1902. O. Passkönig, *Die Psychologie Wilhelm Wundts*, 1912, is a less satisfactory resumé in the form of an abstract of his entire psychology. Th. Ribot in *German Psychology of To-Day*, 1886, dealt with Wundt, but that was before half of Wundt's life as a psychologist had been lived. Hall, *loc. cit.*, has a long account of Wundt's views; the histories of psychology mention him repeatedly, and there are also H. Höffding, *Moderne Philosophen*, 1905, Eng. trans., 1915, 3-37, and G. Murphy, *Historical Introduction to Modern Psychology*, 2 ed., 1949, 149-160, who consider Wundt thus briefly. None of these accounts is, however, satisfactory. Wundt resisted epitomization, partly by the mere bulk of his writing and further by his capacity for integration, which results in the fact that the complete doctrine for any single concept is to be got only from a variety of books and a greater variety of chapters, *i.e.*, from all the various loci where Wundt thought the concept was in context. Without considering articles at all, the last editions of the important books listed above total more than 13,000 pages. Yet these books are of different dates, and, if the summarizer attempts a genetic account of Wundt's thought, he must go to the successive editions and not only to the last. It is no wonder then that Wundt's psychology and philosophy still lack an adequate summary.

Wundt's near invulnerability was due to the mass and speed of his productivity. It was hard for a critic to riddle an argument before Wundt had changed it in a new edition. Nor could an enemy know which to attack among so many kinds of books. James, while appreciating both the power and range of Wundt's campaign, resented both his self-assurance and the fact that his central philosophic theme, if indeed there was one, was lost in the mass of argumentative detail. James wrote to Stumpf of Wundt in 1887: "He aims at being a Napoleon of the intellectual world. Unfortunately he will never have a Waterloo, for he is a Napoleon without genius and with no central idea which, if defeated, brings down the whole fabric in ruin." Speaking of Wundt and his critics James said: "Whilst they make mincemeat of some of his views by their criticisms, he is meanwhile writing a book on an entirely different subject. Cut him up like a worm, and each fragment crawls; there is no *nœud vital* in his mental medulla oblongata, so that you can't kill him all at once." See R. B. Perry, *The Thought and Character of William James*, 1935, II, 68, for this as well as for many other of James' comments on Wundt.

On the nature of Wundt's system and the thesis that his life may be regarded as the carrying-out of the program that he laid down in the *Beiträge*, see E. B. Titchener, *Amer. J. Psychol.*, 1921, 32, 161-178. On Wundt's system as contrasted with Brentano's, see Titchener, *ibid.*, 108-120.

On the psychological systematic fundamentals, the nature of mind, the distinction between psychology and physics, and in particular the theory of actuality, see Wundt, *Physiologische Psychologie*, 6 ed., 1911, III, 733-738; *Logik*, 4 ed., 1921, III, 257-265. On the theory of actuality, *cf.* Eisler, *op. cit.*,

40-49; O. Külpe, *Einleitung in die Philosophie*, 1895, or Eng. trans., sect. 23. In general, see Wundt, *Philos. Stud.*, 1887, 4, 292-309; 1894, 12, 149-182; Eisler, 29-35. On Wundt's doctrine of analysis and elements, see Wundt, *Philos. Stud.*, 1883, 1, 473-494; E. H. Hollands, *Amer. J. Psychol.*, 1905, 16, 499-518; 1906, 17, 206-226.

On psychophysical parallelism, see Wundt, *Physiologische Psychologie*, 1911, III, 739-754; *Logik*, 1921, III, 249-257; *cf.* Eisler, *op. cit.*, 46-51; König, *op. cit.*, 110-119.

Wundt and his contemporaries chose psychophysical parallelism instead of interactionism because nineteenth-century physicists, having come to the new theory of conservation of energy by way of the discovery of the mechanical equivalent of heat, thought of cause and effect as equivalent in energy, as if the cause transferred its energy to the effect. Nowadays it is clear that cause is best defined in Humian terms as what is necessary for the effect or sufficient or both, that multiple causation is the rule in natural events, and that, given a loaded gun, the finger which pulls the trigger is necessary and sufficient without transferring any of its energy to the bullet. Mind-body interaction by release mechanisms would work without involving the conservation of energy, and undoubtedly a great deal of modern mind-body philosophy is just that.

On psychic causality and the specific laws, see Wundt, *Philos. Stud.*, 1894, 10, 1-124; *Physiologische Psychologie*, 1911, III, 755-770; *Logik*, 1921, III, 266-288; *cf.* Eisler, *op. cit.*, 51-58; König, *op. cit.*, 103-107, 120-127, 156-160. At this point the reader may do well to refer again to the discussion of Hume's consideration of the nature of causality (pp. 191 f.). On the Mills and mental chemistry, see pp. 225 f., 229-231.

On association and apperception, see Wundt, *Physiologische Psychologie*, 1911, III, 492-554; *cf.* Eisler, *op. cit.*, 58-69. On the doctrine of association, see also Wundt, *Philos. Stud.*, 1891, 7, 329-361. On the doctrine of apperception, see also König, *op. cit.*, 127-134

W. B. Pillsbury, *Amer. J. Psychol.*, 1897, 8, 315-392.

The development of Wundt's theory of feeling is seen in the *Physiologische Psychologie*, chap. 10 of the first four editions, chap. 11 of the fifth and sixth editions. It is these last two editions that give the new tridimensional theory, which first appeared in the *Grundriss der Psychologie*, 1896, or Eng. trans., sects. 12-13. On Wundt's doctrine of feeling and its development, see Titchener, *Amer. J. Psychol.*, 1908, 19, 213-231. On the tridimensional theory, see Hollands, *ibid.*, 1906, 17, 206-226.

The discussion in the text of the work of the Leipzig laboratory is based upon an analysis of 109 papers in the *Philosophische Studien*. Nearly all of these studies were made in Leipzig under Wundt's personal direction. A few are by Wundt's students after they had gone out from Leipzig to other universities, but these papers are obviously inspired by the Leipzig atmosphere. There are just a few other exceptions. Martius was at Bonn, but his research is integrated with Leipzig. M. F. Washburn was Titchener's first doctoral candidate at Cornell, after Titchener had gone from Leipzig to Cornell. Külpe went from Leipzig to Würzburg and Dürr was his student there; Marbe came later to Würzburg from Leipzig.

The list of names in the text gives some idea of how many important psychologists were trained with Wundt in the early days of the Leipzig laboratory. I do not know where there is a record of all of Wundt's students, but the following list gives the names of most of the important European psychologists who worked with Wundt up to and including 1900. I cite the names approximately in the chronological order of their first association with Wundt: E. Kraepelin (Munich), H. Münsterberg (Har-vard), A. Lehmann (Copenhagen), L. Lange (Tübingen), O. Külpe (Munich), A. Kirschmann (Leipzig), E. Meumann (Hamburg), K. Marbe (Würzburg), F. Kiesow (Turin), G. F. Lipps (Zürich), G. W. Störring (Bonn), F. Krueger (Leipzig), W. Wirth (Leipzig), E. Dürr (Bern), who ends the century.

For an account of the founding and history of the Leipzig laboratory, see W. Wundt, Das Institut für experimentelle Psychologie, *Festschr. zur Feier des 500-jährigen Bestehens der Universität Leipzig*, 1909, 4, pt. 1, 118-133.

America was close behind Germany in adopting the new psychology, and it also took its cue from Wundt. Stanley Hall visited Leipzig in the first year of Wundt's new laboratory and founded in America (six years after Wundt began the *Philosophische Studien*) the *American Journal of Psychology*, thus the second journal of experimental psychology in history. The proportion of Wundt's students from America was very large. Cattell was his first assistant. The following list, arranged chronologically like the other, is, I think, almost complete for Wundt's American students before 1900: G. S. Hall (Clark), J. McK. Cattell (Columbia), H. K. Wolfe (Nebraska), E. A. Pace (Catholic University), E. W. Scripture (Yale), F. Angell (Stanford), E. B. Titchener (Cornell), L. Witmer (Pennsylvania), H. C. Warren (Princeton), H. Gale (Minnesota), G. T. W. Patrick (Iowa), G. M. Stratton (California), C. H. Judd (Chicago), G. A. Tawney (Beloit). Lest the comparison of the nearly complete American list with the highly selected European list imply an incorrect ratio between the two, it may be well to mention that, of the 122 authors who contributed original articles to the *Philosophische Studien*, only thirteen were Americans.

ESTABLISHMENT OF MODERN PSYCHOLOGY IN GERMANY

CHAPTER 17

Hering, Brentano, Stumpf and G. E. Müller

In general, psychology came first, psychologists later. The men who founded and put their marks upon the new experimental psychology had not—at least not at first—regarded themselves as psychologists. For a while psychology's torch had been carried by philosophers, physiologists and an occasional physicist. Lotze, who did so much for the new psychology, still remained a philosopher's philosopher. Fechner, a recognized physicist turned would-be philosopher, was acclaimed a psychologist but not by his own choice. Helmholtz, who contributed more to the scientific status of the new psychology than almost anyone else except Fechner and Wundt, counted as a physiologist who later became a physicist. Wundt began life as a philosopher disguised as a physiologist, published huge tomes on philosophy, logic and ethics and called his new journal of experimental psychology *Philosophische Studien*. We recognize these men as the founders of the new psychology and yet find others following close after them ready to make contributions in the new field. Such men were Hering, the physiologist, the frequent opponent of Helmholtz and a man who within psychology ably supported the phenomenological tradition of Goethe and Purkinje; Mach, the physicist, who contributed so much to both fact and method in psychology as later to be called a psychologist; Brentano, a churchman and philosopher who upheld the Aristotlean tradition within the new context and furnished the antithesis that made the rigor of Wundt's position clear; Stumpf, Lotze's famous pupil, a philosopher who became a psychologist because he wanted to work with music; and G. E. Müller, Lotze's other most distinguished psychologist pupil, who, succeeding Lotze at Göttingen, for forty years maintained a laboratory, the most important in Germany after Leipzig and Berlin, and a tradition of rigorous experimentation.

In general, it is proper to think of Fechner, Helmholtz, Wundt and G. E. Müller together, and of Hering, Brentano, Mach and Stumpf together. The first group stood for rigorous experimental technique, descriptive analysis and the importance of learning in perception. The other group believed in phenomenological description and nativism in perception (the dependence of perception upon the inherited properties of the organism). They argued a little more and experimented a little less, although that is a fine point to attempt to make about the argumentative polemical Germans. The first group has been called, in William James' phrase, tough-minded; the second, tender-minded. It is also said that southern Germany is more tender-minded, more *gemütlich*, in its thought than northern Germany. Such distinctions, however dramatic they may be, never hold without exception. Stumpf turned 'tender' under Brentano's influence while he held the chair in Prussian Berlin which 'should' have been the toughest chair in Germany. Mach, for all his support of phenomenological description, profoundly influenced the chief neo-Wundtians, Külpe and Titchener. The opposition between Wundt and Brentano is clear, but we had better examine the details before we push this dichotomy further.

EWALD HERING

Ewald Hering (1834-1918) was born in Altgersdorf, a small town in Prussia south of Berlin near the German border. When he was about nineteen he matriculated at Leipzig to study medicine, the correct procedure in those days for becoming a physiologist. At Leipzig he came under the instruction of E. H. Weber, Fechner, O. Funke (who twenty-five years later wrote with Hering the chapters on somesthesis in Hermann's *Handbuch der Physiologie*) and P. J. Carus, a young zoologist who had just come to Leipzig. These men were Hering's actual teachers in the years 1853-1858. Hering would have liked also to call himself a pupil of Johannes Müller's, for he was stimulated and guided by Müller's writings without ever having gone to school to him—just as many American psychologists acknowledge James as their teacher when they knew him only through the green cloth-covered volumes of his *Principles*.

For a semester Hering went with Carus to the Gulf of Messina to undertake research on annelids. In 1860 he began practice as a physician in Leipzig and also became a clinical assistant to Ernst Wagner. His important achievements in the 1860s were, however, scientific. Hering barged boldly into the problems of visual space perception. The five parts of his *Beiträge zur Physiologie*, all devoted to the problems of visual space perception, came out in 1861-1864. Then he published *Die Lehre vom binokularen Sehen* in 1868. Helmholtz and Wundt were already active in this field. The first two volumes of Helmholtz's *Optik* had appeared in 1856 and 1860, but the third volume on visual perception came out in 1866. thus following Hering's first volumes. Wundt's first fasciculi on *Sinneswahrnehmung* had appeared in 1858 and 1860, but his completed *Beiträge* was not available until 1863, two years after Hering had started his series. For a little while, then, Hering's volumes were the authoritative handbook on visual perception, although presently one could choose between Hering and Helmholtz. The basic opposition between these two men soon began to become apparent. Quite early there was controversy between them—about the form of the horopter, for instance.

It was in this period that Hering came out as the proponent of nativism in theories of visual space perception. Is the spatial ordering of visual perception given as native endowment or is it learned? That formed the great argument of the late nineteenth century between nativists and empiricists. Hering as nativist found himself in opposition to Helmholtz as empiricist. Hering argued that each retinal point is endowed with three local signs, one for its height, one for the right-left position, and one for the third dimension of depth. To account for stereoscopic vision, Hering held that this third sign can be either positive or negative. Helmholtz, on the other hand, believed that space forms are built up in experience and that the location of the local signs has to be learned. Thus Helmholtz, the empiricist, was following Lotze and the British empiristic tradition. Wundt followed Helmholtz, and Külpe and Titchener, Wundt. On the other side, there was Hering, who did not first conceive nativism, but who owed much of his thinking on that matter to Johannes Müller, who in turn was influenced by Kant's conception of space as a native intuition. Ultimately this dichotomy goes back to Locke's empiricism and Descartes' innate ideas. Hering influenced Stumpf, whose monograph on nativism, coming out in 1873, got him the chair at Würzburg. This line of development—the nativistic line —ends up today in Gestalt psychology, where perception is regarded as dependent more upon the given physical properties of the nervous system than upon the acquired properties that come about with continued experience. The Hering-vs.-Helmholtz difference has not yet fully surrendered to the conception that nature and nurture always work together, neither ever alone.

Having spent one decade on visual space perception, Hering devoted the next to color. He was called to Prague in 1870 to succeed the great Purkinje in the chair of physiology, and he stayed there until 1895. His *Zur Lehre vom Lichtsinne* began to appear in fasciculi in 1872 in the *Sitzungsberichte* of the Wiener Akademie.

It was published as a whole in 1878. Here we find the best known opposition between Hering and Helmholtz, the one that has to do with color theory. Helmholtz had taken over Thomas Young's three-fiber three-color theory. Hering put forward a three-substance six-color theory. In this theory he supposed the retina to have in it a 'red-green' substance, a 'yellow-blue' substance and a 'white-black' substance, each of which can be excited with either of two opposing reactions, dissimilation (or catabolism) and assimilation (or anabolism). The dissimilative reaction gives white, yellow or red respectively in the three substances. Assimilation accounts for black, blue and green—the quieter or less 'violent' colors. There were many other refinements that had to be included in this theory, but its historical importance nowadays is that it represented for almost fifty years an effective alternative to the Young-Helmholtz theory.

In 1870 Hering published a brochure on memory as a characteristic of all organic matter. This was long before Ebbinghaus had brought memory under the experimental method and even before Wundt and James had established psychological laboratories. In its day the paper was often cited as important and was, moreover, translated into English. Now it seems trite.

It was in 1880 that Hering's section on the temperature sense came out in Hermann's *Handbuch*. Here Hering proposed a theory analogous to his color theory. Warmth and cold were to be regarded as *Gegenempfindungen*, mediated by opposed reactive processes. This theory is tempting because for warmth and cold one finds the same relation between adaptation and successive contrast (negative after-image) that holds for the opposing colors. Like the generalization about memory, this view, reinforced by Hering's prestige, had considerable vogue for two decades.

In 1895 Hering was called to Leipzig to succeed another great physiologist, Carl F. W. Ludwig. There he continued with his researches on color, the invention of his many pieces of apparatus for demonstrating color phenomena and the writing of other papers. He began to issue the fasciculi of a revised monograph on color, *Grundzüge der Lehre vom Lichtsinn*, which was finally published in complete form in 1920, two years after its author's death. Hering died in 1918 at the close of the First World War.

Besides his nativism and his color theory, Hering is remembered for his apparatus, of which many of the older laboratories still have specimens as show pieces. There were, of course, the *Hering colored papers* which you could buy, with good permanent *Hauptfarben* of red, yellow, green and blue. There was the series of forty grays, ranging from a pretty good black to a pretty good white. There was the *Hering window* which gave such beautiful colored contrast effects, a double window with a gray (ground glass) opening and another opening for a colored glass. The intensities of the lights from the two halves of the window could be controlled by slides to eliminate brightness contrast, making color contrast maximal. You looked then at the doubled shadow of a vertical rod and you saw for the shadows that physically were green and gray, if you used green and gray glasses, shadows that looked respectively green and bluish red, the complement of the green. Then there was the *indirect-vision color mixer*, a sewing-machine mechanism to operate a horizontal disk-mixer for papers, and above the mixer a campimeter screen, supported on bristle brushes to keep it from being jarred too much by the mechanism, with a hole in the screen through which the mixer could be seen. The eye looked on all down through a ring, and a movable fixation point determined where on the retinal periphery the patch of color would fall. There was also the *color-blindness tester*, where the subject looked down a tube and saw a circular field, half red and half green. By moving reflecting screens he could change the hue of one half, the brightness of the other, and the saturation of both together. He was told to make the two halves match, and, if he succeeded, then he was color-blind. There was a *Hering stereoscope*, a modification of Wheatstone's. There was a *Hering binocular color mixer* where paper patches, a different color for each eye, were combined by a stereoscope-like arrangement. Under the right conditions Hering asserted colors would mix and not rival. All these pieces were beautiful specimens of German manufacture and played their part in earning for the new science the name "brass-instrument psychology."

No account of Hering is, however, complete without noting how he placed his influence behind the phenomenological tradition. Hering believed that sensations lie in consciousness and that the description of conscious phenomena is basic to the understanding of psychological fact. He was, if you like, a psychophysicist, having studied with Fechner, but he was not the believer in elaborate techniques. He belongs in the tradition of Goethe, who had such confidence in what trained observation can see, and of Purkinje, another famous physiologist-observer, who dedicated his book on vision to Goethe. One of Hering's biographers wrote: "Er besass den Goethe'schen Blick in der Anschauung der Naturvorgänge." When one looks forward in time, then he sees how Hering's faith is still with us among the Gestalt psychologists. When they rely on the competence of phenomenological description, when they arrange *experimenta crucis* to demonstrate their principles rather than to extract fact from nature, they are working in the Hering tradition, not only because there is this similarity of basic values between them and Hering, but also because they did actually look to Hering for sanction when, more often than not, they had turned thumbs down on Helmholtz.

FRANZ BRENTANO

Franz Brentano (1838-1917), a descendant of an ancient Italian family, was born at Marienberg on the Rhine, where a branch of the family had settled long before. From early youth he was destined for the priesthood, for which his training began when he was about sixteen years old. He went first to Berlin to study philosophy, and there Trendelenburg taught him to appreciate Aristotle, who came thus to be a dominating influence throughout the rest of his life. A year or so later, in 1856, Brentano went to Munich, where he came under the influence of Döllinger, a Catholic historian and theologian, who was subsequently excommunicated because of his criticism of the Church. This latter fact is interesting in view of Brentano's later difficulties with the Church. Finally he went to Tübingen where he took his degree in philosophy in 1864, completing a decade of preparatory study. In the same year he was ordained a priest at Graz and entered a Dominican convent. He had already published a paper (1862) on the manifold meanings of Being in Aristotle and had dedicated it to Trendelenburg.

In 1866 Brentano left the convent and became *Dozent* at Würzburg, where he was to remain for seven years and throughout the first of the two crises of his life. Here he lectured on philosophy and published half a dozen papers dealing with the history of science within the Church and with the philosophy of Aristotle. For one year (1866-1867) Stumpf, ten years the junior, was Brentano's pupil at Würzburg. Brentano then sent Stumpf to Lotze at Göttingen for his doctor's degree, but Stumpf thereafter returned to Würzburg for two more years of study (1868-1870). It was thus by way of Brentano that the indirect influence of Aristotle finally turned up in the Berlin laboratory.

While Brentano was *Dozent* at Würzburg, there arose within the Catholic Church a controversy concerning the dogma of the infallibility of the Pope. Brentano published in 1869 a memoir in refutation of the proposed doctrine, a memoir so able that he became practically the intellectual leader of the liberal party within the Church. In 1872 Brentano, the priest, was promoted to be professor extraordinary of philosophy, but unfortunately at about the same time the dogma of infallibility was accepted by the Church. The liberal party had lost, and Brentano was placed in an untenable position, for he now came to see clearly a matter that had long troubled him, namely, that allegiance to the Church could come to be incompatible with the integrity of intellectual research. In this dilemma of conscience, Brentano acted with scrupulousness and courage; in March, 1873, he re signed his professorship at Würzburg for the reason that he had been appointed as a priest; he then in April resigned his priest-hood, in so far as he could resign it, and put off the clerical garb.

During the following year, with neither church nor university to occupy him, Brentano wrote the book by which he is best known, *Psychologie vom empirischen Standpunkte*, which was published in 1874. It is a single volume of 350 pages, intended to be but the first volume of two, although the second never appeared. This book is 'empirical' in the sense that Brentano said, "Experience alone influences me as a mistress"; it represents a philosopher's reaction toward experience and away from dogma. It is not an experimental psychology, but seeks a systematic picture in the interest of gaining one psychology to replace the many that were current. Brentano thus took account of Mill, Bain, Fechner, Lotze and Helmholtz, all of whom he mentioned in his preface, but he often wrote of them negatively, respecting their work yet arguing against their conclusions. The first half of Wundt's *Physiologische Psychologie* had been published in 1873 and Brentano cited it more than once. He did not agree that scientific psychology is physiological psychology; he thought that Wundt by this term had stressed method only. Psychology, Brentano argued, is a science, but one that ought not to be limited further.

The year 1874 is important in psychology because it is the date of Brentano's book and of the completed first edition of Wundt's handbook. These two books both represent attempts to formulate the 'new' psychology and to formulate it as a science. The contrasts, however, interest us more than the similarities. Brentano's psychology was empirical but not experimental; Wundt's was experimental. Hence Brentano's method was argumentative and Wundt's was descriptive in intention, although he dropped more into argument, as we have seen in the preceding chapter, than might have been expected. Brentano organized his system about the psychical act; Wundt built his about sensory contents. We shall have more to say of the act presently.

Although Brentano used the leisure gained by his twofold resignation to write his *Psychologie*, it was naturally not agreeable to him, a man thirty-six years old and conscious of his intellectual power, to remain without connection with either church or university, without a formal medium for his service of "the higher interests of mankind," as he once described his mission. Lotze, who was just the sort of person to be concerned about Brentano's predicament, interested himself on Brentano's behalf, and presently, still in 1874 and with Lotze's aid, Brentano secured appointment as a layman to the professorship of philosophy at Vienna. There followed six years of effective teaching during which Brentano's influence increased. It is interesting to note that during this period the youthful Sigmund Freud, in his early twenties, listened to Brentano lecture and even undertook for Brentano the job of translating some of J. S. Mill into German.

The resolution of the first crisis in Brentano's life in 1874 lasted, however, only until 1880 when a second crisis of conscience occurred. Brentano fell in love with a Catholic, who could not in Austria contract a marriage with a man who had been formerly a priest. So once again Brentano resigned his professorship, this time in order that he might assume Saxon citizenship. Then he was married in Leipzig and returned immediately to Vienna, where he was appointed to lecture in the university. All this happened before the end of 1880.

In 1894 his wife died. Disheartened by this event and by the onset of ill health, he resigned his university post. A disease of the eyes threatened the loss of his sight. For more than a year he tried first one place of residence and then another in Switzerland and in Italy. Finally in 1896 he settled in Florence. During the next nineteen years of retirement he was writing, mostly on philosophy and less on psychology. His eyes were growing worse, and an operation on them in 1903 failed. However, ill health never weakened his conscience nor his power to act upon scruples: in 1915 he left Florence for Zürich because he was a pacifist and Italy had entered the World War. His health declined further at Zürich, and he died there of appendicitis in 1917 at the age of seventy-nine.

It is plain that Brentano was primarily a person. Wundt was, in a sense, an institution that prevailed in part by the vigor and mass of its production. Wundt was the first professional psychologist. Brentano was not a professional psychologist. He was a courageous idealist with a mission to seek truth by way of untrammeled research. The volume of his productivity was not great. His bibliography lists but thirty-eight publications during his life, and only eight of these are important for psychology. The first was the famous *Psychologie* written in the interval between Würzburg and Vienna. It was almost two decades before he again published strictly psychological matter. Then, shortly before he finally left Vienna, he wrote three articles on optical illusions, which attracted attention because this was the period when interest in illusions was at its height. After he had settled in Florence, he read a paper on the doctrine of sensation at the Munich Congress in 1896 and published an article on the quality of tones in 1905. Then in 1907 there appeared a small, but important, book on *Sinnespsychologie*, Brentano's second psychological book. Finally, in 1911, he published *Von der Klassifikation der psychischen Phänomene*, an equally important book, a supplement to the *Psychologie* or, as it may be regarded, a substitute for the missing second volume of the *Psychologie*, then thirty-seven years belated.

Brentano's influence is to be explained in part by his personality, in part by the remarkably effective and trenchant character of the little writing that he produced, and in part by the historical accident that it was he who deflected the light of Aristotle into the realm of modern psychology. He thus stood in a sense at the beginning of that full half of modern German psychology which has been empirical, but not wholeheartedly experimental, and which we call the act school.

Since Brentano, living in the days when experimental psychology had arrived, was nevertheless not an experimentalist, we need further only to characterize his act psychology, in order that we may later be able to understand those compromises which the experimentalists made with it.

We have already seen that 'empirical' psychology is not 'experimental' psychology. Brentano had respect for the results of experiment, but he believed that all this stressing of experimentation led to an overemphasis upon method and blindness for the main issue. In this view he resembled William James and, to a lesser extent, all the philosophers who seek to interpret experience. The difference here involved is presumably one of temperament: the philosopher is so keenly interested in the broad interpretation of nature that he lacks the patience for the labor of experimentation which limits his vision for the time being to details. Thus Brentano, in arguing about the optical illusions, was quite ready to draw new forms of old illusions and so pictorially to submit his case on the printed page to the experience of the reader: this is the empirical method in concrete form, the *experimentum crucis*. But Brentano never undertook to measure the amounts of illusions under different conditions by the psychophysical methods; this course would have been the experimental method and would have yielded more precise information about the points in question. The *experimentum crucis* belongs in an argument and is thus apt to be part of the empirical method. Systematic experimentation yields precise description and is the *sine qua non* of the experimental method.

A fundamental test of a system of psychology is the manner in which its author distinguishes psychology from physics. Brentano defined psychical phenomena by their possession of *immanent objectivity*. Phenomena possess immanent objectivity when they refer to a content—are directed upon an object, have that object 'inexisting intentionally' within them. These phrases become intelligible only when it is realized that psychical phenomena are to be thought of as *acts*. When one sees a color, the color itself is not mental. It is the seeing, the act, that is mental. There is, however, no meaning to *seeing* unless something is seen. The act always implies an object, refers to a content. The color as content of the act, 'seeing,' thus 'inexists' by intention within the act. A psychical act is therefore not self-contained but contains its object within itself intentionally; that is to say, it is characterized by immanent objectivity. Physical phenomena, on the other hand, are self-contained because they do not refer extrinsically to objects. Superficially, the difference between psychology and physics seems to be that between act and object; fundamentally, however, this difference lies between the possession of intention or reference by the psychical act and of intrinsic completeness by the physical phenomenon.

It is important to note that physics and psychology are thus related, because it is to the contents of physics that the psychical acts refer. Moreover, Brentano transfers to physics the contents that Wundt, for example, treated as psychological. 'I see a color.' The color is not mental as sensation, but is in itself physical, though it exists in intention within the act of 'seeing.'

We have seen in earlier chapters that with the associationists the problem of matter became the problem of perception. So with Brentano the problem of objective reference disappears as a separate problem, because all psychical phenomena refer to content as part of their ultimate nature.

Brentano divided the acts into three fundamental classes: the acts of *ideating* (sensing, imagining), the acts of *judging* (like acknowledging, rejecting, perceiving, recalling), and the psychic phenomena of *loving* and *hating* (like feeling, wishing, resolving, intending, desiring). The object of an act may be another act, and it does not change the other act for it to become an object of an act. Thus the argument produces an involved system, but the details do not matter to us.

The dilemma for systematic psychology in the late nineteenth and early twentieth centuries lay between act and content, between Brentano and Wundt. Brentano had the sanction of antiquity, Wundt of recent invention. Stumpf began his professional life with the contents (1883, 1890) and then, relegating them to a phenomenology, turned toward Brentano and the acts. Külpe too was a content-psychologist at first (1893), but the negative character of his experiments on thought took him toward Brentano and he ended up with a bipartite psychology (1915), half content and half act. There were other bipartite psychologies about that time too—Witasek's (1908) and Messer's (1914). In England James Ward lined up with Brentano (1886, 1918), and William McDougall, facing Külpe's dilemma, finally created a hormic psychology (1923) which had in it the essence of Brentano's acts which he got from Ward.

Sensations are the best known kinds of contents, and in general it has been easier for psychologists to measure sensations (contents) with psychophysical methods than to treat the acts with equal rigor—the acts which Külpe described as observable only in retrospect, evanescent and impalpable. It is easy to see why the actual experimentalists, the men who really used apparatus to determine the functional relation between two variables, preferred a psychology of content, whereas those who gave lip-service to experimentation and relied basically on argument and personal experience were apt to slip over into a psychology of act, often assigning sensory data to another not-too-clearly defined discipline which they called phenomenology.

CARL STUMPF

Carl Stumpf (1848-1936) was born in the village of Wiesenthied in that province of Bavaria which contains Würzburg. His father was the provincial court physician and his mother's father was also professionally engaged in medical jurisprudence. This grand-father spent the years after retirement in the Stumpf home and was responsible for much of Stumpf's education before and even after he entered the *Gymnasium.* He grounded Stumpf in Latin. Physicians visited the house, and three of them, whom Stumpf came to know, were university professors. Thus the boy came in constant contact with medicine and natural science. Music, how-ever, was his great love. He began the violin at the age of seven, and in the course of the next ten years learned five other instru-ments. At ten he began to compose, even writing the words and music for an oratorio for three male voices; and when eleven years old he went away to a *Gymnasium* for four years. Then, when his family moved to Aschaffenburg, he attended the *Gym-nasium* there for two years more. Thus the first seventeen years of his life were spent in a normal educational development, sup-ported by a home background of science and music—especially music.

In 1865 Stumpf went to the neighboring university of Würz-burg. His dominating passion was for music, but he could not take a degree in music. In the first semester he tried esthetics, which led him toward philosophy; in the second semester he took up law in order to have a profession that would leave him time for music. Then, at the end of this semester, Brentano was habili-tated as *Dozent* at Würzburg. Immediately Stumpf was captured by the vigor of Brentano's personality and the keenness of his thought, and from then on Stumpf became his disciple. Brentano was merciless in the rigor of his thinking, and Stumpf for the first time found himself being disciplined in careful thought. At that time Brentano was absorbed by his aspiration for a philo-sophical and religious renaissance of Christianity, and this idea became Stumpf's dominant motive for four years. Brentano held that the scientific method is the true philosophical method, so his disciple, Stumpf, undertook to learn science in the chemical lab-oratory, even to the extent of causing a fire in the building, for, as Stumpf remarked later, "manual dexterity did not belong to my capacities." (The scientific nineteenth century bred a philosophy that turned to science for its method, and it is an historical commonplace to find its young philosophers attempting to practise science, not because they were experimentally minded—they were not; they were philosophers—but because they wished to put into practice this philosophical belief about method.)

Stumpf had one year with Brentano; then his new master sent him to Lotze at Göttingen for his degree. It was to Lotze, the philosopher, not to Lotze, the psychologist, that Stumpf went. The *Medicinische Psychologie* was then fifteen years old, and Lotze had by that time finished the *Mikrokosmos*. Lotze took a fatherly interest in Stumpf and grounded him more thoroughly in the theory of knowledge. Stumpf also pursued his science, working in physiology with Meissner and in physics with Wilhelm Weber, the brother of E. H. Weber. He received his doctor's degree in the summer of 1868.

Then Stumpf returned to Würzburg for two more years of study. He was still under the dominion of Brentano's conception of the new Christianity; just at the time, it was, that Brentano was writing the famous memoir against the dogma of the infallibility of the Pope. Stumpf schooled himself in theology and scholastic philosophy, until in 1870 he returned to Göttingen to be habilitated as *Dozent* with a dissertation on the mathematical axioms—a topic to which Helmholtz had already appealed in his defense of empiricism directed against Kant.

Stumpf was *Dozent* at Göttingen for three years. He learned to know Lotze well. He became acquainted with E. H. Weber, when Weber was visiting Göttingen from Leipzig, and Weber demonstrated the sensory circles on Stumpf's own skin. He met Fechner in Leipzig in the decade of Fechner's interest in esthetics, and served as an observer for him in the experiments upon the golden section. He played the cello in a little private orchestra. He began work on a critical history of the concept of substance but laid the task by as fruitless when, in 1872, the idea of a study of the origin of space-perception struck him. This idea proved fertile, and Stumpf published his first psychological book, *Ueber den psychologischen Ursprung der Raumvorstellung*, in the spring of 1873. It was a nativistic theory (Hering's nativistic views had been public property since 1864) and argued that both color and extension are equally primitive part-contents of visual sensation. There was a practical timeliness about this publication, for five chairs of philosophy were becoming vacant, and Stumpf used the work as a basis for his application for a better post. He just missed appointment at Vienna, but he was successful at Würzburg, where Brentano had just resigned, and where he was supported by both Brentano and Lotze. Thus, in 1873, for the third time he went to Würzburg, but this time he went as a professor. During his last year at Göttingen, G. E. Müller was also one of Lotze's students, but there seems to have been little contact between Stumpf and Müller.

The next two decades of Stumpf's life were to bring many geographical changes. He spent six years at Würzburg, five at Prague, five at Halle and five at Munich, and then finally went to Berlin in 1894.

The years at Würzburg saw Stumpf turning seriously to psychology but not from philosophy. Philosophy was still "mistress of the house," but, if science were to furnish the method for philosophy, Stumpf conceived that scientific psychology might well be cultivated in the interests of philosophy. In this view he was still following Brentano, whose *Psychologie* had now appeared. He thus became interested in the psychology of association, especially in Mill, for he thought he could use this doctrine in the interest of the concept of substance. Presently, however, it was his love of music that determined him. For a decade philosophy had outrivaled music in Stumpf's life, but now it occurred to him that he could serve philosophy by way of the psychology of music. In 1875 he began work on the *Tonpsychologie*, turning for the first time to psychological experimentation. Stumpf then expected to spend but a few years with the psychology of tone and music and not to devote his life to it, as eventually he did. What really happened was that Stumpf had now found a way of integrating his early inborn love of music with his acquired love of philosophy and, with the conflict resolved, was on the way to becoming effectively productive. He published very little while at Würzburg, but his great work on the psychology of music and tones was already begun.

In 1879 he went, again with Brentano's support, to the chair of philosophy at Prague, replacing the Volkmann who had written the *Lehrbuch der Psychologie* in 1856 (not Fechner's physiological friend, but the Herbartian). At Prague were both Mach and Hering, and Stumpf formed an intellectual contact with the former and a friendship with the latter. William James visited Stumpf at Prague in 1882 (as he did again later in Munich), and a friendly correspondence between the two men began. James had been attracted by Stumpf's book on space-perception. Although worried by the lack of laboratory equipment, Stumpf continued work on the *Tonpsychologie* and finally published the first volume in 1883.

In 1884 Stumpf, anxious to return to Germany, was appointed professor at Halle. A little later Husserl, recommended to him by Brentano, became first his pupil and then *Dozent*. At Halle Stumpf began his investigations of primitive music, but his principal task was the completion of the *Tonpsychologie*. The second volume of this work deals with the combinations of tones and thus reports the results of Stumpf's famous experiments on tonal fusion, historically the most important item in the two volumes. These experiments Stumpf, still lacking laboratory equipment, was able to perform on the cathedral organ. He was publishing little but working persistently.

Then in 1889 Stumpf went to Munich, the fifth university at which he had held an appointment. In a sense, he had here at last a laboratory, although a very small one. It consisted of the attic floor of a high tower and a cabinet in the hall, where he kept tuning-forks that he could use in the lecture-room on Sunday. He got a continuous series of forks by purchasing an old tuning-fork piano from a janitor in the physical institute and disassembling it. These forks helped to complete the *Tonpsychologie*, and the second volume appeared in 1890.

That same year Stumpf criticized at length the work of Lorenz on tonal distances. Lorenz had worked with Wundt at Leipzig, and Wundt had made the results his own in the latest edition of his *Physiologische Psychologie*. A violent and acrimonious controversy ensued between Wundt and Stumpf, in the course of which each published thrice. Stumpf of course began it by his criticism of Lorenz, but it was Wundt who made it personal. The clash seems to have arisen because Stumpf leaned heavily upon his own musical sophistication, while Wundt relied on the laboratory results with apparatus and the psychophysical methods. Whatever is obtained under unprejudiced, carefully controlled experimental conditions must be right, Wundt virtually said. If the laboratory yields results that are obviously contrary to expert musical experience, they must be wrong, was Stumpf's rejoinder. Stumpf, retorting reluctantly to Wundt's personal invective, always remembered the experience bitterly.

In 1894 Stumpf's academic wanderings were ended by his appointment to the chair at Berlin. Ebbinghaus had been at Berlin as *ausserordentlicher Professor* and had started a laboratory there. For some reason or other Ebbinghaus was not advanced and went

to Breslau shortly after Stumpf came. Stumpf therefore had the
most distinguished appointment that Germany could offer. As the
world sees these things, Wundt was undoubtedly then the foremost, as well as the senior, psychologist. His writings were already
enormous; he had founded the first and leading laboratory; the
Philosophische Studien was past maturity, whereas the psychologists outside of Wundt's dominion had only just begun, under
Ebbinghaus' leadership, the *Zeitschrift für Psychologie*. It has been
said that the great and influential Helmholtz opposed Wundt's appointment at Berlin. However this may be, the chair fell to Stumpf,
and he now had a small laboratory and a large future. He also
found himself in what he regarded as the most musical city in the
world and the most intellectually stimulating university in Germany.

With this change, Stumpf's psychological capacities burst into
productivity. The next thirty years saw more than five times
as much publication as the previous thirty. He was drawn into
many activities—"often all too many," he said. The laboratory expanded from three dingy rooms to a large and important institute.
With Lipps he was joint president of the International Congress
of Psychology at Munich in 1896, the only one of the first twelve
congresses that has been held in Germany. In 1897 he was persuaded
to undertake a study of a four-year-old prodigy, a research similar to those on musical prodigies that he undertook some years
later. In 1900 he was the joint founder of the Berlin *Verein für
Kinderpsychologie*. He had considered the writing of a third
volume of the *Tonpsychologie*, but instead he began the *Beiträge
zur Akustik und Musikwissenschaft* (1898 et seq.). In 1900 he
founded the phonogram archives for records of primitive music,
an enterprise for the development of which much of the credit
belongs to von Hornbostel. In 1904 he was diverted into the
investigation of "der kluge Hans," the educated horse that turned
out to be a mind-reader, responding to the small unconscious
movements of his mentor. In 1907-1908 he was honored by the
rectorship of the university. He retired from active work in 1921,
when Wolfgang Köhler was appointed to succeed him, and dis-
continued lecturing in 1923. His eightieth birthday in 1928 was
celebrated by the presentation of his bust to the university. Stumpf
died in 1936 on Christmas Day.

An examination of Stumpf's writings shows that they were
nearly all on the problems of tone and of music. His technical contribution to psychology is thus within a narrow and limited field,

and the debt of psychology to him on this account is less than it is to many other men. His greatest importance to psychology comes in a more general way.

It is apparent that Stumpf's position enhanced his influence, but it is also true that it was his ability that secured for him the position. Stumpf (for all that Wundt had said to the contrary) never forgot the lesson in keen and thorough thinking that Brentano taught him. Stumpf played an important rôle in the revision of the concepts of psychophysics, though no writing of his bears a psychophysical title. His psychophysics is to be found mostly in the first volume of the *Tonpsychologie*. In this volume also is his doctrine of attention and his discussion of other general topics like practice, fatigue, analysis, comparison and surrogation. His erudition is shown in his excellent article on the theory of mathematical probability which he published in 1892. He had an important and influential theory of the feelings as sensations concomitant with the other sensations to which the feeling seems to be attached, and he promulgated and defended it ably in 1907 and in 1916. He had placed himself in opposition to the James-Lange theory of emotions somewhat earlier (1899).

More important than any of these interests, except, of course, his persistent attack upon the problem of music and tone, are Stumpf's systematic contributions. In 1907 he published *Erscheinungen und psychische Funktionen* and *Zur Einteilung der Wissenschaften*. The content of these papers is of course far from matters of experimentation; nevertheless Stumpf affected experimental psychology by them in that he put the stamp of Brentano for the time being upon the Berlin laboratory. One could not then divorce experimental psychology from systematic psychology.

First, before we discuss these papers, it must be said that the new gospel of phenomenology was in the air. There can be no doubt that Husserl, Stumpf's student and *Dozent* at Halle, started phenomenology with his *Logische Untersuchungen* (1900 *et seq.*), which he dedicated "in honor and friendship" to Stumpf. Husserl had been Brentano's pupil before he came to Stumpf, and his life had been devoted to the development of phenomenology, a discipline that claims to deal with pure consciousness by a method of immanent inspection. Neither Husserl nor anyone else has thought that *this* phenomenology should be anyone's psychology. In his psychology Husserl followed Brentano in defining psychology as the empirical science of mental facts (experiences or acts) which intend the material facts (non-experiences), the objects with which physics deals. Husserl's main interest was not psychology, but he worked out differently the view that had been Brentano's, and sometimes, in very un-Husserlian fashion, this view has been called phenomenology. The point is that the word *phenomenology* was in the air, and so were Husserl's views. They were current in Berlin. Later Külpe at Würzburg incorporated some of them into his 'bipartite' psychology of act and content. Külpe may have obtained them directly from Husserl, but it has been said that Bühler took them to him when he went from Berlin to Würzburg about the time that Stumpf was publishing these papers.

In this milieu Stumpf set about a classification of experience, of the immediately given; and he distinguished three primary classes:

1. First there are the *phenomena*, sensory and imaginal data like tones, colors and images, which constitute the subject-matter of *phenomenology*. The phenomena are not the data of physics, and phenomenology is a propædeutic science (*Vorwissenschaft*) to physics and psychology, for it studies this antecedent experimental material. (This was Stumpf's phenomenology, not Husserl's, which—except for the name—was something different, a description of pure Being by immanent inspection.)

2. Then Stumpf brought out the *psychical functions*, like perceiving, grouping, conceiving, desiring, willing. These functions are the equivalents of Brentano's acts; the two words are almost interchangeable: Brentano and Husserl said *Akt*, Stumpf and Külpe said *Funktion*. The psychical functions, of course, are dealt with by *psychology*, to which phenomenology is propædeutic.

3. Stumpf's third class is the *relations*, which belong to *logology*, another propædeutic science. Relations have always made trouble in psychology. They seem to come quite immediately into experience and yet not in the same sense that sensations come; thus it was never clear to the elementists whether they could speak of relational elements or not. Stumpf therefore left the relations in experience and gave them a compartment of their own. It is plain that, like phenomena, they have epistemological priority over the functions, so that logology must also be propædeutic to psychology.

4. There remains finally the problem of immanent objectivity. Brentano had made the phenomena the object of the acts. In the situation *I see red*, it seems as if the red were both a phenomenon and also existent intentionally within the act. In the case of *I like red*, it is not, however, so clear that the red is a phenomenon. The independent existence of the phenomena appears to exclude

their intentional 'inexistence,' not merely for formal reasons but as an actual matter of experience. For this reason Stumpf created a special class for the immanent object of the functions, and called these objects *formations* (*Gebilde*) with a special cognitive, propædeutic science *eidology*, to take care of them.

The two last groups are chiefly advantageous in getting rid of difficulties; the first two groups are of interest in themselves. According to this classification, Wundt might be caricatured as a phenomenologist, Brentano as a psychologist, and Stumpf, if judged by the content of the *Tonpsychologie* as both. As a *Tonpsycholog*, Stumpf was certainly more of a phenomenologist than a psychologist, paradoxical as the words now become. The distinction, however, had the advantage of leaving room for both act and content somewhere and is thus at the basis of the 'bipartite' psychologies of Külpe, Witasek and Messer, who sought later to leave both kinds of data within psychology.

In all this discussion Stumpf by no means lost his empirical habit of mind. If the reader does not understand the difference between a psychical function and a phenomenon, Stumpf gives him examples of their independent variability. The function changes without the phenomenon, when an unnoticed phenomenon becomes noticed without change in itself, as when a musical chord or a touch blend or a taste blend is analyzed. The phenomenon changes without a change in the function, when the room gets darker at twilight without the change being noticed, or when sensations change continuously but we notice the change abruptly and only at intervals of the just noticeable difference.

Formally, then, Stumpf took his stand with the act school, ruling the sensationistic phenomena out of psychology into phenomenology. Actually, however, what he did was the opposite of what he said: he brought phenomenology into psychology. In the first place he legitimatized it as an alternative to the act as a subject-matter for study. In the second place, he never got rid of it, for the reason that he was too much interested in it himself, and, say what he might, the world took Stumpf's interest to be in psychology, as he himself did in 1883 and 1890. It is not surprising then to find Stumpf's pupils at Frankfurt and later at Berlin beginning an experimental phenomenology that formed the basis for the new *Gestaltpsychologie*.

There remains for remark but one other way by which Stumpf's importance in experimental psychology is to be explained. He exerted an influence upon psychology by way of his students, some of whom have been more experimentally active than he. In this manner he has had, however, not nearly so much effect as Wundt, because Wundt was established at Leipzig almost twenty years before Stumpf terminated his wanderings at Berlin, and because Wundt had the beginnings of a formal laboratory fifteen years earlier than Stumpf. Wundt's students were already numerous and going out into positions before Stumpf had left Munich. America took its lead from Wundt because Leipzig, advertised as the new unphilosophical laboratory of psychology, was well established when Americans had to go abroad to become psychologists. By the time Stumpf came to Berlin, Americans were just beginning to take their doctorates in philosophy at home—from other Americans who had been trained at Leipzig.

Of course Stumpf had pupils, but he had settled down in Berlin too late to make of it the Mecca that Wundt had made of Leipzig. Max Meyer, just before he came to America, must have been one of Stumpf's earliest students for the doctorate at Berlin. Stumpf himself especially mentions his assistants, Schumann and Rupp. Friedrich Schumann (1863-1940), who took over the *Zeitschrift für Psychologie* on Ebbinghaus' death in 1909, is an important figure. He went to Göttingen when Müller went there in 1881, took his degree and stayed until 1894; then he went to Berlin when Stumpf went there and was Stumpf's right-hand man for eleven years until he left for Zürich and later for Frankfurt, where he remained from 1910 until his retirement in 1929. Hans Rupp (1880-) is best known to psychologists for his technical skill with apparatus.

Both Köhler and Koffka were Stumpf's students. Koffka took his degree at Berlin with a thesis on rhythm. Köhler's first research was his *Akustische Untersuchungen*. Neither felt much loyalty to Stumpf, and Stumpf had little influence upon them except that Stumpf and the Gestalt psychologists all believed in the phenomenological approach to the problems of perception. Real inspiration came to both Köhler and Koffka at Frankfurt in 1910 from Wertheimer, who had just arrived there and was starting the experiments on seen movement which led to the founding of the school of *Gestaltpsychologie*. Wertheimer was Külpe's pupil, but neither Külpe nor Schumann, who was there at Frankfurt, were ancestors of the new idea. Later, when Köhler succeeded Stumpf in 1921 and Wertheimer, already at Berlin, was made *ausserordentlicher Professor* in 1922, the center for the new Gestalt school was seen to be where Stumpf's laboratory had been, but Stumpf had little to do with that. The Gestalt idea was born at Frankfurt, and then installed at Berlin when Stumpf retired.

Stumpf himself was primarily a philosopher; that is to say, he was a psychologist in the interests of philosophy. He was a musician by native endowment and brought this interest to the service of his psychology. He was an experimentalist by philosophical conviction but not by temperament. Thus for a quarter of a century he regretted his lack of laboratory facilities and then, when he got them, he turned over the technical side, in which he ardently believed, to Schumann and Rupp, although he experimented himself long and patiently with the tones. His position as director of the laboratory at Berlin led him into many administrative acts that benefited experimental psychology, like the founding of the archives for phonograms and the *Verein* for child psychology. Personally, however, he remained a psychological theorist who formulated a system of act psychology friendly to experimentalism, and a student of the psychology of music.

GEORG ELIAS MÜLLER

Georg Elias Müller (1850-1934) was born in Grimma in Saxony, not far from Leipzig. As a boy he received at the *Fürstenschule* at Grimma a humanistic education which included but little mathematics or science. He must, however, have had a philosophical bent, for from this training he extracted a primary interest in philosophy when he was still but fifteen years old. This interest of Müller's was begun by his reading Goethe's *Faust*, the poetry of Byron and Shelley, and Edward Young's *Night Thoughts*, which had been so popular a century before that they had been translated into German. In this way Müller became a youthful philosopher and also somewhat of a mystic. From mysticism, however, he was rescued by the writings of Lessing, the philosophically minded poet, dramatist, and critic. Müller learned from him the value of careful rigorous thought, as Stumpf had learned it from Brentano, and thus initiated the habits of thinking that have been one of his outstanding characteristics throughout his life.

After half a year at the *Gymnasium* at Leipzig, Müller entered the University at Leipzig to study philosophy and history—philosophy because he liked it, history because it might later gain him a post as teacher. This was in 1868, while Wundt was still at Heidelberg beginning his lectures on physiological psychology. At Leipzig Müller came most under the influence of Drobisch, who inducted him into Herbartian philosophy. In 1869 he went to Berlin to study history with the great historians there, archæology and the history of art in the museums, and the philosophy of Aristotle with Bonitz and with Trendelenburg, who had made an Aristotelian of Brentano fourteen years before. For the moment Müller's affections had swung toward history; nevertheless a study of Lotze's writings decided him for philosophy as his *Hauptfach*. Stumpf had been torn between two loves, music and philosophy, and had only much later discovered how to make the latter serve the former. Müller would have liked to make history propædeutic to philosophy, but he was prevented from this decision by the belief of the times, which we have already met, that natural science and mathematics are the proper basis for philosophizing. The struggle between science and history was prolonged in Müller's mind, often, as he said, "until late in the night." The issue was resolved, strangely enough, by the Franco-Prussian War. Müller left his studies and enlisted in a regiment of volunteers. To the young man of twenty years, the life in the army proved an exhilarating vacation from studious routine. Then, after his military year, history seemed to him too narrow a subject to provide the perspective that he desired and he turned readily to the study of natural science, and in particular to Helmholtz's *Physiologische Optik,* which furnished him with the idea of his dissertation.

He therefore in 1871 returned to Leipzig, and in the spring of 1872 he went to Lotze at Göttingen for a year. Lotze, whose writings had decided him for philosophy when he was still at Berlin, now became a close personal friend and exercised a great influence over Müller's thought. He completed the training in precise thinking that Lessing's writings had begun, and he emphasized still further the necessity for grounding philosophy upon science. We have already said that Müller had little contact with Stumpf, two years his senior, although this was Stumpf's last year at Göttingen. At the end of it, Müller received his doctorate on his dissertation, *Zur Theorie der sinnlichen Aufmerksamkeit.*

In tracing the history of experimental psychology, we have to remember (if, for example, we say that it began with Fechner in 1860) that it did not grow up at once. There was in the 1860s a good deal of psychological experimenting going on, mostly in the hands of physiologists. The philosophers, however, owned psychology; they believed that philosophy and thus psychology must depend upon scientific method, but for all of this conviction they could not make themselves into experimentalists. They could, however, be good empiricists; they could use the results of science when the results were available, and they could emphasize experience at the expense of pure reason. Thus the path from philosophy to experimental psychology lay through empirical psychology. Stumpf in 1873 published his nativistic theory of space-perception and Müller in the same year his dissertation on sensory attention. Both monographs were empirical, but not experimental, theses. Müller's discussion was keen and exhaustive (setting the standard for his subsequent style), and it concerned a topic that long resisted experimental attack. So it came about that, thirty-five years later, books on attention were still citing Müller's dissertation profusely.

After receiving his degree, Müller became a tutor in Rötha near Leipzig and later in Berlin. Then he suffered from a severe illness which obliged him to return to the home of his parents. At Leipzig he had become acquainted with Fechner and had since been carrying on a scientific correspondence with him. Thus it happened that, while he was convalescing from this illness, he turned his attention to psychophysics and, with his keen critical sense, to the criticism of Fechner. The result was a revision and extension of psychophysical methodology, which he presented as an *Habilitationsschrift* at Göttingen, where in 1876 he became *Dozent* after three years' absence. This dissertation was published as *Zur Grundlegung der Psychophysik* in 1878 and was supplemented in the following year by an article on the method of right and wrong cases (constant stimuli). These two publications together contained many innovations in method that have since become standard in psychophysical procedure. The book was largely taken up with a discussion of the facts of Weber's law. The later paper contains the table for Müller's weights for the observed frequencies of right and wrong cases, as well as the reasons and rules for their use.

Müller remained at Göttingen as *Dozent* for four years. In 1880 he went for a year to the chair of philosophy at Czernowitz. Then in 1881 Lotze was persuaded to go to Berlin, where he died a few months later, and Müller succeeded Lotze at Göttingen. Here he was to remain for the rest of his life, retiring after forty years of continuous service. Stumpf held appointments at six universities and did not settle down until half his maturity had passed. Except for the year at Czernowitz, Müller never held a university post at any place other than Göttingen. There he added further distinction to an already distinguished chair. In succession, Herbart held it for eight years, Lotze for thirty-seven and Müller for forty.

Thus Müller at Göttingen became in a fashion an institution as Wundt did at Leipzig, but as Stumpf never did at Berlin. He had an excellent laboratory. Visitors have said that he was apologetic for it, but an American surveyor of the German psychological laboratories in 1892 said that it was "in many respects the best for research work in all Germany." Presumably it was then second only to Leipzig. It is not, however, the space and apparatus that count, but the results. Müller, with a critical acumen equal to Stumpf's, was as a psychologist less of a specialist (although as a philosopher more specialized). In the early days he kept on with psychophysics, becoming on Fechner's death the leader in psychophysics. In the 1890s he made the psychophysics of both vision and memory his subjects. He contributed little to general psychophysics after 1903, but the other two topics remained with him throughout his life. In these three fields he took over problems from their originators, criticized them, corrected them, extended them and centered research about them. Psychophysics he inherited from Fechner, the problems of vision from Hering, memory from Ebbinghaus. The men who worked under him at Göttingen furnish the second most distinguished group of names of German psychologists, for the students of Wundt must certainly rank first. Müller, trained in criticism by Lotze, was always theoretically minded, although he never wrote a systematic handbook, as did Wundt, nor published epistemological papers, as did Stumpf. He was purely a psychologist. Stumpf claimed always to be a philosopher who psychologized in the interests of philosophy. Wundt claimed to be a psychologist, but we have seen that the philosopher's mind dominated him. More than either of these men, Müller succeeded in leaving philosophy, his first love, behind him and in sticking to psychology. He may not have succeeded entirely, but for his time he was relatively successful. As he grew older, systematic questions came to interest him more and more, as is the case with old men. In respect of system, it is plain that Müller belonged with Wundt as a psychologist of content. With a background similar to Stumpf's, he ought to have been an act psychologist in belief, if not in practice. The distinction between belief and practice is, however, just the point. Psychologists did not know how to experiment upon acts: they could experiment with contents. In so far as Müller succeeded in being an experimental psychologist, he was bound to move toward Wundt and away from Brentano.

Schumann was Müller's unofficial assistant at Göttingen from the beginning in 1881 until Schumann went to Stumpf in 1894. It is not clear just what was going on in Göttingen in the 1880s. Külpe went there in 1883 for three semesters, after having been at Leipzig and Berlin for a year each. Later he returned to Leipzig to take his degree and to be Wundt's assistant. Alfons Pilzecker came to Göttingen in 1886 and stayed at least fourteen years. He began work on attention and published in 1889, as his dissertation for the doctorate with Müller, *Die Lehre der sinnlichen Aufmerksamkeit,* a work that took its inception from Müller's dissertation of 1873 with a similar title. Müller himself was still busy with psychophysics, for he published with Schumann on lifted weights in 1889 the research from which he concluded that the judgments of 'heavier' and 'lighter' are dependent upon the muscular anticipation of the stimulus, one of the early experimental researches on attitude. It is plain that he was occupied with the problem of muscle, for in the same year his *Theorie der Muskelcontraction* saw the light. It was in 1885 that Ebbinghaus published his classical experiments on the measurement of memory, and in 1887 Müller and Schumann started in to work together on memory with Ebbinghaus' *Erlernungsmethode* (method of complete mastery). Müller was always keen to pounce upon a new method. He and Schumann continued these experiments until 1892 and published them the next year in the classical paper which includes the rules for forming nonsense syllables.

After the publication of this work, Müller immediately undertook its continuation with Pilzecker. This time he worked out the *Treffermethode* (method of right associates). Adolph Jost, another student of Müller's, in the middle of the decade was, however, the first to publish this method. His work resulted in 'Jost's law,' the law that, when two associations are of equal strength, a repetition strengthens the older more than the younger. This was Jost's theory for explaining the advantage of distributing the repetitions in time. Müller and Pilzecker went into print in 1900 in a joint monograph, developing the *Treffermethode* and showing the significance of reaction times as indicating the strength of associations.

Müller had not, however, dropped psychophysics. Lillien J. Martin was a student with him from 1894 to 1898, and they undertook the experiments that appeared later (1899) under their joint authorship as *Zur Analyse der Unterschiedsempfindlichkeit.* After Fechner's *Elemente,* this book is the classical study of the psychophysics of lifted weights, that most thoroughly investigated psychophysical function. At the same time Victor Henri, Binet's pupil from Paris, came to Göttingen, and there performed the experiments that resulted in his *Ueber die Raumwahrnehmungen des Tastsinnes* of 1898. This book is, after E. H. Weber, the classical work on the error of localization and the two-point limen on the skin, and it falls in line with Müller's study in 1879 of the method of right and wrong cases as applied to this sensory problem. Müller did more than open his laboratory to these students. Henri, although he dedicated his book to Binet, was explicit in his appreciation of Müller's ready assistance.

However, psychophysics and memory were not enough for the indefatigable Müller. At the same time that these studies were going on, he was interesting himself in the problems of vision. In 1896-1897 he published four articles called *Zur Psychophysik der Gesichtsempfindungen*, using the term *psychophysics* here in the physiological, rather than the mathematico-methodological, sense. These articles present and defend Müller's theory of color vision—a theory so well known now as often to be called Hering's theory, which it includes. Müller adopted Hering's theory of the three reversible photochemical substances (he held that the processes were chemical rather than metabolic as Hering had thought) and added his concept of cortical gray as the zero-point from which all color sensations diverge. On Hering's theory, when the black-white, blue-yellow and red-green excitations are all in equilibrium, one should see nothing, a visual 'silence,' but actually one sees gray. Müller supposed, bringing some empirical evidence to bear upon his supposition, that there is a constant gray aroused by the molecular action of the cortex, a view that is much more reasonable than Hering's attempt to get around the difficulty by way of experienced composites of sensations of equal weights, in which there is no predominant component to characterize the totality in respect of color.

In these papers Müller also dealt extensively with the problem of qualitative and intensitive series, and further, in the first paper, laid down five psychophysical axioms which must underlie, he thought, the hypothesizing of physiological processes for the purpose of explaining conscious processes. In formulating these axioms Müller was advancing a line of thought which had already been begun by Lotze, Mach and Hering and which was to develop into the isomorphism of Wertheimer and Köhler (pp. 615, 678-680, 690).

In the first decade of the new century, Müller's most important contribution to experimental psychology was undoubtedly his *Gesichtspunkte und Tatsachen der psychophysischen Methodik*, first published in 1903. It was this book that delayed the publication of the second volume of Titchener's *Experimental Psychology*, for Titchener had finished the first volume in 1900-1901 and was ready with both parts of the second, which is concerned entirely with psychophysics, when Müller's new handbook appeared. Titchener had to take account of Müller again all through the *Instructor's Manual* but finally published in 1905. This book of Müller's was his last word on everything in psychophysics, for he did not publish again in this field. It did not change the face of psychophysics or present any large new view; it was simply a thorough revision of the entire field and a summing-up of whither, in Müller's view, psychophysics had come.

There is little else from Müller's own hand that is of importance during this decade. He returned to his color theory in 1904 with a discussion of its bearing upon color-blindness, and in the same year (as again in 1913) to the problem of memory with his account of the mathematical prodigy, Rückle. He must toward the end of the decade have been beginning his large work on *Gedächtnistätigkeit*.

Meanwhile his laboratory was growing in influence. Narziss Ach, who was finally to succeed Müller, was his first official assistant from 1901 to 1904. In 1904 Hans Rupp, with a new doctorate in philosophy from Innsbruck, became assistant for three years, before he went to be Stumpf's assistant for fourteen. We have already seen that most of Stumpf's assistants came from Müller. Eleanor A. McC. Gamble from Wellesley was Müller's student in 1906-1907, and published afterward the classic monograph on the method of reconstruction for the measurement of memory, for which most of the research, however, was done at Wellesley before she went to Göttingen. David Katz became assistant in 1907 and held the post until 1918, almost until Müller's retirement. He had received his doctorate at Göttingen in 1906. In 1909 he published a very important paper, *Die Erscheinungsweisen der Farben*, distinguishing between the characteristics and conditions of volumic colors, surface colors and film colors. The last are the more primitive and from them the others are derived. This paper was really a bit of experimental phenomenology in that it attempted description in a realm where analysis into sensational elements was inadequate. Appearing in the year before Wertheimer's inauguration of what eventually proved to be the school of *Gestaltpsychologie*, it becomes one of the many instances in the history of science which go to show that formally new ideas are almost never actually new: a school can not be founded until its principles are already in existence. Katz went to Rostock in 1919. Then there was also E. R. Jaensch, who took his doctorate at Göttingen in 1908 and stayed for two years. He published from Göttingen *Zur Analyse der Gesichtswahrnehmungen*, with a dedication to Ebbinghaus and Müller. In 1913 he went to Marburg, and his name has been associated with the discovery of eidetic imagery and the related classification of persons into types. Thus the problems of perception were coming to concern Müller through his students, even before *Gestaltpsychologie* had forced perception to the center of the stage.

The next decade was noteworthy because of the publication of Müller's *Zur Analyse der Gedächtnistätigkeit und des Vorstellungsverlaufes*. There were three volumes, issued in 1911, 1913 and 1917, the second volume last. The work, although of a different date in the history of experimental psychology and by an author who relied more upon formal experimentation, may be said to be for memory what Stumpf's *Tonpsychologie* was for tone. The volumes give a mass of new information, especially by way of the prodigy, Rückle, and sum up their author's views in respect of the field. Naturally Müller's thoroughness brought in theoretical topics; almost a third of the first volume is taken up with a discussion of the method of introspection. Yet Müller was not writing a system of psychology; he was holding himself to experimental work and doing only as much theorizing as the experiments required.

Phenomenology and perception would still not down at Göttingen. Müller himself in 1912 published briefly on visual localization and at length in 1915 on an explanation of the Aubert phenomenon in visual localization, a paper which later brought him into conflict with the youthful *Gestaltpsychologen* from Berlin. Edgar Rubin came in 1912 from Copenhagen for a couple of years with Müller to get his degree. He published from Göttingen his *Visuell wahrgenommene Figuren*, a book that was accepted bodily as part of *Gestaltpsychologie* in spite of its source, because it was phenomenological and analyzed visual perceptions into such elements as figure, ground and contour, instead of the more conventional sensory ultimates.

In 1921 Müller retired. In 1923 *Gestaltpsychologie* called forth Müller's criticism in his *Komplextheorie und Gestalttheorie*, a book on methodology in perception that takes the position that *Gestaltpsychologie* is not new; nor does it seem to us to have been entirely new in view of the nature of the research on perception that had issued from Göttingen. In 1924 Müller published a little *Abriss der Psychologie*, his only attempt to treat the entire field of psychology as a whole.

This decade was, however, mostly occupied by Müller's return to the old problems of the psychophysics of color. He had never lost interest in vision and color. By 1930 he completed the 647 pages of his two-volume *Ueber die Farbenempfindungen: psychophysische Untersuchungen*. They were as thorough as his works on memory, but by this time the field was moving away from Müller toward more physical control and less reliance on the facts that introspection yields. With these volumes Müller had, however, fully rounded out his contribution to experimental psychology. The last of the 'giants,' except for Stumpf, he died in 1934.

In a word, then, Müller is the first experimental psychologist, among the men whom we have considered, who was little else than an experimental psychologist. He brought his philosophical acumen into his work by his logical precision and his trenchant criticism, and, by avoiding philosophy and becoming a scientist, he lived up approximately to the teaching of the philosophy of his youth that science must precede philosophizing. Within experimental psychology he exhibited a broad interest and a fertile mind. His students received from him more than their meed of inspiration and help, and through his own work and through theirs he exerted a great influence upon experimental psychology in its formative years. As a power and an institution he was second only to Wundt.

NOTES

Hering

Ewald Hering's full name was Karl Ewald Konstantin Hering, but he always used the shorter form. The text gives the titles and dates of his books. His *Beiträge zur Physiologie*, whose five parts came out in 1861, 1862, 1863, 1864 and 1864 respectively, has the subtitle *Zur Lehre vom Ortsinne der Netzhaut*, which might very well have been the only title since Hering never used the main title again and never extended his concern with physiology beyond the field of vision.

The famous *Zur Lehre vom Lichtsinne* appeared in 1872-1874 and then complete in 1878. Its successor, *Grundzüge der Lehre vom Lichtsinn*, was published in four *Lieferungen* in 1905 (pp. 1-80), 1907 (pp. 81-160), 1911 (pp. 161-240) and presumably in 1920 (pp. 240-294), which was the date of the war-delayed total and posthumous issue. Each of the first three *Lieferungen* ended in the middle of a sentence, and you had to wait years for the verb.

The two general articles mentioned in the text are *Ueber das Gedächtnis als eine allgemeine Funktion der organisierten Materie*, a lecture given on May 30, 1870, to a session of the Kaiserliche Akademie der Wissenschaften zu Wien, and published separately in 1870 and again in 1905; Ueber die spezifischen Energieen des Nervensystems, *Lotos: Jahrbuch Naturwiss.*, 1884, N.F. 5, 113-126. Both of these papers were translated into English and published together in 1895 et seq.

Most of Hering's well known pieces of apparatus are described by E. B. Titchener, *Experimental Psychology*, 1901, I, ii; see, e.g., Figs. 1, 2, 76, and use the index.

For accounts of Hering's life and work, see S. Garten, Ewald Hering zum Gedächtnis, *Arch. ges. Physiol.*, 1918, 170, 501-522; F. Hillebrand, *Ewald Hering: ein Gedenkwort der Psychophysik*, 1918.

Brentano

The full titles of Franz Brentano's three psychological books are: *Psychologie vom empirischen Stand-*

punkte, 1874; *Untersuchungen zur Sinnespsychologie*, 1907; *Von der Klassifikation der psychischen Phänomene, neue, durch Nachträge stark vermehrte Ausgabe der betreffenden Kapital der Psychologie vom empirischen Standpunkte*, 1911. The three short articles on optical illusions, to which the text refers, are to be found in *Zsch. Psychol.*, 1892, 3, 349-358; 1893, 5, 61-82; 1893, 6, 1-7.

On Brentano's life and work, see O. Kraus, *Franz Brentano, zur Kenntnis seines Lebens und seiner Lehre*, 1919. In this book Stumpf contributes his reminiscences of Brentano, which throw light on the relation of the two men, pp. 85-149; Husserl also contributes his reminiscences, pp. 151-167. There is also an excellent brief account of Brentano's life: M. Puglisi, Franz Brentano: a biographical sketch, *Amer. J. Psychol.*, 1924, 35, 414-419. Both Kraus and Puglisi give the bibliography of Brentano's writings, lists differing only in small details.

Titchener has done more than any other writer to introduce Brentano to Americans. On Brentano and the modern systems of act psychology, see E. B. Titchener, Functional psychology and the psychology of act, *Amer. J. Psychol.*, 1922, 33, 43-83, reprinted in *Systematic Psychology: Prolegomena*, 1929, 195-259. For more about Brentano and the contrast between Brentano and Wundt, see Titchener, Brentano and Wundt: Empirical and experimental psychology, *ibid.*, 1921, 32, 108-120. Titchener makes this contrast between the two men identical with the contrast between empirical and experimental psychology, and again echoes this distinction in a retrospect of experimental psychology, Experimental psychology: a retrospect, *ibid.*, 1925, 36, 313-323, esp. 316 ff.

L. Carmichael, What is empirical psychology?, *Amer. J. Psychol.*, 1926, 37, 521-527, criticized Titchener for confusing *empirical* with *rational* in this contrast of Brentano with Wundt. The difficulty seems to be that the empirical method, which strictly speaking includes the experimental, is so unmethodical that its rationalism stands out and relatively it appears to be rationalistic, except when one compares this kind of empiricism with real 'a priorism.' See E. G. Boring, Empirical psychology, *ibid.*, 1927, 38, 475-477. Titchener also made the same point, Empirical and experimental psychology, *J. gen. Psychol.*, 1928, 1, 176 f.; and he noted further the danger of confusion that arises from translating both *empirisch* and *empiristisch* by the English "empirical." Brentano's psychology was empirical, but not empiristic, as it would have been had it been derived from the empiricists and had it described the mind as derived from experience, instead of merely deriving the description of the mind from experience.

On the exposure of the young Freud to Brentano's 'dynamic' psychology, see P. Merlan, Brentano and Freud, *J. Hist. Ideas*, 1945, 6, 375-377; Brentano and Freud—a sequel, *ibid.*, 1949, 10, 451.

Stumpf

Carl Stumpf's important book is called simply *Tonpsychologie*, 1883, I, 1890, II. His *Beiträge zur Akustik und Musikwissenschaft*, beginning in 1898, had run to nine *Hefte* in 1924. *Heft* 1, 1898, is Stumpf's text on consonance and dissonance and is thus in a sense the beginning of a third volume of the *Tonpsychologie*. As a secondary source for this theory, cf. H. T. Moore, *The genetic aspect of consonance and dissonance*, *Psychol. Monog.*, 1914, 17 (no. 73), 11-18. Stumpf also wrote a brief popular summary of his work on primitive music and the origin of music: *Die Anfänge der Musik*, 1911.

Stumpf's first psychological work, that got him the chair at Würzburg, is *Ueber den psychologischen Ursprung der Raumvorstellung*, 1873. His two very important theoretical papers are: *Erscheinungen und psychische Funktionen, Abhl. preuss. Akad. Wiss. Berlin* (philos.-hist. Kl.), 1906, no. 4, 40 pp.; and *Zur Einteilung der Wissenschaften*, *ibid.*, 1906, no. 5, 94 pp. Both are separately paged, and the reprints are dated 1907. For Stumpf's position on the question of mind and body, see his opening address, *III internat. Kongr. Psychol.*, 1897, 3-16; reprinted as *Leib und Seele* in 1903 and 1909.

Stumpf has written his own account of his life and work in R. Schmidt, *Die Philosophie der Gegenwart in Selbstdarstellungen*, 1924, V, 205-265 (also printed and paged separately); Eng. trans., in C. Murchison, *Psychology in Autobiography*, 1930, I, 389-441; and to the German account is attached a bibliography of his writings. This list (to 1924) contains fifty-four entries that concern music or tones, twenty-seven entries for other psychological topics, and fourteen entries for philosophical subjects. In this sense, Stumpf was more of a *Tonpsycholog* than a general psychologist, and more of a psychologist than a general philosopher, but he thought of his psychology as philosophy. For Stumpf's relation to Brentano, see both Schmidt, *loc. cit.*, and Kraus, on Brentano, *loc. cit.*

The more informative necrologies of Stumpf are: H. S. Langfeld, Carl Stumpf: 1848-1936, *Amer. J. Psychol.*, 1937, 49, 316-320; K. Lewin, Carl Stumpf, *Psychol. Rev.*, 1937, 44, 189-194; C. A. Ruckmick, Carl Stumpf, *Psychol. Bull.*, 1937, 34, 187-190. See also E. Becher, Carl Stumpf zu seinem 70. Geburtstage, *Naturwiss.*, 1918, 6, 265-277.

For Stumpf's work in his special field on tones, on fusion, on consonance and dissonance, on combination tones, on primitive music, on vowels and on the analysis of speech sounds, the reader must see, beside the sources mentioned above, Stumpf's bibliography and thence the original studies. This work of Stumpf's has a wide range within a special field.

Stumpf's interest in music led him to the theory of emotion and feeling. On this topic he published three important papers: Begriff der Gemüthsbewegungen, *Zsch. Psychol.*, 1899, 21, 47-99; Ueber Gefühlsempfindungen, *ibid.*, 1907, 44, 1-49; Apologie der Gefühlsempfindungen, *ibid.*, 1916, 75, 1-38. For a discussion of this theory, its motivation, its background and the various criticisms of it, see Titchener, Professor Stumpf's affective psychology, *Amer. J. Psychol.*, 1917, 28, 263-277.

Beside everything that has been mentioned, there are two other theoretical papers of Stumpf's that have attracted especial attention. One deals with the attributes of visual sensation and the much-discussed problem of intensity as a visual attribute: *Die Attribute der Gesichtsempfindungen*, *Abh. preuss. Akad. Wiss. Berlin (philos.-hist. Kl.)*, 1917, no. 8, 88 pp.; the other is a discussion of the relation between sensation and image and of their criteria: *Empfindung und Vorstellung*, *ibid.*, 1918, no. 1, 116 pp.; both are separately reprinted and paged. With respect to the first, cf. Titchener, Visual intensity, *Amer. J. Psychol.*, 1923, 34, 310 f.

Of Stumpf's psychophysics only the psychophysical expert ever hears, and yet scattered through the *Tonpsychologie* is a positive psychophysical theory which contributed to the psychophysical epoch; see Titchener, *Experimental Psychology*, 1905, II, ii, esp. pp. clxi-clxiii, but also the many references in the index. See also Stumpf's papers on the concept of mathematical probability, Ueber den Begriff der mathematischen Wahrscheinlichkeit, *Sitzber. bayr. Akad. Wiss. München (philos.-philol. Cl.)*, 1892, 37-120; Ueber die Anwendung des mathematischen Wahrscheinlichkeitbegriffes auf Teile eines Kontinuums, *ibid.*, 1892, 681-691.

The controversy on tonal distances with Wundt is to be found as follows: for the results criticized, W. Wundt, *Physiologische Psychologie*, 1887, I, 428 f.; C. Lorenz, Untersuchungen über die Auffassung von Tondistanzen, *Philos. Stud.*, 1890, 6, 26-103; for Stumpf's critique of Lorenz, Vergleichungen der Tondistanzen, *Zsch. Psychol.*, 1890, 1, 419-485; for Wundt's three attacks, Ueber Vergleichungen der Tondistanzen, *Philos. Stud.*, 1891, 6, 605-640; Eine Replik C. Stumpf's, *ibid.*, 1892, 7, 298-327; Auch ein Schlusswort, *ibid.*, 1892, 7, 633-636; for Stumpf's interspersed replies, Wundt's Antikritik, *Zsch. Psychol.*, 1891, 2, 266-293; Mein Schlusswort gegen Wundt, *ibid.*, 1891, 2, 438-443. On these polemics, cf. E. G. Boring, The psychology of controversy, *Psychol. Rev.*, 1929, 36, 107-113.

The text makes it clear why it is not possible to compile a list of the influential psychologists who were Stumpf's students before 1900, as we did for Wundt in the last chapter. There is no such list. Stumpf himself mentions (Schmidt, *op. cit.*, 220 f.) as his most important students, first F. Schumann and H. Rupp; then, as especially concerned with the acoustics, O. Abraham, K. L. Schaefer, M. Meyer, O. Pfungst, E. M. von Hornbostel and G. J. von Allesch. He mentions W. Köhler in another connection. Certainly among his more prominent students we should add A. Gelb, K. Koffka, H. S. Langfeld and W. Poppelreuter.

Stumpf himself wrote the history of the Berlin laboratory in M. Lenz, *Geschichte der Friedrich-Wilhelms-Universität Berlin*, 1910, III, 202-207. Ebbinghaus, who had preceded Stumpf at Berlin, had completed his famous experiments on memory there and may be said to have founded the Berlin laboratory. It is plain that Stumpf thought of the actual beginning of the laboratory, although it was called the *Psychologisches Seminar*, as occurring with his coming in 1894. The more formal *Psychologisches Institut* began in 1900. Schumann, coming from Müller, was assistant and *Dozent* from 1894 to 1905. Then von Hornbostel was assistant for a year, and Ach for another year. Ach, like Schumann, came to Berlin from Göttingen. Then Rupp, also from Göttingen, took over the work until Stumpf's retirement.

G. E. Müller

Except for the present chapter in the 1 ed. of this book, there had been published no account of G. E. Müller's life and work until the necrologies began to appear after his death late in 1934, and most of these notices were meager. The more satisfactory are David Katz (a pupil of Müller's), Georg Elias Müller, *Acta psychol.*, 1935, 1, 234-240; also *Psychol. Bull.*, 1935, 32, 377-380; E. G. Boring, Georg Elias Müller: 1850-1934, *Amer. J. Psychol.*, 1935, 47, 344-348

(contains Eng. trans. of letter from Müller to the author describing the early intellectual influences which Müller thought directed his life); E. Claparède, Georg Elias Müller (1850-1934), *Arch. psychol.*, 1935, 25, 110-114.

No bibliography of Müller's writings is readily available, although one is said to have been published in a not easily accessible Dutch journal; J. Van Essen, G. E. Müller ter gedachtenis, *Ned. Tijdschr. Psychol.*, 1935, 3, 48-58. It seems best, therefore, to print again here from the 1 ed. of this book what the present author regards as Müller's more important publications, adding the 1930 item and keeping the references to important comment when such items are known. Here is the list:

1873. *Zur Theorie der sinnlichen Aufmerksamkeit*, 136 pp. Cf. E. B. Titchener, *Lectures on the Elementary Psychology of Feeling and Attention*, 1908, esp. 188-206, 356-359.

1878. *Zur Grundlegung der Psychophysik*, 424 pp. Cf. numerous references in Titchener, *Experimental Psychology*, 1905, II, ii.

1879. Ueber die Maasbestimmung des Ortsinnes der Haut mittels der Methode der richtigen und falschen Fälle, [*Pflüger's*] *Arch. ges. Physiol.*, 19, 191-235.

1889. With F. Schumann: Ueber die psychologischen Grundlagen für die Vergleichung der gehobenen Gewichte, *ibid.*, 45, 37-112. Cf. *Amer. J. Psychol.*, 1889, 2, 650 f.

1889. Theorie der Muskelcontraction, *Nachrichten Gesellsch. Wiss. Göttingen*, 1889, 132-179. Cf. E. C. A., *Amer. J. Psychol.*, 1889, 2, 490-492.

1893. With F. Schumann: Experimentelle Beiträge zur Untersuchungen des Gedächtnisses, *Zsch. Psychol.*, 6, 81-190, 257-339. Cf. J. A. Bergström, *Amer. J. Psychol.*, 1894, 6, 301-303.

1896. Zur Psychophysik der Gesichtsempfindungen, *Zsch. Psychol.*, 10, 1-82, 321-413.

1897. *Idem, ibid.*, 14, 1-76, 161-196.

1899. With L. J. Martin: *Zur Analyse der Unterschiedsempfindlichkeit.*

233 pp. *Cf.* F. Angell, *Amer. J. Psychol.*, 1899, 11, 266-271; Titchener, *Experimental Psychology*, 1905, II, ii, 300-310.

1900. With A. Pilzecker: Experimentelle Beiträge zur Lehre vom Gedächtniss, *Zsch. Psychol.*, Ergbd. 1, 300 pp.

1903. Die Gesichtspunkte und die Tatsachen der psychophysischen Methodik, in L. Asher and K. Spiro, *Ergebnisse der Physiologie*, Jhrg. II, Abth. ii, 267-516. Reprinted with separate paging in 1904. *Cf.* Titchener, *Experimental Psychology*, 1905, II, ii, esp. 310-313.

1904. Die Theorie der Gegenfarben und die Farbenblindheit, *Ber. I Kongr. exper. Psychol.*, 6-10.

1904. Bericht über Untersuchungen an einem ungewöhnlichen Gedächtnis [Rückle], *ibid.*, 46-48.

1911. Zur Analyse der Gedächtnistätigkeit und des vorstellungsverlaufes, I, *Zsch. Psychol.*, Ergbd. 5, 403 pp. *Cf.* Titchener, *Amer. J. Psychol.*, 1912, 23, 490-494 (introspection); J. W. Baird, *Psychol. Bull.*, 1916, 13, 373-375.

1912. Ueber die Lokalisation der visuellen Vorstellungsbilder, *Ber. V Kongr. exper. Psychol.*, 118-122.

1913. Zur Analyse der Gedächtnistätigkeit und des Vorstellungsverlaufes, III, *Zsch. Psychol.*, Ergbd. 8, 567 pp. *Cf.* Baird, *loc. cit.*

1913. Neue Versuche mit Rückle, *Zsch. Psychol.*, 67, 193-213.

1915. Ueber das Aubertsche Phänomen, *Zsch. Sinnesphysiol.*, 49, 109-46. *Cf.* K. Koffka, *Psychol. Bull.*, 1922, 19, 572-576.

1917. Zur Analyse der Gedächtnistätigkeit und des Vorstellungsverlaufes, II, *Zsch. Psychol.*, Ergbd. 9, 682 pp.

1923. *Komplextheorie und Gestalttheorie: ein Beitrag zur Wahrnehmungspsychologie*, 108 pp.

Cf. W. Köhler's reply, *Psychol. Forsch.*, 1925, 6, 358-416; and Müller's rejoinder, *Zsch. Psychol.*, 1926, 99, 1-15.

1924. *Abriss der Psychologie*, 124 pp.

1930. Ueber die Farbenempfindungen: psychophysische Untersuchungen, I and II, *Zsch. Psychol.*, Ergbd. 17 and 18, 647 pp.

The following are all very important researches done at Göttingen with Müller or under his personal direction, which the authors warmly acknowledge:

A. Pilzecker, *Die Lehre der sinnlichen Aufmerksamkeit*, 1889, 84 pp.

Müller and Schumann, 1889, *op. cit.*

Müller and Schumann, 1893, *op. cit.*

A. Jost, Die Associationsfestigkeit in ihrer Abhängigkeit von der Verteilung der Wiederholungen, *Zsch. Psychol.*, 1897, 14, 436-472.

V. Henri, *Die Raumwahrnehmungen des Tastsinnes*, 1898, 228 pp.

Martin and Müller, 1899, *op. cit.*

Müller and Pilzecker, 1900, *op. cit.*

E. R. Jaensch, Zur Analyse der Gesichtswahrnehmungen, *Zsch. Psychol.*, 1909, Ergbd. 4, 388 pp.

Idem, Ueber die Wahrnehmung des Raumes, *ibid.*, 1911, Ergbd. 6, 488 pp.

D. Katz, Die Erscheinungsweisen der Farben und ihre Beeinflussung durch die individuelle Erfahrung, *ibid.*, 1911, Ergbd. 7, 425 pp.

E. Rubin, *Synsoplevede Figurer*, 1915; Germ. trans. as *Visuell Wahrgenommene Figuren*, 1921, 244 pp.

E. A. McC. Gamble's monograph on the method of reconstruction, *Psychol. Monog.*, 1909, 10 (no. 43), does not belong in this list because most of the experiments were completed at Wellesley before she went to Göttingen.

For a description of the Göttingen laboratory in 1892, see O. Krohn, *Amer. J. Psychol.*, 1893, 5, 282-284.

CHAPTER 18

The 'New' Psychology of Content

There was something fresh and exciting in the 1870s about the new experimental psychology that Wundt called "physiological psychology." It had all the status of a new scientific endeavor. It was something more than the sensory experiments of physiologists', like E. H. Weber's and Johannes Müller's discoveries. It was more than the philosophers' turning toward science as an aid, than Herbart's use of mathematics, than Lotze's writing a 'medical' psychology. There was really something new here, a scientific activity with its own name. It is true that most of the new research was on perception, but even so there was hope for a complete experimental psychology as soon as there had been time. Fechner had already provided new methods of measurement. Helmholtz was showing how researches in vision and hearing were to be done, and he was not alone. Before the end of the 1860s Hering and A. W. Volkmann and Aubert and Exner and Delbœuf had published among themselves important work on psychological optics, visual space perception and color sensitivity; Mach and Vierordt had contributed the fundamental experiments on the estimation of time; Donders had invented the compound reaction; and Wundt had extracted the complication experiment from the astronomers' work on the personal equation. *That* was the new psychology which, rumored abroad, aroused the interest of William James in far-off America and later excited him to introduce the new subject to America, and America to the subject.

How much did Wundt have to do with all this? As we have seen, he provided for the 'new' psychology its structure and form, its self-consciousness, its name, its first formal laboratory, its first experimental journal, as well as the systematic pattern with respect to which the experiments could be formulated and given their significance. That was a great deal, even if, without Wundt, history would with a little delay have found itself by 1900 or a little later in the same position which it reached with Wundt's mediation. At any rate—whether the fact be due to Wundt or to the inscrutable ways of history—this new psychology was introspective, sensationistic, elementistic and associationistic. It was *introspective* because consciousness was its subject-matter. Consciousness was then the *raison d'être* of psychology. It was *sensationistic* because sensation shows what the nature of consciousness is. The imageless thoughts were not to claim status until the century had changed. It was *elementistic*, because the whole conception at the start was of a mental chemistry, and it seemed as if sensations, images and feelings might well be the elements which make up those compounds that are the stuff of psychology. And it was *associationistic* because association is the very principle of compounding, and because the British school had shown how you can get perception and meaning out of the association of parts. Later this sort of psychology came to be called the *psychology of content*, in contradistinction to the *psychology of act* which bore Brentano's label.

Within psychology in the nineteenth century the chief division lay between act and content—between Brentano and Wundt, as we usually say. Less clearly, however, that was also the difference between philosopher and scientist and between arguing and experimenting. Experimental psychology knew what to do, more or less, with a psychology of content. The acts—as Külpe found later at Würzburg—were elusive and did not stand up to observation like the contents. To understand the new experimental psychology one needs then to understand the psychology of content.

That demand seems strange to the young American psychologist of 1950. To him what was new and fresh and exciting to James in 1870 is now very old, quite dead and tremendously boring. What has happened is that America has taken over from Germany, and attention within psychology has shifted from sensation and perception to action and conduct. This was in part a change made in accordance with the national temper of America, a change which almost unconsciously transformed the pattern and values of the German psychology in the taking over of it. Later we shall see how this young Lochinvar from out of the west rode away with Wundt's *deutsches Mädchen* and, instead of letting her grow up into the meticulous life of an *akademische Hausfrau*, made a strong practical pioneering woman of her (pp. 506 ff.). But that division between German and American psychology, although it was getting started in the nineteenth century, was not recognized as crucial until the next.

The important thing now is to see what it was that seemed so exciting in the 'new' psychology of the nineteenth century, and that takes us to the parts played by those men who were the leaders in the psychology of content. They are Wundt, Hering, the early Stumpf and G. E. Müller, whom we have already sufficiently considered; Mach, who stimulated the school with his experiments and gave it some simple satisfactory principles of epistemology, principles which turned out later to be essentially the same as those offered by the difficult and almost incomprehensible Avenarius; Ebbinghaus, who was the eclectic and the popularizer in the school of content; Külpe, who, with the impress of G. E. Müller and Wundt upon him, began as a psychologist of content, a clear thinker of succinct thoughts and a man ready to follow whither experiment led, and who ended up, after the researches of his Würzburg school on thought, pretty well over into Brentano's camp, saving his integrity by championing a bipartite psychology of both contents and acts; and finally Titchener, who kept on being an Englishman thinking German thoughts while he lived in America, and who outwundted Wundt, leaving us the paradigm for an introspective psychology of content, one fully as representative of this modern associationism in 1910 as James Mill had been of the older associationism in 1829.

It is then to Mach, Ebbinghaus, Külpe and Titchener, and to some of the other men associated with this kind of psychology, that we now turn. Because of Mach's special relation to Külpe and Titchener, we may begin with Ebbinghaus.

HERMANN EBBINGHAUS

Hermann Ebbinghaus (1850-1909), the son of a merchant, was born in Barmen, not very far from Bonn, the seat of the first university that he attended. He was two years younger than Stumpf and six months older than G. E. Müller. After attending the *Gymnasium* at Barmen, he went, when he was seventeen years old, to Bonn to study history and philology. Thence he migrated, after the custom of German students, first to Halle and then to Berlin. Altogether he spent at these universities three years (1867-1870), and in their course he was won from his earlier interests to philosophy. Trendelenburg at Berlin, who captured Brentano and influenced Müller, may have had something to do with the change. Then came the Franco-Prussian War, and Ebbinghaus, like Müller, joined the army. After the war he returned to Bonn and there, in 1873, received his doctor's degree in philosophy on a dissertation about von Hartmann's philosophy of the unconscious.

The next seven years Ebbinghaus spent in an independent life

of study. First he returned to Berlin for a couple of years, and
there his reading shifted towards science in accordance with the
philosophical tradition of the day. (Brentano had put Stumpf to
studying science; and Lotze, Müller). The three years following
1875 he spent in France and England, studying and engaging in
tutoring. It was during this period that he found a copy of
Fechner's *Elemente* at a second-hand book-shop in Paris. The significance of this work for a scientific psychology caught his attention at once, and in considering the problem Ebbinghaus saw
that experimental psychology had made great advances by Fechner's method in the domain of sensation, but that it had as yet
been unable to attack the 'higher mental processes' that should
make up so large a part of psychology. He must surely also have
known Wundt's *Physiologische Psychologie*, then a few years old,
and, if he did, he would have been confirmed in this conviction, for
neither memory nor thought had yet been brought under experiment.

Ebbinghaus then, alone, without the stimulus of a university
environment, without personal acquaintance with Fechner or
Wundt or Lotze or with such promising younger men as Stumpf
or Müller—with his sole reliance on Fechner's book and his own
interest—set about adapting Fechner's method to the problem
of the measurement of memory. It seems quite probable that his
thought in these years followed actually the exposition of *Ueber
das Gedächtnis*. There, in the first chapter, he worked out the
conditions that must be fulfilled for measurement to be possible.
Then, picking up frequency of repetition as the essential condition of association, he showed how repetitions could be used as
a measure of memory. For the principles of method, he relied on
Fechner. The problem of memory he got from the British associationists, a very natural acquisition for a young philosopher spend-
ing time in study in England. We have seen in earlier chapters
how the laws of association had gradually converged upon frequency as the primary condition of association. It was Ebbinghaus
who fixed this outcome of British associationism, by seizing upon
repetition and making it the basis for the experimental measurement of memory. Although later, in dedicating his *Psychologie* to
Fechner, he could modestly say of his own work, "ich hab' es nur
von Euch," the fact remains that he was in this research highly
original. While he got mental measurement from Fechner, he did
not take over bodily the psychophysical methods; probably he
realized, as later research has shown, that they were unduly laborious when applied directly to mnemonic materials. He invented

the nonsense syllable, it would seem, out of nothing at all in the way of ancestry. If he was to measure the formation of associations, he had to have a material, uniformly unassociated, with which to begin; so he took two consonants and a vowel at random and put them together, like *zat, bok, sid,* and thus found himself in possession of about 2,300 nonsense syllables, which could be associated in lists for learning. Such lists are much more homogeneous than lists of words, for with them the habits of language do not represent associations of unknown degree already formed. With nonsense syllables and poetry as materials, with himself as the sole subject, with the *Erlernungsmethode* and the *Ersparnismethode* (methods of complete mastery and of savings) as instruments, he began his experimental measurement of memory, and some of the experiments were completed before he came out of his academic isolation and into the university world.

In 1880, however, he went to Berlin and was habilitated there as *Dozent.* He kept on with his experiments upon memory, and, unwilling to trust the results that he already had, he repeated the old experiments and verified them. Finally, in 1885, he published the epoch-making report of this work under the title *Ueber das Gedächtnis.* Except for his dissertation, it was his first publication. Beside the matters just mentioned, the book contains the results of measuring the effect upon learning of varying the length of the material learned, of measuring retention as a function of different amounts of repetition, of measuring forgetting as a function of time (the famous 'forgetting curve'), and of measuring the strength of direct and remote, forward and backward associations within a given material. The study is a model of clarity, precision and interesting exposition in scientific writing. It was epoch-making, not merely because of its scope and style, although these features must have helped, but because it was seen at once to be a breach by experimental psychology in the barrier about the 'higher mental processes.' Ebbinghaus had opened up a new field which the patience of G. E. Müller and his associates was soon to develop, and in this way experimental psychology became again vitalized by a sense of progress and of its destiny.

In 1886 Ebbinghaus was made *ausserordentlicher Professor* at Berlin. Undoubtedly his new fame aided his promotion. In this position he remained at Berlin for eight years. He did not continue his work on memory; he was original and an originator, but, with the first task accomplished, he was content to let others, like Müller, work out the method to the end. In the 1880s he published experiments upon brightness contrast and upon Weber's law applied to brightnesses.

Then in 1890 he founded with Arthur König the *Zeitschrift für Psychologie und Physiologie der Sinnesorgane*. In England Bain had founded *Mind* in 1876, but Great Britain was not to be the medium for the new psychology. Then in 1881 Wundt had begun the *Philosophische Studien*, which remained, however, primarily the organ of the Leipzig laboratory; and in 1887 Stanley Hall had started the *American Journal of Psychology*, thus showing that America was not far behind Germany in the development of the new psychology. In this case it was really ahead of the rest of the world, because the *American Journal of Psychology* was not biased in the direction of any one school. Germany needed a general journal for its psychology. By 1890 there was too much going on outside the sphere of Leipzig for Wundt's *Studien* to suffice. So Ebbinghaus, with König's aid, founded the *Zeitschrift*. He was able to enlist in this venture the help, as cooperating editors, of Helmholtz, of such psychological physiologists as Aubert, Exner, Hering, von Kries and Preyer, and of such psychologists as Theodor Lipps (who had just gone from Bonn to a full chair at Breslau), G. E. Müller and Stumpf. Thus the *Zeitschrift* represented in a way a coalition of independents outside of the Wundtian school.

In 1893 Ebbinghaus published his theory of color vision. On the whole, however, he had become a leader without much publication. Although his memory experiments must always remain an historical event, marked by unusual originality, Ebbinghaus' success in general must be ascribed to other factors than the significance and quantity of his scientific publication. We may reasonably assume that, for this reason, he was not promoted at Berlin when Stumpf came in over him to the chair of philosophy in 1894. We have already repeated the rumor that Helmholtz threw his influence against Wundt's call to Berlin. Berlin may have thought that Ebbinghaus lacked the caliber required by its chair, or it may have wanted for the chair of philosophy some one like Stumpf who had less definitely repudiated philosophy for psychology than had Ebbinghaus, or it may simply have had to make its choice between two men of equal age and similar attainments and have chosen Stumpf. However all this may be, the fact is that in 1894, a few months before Helmholtz's death, Stumpf came from Munich to the full chair at Berlin, Lipps went from

Breslau to Stumpf's post at Munich, and Ebbinghaus moved into Lipps's chair at Breslau.

Ebbinghaus remained at Breslau until 1905. He was still susceptible to new ideas. In 1897 he published a new method for testing mental capacity in school-children, a study undertaken at the behest of the aldermen of Breslau, who came to him with an inquiry about the distribution of the hours of study of the school-children. This new method was what came to be called the 'Ebbinghaus completion test,' the method of testing that is utilized in a great many modern intelligence tests and scholastic aptitude tests. Binet had, of course, already begun his researches on the child mind, a fact which may account for Ebbinghaus' publishing a brief account of his work in French, but Binet's *L'étude expérimentale de l'intelligence* did not appear until 1903. A claim can certainly be made that Ebbinghaus' originality penetrated the field of the higher processes not only in respect of memory but also in respect of intelligence as the mental tests came to test it.

In 1897 Ebbinghaus also published half of the first volume of his *Grundzüge der Psychologie*. The second half of this volume, as well as the complete volume, was issued in 1902. The book was a tremendous success. Within two years there was a demand for a revised edition, which Ebbinghaus published in 1905 without having yet written the second volume. The first ninety-six pages of the second volume he put out in 1908, but within a few months he was asked to prepare a third edition of the first volume. He began this revision but was prevented from completing it by his untimely death. Nevertheless, the demand for the book was so great that the first volume was revised and the second volume completed by Dürr after Ebbinghaus' death, and then the first volume was again revised by Bühler after Dürr's death.

The success of this work was largely the result of Ebbinghaus' clear and interesting style as an expositor. He was an effective writer, lucid and precise, scientifically rigorous, but with his human personality showing through withal. As an expositor he was the antithesis of the armored Müller, who marshaled arguments with a general's strategy, or of the host that was Wundt, who overwhelmed his reader with a horde of facts, arguments and dicta. Ebbinghaus was for Germany what William James was for America, the author of the only readable, kindly handbook of psychology, that nevertheless fell not a whit short in scientific care and exactitude.

When Ebbinghaus had completed the first revision of the *Psychologie* in 1905, he went from Breslau to Halle. Here his productive time seems mostly to have been occupied with further revisions. He also undertook another venture in textbook writing. He was asked to contribute the article on psychology to a large compendium on *Die Kultur der Gegenwart*, and this section, appearing in 1907, was reprinted as his *Abriss der Psychologie* in 1908. The *Abriss* was even more popular than the *Grundzüge*, for it went into a second edition in 1909 and then posthumously in the hands of Dürr and Bühler into numerous editions, as well as French and English translations.

Ebbinghaus died of pneumonia suddenly in 1909, when he was just a little over fifty-nine years old. He had been to the end active in his writing of these books, in his participation in psychological congresses and meetings, in his editorial work, and in the many ways in which a keen mind and a sympathetic personality can affect colleagues and contemporaries. The comment of the time reflected the belief that psychology had suffered an irreparable loss, so sudden and unexpected was his death. Everybody remembered the crucial importance of his work upon memory. The comment, nevertheless, was colored by personal admiration. Except for the memory work, Ebbinghaus' influence on psychological thought by way of systematic or experimental contribution was very little, much less than the influence of Stumpf or Müller, his contemporaries, or of Külpe or Titchener, his juniors.

We have here, then, the picture of a man who was important in experimental psychology in spite of a paucity of experimental work. In his list of writings there are only a little over a dozen important publications. The key to his place in the history of psychology is his personality. He had a keen intellect and an unusual sense of relations. He was original in thought, and he preferred to start new things and let others carry them on. Thus we find him working on memory, founding the *Zeitschrift*, experimenting on brightness, theorizing on color, inventing an intelligence test and writing a textbook. It was the success of the textbook that forced him to continue it in successive revisions; but for this external demand, he would probably have been at something else shortly. His dynamic personality was combined with great tolerance and a vivid sense of humor, and all these qualities together made him a leader in the meetings of the *Gesellschaft für experimentelle Psychologie*. His wider reputation was due to his expository style. He was an extremely careful experimenter.

In all these things he was self-made. He had no teachers who determined the course of his thought; he formed his life at the start with no contact other than that with the spirit of the times. He also had no pupils of importance in psychology. He neither founded a school nor wanted to found one. He was content to do well without great ambition and lacked the intolerance that most great psychologists have had. Thus, while personally very influential, he left no deep imprint on the psychological world after his death.

Ebbinghaus was especially important to experimental psychology because he helped to make articulate and effective the spirit of the times that called for an emancipation of psychology from philosophy. The subtitle of *Ueber das Gedächtnis* was *Untersuchungen zur experimentellen Psychologie*, and the title-page carried in Latin the quotation, "From the most ancient subject we shall produce the newest science." This thought he echoed over twenty years later in the often quoted opening sentence of the *Abriss:* "Psychology has a long past, but only a short history."

Ebbinghaus' systematic views are not important. Here his tolerance within the experimental field became eclecticism. He was primarily a psychologist of content because he accepted the psychology that had proved itself amenable to experimentation, but he had no fervid convictions on anything but experimentalism. In his *Psychologie* he avoided the problem of elementism and wrote of the simplest mental "formations" and the general laws of the mental life. He had, without knowing it, a cast toward the sort of psychology of capacity that has characterized America: his memory experiments were more like mental tests than introspective descriptions, and he invented the completion test. The fact remains, however, that one can not take Ebbinghaus' psychology as other than a psychology of the Wundtian tincture, somewhat diluted by tolerance and by a dislike of philosophical argument.

MACH AND AVENARIUS

Mach exerted a great influence on psychology. He was one of the older men, just Brentano's age, a few years younger than Wundt and Hering but a decade older than Stumpf, G. E. Müller and Ebbinghaus. He contributed in the 1860s to the early experimental work in psychology, produced in the 1870s the classical research on the perception of bodily rotation, wrote in the 1880s the famous little book, *Analyse der Empfindungen*, which, in clear and captivating style, laid down the fundamental tenets of scientific positivism and furnished the epistemology of the relation of psychology to physics which Külpe and Titchener later adopted and made the rule for modern parallelists. When this book was out, Avenarius turned up with similar ideas worked out in meticulous detail, and Mach agreed, after deciphering Avenarius' *Kritik der reinen Erfahrung,* that they too were saying the same thing, and then Avenarius agreed. After that, Avenarius died and Mach went on to write more papers on psychology and to contribute more technically to epistemology. We are most vitally concerned here with Mach's positivism and his joint influence with Avenarius upon psychological system making.

Ernst Mach (1838-1916) was born in Moravia, then a part of Austria. He went as a student to Vienna and later became *Dozent* there. At the age of twenty-six he was appointed professor of mathematics at Graz (1864-1867), and then three years later professor of physics at Prague, where he remained for twenty-eight years (1867-1895). Most of his important work was done at Prague. After that he was professor of physics at Vienna for a few years (1895-1901), arriving in Vienna just after Brentano had left. In 1901 he was elected to the Austrian house of peers and in 1905 he published *Erkenntnis und Irrtum,* a book that influenced Karl Pearson. Mach died in 1916.

In the 1860s Mach published research on visual space perception, discussion of the theory of hearing and his experimental work of the time-sense. He was a keen analyst and many of his brief discussions of general principles, tucked away in experimental reports, were brought out and quoted by others, as, for example, his comment of 1865 on mind-body relations, the comment that G. E. Müller picked up in 1896 when he came to formulate the psychophysical axioms.

After Mach went to Prague, he published in 1875 his *Lehre von den Bewegungsempfindungen,* the well known work on the perception of rotation. He described in it his rotation apparatus, the huge rotation frame which used always to dominate a room in those early laboratories that had the space to accommodate it. He also put forth his theory of the functioning of the semicircular canals in the perception of bodily rotation, a theory which, for want of a better, has persisted with modifications until the present day. This book alone would have brought him, a physicist, into the body of psychologists.

His most important work, also published from Prague, was his *Analyse der Empfindungen* (1886), which went into five editions and was translated into English. The epistemological views of this book he later elaborated in his *Erkenntnis und Irrtum* (1905), but it is the earlier book, with its direct simple thinking and its literary charm, which is generally known and which had the greater influence. In this book Mach established what might be called early modern positivism, the kind that was useful to physics and psychology and in distinguishing between them. This sort of positivism—it is safest to call it Machian positivism—is not the later logical positivism of Schlick, Carnap, Feigl and Bridgman, the positivism that runs over into operationism and behavioristics (pp. 653-658). It is the antecedent positivism which Mach expounded and which Karl Pearson took up in his *Grammar of Science*, the view that dates from Hume (pp. 191 f.) and his notion that causality is only what is observed, *i.e.*, concomitance, that asserts that the objects of science are to be understood by reducing them to the experience ("sensations") which constitute the observation of them.

The main thesis of the *Analyse* is Mach's insistence that sensations are the data of all science. He was writing a practical epistemology for scientists, not for philosophers, for his introductory chapter was entitled "Antimetaphysical." Poor metaphysics! Herbart had left it in psychology and had ruled experiment out. Lotze had not avoided it. The 'new' psychologists, even those with philosophical interests like Wundt and Külpe, were never tired of trying to free psychology of philosophy. Thus Mach, adopting the spirit of the times, was an uncritical idealist in his view of science. It is not necessary to go into the intricacies of his views. It is easy to show that all science is observational and that the primary data of observation are sensory. Like Wundt with his immediate and mediate experience, Mach justified introspection by establishing the observational status of conscious data beyond a doubt and throwing upon physics the burden of giving an account of itself. This was before the days of Husserl and Stumpf, who tackled the same problem by setting up phenomenology as a propædeutic science.

Mach quoted Krause, who had framed this paradigm: "Problem: To carry out the self-inspection of the Ego. Solution: it is carried out immediately." That is to say, there is no problem. Sensations are not observed; they are given. Being given, they can not be shown to be in error. Illusions are 'illusory': there are none, or, rather, the straight rod thrust into water is bent, and, if there be any illusion, it is that the rod is still straight. There is no ego; there are only sensory data. If we say, "It lightens," we ought also to say, "It thinks"; *cogitat*, not *cogito*. "The world consists only of our sensations." Dreams are as valid knowledge as perception.

Mach's positivism was his reduction of all the phenomena of both physics and psychology to the immediate data of their observation, to "sensations," as he said. Besides giving Külpe and Titchener a special epistemology for their systems, his views had one other important consequence. Since he thought of all experience as sensation, Mach, who had done his experimentation in visual and somesthetic space perception and in the estimation of times, spoke in the *Analyse* quite naturally of *space-sensations* and *time-sensations*. In that he was far ahead of Wundt who was still thinking of space and time in Kantian terms as the frames in respect of which the sensations are patterned into specific complexes. Wundt did not think of space and time as immediate data of experience, but Külpe, influenced by Mach, wrote them down in 1893 as data of experience, in fact, as two of the attributes of sensation, additional to quality and intensity. Now the elementists tended to think of the elements as differentiated from one another in respect of quality, but not in respect of space and time. This color, if it change hue, is, they thought, a new sensation. but, if it move or recur, then it is not a new sensation but the old sensation in a new place or at a new time. It was Mach's positivism first and Külpe's after him that helped to get these Kantian categories transferred into the class of experiential data. That was an important occurrence because it was preparation for Gestalt psychology, which fully recognized the phenomenal status of both extension and duration.

Mach was a clear, vivid writer, like Flourens, Ebbinghaus and William James, and some of his influence was due to his style. To Külpe and Titchener he seemed to establish the validity of introspection as a scientific method. He was so engrossed with emphasizing the community of psychology and physics that he was somewhat obscure in indicating the distinction, but this deficiency Avenarius, with a similar view, presently supplied.

Richard Avenarius (1843-1896), professor of philosophy at Zürich from 1877 to 1896, was as difficult, uninspiring and involved a thinker as Mach was simple, dramatic and clear. He worked without knowledge of Mach, though at the same time, but both men later agreed that their theories were essentially the same. He too sought to work out a theory of science, to avoid metaphysics and to eliminate the ego from his theory. The two big volumes of his *Kritik der reinen Erfahrung* came out in 1888 and 1890, and were the only work of importance that their author accomplished. They were even more difficult to write than to read, for they broke Avenarius's health and he died not long after their publication.

Avenarius began by hypothesizing a "System C," a bodily system upon which consciousness depends. The system C is practically the central nervous system, but Avenarius avoided the difficulty of defining the limits of the part of the nervous system essential to mind by the unimpeachable circular definition that the System C is whatever is essential to mind. In psychology we have to do with "R-values," the stimuli, and "E-values," statements of experience. The E-values depend directly upon the System C and are direct consequences of its constitution. The System C is constantly undergoing metabolic changes between catabolism and anabolism, but it tends always to maintain a "vital balance" between these two opposing influences. The R-values work toward catabolism and the tendency toward a balance is preserved by opposing S-values. Thus the formula for the vital balance is $f(R) + f(S) = o$, and an inequality means that the balance is destroyed and that there is a "vital difference." The genetic course by which a vital difference approaches balance is a "vital series," and Avenarius gave a very plausible account of the waxing and waning of attention in these terms. We have, however—so the theory goes on—to consider two kinds of vital series. There are *independent* vital series which occur in the System C and are physical. There are *dependent* vital series, which parallel the independent vital series of the System C, dependent upon these latter; they are psychological. The two are covariants, but one can be understood as independent, whereas the other can not be fully described except as dependent upon the first.

It is a travesty on Avenarius to condense his theory into a couple of hundred words, but the important thing for us is to see where Külpe and Titchener got the word *dependent* as applied to the experience which makes up psychological facts, and the word *independent* as applied to the experience underlying physical fact.

KÜLPE BEFORE WÜRZBURG

The German psychologists were professors of philosophy—except, of course, when like Hering they were physiologists or, like Mach, physicists. They believed—the psychologists of content—that psychology must be kept distinct from philosophy, yet few of them in those days were convinced that the separation should be complete. Ebbinghaus did, indeed, keep them separate, and that in itself was a good enough reason for his not getting the Berlin chair when Stumpf did, and it was also a reason for Titchener's great admiration for him, for Titchener also kept psychology and philosophy apart. G. E. Müller, the German critic whom Titchener always had in mind as his audience in the later days, kept the two disciplines separate, but Wundt and Stumpf and eventually Külpe did not.

Külpe, however, began his professional life as a tough experimental psychologist of content. He was tougher than Wundt because he was a positivist on the Mach model. What can not be observed, he thought, does not exist for science. Later he changed —as he matured. The work of his Würzburg school on thought showed him that observation is not so easy to define as the positivists would have you think, that all that exists (thoughts, for instance) is not immediately observable and may have to be caught in retrospect or by some other indirection. We must, therefore, separate the early Külpe from the Külpe of Würzburg, speaking of them successively and watching the contest between act and content for the possession of Külpe's faith.

Oswald Külpe (1862-1915) was born in Candau in Courland, Latvia, in what was then and is now again Russia. The region is very near East Prussia, and, in spite of an ancestor who had been master of the chase to Catherine II, the family was German in thought and interest. His father was a notary and his uncle a clergyman. He attended the *Gymnasium* at Libau on the Baltic coast of Courland. Then he spent two years in private tutoring, beginning his university studies thereafter when he was nineteen.

He went in 1881, not to Königsberg, the nearest university, but to Leipzig in order to study history. At Leipzig, however, he came into contact with Wundt, who diverted him, for the time being, to philosophy and, of course, to experimental psychology, which was still an infant science, for the Leipzig laboratory had been in existence only two years. He was not, however, entirely weaned from his desire to become an historian. He stayed with Wundt a year and then went to Berlin for a semester to study history again. Perhaps he was weighing history against psychology in this turning of his back on Wundt and going to the great Berlin historians like Mommsen, Kirchhoff and Diels. The experience at Berlin did not, however, settle the matter in favor of history. After a single semester he went in 1883, not back to Wundt, but to G. E. Müller at Göttingen, two years after Müller had succeeded Lotze. It would be interesting to know whether Külpe had heard Ebbinghaus lecture at Berlin and whether he went to Müller with Ebbinghaus' new experiments in mind. He spent three very important semesters with Müller. He began at Göttingen his dissertation on feeling, a theoretical study of the kind that Müller himself wrote on attention and Stumpf on space-perception. We lack Külpe's direct word concerning his thought at this time or the way in which he felt Müller's influence, but we have it indirectly that Külpe always regarded Müller as second only to Wundt in the determination of his early life. When his dissertation was published later at Leipzig, Külpe expressed his appreciation of Müller's aid and did not mention Wundt.

Still Külpe was undecided between history and psychology as a life-work. He left Müller to go to Dorpat to study history for a year. Müller had had the same choice to make and could readily have sympathized with him. After a year at Dorpat, for the third time the pendulum swung back to psychology, and Külpe then in 1886 returned to Wundt at Leipzig, where he was to remain for eight years.

In 1887 he took his degree on the dissertation *Zur Theorie der sinnlichen Gefühle*, upon which Müller had started him. In the next year he became *Dozent*. For this advancement his *Habilitationsschrift* was another theoretical study, *Die Lehre vom Willen in der neueren Philosophie*, which Wundt published in the *Philosophische Studien*. At about the same time he became Wundt's second assistant, when Cattell, the self-appointed first assistant, left to return to America. Now Külpe found himself immersed in experimental work of his own and of others. The enthusiasm about mental chronometry—the method of measuring the temporal relations of mental processes by the reaction experiment and the subtractive procedure—was then at its height. Külpe contributed to this movement an important paper (1891) on bimanual reaction times, showing that that hand is favored toward which the attention is directed, and thus supporting the attentional theory of reaction time that had come out of Lange's psychological analysis of the personal equation. In his experimental work he proved himself a careful technician and thus a worthy servant of the 'new' psychology.

In these days Külpe was turning over in his mind the project of a textbook. Wundt's *Physiologische Psychologie*, the only handbook of the new psychology, was in its third edition and about to pass into the fourth, always expanding. Wundt was becoming more and more complicated. There are certain limitations in the progress of thought which an individual cannot readily overcome. He may modify and revise with the utmost honesty, but, the farther he goes on, the less able is he to change direction radically or to check the weightier lines of his development. It is a psychological law of inertia, as against both change of direction and change of speed. What would happen to science if its great men did not eventually die, no one can guess. What does happen is that a new man takes up the work of an older man without the constraint of inertia from his past, that he thinks, works and writes more simply and directly, and that thus from the old he creates something new that gradually itself accumulates inertia. Wundt was becoming too involved, too much at the mercy of his convictions. For instance, he had created and energized experimental psychology, but he had admitted its ineffectiveness against the problems of the higher processes and was turning to *Völker-psychologie* for their solution. It seems as if Külpe must have said to himself: 'Experimental psychology is experimental psychology, and I shall write a book of the new psychology that gives the report of experiments about the mind, and when there are no experiments I will not write.' It is by such naïve judgments of younger men that science is constantly revitalized. So Külpe undertook (as so many after him have undertaken!) to write a clear, simple, direct text of experimental psychology.

At this point we must consider for a moment an important systematic matter. Külpe at Leipzig in the early 1890s was planning and writing what was to become his *Grundriss der Psychologie*. As far as the record goes, he would seem to have been closest in the laboratory to Meumann, Frank Angell and Titchener. Külpe, of course, was *Dozent* and assistant, and these men were but students. Titchener's British brusqueness offended Külpe at first. Nevertheless, there was amongst them much talk of Külpe's book, so much in fact that, when it did appear, Titchener felt a part ownership in it, translated it at once and then wrote a similar book of his own. One of the topics that these men discussed was Wundt's definition of psychology as the science of immediate experience, and of physics as dealing with mediate experience. Wundt's view is easier to understand nowadays with all that has been written since in this vein, but then it seemed unsatisfactory. Moreover, there was the new epistemology of Mach and of Avenarius. Titchener seized especially upon Mach and was ever after greatly influenced by him. Külpe, more given to philosophical intricacies, favored the difficult Avenarius. As we have seen, there is no real difference here, for the two men later agreed that they were both saying the same thing though in very different words. The point is that Mach and Avenarius affected, on the systematic side, Külpe's and Titchener's new psychology.

Having got clear on point of view, Külpe published his *Grundriss der Psychologie* in 1893, dedicating it to Wundt. He defined psychology as the science of "the facts of experience," and he further pointed out that it is characterized by "the dependency of facts on experiencing individuals." This is the idea that he got from Avenarius, and it had for him the advantage of allowing physics also to deal with experience taken as independent of the experiencing individual. Mediate experience, which Wundt assigned to physics, seems, being mediate, not to be experience at all. The new formula was better.

Külpe then proceeded to write his textbook of experimental psychology, omitting the parts where speculation in Wundt had had to take the place of scientific fact. As compared with Wundt, he succeeded pretty well. The first third of the book dealt with the more or less positive knowledge about sensation. A tenth dealt with memory, treating briefly of Ebbinghaus and more liberally of the British associationism. Perhaps Külpe was not yet impressed by the importance of Ebbinghaus' work, although later he gave Ebbinghaus credit for initiating the third great period in the history of experimental psychology. Another tenth of the book covered feeling, somewhat in the older Wundtian manner, for this was before most of the experimental work on feeling that Wundt's new tridimensional theory set off. He had, however, Lehmann's work with the expressive method to which to refer. (It was upon Lehmann's work that Wundt presently founded his new theory.) Then Külpe gave to fusion and colligation as much space as to feeling. Under fusion could go Stumpf's finding on tonal fusion, and something about colors, touch blends and emotions. *Colligation* was Külpe's well-known term for the spatial and temporal forms of combination, and he had all the facts and theories of space-perception to deal with, as well as the work on the time-sense, some of which had been done by Meumann in the Leipzig laboratory. Külpe included the work on reaction under the temporal colligations and made there his criticism of the subtractive procedure in mental chronometry that is supposed to have been its death-knell. He concluded the book with the shortest section of all, on attention. There were five pages on the will and self-consciousness. There was not a word on thought, and thereby hangs the tale of Külpe's life.

KÜLPE AND THE WÜRZBURG SCHOOL

No sooner was the *Grundriss* published than Külpe was advanced to be *ausserordentlicher Professor* at Leipzig, but before the year was out (1894) he went to the full chair at Würzburg, where the famous Würzburg school of imageless thought was to develop under his direction. The psychology of thought was soon to become Külpe's primary concern, but before we turn to this topic we must note that Külpe's interest was also shifting toward philosophy and esthetics.

In 1895 he published his *Einleitung in die Philosophie*, a text similar in style to the *Psychologie* and a very successful one. It had reached the seventh revised edition at the time of Külpe's death and was also translated into English by Pillsbury and Titchener jointly. In 1902 Külpe published *die Philosophie der Gegenwart in Deutschland*, which ultimately went into six editions and an English translation. In 1907 there appeared his treatise on *Immanuel Kant*, which had two more editions. After 1910 there were at least two important articles and two important books on philosophical subjects, which we shall mention later. We are prone to think of Külpe at Würzburg as immersed in the new systematic experimental introspection; but even more he was cultivating his affection for philosophy.

Külpe had always been a great lover of music, and at Würzburg he turned also to writing on esthetics. His first paper (1899) had to do with the objectivity of esthetic laws and their dependence upon stimuli. In the same year he wrote on association as a factor in the esthetic impression. In 1903, in the Stanley Hall commemorative number of the *American Journal of Psychology*, he published a paper on experimental esthetics. The anonymous author of a very complete biographical sketch of Külpe seems to feel that esthetics was one of the dominant interests in Külpe's life.

Meanwhile, however, Külpe was continuing his strictly psychological work. He wrote on attention in 1897 and on psychophysics in 1902. In the summer of 1902, he performed certain experiments on abstraction with W. L. Bryan of Indiana. These experiments raised seriously the question as to whether all the attributes of a sensory impression are simultaneously present in consciousness, since the attentive predisposition for one may lead to a complete failure of introspection with regard to the others. Külpe may not have thought this work important, for he did not report it until 1904; as a matter of fact, Carl Rahn made later use of it in his criticism of Titchener, and Titchener, in the present author's opinion, ultimately revised his views about the observational status of the sensation and the attribute. There was also a related paper of Külpe's in 1902 on the objectification and subjectification of sensory impressions.

As this record goes, it would seem that Külpe was more concerned, during the first decade of the present century, with philosophy and esthetics than with psychology. His only books were philosophical. It is therefore probable that a great deal of his 'leisure' was given to philosophy. On the other hand, publication of the greatest importance was issuing from his laboratory, and Külpe was the inspiration of it all. He was also an observer in most of these experiments, and those who are familiar with the laborious method of introspection can guess how much time he spent upon the mere routine of these researches. However, Külpe was not at this time ready to bring the results together in a theory of his own, and his psychological work of the decade must therefore be regarded as primarily the work of the students of the 'Würzburg school.'

We have noted above that the omission of a section on thought from the *Grundriss* was highly significant in Külpe's later life. In 1893 Külpe could not handle thought in an experimental psychology. He was unwilling to follow Wundt in ruling it out of the laboratory; but, since it had never been in the laboratory, there were no experiments to cite. It is clear that Külpe determined to remedy this deficiency. Ebbinghaus had brought memory, a 'higher mental process,' under the experimental method; why not bring thought into the laboratory too, and round out the new psychology?

The Würzburg school begins technically with the paper by Mayer and Orth (1901) on the qualitative nature of association. Thought seems to be a course of association; if it is, then the introspective method ought to yield a description of thought. We see here, as throughout the work of the Würzburg school, Külpe's positivism coming out. Science is empirical. Observation is its method. If you want to know about thought, why, then have people think and describe—let them describe—their thinking.

In the same year Marbe, then *Dozent* at Würzburg, published his experimental study of judgment. Marbe discovered a very surprising thing. A subject lifts two weights and judges which is the heavier. There is plenty of conscious content, like sensations and images in an associative temporal course, but introspection reveals "no psychological conditions of the judgment." That is to say, the judgments come, they are usually right, and the judger does not know how they got into his mind! Such a view of judgment seemed to contradict the accepted belief of centuries: the laws of logic were supposed to be the laws of thought, and the process of thought was definite, like the process of the syllogism. Now mind was turning out, by the introspective method, to be an irrational associative train of mental contents that nevertheless reaches a rational conclusion. Marbe had good observers, among them Mayer, Orth and Külpe himself; nevertheless, it was possible that all of consciousness did not get into their reports.

This question therefore arose: What other contents can there be in consciousness to account for thought, when the images and sensations which introspection always yields prove inadequate? The answer to the question was *Bewusstseinslagen*, or 'conscious attitudes,' as the German has been translated. Marbe had spoken of conscious attitudes, but it remained for Orth in a new paper (1903) to make them focal. Orth was not working on thought, but on feeling. He had in 1903 either to accept Wundt's new theory of a multiplicity of feelings, and a mind with more affective than sensory content, or else to advance some other hypothesis. His view was that many of these Wundtian feelings and many other contents of the mind are really what may be called conscious attitudes, obscure, intangible, unanalyzable, indescribable contents that are neither sensations nor ideas. He sought under this classification to include many of Wundt's feelings, James' fringes of consciousness, and Höffding's quality of familiarity. The *Bewusstseinslage* was thus a new imageless element of mind that might prove useful for the psychology of thought.

The next research in this series was Watt's. He undertook in 1904 a direct attack upon the problem of thought itself. His observers were asked to form partially constrained associations, like naming a superordinate for a subordinate or a part for a whole. He did not solve the problem of thought by this means, for he came out noting the paucity of consciousness in relation to its thoughtful accomplishment. He contributed, however, three changes to the picture of these researches.

In the first place, he introduced the Hipp chronoscope and its accessories for the securing of accurate reaction times for the associations. In the end, the times did not do him much good, but the presence of the chronoscope must have kept the ghost of the metaphysical Herbart from influencing the results, and moreover it was an evidence of good intentions. If he did not succeed in measuring thought, his failure was not due to indolence.

In the second place, he initiated the introspective method of fractionation. A conscientious observer may use hundreds of words in describing the consciousness of a few seconds, and his memory has faded while he was getting the experience into words. Watt divided the consciousness, therefore, into four periods: (1) the preparatory period, (2) the event of the appearance of the stimulus-word, (3) the period of the search for the reaction-word and (4) the event of the occurrence of the reaction-word. He had his observers confine themselves first to one period and then to another, and thus eventually he got a more accurate and complete account of what had taken place.

In the third place, Watt placed the stress upon the *Aufgabe*, where it has ever since remained. Every one had been expecting to find the key to thought in Watt's third period, the period of the search for the word that would satisfy the conditions, but it was the third period that presented inadequate content. Watt discovered that the thought-process would run itself off at the presentation of the stimulus-word, provided the task or *Aufgabe* had been adequately accepted by the observer in the preparatory period. This was really a remarkable result. So far as consciousness goes, one does one's thinking before one knows what he is to think about; that is to say, with the proper preparation the thought runs off automatically, when released, with very little content. Watt's *Aufgaben* were the various tasks that he set his observers, but so important did this initial preparation become that the word *Aufgabe* has slipped into psychology as a fundamental introspective concept. It is used loosely for any potentiality of consciousness. Strictly speaking, the *Aufgabe* is the conscious task or purpose that precedes a conscious course. The *Aufgabe* may therefore be thought of as setting up in the subject an *Einstellung* or 'set'; and the subject, in accepting an *Aufgabe*, as becoming *eingestellt*.

Ach's work on action and thought (1905) is much better known than Watt's, but its apparently greater importance is due to the fact that he gave definite formulation to many of the results of Watt's work. Ach used the Hipp chronoscope also and verified much of the older work on reaction times. With him it became clear that the problems of thought and action are essentially the same. In both cases one has some specific end to achieve, and the psychophysical process, released by a stimulus, runs its course to that end To name a rhyme for a stimulus-word is psychologically no different from pressing a given finger when a given letter appears.

There are three things of importance that Ach did. In the first place, he invented the term *systematic experimental introspection*, which became the slogan of this school, as it was later of J. W. Baird's laboratory at Clark University. *Systematic* refers most definitely to fractionation, Watt's method which Ach used and so named. *Experimental* undoubtedly refers to the chronoscope among other things. The formula was an insistence on careful scientific technique, even when the method used was introspection.

In the second place Ach invented—or did he merely name?—the *determining tendency*. Watt had tried to account, by way of Müller's 'perseverative tendencies,' for the way in which the initial *Aufgabe* carries over unconsciously to the intended end. Ach preferred a new name to fit the new situation. The concept of the determining tendency implies that the tendency operates superiorly to reinforce associative tendencies. Thus, given a *5* with a *2* below it, printed on paper, the most usual associates would be *7, 3* and *10*. If, however, the subject has been instructed to add, one association will be strengthened so that *7* will almost inevitably occur; or, if the *Aufgabe* has been to subtract, then another association is reinforced and becomes the strongest. This notion of effective predetermination had of course been prepared by Lange and the Wundtians, when they referred the differences in personal equation to the effect of attention. Külpe had taken a hand in the matter when he argued in the *Grundriss* against the subtractive procedure and said that a change in the preparation might change the whole consciousness and not merely add or subtract a factor. However, Ach gave this relation between preparation and end a reality by naming it. It is quite possible that he overdid the matter, for the determining tendency was accepted by opponents of the Würzburg school and has even been called a physiological process, although the only thing that makes it physiological is the fact that it is not conscious. In this way the Würzburg school has taken its place in the history of the psychology of attitude, in the history of dynamic psychology.

The third point that we must note about Ach's work is his invention of the *Bewusstheit* ('awareness'). A *Bewusstheit* is, like the *Bewusstseinslage*, a vague, intangible, conscious content that is not image or sensation. The descriptive word for it is *unanschaulich*, which Titchener has translated "impalpable." The action or thought consciousness lacks enough content adequately to clothe itself, but nevertheless systematic experimental introspection reveals something more than palpable contents; the consciousness has impalpable moments, *Bewusstheiten*. Such was Ach's view. It is not clear that there is any real difference between Orth's conscious attitude and Ach's awareness, although Ach identified the conscious attitude with an awareness of relation, thus making *awareness* the broader term. However, both were imageless elements in thought, and there was little more that could be said about them.

It ought here to be said of Ach that his research was begun in 1900 with Müller at Göttingen and finished at Würzburg in 1904. The book is dedicated to both Müller and Külpe. Moreover, the work was finished before Watt's printed paper was available, so that Ach's apparent crystallization of Watt's ideas was practically an independent discovery. In other words, the *Zeitgeist* was working, and Watt and Ach were its agents. Psychology was ready to find that thinking is not all sensory.

After Ach came Messer of Giessen, whose experimental study of thought was carried through at Würzburg in the summer semester of 1905. In a sense Messer continued Watt's method of constrained associations. The resultant paper is replete with introspective results, and the general conclusion consists of an attempt to classify the conscious data. It served by reiteration to emphasize the general thesis of the Würzburg school, but, viewed from the perspective of many years, it seems not to have developed the position in any radical way.

The last person whom we need to mention in this school is Bühler, who came to Külpe from Berlin in 1907, and shortly thereafter published three papers on the psychology of the thought-processes. Bühler's work is memorable for his use of the *Ausfragemethode* (a very different method from the questionnaire form of the so-called *Aussagemethode*). In the *Ausfragemethode* the experimenter questions the observer and the observer replies; there is free, sympathetic communication between them. It is plain that some such method as this may be necessary in psychoanalysis, but the guardians of 'systematic experimental introspection' have generally criticized a method that is so friendly to suggestion and that makes so little distinction between rigorous description of mind (*Beschreibung*) and the giving of interpretative statements about mind (*Kundgabe*). Bühler was severely criticized by Wundt, by Dürr, who was one of his observers, and by von Aster. Titchener, of course, criticized the entire movement. Bühler, however, like Messer, left the total picture of thought without important change, and we may thus close our account of the Würzburg school and return once again to Külpe.

It is not easy to place Külpe in his own school. The Würzburg period was terminated by his transfer to Bonn in 1909, to Benno Erdmann's chair. He was becoming interested in the relation of psychology to medicine. He published on this topic in 1912, and he had been given an honorary medical degree by the medical faculty of Giessen in 1907. Philosophical problems were continuing to concern him. From Bonn he published papers on epistemology and natural science, on the concept of reality, and on the doctrine of the categories; and his most important book was *Die Realisierung* (1912), a philosophical study of reality, which of necessity dealt with psychological problems. It is plain that he was not yet ready to sum up the status of the psychology of thought.

It is true that in 1912 he published a short article on the modern psychology of thought. In this paper he summarized the work at Würzburg and attempted thus to illustrate the nature of thought. He did scarcely more, and, while summary and illustration are useful, the world was expecting from him some more positive construction. He was lecturing on psychology and preparing his lectures as the basis of a book to replace the *Grundriss*. He died without publishing them, but Bühler published them posthumously in so far as they were complete. They represent what is, in view of human inertia, an astonishing change in Külpe's outlook since he wrote the *Grundriss* twenty years before, and they contain a pretty complete system of psychology. But the chapter on thought was missing! Bühler said that Külpe had not been lecturing on the topic.

What had happened?

In the first place, the work of the school seemed to have failed of its positive purpose. It had yielded determining tendencies and imageless thought. The hypothesizing of the determining tendency was in part a negative and in part a positive result. It was negative in so far as it asserted that the essential conditions of the course of conscious events are not conscious. It was positive in so far as it definitely placed the problem outside of introspection and in so far as it emphasized the discovery that the key to thought, as well as to action, is to be found in the preparation of the subject. For many years the discovery of imageless thoughts was regarded as a purely negative discovery. The conscious attitudes and the awarenesses were never characterized except in terms of what they are not, and it became evident that scientific introspection could not simply admit any statement of an observer about his mind and still keep clear the meaning of conscious actuality. However, Külpe never came to share this view of these critics of the Würzburg school. His letters to friends (*ca.* 1910-1912) show that he felt that the psychology of thought was steadily developing from and beyond these researches which we have mentioned. Apparently he did not stop to sum up the subject because the work was still progressing and was not yet ready for recapitulation and because he had more important work to do, especially the writing of *Die Realisierung,* which he expected to be his greatest book.

It thus seems that Külpe hoped eventually to bring thought into order both by further work upon the problem and by its clarification by philosophical insight. He did not believe that there was any incompatibility between his philosophical and psychological interests, and it appears that Husserl indirectly led him away from Wundt and toward Brentano. Husserl's *Logische Untersuchungen* had appeared in 1900-1901, but the work seems not immediately to have been taken at Würzburg with the seriousness with which Külpe later regarded it. Messer was the first of the school to mention Husserl, and he mentioned him but once, although very favorably. Bühler, however, had read Husserl at Berlin and his paper showed the influence. Bühler may even have introduced Husserl to Külpe. Now we have already seen in our account of Stumpf that the principal effect of Husserl upon psychology was to justify phenomenology, and it is also plain that phenomenology—not exactly Husserl's kind, but the kind that Stumpf and other psychologists could accept— blithely admits awarenesses into the fold when dour introspectionism keeps them out. Here, then, was an opening, but the way beyond was not yet clear.

Another very important effect of Husserl upon psychology was to reinforce Brentano and thus the act. There is room in phenomenology for acts as well as contents; it is a tolerant discipline. If we do not know certainly the exact course of Külpe's thought, at least we know that he leaned more and more toward Brentano and that he came eventually to a bipartite psychology of palpable contents and impalpable acts (or functions, as he preferred to call them). The posthumous *Vorlesungen* contain much of the contents of the old *Grundriss* under "Contents," whereas the new materials of mind come under "Functions." Had the chapter on thought been written, it would certainly have appealed to the functions, or perhaps to both contents and functions, for Külpe once wrote in a letter: "I distinguish between *Gedanken* and *Denken;* the former are contents, the latter, in their different forms, acts or functions."

We must mention this psychology of Külpe's again in the next chapter, but the present account goes to show how it was possible for a man to pass by imperceptible degrees from the psychology of Wundt to the psychology of Brentano.

In our attempt to understand Külpe we must not make the mistake of thinking that he thought he was deserting psychology for philosophy. Psychology was philosophy for Külpe just as much as it was for Stumpf. Külpe's experimentalism was not thought by him to take him outside of philosophy. Thus his eventual search for the key to thought in a more philosophical and a less experimental manner represented for him merely the normal process of research on a single topic, thought, with one method failing and a new method being tried. The course Külpe's views took parallels his philosophical development from the positivism of Mach and Avenarius of his youth to the realism of his maturity.

There is little more to be said of Külpe's life. He was called from Bonn to Munich in 1913, and he died there suddenly of influenza two years later, leaving his psychological work incomplete.

Külpe belongs to the school of content in his early period. He passed imperceptibly to the middle ground which includes both content and act. Between 1893 and 1912 we see the interesting transitional stage of the Würzburg school. The impalpable functions were there, but they were masquerading as mental elements; for all their impalpability they were, being infected with Wundtian elementarism, less fluid than Brentano's acts.

Külpe is quite properly to be considered as one of the chief representatives of the 'new' psychology. He accepted experimentalism. He wrote a book in which he refused to depart widely from experimental results. He could not write in that book on the topic of thought, but he undertook the experimental investigation of thinking, seeking to extend the experimental method to the last stronghold of speculation, as Ebbinghaus had done for memory. He learned much, and he may have thought he had succeeded in producing a positive contribution, but he did not in his life-time convince his critics. At the dramatic moment in this work he died, too early, at the age of fifty-three, without having yet convincingly demonstrated to the world that Wundt was wrong, or that Wundt was right, when he said that one can not experiment upon thought.

So much for then. Now, forty years later, we can see how much more valuable for psychology was Külpe's ability to change his mind than was Titchener's steadfast consistency. The later shift of psychology's focus from consciousness to conduct was furthered immeasurably by Külpe's depreciation of the rôle of consciousness in thinking. Its shift toward the problems of motivation made *set* (*Einstellung, Aufgabe*) and *attitude* (*Bewusstseinslage*) the verbal tools of psychology's next generation.

TITCHENER

Titchener was an Englishman who represented the German psychological tradition in America. We have already seen how close he was to Külpe at Leipzig, and in the early days there was a parallel between these two men. Both were Wundtians; both went out to new laboratories in the beginning of the 1890s and undertook, with modifications, to continue the Leipzig tradition; Külpe wrote his *Grundriss* in 1893, and Titchener translated it in 1895 and wrote a similar book in 1896; each in the new century built a school about himself by concentrating the publications of his students about his own processes of thinking. But there were differences too. Külpe was more of a philosopher in his psychology than was Wundt and definitely opposed himself to the master in the fundamental thesis of the Würzburg school. Titchener avoided philosophy more than Wundt and never opposed him on so crucial an issue. For this reason Titchener really resembles G. E. Müller more than he does Külpe, and he always had for Müller a respect and admiration that rivaled only his feeling for Wundt. Both Müller and Titchener refused to philosophize in spite of an early training in philosophy; both championed the new experimentalism in everything but personal experimentation; both devoted themselves primarily to the theoretical discussion, criticism, and interpretation of experimental results; and both built up an elaborate and penetrating polemical method and attitude. Of this last point it may be said that Titchener was always flexible in his theorizing and rigid in his polemizing, an inconsistency not inconsistent with greatness. We have just noted how Titchener held on to sensory consciousness as the *raison d'être* of psychology, whereas Külpe showed a capacity to change.

Edward Bradford Titchener (1867-1927) was born in Chichester, in the south of England, of an old family in which he took much pride. The family had in his generation little money, and he was forced to rely on his exceptional ability in order to obtain scholarships for his education. One of these scholarships took him to Malvern College, where he must have done well, for it is related that James Russell Lowell (the poet, then American ambassador and the best after-dinner speaker and tablet-unveiler in England), who was distributing the prizes one year and who had already presented several prizes to Titchener, remarked, when the same youth appeared again for still another prize, "I am tired of seeing you, Mr. Titchener." After Malvern he went in 1885 to Oxford, to Brasenose College, where he had obtained a scholarship. His family had arranged for him to go to Cambridge, but he himself had his heart set upon Oxford and managed to have his way. Thus early one gets a glimpse of the insistent independence of thought and action that characterized his whole life.

He remained five years at Oxford. During the first four he was a student of philosophy. We have seen that British empiricism and associationism were the philosophical ancestors of the modern psychology, and it is therefore not unnatural that Titchener should have become interested in Wundt's new physiological psychology. He did not find much sympathy for this interest at Oxford, but Titchener never swam in the social current. He translated into English all of the third edition of Wundt's *Physiologische Psychologie*, which had only just come out. He never published the translation, but took it with him later to Leipzig, where he learned from Wundt that the fourth edition was almost complete (which still later he translated, only to be forestalled by the fifth). The last year at Oxford Titchener spent as a research student in physiology with Burdon-Sanderson, who made a great impression upon him. Whether Titchener turned to physiology because of physiological psychology or whether the process worked the other way, it is impossible to say. At any rate he gained a lifelong respect for the British biology of this time and did his first published research in this field. At the same time he translated Wundt and went, with no encouragement at all from his Oxford friends, to Leipzig to study under him.

At Leipzig in 1890 Titchener found Külpe, Meumann, Kirschmann, Kämpfe, Pace, Scripture and Frank Angell. The next year the last three returned to America, and Warren and Witmer as American students replaced them. Titchener roomed with Meumann, planned with Külpe the *Grundriss* and formed a close personal friendship with Frank Angell. Like Külpe he fell in with the enthusiasm about mental chronometry, and at Wundt's behest completed and published his first psychological research on the reaction times for what was then called 'cognition.' His dissertation was on the binocular effects of monocular stimulation, and he had completed both studies and taken his doctorate in 1892 after but two years with Wundt. Nevertheless, Wundt made a great impression upon him, an impression that was never obliterated.

Titchener would have liked to return then to Oxford, but there was no place and little sympathy at Oxford for physiological psychology or for a physiological psychologist. He lectured there on biology in the summer and then came (1892) to Cornell in America, to the new laboratory which Frank Angell had opened the year before and which he was now leaving in order to go to the newly founded Stanford University. Titchener spent the rest of his life at Cornell, thirty-five years in all, almost, but not quite, as long as Lotze and Müller had successively been active at Göttingen. Only once did he return to Europe: to the International Congress of psychology at Munich in 1896. As the years went on, he left Ithaca less and less frequently, in part because, while he was immersed in psychology, he had little immediate interest in American psychology and thus withdrew more and more from his American contemporaries.

In the 1890s at Cornell Titchener bent himself to the consolidation of the forces of the new psychology. In general, the American and German psychologists of that day felt that they were engaged in a battle to bring old territory under a new authority. We have seen this militancy in Wundt, in Ebbinghaus, and even in Külpe when he sought to justify the experimental method in the field of thought. Locally Titchener felt called upon to secure independence from the Cornell philosophers, and he finally succeeded. He also felt the necessity for establishing psychology more firmly in America, where it had not yet taken firm root; and for this purpose there had to be more psychological books in English. So he translated Külpe's *Grundriss*, joined with others in the translation of Külpe's *Einleitung in die Philosophie* and of Wundt's *Menschen- und Thierseele* and *Ethik*, and, prevented from publishing his translation of the fourth edition of Wundt's *Physiologische Psychologie* by the appearance of the fifth, published his translation of the first portion of the fifth. He wrote in 1896 his *Outline of Psychology*, the book that resembled Külpe's *Grundriss*, and in 1898 his *Primer of Psychology*. He turned, of course, to the building-up of the new laboratory, first on the material side, where he worked with his own hands, and then, as students came, on the side of research, where he worked by way of others. Before 1900, however, M. F. Washburn, W. B. Pillsbury, M. Bentley and E. A. McC. Gamble, to mention only the better-known names, had taken their degrees with Titchener, and more than thirty studies had issued from the laboratory.

The nature of Titchener's militant spirit is shown most strikingly in his large *Experimental Psychology*. Titchener was for having psychology stand upon its own legs, not for bolstering it up with artificial props. The fundamental motive back of the *Experimental Psychology* was the establishment of the new science. Titchener wanted to show what a respectable scientific subject it was. He wanted also to establish laboratory "drill courses," as he called them, in university curricula, not merely to prove that psychology is a science but to provide the proper training that was needed as a basis for research. In writing the *Instructor's Manuals* he must have felt also that he wanted to give the instructor something to live up to, although the thoroughness of these books is undoubtedly primarily a result of Titchener's personality; like Müller he never did anything by halves. The *Student's* and *Instructor's Qualitative Manuals* came out in 1901; the two corresponding *Quantitative Manuals*, delayed by the appearance of Müller's psychophysical text in 1903, appeared in 1905. The books are too well known to need description, although probably no one has ever read either of the *Instructor's Manuals* through. They served rather as encyclopedias. Külpe is said to have called them the most erudite psychological work in the English language, and, though personal opinions about such matters vary, everyone must realize the very great competence and thoroughness of these books against an already large literature and, in psychophysics, a very difficult one. Even now, half a century later, it is hard to name a more erudite set of volumes or single book in English, in psychology, by a single author.

Titchener never became a part of American psychology. Americans were going abroad to study with Wundt; they were coming back filled with enthusiasm for the 'new' psychology, but they were falling inevitably, and often unconsciously, into another kind of psychology, a psychology which concerned itself with human capacities and with individual differences, and one which we must leave for detailed discussion until a later chapter. Titchener's interest lay in the generalized, normal, human, adult mind that had also been Wundt's main concern. He did not desire to initiate research in animal psychology, which, in its experimental phase, really began in America, nor in abnormal and child psychology, nor—and this is perhaps the most important point of all—in individual psychology. He wanted to work on the *mind;* Americans were beginning to be concerned with *minds.*

This difference had already appeared in a controversy with J. M. Baldwin in the 1890s. The trouble arose about reaction times. The fundamental tenet of mental chronometry that the Leipzig laboratory had established is that the sensorial reaction is longer, by about one tenth of a second, than the muscular reaction. Titchener agreed with Külpe's strictures on the subtractive procedure, but he had seen too much of the work with reactions at Leipzig to doubt that the basic difference is obtained with practised observers. Baldwin, however, with others to support him, found a difference in the other direction with some unpractised observers, that is to say, an individual difference between what he then called "sensory" and "motor" observers. There is not necessarily any incompatibility between these two findings, but it is doubtful if either party to the controversy realized this fact. Baldwin argued that Titchener was refusing to open his eyes to a fact of nature, that the classical difference came out only with practice. Titchener argued that science is concerned only with the laws of the generalized mind, that practice in assuming an attitude makes it possible to exhibit the laws for the attitudes, and that a statement of an individual difference is not a law when the difference can be referred to no definite conditions. It was really a controversy between Germany and America, one which served to emphasize Titchener's isolation in America.

The controversy served also to increase this isolation, for Titchener felt rebuffed by the invective and tended to draw away from his American contemporaries. He was an editor of the *American Journal of Psychology* and came to regard the *Psychological Review Publications*, which Baldwin and Cattell began, much as Wundt regarded the *Zeitschrift*. The American Psychological Association had just been organized when Titchener came to America, but it seemed to him to be the medium of the opponent group, and he was never active in it and for many years only nominally a member. Instead he gathered in 1904 an informal group which held, without any organization, meetings in the spring up to the year of his death. This group was known as the "Experimental Psychologists," for already and especially in America the 'new' psychology that was 'experimental' psychology was beginning to subdivide. The word *experimental* was kept for the meaning that Wundt and his contemporaries had given it; animal, child, abnormal and applied psychology, no matter how much they used experiment, were not called 'experimental psychology.' When Titchener died, the Experimental Psychologists reorganized as the present-day Society of Experimental Psychologists and eagerly admitted reports on animal studies into their meetings, but not in general on child, abnormal and applied psychology.

After he had finished with the *Experimental Psychology*, Titchener let himself be drawn into the problems of feeling, attention and thought. His theoretical views on these matters are contained in two books: *Psychology of Feeling and Attention* (1908) and *Experimental Psychology of the Thought-Processes* (1909).

Of feeling he argued that it is an element like sensation with only the two qualities, pleasantness and unpleasantness. Here his discussion was directed against Stumpf, who thought feeling a sensation, against Wundt, who held to the tridimensional view of its qualities, and against others, who had said that it is an attribute of sensation.

To attention Titchener gave attributive status. It is interesting to see how his positivism, his faith in scientific observation, determined his view here. Attention had been a vague and therefore a dangerous concept. It tended, moreover, to bring into the psychology of content the notion of act, for, casually regarded, attention seems to be an activity or capacity. Like the early Külpe starting out to observe thinking, Titchener believed that whatever comes into science must be observable and that attention can certainly come into a scientific psychology. Attention would have to be, therefore, nothing more nor less than that which changes in experience when attention is said to change. Titchener came to the conclusion that this change lies in the clearness of the sensory processes, that sensory processes have therefore an attribute of clearness, just as they have quality and intensity, and that what is changing when attention shifts is this clearness. Later he called the attribute *vividness*, and still later by the univocal new word *attensity*.

Titchener's interest in thought was conditioned upon the work of the Würzburg school. Here he took his stand for the sensory and imaginal nature of the thought-processes. He opposed the belief in imageless thought and argued that, because some thought-processes resist analysis, that fact does not mean that they are not actually sensory-imaginal patterns. Thus at Cornell the 'conscious attitude' came to mean a pattern of the older mental elements. Titchener accepted, however, the determining tendency of Ach and also the premise of the Würzburg school that thought may be unconscious. In the *Thought-Processes* he put forth his context theory of meaning, which makes meaning the conscious sensory or imaginal context that accrues (associatively, it would seem) to the initial sensory core of a perception or the initial imaginal core of an idea. However, this law of meaning holds, he thought, only for new perceptions and ideas; in old habituated ones the core occurs without conscious context and the meaning is "carried unconsciously." It was in this way that he sought to explain the paucity of conscious content in thought at Würzburg. The accrual of the context to the core, or the carrying of the meaning without this conscious representation, he explained as dependent upon the determining tendency.

We have considered these three topics—feeling, attention, and thought—as if Titchener were merely theorizing without recourse to experimentation. Such a view is not at all correct, although some of the experiments at Cornell followed theory and modified it but slightly. On feeling he appealed to the entire experimental literature on affective processes and, as against Wundt, to his own experiments and those of Hayes at Cornell. His view of attention was supported in the laboratory, first by Geissler and then by Dallenbach. His work on thought was at first a criticism of Würzburg which led to the experimental researches of Pyle on expectation, of Okabe on belief, of Clark on conscious attitudes and of Jacobson on meaning and understanding. The last study led to an important paper by Titchener.

In 1909-1910 Titchener published his *Text-Book of Psychology*, a condensed system of experimental psychology, much too difficult for the sophomores for whom it was intended. It is the only book in which Titchener's psychology is worked out to the end and put together between two covers. After its completion he set himself to write a large systematic psychology, but the undertaking still remained uncompleted at his death fifteen years later. A few sections were published in a journal, but somehow or other Titchener found himself unable to work further on the manuscript. In 1915 he had undertaken to revise his *Primer* for publication and with his usual thoroughness rewrote it entirely, renaming it *A Beginner's Psychology*. The work of his laboratory increased after 1910, as did also the number of his students. In the last decade of his life he was greatly impressed by the 'newest' psychology in Germany, the work on perception of the *Gestalt* school and the new method of experimental phenomenology. Titchener had rejected the phenomenology of Würzburg and had remained a conservative; now, however, he was ready to try—and to have his students try—phenomenologizing. He always distinguished between the constrained and rigorous report of introspection and the free reports of phenomenology, but it is plain that he put considerable faith in the new method. Since he never published on this subject, and the papers that have come from his laboratory with his sanction are very specialized, it is useless to try to guess whither Titchener was tending.

In the last decade of his life, Titchener seemed to have less and less energy for his psychology. It is not so much that the frequency of his publication diminished, as that the subjects treated were less important, less often crucial. He developed interests in side-issues like numismatics. He kept his erudition abreast of the times and was always an impressive member of a group. He had great personal magnetism, which made him the master of the group at Cornell and the distant object of admiration of many others. His isolation and his strict interpretation of his code of professional and personal conduct also made him enemies, some from among those who should have been his friends. He died unexpectedly in 1927 after thirty-five years in America.

Titchener stood in America for the 'pure' introspective psychology. The key to his position on almost all crucial matters lies in the word *pure*, which can be used of Titchener's introspection, although he would never have used it himself. What were for Titchener the data of psychology and what were not? The teaching of Mach and Avenarius seems to have been ingrained even into Titchener's everyday thinking. Wundt, we may repeat, drew the distinction between immediate and mediate experience, and this distinction was unsatisfactory because 'mediate experience' seems to be a contradiction in terms. How could physical science be observational, as all science must be, if its data were but mediate? How can data, the givens, be mediate? Avenarius—and thus Külpe and Titchener—talked about dependent and independent experience, avoiding this difficulty. Both psychology and physics work immediately with experience, but they regard it in different ways; physics takes the "point of view" of experience "regarded as independent of the experiencing individual," psychology the "point of view" of experience "regarded as dependent upon the experiencing individual." These terms are Titchener's. Titchener's fundamental theory was that there is a physical point of view, a psychological point of view and perhaps other points of view, like that of common sense or biology. The data of psychology therefore depend upon its point of view, Titchener thought, and the point of view thus becomes all-important in psychology.

This matter first became clear when Titchener coined the phrase *stimulus-error*. The psychologist commits the stimulus-error when he lapses from the psychological point of view into some other, like the physical. What is an error for the psychologist is, of course, not an error for the physicist, but Titchener was thinking only about psychology. Psychologists beyond Cornell's periphery seldom understood this distinction and regarded it as esoteric sophistry; but the distinction may have real meaning. For instance, in the determination of the two-point limen upon the skin, it is quite a serious matter whether the subject observes 'dependent' or 'independent' experience. In the first case, he sets himself to 'introspect'; if he feels only one sensory pattern, he reports *One*. He can, however, take the other point of view and try to say whether one or two points of the stimulus-object are in contact with the skin, and there are certain stretched-out patterns of 'oneness' that mean to him univocally stimulation by two points. In such a case he would report *Two*, meaning one pattern but two points. In other instances the difference is not plain; it is hard to tell in judging a color-match whether one is in his judgment referring to the colored stimuli or to the color sensations. Titchener, however, believed that there is always a difference, that a psychologist can always avoid the stimulus-error, and that the trained psychologist always does. It was the Gestalt psychologists who took the error out of the stimulus-error, who said that perceptual experience consists of objects, not of artifact-sensations. But to Titchener that was experimental phenomenology, not experimental psychology. Always is there the choice, he believed, between viewing the world psychologically and physically.

This distinction was extended when Titchener came to deal with thought. Ach's "awarenesses" were to him, not the data of consciousness but the meanings of those data. Meanings were for Titchener "logical" affairs that should be ruled out of psychology except as the psychologist tries to study the psychology of them. It is plain that Titchener thought of Ach's error as of the more general kind that includes the stimulus-error, in which the experiential data mean the stimulus and the stimulus is a particular meaning. If we avoid meanings altogether, except when they are carefully labeled as such, we shall avoid the stimulus-error in so doing. For this reason Titchener's use of meaning has also been attacked as esoteric and meaningless.

Thus Titchener came to stand for an uncompromising dualism, or perhaps even a pluralism, in scientific methodology. He was not seeking to raise or to answer the epistemological question. He believed, rightly or wrongly, that science could settle its own questions and leave epistemology alone. In the focus there was for him the 'psychological point of view' to be cultivated, a point of view which, while it gave only aspects of experience, seemed to yield a particular kind of data which was psychological and of which sensations, images and feelings are the types. On the periphery there were other kinds of data that could be observed: objects, stimuli, meanings, the data of physics.

The great dichotomy was between physics and psychology, but it is not clear that Titchener intended only a dualism. Meanings would not seem necessarily to belong in physics, but they certainly belonged for him outside of psychology. In these terms one can see what he meant by introspection as the method of psychology. We can see that he rejected animals, children and clinical patients as psychological subjects, because they could not introspect; that is to say, they could not be relied upon to make this dichotomy in their observations. We can see why he rejected behaviorism as abolishing the distinction, and why earlier he had no use for mental tests that deal with physical performance and not with conscious contents. Thus the entire work at Cornell and of those of Titchener's students who held to his teaching fell away from the remainder of American psychology and constituted what is really an independent school, although Titchener never gave it a name. It would have been less isolated in Germany but still quite distinct from the schools of Wundt and Külpe. G. E. Müller was closest to Titchener's position, and Ebbinghaus might have been had he lived.

This underlying 'epistemology' of Titchener's was, of course, not philosophically sophisticated. Ever since Locke, philosophers have concentrated upon this problem, and Mach and Avenarius are regarded today as naïve. Titchener, however, refused to admit that he was philosophizing; he held that he was forming a practical scientific distinction, and it is undoubtedly true that, if his position had been fruitful of scientific progress, the philosophers would have had to interpret it in their own terms.

Titchener was important in the history of American psychology because he staunchly represented this older conservative tradition against overwhelming numbers. West of the Atlantic in psychology there was 'America' and there was Titchener. Names often stand out in history because their owners have opposed something older; movements of thought are always movements away from other thought. However, in Titchener's case the situation was reversed. He has stood out in bold relief because every one near him moved away from him. If all movement is relative, then Titchener moved—backwards with respect to his advancing frame of reference.

To this fortuitous circumstance must be added the effect of Titchener's personality. His erudition, we have said, carried weight afar. At home he was able to impress his will and his views on his associates. His juniors regarded him with a mixture of admiration and fear. While they might glory in their minor heresies, they tended to accept the major structure of his system *ex cathedra*. He gave fifty-four doctorates in psychology during his thirty-five years at Cornell, a great personal achievement because most of these dissertations bore the stamp of his own thought. Some of the names, like Washburn, Pillsbury, Bentley, Gamble, Whipple, Baird, Hayes, Ferree and Dallenbach, later became prominent in the history of American psychology. The volume of Titchener's publication was large. Beside books, his bibliography lists 216 of his own articles and notes and 176 publications from the Cornell laboratory. His professional correspondence was also large. With his personal influence, with many students afield who had once come under it, with all this publication, with the contrast that he presented against the American background, he could not but be the most influential minority in America.

In his later years Titchener had been working on a "systematic psychology." His students envisioned some *magnum opus*, like Wundt's *Physiologische Psychologie*—"the last of the great systematic psychologies," they said. He was being thorough. In the fall of 1917 he announced to them that he had spent one day less than a year in understanding Husserl, that he now understood him, and that "there is nothing in him." Most of this work came out as articles in 1921-1922, and then the whole volume, edited by Weld, was issued posthumously in 1929. It was a little book, not at all an *opus*, and it did not take even Titchener's world by the ears. Somehow Titchenerism in America had been sustained by his magnificent personality. With his death it suddenly collapsed, dwindling rapidly from the status of a vital faith in the importance of consciousness to the equally essential but wholly inglorious state of having been an unavoidable phase of historical development.

THE PSYCHOLOGICAL PHYSIOLOGISTS

Thus far we have sought to catch for ourselves the spirit of the 'new' psychology as it came to life in the minds of certain men: Fechner, Helmholtz, Wundt, Hering, Müller, Stumpf, Ebbinghaus, Külpe, Titchener. For these men it was not merely a profession but also a purpose, no more a fact than an aspiration. In spite of very different temperaments, beliefs and forms of thought, they were all alike in their consciousness of assisting earnestly in the renaissance of psychology. Research might have led on to other research and an accumulating body of fact, and there might yet have been no psychology as we know it today had it not been for this unifying purpose, this conviction, with integrative force, that there was not to be simply more physiology and more philosophy, but a new scientific entity. The 'new' psychology was intensely self-conscious and personal, and it is for this reason that the biographical method of its exposition has seemed best.

Nevertheless it is clear that, while these separate biographical currents show the quality and the course of the stream, they do not truly describe its breadth. There were not a few men but many, not several lines of research but a multitude of experiments, that contributed to the new science and fixed its course. Of the particular researches in the different special fields we can not speak in this book. The histories of psychophysiological optics, of psychoacoustics, of reaction, of learning, of emotion, of thought, require special treatments in other volumes. On the other hand, it will not do for us to leave this whole campaign with only the accounts of what the generals did. We must at least call the roll of the colonels who fought and won or lost particular battles. We are speaking here only of the German campaign of the nineteenth century. What went on in Britain and America and what happened to experimental psychology in the twentieth century in western Europe and in America, all that is the content of subsequent chapters of this book.

In the first place we must note that when Wundt named the new psychology "physiological psychology," he was not merely giving expression to an epistemological conviction, but was describing the actual nature of the new psychology as the child of philosophy and physiology. At the start there were more physiologists than philosophers-turned-psychologist engaged in the new endeavor. The *Zeitschrift für Psychologie*, which began in 1890, had added to its title *und Physiologie der Sinnesorgane*, and its board of editors, picked as the most representative group outside of Leipzig, included six psychologically-minded physiologists (Aubert, Exner, Helmholtz, Hering, von Kries, Preyer), one physicist (König) and only four psychologists proper (Ebbinghaus, Lipps, Müller, Stumpf). Let us therefore call the roll of the physiologists who were also of the 'new' psychology and whom we have not yet met.

The list of course begins before Wundt. The early chapters of this book have dealt with that period. Johannes Müller, E. H. Weber and Helmholtz were psychological physiologists and, for the time being at least, made it respectable for a physiologist to concern himself with problems of mind. Weber would hardly be known today except for his psychological work.

Of Fechner's generation there had been *A. W. Volkmann* (1800-1877), who wrote the physiology of vision (1836) that Johannes Müller referred to in his *Handbuch*, who was professor of physiology at Halle for thirty-nine years (1837-1876), who wrote the section of vision in Wagner's *Handwörterbuch* (1846), who aided Fechner in his experiments on the method of average error (1856-1857) and who wrote a physiological optics (1863).

A little later there was *Karl von Vierordt* (1818-1884), the physiologist at Tübingen, who is known for his work on the time-sense (1868), and his many researches on vision, hearing and somesthesis. Titchener credits him with having formulated the method of right and wrong cases before Fechner. Vierordt comes into the picture more because of his research than because of his personality.

In the same way the Dutch oculist, *F. C. Donders* (1818-1889), requires mention because he made a contribution to the knowledge of visual accommodation and formulated the law of eye-movement that bears his name (1846), because he worked with reaction times (1865-1866) and gave his name to one of the methods of compound reactions, because of his studies of the nature of vowel sounds (1857-1870), and because of his discussion of color theory (1881-1884).

Hermann Aubert (1826-1892) is more nearly of a piece with the 'new' psychology. He was professor of physiology at Breslau and then at Rostock (1862-1892). At Breslau he wrote a *Physiologie der Netzhaut* (1865) and at Rostock a *Grundzüge der physiologischen Optik* (1876). He was noted for his basic research on visual adaptation (1865) and on indirect vision (1857-1865), the demonstration that Weber's fraction in vision varies with intensity (1865), his work on visual space perception (1857), cutaneous space perception (1858) and bodily orientation (1888). He was one of the first editors of the *Zeitschrift für Psychologie*.

Sigmund Exner (1846-1926) spent his academic life (1870-1926) at Vienna, where he was ultimately given the chair in physiology (1891). Beside extensive research on purely physiological problems, he is known for his early work on adaptation to hue (1868), his determination of the rate-threshold for pitch (1875) and his studies of apparent visual movement with two successive sparks (1875-1876). He gave the reaction experiment its name and noted, fifteen years ahead of Ludwig Lange, that reaction is largely automatic and depends on predisposition. That puts him into the history of the psychology of motivation. He too was one of the editors of the *Zeit-schrift*.

Julius Richard Ewald (1855-1921) was a physiologist who spent his academic life (1880-1921) at Strassburg, where he came presently to be the professor of physiology (1900). His special interest was the physiology of the end-organs and thus indirectly of sensation. He gave his name to the 'pressure-pattern' theory of hearing, a theory that is opposed to Helmholtz's, since it avoids the conception of resonating elements in the inner ear (1899-1903). He was another editor of the *Zeitschrift*.

Johannes von Kries (1853-1928) has probably had more influence on psychology than any other person thus far mentioned in this list. In his early days he was associated briefly with Helmholtz at Berlin (1876) and with the famous physiologist, Carl Ludwig, at Leipzig (1877-1880). After that he went to Freiburg (1880-1928), where he stayed for the remainder of a long, useful and influential life until his death in 1928. He is best known for his contributions to the physiology of vision, especially his *Duplicitätstheorie* that relates the retinal rods to twilight vision and the retinal cones to daylight vision (1894). He determined differential thresholds for hue (1882) and worked on color mixture with spectral lights (1881), and he also touched the problem of auditory localization (1878-1890). He wrote *Die Gesichtsempfindungen und ihre Analyse* (1882), more than a third of the sections on vision in Nagel's *Handbuch der Physiologie* (1905), many of the extensive additions to the third and posthumous edition of Helmholtz's *Physiologische Optik* (1910-1911), and finally, when he was seventy years old, an *Allgemeine Sinnesphysiologie* (1923). In spite of being a physiologist, he had a bit of the philosopher in him. As a young man he wrote an excellent but little-known book on the theory of probabilities (1886) and as an old man a logic (1916). He too was an original editor of the *Zeitschrift* and he really belongs more to the 'new' psychology than to physiology.

Arthur König (1856-1901) was a physicist at Berlin, Helmholtz's loyal supporter, who joined with Ebbinghaus in the foundation of the *Zeitschrift*. He published many careful measurements of color vision, the most noteworthy being his determination of the way in which the Weber fraction varies with visual intensity (1888), his working out of the curves of brightness as a function of wavelength (1884, 1891), and his establishment of curves of color sensitivity for trichromatic vision and for dichromatic (color-blind) vision (1886, 1892). It was he who established the function of visual purple in rod vision (1894). His many researches were collected and published posthumously. Immediately after Helmholtz's death he undertook the publication of the second edition of Helmholtz's *Physiologische Optik* (1896) and added to it his famous bibliography of vision, consisting of almost 8,000 titles. The range of this subject, even at that time, shows why so many of the psychological physiologists were primarily interested in problems of vision. König died when he was but forty-five years old before the full promise of his early work had been realized.

König was succeeded as the physiological editor-in-chief of the *Zeitschrift* by *Wilibald A. Nagel* (1870-1910), who was then at Berlin, but who later went to Rostock. He too was primarily interested in the topic of vision, as his many articles in the *Zeitschrift* attest, but he also accomplished considerable research in the sense-departments of taste, smell and touch. He edited an important *Handbuch der Physiologie*, of which the third volume (1905) is the standard handbook for the psychophysiology of sensation for that period. In it he himself wrote a small portion of the section on vision, and the sections on taste, smell, organic sensation and the specific energies of nerves. With von Kries and Gullstrand he was an editor of the third edition of Helmholtz's *Optik* and wrote some of the additions to the second volume (1911). He died when he was only forty.

We should also mention here *Armin von Tschermak* (1870-   ), who, after being *Dozent* at Leipzig and Halle, became *ausserordentlicher Professor* of physiology at Vienna (1906-1913) and professor at Prague (1913-   ). He was also on the board of the *Zeitschrift für Sinnesphysiologie*. He has contributed mostly to the psychology of vision and is best known for his work on light and dark adaptation (1902).

The authority on smell was the Dutch physiologist, *Hendrik Zwaardemaker* (1857-1930) who spent practically his entire academic life at Utrecht. He published the classical work on smell, *Die Physiologie des Geruchs* (1895). As we have already seen (pp. 113-114), there had up to that time been almost nothing scientific to say about smell. Now there was something, and Zwaardemaker, except for Hans Henning, has remained the authority on olfaction practically until the present. He published again on the subject thirty years later: *L'odorat* (1925). He was always in close touch with the 'new' psychology and became an editor of the *Zeitschrift für Sinnesphysiologie*, when that began as the second division of the *Zeitschrift für Psychologie*.

The authority on touch was the physiologist *Max von Frey* (1852-1932), a contemporary of Stumpf, Müller and Ebbinghaus. In 1882 he was habilitated as *Dozent* in physiology at Leipzig, where the great Ludwig was professor, being made *ausserordentlicher Professor* in 1891. He remained there until 1898, and during that period (1894-1897) he published his classical papers on cutaneous sensibility. Blix (1882) and Goldscheider (1884) had discovered the sensory spots in the skin. Von Frey confirmed their results, established pain as a fourth sense modality in addition to pressure, cold and warmth, suggested the identity of the sense organs for each of these four qualities (he was wrong; that was one of the lost battles), and established a number of important quantitative functions for cutaneous sensitivity. After a year at Zurich, von Frey went to Würzburg in 1899, where he continued to publish frequently on cutaneous and other somesthetic problems. It was, however, his early work which had the most influence for it gave a clear picture of the sense-physiology of the skin, which had theretofore not even had its problems clearly defined. After von Frey, the writers of psychological textbooks all knew what to say, by section and almost by paragraph, about the skin.

There was also the physiologist *William Preyer* (1842-1897), another original editor of the *Zeitschrift*. In his research he was more of a psychologist than a physiologist. He was one of the older men, younger than Wundt, older than Stumpf, Müller and Ebbinghaus. As a student he had worked at Bonn and then at Paris with Claude Bernard (1862-1865). He was *Dozent* at Jena (1866-1869) and then became professor of physiology there (1869-1888). Then he did an unusual thing; he resigned his chair at Jena because he preferred the intellectual atmosphere at Berlin and became *Dozent* there (1888-1893). Five years later he was overtaken by ill health and he died after four years of illness. His most important book is *Die Seele des Kindes* (1882 and later editions), and thereafter he occupied himself primarily with child psychology. In the earlier years he published research on color vision (especially 1868, 1881) and on hearing (1876, 1879). His determinations of the lower limits of hearing (with forks, reeds and difference tones) are classic. He was a friend of Fechner, and the correspondence between the two men from 1873 to 1882 has been published (1890).

It is plain that the 'new' psychology was really physiological psychology. The physiologists were having almost as much to do with it for a time as the psychologists proper. We have mentioned only those physiologists who were seriously involved in the new movement. There were many others less closely connected with it. For instance, in the volume of Hermann's *Handbuch der Physiologie* that deals with sensation (1879-1880), A. Fick of Würzburg and W. Kühne of Heidelberg supplemented Hering in the chapters on vision; V. Hensen of Kiel wrote the chapters on hearing and suggested a theory of hearing that is still cited; M. von Vintschgau of Innsbruck wrote the portion on taste and smell and is thus one of the classical sources for these modalities; and O. Funke of Freiburg wrote all of the section on touch except temperature, which Hering took.

THE PERIPHERY OF THE 'NEW' PSYCHOLOGY

Beside the physiologists, there were a number of psychologists who may be described as belonging more or less on the periphery of the new experimental psychology. There was Münsterberg, who began at the core but was lured to other interests in America. There were others of Wundt's students, who, for the most part, came after the newness of this movement had begun to wear off, or who were less important, or who settled down in some special field. There were also others like Lipps and Ziehen who were not experimental psychologists but were infected by the spirit of the times. And then there were the French psychologists, like Ribot and Binet, who belong properly in the French tradition, but who nevertheless were on the outskirts of the German movement. Let us call this roll, as we have called the roll of the physiologists.

Next to Fechner and Müller, the Belgian, *J. L. R. Delbœuf* (1831-1896) of Liège played the most important rôle in psychophysics. His important books were *Étude psychophysique* (1873) and *Théorie générale de la sensibilité* (1876). These two monographs were reprinted together as *Éléments de psychophysique* (1883) and followed by *Examen critique de la loi psychophysique* (1883). Psychophysics is a special field and we cannot enter into Delbœuf's work here. Perhaps the most important thing that came out of it was the new conception of the sense-distance, a conception that disposed of the objection to Fechner's measurement of sensation. Fechner had thought of sensations as magnitudes, quantities definitely related to a zero-point; and much of the resistance to Fechner, and thus to quantitative experimental psychology, was based upon the introspective fact that sensations are not given in consciousness as large or small (pp. 289-291). Delbœuf's notion that sensations, without being magnitudes, can nevertheless be arranged in a continuum so that there are observable degrees of distance between them met this objection;

and Titchener made much of the point when he came to write the *Experimental Psychology*. Actually Delbœuf's notion of sense-distance (*contraste sensible*) is basic to all measurement of sensation.

Theodor Lipps (1851-1914) was the only psychologist of the act school (unless we are to count Stumpf) who was included in the original editorial board of the *Zeitschrift*, the organ of the 'new' psychology outside of the sphere of Leipzig. Perhaps Lipps does not belong in this chapter, but in the next. It is hardly proper, however, to omit him, because his *Grundtatsachen des Seelenlebens* (1883) was a very important book that took account of all the 'new' psychology of that date and because his *Raumaesthetik* (1897) played into all the other work on optical illusions. He is best known for his esthetics. He was by temperament more of a logician than an experimentalist, and he wrote a logic (1893). He was very prolific. He was first at Bonn (1877-1890), then at Breslau (1890-1894) and then at Munich (1894-1914).

Theodor Ziehen (1862-   ) was a philosopher by predilection and for many years a psychiatrist by training and occupation. After studying philosophy at Würzburg (1881-1883) he turned to medicine at Berlin (1883-1885) and was appointed on the basis of his doctor's dissertation assistant in the psychiatric clinic at Jena, where he was also *Dozent*. He was at Jena for fourteen years as *Dozent* and *ausserordentlicher Professor* (1886-1900), and then became professor of psychiatry successively at Utrecht (1900-1903), Halle (1903-1904), and Berlin (1904-1912). During all this time he tried to lead the double life of a psychiatrist and a philosopher, but presently retired to Wiesbaden for five years (1912-1917) to devote himself entirely to philosophy. After that he became professor of philosophy at Halle until his final retirement in 1930. In the early days at Jena, he published a *Leitfaden der physiologischen Psychologie* (1891), a textbook of physiological psychology that, because of its clear and forceful style, reached a twelfth edition (1924). He signalized his return to philosophy by writing *Die Grundlagen der Psychologie*, 1915, a book which deals with the philosophical and epistemological bases of psychology. As a psychologist he was not a Wundtian, although he did much to popularize physiological psychology. He might be called an associationist but not an elementist. He wrote much in psychiatry and much in philosophy, as well as these two books about psychology.

Hugo Münsterberg (1863-1916) began his academic life as if he were to be one of the leaders of the new movement. Actually he was Wundt's student (1882-1885), although he showed the impress less than many others. After Leipzig he went to Heidelberg for study (1885-1887) and then selected Freiburg for his habilitation as *Dozent* (1887-1892). At Freiburg he published his *Beiträge zur experimentellen Psychologie* (1889-1892). He had developed a laboratory there, and his experiments were highly original and attracted considerable attention at the time. Much of the criticism was negative, and Titchener, then at Leipzig, took him to task for his misunderstanding of Wundt. G. E. Müller attacked him vigorously. On the other hand, William James, who had just published his famous *Principles of Psychology*, wrote Münsterberg congratulating him on his "sense for the perspective and proportion of things" which his critics lacked. James was so well impressed with Münsterberg that he finally succeeded in arranging to have Münsterberg come to Harvard for three years (1892-1895) with the hope that the appointment could be made permanent. The plan worked well; Münsterberg was offered a permanent professorship; he took two years in Germany to think it over, and finally he came to Harvard for the rest of his life (1897-1916). At Münsterberg's coming, James had his own title changed from "professor of psychology" back to "professor of philosophy," in order to give Münsterberg a clear field. Thus Münsterberg became the exponent of the new psychology at Harvard. As it happened, however, the original plan never worked out. Münsterberg regressed toward philosophy and the problems of theoretical psychology (his *Grundzüge der Psychologie* of 1900 is a thorough and 'sound' book) and progressed toward the application of psychology. There is, however, almost nothing of importance in experimental psychology connected with Münsterberg's name since the experiments in the *Beiträge* of the Freiburg days. What happened was that Münsterberg was too original; his energetic mind went on at once from experimental to still newer psychologies. He broke ground in psychotherapeutics, in juristic psychology and in industrial psychology. In a sense he 'founded' applied psychology. He was at times deep in the investigation of psychic research. Partly because of this and partly in addition to it, he became a public character, widely known and quoted. He was even sent abroad for a year (1910-1911) to help in founding an American Institute in Berlin, a quasi-diplomatic mission. Like many another important scientist Münsterberg was lured by public service and applause away from the narrowed life of a scientist, and the promise of Freiburg was never realized, although many other achievements were. Münsterberg died during the First World War, broken in spirit by the shattering of his dreams of *rapprochement* between

Germany and America and by the hostility of Americans to him in that period of fear of Germany.

None of Wundt's students played so important a rôle in establishing the new psychology as Külpe and Titchener. There was *Emil Kraepelin* (1856-1926) of Heidelberg (1890-1903) and Munich (1903-1926), but he was a psychiatrist. In fact, he had written a psychiatry (1883) when he was only twenty-seven years old, one that went into many editions. He was as distinguished as any of Wundt's pupils but not as an experimental psychologist, as the phrase is used.

There was *Ernst Meumann* (1862-1915), another pupil of Wundt's who, after moving from Leipzig to Zürich, to Königsberg, to Münster, to Halle, to Leipzig again, finally settled down at Hamburg (1911-1915); but he was claimed by educational psychology. His *Oekonomie und Technik des Lernens* (1903, with two revised editions and an English translation) was a classic in its field and showed the Wundtian tradition throughout. Nevertheless he never was assimilated by pedagogy. He founded the *Archiv für die gesamte Psychologie* in 1903, when Wundt gave up the *Philosophische Studien*. With Wundt he had worked on the time-sense, and an important piece of apparatus from this experiment bears his name. In his later years he published on esthetics. His death from influenza at the age of fifty-two was unexpected and cut short a life that promised much more than had been realized.

Then also among Wundt's pupils there were *Alfred Lehmann* (1858-1921) of Copenhagen, distinguished for his work on the method of expression; *August Kirschmann* (1860-1932), for a long time at Toronto, but later at Leipzig, and still remembered for his work with Wundt on color contrast; *Gustav Störring* (1860-1947), after Leipzig at Zürich, Leipzig, and Bonn, known to psychologists best for his psychopathology, but much more of a philosopher than anything else; and *Friedrich Kiesow* (1858-1940), for many years at Turin, known originally for his work with Wundt on taste, and after that for his studies in the tactual field.

Besides the Wundtians, there was *Friedrich Schumann* (1863-1940), whom we have already mentioned as Müller's and Stumpf's assistant. He is best known for his work on memory with Müller and for his studies of visual space-perception (1900-1904). For eighteen years he was at Frankfurt (1910-1928) and had there a very influential laboratory. It was in his laboratory that Wertheimer, supported presently by both Köhler and Koffka but not by Schumann, brought Gestalt psychology forth in 1912. There was also *William Stern* (1871-1938), who did not come from Leipzig but studied at Berlin successively with Ebbinghaus and Stumpf. He is noted for his differential psychology and his educational psychology, but experimentalists also remember his psychophysical work and his invention of the tone-variator that bears his name (1898).

Outside of Germany, the new psychology was welcomed in America, and that story we leave to later chapters. In England it has never been truly welcomed, although Cambridge has at last accepted it, University College, London, admits it, and even conservative Oxford has finally given it a chair (1947). In France it has always also been somewhat out of place, for France plays its major part in the history of psychology within the more strictly physiological psychology and in psychopathology, where she assumes a leading rôle. France had *Théodule Armand Ribot* (1839-1916), who undertook to interpret the new psychologies of England (1870) and Germany (1879) to his country, and who wrote many books on psychology thereafter. He was not an experimentalist. He knew Charcot, and Janet was his pupil. *Alfred Binet* (1857-1911), director of the psychological laboratory at the Sorbonne (1892-1911), came a little nearer the German tradition in some of his experimental work. On the whole, however, he is rightly placed by his early concern in the psychology of reasoning (1886), which led him to his famous study of intelligence (1903) and thus to the Binet scale for measuring intelligence, an achievement that has made his name familiar to laymen all over the world.

This ends our lists. These vignettes show the range and the ramifications of this 'new' psychology. It seemed then a great new thing. Some men were immersed in it. Others were drawn but partly into it. Still others, indisposed for it by temperament or training or environment, were, nevertheless, forced to take account of it. No one could write psychology and ignore it. Brentano harked back to Aristotle, but he drew pictures of optical illusions. Empiricism had become experimentalism, and the world had to go along, for the times do not stand still and a man writes more or less of the age in which he writes.

NOTES

The text encounters a difficulty of terminology. The 'new' psychology was experimental, physiological psychology, but it was in a great degree linked with a systematic position that has never been given a generally accepted name. This position is typified by the systematic position of Wundt, but in the hands of others it became a much broader thing than Wundt alone made it. To call it 'sensationistic' or 'associationistic' psychology is to limit it too narrowly; to call it 'elementistic' is to include too much and also to give it the wrong emphasis. The author has chosen the word *content*, because content (*Inhalt*) has historically been opposed to act. Külpe and Messer finally tried to resolve the division within psychology by placing content and act (or function) side by side within psychology. If the reader prefers another name for this position, the author will have no quarrel with him, and he therefore undertakes to list the possible choices.

G. E. Müller at one time placed the word *Komplextheorie* in opposition to *Gestalttheorie*, but the word *complexes* has a meaning pre-empted by psychoanalysis and lacks the general sanction of *contents*. Titchener similarly once used for this position the term '*structural*' *psychology;* unfortunately, however, this term has become ambiguous, because *Gestaltpsychologie* has been called *Strukturpsychologie,* and (alas for clarity!) *Gestaltpsychologie* was even once translated into English as "structural psychology," thus adopting the name of its chief enemy. *Verbindungspsychologie* stresses Wundt's fundamental principle of mental connections, but the term does not pass well into English. The psychologist of this school usually talked about his data as 'conscious processes,' and the school might be called 'process' psychology. The author dislikes this term because the word *process* (*Vorgang*) was invented as a persistent assertion of the fluidity of the mental elements, that is to say, as an answer to the criticism of elementism; and yet the conscious data in the hands of this school were always becoming more or less fixed and stable in spite of being called 'processes.' In America the adjectives *introspective* and *introspectional* were frequently used by behavioristically minded psychologists for their opponents, but it does not seem desirable to go to America for a name when America, except for Titchener, held so inconstantly to the German tradition. There is no similar stress upon the word *Selbstbeobachtung* in Germany. There remains

existential, an adjective which Woodworth has applied to Titchener's psychology, because Titchener was arguing that the content of consciousness which exists (in the sense of standing up under observation like the sensory processes and unlike the acts) is best characterized as existential; but the term has not caught on and is meaningless until explained.

The whole difficulty arises because this school, that took its origin from Wundt, never regarded itself as a school of psychology, but simply as one with experimental psychology. All heretics need names in order to set themselves off from orthodoxy; but the conservatives need no name for themselves and never recognize the imminence of a revolution by adopting one. It is impracticable to name a group which will not accept the name. This very fact is, however, an important historical datum. Orthodox experimental psychology, even in its systematic tenets, was a self-conscious school only as against philosophy. It never felt the need of any other name than "psychology," which it carried away from philosophy when the two separated. The enemies of this orthodox psychology came it, but always in accordance with what they most dislike in it.

Ebbinghaus

On Hermann Ebbinghaus' life, see the memorial in *Chronik vereinigten Universitäts Halle-Wittenberg,* 1908-1909, 21-24; E. R. Jaensch, *Zsch. Psychol.,* 1909, 51, iii-viii; D. Shakow, Hermann Ebbinghaus, *Amer. J. Psychol.,* 1930, 42, 505-518; R. S. Woodworth, *J. Philos.,* 1909, 6, 253-256. Woodworth gives the essential bibliography. On Ebbinghaus' place in psychology, see also G. Murphy, *Historical Introduction to Modern Psychology,* 2 ed., 1949, 174-181.

Ebbinghaus' dissertation is *Ueber die Hartmannsche Philosophie des Unbewussten,* 1873, the year of Stumpf's *Raumvorstellung* and G. E. Müller's *Aufmerksamkeit.*

Ueber das Gedächtnis, 1885, was translated in 1913 into English under the title *Memory*, and valuable excerpts from the Eng. trans. are reprinted by W. Dennis, *Readings in the History of Psychology*, 1948, 304-313. The two pioneers in the experimental investigation of memory are Ebbinghaus and G. E. Müller. Ebbinghaus got his inspiration from Fechner; Müller inherited the leadership in psychophysics from Fechner. It has been a matter of comment, therefore, that neither of these men transposed the psychophysical methods intact upon the problem of memory, determining by them mnemonic limens and thus securing much greater mathematical precision for their measurements. Attempts to use the psychophysical *Konstanzmethode* for memory have, however, shown that the work involved is tedious and thus often impracticable; perhaps both Ebbinghaus and Müller knew this fact. Cf. H. D. Williams, On the calculation of an associative limen, *Amer. J. Psychol.*, 1918, 29, 219-226.

The two experimental papers on brightness and the paper on color theory are: Die Gesetzmässigkeit des Helligskeitscontrastes, *Sitzungsber. preuss. Akad. Wiss. Berlin*, 1887, 995-1009; Ueber den Grund der Abweichungen von dem Weber'schen Gesetz bei Lichtempfindungen, *[Pflüger's] Arch. ges. Physiol.*, 1889, 45, 113-133; Theorie des Farbensehens, *Zsch. Psychol.*, 1893, 5, 145-238.

The paper on the completion test is Ueber eine neue Methode zur Prüfung geistiger Fähigkeiten und ihre Anwendung bei Schulkindern, *Zsch. Psychol.*, 1897, 13, 401-459. For the brief French account, see *Rev. sci.*, 1897, 4 sér., 8, 424-430.

The big textbook is *Grundzüge der Psychologie*. The first half of vol. I appeared in 1897; the whole of vol. I in 1902, the 2 ed. of vol. I in 1905; the first *Lieferung* of vol. II in 1908; the 3 ed. of vol. I, ed. by E. Dürr, in 1911; what is really the 1 ed. of vol. II, completed by Dürr, in 1913; the 4 ed. of vol. I, ed. by K. Bühler, in 1919.

The little textbook is *Abriss der Psychologie*. It was first published as the section on psychology in P. Hinneberg's *Die Kultur der Gegenwart*, 1907, I, vi, 173-246. The 1 ed. of the *Abriss*, so entitled, is 1908; 2 ed., 1909; Eng. trans., 1908; French trans., 1910. Dürr published 3, 4 and 5 eds. (1910-1914), and the series kept on to the 8 ed. in 1922. Many American psychologists used it for learning German.

The high esteem in which Ebbinghaus was held by contemporary psychologists is shown by the eulogistic remarks of the conservative E. B. Titchener, The past decade in experimental psychology, *Amer. J. Psychol.*, 1910, 21, 404-421, esp. 405. This was Titchener's address at Clark University's vigentennial celebration in 1909, when Stanley Hall invited Freud and Jung to America to make American psychologists aware of the meaning of psychoanalysis. Ebbinghaus was also to have been present and to have spoken. Titchener had in his audience, besides Hall, Freud and Jung, William James, J. McK. Cattell, Franz Boas, Adolph Meyer, H. S. Jennings, C. E. Seashore, Joseph Jastrow, Ernest Jones and E. B. Holt. He said: "When the cable brought the news, last February, that Ebbinghaus was dead, just a month after the celebration of his fifty-ninth birthday, the feeling that took precedence even of personal sorrow was the wonder what experimental psychology would do without him." Titchener spoke of Ebbinghaus' "instinctive grasp of the scientific aspect of a problem," his "perfect clarity of thought and language," his "easy mastery of the facts." "There was about Ebbinghaus," said Titchener, "a sort of masterfulness; he never did violence to facts, but he marshalled them; he made them stand and deliver; he took from them, as of right, all they contained; and with the tribute thus exacted he built up his theories and his system." Had Ebbinghaus lived, Titchener thought, his place in psychology would have been comparable to Wundt's and to Brentano's.

Mach

On Mach in general, see H. Henning, *Ernst Mach, als Philosoph*

Physiker und Psycholog, 1915. The book gives a bibliography.

Mach's important experimental contribution to psychology is the *Grundlinien der Lehre von den Bewegungsempfindungen*, 1875.

By far his most important book is *Die Analyse der Empfindungen und das Verhältnis des Psychischen zum Physischen*, 1886, 2 ed., 1900, 6 ed., 1911, Eng. trans. of 1 ed., 1897, of 5 ed., 1914. Less well known is *Erkenntnis und Irrtum, Skizzen zur Psychologie der Forschung*, 1905, 2 ed., 1906.

We ought also to mention here Mach's popular scientific lectures, which were popular in form and enjoyed popularity among the public: *Populär-wissenschaftliche Vorlesungen*, 1895, 5 ed., 1923, Eng. trans. of 1 ed., 1895, of 4 ed., 1910. These lectures contain, however, only a little psychological material.

Mach openly acknowledged the practical identity of his theory with Avenarius' by devoting chap. iii of the 2 ed. of the *Analyse der Empfindungen* to the subject.

Limits of space have made it impracticable to illustrate in the text Mach's vivid manner of arguing for sensations as the only materials of science. The reader must go to the *Analyse* for himself; for instance, to the classic picture (chap. 1, fig. 1) of Mach's real world as he lies on his sofa: parts of the room, framed above by an eye-brow and below by a mustache.

On Mach and Pearson, on their notions of correlation in relation to Humian causality, see the notes on Hume, p. 202 *supra*. Mach recognized his debt to Hume in the dedication of *Erkenntnis und Irrtum*.

For a clear and interesting modern treatment of Mach's philosophy of science and his relation to positivism and the unity-of-science movement, see Philipp Frank, *Modern Science and Its Philosophy*, 1949, 6-19, 61-89.

Avenarius

There is a brief, partly biographical account of Richard Avenarius in H.

Höffding, *Moderne Philosophen*, 1905, 117-127, Eng. trans., 130-140.

As the text has already said, Avenarius' great book was the *Kritik der reinen Erfahrung*, 1888, I, 1890, II. Secondary sources upon this difficult work are: F. Carstanjen, *Mind*, 1897, N.S. 6, 449-475; H. Delacroix, *Rev. métaphys. morale*, 1897, 5, 764-779; 1898, 6, 61-102; W. T. Bush, Avenarius and the standpoint of pure experience, *Columbia Univ. Contrib. Philos. Psychol.*, 1905, 10, no 4 (also recorded as *Arch. Philos.*, no. 2).

For Wundt's polemic against Avenarius, see *Philos. Stud.*, 1896, 13, 1-105.

Külpe

For biographical accounts of Oswald Külpe, see C. Bäumker, *Jhrbh. bayr. Akad. Wiss.*, 1916, 73-102, which contains a bibliography of sixty titles compiled by Bühler; K. Bühler, *Lebensläufe aus Franken*, 1922, II, 243-255; and an anonymous memorial, presumably by a colleague, in the *Jhrbh. Ludwig-Maximillians Universität München*, 1914-1919 (publ. 1927), 25-29. Unfortunately all these sources are relatively inaccessible. More accessible, but less complete, is A. Fischer, *Zsch. päd. Psychol.*, 1916, 17, 96-99. Külpe's doctoral dissertation, when published as a separate, has a *Vita*.

Certainly there is no readily available bibliography. The author therefore gives below a list of twenty-seven publications, which are mentioned directly or indirectly in the text or are items that seem generally to be considered important.

1887. Zur Theorie der sinnlichen Gefühle (dissertation), *Vtljsch. wiss. Philos.*, 11, 424-482; also separate with *Vita*.

1888-1889. Die Lehre vom Willen in der neueren Philosophie (Habilitationsschrift), *Philos. Stud.*, 5, 179-244, 381-446.

1891. Ueber die Gleichzeitigkeit und Ungleichzeitigkeit von Bewegungen, *Philos. Stud.*, 6, 514-535; 7, 147-168.

1893 *Grundriss der Psychologie;* Eng. trans., 1895.

1894. Aussichten der experimentellen Psychologie, *Philos. Monatshefte*, 30, 281-294.

1895. *Einleitung in die Philosophie;* successive editions in 1898, 1903, 1907, 1910, 1913, and (7 ed.) 1915; also posthumous eds. by Messer; Eng. trans., 1897 and 1901.

1897. Zur Lehre der Aufmerksamkeit, *Zsch. Philos. u. philos. Kritik,* 110, 7-39.

1899. Die ästhetische Gerechtigkeit, *Preuss. Jhrbh.,* 98, 264-293.

1899. Ueber den associativen Faktor des ästhetischen Eindrucks, *Vtljsch. wiss. Philos.,* 23, 145-183.

1900. *Welche Moral ist heutzutage die beste?*

1902. *Die Philosophie der Gegenwart in Deutschland;* successive editions in 1903, 1905, 1911 and (5 ed.) 1914; Eng. trans., 1913.

1902. Zur Frage nach der Beziehung der ebenmerklichen zu den übermerklichen Unterschieden, *Philos. Stud.,* 18, 328-346.

1902. Ueber die Objektivierung und Subjektivierung von Sinneseindrücken, *Philos. Stud.,* 19, 508-556.

1903. Ein Beitrag zur experimentellen Aesthetik, *Amer. J. Psychol.,* 14, 479-495 (Stanley Hall Commemorative Volume).

1904. Versuche über Abstraktion, *Ber. I Kongr. exper. Psychol.,* 56-68.

1907. *Immanuel Kant, Darstellung und Würdigung;* 2 ed., 1908; 3 ed., 1912.

1908. Ein Beitrag zur Gefühlslehre, *III internat. Kongr. Philos.,* 1909, 546-555.

1909. Zur Psychologie der Gefühle, *VI Congr. internat. psychol.,* 1910, 183-196.

1910. Pour la psychologie du sentiment, *J. psychol. norm. pathol.,* 7, 1-13.

1910. *Erkenntnistheorie und Naturwissenschaft.*

1912. *Die Realisierung: ein Beitrag zur Grundlegung der Realwissenschaften,* vol. I. Vols. II and III were published posthumously under Messer's editorship in 1920 and 1923, respectively

1912. Contribution to the history of the concept of reality, *Philos. Rev.,* 21, 1-10.

1912. *Psychologie und Medizin.*

1912. Ueber die moderne Psychologie des Denkens, *Internat. Monatschr. Wiss., Kunst Technik,* 6 1069-1110. Reprinted in 2 ed. of *Vorlesungen,* 1922, *v. infra.*

1915. Zur Kategorienlehre, *Sitzber. bayr. Akad. Wiss. München (philos.-philol. Kl.),* 1915, no. 5.

1915. *Die Ethik und der Krieg.*

1920. *Vorlesungen über Psychologie,* posthumous, edited from MS. by K. Bühler. The 2 ed., 1922, pp. 297-331, has added the article Ueber die moderne Psychologie des Denkens (1912, *supra*) in lieu of the missing chapter on thought.

For Külpe's work in esthetics, see A. A. Bäumler and Th. Ziehen, *Zsch. Aesthetik,* 1916, 11, 193-197.

The reader can discover the effects of Külpe's experiments on abstraction (1904) by reference to C. Rahn, *Psychol. Monog.,* 1913, 16 (no. 67), esp. 76-85; and to E. B. Titchener, *Amer. J. Psychol.,* 1915, 26, 262-264.

On the similarity of Külpe to Husserl, see H. Schräder, *Die Theorie des Denkens bei Külpe und bei Husserl,* 1924.

The author here makes acknowledgment to Professor R. M. Ogden of Cornell for the transcription of certain of his letters from Külpe about the psychology of thought.

Würzburg School

The publications cited in the text as constituting the printed record of Külpe's 'Würzburg school' of imageless thought are as follows:

A. Mayer and J. Orth, Zur qualitativen Untersuchung der Associationen, *Zsch. Psychol.,* 1901, 26, 1-13.

K. Marbe, *Experimentell-psychologische Untersuchungen über das*

Urteil, eine Einleitung in die Logik, 1901.

J. Orth, *Gefühl und Bewusstseinslage,* 1903.

H. J. Watt, Experimentelle Beiträge zur einer Theorie des Denkens, *Arch. ges. Psychol.,* 1905, 4, 289-436.

N. Ach, *Ueber die Willenstätigkeit und das Denken,* 1905.

A. Messer, Experimentell-psychologische Untersuchungen über das Denken, *Arch. ges. Psychol.,* 1906, 8, 1-224.

K. Bühler, Tatsachen und Probleme zu einer Psychologie der Denkvorgänge: I. Ueber Gedanken, *Arch. ges. Psychol.,* 1907, 9, 297-305; II. Ueber Gedankenzusammenhänge, *ibid.,* 1908, 12, 1-23; III. Ueber Gedankenerrinerungen, *ibid.,* 24-92.

It was Bühler's papers that touched off the criticism. Wundt specifically objected to Bühler's method: *Arch. ges. Psychol.,* 1908, 11, 445-459. E. Dürr, one of Bühler's observers, was moved to differ from Bühler in his interpretations: *Zsch. Psychol.,* 1908, 49, 313-340. E. von Aster criticized the entire movement: *ibid.,* 56-107. To these papers Bühler replied: *ibid.,* 1909, 51, 108-118.

In America the effect of the work of the school as a whole was considerable. E. B. Titchener at Cornell summarized and criticized the work in his *Lectures on the Experimental Psychology of the Thought-Processes,* 1909, esp. lectures iii and iv, and he undertook constructive research by way of his students in 1909-1911. Subsequently J. W. Baird, once regarded as Titchener's most representative follower, made 'systematic experimental introspection' of the 'higher mental processes' the central topic of the Clark laboratory.

On the distinction between *Beschreibung* and *Kundgabe,* which is mentioned in the text, see Titchener, Description vs. statement of meaning, *Amer. J. Psychol.,* 1912, 23, 165-182.

In general on the Würzburg school, besides Titchener, *loc. cit.,* see G. Murphy, *Historical Introduction to Modern Psychology,* 2 ed., 1949, 225-233; J. C. Flugel, *A Hundred Years of Psychology,* 1933, 233-240.

Titchener

The most complete biographical sketch of Edward Bradford Titchener is the author's, *Amer. J. Psychol.,* 1927, 38, 489-506. (On the similarity of Titchener to Wundt, mentioned in the text, see pp. 442 f.) See also the sketches by H. C. Warren, *Science,* 1927, 66, 208 f., and C. S. Myers, *Brit. J. Psychol.,* 1928, 18, 460-463; and for a picture of Titchener at Leipzig, F. Angell, *J. Gen. Psychol.,* 1928, 1, 195-198.

For a complete bibliography of Titchener's publications and the publications from the Cornell laboratory, see W. S. Foster, *Studies in Psychology: Titchener Commemorative Volume,* 1917, 323-337 (which extends to 1917) and K. M. Dallenbach, *Amer. J. Psychol.,* 1928, 40, 120-125 (which brings the list up to the time of Titchener's death).

For a list of the students who took the doctorate with him, see K. M. Dallenbach, *Amer. J. Psychol.,* 1927, 38, 506.

For the comments of other authors on Titchener and his school, see esp. R. S. Woodworth, *Contemporary Schools of Psychology,* 1 ed., 1931, 18-42 (the 2 ed., 1948, 26-30, is skimpy because Titchener was ceasing to be contemporary); E. Heidbreder, *Seven Psychologies,* 1933, 113-151. G. Murphy, *Historical Introduction to Modern Psychology,* 2 ed., 1949, 210-216, is too brief, as are most of the other accounts.

Titchener's books are: *An Outline of Psychology,* 1896, 2 ed., 1899, Russian trans., 1898, Italian trans., 1902; *A Primer of Psychology,* 1898, 2 ed., 1899, Spanish trans., 1903, Japanese trans., 1904, 1907; *Experimental Psychology: A Manual of Laboratory Practice,* I, i (*Qualitative, Student's Manual*), 1901; ii (*Qualitative, Instructor's Manual*), 1901; II, i (*Quantitative, Student's Manual*), 1905; ii (*Quanti-*

tative, Instructor's Manual), 1905; Lectures on the Elementary Psychology of Feeling and Attention, 1908; Lectures on the Experimental Psychology of the Thought-Processes, 1909; A Text-Book of Psychology, 1909-1910, German trans., 1910-1912, Russian trans., 1914; A Beginner's Psychology, 1915. For his diligent translation of the work of others in his younger days Titchener was rewarded by much translation of his own books when he came to write them.

Titchener's first psychological research is Zur Chronometrie des Erkennungsactes, Philos. Stud., 1892, 8, 138-144; and his doctor's dissertation is Ueber binoculare Wirkungen monocularer Reize, ibid., 231-310. There is a separate of the dissertation with a Vita.

For Titchener's controversy with Baldwin on the reaction times, see J. M. Baldwin, Psychol. Rev., 1895, 2, 259-273; Titchener, Mind, 1895, N.S. 4, 74-81, 506-514; Baldwin, ibid., 1896, N.S. 5, 81-89; Titchener, ibid., 236-241. This controversy was resolved in a wise and, after the fact, an obvious manner by J. R. Angell and A. W. Moore, Psychol. Rev., 1896, 3, 245-258. On this belief and its implications, see E. G. Boring, The psychology of controversy, Psychol. Rev., 1929, 36, 97-121, esp. 111 f.

Weld entitled Titchener's posthumous volume Systematic Psychology: Prolegomena, for that is all it was. It came out in 1929, and parts already printed were in Amer. J. Psychol., 1921-1922, vols. 32-33.

The history of Titchener's fundamental dichotomy between psychology and not-psychology has not been fully worked out. It begins with Mach and Avenarius whom Titchener read in Leipzig. The text has omitted mention of the next step, Titchener's opposition of "structural psychology" to the "functional psychology" which was formulated at Chicago. The casus belli was John Dewey's Reflex arc concept in psychology, Psychol. Rev., 1896, 3, 357-370. Titchener replied with The postulates of a structural psychol-

ogy, Philos. Rev., 1898, 7, 449-465, and later, Structural and functional psychology, ibid., 1899, 8, 290-299. The first of these papers is reprinted by W. Dennis, Readings in the History of Psychology, 1948, 366-376.

The next dichotomy was that implied in the use of the term stimulus-error. On it see Titchener, Experimental Psychology, II, i, pp. xxvi f.; Text-Book of Psychology, 202 f. The author has discussed the meaning of the stimulus-error in E. G. Boring, The stimulus-error, Amer. J. Psychol., 1921, 32, 449-471, but the reader must be warned that Titchener expressly repudiated this interpretation of the stimulus-error, although not in print. Cf. also M. Bentley, Field of Psychology, 1924, 411 f. Titchener referred the notion of the stimulus-error to von Kries, but he was only modestly seeking the inevitable historical antecedent for his own idea. For other references to Titchener's use of the "stimulus-error" and for the reference to von Kries, see Boring, op. cit., 451.

On the dichotomy between mental process and meaning, and therefore for the context theory of meaning, see Titchener, Thought-Processes, 174-194, esp. 174-184; Text-Book, 364-373; also for a terse statement that had Titchener's approval, H. P. Weld, Titchener Commemorative Volume (op. cit.), 181 f. Jacobson's experiments left an opening for an attack from Würzburg, and Titchener sought to repair the gap in his clearest presentation of this dichotomy, Description vs. statement of meaning, Amer. J. Psychol., 1912, 23, 165-182. This entire matter becomes clearer in connection with Titchener's contemporaneous articles on introspection: Prolegomena to a study of introspection, ibid., 427-448; The schema of introspection, ibid., 485-508. It has been complained that Titchener and other psychologists have tended to use the word meaning ambiguously and too generally, as an escape from trouble; cf. M. W. Calkins, ibid., 1927, 39, 7-22.

There is no printed record of what Titchener conceived phenomenology to be; but for what Titchener thought Husserl thought, see Titchener, Sys-

tematic Psychology (op. cit.), 213-218.

The student of Titchener's psychology will find many articles relevant to the subject-matter of the text which are not mentioned here. He should consult Titchener's bibliography, *locc. citt.* Here too he can find the references to the Cornell experimental studies cited, or in the index of the *Amer. J. Psychol.* (vols. 1-30, 1926; 31-50, 1942).

Psychological Physiologists

It would unduly encumber these notes to give here the references to the important psychological publications of all the men mentioned in the text as psychological physiologists. The text gives some titles and many dates. The student who wishes to go further can find most of the references for the nineteenth century by author and date in B. Rand's bibliography in J. M. Baldwin's *Dictionary of Philosophy and Psychology*, 1905, III, ii. For titles after 1894 he can consult the *Psychological Index*. For the period after 1890, the indices of the *Zsch. Psychol.* are a great help to the many articles published or reviewed there. These indices were published for successive groups of twenty-five volumes in 1902, 1909, 1918 and 1927. A surprising number of these references can also be found by way of the author indices in E. B. Titchener's *Experimental Psychology*, 1901, I, ii, and 1905, II, ii; R. S. Woodworth's *Experimental Psychology*, 1938 (see also the 1729 titles in the bibliography); E. G. Boring's *Sensation and Perception in the History of Experimental Psychology*, 1942. On vision, *cf.* König's bibliography in H. v. Helmholtz, *Physiologische Optik*, 2 ed., 1896, 1017-1310.

The text names thirteen psychophysiologists or psychophysicists who belong in this section. The author does not know of good, readily accessible biographies of Volkmann, Vierordt, Donders, Aubert, Exner, Nagel and Tschermak. Before 1890 there was not the same care given to *Nachrufe* for psychology's great as there was after

the professional journals had got going. There are, however, six men for whom biographical references can be given.

Ewald: M. Gildmeister, Julius Richard Ewald, *Zsch. Sinnesphysiol.*, 1921, 53, 123-128.

Von Kries: E. v. Skramlik, Johannes v. Kries, *ibid.*, 1929, 60, 249-255.

König: H. Ebbinghaus and J. A. Barth, Arthur König, *Zsch. Psychol.*, 1901, 27, 145-147.

Zwaardemaker: there is an autobiography in C. Murchison, *Psychology in Autobiography*, 1930, I, 491-516; see also G. Grijns, In memoriam H. Zwaardemaker, *Arch. néerl. physiol.*, 1931, 16, 1-5; A. K. M. Noyons, Hendrik Zwaardemaker 1857-1930, *Amer. J. Psychol.*, 1931, 43, 525 f.

Von Frey: E. G. Boring, Max von Frey 1852-1932, *Amer. J. Psychol.*, 1932, 44, 584-586; R. Pauli, Die Erforschung der Haut- und Muskelempfindungen: Max v. Frey zum Gedächtnis, *Arch. ges. Psychol.*, 1933, 88, 231-252.

Preyer: his letters with Fechner bear on this early period before he turned to child psychology; see K. v. Vierordt, *Wissenschaftliche Briefe von Gustav Theodor Fechner und W. Preyer*, 1890.

Periphery of the 'New' Psychology

In general see the bibliographical sources cited in the preceding section of these notes.

It is easy to find some bibliographical material on all fourteen of the men named in the text except Lehmann.

Delboeuf: on his work, see E. B. Titchener, *Experimental Psychology*, 1905, II, ii, using the index but noting esp. pp. cxvii-cxxii, 211-218; for G. S. Hall's casual biography, see *Amer. J. Psychol.*, 1896, 8, 142; 1897, 8, 312.

Lipps: G. Anschütz, Theodor Lipps *Arch. ges. Psychol.*, 1915, 34, 1-13 (bibliography of 53 titles); E. v. Aster, Theodor Lipps, *Zsch. Psychol.*, 1915, 70, 429-433. A brief anonymous note in English occurs in *Amer. J. Psychol.*, 1915, 26, 160.

Ziehen: there is an autobiography in R. Schmidt, *Philosophie der Gegen-*

wart in Selbstdarstellungen, 1923, IV, 219-236 (also separate; bibliography of 36 titles); Eng. trans., in C. Murchison, *Psychology in Autobiography*, 1930, I, 471-489.

Münsterberg: Margaret Münsterberg (his daughter), *Hugo Münsterberg: His Life and Work*, 1922, which gives a personal rather than academic account but adds an appendix on his writings. There is an instructive review of this book by Frank Angell, *Amer. J. Psychol.*, 1923, 34, 123-125. War feeling forestalled eulogy when he died.

Kraepelin: W. Wirth, Emil Kraepelin zum Gedächtnis, *Arch. ges. Psychol.*, 1927, 58, pp. i-xxxii.

Meumann: G. Störring, Nachruf für E. Meumann, *Arch. ges. Psychol.*, 1915, 34, pp. i-xiv (bibliography of 51 titles); Ernst Meumann 1862-1915, *Amer. J. Psychol.*, 1923, 34, 271-274; also a little anonymous note in *Amer. J. Psychol.*, 1915, 26, 472.

Kirschmann: W. Wirth, Zum Gedächtnis August Kirschmann, *Arch. ges. Psychol.*, 1933, 88, 321 f.

Störring: W. Wirth, Gustav Störring zum 80. Geburtstag, *Arch. ges. Psychol.*, 1940, 107, 384-391; K. Fischer, Ueber Gustav Störring's Lebenswerk, *ibid.*, 392-410.

Kiesow: the autobiography is in Murchison, *op. cit.*, I, 163-190; then there are W. Wirth, Friedrich Kiesow zum 70. Geburtstag, *Arch. ges. Psychol.*, 1928, 65, 1-6; M. Ponzo, Friedrich Kiesow Nachruf, *ibid.*, 1941, 108, pp. v f.

Schumann: W. Metzger, Friedrich Schumann ein Nachruf, *Zsch. Psychol.*, 1940, 148, 1-18.

Stern: the autobiography is in Schmidt, *op. cit.*, 1927, VI, 129-184 (also separate); Eng. trans. in Murchison, *op. cit.*, 1930, I, 335-388; see also G. W. Allport, William Stern 1871-1938, *Amer. J. Psychol.*, 1938, 51, 770-773.

Ribot: the accounts of him are short and inadequate as they are for many who died during the First World War. E. Claparède, Théodule Ribot, *Arch. psychol.*, 1916, 16, 194-196; J. W. Baird, Théodule Armand Ribot 1839-1916, *Amer. J. Psychol.*, 1917, 28, 312 f.

Binet: E. Claparède, Alfred Binet 1857-1911, *Arch. psychol.*, 1911, 11, 376-388; T. Simon, Alfred Binet, *L'année Psychol.*, 1912, 18, 1-14; J Larguier des Bancels, L'œuvre d'Alfred Binet, *ibid.*, 15-32; R. Soucek, Alfred Binet et l'école de Brentano, *J. psychol. norm. pathol.*, 1924, 21, 883-888.

CHAPTER 19

Act Psychology and the Austrian School

Systematically the two foci of German psychology at the end of the last century were, as we have seen, act and content, the one represented by Brentano, the other by Wundt. The preceding chapter has shown how the psychology of content and the experimental method came to be associated. The historical fact is that content has lent itself persistently to experimentation, whereas act has not. It is tempting to imagine that this difference is fundamental to the nature of act and content, but one must not conclude too readily that the accidents of historical association are necessary and causal. The fact is that the acts were the older concepts and thus associated with philosophy which, when it deals with the mind, is nonexperimental. The contents, on the other hand, had come out of the newer analytical empiricism and so in the new psychology turned up in the hands of the experimentalists. Presumably act psychology could have developed into the modern dynamic psychology of behavior and purposive conduct without there ever having been a psychology of content. There might then never have been those many years of introspective experimentation when observers spent long hours learning to label the bits of their consciousnesses as these and those sensations, images and feelings.

Sometimes this school of act has been called the *Austrian school*. Geographical distinctions of this sort are seldom precise, and yet there is no doubt that the proper home of the act, in the period of which we are speaking, was in Austria and adjacent southern Germany.

When the Austrian school went beyond systematization and argument to fields that more properly belong within experimental psychology, it generally worked with the problems of space-perception and such related problems as esthetics. There is no mystery about this specialization. The problem of perception is the fundamental psychological problem that immediately lends itself to experimental and quasi-experimental demonstration. The school of content, by its union with sensory physiology, was led thence to the investigation of sensation and then went on to other subject-matters, endeavoring to bring all problems under the experimental method. Act psychology, with no conscious desire to be always physiological or experimental and with no heritage of analysis from associationism, could afford to experiment with perception and then to leave off.

The most definite point of contact at the end of the last century between the Austrian psychology and experimental psychology lay in the doctrine of form-qualities (*Gestaltqualitäten*). This doctrine, which we shall consider presently, both met and criticized the view of perception as a composite of elementary sensations, the view that represented the current position of the school of content. Out of the school of form-qualities came systematically the modern Gestalt psychology and also some of the experimental work on perception that properly belongs to this school. Lipps at Munich represented another connection, because of his broad interests, his influence in the 'new' psychology, and his work in space-perception and in esthetics. Later we find at Graz the experimental work of Benussi on perception and the development of those bipartite psychologies of act and content that we came across in our account of Külpe in the preceding chapter.

One sees what is meant by the Austrian school if one considers both men and universities. The important names are Brentano, Lipps, Meinong, Ehrenfels, Cornelius, Witasek and Benussi. Stumpf comes into the list incidentally as Brentano's pupil, leaning systematically toward the act. Külpe comes in on the periphery, and with him Messer, because of their later systematic views. Mach had something to do with the form-qualities because he wrote of 'sensations of space' in his *Analyse*. The Austrian universities important for psychology were Vienna, Graz and Prague. (The only others in Austria were Innsbruck and Cracow.) Munich in southern Bavaria in Germany must be added to this list. It is tempting to add Würzburg, also in Bavaria, because of the relation of Brentano, Stumpf and Külpe to Würzburg, but one must beware of placing too much emphasis upon the relation of geography to philosophical point of view. Now let us sketch the picture.

Brentano was in Vienna from 1874 to 1894. Mach was at Prague, where he wrote his books that have influenced psychology the most, and he came to Vienna just after Brentano left. Meinong was a student of Brentano's at Vienna from the time that Brentano went there; he was *Dozent* at Vienna; he went to Graz in 1882, established there the first Austrian psychological laboratory in 1894, and remained there until his death in 1920. Ehrenfels was a student of

Brentano's at Vienna about the time Meinong went to Graz; then he was *Dozent* at Graz, then *Dozent* at Vienna, and finally professor at Prague. Witasek and Benussi were younger and studied with Meinong, not with Brentano. Witasek was at Graz from about 1900 until his death in 1915; Benussi was at Graz a little later, and went to Italy before his death in 1927. These men—Brentano, Meinong, Ehrenfels, Witasek and Benussi at Vienna, Graz and Prague—are the outstanding figures of the Austrian school. Closely allied to them, however, are Lipps and Cornelius. Lipps succeeded Stumpf at Munich in 1894 and remained there until his death in 1914. Cornelius had been at Munich in Stumpf's time and remained there with Lipps until 1910 when he went to Frankfurt.

As we have said, the first important thing that came out of this skein of relationships was the doctrine of form-qualities. We must now see what this doctrine was.

FORM-QUALITIES

The elementism of the psychology of content led to an equivocal conception of perception. On the formal systematic side, perception was thought of as a composite of sensations. Perception was the compound and sensations were the elements. This view of perception is quite clear in the fusions and in the complications. A tone is a sensation, but, if two tones are given simultaneously, there is something new, the perception of a tonal fusion. Add to the sensations from the retina the sensations of accommodation and convergence of the eyes, and one gets the visual-kinesthetic perception of seen depth, a complication.

This chemical view of perception—what Wertheimer later called an *Und-Verbindung*, meaning mere addition of elements without integration—might have been satisfactory for a time had it not been for the fact that most of the problems of perception have actually been problems of space-perception, and that there were some problems of temporal perception that presented the same difficulties as did the spatial ones. Space and time have troubled the psychologist as well as the philosopher. Külpe made for them the separate perceptual class of colligations. Titchener derived them from sensory attributes coordinate with quality and intensity. Other psychologists have given them special status.

The difficulty is at once apparent if one considers the case of spatial form in two dimensions—that is to say, independently of its complication by the factors that yield depth and distance. Sensations have ordinarily been distinguished by the elementists in terms of quality. If one sees a red dot near a black dot, one would be said to have two sensations simultaneously. But suppose that one sees two black dots near each other. Does one have two sensations of the same quality? It seems incorrect to say that the two black dots are one sensation and the white background a second. Yet if one calls the two black dots different sensations, then it is plain that we are distinguishing between elements on the basis of spatial separation and not on the basis of quality. The difficulty is not solved if we agree to base elementism on space as well as quality. Join the black dots by a black line, and what does one have? One sensation instead of two, or a row of sensations? If a row, how many sensations are there? What limits an element spatially?

This dilemma was never finally resolved by elementism, and in fact it was ordinarily not even clearly realized until modern Gestalt psychology pointed it out. Research in perception went on, and the results were in general cast as nearly in the terms of sensational compounds as proved possible.

Ernst Mach, as we have seen, wrote the *Analyse der Empfindungen* at Prague in 1886 (p. 395). In this influential book, Mach identified experience with sensations, making sensations into the observational data of both physics and psychology. Such a course is plainly an uncritical use of the term *sensation,* and Mach felt no hesitation in extending the concept to include differences in space and in time as well as in quality. He spoke of "sensations of space-form," like a circle, and "sensations of time-form," like the succession of intervals in a melody. What he meant was, of course, that form is in itself an experience independent of quality. You can change the color or the size of a circle without changing its circularity, its space-form; you can change by transposition the actual notes of a melody without changing the melody, its time-form. Form is independently experienced; experience is sensation; therefore there are sensations of form.

It remained for *Christian von Ehrenfels* (1859-1932) to give this naïve theory systematic formulation. Ehrenfels had been with Brentano at Vienna and with Meinong at Graz, and had returned again to Vienna as *Dozent* when in 1890 he published a paper that created the concept of form-quality (*Gestaltqualität*). His problem was to answer the question as to whether form in space and time is a new quality or a combination of other qualities, and he decided in favor of the former view. A square can be formed of four lines. They are the sensations that underlie the perception of the square and can thus be called for this perception the *Fundamente;* or, all together, they may be said to constitute the *Grundlage*. However, 'squareness' inheres in no one of these elementary *Fundamente*. Only when they are brought together as a *Grundlage* does squareness appear, and, since the form is obviously immediately experienced, it must be a new element, a form-quality.

Ehrenfels elaborated the system much further. He distinguished two classes of form-qualities, the temporal and the non-temporal. The temporal form-qualities included musical melody, 'color-melody' and any changing temporal course of sensation, like reddening or cooling. The non-temporal form-qualities were mostly spatial but included also tonal fusions, clang tints, flavors and the perception of movement. In all these cases the existence of form-qualities can be demonstrated by independent variability: if the qualities of the *Fundamente* can change without changing the form, then there must be an independent form-quality.

Ehrenfels also noted that the relationship of *Grundlage* to form-quality occurs at various levels. There are higher orders of form-qualities, which may have as their *Fundamente* the form-qualities of lower levels. One may get the higher orders by comparison, as of one melody with another, or by combination, as of melodies in a polyphonic composition. These complications of the system need not concern us further than to indicate the great scope of the new conception.

This theory of Ehrenfels is a logical analysis of certain perceptions, based upon argument with an empirical, but not an experimental, basis. Such a method is the usual method of act psychology, but there is no immediate necessity for a relationship between form-qualities and psychical acts. The form-qualities themselves were really new elementary contents and might have been created by the other school. As a matter of fact, however, Ehrenfels, in the Austrian environment, related them to the acts. It is, he thought, the mental activity of comparing or of combining that elicits the form-quality from the *Grundlage*. One can see how real these acts can become to the psychologist by mentally creating a square out of four dots and noting the experience of combining that is involved.

It is important to note at this point that Ehrenfels did not say that the form-quality arises out of the relations among the *Fundamente*. It is obvious that four lines do not yield a square unless they are given in a certain relation to one another, and it is tempting therefore to conclude that the form-quality is the relation and is given independently of the *Fundamente*. Ehrenfels, however, thought of the form-quality as distinctly secondary to the *Funda-*

mente, as variable independently of them but not independently given. He may have been wrong, but that is not the point.

It is also interesting to note here the inertia of the *Zeitgeist.* Ehrenfels had the insight that Wundtian elementism will not work, and he might have thrown the whole business of analysis overboard then and there as Wertheimer did twenty years later—he might have done that had it not been too big a step for him to take. He advanced psychology a little but kept a firm hold on the past. He was not a phenomenologist and could not see how to get along without elements. So he kept the primary elements and added new secondary elements, thinking of the properties of the wholes as if they were added on to the parts of which the wholes are made. That is why Gestalt psychology later insisted that the original parts disappear in the whole, are not simply added to by whatever it is that emerges new when the whole is formed.

Ehrenfels' system was next elaborated by *Alexius Meinong* (1853-1920), Brentano's pupil and the leader of the school at Graz. Meinong's view differed in its fundamentals but little from Ehrenfels', but it used a new terminology. Meinong spoke of founding contents (*fundierende Inhalte*) and of founded contents (*fundierte Inhalte*). Ehrenfels' *Fundamente* were Meinong's founding contents, and his form-quality was Meinong's founded content. The relation of the two kinds of contents is relative and hierarchical, and the founding contents may be called *inferiora* and the founded content a *superius.*

In Meinong's view the founding and founded contents together may be said to form a complexion, and he spoke of both real complexions which are equivalent to perceptions and ideal complexions which are equivalent to conceptions. Complexions, he thought, are formed by acts of founding, but the real complexion (perception) is dependent primarily upon the relationships inherent in the perceived object, whereas the ideal complexion (conception) depends primarily on the act of founding. Here, then, we get the recognition of the importance of the relationships between the primary members of the perception, a recognition that was lacking in Ehrenfels. We get also, in the ideal complexions, a further emphasis upon the importance of the act.

Meinong recognized the relativity of this mental hierarchy. There may be, he thought, complexions of higher orders in which the *superiora* of lower complexions become the *inferiora* of higher complexions in the founding of a still higher *superius.*

Meinong, for all that he founded the first Austrian laboratory at Graz (1894), was a philosopher and not an experimental psychologist. He was a man of great ability and influence, and his espousal of the form-qualities did much to establish them in psychology.

On this showing it begins to look as if the psychology of perception might have been getting out of the hands of the psychologists of content. It is true that the form-quality was only a new elementary content, but it seemed to require an act of founding to account for it. However, the argument was brought back nearer the traditional position of the experimentalists by *Hans Cornelius* (1863-) at Munich. Munich was just beyond the periphery of Austria, intellectually as well as geographically. Cornelius was at Munich when Stumpf was there and became *Dozent* when Lipps came there from Breslau. He is a philosopher and not a psychologist, but the fact was no bar to his participation in this argument.

In general Cornelius supported Meinong, but he suggested two significant changes in the system. In the first place, he held that the form-quality is not a founded content but a *founded attribute*. In the second place, he said that it is not so much that these attributes are founded by an act of founding as that they are disestablished by analytical attention. Experience is ordinarily given, he observed, in great unanalyzed wholes which possess characteristics that pertain to the wholes. Attention to the parts destroys the whole and abolishes its founded attributes.

There may seem to be little more than a verbal difference between Meinong and Cornelius, but words can be important. The school of content claimed the ability to deal with attributes and with attention, whereas it denied the existence of new non-sensory elements and of acts, like the act of founding. There was nothing incompatible with orthodox elementism in saying that the compounds may have secondary attributes that belong only to the compounds or to admit attention into the system as a principle of explanation. Attention, of course, could not by a Wundtian be thought of as an act; nevertheless it is true that it has always occupied an equivocal status between act and content, a fact that modern Gestalt psychology has used as a criticism of orthodox elementism.

Thus it was possible for Schumann, then Stumpf's assistant at Berlin, to seem effectually to dismiss the heterodox form-quality by his classical experimental studies of visual form. These papers study and analyze into their conditions a very great many visual forms and illusions without finding a necessity for appealing to the concept of form-quality. Schumann referred the phenomena in gen-

eral to the objective conditions in the stimulus and to the effect of
attention. His results were not speculative but an interpretation of
experimental observations. Thus he came to the conclusion that a
visual perception of form is a grouping under the laws of attention,
a grouping which is dependent in part upon the objective conditions and in part on the attentional attitude of the observer. It may
involve certain subjective additions, like the tied images of perceptual completion, and a certain subjective selectiveness. Many
perceptions depend upon the direction of attention to the 'total impression' and are altered by an analytical attention. Eye-movements
may play a rôle, but in general Schumann thought them much less
important than did Wundt. The perception, then, is a composite,
but it has unity because attention tends to combine it into a group
and also to abstract from those parts that are not essential to the
perception.

It is true that Schumann called attention an act. It is also true
there was nothing fundamentally incompatible in his findings with
the Austrian position. Nevertheless, because he was experimental in
his method, because he used familiar terms, because he avoided speculation and pure argument and did not seek to establish a system of
act, his work, which is hardly more than the experimental test and
extension of Cornelius, was taken as a refutation of the doctrine of
the form-quality.

The school of form-quality belongs to the 1890s, when Ehrenfels, Meinong and Cornelius wrote their papers. The point of view
was kept alive in the next decade by Meinong's pupils, Stephan
Witasek (1870-1915) and Vittorio Benussi (1878-1927). In general Witasek's contributions were systematic, both in his textbook
of psychology and in his handbook on visual space-perception. His
psychology of perception was built around the effect of the psychical act of producing. The resulting complexions may be, he
thought, simple (as in clangs or simple melodies) where the founding is practically automatic, or they may be complex (as in polyphonic composition). In the latter case the complexion is determined
both by external factors in the stimulus-object and by the internal
act of producing. Benussi was an able experimenter, in fact, the
most productive and effective experimental psychologist that
Austria had had. His researches were almost entirely upon problems of visual and somesthetic perception, and there is a long and
important list of them. They contain a theory of perception, but
for the most part they represent simply psychophysical work
placed in the systematic setting of the Austrian school.

If one takes the larger view of this movement, it becomes apparent that, although it was checked at the end of the century, its force persisted. The movement, within act psychology, attracted the attention of the elementists because it claimed the discovery of a new element. It seemed for the time being that the movement had failed, because the alleged element did not gain acceptance, because alternative modes of explaining the fact presented themselves, and because the members of the Austrian school itself shifted from an emphasis upon form-qualities to a discussion of complexions which, except for their dependence upon acts, were not necessarily unlike the composite perceptions of the school of content.

On the other hand, it is apparent now that the doctrine of form-quality was at bottom a criticism of elementism, which failed in its original form because it added merely a new element instead of offering a new view of psychological analysis. The same criticism of elementism with a new remedy was offered in 1912 by Gestalt psychology. Thus the movements of *Gestaltqualität* and *Gestaltpsychologie* have a common negative motivation in seeking to correct an untenable psychological chemistry, and a common positive aspect in choosing the field of perception as the ground of controversy. They are quite unlike in that the former sought to solve the dilemma by finding a new element, whereas the latter denies the validity of assuming the existence of real elements. The reader may take his choice as to whether he will consider the new school as the improved form of the old or as an entirely new movement. There can, however, be no question that Gestalt psychology was a new and independent movement in both thought and personnel, in so far as anything is ever new in the slow but sure evolution of the *Zeitgeist*. Ehrenfels made progress; Wertheimer made more; but J. S. Mill and Wundt had already begun to move in this direction. The most '*undlich*' of *Und-Verbindungen* are to be found in James Mill.

PSYCHOLOGIES OF ACT AND CONTENT

Act and content were in Europe the two horns of a dilemma. The empiricist, who has his attention always on the nature of his own consciousness, is driven to accept activity as the essence of mind. The experimentalist accepts content because he can work with it, and, having accepted it, introspection of his own consciousness may fail to convince him of the validity of the act as mental stuff. The empiricist accuses the experimentalist of being prejudiced by his method. The experimentalist replies that casual empirical observation has always failed to yield the truth and that science resorts to experiment for this reason. The difference arises because the act is impalpable and the content palpable. The act eludes direct observation but comes to consciousness in retrospect with the assurance of its just having been there. The content, being sensory in its essence, stands up for introspection. But this difference was not recognized at first when the *impasse* between the two contentions developed. Let us see how resolution of the contradiction came about.

In the first place, we must note that there was some movement of act psychologists toward the experimental method. Brentano was sympathetic with the new experimental psychology. Meinong founded a laboratory. Witasek's psychology, like Lipps', tended to deal with the data of experimental psychology. Witasek was definitely of the school of Brentano and Meinong, although he granted contents as well as acts in psychology. His experiments on space perception are especially interesting, for the results were translated into terms of act. Benussi, as we have said, carried this tendency further. He also was of the school of Brentano and Meinong, but he was primarily an experimentalist and only indirectly a systematist. In Witasek and Benussi it becomes clear that most of the data of perception can be expressed in terms of act. One needs only to consider the ordinary psychophysical experiment to see what happens. Such an experiment involves judgments as its data. The psychologist of content treats these judgments as observations of what is judged. The psychologist of act stresses the judging and not its content. Even Wundt thought that Weber's law holds between sensations and the judgments of them, not between stimuli and their sensations. Nevertheless, for all this work, integration of the two opposing views never went far in the hands of the Austrians.

A movement that has progressed further has been the forced marriage between act and content. Külpe led in this movement, although Messer gave the most complete example of it. The influence of Husserl was behind it, largely because Külpe and Messer took Husserl very seriously. This new view simply brings both act and content into psychology and leaves them there, to be dealt with, side by side. The result might be called a bipartite psychology, since there are now two kinds of very different materials, impalpable acts and palpable contents, to be wrought into a systematic whole. We may examine such a union in the hands of Messer, who wrote the only complete book from this dual point of view.

August Messer (1867-1937) was a philosopher with psychological interests, who as a student at Giessen came under the influence of the philosopher Schiller. After his student days, he occupied for a few years teaching posts in several *Gymnasien* and then, in 1899, became *Dozent* in philosophy at Giessen. He was made *ausserordentlicher Professor* there in 1904 and professor in 1910. The first *Kongress für experimentelle Psychologie* met at Giessen in 1904, and there Külpe read his paper on *Versuche über Abstraktion*, to which we have already referred (pp. 401 f.). Messer was much impressed by Külpe's outlook on philosophy and psychology and decided to engage in work under his direction. Accordingly he spent the summer semester of 1905 with Külpe at Würzburg, and, as we now know, his *Experimentell-psychologische Untersuchungen über das Denken* (1906) was the result, one of the important studies of the Würzburg school (p. 406). Messer's interests lay as much in epistemology as in psychology, and Külpe's interests were then becoming very much the same. Messer was only five years Külpe's junior and an intellectual friendship sprang up between the two men. In 1908 Messer published *Empfindung und Denken*, a book that grew out of his work at Würzburg. In it he attempted to formulate the alternative to sensationism by a discussion of such problems as perception, meaning, attention, abstraction, judgment and thought—topics which can be made to fall within the borderland between psychology and epistemology. One gets the beginning of his dichotomy between content and act in his chapters on sensory elements and thought elements in perception. Thus Messer was greatly impressed by Külpe's *Die Realisierung*, of which Külpe published the first volume, the only volume which he himself completed, in 1912. In these days Külpe had come over to the dual point of view, as his posthumous *Vorlesungen* show. Messer made that approach to psychology explicit in his *Psychologie* of 1914 (second edition, 1920). Priority of explicit publication is therefore Messer's. Külpe originally was his inspiration. We do not know how much each got from the other in their friendly intercourse between Giessen and Würzburg, seventy-five miles apart, and, since no one else has raised the question, we do not need to raise it ourselves.

The marriage of act and content, which Messer accomplished, was somewhat more than a mere juxtaposition of incompatibles. Messer held that psychology deals only with intentional experiences, 'acts' taken in a broad sense. However, he argued, such experiences involve both an impalpable activity ('act' taken in a narrower sense) and the palpable content of the act. Psychology must therefore consider both, extending its scope from the contents to include the acts.

He distinguished three kinds of intentional experiences: knowing (consciousness of object), feeling (consciousness of state) and willing (consciousness of cause). For each of these classes he discussed both the elements of content and the elements of act that enter into them.

The contents of knowing were for him the sensations, the images, the temporal and spatial contents, and the impressions. Sensations and images are the obvious sensory material of which he was trying to take account. To spatial and temporal experience, always trouble-makers for the systematist, he gave palpable status, much as Külpe had done in making them sensory attributes. Messer's impressions were the palpable relations, experiences like *similar, different, greater, less* and their kind. Even the experimental psychophysicist has been bothered by the exclusion of such data from the inventory of the palpable, for they seem introspectively to be more like immediate experience than mere judgments of contents. Messer, then, was very generous to the contents, but he could afford to be because he had so much left to say about the acts. To the acts of knowing he gave an elaborate logical treatment. They are perception and its two opposites, memory and imagination, all of which are characterized by having a content; and there is also the coordinate system for thinking of present object, of past object and of a construct, which have, however, no content. At the higher levels of complexity the acts become involved. Relating and comparing are simple acts of knowing; so are the paired opposites, affirmation and negation; so too would seem to be the series of acts from conviction to conjecture, a series which marks affirmation or negation with its degree. Judgment involves all of these acts, as does also its opposite, supposal.

Feeling has sensations as contents, and affective preference and feelings of value as acts. The simple feelings, which have made so much difficulty for the psychologists of content, are placed by Messer on the border-line, as being sometimes contents, but sometimes also, in so far as they are impalpable, acts.

Willing has sensations for contents. It has appetition, desire and will for acts. Conation is equivocal, like the simple feelings; in part it is sensation, in part act.

Such is Messer's 'bipartite' psychology. The term is applicable, for act and content are for him not only as different as the impalpable and the palpable, but in particular cases they may be separable. If you wish to know what content is like without act, you have only, Messer thought, to consider the margin of consciousness where bare, meaningless content occurs. If you wish to know act without content, you need only examine imageless thought.

The relevancy of such a system to experimental psychology lies not in any positive contribution, but in the removal of constraints. As long as mind was thought to have to be all act or all content, act psychology came to be, for the most part, opposed to experimental psychology. In a system like Messer's, content psychology, and thus the traditional experimental psychology, is given a clean bill of health and allowed to go about its business as long as it does not interfere with its partner in psychology.

It is plain from Külpe's posthumous and incomplete *Vorlesungen* (1920) that he was going the same way as Messer. One gets in this book very much more of the Wundtian tone, as one would expect from the author of the *Grundriss*, written in Leipzig in 1893. However, Külpe had come a long way in twenty years. The outcome of Würzburg had driven him toward Brentano and Husserl. To his earlier psychology Külpe added the acts (although, like Stumpf, he called them functions), just as Messer had added contents to acts.

To the present author, the most interesting thing in Külpe's book is his effort to give the criteria of difference between content and function. Here it seems almost as if Külpe, the experimentalist, had caught the will-o'the-wisp of all experimentalists, the impalpable moment of mind.

In brief, Külpe's argument runs thus. Content and function are different facts of mental life. (1) They must be different because they are demonstrably separable in experience. Content occurs with but little function in dreams and in the bare givenness of an object; and function occurs with but little content in acts like bare noticing or bare expecting where there is no object. (2) Moreover, the two are independently variable. Content changes without function when one perceives one sense-object and then another, keeping on perceiving all the time. Function changes without content when one successively perceives, recognizes and judges the same sensory content. (This is not Brentano's doctrine, where the separation of act and content is much less sharp.) (3) Moreover, content and function are characteristically different. Contents are analyzable in consciousness, whereas functions are not, for analysis alters the function but not the content. Thus contents are observable by introspection, but functions only by retrospection. Moreover, contents are relatively stable and functions are relatively instable. In these characteristics one comes to see just what has been meant by the impalpability (*Unanschaulichkeit*) of the functions or acts. (4) Contents and functions alike have both intensity and quality, but there is no relationship between the two classes. Qualitative differences among functions mean nothing for qualitative differences among contents, nor is an intense tone in any way comparable to an intense desire. Duration, however, they possess in common: the tone and the desire may be compared in their temporal persistence. (5) Finally, Külpe tells us that contents and functions can be distinguished because they obey different laws. The laws of content are association, fusion, contrast, relation to stimulus and sense-organ, and psychological correlation in general. The laws of function include the facts of the effect of a point of view or *Aufgabe*, the laws of the determining tendency. Here Külpe had only the discoveries of the Würzburg school to draw upon for the laws of function, but he doubtless thought that these laws would multiply when more experiments had been undertaken upon the impalpable functions.

Külpe's early death is much to be regretted. One feels that, if he had lived to complete and work over this new psychology, he might have ended by making the acts seem much more reasonable. As it is, one gets glimmerings of what might have happened, but no clear insight. Of course what did happen is another matter: experimental phenomenology and Gestalt psychology sprang up. These movements worked experimentally with acts and contents without so naming them because they admit all classes of experience into consideration. We shall come back to Gestalt psychology later (pp. 587-619). We must turn next to modern British psychology, where the Austrians were not without influence.

We may close the present chapter with a semantic key to the varying terminology of the act psychologists and to their epistemo-

Semantic Key

THE SUBJECT-MATTER OF PSYCHOLOGY IS PRINTED IN CAPITALS.

Thus the lines inclose the field of psychology.
The subject-matter of physics is printed in italics.
The subject-matter of phenomenology is printed in roman.

	SUBJECT-MATTER OF PSYCHOLOGY	Intentional Data	Other Available Data	
			Content as data	Other data not within psychology
BRENTANO	ACT	= ACT	→ *Content*	
STUMPF	FUNCTION	= FUNCTION	↔ Phenomena	
WITASEK	MIND	= ACT	+ CONTENT	*Physical da*
HUSSERL	ACT	= ACT	→ *Content*	Phenomena
MESSER	ACT (broadly)	= ACT (narrowly)	+ CONTENT	*Physical da*
KÜLPE	CONSCIOUSNESS	= FUNCTION	+ CONTENT	*Physical da*

logical views as to what constitutes the subject-matter of psychology. The different views are confusing and a schema aids clarity even though it may imply a false rigidity. Lipps is omitted from this table because he called the subject-matter of psychology content and described it as act, so that it is impossible to decide in which column to place him.

Now from the perspective of the present we can see that the bipartite psychologies were never destined to persist. They had in them the lethal gene of elementism. To settle the problem of whether psychology deals with contents or acts by saying merely that we will compromise by having both is sheer eclectic laziness. It remained for the Gestalt psychologists to pay the price of content in order to have the prize which Külpe and the others sought.

NOTES

It is interesting to study Austro-German psychology with one's eye on the map. The tendency has been for experimental psychology to thrive better in the north and for act psychology to flourish in the south, although of course act and experiment are not necessarily incompatible. For instance, one can arbitrarily draw a line from Metz to Warsaw, leaving Vienna, Graz, Prague, Munich and Würzburg to the south, and Leipzig, Göttingen, Berlin, Frankfurt and Marburg to the north. If one tried to draw a picture of the psychology of each of these artificial groups, one would draw very different pictures, although one would by no means have created a clear dichotomy. It is Stumpf at Berlin who spoils this generalization. A *gemütlich* act psychologist did not fit in Prussia.

In Austria and southern Germany the influence of the Catholic Church is great. The psychology of Aristotle adapted to the modern world by Brentano is the appropriate psychology for this region. Act fits the Church better than content, for it tends less toward a mechanistic and therefore a deterministic psychology. Experimental psychology has to be deterministic. It is impossible to know just how much religious faith and scientific faith are connected, but one should not expect complete dissociation in psychology.

We have already seen how Brentano's psychological career was twice dramatically affected by the Church, and Stumpf also felt its influence.

Ehrenfels

Christian von Ehrenfels (1859-1932) was Brentano's student at Vienna (1882-1885), then associated with Meinong as *Dozent* at Graz (1885-1888), then *Dozent* at Vienna (1889-1896), then *ausserordentlicher Professor* at Prague (1896-1900) and professor (1900-1932). He was a man of broad cultural interests, and his important writings have to do with the drama, Wagner, sexual ethics, the theory of values and cosmogony. He comes into the history of psychology only incidentally as the originator of the doctrine of form-qualities. This paper of his is: Ueber Gestaltqualitäten, *Vtljsch. wiss. Philos.*, 1890, 14, 249-292.

When Ehrenfels died in 1932, the Gestalt-psychologist editors of the *Psychologische Forschung* printed this tribute: "Sadly we note the death of Chr. von Ehrenfels. For him no separate memorial is required, for in most of the psychological work of the present day there live the consequences of his work"; *Psychol. Forsch.*, 1933, 18, 1.

Meinong

Alexius Meinong (1853-1920) was a student at Vienna (1870-1878), whom Brentano, when he came there in 1874, interested in philosophy. Meinong, after he had taken his degree in philosophy, remained at Vienna as *Dozent* (1878-1882), and then was *ausserordentlicher Professor* (1882-1889) and later professor (1889-1920) at Graz, where he founded the first Austrian laboratory of psychology (1894). For his own sketch of his life and evaluation of his work, see R. Schmidt, *Philosophie der Gegenwart in Selbstdarstellungen*, 1923, I, 101-160 (also separate). This gives a selected bibliography; for a complete bibliography, see his *Gesammelte Abhandlungen*, 1914, I, 631-634, or 1913, II, 551-554 (the two lists are the same). This first volume is *Abhandlungen zur Psychologie* and contains most of the psychological papers. See also A. Höfler's account, Meinongs Psychologie, *Zsch. Psychol.*, 1921, 86, 368-374.

Meinong's field was theoretical psychology and the theory of knowledge. A very great deal of his work was psychological, and he has had much influence wherever the Austrian school has been influential (*e.g.*, on Ward and Stout in England). He was one of the editors of the *Zeitschrift für Psychologie*. His name is associated with psychophysics because of his discussion of Weber's law and of mental measurement in general, for mental measurement raises an epistemological problem. His contributions to the doctrine of form-qualities are to be found in Zur Psychologie der Komplexionen und Relationen, *Zsch. Psychol.*, 1891, 2, 245-265; Ueber Gegenstände höherer Ordnung und deren Verhältnis zur inneren Wahrnehmung, *ibid.*, 1899 11, 180-272.

Incidentally it may be remarked that *fundirende und fundirte Inhalte* should be translated as "founding and founded contents" and not as "funding and funded contents" (*cf.* Bentley, *op. cit. infra.*). It was tempting to the elementists to think that Meinong meant by his verb "founding" (as in a foun-

dry)=fusing, and hence a fusion=fund (*fundo, fundere, fusum*), whereas he really meant "found" in the sense of forming a fundamental basis or foundation (*fundo, fundare, fundatum*).

Cornelius

Hans Cornelius (1863-   ), after studying first mathematics and physics and then chemistry, became *Dozent* in philosophy at Munich (1894-1903) in the year that Lipps replaced Stumpf at Munich. Stumpf brought him to philosophy, but there was no sympathy between Lipps and Cornelius. The latter was later *ausserordentlicher Professor* of philosophy at Munich (1903-1910) and then professor of philosophy at Frankfurt (1910-   ). For his own account of his life and work, see Schmidt, *op. cit.*, 1923, II, 83-102 (also separate), which includes a short bibliography of his writings. His chief work was epistemological and philosophical, but he thrice contributed importantly to theoretical psychology. For his views referred to in the text, see especially Ueber Verschmelzung und Analyse, *Vtljsch. wiss. Philos.*, 1892, 16, 404-446; 1893, 17, 30-75; but for the more general systematic discussion of these matters, see his *Psychologie als Erfahrungswissenschaft* (a general textbook of psychology), 1897, 128-235, esp. 164-168; *Zsch. Psychol.*, 1900, 24, 117-141.

Schumann

We have already referred to Friedrich Schumann (1863-1940) in the two preceding chapters (pp. 370, 429). He was at Göttingen (1881-1894), Berlin (1894-1905), Zürich (1905-1910) and Frankfurt (1910-1928). His classical papers on visual space-perception are: Beiträge zur Analyse der Gesichtswahrnehmungen, *Zsch. Psychol.*, 1900, 23, 1-32; 1900, 24, 1-33; 1902, 30, 241-291, 321-339; 1904, 36, 161-185.

Witasek

Stephan Witasek (1870-1915) spent his academic life at Graz. He was *Do-*

zent there (1900) and was later given the title of professor. The author knows of no account of his life or work. He was primarily a psychologist, with incidental interests in educational psychology, esthetics and ethics. His most important writings are his textbook of psychology and his psychology of visual space-perception (both cited below). For his views on complexions and the act of producing, see his Beiträge zur Psychologie der Komplexionen, *Zsch. Psychol.*, 1897, 14, 401-435; *Grundlinien der Psychologie*, 1908, 222-246; *Psychologie der Raumwahrnehmung des Auges*, 1910, 291-338. It is the *Grundlinien*, of course, that most clearly represents his bipartite psychology of act and content, on which *cf.* E. B. Titchener, *Systematic Psychology: Prolegomena*, 1929, 197-201, 226-235.

Benussi

Vittorio Benussi (1878-1927) was at Graz from about 1902 until the First World War, and he died at Padua. The author knows of no biographical record of him. His more productive period was before the war at Graz. He was unlike the other Austrians in that nearly all his papers were experimental and in that the list is long. He worked on the perceptions of time, of weight, of solidity, of optical illusions, of visual movement and of tactual movement. There are fifteen such articles in the *Zsch. Psychol.* and the *Arch. ges. Psychol.* between 1902 and 1920.

Benussi's theory of perception is scattered through these experimental papers. K. Koffka has attempted to present it and examine it in Zur Grundlegung der Wahrnehmungspsychologie: eine Auseinandersetzung mit V. Benussi, *Zsch. Psychol.*, 1915, 73, 11-90, and lists there twelve important articles. There is much informative exposition of Benussi scattered through H. Helson's Psychology of Gestalt, *Amer. J. Psychol.*, 1925, 36, 342-370, 494-526; 1926, 37, 25-62, 189-223 (also separate with an index). Helson gives a list of sixteen articles,

pp. 217 f. In general Benussi followed Meinong, and the act of producing looms large, a fact to which Koffka, as exponent of modern Gestalt psychology, took exception.

Form-Qualities in General

The doctrine of form-quality is excellently expounded and criticized by M. Bentley, The psychology of mental arrangement, *Amer. J. Psychol.*, 1902, 13, 269-293. G. F. Stout adopted the view and presented his version of it in his *Analytic Psychology*, 1896, I, 66-77. Seyfert, Schumann, and von Aster are all regarded as criticizing the doctrine of form-quality because they made experimental analyses of the perception of simple forms without appealing to this concept or to the concept of the act, but the reader will not find that their papers directly attack the Austrian view. See R. Seyfert, Ueber die Auffassung einfachster Raumformen, *Philos. Stud.*, 1898, 14, 550-566; 1902, 18, 189-214; Schumann, *opp. citt.*; E. von Aster, Beiträge zur Psychologie der Raumwahrnehmung, *Zsch. Psychol.*, 1906, 43, 161-203.

Lipps

Discussion of the psychology of Theodore Lipps (1851-1914) is omitted from the text because, although an act psychologist, he does not seem in that capacity greatly to have influenced the course of psychology. See p. 427 for a brief statement of his place in the 'new' psychology, and p. 437 for a biographical note and an account of his work. This entry in these notes serves the purpose of reminding us that Lipps was a psychologist of importance and an act psychologist, even if not so important as an act psychologist. On Lipps' conception of act and content, see Titchener, *op. cit.* 206-212, 238-242, 248 f.

Lipps is, of course, best known for his theory of empathy (*Einfühlung*), the theory that a perceiving subject projects himself into the object of perception. He perceives the huge object as pressing down, the bridge span as straining or in tension, the arrow as moving or striving forward. Lipps' theory of esthetic feeling is based on empathy, and for him empathy is an act. The theory could, however, have been readily restated in terms acceptable to a psychologist of content, and, as Titchener indicates (*loc. cit.*), Lipps himself at different times was not always consistent about what is act and what content.

Messer

For August Messer's (1867-1937) own account of his life and work, see Schmidt, *op. cit.*, 1922, III, 145-176 (also separate). Here a list of twenty-nine of his important publications is given. The text mentions explicitly those with which it is concerned. *Cf.* the mention of Messer in the preceding chapter (p. 406). On Messer's system, see Titchener, *op. cit.*, 219-235.

Külpe

See notes to the preceding chapter, pp. 433 f.

Act Psychology in General

See Titchener, *op. cit.*, 194-259. The reader may also here be referred again to Titchener's discussion, Brentano and Wundt: empirical and experimental psychology, *Amer. J. Psychol.*, 1921, 32, 108-120; Experimental psychology: a retrospect, *ibid*, 1925, 36, 313-323. Titchener has been the chief expounder of the act school in English.

ESTABLISHMENT OF MODERN
PSYCHOLOGY IN GREAT BRITAIN

CHAPTER 20

British Psychology

From time to time throughout the preceding chapters we have gained insight into the manner in which science advances. At close view, the course of science seems discontinuous; all at once a 'genius' makes a discovery or formulates a theory, and productive research follows on immediately. At the greater range of historical perspective, the course of science seems to be continuous, and the 'genius' appears as an opportunist who takes advantage of the preparation of the times. Chance also plays a rôle, but the history of science selects for record those endeavors that have been fruitful and neglects the promising failures, thus obscuring the operation of chance. However, in addition to these primary factors in scientific progress, there has been another force especially evident during the last century, namely, the support of society. We have seen repeatedly how young men, faced with the problem of earning a living, have nevertheless in one way or another managed to become psychologists or philosophers of note, but we have seen nothing of those who did not become eminent psychologists because of economic handicaps. In psychology the usual social support has come by way of university appointments, until the great professionalization of psychology in America in the 1940s. In Germany there had been no chairs of psychology, but men holding chairs of philosophy had been able to devote themselves to psychology and even to experimental psychology. Had there been no appointments at all for psychologists, psychology could scarcely have prospered. As it is, this economic factor led to a German psychology much less free from philosophy than was the case in America, where the same relationship in professional appointments from the first held much less rigidly. In America, chairs of psychology were created early and the economic resources of the universities were placed directly behind the new science. In Great Britain there has never been the same support from universities. The result has been that, in general during the half century from 1885 to 1935, Germany and America led the way in the new psychology, and Great Britain followed.

In Germany and America the course of development was from philosophical psychology to experimental psychology and then on to applied psychology. Experimental psychology came to Germany before it came to America, but America was the first to make substantial progress in applied psychology. In Great Britain philosophical psychology in the hands of Ward and Stout remained in the saddle for a long time, but after the First World War applied psychology sprang up and flourished with the economic support of industry. Experimental psychology, which had been supposed in Germany and America to constitute a necessary intermediate stage, was not wholly lacking, but it had to work against difficulties. Oxford long resisted modern psychology and had no psychological laboratory until 1936, no chair of psychology until 1947. In fact, it was only after the most bitter controversy in 1882 that this stronghold of the classics was brought to the establishment of a physiological laboratory. At Cambridge, Ward, as professor of moral philosophy since 1897, was as much the psychologist as the philosopher, but there was almost nothing of the experimentalist about him. Nevertheless, Cambridge had under Rivers a psychological laboratory of sorts from as early as 1897 and a good one under Myers from 1913 on. In experimental psychology Cambridge has always led Britain. Spearman was professor of mind and logic at London; but, although trained in Germany and sympathetic to the new psychology, he was not an experimentalist after the manner of Germans and Americans. Sully wrote about experiments but did not experiment. Stout, professor of logic and metaphysics at St. Andrews, was not an experimentalist. Galton in a sense initiated experimental psychology in England as he initiated so many other things, but he was independent of the universities. McDougall was an experimentalist and did much to establish experimental physiological psychology in Great Britain, but he never held an important post at a British university. Lloyd Morgan was professor of psychology and education at Bristol. Myers was once professor of psychology in King's College, London, but Rivers was never more than lecturer in physiological and experimental psychology at Cambridge. From 1890 to 1920, when Germany and America were teeming with laboratories and professional experimental psychologists, Great Britain was advancing slowly in the new science only by way of the work of a few competent men. Nowadays, the Cambridge Laboratory, since 1922 under the direction of F. C. Bartlett, still asserts leadership in research and productivity. A number of professorships of psychology have been established, even Oxford coming in at last (1947).

University College, London, has a small old laboratory dating from the 1890s, and Edinburgh a good newer one. All in all, Britain lags far behind America and came finally to lead Germany only because Nazi culture strangled scientific activity in Germany.

Not only in magnitude and rate of progress but also in quality did the new British psychology differ greatly from the new German psychology, and in no way is this contrast so clearly seen as between Francis Galton and Wundt. Wundt we already know.

Galton was a genius. He was a genius in the technical sense that his youthful precocity was such that his intelligence quotient, had he been tested for intelligence, would probably have approached 200; that is to say, he belonged on this basis with the most intelligent persons who have been tested or whose biographies have been examined, with John Stuart Mill, Goethe and Leibnitz. He was also a genius in the popular sense, for he was a brilliant, original, versatile, stimulating scholar, whose research opened large new fields of investigation. He had independent means and he never held an academic appointment. He was a free-lance and a gentleman scientist. In fact, the question as to whether he should continue creative work or settle down, like his brothers, as a country gentleman was once the serious dilemma of his life. His scientific contributions, besides his early ventures in exploration, include investigations in simple mechanics and the invention of apparatus, his persistent interest in meteorology, his continued study of inheritance and his foundation of the art of eugenics, his development of Quetelet's methods of statistics and their application to anthropological and psychological problems, his numerous researches in anthropometry, and his initiation of the experimental psychology of tests in England. He was forever seeing new relationships and working them out, either on paper or in practice. No field was beyond his possible interest, no domain was marked off in advance as being out of his province. A restless interest and a vivid imagination had Francis Galton.

How different he was from Wundt! Was Wundt a genius? We hardly use this phrase of him in spite of his great erudition and his remarkable productivity. Wundt was erudite where Galton was original; Wundt overcame massive obstacles by the weight of his attack; Galton dispatched a difficulty by a thrust of insight. Wundt was forever armored by his system; Galton had no system. Wundt was methodical; Galton was versatile. Wundt's science was interpenetrated by his philosophy; Galton's science was discursive and unstructured. Wundt was interminably arguing; Galton was forever observing. Wundt had a school, a formal, self-conscious school;

Galton had friends, influence and effects only. Thus Wundt was personally intolerant and controversial, whereas Galton was tolerant and ready to be convicted of error. Wundt, as we have said in an earlier chapter, was a professional psychologist, the first; Galton had no profession. Thus Wundt in his scientific affairs tended to be unsocial, but Galton, in close personal touch with his eminent contemporaries, was distinctly social. It is impossible to get the entire difference expressed in a phrase, but the important thing that Galton lacked was Wundt's professionalism. As a professional psychologist Wundt always bore upon himself the weight of his past, of the logic of his systematic commitments and of his philosophical predilections. He could work only within the shell of what he had made psychology to be. Galton was free. He had no major commitments. He was not a psychologist nor an anthropologist nor anything at any time except what his vivid interests made him. He had the advantage of competence without the limitation of being an expert.

This contrast between Galton and Wundt shows in the extremes the general difference between German and English science. Individuals, however, may vary from the national type. Helmholtz, as we noted in our discussion of him, was more like the British investigator. Brentano's influence was partly due to his personality. Nevertheless, the gross difference holds. German psychology was institutionalized, and for it we find schools and their leaders. In Great Britain, we have to deal more with persons.

SYSTEMATIC PSYCHOLOGY

We have already seen that it was British empiricism and associationism which furnished a full half of the preparation for experimental psychology. Experimental psychology resulted from this marriage of philosophical psychology and physiology. Although Herbart and Lotze were extremely important in preparation for the new psychology, in general it is true that Wundt got experimental method from physiology and systematic structure from Mill and Bain and their British predecessors. Thus the pattern of the 'new' psychology in Germany came from England. Since Great Britain was not backward in its pursuit of physiology, we might have expected this marriage to have taken place there; but the facts are otherwise. Experimental psychology began in Germany and came only by adoption to Great Britain.

After Bain the philosophical tradition in psychology was continued in Great Britain by Ward and Stout. *James Ward* (1843-1925), who acknowledged his psychological debt to Brentano, was, in a sense, an act psychologist. He built up an elaborate and brilliant system about the relation of the active subject to the object. He first presented his psychological views in the article on psychology in the ninth edition of the *Encyclopædia Britannica* (1886), and elaborated and perfected them for the eleventh edition (1911). Subsequently he rounded out the picture in his *Psychological Principles* (1918), a work which he characterized as having been in preparation for forty years. To the experimentalist this system seems almost an anachronism, so logically perfect is it, and so devoid of dependence on the accumulating mass of experimental fact. Ward was, however, primarily a philosopher, and his interest in psychology was philosophical after the English tradition. For all this, his influence was great, and he was after Bain the senior psychologist in Great Britain, for his contemporary, Sully, was less influential. It must not be thought, however, that Ward was hostile to experimental psychology. He was trained at Cambridge, but he also studied abroad at Berlin and Göttingen (in Lotze's day; *ca.* 1874), where he learned to respect the new movement. When he returned to Cambridge (1875), he wanted to start a psychological laboratory, but was prevented by an opposition that identified a laboratory for the study of mind with the support of materialism. Ward was, however, not fitted by temperament for the technique of experimental research, any more than Brentano, who would have liked to found a psychological laboratory at Vienna. Presently we shall see how hard Ward worked to get the Cambridge laboratory established (pp. 489-493).

Ward divided the subject-matter of psychology into cognition, feeling and conation, and the schema whereby he distinguished these phases follows. Psychology deals with "a Subject, (1) nonvoluntarily attending to changes in the sensory continuum [*Cognition*]; (2) being, in consequence, either pleased or pained [*Feeling*]; and (3) by voluntary attention or 'innervation' producing changes in the motor continuum [*Conation*]." This is the subjective schema which implies its objective complement. From the point of view of the object, we find that (1) cognition is the presentation of sensory objects, that (3) conation is the presentation of motor objects, and that (2) feeling is not a presentation, because it does not lie in experience but is the primordial consequent of sensory presentation and the condition of motor presentation, an explanatory middle term between the two kinds of presentation. The presentation, the experimental stuff of mind, is an *Erlebnis*, the modern equivalent, Ward thought, of Locke's idea; and, we must note, conation is just as much within experience as cognition. The presentation implies the subject-object relationship, the subject-matter of psychology. We need not go into this system. It is sufficient to see the sort of interest that dominated Ward and how far he was from the psychology of the laboratory.

Ward was not a popular psychologist, for his ideas were too difficult of comprehension and for the most part found definite expression after psychology had already taken on an explicit form in England. The effective presentation of a similar point of view was left to *George Frederick Stout* (1860-1944), who studied at Cambridge (1881-1883) but not abroad. Stout, in the middle of his life, gained a great influence by writing systematic textbooks of psychology: his *Analytic Psychology* (1896), a *Manual of Psychology* (1899) with many revised editions, and a *Groundwork of Psychology* (1903). These books, although written from different points of view and using different terminology, all present an act psychology resembling Ward's. Stout recognized primarily Ward's influence, and secondarily the influence of the English school and of Herbart. It would also appear that the Austrians, especially Meinong, had something to do with his thinking. Activity comes into Stout's system in the famous doctrine of conation, the fact and the experience of striving. His *Manual* has been very widely used in Great Britain, and without a successful competitor it determined for many years the pattern of British systematic psychology. Stout's influence was also increased by the fact that he became Croom Robertson's successor as editor of *Mind* in 1892.

Stout held that psychology deals with psychical processes that are in themselves subjective and that have mental objects like sensations. He resembled Ward in insisting that the subject-object relationship gives psychical processes their mental character. He was like Brentano in making sensations objects of the processes. He divided these processes into cognition and interest, and subdivided interest into conation and feeling-attitude. Conation he described as the equivalent of craving, desire or will; it is characterized by its relation to its satisfaction or fulfilment and disappears in its satisfaction. The object of conation is whatever appears as its end or as the means to the end. Here one must carefully distinguish between what appears as an end and the actual end. The object of conation that gives it its driving force is not necessarily the terminus to which the activity leads. One may seek salvation, but go to church. Thus Stout did not think that conation explains all activity. He had a great deal to say about unconscious psychical dispositions, which are known only by their effects and which must therefore be localized in the brain. In general Stout's views, especially his doctrine of conation, interest us because they lead up to McDougall's systematic position.

William McDougall (1871-1938) was next in the systematic line after Stout, even though he developed his systematic views most explicitly after he left England for America in 1920. McDougall has been called a 'purposivist,' because he has organized his view of mind about the rôle that purposive striving, a child of conation, plays in mental activity. He was thus really an act psychologist like Ward and Stout, but his descent from Brentano was so remote as to leave little resemblance. Perhaps the difference is largely due to the fact that McDougall, unlike Ward and Stout, had been an experimentalist. Moreover, William James had a great influence upon him, and systematically he took an inheritance more from the Scottish tradition of Dugald Stewart than did Bain, another Scot, who fell under the English influence of the Mills.

McDougall had a medical training in Cambridge and London, as well as a brief contact with G. E. Müller at Göttingen. He was a member of the Cambridge Anthropological Expedition to Torres Straits and undertook independent anthropological work in Borneo (1899-1900). On returning to England he became, at Sully's recommendation, a reader in University College, London, where he commanded the very small psychological laboratory of which mention is made later. He was Wilde Reader in Mental Philosophy at Oxford (1904-1920), where he had, by informal personal arrangement with Gotch, the physiologist, a laboratory up to the time of the First World War. Then he came to Harvard University in America, where psychologists were supposedly better treated than in England, but it can hardly be said that America accepted him. His faith in the superiority of a Nordic race, his belief that determinism does not wholly control the mind which still has an element of freedom left to it, his persistent interest in psychic research and his insistence on tolerance for it, all tended to throw him out of mesh with the culture that was natural to the American psychologists. Still thinking of himself as an Englishman in the British Colonies, he shifted scene again, going to Duke University in 1927, where he died in 1938.

In the early days, McDougall published numerous experimental researches, many of them on problems of vision, as well as a small *Physiological Psychology* (1905). His *Body and Mind* (1911), an examination of the theories of the mind-body relation, is a classic. During the First World War he was engaged in psychomedical work in the British armies, and later he published an extensive *Outline of Abnormal Psychology* (1926). He was also concerned with anthropology and social psychology, and his text on *Social Psychology* (1908, and later editions), was extremely influential. He wrote a small general text, *Psychology, the Study of Behaviour* (1912), but the subsequent rise of behaviorism in America led him to abandon this term as no longer descriptive of his own point of view toward mind. His systematic position was put forth in his *Outline of Psychology* (1923), a book that contrasts with American behaviorism. He also published several books dealing with practical social problems. Thus McDougall typifies the broad discursive interests of the Englishman that differ so strikingly from German professionalism. He enters the picture of British psychology both because of his experimental contributions and because his systematic position is derived directly from Ward (and so indirectly from Brentano), but he also belongs intellectually in the American tradition because his purposive psychology relates systematically to the behaviorism of E. B. Holt and E. C. Tolman and thus indirectly to what eventually became dynamic psychology. He was a great admirer of William James, who may indeed have had something to do with these views.

McDougall's purposive psychology resembles Ward's in its fundamental systematic assumption, that is to say, in respect of the subject, the object and activity. There is, however, less of the philosopher and more of the experimentalist about his emphasis. He defined psychology as "the positive empirical science of the mind" and the mind of an individual organism as "that which expresses itself in his experience and in his behavior." As against introspectionism and behaviorism he represented a third corner of a triangle. His emphasis was always upon the purposive activity of the organism, and he was thus led to stress the behavior of the organism as resulting from the interaction of mind and body. Still he was not a behaviorist in the Watsonian sense, for he thought of behavior as something different from mere movement and mechanical reflexes. In America he was forced to find objective criteria for the behavior that is peculiarly psychological and not merely physical. His seven marks of behavior are: (1) "spontaneity of movement," (2) "persistence of activity independently of the continuance of the impression which may have initiated it," (3) "variation of direction of persistent movements," (4) "coming to an end of the animal's movements as soon as they have brought about a particular kind of change in its situation," (5) "preparation for the new situation toward the production of which the action contributes," (6) "some degree of improvement in the effectiveness of behavior, when it is repeated by the animal under similar circumstances," and (7) the totality of reaction of the organism. Action which meets these criteria is purposive; a reflex does not meet them.

It is plain that, in making purposive striving the central fact of mind, McDougall was appealing both to the observation of animal and human behavior and to human introspection. Every man finds that the obvious thing about his own mind is 'what he wants to do,' and when he comes to interpret the minds of others they appear to be similar. Effort and volition and freedom are everywhere apparent when mind is in question, and a careful examination of McDougall's criteria of purposive behavior reveals the fact that they involve some degree of indeterminateness, of freedom, that they are in part negative as against the observation of their necessary conditions or causes. Nor can there be any doubt that this element of freedom is exactly what McDougall wished to preserve as the distinguishing mark of mind. There is and must always be a certain indeterminateness about phenomena, and thus there is ample warrant for a view opposed to the deterministic conception of science. When McDougall had developed this view in America, he met with scant sympathy, because of the dominance of mechanistic behaviorism, and even more because freedom was out of fashion in science. However, the mechanistic experimental psychologist is never freed of his indeterminate probable error, and to the author it seems that all the controversy which arose was about nothing more than McDougall's calling 'freedom' what the determinist calls a 'probable error.'

In America, McDougall undertook, by breeding successive generations of white rats trained in a special discrimination, to demonstrate the inheritance of acquired characters. In thus supporting the Lamarckian hypothesis, he was in a way supporting freedom or at least arguing against the narrow genetic determinism of Weismann's. His conclusions favoring Lamarck raised a storm of protest and are unlikely to be accepted until they have been verified in other laboratories. In this, as in his tolerant interest in psychic research and telepathy, he was keeping an open mind against conservatism, mistrusting the constraints of modern mechanistic psychology.

At this point we must make mention of *James Sully* (1842-1923), older than McDougall and a contemporary of Ward's, who played a prominent rôle in English psychology as a writer of textbooks. Sully was a man of modest means who thrice applied vainly for university chairs and was at last appointed Grote professor of mind and logic at the University of London, on Croom Robertson's death in 1892, and largely as a result of the publication of the two volumes of his *Human Mind*. He was a close younger friend of Bain, who took a paternal interest in him. He was personally acquainted with the men of science and letters of his day and was one of the lesser members of the group of friends and correspondents that centered about Darwin and the great intellectual topic of the day, the theory of evolution. Sully's primary interests were psychology and esthetics. He studied abroad at Göttingen (1867-1868), where he came into but superficial contact with Lotze, and at Berlin (1871-1872), where he sought to learn psychology from Helmholtz and anatomy from du Bois-Reymond. He became a writer, not a scientist. His first book of essays, called *Sensation and Intuition* (1874), received favorable comment from Darwin, and his second on *Illusions* (1881) from Wundt. After these publications he set himself definitely to supply the need for textbooks of psychology, for there had been nothing suitable since Bain's two volumes twenty-five years earlier. He published his *Outlines of Psychology* in 1884 and the book, very well written, was immediately successful. He followed it with a psychology for teachers, and then in 1892 his more ambitious *Human Mind*. After that he turned to writing on child psychology, following the example of Preyer in Germany but drawing material in part from anthropological sources. Sully's texts fill in the gap between Bain and Stout. A writer of good textbooks is not without his place in the history of science, since he gives knowledge explicit form and diffuses it. On the other hand, Sully's name is probably better known than his real importance to psychology would warrant, simply because he was the author of such widely used books.

Now we must turn from systematic questions to consider the influence of Charles Darwin and the doctrine of evolution upon British psychology.

THEORY OF EVOLUTION

The eighteenth century believed in the special creation of every species, that is to say, of "every living creature after his kind"—a belief quite consistent with the Biblical account of the creation of animal life and its preservation in the ark at the time of the deluge. There were occasional men who toyed with the idea of the development of one species from another and of intermediate forms, but no real progress toward the solution of the problem of the origin of species was made during the century. Toward the end of the century the problem had become acute, for geographical exploration had so multiplied the number of known species that it was no longer possible to conceive that Noah had crowded a pair of each into the ark.

The first steps toward the solution came from Goethe, the poet, whose flair for scientific observation we have already noted (p. 20), and from Erasmus Darwin, the grandfather of Charles Darwin. Goethe (1749-1832) is responsible for the theory of the metamorphosis of parts (1790). As the result of a great deal of careful observation of plants, he came to the conclusion that, apparently, different forms of a plant can be created by the change of one part into another form: for example, in the double flower, stamens of the single flower may have been transformed into petals. Later, Goethe participated in extending the theory to animal life, suggesting, for example, that the vertebrate skull is essentially a modified and developed vertebra. Erasmus Darwin (1721-1802) independently formulated the notion of the transmutation of species. The idea is similar to Goethe's and touches more directly upon the problem of the origin of species. Erasmus Darwin was, however, a lover of nature who rhymed about it, and his views lost force when presented in verse. Nevertheless, the idea was there at the end of the eighteenth century, when most thoughtful men took the special creation of species for granted.

The first great figure in the history of the theory of evolution is the French naturalist, Lamarck (1744-1829), who belongs in the nineteenth century because he first published his views on this topic in 1809. A Lamarckian nowadays is a man who believes in the inheritance of acquired characteristics, but what Lamarck stressed was the modification of animal form through effort, on the animal's part, further to adapt to its environment, and the inheritance, by its progeny, of these acquired modifications. If a short-legged bird gains a living by fishing, standing in shallow water, presumably it will, when the fish are scarce near shore, wade in just as far as the length of its legs allows. Lamarck's belief was that, by thus trying ever to go deeper, it would stretch its legs a tiny amount, perhaps strengthening them by straining them and thus causing them to grow a bit longer. If its progeny were to inherit this tiny increment and to continue the same adaptive effort, the cumulative result would be a long-legged bird like a heron.

In this view Lamarck was vigorously combated by another and very famous French naturalist, Baron Cuvier (1769-1832), who

argued for fixity of species. Cuvier had earlier enunciated the
doctrine of the correlation of parts, the doctrine that the adaptation
of a species to its environment and mode of living was reflected in
certain relationships of use among its parts. Thus a flesh-eating
animal must have not only sharp teeth but also legs for the swift
movement of attack. An animal that carries its prey in its mouth
must have not only strong teeth but also strong neck-muscles. Cuvier
claimed that by a knowledge of these relationships the form of an
entire animal could be reconstructed from a single fossil bone, but
this extreme boast has never been made good. Cuvier thought, of
course, of the adaptation of the species as given in its creation and
not as acquired through its own adaptive efforts. Although Lamarck
seems to have made the more thoughtful argument, Cuvier's influence was so great as effectually to hinder a wide acceptance of
the Lamarckian view.

To Charles Darwin (1809-1882) belongs the credit for the far-
reaching and plausible theory of the evolutionary origin of species,
which took the world by storm, raised immediately a tempest of
protest, and is considered by many as the greatest scientific achievement of the century, because of its profound effect upon thought
and the culture. Like many great ideas, it is extremely simple when
viewed in retrospect; its greatness lies in its adequacy, its novelty,
and in the degree to which it ran counter to the accepted belief of
the time. The fact of variability among individual animals of the
same species is obvious. Darwin believed that this spontaneous
variability is sometimes of such a nature as to be inheritable. By
selecting in accordance with such 'chance' variation, animal breeders
can, cumulatively through many generations, produce great changes
in a breed. Presumably, therefore, in nature we have a natural
selection by way of the survival of the animals best fitted for their
environment and requirements of living. Thus ultimately, in æons
of time, natural selection taken together with gradually changing
environmental conditions may give rise to new species. The species
would not be so discrete as was originally supposed; they would
form continuous orders; and their present relative discreteness
would mean simply that, in a cross-section of time, the various
animal forms would exist as approximately adapted to the conditions under which they live. Darwin's theory differed radically
from Lamarck's only (1) in assuming that inheritable variation
occurs spontaneously or by chance rather than by the adaptive
effort of the organism, (2) in recognizing that selection is natural
to the struggle for existence in which all animals engage (Darwin

had been impressed by Malthus' theory of the limitation of population by natural conditions), and (3) in substituting the chances of variation and of survival for definitely directed adaptive effort. Of course, Darwin's theory made it necessary to assume a much longer time for the emergence of a new species.

It is important to notice that there is no final incompatibility between the beliefs of Darwin and Lamarck. To call the inheritable variation spontaneous or 'chance' is not to forbid its explanation by adaptive effort, and Herbert Spencer (pp. 240-243) championed this synthetic view. *Chance* is often a term for ignorance of causes where a belief in the existence of determinative cause still persists. The Lamarckian view can, therefore, be made to complete the Darwinian theory. Weismann (1834-1914), however, in 1883 seriously challenged the belief in inheritance of any acquired characteristics, and the issue between Weismann and Lamarck is still today in dispute. We have just seen how McDougall supported the Lamarckian view and how most scientists, at least in western culture, have rejected it.

Darwin's great work, *The Origin of Species*, was published in 1859. The compendious and elaborately revised notes upon which it was based he began to make in 1837 as a young man of twenty-eight in his trip around the world in the *Beagle*. He came rather quickly, as the result of his observations, to his theory in outline. In 1844 he made a manuscript abstract of the conception, but stored it away, with provision for its publication in event of his death, while he collected more observations and revised his notes again and again. And then, just as he was preparing to publish, his friend Alfred Russell Wallace (1823-1913) sent him for publication a paper putting forth the same view in brief, though without the same full observational background. Darwin published Wallace's paper and his own simultaneously, and his book the following year. In the storm of criticism that followed, Darwin remained imperturbable, ably defended by many men of science, of whom Herbert Spencer and Thomas Henry Huxley (1825-1895) were perhaps the most notable.

The effect of this theory upon the development of psychology was tremendous. Not only did the theory challenge the authority of Genesis in respect of the special creation of species, suggesting that man has inherited his body from animal ancestors, but it also raised the question as to whether there is continuity in respect of mind between animals and man. Darwin believed in this continuity and his *Expression of the Emotions in Man and Animals* (1872)

furnished evidence for his view, although it must be admitted that
the animal emotions which he cited consisted of behavioral attitudes
(the friendly cat, the angry dog) and not any animal consciousness
resembling what might serve as an ancestor for a human soul—an
unextended, immortal Cartesian soul, the kind of soul which nineteenth-century religious orthodoxy required.

As we shall see presently, Francis Galton seized at once upon the
notion of mental inheritance and brought out evidence in favor of
it. Out of that activity grew the whole business of studying individual differences in mental capacities and of psychological assessment by means of mental tests, the business which the Americans
took over and promoted. Animal psychology and comparative psychology, as well as the conception of mental evolution in animals
and in man, began in England under Darwin's influence. All of these
interests were soon translated to America and flourished there. Later
we shall be discussing the question as to whether the theory of
evolution played an important rôle in determining the nature of
American psychology and in differentiating it from the German, or
whether it was the pioneer culture of America which determined
both the popularity of the theory of evolution and the kind of
functional psychology which is characteristic of America.

ANIMAL PSYCHOLOGY

It was the theory of evolution which gave rise to modern animal
psychology. When animals were automata and men had souls, there
was not so much reason for scientific interest in the animal mind as
there was when it became clear that there is no break in continuity
between man's mind (which by that time was being distinguished
from his soul) and whatever it is that animals have for minds. So it
comes about that we may properly regard Darwin as starting the
modern era in animal psychology by the publication of his *Expression of the Emotions in Man and Animals* (1872), where he drew
upon his great wealth of observational knowledge to point out the
dependence of emotional behavior in man upon the inheritance of
behavior which was useful in animal life but no longer immediately
useful to man. His explanation of the curling of the human lips in
the sneer as a remnant of the useful habit of the carnivorous animal
that bares its canine teeth in rage is only one of the very many
examples with which this book is filled. In modern terminology we
can say that the book is a discussion of conditioned emotional responses in men and animals, with many examples of individual conditioning, but also many others of what can be made to appear as

racial or phylogenetic conditioning by an extension of Lamarckism.

The next step in this scientific development was taken by *George John Romanes* (1848-1894), who published in 1882 his *Animal Intelligence*. Romanes was a friend of Darwin's, a writer, and one of the group of English intellectuals who rallied to Darwin's standard. He wrote mostly on zoological topics and, in the interests of squaring religion with evolution, on theological topics.

Romanes' book on animal intelligence is the first *comparative psychology* that was ever written, and its author used this term believing that comparative psychology would come to rank alongside of comparative anatomy in importance. In this book Romanes did not deal directly with the problem of mental continuity between animals and man, but was content to present a great mass of data on animal behavior, thus laying the groundwork for a subsequent argument on the relation of animals to man. He got his material from an exhaustive combing of both the scientific and popular accounts of animal behavior, and his method has thus come to be called the 'anecdotal method.' In view of the fact that this procedure is regarded with disapproval today, it is only fair to Romanes to say that he himself was aware of the danger of "mongering anecdotes" and laid down certain rigorous principles of selection to which he strictly adhered. However, in observation the line between fact and interpretation is never clear, and the untrained observer too often reports his own interpretation of the animal's mind instead of describing what he observed in the animal's behavior. In general he tends to 'anthropomorphize' the animal, and this tendency played into the hands of Romanes, who was seeking to find accounts of the highest levels of intelligence in animals in order later to demonstrate the mental continuity from animals to man. For this reason the anecdotal method of Romanes has not only been discarded, but has become a term of opprobrium in animal psychology. However, in eschewing the anecdotal for the experimental method, psychologists should remember that Romanes got comparative psychology on its feet in that observational period which, in so much scientific work, precedes the development of experimental technique.

Romanes did not regard this first book as his most important venture, successful and popular as it was. He meant in it simply to lay the factual groundwork upon which he could erect his defense of mental evolution. Nor did his second book, *Mental Evolution in Animals* (1883), give, as he had originally intended, the complete argument. It was devoted more to the demonstration of continuity among animal forms. The third book, *Mental Evolution in Man* (1887), completed the series and was the most important from the point of view of the argument about evolution. To us neither of these latter books seems as important as the first, because Romanes lacked a satisfactory classification of human faculties with which to work. He was thrown back upon Locke and the associationists for his terms. His general conclusion was that "simple ideas," like sensory impressions, perceptions and the memories of perceptions, are common to all animals and man; that "complex ideas," the associative compounds, with which associationism dealt (and he might have added Wundt), belong to some animals and to man; and that "notional ideas," the concepts of abstract and general thinking, are the "unique prerogative of man." Again we should be lenient toward Romanes' analytical difficulties; comparative psychology is still struggling with vague concepts, like 'free images,' 'delayed reactions,' 'symbolic processes' and 'insight,' to establish a conceptual framework with respect to which the differences between human and infrahuman minds can be specified.

The dangers of the anecdotal method were recognized by C. *Lloyd Morgan* (1852-1936), who undertook to offset the anthropomorphic tendency in the interpretation of the animal mind by an appeal to the 'law of parsimony.' This law as applied to animal psychology is often known as 'Lloyd Morgan's canon,' and his formulation of it (1894) was as follows: "In no case may we interpret an action as the outcome of the exercise of a higher psychical faculty, if it can be interpreted as the outcome of the exercise of one which stands lower in the psychological scale." The justification of the canon lies in the need for offsetting one constant error by introducing another with the opposite effect. At the end of the last century, when the proof of the theory of evolution was uppermost in everyone's mind, such a course was sound: if evolutionary continuity could be proved in spite of the adoption of the canon, then evolution must be true. If the proof had failed with the use of the canon, no harm would have been done; we should have had simply a failure of proof, not a falsification of fact. Today, however, when our interests center primarily in the description of the animal mind, the canon is less of a safeguard; nature is notoriously prodigal; why should we interpret only parsimoniously?

Lloyd Morgan's reaction against Romanes was represented first by his *Animal Life and Intelligence* (1890-1891), which was later revised under the title *Animal Behaviour* (1900). His best-known book of this period is his *Introduction to Comparative Psychology*

(1894), a quite general psychology that deals in detail with the relation of the animal mind to the human. It is this book that gives the methodological principles and the canon of interpretation. All these books contain many accounts of the author's own experiments upon animals, experiments which lie midway between the observation of the naturalist in the field and observation by way of artificial but controlled situations in the laboratory. They consist in the careful observation of animal behavior when the usual environment has been modified so as to create special situations. Thus, to say that experimental animal psychology began with Thorndike's use of puzzle-boxes in 1898 is to limit the meaning of the word *experimental* to the formal laboratory with apparatus.

The conservative view of Lloyd Morgan received support at this time from Jacques Loeb (1859-1924), then in Germany, who put forth his theory of the tropism in 1890. In part Loeb's theory represented a return to the mechanistic view of Descartes that animals are automata, but Loeb was not so sweeping. He held that the possession of "associative memory" is the criterion of consciousness and that only the lower animals are therefore unconscious. He was not reacting against Darwinism but supporting his faith in the adequacy of physico-chemical methods for scientific study of physiology and behavior. As a matter of fact, it has proven impracticable to establish a criterion for mind. The behavior of even the lowest animals (and perhaps of some machines) is slightly modifiable through experience and might therefore depend on 'associative memory.' Nevertheless Loeb's theory and researches reacted against the anecdotal method, although more in America than in England.

In England there was other research of importance to support the work of Romanes and Lloyd Morgan. Sir John Lubbock (1834-1913) published *Ants, Wasps, and Bees* (1882) in the same year that Romanes' first book appeared. This book is full of information about the social insects, whose high order of civilization seems, except for the fact that it is not readily modified, to establish the existence of mind in animals. Leonard Trelawney Hobhouse (1864-1929) also belongs in the English picture because of his *Mind in Evolution* (1901), a book in which he argued out the whole matter and presented some of his own experiments. These experiments were of the same type as Lloyd Morgan's, and are not unlike Köhler's on apes (1917), although they lack the added significance of being related to a new system of psychology.

Outside of England there was also important work in progress, especially on the insects. J. Henri Fabre's (1823-1915) studies of entomological behavior ran in successive volumes from 1879 to 1904. The work of Auguste Forel (1848-1931), principally on ants, dates from 1874 to 1922, and his first important book on the sensations of insects came out while Romanes was publishing (1887). Albrecht Bethe (1872-1931) published his well-known research on ants and bees in 1898, a study which presented the mechanistic interpretation of the complex behavior of these social insects. Binet had published on the psychic life of micro-organisms in 1888; and this research was taken up very effectively in America by H. S. Jennings at the very end of the century and later. All this work had its roots in the new interest in the animal mind that Darwin's theory aroused.

At the beginning of the present century, the initiative in animal psychology passed to America, where Thorndike's subjection of animals to formal laboratory technique began a very active period of research with mazes, puzzle-boxes, and physical apparatus for testing sensory discrimination, as well as the organization of special laboratories of comparative psychology. We shall return to this topic again when we come to consider the rôle of animal psychology in the development of behavioristics (p. 626).

MENTAL INHERITANCE

Another way in which Darwin stimulated the thought of his times was by arousing interest in the problems of heredity and mental inheritance. Galton, his half-cousin, became the leader in the latter field. In 1869 Galton published *Hereditary Genius*, a careful biographical study of the tendency of genius to run in families. His argument that reputation is a reliable measure of the mental capacity that is genius can be questioned; nevertheless his work has preserved its importance for a half century because, in spite of disagreement about the inheritance of 'intelligence' (as the tests test it), no one can question Galton's primary findings that eminent men tend to have eminent offspring, however distinction is transmitted, socially or biologically. This book also represents the beginning of Galton's influence on statistical work, not only in respect of the collection of data but also with regard to their method of treatment.

Galton got his ideas on statistical method from the Belgian statistician, Adolph Quetelet (1796-1874), who was the first to apply Laplace's and Gauss' normal law of error to the distribution of human data, biological and social. Quetelet found that certain anthropometric measurements, like the heights of French army conscripts and the girths of the chests of Scottish soldiers, were distributed in frequency approximately in accordance with this normal law, the bell-shaped probability curve. The law had been developed originally in connection with the theory of probabilities in games of chance. It had also been applied to other cases of chance variation and had been used by Gauss to express, among other things, the distribution of errors in observation. The coupling of this mathematical function with the notion of error seemed to imply that the law shows the variability that occurs when an ideal is aimed at and achieved only with varying degrees of success, like the distribution of shots on either side of a line at which aim has been taken. Thus Quetelet assumed, from the approximate applicability of the law to human variability, that we might regard such human variation as if it occurred when nature aimed at an ideal and missed by varying amounts. Since the curve is symmetrical, its average is medial and gives, from the distribution of errors alone, the position of the ideal that nature sought. In this manner we can understand Quetelet's doctrine of *l'homme moyen*, in which the average man appears as nature's ideal, and deviations toward the good as well as toward the bad (when human characters can be thus evaluated) appear as nature's mistakes of different degree. The average is the most frequent value and nature's large errors are rare.

Galton believed that quantitative measurement is the mark of a full-grown science and he adopted Quetelet's use of the normal law in order to convert the frequency of occurrence of genius into measures of its degree; that is to say, he set up a scale of lettered grades of genius from "A," just above the average, up to "G," and to "X" which represented all grades above "G." For example, ability "F" he defined as that level attained by one man in 4,300, "G" as the attainment of one man in 79,000, and "X" as one in 1,000,000. Similarly there must be a descending scale from "a," below the average, to "idiots and imbeciles" at "f," "g" and "x." This procedure is a method of transforming observed statistical frequencies into another scale, one in which adjustment has been made for the fact that cases pile up about the average and that two adjacent cases near the average are presumably separated by a smaller interval than two cases near the extreme. Nowadays, statisticians are not so naïve as to assume that nature holds to a particular law of variation no matter what scale of measurement man chooses to use, but in those days the normal law was supposed really to be normal—nature's rule.

Galton followed *Hereditary Genius* with his study of *English Men of Science* (1874) and then *Natural Inheritance* (1889). These were his books, packed full of biographical research and ingenious treatment and interpretation. Beside them he published between thirty and forty papers on problems of inheritance, of which the most important is a study of the dependence of the resemblances of twins upon "nature and nurture" (1876). This paper is the source of those two convenient synonyms—*nature* for heredity and *nurture* for the environment.

In *Hereditary Genius* Galton had concluded that Athenian civilization was, in mental ability, about as far above present-day British civilization as the British are today above the Negro, and his mind was constantly occupied with the problem of improving the race. To the project and science of substituting for natural selection an intelligent selection in the interests of racial improvement Galton gave the name *eugenics* in 1883, and the matter was much mooted at that time and later. Finally in 1904 he endowed at the University of London a research fellowship in eugenics, and Karl Pearson became the incumbent. The resulting Francis Galton Laboratory for National Eugenics was in University College and was conducted in connection with Pearson's older Biometric Laboratory. In 1911 the two were combined in a department of applied statistics under Pearson as Galton professor. Pearson's work is another story. It is well known how his development of the statistical methods for more than two decades dominated the work in individual psychology in England and America.

STATISTICAL METHOD

In general, experimental psychology and individual psychology developed independently of each other. The results of laboratory investigations had little effect upon research by the method of the mental test. It is for this reason that the histories of the psychophysical methods and of the statistical methods have been largely independent of each other, although it is true that their relationship has been evident to William Brown and G. H. Thomson in England, and more recently to L. L. Thurstone and J. P. Guilford in America. In this book, however, we can touch upon individual psychology and the mental tests only incidentally. Mental testing is, of course, fundamentally experimental; it is an historical artifact that the word *experimental* has come to possess a more circumscribed meaning.

The statistical methods, the chief tool of individual psychology, may be said to have their historical beginning in the work of Quetelet, of whom we have just spoken. We have seen how Galton took from him the use of the normal law of error and applied it to the measurement of mental ability. It is impossible for us to review here the many varied, if trivial, uses to which the ingenious Galton put this law. An example must suffice. Galton used the law to determine the proper proportion between the amounts of the first and second prizes in a competition. As we have said, this law requires that individuals near the average of a group should differ from each other less than individuals at the extremes. Moreover, the differences at the extremes become relatively greater in larger groups. Galton's analysis indicates that ability would be fairly rewarded if (in groups of from ten to 100 persons) the first prize were about three times as large as the second prize.

It was Galton who first worked out the method of statistical *correlation*. The idea was forming in his mind as early as 1877. He came at the concept by way of his principle of "reversion" or "regression toward mediocrity" that appears in the phenomena of inheritance. In studying, for example, the dependence of the stature of sons upon the stature of their fathers, one can think of a son's stature as partly derived from his father's and partly the result of other causes which are indeterminate from the available data. The sons' statures ought thus to be found more closely grouped about the mean than were the fathers', for the concurrence of the extremes in these two components would be much less frequent than the occurrence of an extreme in one alone. Galton's work in inheritance made him familiar with scatter diagrams of frequencies showing the relationship between paired measures, and he finally came, with some mathematical aid from J. D. H. Dickson, to a knowledge of lines of regression and of the nature of the frequency surface in such a diagram with its elliptical contour-lines, and to the expression of the relationship by a simple coefficient. He dealt with the law of "regression toward mediocrity" in his presidential address before Section H of the British Association in 1885, reprinting the paper in part the next year. Here he illustrated regression with a mechanical model. He also described an actual experiment with seeds, where the first generation showed the regression toward mediocrity that was required. It was in another paper in 1886 that, with Dickson's slight aid, he developed the "index of co-relation," which came presently to be called ' Galton's function,' until F. Y. Edgeworth christened it in 1892 the "coefficient of correlation." This coefficient has ever since been conventionally represented by the symbol r (regression).

It was *Karl Pearson* (1857-1936), however, who gave the theory of correlation its present mathematical foundation. It is true that the fundamental theorems had been worked out much earlier (1846) by the French mathematician, A. Bravais, but it was Pearson who used them in 1896 to develop the solution of Galton's problem. Pearson's investigations of the normality of biological distributions began two years earlier. He possessed more capacity for a technical and elaborate mathematical treatment of statistics than did Galton, and the promise of his later brilliance was already apparent at the first. In 1901 Galton, Pearson and W. F. R. Weldon founded the journal *Biometrika* for mathematical researches in biology and psychology. The Biometric Laboratory under Pearson was also begun at the University of London in the same year.

Pearson's subsequent contributions to biometrical method are too extensive to find mention in this book. He and Galton established statistical investigation of psychological problems as one of the fundamental methods and other British investigators have employed them. Subsequently G. Udny Yule (1871-   ), because of his text on statistical method, became well known and represented a more cautious view about the potency of statistics than did Pearson and his immediate followers. It seemed at times as if Pearson believed that inaccurate data could be made to yield accurate conclusions by statistical treatment, a view which the experimentalist seldom shares and which was criticized by Yule.

Charles E. Spearman (1863-1945) comes into this history at this point because in 1904 he made the next significant step in the use of the method of correlation. He published then his now famous paper on *General Intelligence, Objectively Determined and Measured*, the paper in which he laid down the two-factor theory of human capacity. Just as Galton had explained regression by reference to two components, a determinate and an indeterminate element, so Spearman undertook to interpret correlation between two variables as signifying the existence of a common factor and, in each variable, a specific factor. Measures of apparently different mental abilities are habitually, at first to the surprise and dismay of the psychologist, found to show correlations. Spearman concluded that the prevalence of positive correlations must be due to the presence of a *general ability* common to all kinds of performance. He called the general factor G, and it came to be thought of as *intelligence*. It seemed natural enough to analyze two abilities into three factors—what is common to both and what is specific in each. In 1912 Spearman and Hart worked out a technique of a hierarchal matrix of correlation coefficients which would separate a variety of performances into the general factor, G, and the various specific factors, S_1, S_2, etc. In 1916 and immediately afterward, Godfrey H. Thomson pointed out that when you have more than two performances there can be other overlappings besides G. Three performances, for instance, could have what is common to all (G), what is common to each pair (R_1, R_2, R_3), and what is specific for each of the three (S_1, S_2, S_3). There was controversy, for the two-factor theory and the theory of group factors, as it was called, seemed incompatible, until J. C. Maxwell Garnett undertook to show that the two-factor theory is but the simplest case of group factoring. By 1927, Spearman had come to accept the validity of certain other common factors, which he discussed in his *The Abilities of Man*.

Then, in the 1930s, *factor analysis* developed under the leadership of Thomson at Edinburgh, Cyril Burt at London and, in America, L. L. Thurstone at Chicago. Factor analysis is a method for analyzing a set of intercorrelated performances into as many independently variable factors as justify the labor of computation. Each factor is defined by the degree to which it participates in each of the various original performances. You get the most important factor analyzed out first, and presently you stop with some residuals that are too small to merit consideration. This technic is used mostly with mental tests and is not appropriate when the problem-situation can be separated in advance into various parameters which are subject to independent experimental control and variation. For that reason this book must do without any fuller exposition of this important development in psychology. We may note the line of descent for factor analysis, noting only the prominent ancestors: Laplace—Quetelet—Galton—Pearson—Spearman—Thomson—Garnett—Burt—Thurstone.

Although America carried on with factor analysis, England by no means lost her leadership in statistical method. Besides the continuing work of Godfrey Thomson and of Cyril Burt, R. A. Fisher appeared on the scene in the 1930s. He succeeded to Pearson's chair, the Galton Professorship of Eugenics in the Francis Galton Laboratory in University College, London. He is known for his development of the techniques for the analysis of variance and for the use and validation of small samples. He has, for instance, put the *null hypothesis* into the vocabularies of thousands of graduate students of psychology in Great Britain and America, and he has also changed their thinking so that they now know that there is no sharp line between a significant and an insignificant difference, but that significance in statistics varies continuously between extremes as it does elsewhere in the universe of values.

GALTON AS A PSYCHOLOGIST

There can be no doubt that Sir Francis Galton (1822-1911) was the pioneer of a 'new' psychology in Great Britain, that is to say, of an experimental psychology that was primarily, though not entirely, concerned with the problem of human individual differences. Karl Pearson would make of Galton a British Wundt, conceiving Galton as working independently of Wundt and concurrently, and as falling short of being the 'father' of British psychology only because the younger generation of psychologists unfortunately chose German parentage. Into this claim we need not enter. We have already compared Galton with Wundt at the beginning of this chapter. We have seen something of Galton's versatility and that psychology was but one of his many interests. There is no question as to his originality and the fact that his inspiration did not come from the Continent, although he was sufficiently conversant with the German work to make use of it and paid considerable attention to the implications of the Weber-Fechner law. As to Pearson's lament that modern experimental psychology has neglected most of Galton's work except the theory of correlation, it is quite true that many of Galton's ingenious ideas might have given rise to important methods and results had they been fostered by an enthusiastic band of followers, although one can only guess as to what fertile germs lie hidden away in the many written words which this restless, inventive mind scattered so widely that a complete bibliography is extremely difficult to achieve. On the other hand, it is the author's opinion that the important psychological research of Galton's, both as regards apparatus and as regards fact, has been fully assimilated by modern psychology, and that Galton's influence has not been greater for the simple reason that, with attention dispersed in so many other directions, his psychological productivity was not greater. After all, Galton was but half a psychologist and that for only fifteen years. Wundt was nothing but a psychologist for sixty years.

Galton's psychological researches were entirely ancillary to his deep concern with the problems of human evolution, and thus he furnishes an excellent example of the far-reaching stimulation of Darwin and his theory. *Hereditary Genius* (1869), although published when Galton was forty-seven years old, stands almost at the beginning of its author's period of great productivity, and it appears that it was the problem of mental inheritance and the improvement of the race—or at least of the British portion of the race—which concerned Galton most from the beginning. During the next fourteen years his interest in the measurement of human faculties grew, and finally culminated in the *Inquiries into Human Faculty and its Development*, published in 1883. This famous book has sometimes been regarded as the beginning of scientific individual psychology and of the mental tests. Galton's own intention regarding the book was, however, different. The conflict between evolutionary doctrine and theological dogma was in those days acute, and the scientific men of England who upheld Darwin's view were generally regarded as religious agnostics. Galton, with that degree of scientific objectivity which characterized all his thought, weighed the question quite without emotion and concluded that he could find no evidence that the intensity of a belief measures its validity. A case in point is his discussion in the *Inquiries* of the objective efficacy of prayer and his conclusion that there is no evidence that physicians can take prayer into account as a therapeutic agent, or that meteorologists should consider prayer in predicting the weather, or that clergymen prosper more than others in business affairs. Galton convinced himself that there is very little difference between the lives of Roman Catholics, Protestants, Jews and agnostics, either in their relations to humanity or in their own mental calm, and he was seeking in the *Inquiries* for a new scientific Creed to give the world. He would have had the world substitute for current religious dogma a belief in evolutionary progress as the end toward which men should strive, and he held up as the goal of human effort, not heaven, but the superman.

Thus the *Inquiries* became an attempt to measure man as he is today with the emphasis, not upon his attainment as the lord of creation, but upon his limitations as the defective ancestor of better generations. One finds Galton assuming an almost religious attitude and substituting human defect for sin. Galton's visions of the future did not, however, take him from the laborious and careful examination of the present. In part, the *Inquiries*, which includes the first formulation of the program of eugenics, presents this vision; but mostly it is a description of man with primary emphasis upon his mental faculties. Sometimes Galton wrote general psychology, as if to show the limitations of humanity taken altogether; but usually his emphasis was upon individual differences, because these show the variation that already is in existence and so provide the immediate possibility of the intelligent selection of the more fit.

Intelligent selection, however, requires in the first place a survey of available human assets. Here Galton's statistics and psychology went hand in hand. To measure the capacities of a large number of persons, and thus to sample the population, requires as a practical matter the development of apparatus and methods by which the measurements of a single individual can be easily and quickly made; such errors as are introduced by the casual procedure are expected to cancel out in the mass results. For this purpose Galton invented the *test*, and in particular the *mental test*, an experimental method of measurement which is characterized by its brevity and which contrasts with the elaborate psychophysical procedure of German psychology. Since the mental test is the tool of individual psychology and not of general psychology, it aims to exhibit human differences and not to gain an exhaustive analysis of some mental phenomenon with a few subjects considered as typical of all persons. This fact also leads to the result that the test deals ultimately with performance and not with the detailed physiological or conscious conditions that lie back of the performance. In America, behaviorism was able readily to assimilate the mental test because both are primarily concerned with performance without regard to its conscious causes. Galton anticipated this view; he wrote: "We do not want to analyze how much of our power of discriminating between two objects is due to this, that or the other of the many elementary perceptions called into action. It is the total result that chiefly interests us."

In spite of this very practical trend in Galton's psychology, he was also a good introspectionist. He argued, against the philosophers, that the report of a man as to what goes on in his own mind is as valid as the report of a geographer about a new country. He was himself an excellent observer of conscious as well as of objective events. By observing his own mind as he walked along the streets of London, he came to his first conclusions about the variety of its associative processes, and also as to the great extent with which unconscious processes occur in "the antechamber of consciousness." On the basis of such careful introspection, he also formed his own conclusion against the freedom of the will, noting how, in choice, ideas fluctuate until one of them dominates without any conscious act of will. This conclusion he reached independently of the introspective work of the German laboratories, but of course not without the influence of his predisposition toward deterministic science and away from current theology. He attacked the problem of the religious consciousness introspectively, for he put up a comic picture of Punch and made believe in its possession of divine attributes, addressing it "with much quasi-reverence as possessing a mighty power to reward or punish the behaviour of men toward it"; and he was

finally rewarded by the acquisition of a superstitious feeling toward
the picture and the possession in "a large share of the feelings that
a barbarian entertains towards his idol." This result must have been
a great triumph for a nature so little subject to superstition. Galton
also tried a personal excursion into insanity. He undertook to invest
everything he met, "whether human, animal, or inanimate, with the
imaginary attributes of a spy"; and he succeeded in establishing in
himself a paranoid state "in which every horse seemed to be watching him, either with pricked ears or disguising its espionage."

Galton's greatest contribution to introspective psychology was,
however, his study of imagery and of individual differences in imagery. With Fechner in Germany and Charcot in France he is one of
the three originators of the conception of ideational types. His questionnaire for determining types and for measuring the vividness of
the imagery for the different senses is known to every psychologist.
He was astonished at the differences that he found among individuals. He discovered synesthesia, and his examples of 'color associations' are well known. He discovered the existence of number-forms
and collected a great mass of representative data about them.

Galton's other contributions to psychology consist for the most
part in the invention of apparatus for mental tests. He constructed
a whistle for determining the highest audible pitch and tested not
only people but also animals. He had one whistle set at the end of
a hollow walking-stick with a rubber bulb for its operation in the
handle at the other end, so that he could experiment with animals
at the Zoological Gardens and on the street. For very high tones—
some animals have a limit of hearing above the human limen—he used
coal-gas or hydrogen with the whistle. The 'Galton whistle' in
much improved form later became a standard piece in all psychological laboratories until the electronics of the 1930s displaced it.

He invented a bar with a variable distance upon it for testing the
ability of persons to estimate visual extension, and also a disk to
test capacity for visual judgment of the perpendicular. The 'Galton
bar,' although generally used with the elaborate psychophysical
procedure which Galton avoided, later became standard in psychophysical laboratories.

For the muscular sense he arranged sets of three weights each,
which the subject was, in every case, to arrange in order of heavi-
ness. Originally he made the weights of cartridge cases, but later
they were put on the market, beautifully finished, in brass. This particular test is no longer used, but it has its descendant in the discrimination test for nine-year-old intelligence in the Binet scale. Its inclu-

sion in the intelligence test would seem to be one of the few instances of a practical acceptance of Galton's contention that tests
of sensory discrimination are indicative of judgment and thus of
intelligence.

Galton's other apparatus for tests has had less subsequent history.
He had a pendulum device of his own design for measuring reaction
times. He devised an ingenious apparatus for measuring the speed
of a blow struck with the arm. He made an instrument for measuring discrimination of difference in the depth of color, cards for the
determination of visual acuity, and a set of wools for the discrimination of colors. He planned an apparatus for testing color-blindness.
He was also intimately concerned with the problem of establishing
a standard scale of colors, and at one time planned to appeal to the
Vatican for samples of its 25,000 differently colored pieces used for
mosaics. He employed for olfactory discrimination sets of bottles
containing different substances, an obvious procedure that is still
the usual technique; and he adopted the esthesiometer for testing
tactual spatial discrimination—the compass test originally used by
E. H. Weber. After the publication of the *Inquiries*, we find him taking up Jacobs' work on memory span (published in *Mind* in 1887) as
a measure of "prehension," and working out ways of measuring
fatigue in schoolchildren.

Outside of psychology proper lies all of Galton's work in composite portraiture. He developed photographic methods for super-
posing a large number of portraits to form a single picture of the
'type,' using many checks to show that every element had equal
value. Thus he secured many pictures of 'generalized' criminals,
families, races, thoroughbred horses and so forth. The technique was
excellent, but differences of physiognomy do not clearly appear.
He also at one time concerned himself intensely with the identification of criminals and other human beings, and especially with the
problems of fingerprints. This matter is, however, primarily anthropometric and not psychometric.

One sees most clearly what Galton intended in his psychological
work in an account of the demonstrational Anthropometric Laboratory, which he opened in 1884 at the International Health Exhibition
and later transferred to the South Kensington Museum in London,
where it was maintained for six years. Instruments were provided for
making a number of anthropometric and psychometric measurements. They were arranged on a long table at one side of a narrow
room. Persons were admitted for threepence at one end and passed
along the table with the superintendent, who filled up a schedule

card as the measurements were successively made. An account of the laboratory lists the data as "height, weight, span, breathing power, strength of pull and squeeze, quickness of blow, hearing, seeing, color sense, and other personal data." Data for 9,337 persons were recorded during the life of the laboratory. The relation of this work to Galton's eugenic program is obvious. Galton wished to get the statistics of the range of human capacity in a large number of attributes and faculties. No important generalizations as regards human individual differences appeared, however, unless we should note Galton's erroneous conclusion that women tend in all their capacities to be inferior to men. The Anthropometric Laboratory was, nevertheless, a grand and dramatic experiment. It represents the psychologist's ideal, one which he never quite achieves. The test is too brief, the sample too small. Galton trusted his tests and would have liked to examine the whole population of Great Britain. Then, he thought, the nation would know for the first time the exact extent of its mental resources.

Although Pearson complained that experimental psychologists have accepted the Wundtian tradition as the pattern for their activities and have overlooked or forgotten Galton, England's pioneer in experimental psychology, he is hardly correct. Wundt can count as the founder of general psychology—the psychology of the generalized, human, adult, normal mind—whereas Galton is founder of individual psychology—the psychology of individual differences in human capacity. Everyone recognizes Galton's genius and initiative in this field, the significance and versatility of his insights and their important consequences in mental testing and in the growth and use of a psychology of human capacities. It would not be quite correct to call Wundt a 'pure' and Galton an 'applied' psychologist, and yet there is the difference that Wundt favored description and generalization, whereas Galton was constantly aware of the practical uses of psychology and was diligent in promoting their use. Wundt wanted to improve psychology; Galton, the human race.

It is true that general psychology and the German tradition came first and that applied psychology and the American tradition came later. It is not true that applied science has to follow generalized science; the order is more often the reverse. What happened was that the British failed to support adequately either kind of psychology, while the Germans and Americans were forging ahead. Later, as Cambridge University got well into experimental psychology and other British universities began to get laboratories, it is clear that the universities followed the accepted German tradition; but it is also true that applied psychology caught on in Great Britain more rapidly, as compared with the development of experimental general psychology, than it did in America. At the Oxford International Congress of Psychology in 1923, it was easier to find a British psychologist from a coal mine than from a psychological laboratory. Thus Galton might well have been pleased at the way things were going with British psychology, but Pearson would still have been disappointed because the applied psychologists did not form a self-conscious guild, write up their history and erect the image of Galton as their ancestral Prime Mover.

Perhaps it is true that America, while giving homage to Wundt, has overlooked Galton, to whom it owes a greater debt. Americans, never insufficiently self-conscious, have looked to Cattell, Wundt's recalcitrant student who insisted on working on individual differences, as their great pioneer in the tests. Cattell himself recognized Galton's priority and genius, but Galton seemed remote to the American testers. If only he had come with Helmholtz to the Chicago World's Fair in 1893! They were within six months of each other in age; but Galton did not come. Then, shortly after, Galton lost out to Binet in the matter of the kind of tests that were going to bring out the individual psychological resources most useful to a nation. The testers concentrated upon intelligence, Spearman's G, not on assessing the variety of capacities which were listed in Galton's inventory of human abilities.

EXPERIMENTAL PSYCHOLOGY

As we have seen, experimental psychology, never greatly encouraged by the British universities, was late in making its beginning in England. Galton's work led to no school of the psychological laboratory. The last fifteen years of the nineteenth century gave rise to little human psychology in Great Britain other than the varied contributions of Galton, the biometrics and statistics of Pearson and his associates, the system-making of Ward and Stout, the textbook writing of Sully and Stout, and the animal psychology and evolutionism of Romanes and Lloyd Morgan.

As the scene recedes into perspective, it becomes clear that the Cambridge laboratory and experimental psychology at Cambridge contribute a full half the history of British experimental psychology. The efforts, successes and failures of Ward, Rivers, Myers and Bartlett at Cambridge provide a continuity against which the extent of British progress in this line can be measured. McDougall's rôle at London and at Oxford was important but peripheral. Other persons, laboratories and events enter the history, but they appear as symptoms of what was going on. The whole genesis of the practice of experimental psychology in Britain is not, however, so complicated but that we may sketch the chief events in the order of their occurrence from James Ward on.

James Ward, the difficult philosopher-systematist, was not innocent of the new physiological psychology. He had been abroad to work in the laboratory of the great physiologist, Ludwig, at Leipzig, and to be instructed by the man who sponsored Brentano, Stumpf and G. E. Müller, the philosopher-psychologist Lotze at Göttingen. Ward, taking the experiments on the Weber-Fechner principle as the background, offered as a dissertation for a Fellowship at Trinity College, Cambridge, an essay entitled *The Relation of Physiology and Psychology*. That was in 1875, and he got the appointment. In 1877 he and John Venn, the Cambridge logician, proposed that the University should establish a laboratory of psychophysics. The proposal failed. A mathematician protested that the undertaking would "insult religion by putting the human soul in a pair of scales." In 1879 Ward tried again and failed again. Then G. F. Stout arrived at St. John's College and became Ward's student.

Ward was working on his Britannica article, which was published in 1886. That was the year when Cattell, en route to America with a fresh PhD from Wundt in hand, stopped off at Cambridge. In 1888 Cattell was back briefly, became a Fellow Commoner at St. John's, undertook some experiments on color in Clerk Maxwell's laboratory of physics (the paper disks for color mixing were called Maxwell's disks in those days), and generally impressed the Fellows at St. John's (as indeed he had impressed Wundt) with his American verve and freedom. After that, they knew at St. John's that experimental psychology existed—elsewhere. In 1887 Stout had been made a Fellow at St. John's, the first to be appointed as a psychologist. Then in 1890 McDougall arrived at St. John's for four years of study.

In 1891 Ward tried again and got £50 from the University for psychological apparatus and other sums in later years. Thirty years later Bartlett found a Helmholtz double siren and a Hipp chronoscope in the Cambridge laboratory left over from these times. Then, in 1893, Michael Foster, the physiologist, managed to get established a Lectureship in the Experimental Psychology and Physiology of the Senses, and *W. H. R. Rivers* (1864-1922), who had been working on the Continent with Hering and Kraepelin, was appointed—as "a ridiculous superfluity," said one member of the Senate. Four years later, in 1897, Michael Foster was able to assign a single room in the old Physiology Department as a psychological laboratory and Rivers was put in charge. At the same time Ward was made Professor of Moral Philosophy and thereafter he left the active interest in laboratory psychology to others. Rivers, who had been with Hering at Prague, worked on problems of vision, and *Charles S. Myers* (1873-1946) turned up as a student. In the next year McDougall became a Fellow of St. John's.

Meanwhile the Cambridge anthropologist, A. C. Haddon, had been planning an anthropological expedition to the Torres Straits (New Guinea), and he asked the psychologists of St. John's—Rivers, Myers and McDougall—to go along to make anthropological and psychological measurements and observations of primitive people. They all went. Myers and McDougall assisted Haddon and Rivers, inventorying the senses and the perceptions. They were conscious that they were doing a more thorough job than Galton had been able to undertake in his inventory of British capacities, but their methods seemed crude later. Myers went on to Borneo for more work, but they all got back before the end of 1899.

In England the physiologist, *Charles S. Sherrington* (1857-   ), then at Liverpool, had been getting interested in sensory psychology. His researches on color vision and flicker in the 1890s were often cited, and he wrote the chapters on tactual and muscular sensibility in E. A. Schaefer's *Text-Book of Physiology* which came out in 1900. Rivers wrote the chapter on vision.

Another event of importance outside of Cambridge was the establishment of a laboratory at University College, London, in 1897, the same year that the laboratory at Cambridge was 'founded.' This was also the year that Münsterberg finally left Freiburg to come permanently to Harvard, and friends of University College purchased a great deal of his Freiburg apparatus for the College. Galton was one of this group of purchasers, but the project was Sully's. Rivers assumed responsibility for the laboratory at first in addition to his Cambridge charge, and then E. T. Dixon took over when Rivers went to Torres Straits. Later, with the psychologists all back in England, McDougall went to University College as Reader (1900). He found the Freiburg apparatus in a room in a top story, a small unsuitable place, which he nevertheless continued to use as a laboratory until Spearman inherited it in 1906.

The one-room laboratory in Cambridge was also unsatisfactory, and Rivers in 1901 asked the University for £35 per annum for apparatus and "more adequate accommodations for experimental psychology." He got the grant and a little building, the rooms of which were presently being described as "dismal." Rivers, however, had lost his heart to anthropology and was off in 1902 for research in Southern India, with papers on the Todas later to show for his work. Then he was back in Cambridge, asking this time (1903) for £50 per annum and "the decent small cottage" on Mill Lane. Again he got both. He and Myers and other students worked there for six years, but by that time the "decent small cottage" had come to be called "damp, dark, ill-ventilated." The next step, however, had to be made by Myers.

Meanwhile Henry Head (1861-1940), soon to be the renowned neurologist, had become interested in the effects of lesions in peripheral sensory nerves and associated Rivers with him in what later became the classical experiment which distinguished between protopathic and epicritic cutaneous sensibility. In 1903 Rivers had two nerves severed in his left forearm, so that he and Head could study returning sensibility in his hand and wrist as the nerves regenerated. They published with the surgeon, James Sherren, their first report in 1905, and then Head and Rivers together got out the long report in 1908, freeing Rivers at last to run off to Melanesia for more anthropologizing.

When Rivers got back again in 1909, he resigned his Lectureship, keeping his Fellowship at St. John's, where he remained, until his death in 1922, a constant source of intellectual stimulation and a beloved friend to younger scholars. Myers succeeded him in the laboratory, and Bartlett turned up as a student just in time to hear Rivers lecture. Myers had had an appointment as Professor of Psychology at King's College, London. In 1908, with the physicist, H. A. Wilson, he had published the classical research on the effect of relative phase on the binaural localization of tones; and then, in 1909, he had got out his *Text-Book of Experimental Psychology*, which was intended to be and actually was just what the title says, and not a manual of methods like Titchener's. Myers was fully prepared to take over at Cambridge.

McDougall meanwhile went on with his psychophysiological experimentation at University College, until in 1904 he was appointed Wilde Reader at Oxford, a post which he held until he went to Harvard in 1920. It is an interesting fact that the Wilde Readership excludes from its functions experimental psychology, which was then McDougall's chief interest, and psychic research, which became later one of his greater interests. Still it localized McDougall at Oxford at a time when places for psychologists were scarce, and presently in 1907 the Oxford physiologist, Francis Gotch, gave

McDougall the use of three rooms in his laboratory, where he worked with such later distinguished persons as William Brown, Cyril Burt, J. C. Flugel and May Smith. McDougall published his *Physiological Psychology* in 1905, and then in 1908 his *Social Psychology*, the book which practically began a new field of university instruction and which made the classification of instincts a never-failing source of discussion for arm-chair psychologists.

Up in Edinburgh at this same time the new psychology was being discovered. W. G. Smith was appointed Lecturer in Experimental Psychology in 1906 and had established a laboratory there in 1907. A laboratory of educational psychology was set up later—in 1912. Smith died in 1918. Drever succeeded him.

In 1904 Sherrington was invited to America to Yale to give the Silliman Lectures, which were published later (1906) as *The Integrative Action of the Nervous System*. Probably no single volume had stimulated physiological psychology so much as this one, which developed the concepts of the reflex and of the integration of reflexes in complex behavior, outlined what was for years the gospel on the properties of the synapse, and contributed the notion of *adequate stimulation* to what Johannes Müller had called *specific irritability*.

In 1902 the British Psychological Society was organized. In 1904 Ward, Rivers and Myers founded the *British Journal of Psychology*, and Ward and Rivers became its editors for the first three volumes (1904-1910). British psychology was becoming self-conscious, twenty years after Germany, fifteen after the United States.

And it was spreading as well as becoming self-conscious. In 1901 Lloyd Morgan, famed for comparative psychology, was appointed Professor of Psychology and Education at Bristol. In 1906 Spearman, back from study at Leipzig, Würzburg and Göttingen, was made Reader at University College, London, and then in 1911 advanced to the Grote Professorship of Mind and Logic. In 1908 Henry J. Watt (1879-1925), known to us as one of the important members of Külpe's Würzburg school, was appointed Lecturer at Glasgow. He presently published *The Economy and Training of Memory*. In 1909 T. H. Pear went to Manchester as Lecturer.

Now we may return to Cambridge. In 1908 Myers appealed for money to build a laboratory that was not dismal, damp or dark. He got it, mostly from relatives and himself, and the donors of J. N. Langley's new physiological laboratory were pleased to have the psychological laboratory added as a wing. The foundations were laid in 1911 and the Laboratory was opened in 1913. Myers was made the

Director—the unpaid director, for Great Britain had hardly yet learned to tolerate experimental psychology, much less support it. Cyril L. Burt (1883-   ) now worked with Myers, as did G. Dawes Hicks (1862-1941). Ward dropped out as editor of the *British Journal of Psychology* and Myers replaced him in 1911 for two volumes. Then Rivers dropped out in 1913 and Myers carried on alone for nine volumes (1913-1924). Rivers published *The History of Melanesian Society* and immediately ran off to Melanesia again. He did not get back until after the First World War had begun. Myers was made Reader in Experimental Psychology in 1914, but soon both he and Rivers were off for four years of war, Myers in the Army Medical Corps in France, Rivers as psychologist in the Royal Air Force. Watt found himself interned in Germany, but used his internment to publish two excellent works, *The Psychology of Sound* in 1917 and *The Foundations of Music* in 1919.

In 1919, after the War, *T. H. Pear* (1886-   ) was made Professor of Psychology at Manchester. *James Drever* (1873-   ) was appointed Lecturer in Psychology at Edinburgh (1919-1931) in place of W. G. Smith, who had died. McDougall went to Harvard, and *William Brown* (1881-   ) succeeded him as Wilde Reader at Oxford (1921-1946). Rivers began feverishly publishing books: *Instinct and the Unconscious, Conflict and Dream, Psychology and Politics, Principles of Social Organization.*

In 1922, the year in which Rivers died, Myers left Cambridge to devote himself in London to the new National Institute for Industrial Psychology "for the application of psychology and physiology to industry and commerce." He was its Director. Applied psychology, finding support in England in the postwar period, soon outstripped its academic parent. Myers had, however, gone back to Cambridge from the War, the war where psychology and psychologists had been used and sometimes welcomed. He wrote: "I found that the wild rise of psychoanalysis had estranged the Regius Professor of Physics; I received little encouragement from the Professor of Physiology; and the Professor of Mental Philosophy [that was Ward, who approved of experimental psychology but still claimed psychology proper for philosophy], to my surprise, publicly opposed the exclusion of the word *experimental* in the title now about to be conferred on me." In other words, Ward wanted to limit Myers to experimental psychology, something less than all of psychology. Suddenly Myers found he was tired of fighting academic bigotry and moved to more friendly fields.

Bartlett, however, was ready to carry on where Myers left off.

Frederic C. Bartlett (1886-   ) accepted the title of Reader in *Experimental* Psychology (1922-1931) and Director of the Psychological Laboratory. A decade later Cambridge at last created a chair for psychology, but with the disputed word *experimental* still in the title: in 1931 Bartlett became Professor of Experimental Psychology. By that time, however, there was at London another professorship of psychology. Spearman, retiring from the Grote Professorship of Mind and Logic in 1928, had a chair as Professor of Psychology created for him, one which Cyril Burt inherited in 1931—presumably along with some old pieces of Freiburg apparatus in a top room somewhere. D. W. Harding succeeded Burt in 1945. Drever was appointed Professor of Psychology at Edinburgh in 1931, a chair which he held until his retirement in 1945.

Oxford had had only its Wilde Readership in Mental Philosophy, a post which excluded experimental psychology. It was founded in 1898 and held successively by Sully (1898), Stout (1899-1903), McDougall (1904-1920) and William Brown (1921-1947). Then, with the establishing of a chair of psychology, the readership was turned over to the philosophers. Oxford was even more reluctant than Cambridge to move with the times. The VIIIth International Congress of Psychology, with Myers as President, was held in 1923, not at Cambridge, as you would expect, where psychology was fairly well established, but at Oxford, where psychology was still confined to the Wilde Readership and such charity as McDougall's one-time borrowing of a bit of laboratory space from the physiologists. It was hoped in 1923 that Oxford would be aroused by all the visiting scholars at the Congress to discover the existence of its missing field—just as Cambridge was awakened (a little) by Cattell's visit in 1888. Perhaps Oxford did stir in 1923. At any rate, in 1936 it established, with William Brown as director, an Institute of Experimental Psychology, initially a small affair which came, after a decade, to have really adequate support. And then, at last, in 1947 a chair of psychology was created, the chair which that loyal Oxonian, Titchener, then twenty years dead, would have wanted more than anything else in life if it could have come to him in 1917 (instead of the Harvard offer) or in 1907. To the new chair Oxford called George Humphrey, a Canadian, schooled at Oxford, Leipzig and Harvard, at one time a tutor in Greek and Latin, and thus prepared to show his new colleagues that scientific psychology can come adorned with scholarship as well as not. It was in this deliberate fashion, with much unpublished painstaking effort, that Oxford was won over. It now has laboratory support, and you can take

Honours there either in Psychology and Philosophy or in Psychology and Physiology. The good Oxonians hope that philosophy will remain more important than physiology and that an Oxonian psychologist will for that reason not be confused with a Cantabrigian one.

As in America, the British psychologists participated heavily as psychologists in the Second World War. This activity was greatest in the Cambridge laboratory. Innumerable reports were issued, but the assessment of the success of this phase of the struggle for freedom on both sides of the Atlantic awaits the perspective of time.

A still earlier sign that British psychology was beginning to receive general scientific recognition lies in the election of Fellows of the Royal Society. Rivers was elected in 1908, McDougall in 1912, Myers in 1915, Spearman in 1924, and Bartlett in 1932. Sir Cyril Burt was knighted in 1946, Sir Frederic Bartlett in 1948, Sir Godfrey Thomson in 1949.

NOTES

Ward

James Ward (1843-1925) received his philosophical education (1872-1875) primarily at Cambridge, but also at Berlin before Ebbinghaus went there, and at Göttingen in Lotze's later days, just after Stumpf and Müller had left and before Müller returned as *Dozent*. His contact with the 'new' psychology was thus no greater than what Stumpf and Müller also had with Lotze; and the study in Germany was not entirely without effect on Ward, as his article on Fechner's law in the first volume of *Mind* (1876) shows. In England he was appointed successively at Trinity College, Cambridge, fellow (1875), lecturer (1881), and professor of moral philosophy (1897). There is a short and inadequate account of his life by W. R. Sorley, *Mind*, 1925, N.S. 34, 273-279. For an appreciation of Ward and an account of how Ward tried to get experimental psychology and a laboratory started at Cambridge, see F. C. Bartlett, James Ward 1843-1925, *Amer. J. Psychol.*, 1925, 36, 449-453; Cambridge, England, 1887-1937, *ibid.*, 1937, 50, 97-110, esp. 97-101.

There is a bibliography of Ward's writings by E. B. Titchener and W. S. Foster, *Amer. J. Psychol.*, 1912, 23, 457-460, which has been reprinted with corrections and extension to the date of Ward's death in *Monist*, 1926, 36, 170-176. One sees from these lists that psychology dominated Ward's thought up to about 1880 and became increasingly less important to him thereafter. On the other hand, he kept the subject with him throughout his life. He wrote the article "Psychology" for the ninth edition of the *Encyclopædia Britannica* (1886) and then rewrote it, a masterpiece of difficult systematic work, in the eleventh edition (1911). His one book on the subject is *Psychological Principles*, 1918, for which he says he had laid down the plan forty years before (1878), presumably after reading Brentano's text of 1874. For an excellent account of Ward as a psychologist by the man best fitted to write it, see G. F. Stout, *Monist*, 1926, 36, 20-55. See also J. Laird on Ward and the Ego, *ibid.*, 90-110.

On Ward's philosophy, see the six other articles in *ibid.*, 1-159; also G. Dawes Hicks, *Mind*, 1925, N.S. 34, 280-299.

Stout

George Frederick Stout (1860-1944) studied in philosophy and psychology at Cambridge (1881-1883), primarily with Ward. He was appointed fellow in St. John's College, Cambridge (1884) and later lecturer in moral science (1894-1896). Then he went for two years to Aberdeen as Anderson lecturer in comparative psychology. He was Wilde Reader in mental philosophy at Oxford (1898) and subsequently examiner for the University of London. These were the years when he was able to employ his leisure for the production of psychological textbooks (1896-1903). After 1903 Stout became professor of logic and metaphysics at St. Andrews in Scotland. See C. A. Mace, George Frederick Stout 1860-1944, *Brit. J. Psychol.*, 1946, 36, 51-54.

As the text has made clear, Stout's importance to psychology comes by way of his textbooks: *Analytic Psychology*, 2 vols., 1896; *Manual of Psychology*, 1899, 3 ed., 1913, 10th impression, 1924; *Groundwork of Psychology*, 1903. On Stout as an act psychologist, see E. B. Titchener, *Systematic Psychology: Prolegomena*, 1929, 236-238, 243, 245. Stout was editor of *Mind* from 1892 to 1920.

McDougall

William McDougall (1871-1938) studied at Manchester (1886-1890) and Cambridge (1890-1894), at St. Thomas' Hospital in London (1894-1898), and also in Göttingen (1900). He had a medical degree from Cambridge. He worked with Müller at Göttingen. He was appointed fellow in St. John's College, Cambridge (1898-1904), reader in University College, London (1900-1906), Wilde Reader in mental philosophy at Oxford (1904-1920), and extraordinary fellow in Corpus Christi College, Oxford (1912). During the First World War he was engaged in psycho-medical work. In 1920 he accepted a call to Harvard University in America as professor of psychology, the chair made vacant by Münsterberg's death in 1916. In 1927 he went to the newly endowed Duke University in North Carolina.

McDougall published an autobiographical sketch in C. Murchison, *Psychology in Autobiography*, 1930, I, 191-223. Eight "appreciations" of McDougall are listed by A. L. Robinson, *William McDougall, a Bibliography*, 1943, items 203-210. See especially D. K. Adams, William McDougall, *Psychol. Rev.*, 1939, 46, 1-8; C. L. Burt, William McDougall, an appreciation, *Brit. J. educ. Psychol.*, 1939, 9, 1-7; J. C. Flugel, Professor William McDougall 1871-1938, *Brit. J. Psychol.*, 1939, 29, 320-328; F. A. Pattie, William McDougall 1871-1938, *Amer. J. Psychol.*, 1939, 52, 303-307; C. E. Spearman, The life and work of William McDougall, *Char. and Personal.*, 1939, 7, 175-183.

McDougall was very prolific. Robinson, *op. cit.*, lists 24 books and 167 articles and notes. His more important books from our point of view are: *Physiological Psychology*, 1905; *Introduction to Social Psychology*, 1908, 14 ed., 1919; *Body and Mind*, 1911; *Psychology, the Study of Behaviour*, 1912, 2 ed., 1914; *The Group Mind*, 1920, 2 ed., 1927; *Outline of Psychology*, 1923; *Outline of Abnormal Psychology*, 1926. There are seventeen other books, beginning with *Is America Safe for Democracy?*, 1921, and ending with *The Riddle of Life*, 1938, published in the year of his death. McDougall was a prophet, writing with a sense of mission.

For McDougall's systematic position, see *op. cit.*, 1923; also Purposive or mechanical psychology?, *Psychol. Rev.*, 1923, 30, 273-288; Fundamentals of psychology, *Psyche*, 1924, 5, 13-32; Men or robots?, *Psychologies of 1925*, 1926, 273-305.

For McDougall's work on the inheritance of acquired characters, see his An experiment for testing the hypothesis of Lamarck, *Brit. J. Psychol.*, 1927, 17, 267-304; Second report on a Lamarckian experiment, *ibid.*, 1930, 20, 201-218; (with J. B. Rhine) Third report, *ibid.*, 1933, 24, 213-235; Fourth report, *ibid.*, 1938, 28, 321-345. He stuck to this faith until his death.

McDougall's experimental work is discussed briefly in the last section of the text. His theory of nervous inhibition by drainage appeared originally as The nature of inhibitory processes within the nervous system, *Brain*, 1903, 26, 153-191. For his work on retinal rivalry, see The physiological factors of the attention-process, *Mind*, 1903, N.S. 12, 473-488. He developed a method for the measurement of attention with G. E. Müller at Göttingen; see On a new method for the study of concurrent mental operations and of mental fatigue, *Brit. J. Psychol.*, 1905, 1, 435-445. For his 'spot-pattern' test, see *Physiological Psychology*, 129-134.

Sully

James Sully (1842-1923) studied principally at London. The text mentions his visit to Göttingen and to Berlin. In 1892 he succeeded Croom Robertson as Grote professor of mind and logic at University College, where he was later in turn succeeded by Spearman. For many years this chair was the nearest appointment to a professorship of psychology that Great Britain had. For biography, see Sully, *My Life and Friends*, 1918, which is unfortunately more a book of reminiscences than an account of his intellectual development, with side-lights on British psychology.

Sully's important psychological texts are: *Sensation and Intuition*, 1874, 2 ed., 1880; *Illusions*, 1881; *Outlines of Psychology*, 1884, 3 ed., 1896; *Teacher's Handbook of Psychology*, 1886, 5 ed., 1910; *Human Mind*, 1892; *Studies of Childhood*, 1896, 2 ed, 1903; *Children's Ways*, 1897; *Essay on Laughter*, 1902.

Evolution

The reader will readily find a large literature on organic evolution. The views of Buffon, Erasmus Darwin and Lamarck, especially as related to the views of Charles Darwin, are considered in a readable and interesting manner by S. Butler, *Evolution, Old and New*, 1879, 3 ed., 1911. The modern theory is presented by T. H. Morgan, *Critique of the Theory of Evolution*, 1916, in which the relation of the present view to its early history is indicated (pp. 27-39). A very thorough work, dealing with cosmological as well as organic evolution. is H. Smidt, *Geschichte der Entwicklungslehre*, 1918. An excellent briefer account in English is E. Nordenskiöld, *History of Biology*, 1928, 453-616.

For a life of Charles Darwin, see Francis Darwin, *Life and Letters of Charles Darwin*, 1887. The dates of Darwin's three most important books are: *Origin of Species*, 1859; *Descent of Man*, 1871; *Expression of the Emotions in Man and Animals*, 1872. An "Essay on Instinct" was published posthumously in Romanes' *Mental Evolution in Animals* (*infra*).

Romanes

For Romanes (1848-1894), see *Life and Letters of George John Romanes*, 1896, by his wife. His three books on comparative psychology are: *Animal Intelligence*, 1882; *Mental Evolution in Animals*, 1883; *Mental Evolution in Man*, 1888.

Romanes fills a chronological gap between Darwin and Lloyd Morgan. His first book, *Animal Intelligence*, appeared in the year of Darwin's death. Lloyd Morgan's second book, the *Comparative Psychology*, appeared in the year of Romanes' death.

Lloyd Morgan

Conwy Lloyd Morgan (1852-1936), after holding a lectureship in South Africa (1878-1883), first became professor of zoology and geology at University College, Bristol (1884) and then principal of the college (1887-1909). His autobiography is in C. Murchison, *Psychology in Autobiography*, 1932, II, 237-264. His important contributions to comparative psychology, in the period we have discussed, are *Animal Life and Intelligence*, 1890-1891; *Introduction to Comparative Psychology*, 1894; *Habit and Instinct*,

1896; *Animal Behaviour*, 1900, 2 ed., 1908. Of his later books *Emergent Evolution*, 1923, is best known.

For Lloyd Morgan's canon, see chap. 3 of his *Comparative Psychology*. The law of parsimony has sometimes been referred to as William of Occam's 'razor': "Entia non sunt multiplicanda, praeter necessitatem." *Cf.* Karl Pearson, *Grammar of Science*, 1908 or 1911, appendix, note iii. On the question of the exact origin of the phrase, *cf.* the discussion in W. M. Thorburn and C. D. Burns, Occam's razor, *Mind*, 1915, N.S. 24, 287 f., 592. Sir William Hamilton called it the "law of parsimony"; *cf.* his *Discussions on Philosophy*, 2 ed., 1853, 628-631. For all its antiquity the 'razor' is hardly a useful tool of science except for its uncertain use in offsetting a bias of interpretation. Lloyd Morgan was justified in employing it against the tendency to anthropomorphize animals, a tendency reinforced by the desire to prove the Darwinian theory; but conditions have changed today in comparative psychology. *Cf.* D. K. Adams's criticism of the use of the law, The inference of mind, *Psychol. Rev.*, 1928, 35, 235-252. Entia sunt multiplicanda propter necessitatem.

Animal Psychology in General

Jacques Loeb's (1859-1924) theory of the tropism was promulgated in *Der Heliotropismus der Thiere und seine Ueberstimmung mit dem Heliotropismus der Pflanzen*, 1890. Loeb published later *Einleitung in die vergleichende Gehirnphysiologie und vergleichende Psychologie*, 1899, Eng. trans., 1900.

As bearing on the question of historical priority, it is important to mention that Spalding performed experiments on chicks even before Romanes began writing and before he himself had read Darwin's *Expression of the Emotions*. The reference is D. A. Spalding, Instinct: with original observations on young animals, *Macmillan's Mag.*, 1873, 27, 282-293; reprinted in *Pop. Sci. Mo.*, 1902, 61, 126-142.

Leonard Trelawney Hobhouse (1864-1929) published *Mind in Evolution* in 1901, 2 ed., 1915. Most of his work has lain in metaphysics, epistemology, the philosophy of the state and sociology.

The classical papers on the social insects are: J. Henri Fabre, *Souvenirs entomologiques*, 1879-1904; Sir John Lubbock, *Ants, Bees, and Wasps*, 1882; Auguste Forel, *Expériences et remarques critiques sur les sensations des insects*, 1887, Eng. trans., 1908; Albrecht Bethe, Dürfen wir den Ameisen und Bienen psychische Qualitäten zuschreiben? [*Pflüger's*] *Arch. ges. Physiol.*, 1898, 70, 15-100; 1900, 79, 39-52.

On the psychic life of protozoa, see A. Binet, *Étude de psychologie expérimentale: la vie psychique des microorganismes*, 1888, 2 ed., 1891, Eng. trans., 1889. H. S. Jennings took up this point of view in America in 1897 *et seq.*: see *J. Physiol.*, 1897, 21, 258-322; *Amer. J. Psychol.*, 1899, 10, 503-515; *Amer. Natural.*, 1899, 23, 373-390; *Amer. J. Physiol.*, 1899, 2, 311-341, 355-393; 1899, 3, 229-260; etc. See also his monograph, *Contributions to the Study of the Behavior of the Lower Organisms*, 1904 and 1906. On Jennings, *cf.* also pp. 625 f.

On Thorndike's use of formal laboratory technique with animals, see E. L. Thorndike, *Animal Intelligence*, *Psychol. Monog.*, 1898, 2, no. 4; reprinted outside the monograph series, 1911.

For a bibliography of comparative psychology, see M. F. Washburn, *Animal Mind*, 1908, 3 ed., 1926. On the history of comparative psychology, see C. J. Warden, *Psychol. Rev.*, 1927, 34, 57-85, 135-168; esp. 145-164, which deals with this period.

Mental Inheritance

See notes on Galton, *infra*.

Statistical Method

The best text on the history of the development of the statistical methods is H. M. Walker, *Studies in the History of Statistical Method*, 1929. The theory of probabilities underlies all statistical method, and on the history of this theory see I. Todhunter, *History of the Mathematical Theory of Probability*, 1865, the standard historical work beginning with Pascal and Fermat (1654) and extending to Laplace (1812). The normal law of error, which gives the bell-shaped curve of distribution, is properly accredited to Laplace (1786) and was known to de Moivre in 1733. Gauss (1809) dealt with the applications of the law, as well as deriving it from a new principle, and his name became attached to it in the way that promoters are often confused with discoverers in the history of science.

On the application of the law to anthropometric and social data by Adolphe Quetelet (1796-1874), see É. Mailly, *Essai sur la vie et les travaux de L. A. J. Quetelet*, 1875; F. H. Hankins, *Adolphe Quetelet as Statistician*, 1908. Quetelet's statistical researches, which began about 1825, culminated in his *Essai de physique sociale*, 1835, which contains the doctrine of *l'homme moyen*. Almost equally important for our interest is his *Lettres sur la théorie des probabilités*, 1846, Eng. trans., 1849. On the history of the use of the normal law, see Walker, *op. cit.*, 4-70, which includes 84 references to more important articles.

Quetelet was a mathematician and astronomer of Brussels. He was the founder of modern statistics, and in his hands the word broadened its meaning from denoting data concerning the state to its present significance. He has also been looked upon as the founder of modern sociology. On the history of the word and its relation to the data of the state, see Walker, *op. cit.*, 31-38.

Not only did Galton in *Hereditary Genius* adopt Quetelet's use of the normal law and turn it into a more effective instrument of measurement, but he became in a sense Quetelet's successor, building up in England a gospel of statistical science, which culminated in part in his advocacy of eugenics and his foundation of the Research Laboratory for National Eugenics. For Galton, statistics and anthropometry were inseparable, and his anthropometry included such a large measure of the study of mental faculties that his individual psychology and statistics become inseparable also.

For Galton on regression, see first his paper, Regression towards mediocrity in hereditary stature, *J. Anthropol. Inst.*, 1886, 15, 246-263 (reprint of part of his presidential address of 1885). The conception of correlation becomes clearer in Family likeness in stature, *Proc. Roy. Soc.*, 1886, 40, 42-73 (a paper which includes the mathematical appendix by J. D. H. Dickson, 63-66), and in Family likeness in eye-colour, *ibid.*, 402-406. Finally the shift of emphasis from regression to correlation is complete in Co-relations and their measurement, *Proc. Roy. Soc.*, 1888, 45, 135-145. Here Galton called *r* the "index of co-relation." For a general discussion of regression, see Galton, *Natural Inheritance*, 1889, 95-110. In general, see K. Pearson's chapter, Correlation and the application of statistics to the problems of heredity, in his *Life, Letters and Labours of Francis Galton*, 1930, III, 1-137.

F. Y. Edgeworth established the term, *coefficient of correlation*, for *r* in a mathematical paper in *Philos. Mag.*, 1892, 5 ser., 34, 190-204.

For Karl Pearson's development of the method of correlation and its establishment in the form of 'product-moments,' see his Mathematical contributions to the theory of evolution: regression, heredity, and panmixia, *Philos. Trans.*, 1896, 187A, 253-318. What we have here is the application to observed data of the old principles of the problem of "the laws of error of a point in space." Bravais' theorems, which Pearson applied, are to be found in A. Bravais, *Mém. l'Acad. roy. sci. l'Inst. France, sci. math. et phys.*, 1846, 9, 255-332.

On the history of the theory of correlation in general, see Walker, *op. cit.*, 92-147, with an annotated bibliography of 81 important titles.

G. Udny Yule's well-known text is *Introduction to the Theory of Statistics*, 1911, 6 ed., 1922. His remarks about the limitations of statistics were directed specifically to Brown and Thomson in his review of their book, *op. cit. infra, Brit. J. Psychol.*, 1921, 12, 105-107.

William Brown published the *Essentials of Mental Measurement*, 1911, and the book, revised by Godfrey H. Thomson, appeared under their joint authorship in 1921. The volume represents the attempt to combine psychophysical and psychological statistical methods under a single treatment.

The classic papers by C. E. Spearman are The proof and measurement of association between two things, *Amer. J. Psychol.* (the *Brit. J. Psychol.* was not founded until the next year), 1904, 15, 72-101; "General intelligence" objectively determined and measured, *ibid.*, 200-292. The mathematical treatment for determining the hierarchical arrangement of coefficients of correlation is B. Hart and Spearman, General ability, its existence and nature, *Brit. J. Psychol.*, 1912, 5, 51-84. For an annotated bibliography of 35 important titles up to 1929 (before factor analysis), see Walker, *op. cit.*, 142-147, where most of the papers are by Spearman, G. H. Thomson and J. C. M. Garnett. Spearman's *Abilities of Man, Their Nature and Measurement*, 1927, is really a summary of this work replete with references and appendices showing how to make the computations. Another good summary is S. C. Dodd, The theory of factors, *Psychol. Rev.*, 1928, 35, 211-234, 261-279, which gives references to 39 of the important articles. Spearman's earlier book on this general topic is *The Nature of Intelligence and the Principles of Cognition*, 1923, 2 ed., 1927; and his later book, *Creative Mind*, 1931.

Thrice after 1931 Spearman held teaching posts in America. He wrote an autobiography in C. Murchison, *Psychology in Autobiography*, 1930, I, 299-333. Two appreciations of Spearman are: E. L. Thorndike, Charles Edward Spearman 1863-1945, *Amer. J. Psychol.*, 1945, 58, 558-560; J. C. Flugel, Charles Edward Spearman

1863-1945, *Brit. J. Psychol.*, 1946, 37, 1-6.

As for the complications of factor analysis, see G. H. Thomson, *The Factorial Analysis of Human Ability*, 1939; C. L. Burt, *The Factors of the Mind*, 1941; L. L. Thurstone, *Multiple-Factor Analysis*, 1947.

R. A. Fisher's two important books are *Statistical Methods for Research Workers*, 1925, 10 ed., 1946; *The Design of Experiments*, 1935, 4 ed., 1947. For what modern statistics is like (including the Fisher contributions), see any of the good texts, like C. C. Peters and W. R. Van Voorhis, *Statistical Procedures and Their Mathematical Bases*, 1940, or Quinn McNemar, *Psychological Statistics*, 1949.

Galton

On the life and work of Francis Galton (1822-1911), there is first his *Memories of My Life*, 1908, which contains an incomplete and often inaccurate bibliography of 183 titles. (This book is referred to hereinafter as *M*.) Then there is Karl Pearson's account of his hero, *Life, Letters and Labours of Francis Galton*, 1914, I, 1924, II, 1930, III. The first volume includes the story of Galton's early life and the account of his ancestry. The second volume (referred to hereinafter as *P*) includes the account of his geographical, his anthropological, his psychological and, in part, his statistical work, and is important for us, especially the chapter on "Psychological Investigations" (chap. 11, 211-282). The third volume contains the story of the development of the method of correlation and its use in the problems of heredity, Galton's contributions to the problems of personal identification and fingerprinting, Galton on eugenics, and—most important for the account of so discursively versatile a mind—the index for all three volumes.

On Galton's remarkable intelligence, as estimated posthumously by those experienced in testing intelligence, see L. M. Terman, *Amer. J. Psychol.*, 1917, 28, 209-215; and *cf.* C. M. Cox, *Early*

Mental Traits of Three Hundred Geniuses (*Genetic Studies of Genius*, II), 1926, for Galton's parity with the most intelligent men of this list: Leibnitz, Goethe and J. S. Mill.

Galton's important books were all on the subject of inheritance, for the *Inquiries* should be included in the list. They are: *Hereditary Genius*, 1869, 2 ed., 1892; *English Men of Science, Their Nature and Nurture*, 1874; *Inquiries into Human Faculty and Its Development*, 1883 (referred to hereinafter as *I*), reprinted with the omission of two chapters, 1907; *Natural Inheritance*, 1889. Galton's important paper on the history of twins is The history of twins, as a criterion of the relative powers of nature and nurture, *J. Anthropol. Inst.*, 1876, 5, 324-329. *Cf. I*, 216-243.

For Galton's attitude on religion, see the memorandum which Pearson publishes for the first time, *P*, 425. For Galton on the "objective efficacy of prayer," see *I*, 277-294; *P*, 249 f. For Galton on the doctrine of evolution as (practically) a religious creed, see esp. *I*, 331-337.

Three readily available excerpts from Galton's writings are to be found in W. Dennis, *Readings in the History of Psychology*, 1948, 231-247 (chap. 3 of *Hereditary Genius*, 1869), 277-289 (Galton whistle, imagery questionnaire, association of ideas, from *Inquiries*, 1883), 336-346 (co-relations an! their measurement, 1888).

Pearson's volumes furnish a great mass of material about Galton upon which it has been impracticable for the text to touch. It is also not practicable to burden these notes with the original references to all of Galton's scattered contributions to psychology: the reader can find most of them in Pearson. The following list of references to three secondary sources may, however, be of aid to the person who seeks immediate information about some one of the many items mentioned but briefly in the text.

Mental tests for performance, without analysis of conscious conditions: *P*, 373.

Introspection as observation: *P*, 243.

The antechamber of consciousness: *I*, 203-207; *P*, 256.

Free will: *P*, 245-247.

Introspective experiments on [paranoid] insanity and the religious attitude: *M*, 246 f.; *P*, 247 f.

Imagery, the questionary, synæsthesia, and number-forms: *I*, 83-203, 378-380; *P*, 236-240, 252-256.

The Galton whistle: *I*, 38-40, 375-378; *M*, 247 f.; *P*, 215-217, 221 f.

Discrimination of visual distance (Galton bar) and of the perpendicular: *P*, 222 f.

Discrimination of lifted weights: *I*, 34-38, 370-375; *P*, 217 f.

Reaction time and chronoscope: *P*, 219 f., 226.

Speed of a blow: *P*, 220 f.

Visual acuity and color discrimination: *P*, 222 f.

Color-blindness: *P*, 227.

Color scale and standards: *P*, 223-226.

Discrimination of smells: *P*, 223.

Tactual space-discrimination (compass test): *P*, 223.

Memory span (prehension): *P*, 272.

Mental fatigue: *P*, 276-278.

Composite portraiture: *I*, 8-19, 340-363; *M*, 259-265; *P*, 283-333.

Fingerprints and personal identification: *M*, 252-258.

The Anthropometric Laboratory: *M*, 244-251; *P*, 357-362, 370.

Women inferior to men: *I*, 29 f. (but cf. 99); *P*, 221 f.

In not all cases do these sources furnish the original reference.

Experimental Psychology

For the history of experimental psychology at Cambridge, see F. C. Bartlett, Cambridge, England, 1887-1937, *Amer. J. Psychol.*, 1937, 50, 97-110. On the laboratory at University College, London, see G. Dawes Hicks, A century of philosophy at University College, London, *J. philos. Studies*, 1928, 3, 468-482.

On Ward, Stout and McDougall, see the respective sections in these notes *supra*. On Spearman, see Statistical Method in these notes *supra*.

On W. H. R. Rivers, see Bartlett,

William Halse Rivers Rivers 1864-1922, *Amer. J. Psychol.*, 1923, 34, 275-277; Bartlett, *op. cit.* (1937), 102-107.

On C. S. Myers, see his autobiography in C. Murchison, *Psychology in Autobiography*, 1936, III, 215-230; Bartlett, *op. cit.* (1937), 102-104, 107 f.; T. H. Pear, Charles Samuel Myers 1873-1946, *Brit. J. Psychol.*, 1947, 38, 1-6; *idem, Amer. J. Psychol.*, 1947, 60, 289-296.

On F. C. Bartlett, see his autobiography in C. Murchison, *op. cit.*, 1936, III, 39-52; Bartlett, *op. cit.* (1937).

On James Drever and the history of psychology at Edinburgh, see Drever's autobiography, in Murchison, *op. cit.*, 1932, II, 17-34.

Psychopathology, Psychic Research and Philosophical Psychology

There were in Great Britain some important influences that lay just at the periphery of experimental psychology. The text has shown how the experimental psychologists tended, when they did not go over into anthropology, to work in medical psychology or physiological psychology. The relation of Sherrington to psychology is an example of the influence of physiologists. There is, however, also a definite *psychopathological* tradition. John Hughlings-Jackson (1835-1911) affected psychology by way of his doctrine of the evolutionary strata of the brain and the mind. Henry Maudsley (1835-1918) quite early published a very influential book, *The Physiology and Pathology of Mind*, 1867. In the third edition it was entirely rewritten and divided into two books, *The Physiology of Mind*, 1876, and *The Pathology of Mind*, 1879. Maudsley also wrote on other psychological topics; *cf.* his *Body and Mind*, 1870. Henry Head

(1861-1940) has had great influence, not only in his theory of cutaneous sensibility, but in his work on aphasia and on the functions of the thalamus in feeling and emotion. See his *Studies in Neurology*, 1920; *Aphasia and Kindred Disorders of Speech*, 1926. On brain physiology in England, see pp. 74-76, 683 f.

Psychic research has also lain at the periphery of the new psychology in England. F. W. H. Myers (1843-1901) was very influential. *Cf.* his *Science and Future Life*, 1893; *Human Personality and Its Survival of Bodily Death*, 1903. Edmund Gurney (1847-1888) was another leader. *Cf.* E. Gurney, F. W. H. Myers, and F. Podmore, *Phantasms of the Living*, 1886. Gurney also contributed to the experimental research on hypnosis. Henry Sidgwick (1838-1900), also involved in the investigation of 'supernormal' phenomena, was the president of the second International Congress of Psychology which was held in London in 1892. In fact the emphasis placed upon psychic research at this congress led to a definite reaction away from the topic in the succeeding congresses.

Finally there were always on the periphery of psychology the *psychological philosophers*. Men like Ward straddled the two fields. Some others of the philosophers, however, were definitely concerned with writing psychology, as the foundation of *Mind*, and subsequently its contents, attest. In addition to the names that receive mention in the text, we should call attention to the writings of F. H. Bradley (1846-1924) and Bernard Bosanquet (1848-1923), both of whom sought to contribute to the new psychology and were influential in determining its thought. Since 1930, however, the line between psychology and philosophy in England as in America has become quite distinct—except, of course, at Oxford.

ESTABLISHMENT OF MODERN
PSYCHOLOGY IN AMERICA

American Psychology: Its Pioneers

I t is well for us to outline the beginnings of American psychology
before filling in the details.

James began psychology in America with his recognition of the
significance of the new experimental physiological psychology of
Germany. He was not by temperament an experimentalist himself,
but he believed in experimentalism; he introduced it to America, and
he put upon this new psychology the seal of America by emphasizing the functional meaning of mind. Stanley Hall was technically
James's pupil, although they breathed different atmospheres, and
he was the pioneer of the psychological laboratory, of educational
psychology and, in fact, of everything new. Like the pioneer, he
moved with the frontier and left others to settle in. Ladd was the
Sully of America and gave it its early texts, even before James put
out his famous *Principles*. He too was a functional psychologist before there was any such school. From about 1888 to 1895 a wave of
laboratory-founding swept over America, lagging only a little in
phase behind a similar wave in Germany. Americans were going to
Germany, mostly to Wundt at Leipzig, and coming back filled with
enthusiasm for making American psychology secure in experimentalism. Titchener and Münsterberg were imported in 1892. On the
face of things, America was attempting to duplicate Germany; but
under the surface, quite unrecognized at first, a psychology that resembled Galton's more than Wundt's was being formed. Cattell,
the senior after James, Ladd and Hall, had returned from Leipzig
but little impressed with the importance of the generalized normal
human adult mind and bent upon the investigation of individual differences in human nature. Baldwin supported him. Finally, under
the influence of William James, John Dewey and pragmatism, and
with direct instigation by Dewey, the systematic structure of American psychology began to show above the surface at Chicago, where
philosophers and psychologists (the future pragmatists and functionalists) were working together. American functionalism came
into being, in bold relief against the Wundtian background which

Titchener was there to provide. Cattell himself never had a system, but the influence of Columbia was with functionalism as Galton's would have been.

By 1900 the characteristics of American psychology had become well defined. It had inherited its physical body from German experimentalism, but it had got its mind from Darwin. American psychology was to deal with mind in use. Cattell himself never had an explicit system, but his faith filled out part of the picture. Thorndike brought the animals into the laboratory, and an experimental animal psychology began forthwith. Thorndike then took himself over to the study of school-children, and the mental tests increased. Hall helped here too with his pioneering in educational psychology. In 1910 American psychology had embraced experimental human psychology, animal psychology and mental tests and was beginning to discover Freud. Some conservatives were Wundtians, some radicals were functionalists, more psychologists were middle-of-the-roaders. Then Watson touched a match to this mixture, there was an explosion, and behaviorism was left. Watson founded behaviorism because everything was all ready for the founding. Otherwise he could not have done it. He was philosophically inept, and behaviorism came into existence without a constitution. Immediately, however, the more philosophically-minded psychologists undertook to write a constitution for it. E. B. Holt and his pupil E. C. Tolman turned behaviorism in the direction of what was much later to be a new dynamic psychology—after Freud and Watson had been fused. By the 1930s the relation of psychology to the new Austrian positivism was recognized, and it became apparent that psychology ceases to be a body-mind dualism if you but remember that all psychological data of behavior or of consciousness are reducible to comparable observational operations. Since what you directly observe in another person is behavior, even though he be introspecting, positivistic psychology turns into a behavioristics or an operationism. Although most American psychologists have not accepted such terms, many have believed that these formulas of the 1940s provide a working constitution for what most Americans are actually doing.

Meanwhile Gestalt psychology, which originated in Germany in 1912 and which had an ancestral line leading back to von Ehrenfels in 1890, had been transplanted to America by Nazi intolerance. It continued there, setting off American behavioristics by contrast, much as Titchener's introspectionism had done twenty years before. To see a figure clearly, you need a ground.

It is an interesting question why American psychology went

functional in this broad sense instead of following the German pattern. The Americans travelled to Leipzig to learn about the new psychology from Wundt; they came back fired with enthusiasm for physiological psychology and experimental laboratories; they got their universities to let them give the new courses and have the new laboratories; they extolled their German importation; and then, with surprisingly little comment on what they were doing and probably but little awareness of it, they changed the pattern of psychological activity from the description of the generalized mind to the assessment of personal capacities in the successful adjustment of the individual to his environment. The apparatus was Wundt's, but the inspiration was Galton's. Why?

The simple answer is to say that the theory of evolution determined the change. We have already discussed this question once in connection with evolutionism and Herbert Spencer (see pp. 240-244), but now is the time to make as definitive a statement about the matter as is possible with our available knowledge. In general, America accepted the theory of evolution with avidity; so, we might say, a psychology of adaptation and survival-value was the result. Galton and Cattell, this theory runs, were agents of the *Zeitgeist* but neither necessary nor sufficient causes. Even Darwin was not an essential link in the chain but a symptom of the times, as we see by the simultaneous invention of the theory of natural selection by both Darwin and Alfred Russell Wallace. That view is correct, but it is not enough. Why, we ask further, was the effect of the theory of evolution so great upon American psychology, so little upon German psychology? There must have been a difference between America and Germany. Why did not England, with such a good head start, keep far ahead of America in functional psychology instead of dropping behind? There must have been a difference between America and England.

The complete answer is that America was ready for evolutionism —readier than Germany, than England even. America was a new pioneer country. Land was free—to the strong pioneer who was ready to take it and wrest a living from nature. Survival by adaptation to environment was the key to the culture of the New World. America's success-philosophy, based on individual opportunity and ambition, is responsible for shirt-sleeves democracy ("every man a king"), for pragmatism ("the philosophy of a dollar-grubbing nation") and functionalism of all kinds, within psychology and without. These forces in this *Zeitgeist* were, however, simply the present forms of old forces for change that we know were operating in the

Renaissance, the forces that were against hereditary right and for the recognition of personal achievement, against theological dogma and for scientific inquiry, forces that were reinforced, many believe, by the discovery of new land and wealth in the New World and the Far East. It was this trend which, in a mere three centuries, made the invention of the theory of evolution both possible, and, we have a right to believe, probable. The theory had to be born in England where well-to-do scholars had leisure for scientific pursuits, not in gauche America which was still too busy adapting and surviving to speculate wisely on the origin of species. Later indeed, when the American frontier had moved west to the Pacific, and the railroads were built, and the free land for settlers had disappeared, there came the time for consolidation and thinking. Then it was that the new theory of evolution was taken over in energetic America with an enthusiasm that in some savants, like Stanley Hall, amounted to religious fervor. This is just the way that the *Zeitgeist* works. No person invented functional psychology—James, Dewey, Ladd, Baldwin, Cattell—nor gave it to America as a gift. It was there when it was there because the time and the place required it. The time—the necessary yet insufficient conditions for functionalism have been forming since the sixteenth century and, for that matter, since the beginning of eternity. The place—the New World was the only large sparsely populated area left for pioneering, the only one with huge fertile regions existing in a climate (25 to 50 degrees latitude) where intellectual work is so easy that it occurs in large amounts.

In brief, then, American psychology went functional because functionalism and thus evolutionism were both natural to the temper of America. Each of these conceptions, moreover, helped the other because both were but different aspects of a same basic attitude toward human nature.

Now we may go back to the details of our history and begin, as we so easily can because of his originality, with William James.

WILLIAM JAMES

William James (1842-1910) is an important figure in the history of experimental psychology, although he was not by temperament nor in fact an experimentalist. He was, nevertheless, the pioneer of the 'new' psychology in America, and he was its senior psychologist. Because James in America was interpreting and criticizing the new psychology of Germany, we are apt to forget how early he seized upon the new movement. In age he was only ten years Wundt's junior, and he was almost as much again older than Stumpf and G. E.

Müller. With an appointment in physiology at Harvard, he was offering instruction in physiological psychology as early as 1875, the year that Wundt went from Zürich to Leipzig. In that year James got Harvard to spend three hundred dollars on "physiological" apparatus and to set aside two rooms in the Lawrence Scientific School where the students in his graduate course, *The Relations between Physiology and Psychology*, could repeat experiments and see for themselves what the lecturer was talking about. Beginning in 1877 James for his own experimentation had additional space in Harvard's Museum of Comparative Zoology. All this was very early, for it is conventional to say that Wundt founded the world's first psychological laboratory at Leipzig in 1879, although Wundt himself had facilities for experimental demonstrations at Leipzig soon after he arrived there in 1875. In short, both James and Wundt had informal demonstrational laboratories (not research laboratories) in 1875 and thereafter.

With James the laboratory never was, however, anything more than a personal conviction; it never with him became a personal habit. He thoroughly appreciated its significance and often made light of its actual working. This paradox becomes quite clear in James' *Principles of Psychology*, published after twelve years of laborious work interrupted by much ill health, in 1890, and after Ladd had already published a textbook of physiological psychology. The *Principles* both supported and condemned the new German movement. It supported it by presenting with painstaking care a great many of its experimental findings to American readers and by interpreting them in the light of James' systematic views. It condemned it often in the interpretation of these results and in the fact that it was a presentation of a different approach to psychology. In this point of view, James was consistent with the functional spirit of American psychology, and we have already seen how difficult it is to say whether James determined this spirit or only reflected it, whether he was a cause or a symptom. The key to his influence lies, however, in his personality, his clarity of vision and his remarkable felicity in literary style. His books, in fact, contain his personality, and there is no reason for us to distinguish between the man and his writings. James was both positive and tolerant. He was clear and gifted in happy expression; thus he was persuasive. The operation of a brilliant mind through assurance and good humor upon a great fund of positive knowledge was bound to be effective through the medium of personal contact and of publication. There can be no doubt that James is America's foremost psychologist, in spite of the fact that he was but a half-hearted experimentalist influencing a predominantly experimental trend.

William James, after some schooling abroad and a year in studying art in America, entered the Lawrence Scientific School of Harvard University when he was nineteen. Here he studied chemistry under Charles W. Eliot (later the president of Harvard) and comparative anatomy. Two years later he entered the Harvard Medical School. When he was twenty-three, he accepted the unusual opportunity to go with Louis Agassiz on a naturalist's expedition to the Amazon. James contributed little to the work of the expedition, but he made in Brazil one important discovery: he found that he was a philosopher. He always admired Agassiz, but he could not bring himself to any degree of enthusiasm for mere observational fact divorced from speculation as to causes and meanings. In other words, James, educated in America, was more functionally minded than Agassiz, educated in Europe. After the expedition, James returned to Cambridge, Mass., for a year's continuation of his medical studies, and then went for the same purpose to Germany for a year and a half. His health was poor and failed him almost completely while abroad, so that he did not accomplish his purpose in medical study except for a limited private reading. He was becoming more and more the philosopher, but planning, if possible, to teach physiology. After his return to America, he obtained his medical degree from Harvard in 1869, but he was condemned for three years to an invalidism, which he improved by extensive systematic reading. His always restless, creative mind was restricted by his health but was in no way diminished in quality.

In 1872 James was appointed an instructor in physiology in Harvard College. The appointment led him presently to decide between philosophy and physiology as his life-work, or at least so it seemed to him. The life of the philosopher seemed to James the larger and also the more difficult undertaking, and he determined to content himself with physiology, intending that, within physiology, physiological psychology should be his field and that in this way he could be indirectly a philosopher; for James, like Stumpf, saw in the 1870s no valid demarcation between philosophy and physiological psychology. James' instruction at Harvard was very successful, and it was in connection with his course that he offered laboratory work in that early, informal and unchristened psychological laboratory that was at least as early as Wundt's. His health had improved greatly under the stimulus of definite teaching and his success. In 1876 he was made assistant professor of physiology. In 1878 he actually contracted with the publishers for what was to become his *Principles of Psychology*, hoping to finish in two years the book that finally took him twelve. By 1880 James, the philosopher, was recognized as such: he was made assistant professor of philosophy; and in 1885 he was appointed professor. All through this decade he was working steadily on the *Principles*, reading philosophy, psychology and physiology, becoming enthusiastically interested in other affairs like psychic research, and exhibiting an irrepressible vitality irregularly limited by an uncertain health. In 1889 his title was changed to professor of psychology, and in the following year the *Principles* appeared, to score an immediate triumph. In the sixty years that have elapsed since its publication, its vigor and freshness have remained undimmed, and its insight has refused to become anachronistic.

The changing of James' title from professor of philosophy to professor of psychology was out of phase with his mental development. The completion of the *Principles* marked for him the close of the domination of his philosophical life by psychology. He had begun the *Principles* as a manual of the new scientific psychology; when he had finished he wrote in letters that it proved nothing but "that there is no such thing as a science of psychology" and that psychology is still in "an ante-scientific condition." He believed in the laboratory, but he did not like it. He wrote to Münsterberg in 1890: "I naturally hate experimental work, but all my circumstances conspired (during the important years of my life) to prevent me from getting into a routine of it, so that now it is always the duty that gets postponed."

James had been attracted to the first parts of Münsterberg's *Beiträge*. He felt that there was a freshness and originality about Münsterberg's work. He disliked, as strongly as his kindly tolerance allowed, the pedantry of Wundt and Müller; and Müller's "peculiarly hideous" attack upon Münsterberg's researches drew him even closer to the young psychologist at Freiburg. He schemed to get Münsterberg to Harvard and finally succeeded. Münsterberg came for three years (1892-1895) on trial, as it were, and then, after two years to think over a change of country, came to stay in 1897. In this year James' title was changed back to professor of philosophy, and Münsterberg was left in command of the laboratory.

The last twenty years of James' life saw his development as a philosopher, against the odds of a precarious health. He never ceased to be a psychologist, but he grew away from psychology. The *Principles* were rewritten briefly for textbook purposes—the "Briefer Course"—in 1892. The *Talks to Teachers* came out in 1899 and the

Varieties of Religious Experience in 1901-1902. In 1907 he resigned his active duties at Harvard and at that time his more important philosophical books began to appear: *Pragmatism* (1907), *A Pluralistic Universe* (1909), *The Meaning of Truth* (1909). The conflict of the mind with the body was terminated by his death in 1910 at the age of sixty-eight, but he left behind him a tradition, an influence, and an intellectual ideal of personality, of literary style, and of thought, much more effective than a formal school could have been. His influence was very great, often entirely by way of the *Principles*. Both John Dewey and William McDougall have said how James affected the early development of their thinking, how they went to school to the *Principles* before they had ever seen the author.

If James was not an experimentalist, why then did he exercise such an influence upon psychology in an age when psychology was dominated by experimentalism? Why is he so often regarded as the greatest of American psychologists? There are three reasons. The first is personal: a crabbed personality, a pedantic, obscure writer, might have said the same things with but little effect. Such a man could have been ruled out of consideration as an anachronism in the experimental movement. The second reason is negative in the way that all movements and schools are negative: James opposed the conventional elementism of the current German psychology, offering an alternative picture of the mind. The third reason is positive: this alternative picture contained implicitly the possibilities of the new American psychology which has since come into being, that is to say, functional psychology, with its cousin, the mental tests, and its child, behaviorism. James was telling others how to get where they already wanted to go.

Of James' personality we need say no more. The reader who has never read James will discover it for himself when he does. James remains a human being even when screened by paper and ink.

James' opposition to the elementism of Wundt and all the others appears most clearly in his discussion of the 'stream of thought.' There was no question in James' mind but that analysis is the necessary scientific method; he believed, however, that the analytic description of mind should not be taken to mean that the real mind is a mere congeries of elements. Psychology had, he thought, lost the real whole in seeing only the elementary artifacts of its method. The main thing about consciousness is that it "goes on"; it is a stream. For this same reason Wundt had argued that mind is process, but we have seen that the elementists did not always remember this

principle, and that processes in their hands had a way of getting
fixed. James had valid grounds for objection.

Beyond this primary datum we can find, James said, other essential characteristics of consciousness. (1) In the first place, it is obvious that consciousness is *personal*, that every thought "is owned"
by some one, and that we have here an essential fact about consciousness. Thus James was agreeing with subject-object psychologists like Ward and Stout and was laying a foundation for self-
psychology; on the other hand, he was doing little more than giving
an alternative to Avenarius' principle that some experience is dependent upon the individual.

(2) Next James pointed out that consciousness is forever *changing*. He took the extreme view. "No state once gone can recur and
be identical with what was before"; nor did he mean here simply
the logical point that a recurrence is not an identity because time is
different. He meant that every conscious state is a function of the
entire psychophysical totality and that mind is cumulative and not
recurrent. Objects can recur, but not sensations or thoughts. Here
James anticipated Gestalt psychology, and especially its objection to
what Wertheimer called the 'constancy hypothesis': when the stimulus-object comes again it finds a different mind, and together the
old object and the new mind yield a brand-new conscious state.
James' objection to elementism on this score is so clear and complete
that it has been said that he began Gestalt psychology a quarter of a
century before its birth. For instance, he wrote: "A permanently
existing 'Idea' which makes its appearance before the foot-light of
consciousness at periodical intervals is as mythological an entity as
the Jack of Spades."

(3) Moreover, James continued the argument, consciousness is
sensibly *continuous*. There may be time-gaps, as in sleep; nevertheless, when Peter and Paul awake after sleep, Peter is still Peter, and
Paul still Paul; they never get mixed. In waking life the changes in
consciousness are never abrupt. It is true that there are relative differences: there are relatively stable substantive states of consciousness, where the stream of thought is quiet or caught in an eddy; and
there are fleeting, instable, transitive states where the flow of the
stream is rapid and defies description. These states are, of course,
comparable to the palpable contents and the impalpable acts of
which we have had so much to say. We must note further that the
complication of the conscious stream is, in James' view, bidimensional; change occurs, not only in time, but also in cross-section.
The states of consciousness have overlapping "fringes," "halos of

relations," "psychic overtones." Usually this extra dimension of consciousness (which is related to time as space is related to time in the
physical world) is thought of as an attentional dimension, and James
is here talking about the range and degree of awareness, which come
perhaps to about the same thing.

(4) Finally James laid down as an essential characteristic of consciousness—the fact that it is selective, that it "chooses." Here he
was thinking less of freedom, which has to do with the grounds of
choosing, than with the nature of selection and thus with attention.
It is plain that only a small part of the potentially effective world of
stimulus comes to consciousness, and the principle of selection is,
James thought, "relevance." Hence, consciousness selects so that it
tends to run in logical grooves, and trains of thought arrive at rational ends. Wundt would have abhorred this view of mind, but we
shall see in a moment that James was considering the mind as containing 'knowledges' (or 'meanings,' as we sometimes say), and he
had therefore to take account of its logical nature. Philosopher-psychologists seldom separate the laws of thought from the laws of
logic. Of especial interest to us is that James in this concept of relevance anticipates the Würzburg concept—Watt, Ach, Külpe—of
set and determining tendency.

Such was James' picture of mind. In itself it was positive. In its
effect upon experimental psychology it was negative, for it was an
argument against the accepted view and yet gave no suggestion as
to how experimental research should be altered to meet the objection. What is one to do scientifically with this stream of mind except
to analyze it, except to fix it photographically in its various states?

This question was not asked of James and he did not have to
answer it; however, there is a more positive aspect to James' psychology, which has turned out to constitute an answer. James'
point of view has never been given a class name. Titchener once
called his psychology a "theory of knowledge"; he would have done
better, in view of James' reliance upon the empirical method, to have
said a "science of knowledge." It is quite true that James in his
psychology was facing the problem of conscious knowledge or
awareness, and this fact puts him partly in the Austrian tradition
along with the modern British systematists like Ward and Stout.
Consider, for example, James' formula for the "irreducible data of
psychology." They are (1) the psychologist, the subject who
knows, who makes the consciousness personal; (2) the thought studied, the material of psychology, but only, as it turns out, its part-
object; (3) the thought's object, which is implicit in the thought,

just as Brentano believed that a content is intended by an idea; and finally (4) the psychologist's reality, which is the psychological fact, the generalized relation between and among thoughts and their objects, the essential if artificial, scientific construct. This is a schema of knowledge and not of content, as that term came eventually to be used. It gives the data *of* consciousness, but not the data *in* consciousness, either Titchener or Külpe might have said. For twenty-five years after the *Principles* was published, most experimental psychologists disagreed with James. Then came a change. The Gestalt psychologists were successful in their claim that consciousness contains knowledge rather than sense-data. The behaviorists prevailed in their claim that the important thing about man is what he is capable of doing, that is to say, what he knows. Both groups were functionally minded, and under their influence psychology came around to being what James long before had said it should be.

The conception of function was explicit in James' psychology— not the *Funktion* that is like the *Akt* of the act psychologists, but the biological function that derives from Darwin and not from Brentano. Mind has a use and it can be observed in use. Thus we find in James what came later to be the central tenet of American functionalism. James thought of consciousness as if it were an organ with a function in the psychophysical economy. "The distribution of consciousness," he wrote, "shows it to be exactly such as we might expect in an organ added for the sake of steering a nervous system grown too complex to regulate itself." "Consciousness... has in all probability been evolved, like all other functions, for a use —it is to the highest degree improbable *a priori* that it should have no use."

We have spoken successively of these cognitive and functional aspects of mind in James' psychology, but they really belong together. Cognition is a primary function of mind. Even sensations, James believed, are cognitive and have their objects, the sensible qualities; the function of sensation is that "of mere *acquaintance*" with its homogeneous object, the quality; and "perception's function is that of knowing something *about* the fact." It is plain that the principal use of mind to the organism is knowledge, and that knowledge about the external world (perception) is one very important kind of knowledge. James was dealing with consciousness; he was writing, if you like, introspective psychology. But he was not ignoring the nervous system, nor the organism, nor the world in which the organism lives. For this reason, in spite of his preoccupation with consciousness, we see in him an ancestor to behaviorism. In observing the relation between stimulus and response, one observes essentially a cognition. It was some time before behaviorists recognized this fact. They came to it eventually because Holt got the idea from James, and Tolman from Holt.

It is not possible to press many finer points of definition against James. Unlike Wundt, he had the courage to be incomplete. The justification for this course he made later when he espoused pragmatism. In his psychology he was a pragmatist. He threw himself *in medias res* and went ahead, trusting to results for his final sanction. He was thus freeing himself from formal, traditional constraints, accepting the obvious about mind and attempting to show the use to which he could put the new freedom. It is no wonder then that he anticipated in some ways Gestalt psychology and in others behaviorism, both of which are revolts against the same traditional dogmas. More immediately, James prepared the way for American functionalism, and his fellow pragmatist, John Dewey, presently officiated at the birth of the school.

There was only one specific psychological theory of James' that ever became famous and led to extended discussion and research, and that was his theory of emotion. James first formulated the theory in 1884. He argued then that there are certain innate or reflex adjustments of the nervous system to emotional stimuli, adjustments which lead automatically to bodily changes, mostly in the viscera and the skeletal muscles, that some of these changes can be felt, and that the perception of them *is* the emotion. His schema is that an object in relation to a sense-organ gives rise to the apperception of the object by the appropriate cortical center, that this apperception is the "idea of object-simply-apprehended," that this idea gives rise to reflex currents which pass through preordained channels and alter the condition of muscle, skin and viscera, and that there is an apperception of these changes which is the "idea of object-emotionally-felt." In 1885 Carl Lange (1834-1900) of Copenhagen published a theory that was quite similar, except that it did not go so far, and that it stressed the vasomotor changes. James republished his theory, taking account of Lange and making some changes and amplifications, in the *Principles* in 1890. There was much criticism. Some of it was based upon the oversimplification that resulted from James' picturesque style. James made the emotion the result, and not the cause, of the bodily changes, and it was easy to summarize his view in such phrases as "we feel sorry because we cry, afraid because we tremble"—forceful catch-phrases in view of the well-established belief in the opposite causal order. James took account of various objections in a second paper in 1894, a paper in which he modified the simple theory in the direction of its necessary complications. He argued then, in the first place, that the stimulus to the bodily changes is not a simple object but a "total situation": we may run from a bear, but we do not run if the bear is chained or if we are hunting him with a rifle and are skilled in shooting. In the second place, James distinguished emotion definitely from feeling-tone; in fact he practically defined emotion as the kind of seizure that includes these bodily changes. These modifications limited the theory but doubtless brought it nearer the truth.

Recent physiological research by W. B. Cannon, Henry Head, Phillip Bard and others has exhibited the rôles of the sympathetic nervous system and the hypothalamus in emotion, and nearly every new discovery of fact has been used to emphasize some deficiency in the James-Lange theory. The fact remains, nevertheless, that the James-Lange theory is a behavior theory of emotion. As such it makes awareness depend upon response, thus anticipating modern behavioristics.

G. STANLEY HALL

It would be hard to find two psychologists more different in personality and in the character of their work than G. Stanley Hall and William James, and yet there is one point of resemblance. Both were pioneers in the new psychology, and both through their personalities exerted a very great influence upon American psychology in its formative period. Neither had a school, but each had a large following. There were in America until recently many psychologists whose chief intellectual debt was to James and many others who derived their origin from Stanley Hall. There may have been none who acclaimed both as great: the disciple of Hall could hardly appreciate the narrower depth of James nor his philosophical bent; the disciple of James would find Hall superficial and discursive. Yet both men were very important.

Hall, always in excellent health, led a life of action. He was for thirty years a university president, but he was not led away from psychology to administration or he would have no place in this history. He was an 'inside' president and a teaching president with little time for raising money or for creating academic administrative structures. He was a 'founder,' if there ever was one in psychology. His life was punctuated with the foundation of laboratories, journals, and institutes. More important is the fact that he was, in a sense, forever 'founding' ideas, that is to say, he would, under the influence of a conviction, bring together certain new ideas that were not original with himself, add to them a supporting mass of other ideas drawn from his omnivorous reading, and then drive the resultant mass home in a book, on the lecture-platform, in his seminary, and on every other occasion that presented itself. Hall himself admitted that his intellectual life might be viewed as a series of "crazes"; nevertheless, his biographers have managed to find more continuity in the discursive chain than the casual student would expect. James philosophized, but Hall speculated—for there is a difference. Both were enthusiasts, but, where James' penetrating, sympathetic whimsicalities won him a quiet supporter, Hall's torrential, fervid vividness won him an ardent disciple.

Granville Stanley Hall (1844-1924) was born on a farm at Ashfield, Massachusetts, and passed his youth there, attending the country school. He had an isolated boyhood, for he was already beginning to develop intense interests, one after the other, and for them he found no sympathy among his natural companions. Quite early he revolted against becoming a farmer, and finally, with his mother's support and his father's opposition, it was decided that he should go to college and prepare for the ministry, which in Ashfield appeared to be the most obvious of the learned callings. He went away to a seminary for further study, taught school for a term in Ashfield, and then entered Williams College (1863-1867). At first he shone neither scholastically nor socially, a country boy, the only one of his community to go to college; but by the time of his graduation he had won a number of scholastic honors. He also achieved an enthusiasm for philosophy, especially for John Stuart Mill, and an admiration for the theory of evolution, an attitude that is one of the unifying threads of his varied intellectual life. He took his philosophy with him to the Union Theological Seminary in New York City, and so much the philosopher and so little the theologian was he that, after his trial sermon, the member of the faculty whose custom it was to criticize, despairing of mere criticism, knelt and prayed for his soul. Henry Ward Beecher was more sympathetic; he advised Hall to go to Germany to study philosophy.

Hall went, on borrowed money (1868-1871). He studied first at Bonn and then at Berlin, where he was particularly impressed by the great Trendelenburg (the man who made an Aristotelian of Brentano) and where he took du Bois-Reymond's course in physiology. Presently he returned to New York, took his degree in divinity, was for ten weeks a preacher in a little country church, and after that was a tutor in a private family. The future course of his life was anything but clear. However, he shortly secured a professorship at Antioch College in Ohio (1872-1876) where he taught at different times English, modern languages and philosophy. Philosophy was still his *métier*, but the appearance in 1874 of Wundt's *Physiologische Psychologie* brought his interest about to the new psychology. Like so many others, in those days at least, Hall felt that philosophy was impractical; yet he lacked the technique for science. To such men the new psychology opened a *via media*.

Hall wanted to go to Germany at once to study with Wundt. He was persuaded to stay a year at Antioch. Then, on his way to Germany, President Eliot side-tracked him at Harvard with the offer of a tutorship in English, which the impecunious Hall could not afford to refuse. So he stayed at Harvard for two years, tutoring in English, studying philosophy and, with William James, psychology. That was in the days when James had started his little student laboratory in the science building and his own laboratory room in the museum building, all before Wundt had opened the formal laboratory at Leipzig. In 1878 Hall took his doctorate with a dissertation on the muscular perception of space. The experimental work was performed in the laboratory of the physiologist, H. P. Bowditch, who was close to James and cooperated in more ways than one. Hall received at the hands of James what is presumably the first doctorate of philosophy in the new psychology to be granted in America. There was almost no difference in age between these two men, but great difference in temperament. Each appreciated the other's qualities, but they were already on different tracks and drew far apart in later years. Hall was a comet, caught for the moment by James' influence, but presently shooting off into space never to return.

After Harvard, Hall went to Germany as he had originally planned (1878-1880). First he went to Berlin, where he worked with von Kries and Kronecker. Then at last he came to Leipzig, where he lived next door to Fechner, studied physiology in Ludwig's laboratory, and became Wundt's first American student in the year of the founding of the Leipzig laboratory. He was sampling everything, not so superficially but that he published jointly with von Kries and Kronecker.

After his return to America, Hall was still without a position.

He settled near Cambridge and was asked by President Eliot of Harvard to give a course of Saturday morning lectures on educational problems. The lectures were a great success, and Hall came into public notice.

In 1881 he was invited to lecture at the new graduate university, Johns Hopkins (founded 1876). Again he was successful, and he was given a lectureship in psychology in 1882 and a professorship in 1884. At Hopkins he found a group of younger men who were later to become famous in psychology: John Dewey, J. McK. Cattell, H. H. Donaldson, E. C. Sanford, W. H. Burnham, Joseph Jastrow and others. He 'founded' in 1883 what is called "the first psychological laboratory in America." Of course, as we have seen, experimental work in psychology brings laboratories into existence wherever it occurs, and James had for several years had space for experimental instruction and thus a laboratory at Harvard. However, James' laboratory came into being, whereas Hall founded his. The difference between *having* and *founding* is a difference between the temperaments of the two men. In 1887 Hall began— 'founded'—the *American Journal of Psychology*, the first psychological journal in America, and the first in English except for *Mind*, to which the few American experimental psychologists had been contributing their papers. The laboratory and the journal were the first of his many foundings.

In 1888 Hall accepted the unexpected call to become the first president of the new Clark University at Worcester, Massachusetts. Hall more or less determined the nature of the initial undertaking at Clark, and the university was organized along the lines of Johns Hopkins and the Continental universities, a graduate institution with its primary stress upon investigation and not upon instruction. Hall spent a year abroad, studying universities and visiting almost every country in Europe. The story of his great disappointment after his return does not belong in this history. He had expected large funds from the founder, who, instead of giving more and more, gave less and less, leaving at death in 1900 an endowment which was largely diverted to the founding of an undergraduate college. The university was constituted of five scientific departments, and Hall remained professor of psychology, in fact as well as name, while he was president. The laboratory at Clark he gave over, however, to E. C. Sanford, who came to Clark from Hopkins. Quite early, a department of pedagogy, which in the Clark atmosphere was almost synonymous with educational psychology, was established under W. H. Burnham, another man who had been at Hopkins with Hall. Thus psychology prospered at Clark.

Stanley Hall's rôle in child study and the promotion of educational psychology in the 1880s and 1890s is discussed in the next chapter (pp. 567-569).

The *American Journal of Psychology* came, of course, to Clark with Hall. It was his personal property. In 1891 Hall founded the *Pedagogical Seminary* (now the *Journal of Generic Psychology*), the second psychological journal in America, for it really was as much psychological as Hall was a psychologist. The American Psychological Association was planned in 1892 in a conference in Hall's study and began its career later in the year with Hall as its first president. In 1904 he founded the *Journal of Religious Psychology*, which, however, lapsed after a decade of publication. He attempted to organize an institute of child study about 1909, but sufficient funds were not available and the institute, much to Hall's sorrow, never came into independent being, except as a museum of education. Then in 1915 he founded the *Journal of Applied Psychology*, but psychological journals were no longer new; there were already fifteen others in existence in America.

Hall was elected for the second time president of the American Psychological Association in 1924. Only to James had the honor of re-election previously been given. However, Hall died before the year was out, at the age of eighty.

For all his 'foundings,' Hall was not primarily an administrator. The journals and other organizations were but deposits of his restless mind. It seemed, rather, that he developed a new interest, carried it through the pioneer stage, and then, already caught by the next topic, tried to perpetuate the old by creating for it a new professorship, a journal or an institution. Let us turn to this torrent of interests.

Hall's earliest serious intellectual concern was, as we have seen, philosophy. Within it he came upon psychology and, ultimately, turned the tables by saying that psychology furnished the true approach to philosophy; that is to say, the psychoanalysis of men is the key to the significance of their opinions. Within philosophy he also assimilated the doctrine of evolution, and thus his psychology was always an evolutionary psychology or, as he called it, genetic psychology. When Hall first came into direct contact with the new psychology, it was the problem of movement that fired his imagination. His thesis, showing the influence of the associationists and of Wundt, held that sensations of movement are the basis of all space-perception. The muscle sense, he argued, is the organ of will. The reaction experiments seemed to him, as they did to most other psychologists at that time, to be a remarkable tool for the measurement of the mind. Hall took this view with him to Hopkins and its new laboratory, and there we find him working on motor sensations, bilateral asymmetry, rhythm and dermal sensitivity, topics dull enough in themselves but furnishing in Hall's hands material for vivid pictures of the human mind as the agent of civilization. Nevertheless, Hall felt that the laboratory work of the new psychology was proving too narrow. Certainly it lacked the breadth and the broad significance that he demanded and that he forced upon it when he dealt with it. He was also impatient of the psychology of consciousness that was characteristic of the new psychology, and he had quite early, long before he became interested in Freud, come to the conclusion that introspection is inadequate to account for many psychological phenomena. So he continued to draw freely upon a very wide field for his psychological data and came to uphold what he called "synthetic psychology." This phrase was simply Hall's name for the eclectic view with the broadest possible scope. It is a negative characterization. Positively Hall was a genetic psychologist, that is to say, a psychological evolutionist who was concerned with animal and human development and all the secondary problems of adaptation and development. When he died, he left his money to Clark for founding a chair of genetic psychology—a chair now named after him.

At Clark, with the laboratory safely in Sanford's hands, Hall's geneticism brought him to child psychology, to pedagogy and, presently, to the special study of adolescence. His most important work is the two huge volumes called *Adolescence: Its Psychology, and Its Relations to Physiology, Anthropology, Sociology, Sex, Crime, Religion, and Education* (1904). This work, coming at the time when psychology was supposed to be about to unlock the door to scientific education, had a tremendous vogue. After its publication, his interest in child study increased still further. Growth, imagination and play were some of the topics that especially engaged his attention. He made extensive use of the questionnaire for collecting statistical data, so that this psychological method came in the early days to be particularly associated in America with Hall's name, although Galton invented it. All this work should have culminated appropriately in a Child Institute, but, as we have seen, the project failed for lack of funds.

From boyhood Hall had an intense interest in animals, and along with the child study went his lectures on animal life, habits and instincts.

When psychoanalysis and the work of Freud and Jung came to be known in America, Hall took up with the new doctrines. In fact Hall had a great deal to do with psychoanalysis' becoming known in America, for he brought Freud and Jung from Europe for Clark's vigentennial celebration in 1909, letting James, Titchener, Cattell and the others meet them and listen to their views. The psychoanalytic doctrine fitted in with Hall's belief in the inadequacy of introspection as the sole psychological method and with many of his dicta that had a behavioristic sound long before behaviorism was ever heard of. Psychoanalysis led Hall still further into the psychology of sex than had his concern with adolescence, and he often suffered from the *odium sexicum* that was thus attached to his name. However, he was dauntless when driven by one of these intellectual curiosities of his, and he was not deterred from filling out a new portion of the synthetic psychology. Another incidental interest of these years was his concern with the psychology of alimentation and presently with the work of Pavlov. For a time this topic assumed tremendous importance as the others had done: temporarily the mind migrated to the stomach and Hall concerned himself with the "pyloric soul."

One of Hall's later fields of concentration was the psychology of religion, a revival of an old interest which culminated in his publication of *Jesus, the Christ, in the Light of Psychology* (1917). And this book brought to him the *odium theologicum*. In old age, still feeling young, Hall met the problem of his retirement from the presidency of Clark as he had met all other problems: by trying to understand old age psychologically. He wrote his *Senescence* (1922).

Looking back on this crowding host of enthusiasms, we can see that Hall contributed mostly to educational psychology in America, and much less to experimental psychology, which represented but an early phase of his productive life. The laboratory could never have become his professional locus; it was too far removed from the living problems of human nature that fascinated him. On the other hand, experimental psychology was never removed from his synthetic view, and while as professor of psychology at Clark he might be impatient of it, as president he supported it, and the work of Sanford and of J. W. Baird, who successively directed the laboratory. His work in founding the early laboratory at Hopkins and its subsequent work were very important in the pioneer days of

psychology. His leadership in the founding of the American Psychological Association "for the advancement of psychology as a
science" was an event in the formal history of psychology. So was
the founding of the *American Journal of Psychology*. At one time
it seemed as if the majority of American psychologists had been
associated with Hall either at Hopkins or at Clark, although they
did not all derive their primary inspiration from him. In 1890, just
before the wave of laboratory-founding had reached its height,
there were probably not more than ten psychological laboratories
in America, and at least four of these, beside Hopkins itself, had
begun life under the direction of a pupil or associate of Hall's at
Hopkins. Hall's personal influence lies, therefore, mainly outside of
experimental psychology; nevertheless, the laboratory in America
is indebted to him as a promotor and a founder.

LADD AND SCRIPTURE

We have called Ladd the Sully of America because it is his textbooks that are his contribution to psychology. His importance is a
function of the time at which he wrote. In the 1880s James, Hall
and Ladd were the only psychologists in America who had as
yet 'arrived.' Persons like Baldwin, Cattell, Jastrow and Sanford
belong just a bit later. Hall was the first president of the American
Psychological Association, Ladd the second, and James the third.
Before 1890 there were few general textbooks of the new psychology to read. In German, beside Volkmann, there were three
editions of Wundt, and there was Brentano. In English, Bain and
Spencer were out of date, and there was Sully's *Outlines* but not
yet his *Human Mind*. In America there was nothing, except Dewey,
until Ladd began. James in his Harvard courses used Spencer (1878-
1883), Sully (1884), Bain (1885-1888) and Ladd (1887).

George Trumbull Ladd (1842-1921) was just as old as James and
two years older than Hall. He graduated from Andover Theological Seminary (1869) and spent ten years in the ministry in the
Middle West. Then he was appointed professor of mental and moral
philosophy at Bowdoin College (1879-1881), and while there he
began the study of "the relationships between the nervous system
and mental phenomena," just as an up-to-date professor of mental
philosophy ought in those days to have done. From Bowdoin Ladd
went to Yale (1881-1905) without change of title. He said that at
Yale he continued to study physiological psychology in the laboratory, but it is doubtful if he had any laboratory of importance at
Bowdoin. At Yale, however, he did have an informal laboratory

where he worked with the assistance of J. K. Thatcher, the physiologist. This statement means essentially that Yale was started in practical experimental psychology at the time that Hopkins was getting under way, but not that Ladd anticipated Hall in 'founding' a psychological laboratory. In general these dates are unimportant: the laboratories came into being because they had to come, not because Hall, shortly after Wundt and James, had set the custom. Ladd's principal interest lay, however, in working up his lectures on physiological psychology, and it was from them that his first psychological book issued.

This book was the *Elements of Physiological Psychology* (1887). It met with a warm welcome. Ladd said that he had had only Wundt to point the way as he wrote, and Wundt, beside being in German, was difficult for most readers. The literature of the new psychology was becoming large. Ladd went through it carefully and conscientiously and presented the first English handbook for the scattered subject-matter. In America and England the volume made a great impression. In fact it long remained almost alone among psychological compendia in the stress which it laid upon the physiology of the nervous system; and for this reason it was revised in 1911 by R. S. Woodworth and became again a standard text.

Ladd published an abbreviated edition of this book in 1891. In 1894 he published a little *Primer of Psychology* and a big *Psychology, Descriptive and Explanatory*. The latter reappeared in abbreviated form four years later. The large text of 1894 met with a less cordial reception than its predecessor of 1887. For one thing there were more books now—James and Baldwin in English, and Külpe and Ziehen in German, besides others less important. James found Ladd's second compendium "dreary." Hall denied that it was dreary, but he found no stimulus in it, and, while admiring its accurate thoroughness, deplored, all unconscious of what the future was to bring forth in America, the multiplication of textbooks. However, viewed historically, this book has the advantage of being a systematic text that is really a functional psychology in the American sense. It is one of several events that show that functional psychology was of the American atmosphere and not simply a unique discovery at Chicago. Here was Ladd by himself at Yale 'getting up' the new psychology for lectures and books, making an excellent job of it, and writing, not as Wundt wrote, but of mind as a useful organ. We shall return to this point in a moment.

During Ladd's first decade at Yale the work in the psychological laboratory was increasing and getting out of hand. Accordingly in 1892 Scripture was appointed instructor and the laboratory given into his charge, that is to say the Yale laboratory was, after an informal existence, at last ready to be 'founded.' Ladd kept on with his books for a bit, but, with his theological background, he was never an ardent promotor of the new and mechanistic (materialistic) psychology. He reverted to philosophy. On three occasions he went to the Orient to lecture. In 1905 he retired and became *professor emeritus.* As a psychologist his influence really belongs only to the eight years during which his psychological books were appearing, or at most to the twenty years from the time when he first was 'getting into' physiological psychology at Bowdoin to the end of the century, when he faded out of the active scene.

In calling Ladd a functional psychologist, it is necessary for us to see just what is meant by the term. (1) In the first place, it appears that Ladd, like Ward and Stout and James, accepted the necessity for a self within psychology, for a subject which is active. In this way consciousness is seen to be a matter of activity, the activity of a self. Ladd, however, was trying to mediate between his convictions about the soul and the contents of Wundt, so that we find him describing and explaining consciousness in two ways, as active function and as passive content. This dual psychology is not like the bipartite psychology of Messer or Külpe, where acts lie on the one hand and contents on the other; for Ladd every conscious fact, even a sensation, was completely described and explained only by both accounts.

(2) The notion of the active self—the fact, as James said, that consciousness is personal—led Ladd into the biological notion that the function of consciousness is to solve problems. Mind is to be explained in terms of its use. This was physiological psychology, and it is perhaps not strange that the biological point of view should come out of the physiological. Psychologically, consciousness is the activity of a self. Physiologically, there are the nervous system and the organism to represent the self. If consciousness is thus tied up to a person, it would be the most natural thing in the world—after Darwin—to explain it on evolutionary grounds, that is to say, in terms of its use to that person. The function of mind is adaptation.

(3) If mind, however, has adaptive value for the organism, then it has a purpose; and psychology becomes teleological. Teleology is the third mark of functional psychology and was a principle that the theologically minded Ladd was glad to admit.

(4) Finally, we find that the result of the biological point of view is to make psychology practical. You have a person (the self, the organism) with a mind (content) acting (function) to adapt him to his environment (biology) in the ways for which his mind is fitted (teleology). For something to be practical is for it to have a use in the business of life, and the science of living is the one great applied science. In general, functional psychology in America has thus led with the utmost facility directly into applied psychologies. Ladd, however, was content to let psychology be propædeutic to philosophy, which demanded then (as well as now) a psychology of human nature.

These four points are really not independent. Given the evolutionary atmosphere, one follows from the other. They are all in Ladd at the level of theoretical systematization. The history of American psychology is little more than their working-out in reality.

We may now return to Scripture, who took from Ladd's shoulders the burden of the Yale Laboratory.

Edward Wheeler Scripture (1864-   ) we have mentioned in an earlier chapter as one of Wundt's students. He spent three semesters with Wundt at Leipzig, a semester at Berlin where he heard Ebbinghaus, Zeller and Paulsen, and a semester at Zürich, where Avenarius taught him pedagogy. He took his degree with Wundt in 1891 with a thesis on the association of ideas. After that he was a fellow at Clark for about a year (1891-1892). Then Ladd brought him to Yale as instructor in experimental psychology (1892-1901). He was in charge of the laboratory from the start, and its official director later (1898-1903). He was assistant professor during these last two years (1901-1903).

Scripture spent an energetic and effective decade at Yale. He was a great contrast to the theological and philosophical Ladd, coming into the laboratory with a strong conviction as to the scientific nature of psychology and its mission to work quantitatively upon the mind, ever approaching more and more nearly to the precision of measurement that obtains in physics. Most of the younger men of this period were devotees of the laboratory, but in none does the spirit of the times show more clearly than in Scripture's writings. He wrote in this period two popular books, *Thinking, Feeling, Doing,* (1895) and *The New Psychology* (1897). They are both packed full of pictures of apparatus, graphs, and other apt illustrations. The style is terse; the content is factual. Figures are given wherever possible. There is no argument, no theory, no involved discussion. The books still carry the fervor of the 1890s: a *new* psychology, soon to be as accurate as physics!

Under Scripture's leadership the Yale laboratory grew, at least in apparatus and technique. Scripture began at once the *Studies from the Yale Psychological Laboratory*, of which ten annual volumes were issued during his decade there. Their emphasis was at first upon reaction times and the sensory problems of tone. An examination of the studies shows, however, that Scripture was himself the chief contributor and that the Yale laboratory drew no large group of students who were later to become distinguished, as Hall did in the corresponding period. Of the forty-five studies published during the ten years, eighteen were by Scripture alone, five were contributed by him with some other person, and the other half were by investigators in the laboratory. C. E. Seashore (1866-1949), who later devoted his life to the psychology of tone, is easily the most distinguished of the group. He took his degree at Yale in 1895. The only other names that were generally known later are J. E. W. Wallin and M. Matsumoto.

After this period Scripture dropped out of American psychology. His interest in acoustics had already been passing to phonetics, and for the next three decades he devoted himself primarily to the problems of speech and its defects. He took his medical degree at Munich in 1906 and he was Professor of Experimental Phonetics at Vienna from 1923 to 1933. C. H. Judd (1873-1946) followed him at Yale.

JAMES MARK BALDWIN

Generations among psychologists are measured by decades. James, Hall and Ladd were in the 1880s the first generation of the 'new' psychologists in America. In the 1890s other leaders appeared: Sanford, Cattell, Baldwin, Jastrow, Münsterberg, Scripture and Titchener—to name them in order of age. Titchener was eight years younger than Sanford; and in 1892, when they had all in a sense 'arrived,' Sanford was thirty-three and Titchener twenty-five. Beside these men there were, of course, others, who were then and later philosophers, or who were drawn off from psychology to administration or to other activities. The seven men in the list all left their impress upon psychology, and we see that the new science was at first in the hands of very young leaders. Perhaps this is the reason why every one of them tried to lead in a different direction. Youth is energetic, ambitious, egotistical and even quarrelsome. Sanford, the oldest, was the only pacifist in this group and left perhaps the faintest impression. Most of the others mellowed with time in greater or lesser degree, but the 1890s were a furious decade in American psychology. Perhaps youthful ambition was enhanced by the polemical spirit of Germany, from which America obtained, with its doctorates, its psychological etiquette.

When Cattell died in 1944, only Scripture of the ten men named in the preceding paragraph was still living. Cattell had become the senior American psychologist, not only in age but also by right of achievement. We may, however, turn first to Baldwin as making the readiest transition from Ladd.

James Mark Baldwin (1861-1934) was primarily a psychological theorist and writer, who, like Hall and almost all of the native-born American psychologists, was impressed by the bearing of the theory of evolution upon psychology. He was also half a philosopher, or, to be more exact, somewhat of a philosopher-psychologist in the 1890s, and mostly a philosopher in his later professional life. He was an experimentalist, quite as much as the philosopher-turned-psychologist is ever an experimentalist, and he founded the Toronto laboratory, and the Princeton laboratory, and then re-established Hall's lapsed laboratory at Hopkins. He was a man of the world, and he had both the ability and the will to meet and mingle with important persons—and finally to write his reminiscences of them. However, while he was one of the 'new' psychologists, his skill was the philosopher's ability in speculative theorizing. In 1895 he wrote of "that most vicious and Philistine attempt, in some quarters, to put psychology in the strait-jacket of barren observation, to draw the life-blood of all science—speculative advance into the secrets of things,—this ultra-positivistic cry has come here as everywhere else and put a ban upon theory. On the contrary, give us theories, theories, always theories! Let every man who has a theory pronounce his theory!" This cry was not the slogan of the laboratory men, and one can guess how Scripture and Titchener, for example, received it. Moreover, Baldwin was a writer as well as a theorist. It is not merely that his theories found their way into print; it is rather that he wrote them out of himself. His reader is present at the scientific act of creation, and thus theory and its verbal expression were closely associated in Baldwin's mind.

Baldwin was born in South Carolina, at the outset of the Civil War, of a prominent family of Northern descent and Northern sympathies. After an undergraduate course at Princeton, he spent a year abroad at Berlin and Leipzig (1884-1885) studying philosophy, but gaining from Wundt what he particularly wanted, an introduction to the 'new' psychology. After two years at Princeton as instructor in modern languages and as a student in the theological seminary, he was appointed professor of philosophy at Lake Forest University in Illinois. His doctorate was in philosophy; in his thesis, at the insistent direction of President James McCosh (1811-1895) of Princeton (one of the last of the old school of philosopher-psychologists who therefore finds no other mention in this book), Baldwin refuted materialism, although his inclinations took him to no such topic. In 1889 he went to Toronto to the chair of metaphysics and logic, but with a growing interest in psychology which led him to inaugurate a small laboratory there. In 1893 he was called back to his *alma mater* as professor of psychology, and he spent at Princeton the ten most effective years of his life, organizing again a new American laboratory, writing books and making several visits to Europe. He spent the winter of 1900 at Oxford, where he was one of the two first to receive the new honorary degree of Doctor of Science. In 1903 he went to Hopkins to revive the laboratory that had lapsed when Hall left for Clark; nevertheless he was in these days becoming more of the philosopher than the psychologist. Twice he visited Mexico to advise on the organization of the National University. Then in 1908, after five years at Hopkins, he resigned to spend five years in Mexico in this advisory capacity and then five years in Paris as professor at *L'école des hautes études sociales*. He died in Paris in 1934.

After Hopkins, Baldwin seemed first to have divided his time between Mexico and Paris, and then to have settled down abroad, mostly in France. There was in this period only one excursion into psychology, a very clear and readable little *History of Psychology* in 1913. His more philosophical writings began to give place to the consideration of the problem of the relation of France to America, and these interests were suddenly intensified by the First World War and, for a while, by American neutrality. He supported the cause of the Allies vigorously and won recognition from the French government.

His first work was his *Handbook of Psychology*, divided into two volumes, *Senses and Intellect* (1889) and *Feeling and Will* (1891). The former appeared just as he was going to Toronto, and there was a second edition of it in the next year. After the custom of Ladd and James, he also got up a briefer course, which came out as *Elements of Psychology* just as he was about to leave

Toronto. It was these books that first made Baldwin's reputation. They were meant to be just what they claimed, handbooks; but they contained too much theory and too little experimental fact to make a lasting impression in the days of the 'new' psychology. Baldwin's felicitous literary style, surpassed only by James', gave a transient vitality to his ideas; but his effect was not permanent.

At Princeton he published his two books on mental development: *Mental Development in the Child and the Race* (1895) and *Social and Ethical Interpretations in Mental Development* (1897). These books present clearly and forcibly the evolutionary principle in psychology, and even seek to modify Darwin's theory by the conception that Baldwin called "organic selection." The evolutionary view permeated American psychology and dominated Hall. Hall, however, had not given it clear or elegant expression; his *Adolescence* was still more than half a dozen years away. James adopted the point of view only in so far as he dealt with the organism in relation to its environment. Baldwin made it his theme. The group at Clark looked askance at these books because they contained so much personal speculation and so little observational fact, but then, of course, these were the days when most psychologists looked askance at most of the others.

In 1898 Baldwin published a little book that went into many editions: *The Story of the Mind*—"my only novel," he called it later.

He was also engaged in two very important cooperative undertakings. The first was the founding of the *Psychological Review* in 1894, with its supporting members, the *Psychological Index* and the *Psychological Monographs*. The *Psychological Bulletin*, a shoot from the same stem, came a decade later. Cattell and Baldwin began this venture together, two very positive personalities, both unaccustomed to brook interference. They got along for a time. When neither succeeded in compromising without yielding, they first agreed that each should assume primary responsibility in alternate years, and then in 1903 they agreed to part company. So they bid against each other. After a while Cattell bid $3400, Baldwin bid $3405, Cattell $3500, Baldwin $3505. Since Cattell had set $3500 as his top bid, Baldwin got the journals. Later, when Baldwin went to Mexico, the journals became the property of H. C. Warren and were finally purchased by the American Psychological Association.

The other cooperative venture was Baldwin's *Dictionary of Philosophy and Psychology*. It was a huge undertaking, involving the work of more than sixty philosophers and psychologists in Europe and America. Two large volumes, comprising more than 1,500 pages, were issued in 1901-1902, and Benjamin Rand's bibliography of almost 1,200 pages followed in 1905.

There remains only the question of Baldwin's actual experimental work. There was little of importance. Of course there were experiments which he and his assistants conducted and published, but Baldwin's genius did not lie in experimentation. He was a philosopher at heart, a theorist. In discussing Titchener in an earlier chapter (pp. 413 f.), we have already examined his controversy with Baldwin about the reaction times. Some of the data on Baldwin's side of this argument were of his own acquisition, but they were meager. In this argument a principle, not a fact, was primarily at stake: Should psychology study human nature and therefore individual differences (Baldwin) or should it study the generalized mind (Titchener)? The influence of Darwin upon psychology has always been to favor the study of individual differences, as we have seen with Galton and as was equally true with Hall and Baldwin. Baldwin took the American, the functional, point of view, while Titchener remained true to the German set of values.

JAMES MCKEEN CATTELL

In some ways Cattell is a contradiction: his influence upon American psychology has been so much greater than his individual scientific output. It follows that his influence has been exerted in personal ways. He was for twenty-six years in charge of psychology at Columbia, then America's largest university, where undoubtedly more students of psychology came into contact with him than had been the case with any other American psychologist. He had, moreover, the executive temperament, a man of many affairs in the psychological and scientific world, so that a great number of organized projects within American psychology felt his touch. He was editor of at least six important journals in psychology or in general science. It would be easy to say that this man of pronounced ideas and fearless aggression did more than any one other to make American psychology what it is; however, Cattell might not have seemed so effective had he been a voice in the wilderness, like Titchener, instead of an able representative of the American trend. Leaders may make the times, but the times also select the leaders. Let us see how Cattell was the man for his generation in America.

In the 1880s and 1890s psychology was new. It needed young

aggressive leaders, and Cattell was just such a man. So too were Hall, Baldwin, Münsterberg, Scripture and Titchener.

Evolution had taken hold of American thought, and evolution, as we have seen, meant in psychology an emphasis upon individual differences. Cattell was convinced of the importance of the psychology of individual differences even before he went to Wundt, and he stuck to his belief. He did not get this idea from Galton, but presumably got it out of the same atmosphere that gave it to Galton.

We have seen that the psychology of individual differences, because it tends to deal with the particular rather than with the general, is apt to be practical. The mental test became its chief method. We have already discussed America's practicality and its bias toward functionalism (pp. 506-508), the temper that made the theory of evolution accepted with enthusiasm, that is proper to a new pioneer country, and that could be seen already emerging in western culture after the Renaissance. Cattell, who invented the term *mental test* and was the first American to promote mental testing, was aptly fitted to become a leader in the American development. Representing the spirit of America, he was prepared to lead. His vigorous personality and his contacts with many persons and many affairs provided his opportunity. The Columbia laboratory was the most important single factor in distributing his effect. He never wrote a psychological text. His own research is small as compared with his influence. Nevertheless his influence spread because the Americans wanted it. That is clearly the explanation of Cattell.

James McKeen Cattell (1860-1944), after an undergraduate course at Lafayette College, went abroad for two years to study (1880-1882). His interest in human capacities was fixed at this time by Lotze at Göttingen (the year before Lotze's death) and by Wundt at Leipzig. Cattell then returned to America for a year's study at Hopkins, and while he was there Stanley Hall arrived to take command of psychology. Thus Cattell was a student of Hall's by accident for a semester. In 1883 he returned to Leipzig and, as we have already seen, informed Wundt in *ganz amerikanisch* fashion that he needed an assistant and that he, Cattell, would be it. His three years at Leipzig were very productive. He published over half a dozen articles in the *Philosophische Studien*, in *Mind*, and in *Brain*, all of them about reaction times or about individual differences. Some of these papers are now classic. The excitement about the reaction experiment as a tool for mental measurement

was then at its height, and Cattell combined his conventional interest in reaction times with his unconventional concern about the
individual, so that some of the papers were contributions to both
topics. He took his doctorate with Wundt in 1886.

In 1887 he was lecturer in psychology at the University of
Pennsylvania and at Bryn Mawr College. In 1888 he was lecturer
at Cambridge University (p. 489), and at that time he came first
into contact with Galton. The similarity of their views drew them
together, although they had come independently at the problem
of individual differences. Then Cattell became professor of psychology at Pennsylvania for three years (1888-1891) and began
the psychological laboratory there.

The most important outcome of this period was his monograph
On the Perception of Small Differences (1892), which he published
with G. S. Fullerton, a philosopher temporarily bewitched by experimental psychology. This paper, supported by another on errors
of observation in the following year, shows Cattell already bringing
statistical method to bear upon the conventional procedures in psychophysics, his revolt against the fine distinctions of introspective
psychology, and his respect for the probable error. Here we find
Cattell and Fullerton introducing the functional point of view
into psychophysics and the problem of the differential limen.
Orthodox psychophysics had accepted the limen as a fact to be
described: there is a critical difference—the "just noticeable difference"—below which the observer is more often unable to make discriminations than able. His sensitivity varies inversely with this difference. The functional formula, on the other hand, assumes that the
subject is trying to discriminate every difference and failing only
when it is too small. Hence it treats of the size of the average error
instead of the magnitude of the just noticeable difference. One value
can be reduced to the other and Fechner used both kinds. Nevertheless there is a difference in orientation as to whether the problem is
the determination of a critical difference or the measurement of a
degree of error. Quetelet had spoken of human variability as Nature's
errors in aiming at Nature's ideal. These functionalists were describing sensory variability as man's error in aiming at perfect discrimination.

From Pennsylvania Cattell went to Columbia, leaving Witmer
in control of the new laboratory. He founded another laboratory
at Columbia and remained in charge of it for twenty-six years
(1891-1917). His earlier interests in reaction times had now lapsed,
and he found himself in the 1890s promoting mental tests. In 1896

he published with Livingston Farrand the classical study of physical and mental measurements of the Columbia students, the research which was planned along Galtonian lines but which failed to set the pattern when Binet's intelligence tests succeeded later. About 1903 his interest in scientific eminence began, first with his ranking of psychologists in order of merit, and then, when the first edition of *American Men of Science*, which he compiled, came along, with the ranking of men of all sciences and the printing of stars after the names of the most eminent. He published eight important papers on this topic in thirty years.

We have already seen that Cattell began the *Psychological Review* with Baldwin in 1894 and remained an editor until Baldwin bought him out for $3505 in an auction in 1903. Cattell's bereavement was, however, brief. He had already started *Popular Science Monthly* in 1900, which he continued as *Scientific Monthly* after he sold the first name in 1915. From 1906 to 1938 he edited six editions of *American Men of Science*. He was editor of *Science, School and Society* and the *American Naturalist*. He was a good editor, and no other psychologist has equalled him in both the range and quality of his work.

In 1917, at the time of America's entry into the First World War, Cattell was dismissed by Columbia University because of his pacifistic stand. He had always been fearless in his frank expressions of opinion, though often in the minority, and there was an emotional background to this occurrence which was brought to a focus by the new emotions induced by the war.

In later years Cattell was active in his editorships, in the Psychological Corporation, an organization that he promoted for the sale of expert psychological services to industry and to the public, and in many organized projects where his advice was sought. He became by the death of others or their deflection from psychology, America's senior psychologist, and was elected president of the Ninth International Congress of Psychology, the first of these congresses to meet in America (1929). In his later years he remained active as an editor until his death in 1944.

Cattell's research is scattered among many topics in many books and journals. In 1914 six of his students undertook to bring it together and to point out its significance under six topics: reaction time, association, perception and reading, psychophysics, determination of order of merit, and individual differences. In 1947, three years after his death, his colleagues printed in two volumes a collection of his more important psychological researches

(29 items), his addresses and formal papers (41 items), and his bibliography (167 items). We follow now the assessment of his work by his six students in 1914.

With respect to research on *reaction times,* Henmon classed Cattell with Wundt. Cattell began his investigations at Hopkins and took them with him to Leipzig. By 1902 he had touched almost the entire field. On the side of apparatus he made various improvements in the chronoscope and in its control apparatus, and he invented a lip-key and a voice-key for vocal reactions. In the interests of objectivity of method he established the practice of disregarding extreme deviates in times in accordance with a statistical rule, instead of intuitively on the assumption that all seemingly wide deviates must have been due to lapse of attention. His investigation of times of reaction as dependent upon sense-organ and the peripheral location of tactual stimuli was begun at Leipzig and finished in a thorough study with C. S. Dolley at Columbia. This was Helmholtz's old experiment of the rate of conduction of sensory and motor impulses. Cattell and Dolley did not, however, arrive at a simple conclusion because so many other factors affected their results, as one can readily understand from the results of Cattell's other investigations. Cattell worked further with the times for discrimination and cognition (between which he did not, like the good Wundtians, distinguish) and with the times for choice ("will"); and his resultant table for "perception-times" and "will-times" for lights, colors, letters, pictures and words has often been cited. Nevertheless he was himself doubtful of the validity of the 'subtractive procedure' by which these times are got, a procedure which went out of fashion even in Leipzig with Külpe's criticism of it. Cattell was also skeptical of Lange's classical distinction between the sensorial and muscular reactions and of the standard difference between them of one tenth of a second. He characterized the muscular time as a subcortical reflex, and later, as we have seen, he contributed results which lent aid to Baldwin in his controversy with Titchener (pp. 413 f). The sensory type of observer gives the sensorial reaction more quickly than the muscular, Baldwin's argument ran; and Cattell of course was glad to find an individual difference here. Cattell also investigated association times, first constrained associations and then free associations. These results are also classical in the literature of this experiment. He studied the relation of reaction time to intensity of stimulus, to attention and to discrimination, and his results indicate a possible measure, by way of reaction time, of each of these factors. The last two studies have led to researches at the hands of others in which degree of attention or the amount of differences between sensations is measured by the reaction experiment. The latter measurement was a new psychophysical method.

Cattell's work on *association* has just been mentioned. The paper on controlled association is of 1887, and the paper on free association of 1889. These papers, however, share with only a few others the distinction of being the foundation for the whole association method as it is used today. Cattell vaguely realized their significance when he remarked that the association reactions "lay bare the mental life in a way that is startling and not always gratifying." He also anticipated the work that has had its culmination in the lists of Kent and Rosanoff of normal associations, for he prepared such lists for a small group. The investigation of the association method was carried much further by his students at Columbia.

In the matter of the times of perception and of reading, Cattell was also a pioneer. He investigated the retinal time of visual perception. Then he studied "the time it takes to see and name objects," forms, colors, letters, sentences. He used the tachistoscopic procedure and found that the time for each item decreases when the number of simultaneously presented objects is increased up to a small number, say five. These data have been the classical data for the *range of attention*, although Cattell's interest was not in this systematic point but in the relation of the times to familiarity. More letters can be perceived in a short time when they form a word, or more words when they form a sentence, because the combination is familiar. Similarly Cattell showed that the reading time for different languages varies with the familiarity of the language, without the knowledge of the reader that the times are different. Cattell also investigated by this method the legibility of different letters of the alphabet and of different types, a study that has been carried on by others subsequently with some important practical results.

In *psychophysics* Cattell, in Galtonian fashion, brought the law of error to bear. He was quite out of sympathy with the classical German work of Fechner, Müller and Wundt because of the stress that it laid upon introspection. He did not believe that reliable judgments of a sense-distance, with introspection supplying the only criterion, can be made, and he would have taken his stand against the distinction that is implied by Titchener in the phrase *the stimulus-error*, had that term then been coined. One judges stimuli, he thought—not sensations, which are something different; and the problem is one of the accuracy of the judgments. To such a problem the law of error can be applied because it is—or has been supposed to be ever since Gauss—a law of errors of observation. "It seems to me," he said in 1904, "that most of the research work that has been done by me or in my laboratory is nearly as independent of introspection as work in physics or zoology." Cattell's classic monograph, on which we have just commented (p. 534), is the one with Fullerton in 1892. In it they criticized the method of average error on the ground that the time of the adjustment of the equating stimulus by the subject is not controlled and many variable elements are thus introduced. They criticized the method of just noticeable differences on the ground that the category *equal*, applying to a range of stimuli, is dependent solely upon introspection and in practice yields great variability. They were left with the third Fechnerian method, the method of constant stimuli. This is the method that makes use of the normal law of error, and Cattell may have been favorably disposed toward it on this account. It also uses the category *equal*; but Cattell and Fullerton got rid of this source of 'error' by dividing the 'equal' judgments equally between the other two categories. The result was not the limen which measures the range of the region of equality but probable errors of judgments, a result which harmonizes with Galton's work much more than with Fechner's. Baldwin had remarks to make about Cattell's reverence for the probable error; certainly he raised it to a high office when he substituted it for the reigning limen.

Beside the construction of psychophysical apparatus, Cattell made two other important contributions to this field. He and Fullerton proposed, as a substitute for Weber's law, a law of the square root— for $S = k \log R$, $S = k \sqrt{R}$—although it was not sensation S, but the error of observation that they were describing. The substitution of this formula for the other seemed to be indicated, partly on theoretical grounds connected with the law of error and partly by their empirical results. Here, too, we see that no tradition was too sacred for Cattell's iconoclastic hand. The other contribution we have mentioned; it is Cattell's new psychophysical method whereby the amount of sensory difference is measured inversely by reaction time.

Just outside of psychophysics lies Cattell's invention of the *method of order of merit* or of relative position. This method he first developed in 1902 in connection with the placing of grays in order—a happy case for a first use, since the true order could be determined photometrically as a check. The subsequent history of the method in Cattell's hands has lain, however, with his studies of eminence, especially in the case of American men of science. On the basis of many rankings by different judges, he determined the central tendency of position for each individual and its probable error. The central tendency he took, of course, as the true position. The method has had wide use, especially in the hands of Cattell's students, and he himself has carried his studies of eminence, periodically publishing lists of the most distinguished scientists.

All these studies, it will be seen, have for their central theme the problem of *individual differences*. Cattell published in 1890 a paper on mental tests and measurements, and another in 1893 on tests of the senses and faculties. In general, however, his own research on the subject has been the work cited and his study of *Homo scientificus Americanus*. "It is surely time," he wrote, "for scientific men to apply scientific methods to determine the circumstances that promote or hinder advancement of science." This was his motive. His influence, however, has been very much wider in support of the *mental tests*. E. L. Thorndike was his student. After devising mental tests for animals in the form of the puzzle-boxes of his doctoral dissertation, he was advised by Cattell to undertake the same sort of thing with children at the new Teachers College founded at Columbia. Thorndike has been the leader in the psychology of mental tests in America. Columbia was for years the leading university in this movement. Between them Cattell and Thorndike created at Columbia an irresistible atmosphere, and Cattell, who refused to follow Wundt, could later see his own influence all over America spread by Columbia students—his children, his grandchildren by way of Thorndike, and even his great-grandchildren. Of course the American atmosphere helped. As we have said, it was ready for just this kind of psychology.

Cattell's psychology is, however, something more than mental tests and reaction times and statistical method and the resultant objective judgments that are not introspections. It is a psychology of human *capacity*. It is motivated by the desire to determine how well men can do in this or that situation. It is concerned little with an analysis of capacities into conscious causes, and only a little more with the physiological causes. It seeks a description of human nature in respect of its range and variability, just as Galton sought the same end. This psychology of capacity is, of course, functional psychology, though it may not be wise to give so unphilosophic a movement this formal systematic name. Nevertheless, it is important to realize the significance of the movement, because it, almost more than any other 'school,' has been typical of the American trend. To the description of this trend, this American functional psychology, the next chapter is devoted.

It is difficult to give a picture of Cattell's effect upon American psychology by way of his students. During the sixty-five years from 1884 to 1948, Columbia University gave 344 doctor's degrees in psychology, more than any other university. (Iowa was second with 269.) In the latter part of Cattell's incumbency, however, many of these doctorates represent Thorndike's and Woodworth's influence. Out of a list about four times as large and one that contains many other well-known names, we may mention those psychologists who received their doctorates in psychology at Columbia while Cattell was in command and who have been at some time placed by Cattell in his lists of leading American psychologists, lists determined at intervals by Cattell's statistical treatment of judgments of order of merit. (The date of the doctorate is given with each name.) Here is the list: E. L. Thorndike (1898), who began the formal laboratory work upon animals and who became America's most distinguished leader in the field of the mental tests; R. S. Woodworth (1899), who was long Cattell's support at Columbia and who succeeded him in his position there and eventually in his relation to American psychological thought; S. I. Franz (1899), famous for his work on the localization of cerebral functions; Clark Wissler (1901), anthropologist and psychologist; W. F. Dearborn (1905), Harvard's educational psychologist; F. L. Wells (1906), the champion of psychometrics at Harvard; Warner Brown (1908), the senior experimentalist at the University of California; H. L. Hollingworth (1909), at Barnard College and the author of many books on a wide range of psychological topics; E. K. Strong (1911), known for his work in industrial psychology and vocational interests; A. T. Poffenberger (1912), later Woodworth's successor at Columbia as Woodworth was Cattell's; J. F. Dashiell (1913), the behaviorist at North Carolina; T. L. Kelley (1914), Thorndike's pupil and for some years America's leading psychologist-statistician; A. I. Gates (1917), professor of psychology at Teachers College and the youngest of this distinguished list.

OTHER PIONEERS

We have considered the more influential of the American 'pioneers' in experimental psychology. Now let us mention the other men who loomed large in the 1880s and 1890s.

Joseph Jastrow (1863-1944), born in Warsaw, Poland, was a student at Hopkins when Hall went there, and received his doctorate in 1886 for work done with Hall. He then went in 1888 to Wisconsin as professor of psychology, began a laboratory there and remained in this position until his retirement in 1927.

Jastrow's original work was in psychophysics and he got his first interest in psychology from C. S. Peirce and not from Hall. While he was at Hopkins, he presented to the National Academy of Sciences in collaboration with Peirce an important paper on the method of determining the differential limen, and a little later he published a general critique of the psychophysical methods. In his work he anticipated Fullerton and Cattell in recommending the substitution of the probable error for the conventional limen, and thus the notion that the critical frequency in differential sensitivity is 75 per cent and not 50 per cent. In the method of constant stimuli, the limen had been defined as the point where the judgment *greater* (or *less*) is given as often as it is not, *i.e.*, at 50 per cent. This criterion, however, implies the acceptance of the category *equal,* for, if there be only two categories, *greater* and *less,* then, when *greater* is given 50 per cent of the time, *less* must be given the other 50 per cent, the two liminal points coincide, and there is not the interval between them that the concept of the limen requires. Jastrow, like Cattell, mistrusted the subjective criterion for the equality judgments, and he had to choose the probable error (the judgmental frequency of 75 per cent) in order to preserve the fundamental psychophysical notion.

The 1890s were the heyday of the 'minor studies.' Experimental psychology was very new. Almost any one with patience and a little knowledge or advice might, according to the faith of the times, contribute important experimental data. Little formal training was required because there was little to be had. In some measure this faith was justified. Many important studies have appeared thus labeled "minor." It was Jastrow who started this custom with twenty-five minor studies published from Wisconsin in three years (1890-1892). Clark and Cornell soon followed suit; later Michigan had such a series for a time; still later Vassar under M. F. Washburn began the long series of her sixty-seven minor studies (1905-1934). Jastrow did not continue with what he started, but the early series contained many short psychophysical studies which had to be taken into account at the time.

Jastrow is also known for his popularization of scientific psychology, which he accomplished in a much more dignified manner than did Scripture. Many of his essays and lectures were finally brought together in his *Fact and Fable in Psychology* (1900), a book that considers the psychology of the occult, psychic research, mental telepathy, deception, spiritualism, hypnotism, the dreams of the blind, and similar topics. His sobriety of judgment he dispensed in easy English prose.

Edmund Clark Sanford (1859-1924) went to Hopkins to study psychology with Hall and received his degree there in 1888. Then he migrated with Hall to Clark, where, as we have seen, Hall turned over to him the new laboratory. His psychological life was cut short by his appointment in 1909 to the presidency of Clark College, the undergraduate addition to the graduate Clark University.

He began, and maintained at an excellent standard, the minor studies from Clark. He was something of a technician and constructed with his own hands many original pieces of psychological apparatus. His vernier pendulum chronoscope became for a while the standard instrument for elementary work with reaction times. His publications were often of a literary nature with a strain of whimsicality in them. His health was never good, and that fact probably accounts for his lack of aggressiveness, both in productivity and in the professional quarrels that were characteristic of his generation.

Sanford accomplished one very important service for psychology. He wrote the first laboratory manual for the new science, antedating even Titchener. This *Course in Experimental Psychology* began to appear in the *American Journal of Psychology* in 1891, and the book, altered from these advance issues, appeared in 1898, three years before Titchener's first manual. Sanford's book covered only the topics of sensation and perception; it was supposed to be the first volume of a complete work, but he never wrote Part II. Within the most highly developed field of the new psychology, this handbook, however, was pioneer work of exceptional merit. For thirty years, in spite of the other manuals that followed upon it, the psychologist would still turn to Sanford's *Course* for references, for experiments and for apt lecture demonstrations.

Titchener was another pioneer in America, but not in American psychology as we have used the phrase in this chapter. Titchener, though not a German, worked always in the German tradition and stood apart from the American trend. For this reason we have already discussed his contribution to psychology along with Külpe's (pp. 410-420). He had the closest association with Sanford, who was one of the few prominent American psychologists, all older than Titchener, who welcomed the young Englishman to America in 1892.

Münsterberg was the other foreign importation into America in 1892. He was a German, but did not continue the tradition which he had begun at Freiburg. Instead he turned to promoting, in the broadest sense, applied psychology in America. His should be one of the names to associate especially with the mental tests, but on the whole his scientific influence was much less than Cattell's. His philosophy was explicit and it was not American functionalism. He never belonged to America. His popularization of applied psychology only brought him into disrepute with his colleagues. Here lies presumably the reason why Münsterberg's influence died with him, as Cattell's, passed beyond his own control, did not. We have already mentioned Münsterberg (pp. 427-429) and must be content to let our acquaintance with a forceful, farseeing enthusiast rest thus.

There were still other men of the early days in America. There was E. B. Delabarre, an American student of Münsterberg's at Freiburg, who had been at Brown University since 1891 and who ran the Harvard laboratory for James the year Münsterberg was away deciding whether to come back (1896-1897). He contributed early experimental work on muscular sensation. There was W. L. Bryan from Clark, who worked with Külpe at Würzburg on the abstraction experiment (p. 401) and who was once president of the American Psychological Association; but very early in his career he lapsed into the presidency of Indiana University. There was Livingston Farrand, the anthropologist, who was associated with Cattell in testing the students at Columbia, and who later became the president of Cornell. There were the philosophers in the days when psychology, even experimental psychology, was still part of philosophy: J. G. Schurman and J. E. Creighton of Cornell; G. S. Fullerton, who experimented with Cattell at Pennsylvania; Josiah Royce of Harvard, who wrote a psychology; and John Dewey, who also wrote a psychology and who played an important rôle in the movement of functional psychology, which we shall consider later (pp. 552-554). All these men were actively concerned with the new psychology in its early days; all were members of the American Psychological Association, which was founded in 1892, and played active parts in its affairs. Nevertheless, except for Dewey, the perspective of the present does not show that they influenced greatly the course of psychology, which in America continued to move steadily away from philosophy.

NOTES

The great-man theory of scientific progress and the *Zeitgeist* theory have been discussed on pp. 8 f.; see also p. 745. The relation of English evolutionism to American functional psychology has been anticipated in Chapter 12, pp. 242 f.

James

A very great deal has been written about William James. The best source is R. B. Perry's Pulitzer Prize volumes, *The Thought and Character of William James*, 2 vols., 1935. These volumes quote many letters and add wise commentary. See II, 3-204, for James as psychologist. See also Henry James, *The Letters of William James*, 1920. James could hardly put his pen to paper without leaving some record of his vivid personality, and the *Letters* well repay reading by whoever would catch the flavor of the man. Another earlier book about James is E. Boutroux, *William James*, 1911, Eng. trans., 1912. See also the seven reminiscences by E. L. Thorndike, G. W. Allport, John Dewey, R. B. Perry, E. B. Delabarre, E. D. Starbuck and R. P. Angier, Centenary of the birth of William James, *Psychol. Rev.*, 1943, 50, 87-134.. There is also an excellent discussion of James' rôle in G. Murphy, *Historical Introduction to Modern Psychology*, 2 ed., 1949, 193-209; and another in E. Heidbreder, *Seven Psychologies*, 1933, 152-200. See also E. G. Boring, Human nature vs. sensation: William James and the psychology of the present, *Amer. J. Psychol.*, 1942, 55, 310-327, which is another paper written to honor the centenary of James' birth.

James' writings were widely scattered, and often original writing is almost lost in book reviews. This difficulty is relieved by the annotated bibliography of some 300-odd excursions into print, by R. B. Perry, *The Writings of William James*, 1920. Henry James' *Letters* gives a list of books, II, 357-361. Perry's list is based originally upon the less complete, unannotated,

but more available list in *Psychol. Rev.*, 1911, 18, 157-165.

James' important psychological books are: *Principles of Psychology*, 1890; *Text-Book of Psychology: Briefer Course*, 1892; *Talks to Teachers on Psychology*, 1899; *Varieties of Religious Experience*, 1901-1902. The philosophical books are: *Pragmatism*, 1907; *A Pluralistic Universe*, 1909; *The Meaning of Truth*, 1909; and four posthumously printed books, three of which are collections of essays, largely reprinted.

That in 1927 American psychologists rated James as the most important psychologist in all history is indicated by M. A. Tinker, B. D. Thuma and P. R. Farnsworth, The rating of psychologists, *Amer. J. Psychol.*, 1927, 38, 453-455.

On the beginnings of experimental psychology with James at Harvard and the question of who founded the first psychological laboratory—James at Harvard in 1875 or Hall at Hopkins in 1883—see Perry, *op. cit.* (1935), II, 6-15; R. S. Harper, The laboratory of William James, *Harvard Alumni Bulletin*, 1949, 52, 169-173.

On the stream of thought, see *Principles*, I, 224-290. On consciousness as cognitive and functional, see *Principles*, I, 144; *Text-Book*, 103 and 13 f. On James' use of the word *function*, see C. A. Ruckmick, The use of the term *function* in English textbooks of psychology, *Amer. J. Psychol.*, 1911, 24, 99-123, esp. 111.

On James' theory of emotion, see his writings: *Mind*, 1884, 9, 188-205; *Principles*, 1890, II, 442-485; *Psychol. Rev.*, 1894, 1, 516-529. C. Lange's paper is *Om Sindsbevoegelser*, 1885; *Ueber Gemütsbewegungen* (German trans.), 1887. James' paper of 1884 is reprinted in his *Collected Essays and Reviews*, 1920, and in W. Dennis, *Readings in the History of Psychology*, 1948, 290-303. It and the chapter from the *Principles* (but not the important paper of 1894) have been reprinted with the first English trans. of Lange's monograph, Lange and James, *The Emotions* (Psychology Classics, I), 1922.

E. B. Titchener has argued that the James-Lange theory was not new, but clearly had its origin in the writings, for the most part, of the earlier French philosopher-physiologists: see his An historical note on the James-Lange theory of emotion, *Amer. J. Psychol.*, 1914, 25, 427-447.

On the immediate critical discussion which James' theory of emotion produced, see E. Gurney, *Mind*, 1884, 9, 421-426; W. L. Worcester, *Monist*, 1893, 3, 285-298; D. Irons, *Mind*, 1894, N.S. 3, 77-97.

Hall

There is a great deal of information available about the life and work of G. Stanley Hall, but there is no very full direct biographical account. The most direct is L. N. Wilson, *G. Stanley Hall: a Sketch*, 1914, but there are many omissions in it. It may be supplemented by *Publications of Clark Univ. Library*, 1925, 7, no. 6, which contains a further sketch by Wilson, sketches by E. C. Sanford (reprinted from *Amer. J. Psychol.*, 1924, 35, 313-321) and W. H. Burnham (reprinted from *Psychol. Rev.*, 1925, 32, 89-102), extracts from the letters of numerous psychologists about Hall, a list of 81 persons who took their doctor's degrees with Hall at Clark, and a bibliography. Very informative is Hall's own *Life and Confessions of a Psychologist*, 1923, which exhibits Hall's characteristic inaccuracy as to detail, but gives the inner picture of the man, and also reveals for the first time the inside history of the difficulties at Clark in 1890-1900 when the founder, the president and the faculty were all at odds. Then there is L. Pruette, *A Biography of a Mind*, 1926, which is a collection of sketches without an index and is interesting reading but inconvenient for reference. S. C. Fisher, The psychological and educational work of Granville Stanley Hall, *Amer. J. Psychol.*, 1925, 36, 1-52, really deals with Hall's psychology and only incidentally with his biography. Under her

hand Hall begins to show some signs of systematic stability beneath the turbulent surface of his stormy interests. On the relation of Hall to Bowditch, *cf.* W. R. and C. C. Miles, Eight letters from G. Stanley Hall to H. P. Bowditch, *Amer. J. Psychol.*, 1929, 41, 326-336.

For a bibliography to 1914 (339 titles), see Wilson, *op. cit.*, 119-144; to 1922, *Life and Confessions*, 597-616; *complete* (439 titles), *Publications of Clark Univ. Library, op. cit.*, 109-135. Hall was prolific.

For an excellent picture of Hall as a man, see Burnham, *op. cit.* For an estimate of him as a psychologist, based on his own method of the questionnaire and thus summarizing the opinions of American psychologists, see E. D. Starbuck, G. Stanley Hall as a psychologist, *Psychol. Rev.*, 1925, 32, 103-120.

If the reader questions the propriety of including an extended account of Hall in a history of experimental psychology, he should refer to the editorial in *Amer. J. Psychol.*, 1895, 7, 1-8, esp. 1 f. Here he will discover that the enthusiastic group about Hall at Hopkins and Clark thought of him as the prime mover in the new psychology in America and thus in American experimental psychology. Of course their enthusiasm ran away with them and they were properly spanked by James, G. T. Ladd, J. M. Baldwin and J. McK. Cattell in Experimental psychology in America, *Science*, 1895, N.S. 2, 626-628 (though *cf.* here Hall's rejoinder, *ibid.*, 734 f.). For Hall as the propagandist of the new psychology, see The new psychology, *Andover Rev.*, 1885, 3, 120-135, 239-248; Experimental psychology, *Mind*, 1885, 10, 245-249. It must be remembered that Clark University was only a scientific institute and that psychology was the dominant department in it. This unique reversal of the usual academic situation made psychologists think of Clark as a psychological university, and Clark and Hall are inseparable in thought. Moreover, Titchener, relatively isolated in American psychology, threw in his lot, *faute de mieux*, with Hall in the *American Journal of Psychology,* and Clark and Cornell standing together formed a strong party.

Hall's paper of 1883, The content of children's minds, shows him in the pioneering rôle in child psychology. It is reprinted by W. Dennis, *Readings in the History of Psychology,* 1948, 255-278. But on this matter see the discussion of educational psychology in the next chapter (pp. 567-570, 581).

Hall's influence is further shown by the long list of his pupils and their record of productivity in afteryears. Of the eighty-one doctorates that he gave at Clark, the author ventures here to list twenty-five names which in 1929 seemed to him best known to psychologists. (Alas, some of the glamour had already gone!) The list is chronological and naturally includes mostly the older persons. All but one of them received their degrees before 1912, and two thirds of them before 1900. The list: H. Nichols, W. L. Bryan, A. H. Daniels, J. A. Bergström, F. B. Dresslar, T. L. Bolton, J. H. Leuba, C. A. Scott, E. H. Lindley, E. D. Starbuck, L. W. Kline, F. E. Bolton, H. H. Goddard, E. B. Huey, H. D. Sheldon, W. S. Small, N. Triplett, A. W. Trettien, J. Morse, L. M. Terman, D. S. Hill, G. Ordahl, H. W. Chase, E. S. Conklin, F. Mateer. Hall's executive personality made him a practical psychologist, and thus an educational psychologist, and thus a president. Do pupils take after their 'master'? Well, the foregoing list contained in 1929 four college presidents, four college deans, and one superintendent of schools—a third altogether.

Ladd

No list of Ladd's very many books on philosophy and topics connected with his interest in the Orient is necessary here. He was a persistent writer, and Stanley Hall complained in 1894 that his new book was "the eighth large volume put forth by the author within the last few years, to own all of which now costs the devoted reader twenty-five dollars and fifty cents": *Amer. J. Psychol.,* 1894, 6, 477 f. Hall

had been much more cordial to the first book: *ibid.,* 1887, 1, 159-164. Two of these eight books are unimportant outlines of Yale courses; one can not be readily identified; the others and two that came out later are: *Elements of Physiological Psychology,* 1887, revised by R. S. Woodworth, 1911; *Introduction to Philosophy,* 1890; *Outlines of Physiological Psychology* (the abridged *Elements*), 1891, 8 ed., 1908; *Primer of Psychology,* 1894; *Psychology, Descriptive and Explanatory,* 1894; *Philosophy of Mind,* 1895; *Outlines of Descriptive Psychology* (abridged from the book of 1894), 1898.

George Trumbull Ladd was a distinguished person, but there seems to be no adequate account of his life and work. For short necrological sketches, see A. C. Armstrong, *Philos. Rev.,* 1921, 30, 639 f.; and esp. E. B. Titchener, *Amer. J. Psychol.,* 1921, 32, 600 f.

For an analysis and criticism of Ladd's system, see E. B. Titchener, *Systematic Psychology: Prolegomena,* 1929, 158-194. This chapter deals with functional psychology in general, and the four characteristics of a functional psychology, which the text gives, are derived from Titchener.

Scripture

For Edward Wheeler Scripture, the text cites the two important books and the *Studies from the Yale Psychological Laboratory* which make up the more important part of his psychological work from 1892-1902. After 1902 the trend of his work in phonetics is shown by *Elements in Experimental Phonetics,* 1902; *Researches in Experimental Phonetics: the Study of Speech Curves,* 1906; and *Stuttering and Lisping,* 1912, 2 ed., 1923. There were many other publications within the same field.

It is perhaps well to add to the comment of the text that Scripture's enthusiasm for the 'new' psychology contained an element of exaggeration and another of egotism (*cf.* the account of John Elliotson, pp. 119-121). It thus made him few friends and perhaps explains why the productivity of the Yale laboratory was limited so nearly to his own. Both his early books revealed a faith in the Yale laboratory similar to that of the modern 'booster' in an American town. The conservatives—and even Hall is a conservative in this context—disliked such popular appeals as a picture of all the European monarchs holding hands in a chain reaction. It was Scripture who invented the term *arm-chair psychology*. His first book was "written expressly for the people" with the hope that it could "be taken as evidence of the attitude of the science in its desire to serve humanity," a statement that is not wholly without diagnostic value for the American trend. Scripture's confidence in himself is shown by his statement in the preface of this book that Wundt is the greatest of psychologists but intelligible only to the expert, and that "no one else has produced a book explaining the methods and results of the new psychology." He added: "This is my reason for writing one"—in 1895!

For more about Scripture, see his autobiography in C. Murchison, *Psychology in Autobiography*, 1936, III, 231-261.

Baldwin

The text fits Baldwin into his rôle in the American scene. Much more about the development of his thought is to be obtained from his autobiography in Murchison, *op. cit.*, 1930, I, 1-30.

Baldwin's more psychological books were: *Handbook of Psychology: Senses and Intellect*, 1889, 2 ed., 1890; *Handbook of Psychology: Feeling and Will*, 1891; *Elements of Psychology* (the abbreviated *Handbook*), 1893; *Mental Development in the Child and the Race*, 1895, 3 ed., 1907; *Social and Ethical Interpretations in Mental Development*, 1897, 4 ed., 1907 (the word *Ethical* was added to the title after the MS. was completed, enabling the author to win the decennial gold medal of the Royal Academy at Copenhagen which prescribed the social foundations of ethics as the field for compe-

tition that year); *The Story of the Mind*, 1898; *Fragments of Philosophy and Psychology* (collected essays), 1902; *History of Psychology*, 1913. Baldwin's most important undertaking in the Hopkins days was the writing of *Thought and Things or Genetic Logic*, 3 vols., 1906-1911. There are four other books dealing with the philosophy of evolution and four about America, France, the Allies and the First World War.

For Baldwin's life and much personal information about the psychology of 1890-1905, see his *Between Two Wars: 1861-1921*, 1926. The first volume is *Memories* and is the more important in this connection. The second is *Opinions and Letters*. The *Memories*, although somewhat discursive, make capital reading, for Baldwin writes in a detached, half-humorous way about himself and others—many others. He probably holds among psychologists the record for close approach to persons of royal blood.

In this book Baldwin chuckles over the incident of having to pay duty on Bain's gift of the two large volumes of his *Psychology*. Baldwin protested the duty on the ground that scientific books were then duty-free, and Washington replied: "Our experts report that these books are in no sense scientific." One wonders at once whether Baldwin's books might not have evoked the same judgment.

The text asserts that Baldwin was essentially a writer in the sense that his theories were closely associated with their verbal expression. The grounds for this statement lie in Baldwin's tendency to quote verbatim his own statements and *bons mots*. Cf. Baldwin's own discussion of this point in the preface of the *Story of the Mind*.

The flavor of the reaction of the more experimentally or empirically minded group to Baldwin's theorizing is given in T. L. Bolton's review of Baldwin's *Mental Development in the Child and Race*; see *Amer. J. Psychol.*, 1895, 7, 142-145. On the controversy with Titchener, see pp. 413 f.

For Baldwin's account of his Toronto laboratory, see *Amer. J. Psychol.*, 1890, 3, 285 f.

Cattell

There is now available *James Mc-Keen Cattell—Man of Science*, 2 vols., 1947. Vol. I, *Psychological Research*, reprints 29 scientific papers and gives the bibliography, thus making it unnecessary to print again here the selected bibliography which seemed necessary in the 1929 edition of this book. Vol. II, *Addresses and Formal Papers*, reprints 41 items on the progress of psychology, accounts of early psychological laboratories, the growth and administration of scientific organizations, educational and administrative problems of colleges, universities and foundations, studies of eminent men, of the birth-rate among scientists, of their biographies, and the rôle of applied psychology in the welfare of the nation. These volumes also reprint two excellent necrologies which had appeared elsewhere: R. S. Woodworth, James McKeen Cattell 1860-1944, *Psychol. Rev.*, 1944, 51, 201-209; F. L. Wells, same title, *Amer. J. Psychol.*, 1944, 57, 270-275. There is also an appreciation by eleven distinguished scientists with whom Cattell had worked in one capacity or another: James McKeen Cattell—in memoriam, *Science*, 1944, 155-165. These sketches describe Cattell as a scientist, a psychologist, an educationalist, a promoter, a humanitarian, a leader, and his work in the American Association for the Advancement of Science, in Science Service, in the Psychological Corporation and in certain of the learned societies.

The early article by six of Cattell's students is The psychological researches of James McKeen Cattell, *Arch. Psychol.*, 1914, no. 30. Here V. A. C. Henmon treats of reaction time, W. F. Dearborn of reading and perception, F. L. Wells of association, R. S. Woodworth of psychophysics, H. L. Hollingworth of the method of order of merit, and E. L. Thorndike of individual differences. Henmon's chapter is an excellent account of the entire history of the reaction experiment.

Cattell's editorships were: *Psychological Review* (1894-1903); *Popular Science Monthly* (1900-1915), continued as *Scientific Monthly* (1915-1943); *Science* (1904-1944); *American Naturalist* (1907-1944); *School and Society* (1915-1939); *American Men of Science*, 6 eds. (1906-1938).

The articles on the ranking of men of science are variously printed in the editions of *American Men of Science*. See the 4 ed., 1111-1117, for the selection of fifty psychologists of which account is taken in the text in naming Cattell's more eminent students. Cattell's starring of scientists has resulted in a book analyzing the selections: S. S. Visher, *Scientists Starred 1903-1943 in "American Men of Science,"* 1947. See pp. 141-143 for the lists of psychologists and for the rank-order of the first fifty who were starred in the first edition (1903). The first ten in order were then James, Cattell (ipse), Münsterberg, Stanley Hall, J. M. Baldwin, Titchener, Royce, G. T. Ladd, Dewey and Jastrow. The second ten were Sanford, Calkins, W. L. Bryan, Fullerton, Stratton, Thorndike, E. B. Delabarre, Scripture, Ladd-Franklin, H. R. Marshall. The third ten were Judd, J. R. Angell, Witmer, Patrick, Warren, W. T. Harris, Dodge, Hyslop, Seashore, C. A. Strong. In the last twenty the best known names are Max Meyer, Leuba, Frank Angell, Pillsbury, Washburn, Woodworth, Franz. There were three women—Calkins, Ladd-Franklin, Washburn.

On Cattell's and other psychologists' students, see M. D. Boring and E. G. Boring, Masters and pupils among the American psychologists, *Amer. J. Psychol.* 1948, 61, 527-534. On the Ph.D.s from Columbia and other universities, see R. S. Harper, Tables of American doctorates in psychology, *ibid.*, 1949, 62, 579-587; also this book, p. 581.

On Cattell's first laboratory see his Psychology at the University of Pennsylvania, *Amer. J. Psychol.*, 1890, 3, 281-283. On other early laboratories.

see his Early psychological laboratories, *Science*, 1928, N.S. 67, 543-548, or in M. L. Reymert, *Feelings and Emotions (Wittenberg Symposium)*, 1928, 427-433 (the two articles are identical).

Four papers of Cattell's in the period 1885-1890 on reaction, perception, association and the mental test, respectively, are reprinted by W. Dennis, *op. cit.*, 323-335, 347-354. The last paper is the one that coins the term *mental test:* Mental tests and their measurement, *Mind*, 1890, 15, 373-380.

Jastrow

Joseph Jastrow's important psychophysical contributions are: C. S. Peirce and Jastrow, On small differences of sensation, *Mem. Nat. Acad. Sci.*, 1884, 3; Jastrow, Critique of psychophysic methods, *Amer. J. Psychol.*, 1888, 1, 271-309.

The 25 minor studies from the Wisconsin laboratory are scattered through the *Amer. J. Psychol.*, 1890-1892, vols. 3-5.

For an account of the early Wisconsin laboratory, see Psychology at the University of Wisconsin, *ibid.*, 1890, 3, 275 f.

On Jastrow's life, see C. L. Hull, Joseph Jastrow, 1863-1944, *Amer. J. Psychol.*, 1944, 57, 581-585; W. B. Pillsbury, same title, *Psychol. Rev.*, 1944, 51, 261-265.

Sanford

For accounts of Edmund Clark Sanford's life and work, see W. H. Burnham, Edmund Clark Sanford, *Ped. Sem.*, 1925, 32, 2-7; E. B. Titchener, Edmund Clark Sanford 1859-1924, *Amer. J. Psychol.*, 1925, 36, 157-170; also *Publications of Clark Univ. Library*, 1925, 8, no. 1, which reprints the first two articles and adds others. The Clark pamphlet gives a bibliography, including a list of the minor studies. Titchener gives the same, and also a list of articles that resulted from Sanford's work with students. The 22 minor studies occur in *Amer. J. Psychol.*, 1893-1908, vols. 5-19 (and one in vol. 35 after Sanford had retired from the presidency of Clark College and returned to psychology for his few remaining years).

The *Course in Experimental Psychology, Part I: Sensation and Perception*, 1898, had been appearing in the *Amer. J. Psychol.*, 1891-1896, vols. 4-7. These dates are important: Sanford was much more of a pioneer in the matter of a laboratory course in experimental psychology in 1891 than he was in 1898. Psychology moved rapidly in that decade, and Titchener's *Manuals* began coming out in 1901.

On Sanford's vernier chronoscope, see *Amer. J. Psychol.*, 1890, 3, 174-181; 1898, 9, 191-197; 1901, 12, 590-594.

Laboratories

C. R. Garvey, List of American psychological laboratories, *Psychol. Bull.*, 1929, 26, 652-660, lists in the order of their founding with their dates and their first directors 117 American laboratories, and he appends a bibliography of 28 articles about laboratory founding in the United States.

CHAPTER 22

American Functional Psychology

We have now followed the development of 'general psychology,' the matrix of experimental psychology, up to, and in some cases into, the twentieth century. We have seen how general psychology emerged from physiology and philosophy, we have seen it get organized as an independent science and establish itself in Germany, Great Britain and America. So far we have spoken mostly of the contributions of great men to this development, as if the great-man theory of history were true. Altogether we have studied the effects and contributions of almost four score great men, among whom some of the most prominent are John Locke, Johannes Müller, the Mills, Lotze, Fechner, Helmholtz, Wundt, Külpe, Titchener, Galton, James and Cattell. The thoughts and actions of all these men occupy the preceding pages of this book. We have seen how they affected history and also, to some extent, how history affected them. This personal approach to history is the most natural and the most congenial. The *Zeitgeist* becomes comprehensible when it is analyzed into the interactions of persons, one with another. The action may be positive as when disciple follows master, or negative as when in-group opposes out-group. In the twentieth century, however, psychology gets too big to be understood as personal interaction—at least in so small a book as this one. There are too many great men for us to consider each as a separate personality. It is, moreover, unsafe to assess the influence of the recently great. We need to let time make the first assessment for us. From this point on, therefore, we are obliged to concentrate more on the movements which constitute the background of experimental psychology and less on the personalities which made the movements move. We must, however, continue to be as personal as possible, for the individual is still the crux where culture and social pressures can be seen determining the choices which later will have made the future what it will have turned out to be.

Our business now in the remaining chapters is (1) to continue the discussion of functional psychology, (2) to see how Gestalt psychology came out of the act and content psychologies and what it was, (3) to trace behavioristics from materialistic psychology through behaviorism down to modern operationism, (4) to examine the basic trend in physiological psychology which shows how thought changed on the matter of how the brain functions, and finally (5) to bring into the orbit of experimental psychology a précis of the history of dynamic psychology in order to see how an unexperimental psychology eventually affected the experimental psychology of motivation.

We begin with *functional psychology*, and for the most part American functionalism, partly because the American temper fostered functionalism and partly because the functional point of view is close to common sense. The alternative to function is structure. If, influenced by the culture, you conclude that you should devote yourself to the description of nature, content to say *what* happens and *how* it happens, without asking the question why, then you are concerned with structure, are working in the descriptive tradition of the taxonomists and, in psychology, the tradition of Wundt, Külpe and Titchener. But if you ask *why*, if you try to understand causes, then you are interesting yourself in capabilities, in capacities, and are being a functionalist. It is as natural to be a functionalist as it is to want to predict, to be more interested in the future than the past, to prefer to ride facing forward on the train. The future concerns you because you think you might change it if you had the ability. The past has gone by, lies there open to description but unalterable. The theory of evolution took people by storm not so much because it described the descent of current man, as because it opened up the astonishing possibilities for the future, which Galton saw at once. The functional view is the natural view. Even such a descriptive word as *sensation* used to be functional to the physiologist Albrecht von Haller, who identified sensation with awareness. He wrote in 1747: "We are solicited to take food, as well from a sense of pain which we call hunger, as from that pleasure which is received by taste." That is a functional view of hunger-pangs and taste. It takes a sensation to tell you what you want, or what you need.

From this it follows that *applied psychology* is functional. So too is that basic applied psychology functional, the one which has to do with success in living, with the adaptation of the organism to its environment, and with the organism's adaptation of its environment to itself. It did not require the invention of the theory of evolution to make man interested in his own survival or in getting what he wants. Any conception of the conscious or behavioral capacities of the organism as means for achieving success is part of a functional psychology. But sheer description is not functional, unless it be description of capacities or functional potentialities and relations. If applied psychology is functional, its subdivisions and tools will be functional—child psychology, educational psychology and the mental tests.

Now let us take stock of what we already know about functional psychology. In connection with the evolutionary psychology of Herbert Spencer, we have discussed the relation of the theory of evolution to functionalism (pp. 240-243). We have seen how Galton presently became the perfect example of a functional psychologist (pp. 482-488) and how British psychology, except for the systematists like Ward, was essentially functional. And then in the preceding chapter we have seen how James, Hall, Ladd, Scripture, Baldwin and Cattell, the pioneers of American psychology, got the functional psychology of the New World under way. James and Ladd outlined the nature of their functional systems (pp. 508-517, 523-527). Baldwin was an evolutionary psychologist (pp. 528-532). Hall and Cattell acted out the functional rôle (pp. 517-524, 532-540). Everything was ready for a formal school of functional psychology, which arose at Chicago about 1896, under the influence of John Dewey and his associates.

CHICAGO'S FUNCTIONAL PSYCHOLOGY

John Dewey (1859-   ), the organizing principle behind the Chicago school of functional psychology, was one of the men whom Stanley Hall found at Hopkins when he went there in 1882. There Dewey took his degree in philosophy at Hopkins two years later, moving on to Michigan to a series of appointments in philosophy. Except for an intervening year at Minnesota, he stayed at Michigan for ten years (1884-1894). In 1886 he published a textbook, *Psychology*, the first attempt by an American to write a text for the 'new' psychology and the first in English except for Sully's *Outlines* of 1884. This text was popular for a time, reaching a third edition within five years. It was, however, soon overshadowed by the other texts which appeared—Ladd (1887), Baldwin (1889-1890), James (1890) and the later ones. Dewey wrote his psychology as a philosopher. He said then, as philosophers say now, that an exposition of psychology depends upon the philosophical assumptions implicit in it and that it is better to have these implications out in the open than to go ahead pretending they do not exist. Seldom do the psychologists accept this admonition. They point out that psychology might be expected to get along as well as other sciences with philosophical naïveté. So Dewey, aged twenty-seven, did not get the psychologists to pay much attention to his philosophically sophisticated *Psychology*. In fact, his views were not yet very clear. A decade later he was listened to.

In 1894 Dewey went to the University of Chicago for ten years as professor of philosophy. G. H. Mead came with him from Michigan as assistant professor of philosophy. A. W. Moore was assistant in philosophy the next year. In 1894 James R. Angell also came to Chicago as assistant professor of psychology and director of the psychological laboratory which had been started the year before. Dewey, the oldest, was then thirty-five; Angell, the youngest, was but twenty-five. Dewey was at the time half a psychologist; Mead and Moore were interested in psychology; and Dewey's brilliance was able to exert considerable influence on the systematic tenets of the others. They were all young. It was just the situation that might lead to a school based on a systematic point of view. What was it that Dewey wanted?

John Dewey's great influence in the American scene—we can see this now after fifty years of his effective propaganda—was due to the fact that he was consistently and persistently the philosopher of social change. Thinking men usually think about change, for the *status quo*, being already present, does not need thought. Dewey was against *laissez-faire*, against things as they are. He was for that progress which can be gained through the struggle of intelligence with reality. He was for experiment, and use, and innovation. "Philosophy," he wrote, "recovers itself when it ceases to be a device for dealing with the problems of philosophers and becomes a method, cultivated by philosophers, for dealing with the problems of men." That is a pragmatism which gives you a functional psychology, and, although Dewey's faith was not so clear in the early days, it was just exactly his faith in use-value, his mistrust of conventional stereotype, that made him able to give definition in psychology to the American temper and successfully to depreciate the German model.

It may also be said that Dewey was a democratic evolutionist. He was greatly influenced by Darwin's theory, but he saw the survival of the fittest as meaning that use and functional practicality are basic to progress, that struggle is fundamental in human life, that kings have no divine right because nature rules by selection among random individual differences, and that even this aristocracy of chance can be overcome by social inheritance and social evolution. In short he was for evolution because the alternative view of special creation gives divine rights to species. Why should not an ape conceive the possibility of manhood for his descendants?

The first important paper in this young Chicago school was Dewey's in 1896. *The Reflex Arc Concept in Psychology*, he called it. In this paper Dewey took a stand against the elementism of his day, not against the current sensationism but against its physiological counterpart, reflexism. We are interested, he insisted, in total coordinations which are not properly to be reduced to a sum of constituent reflex arcs. Nor is the reflex arc itself to be properly understood as a stimulus followed by a response, with perhaps a sensation occurring in between them. The reflex is an indivisible coordination, for the response is *to* the stimulus, and how could it be a response without the stimulus? And the stimulus is *to* the response and would not be stimulus unless it aroused response. Sound is not a stimulus if it falls on a plugged or an inattentive ear; there must have been response or it has not stimulated. Movement is not a response if there is no stimulus; being caught up by a tornado is movement but not response. What is the stimulus? The reflex, Dewey said, is an instrument for "effecting a successful coordination." The stimulus and the response are "strictly correlative and contemporaneous." The stimulus to a response is just as much "something to be discovered" as is the response to a stimulus. In his stress on total coordinations Dewey was anticipating the position of Gestalt psychology. In his insistence that the coordination is adaptive or purposeful, being directed toward success, he was also occupying a position in the history of dynamic psychology.

The next ten years saw the new school of functional psychology emerge at Chicago. Presently Angell took over from Dewey.

James Rowland Angell (1869-1949) had worked at Harvard in James' day (1892), accepted James as his chief mentor, and was already functionally minded when he got to Chicago later. After Harvard he studied abroad, but without staying long enough in one place to receive a German impress. Then he had a year at Minnesota and came to Chicago in 1894, the year that Dewey arrived from Michigan. He was to stay at Chicago until 1920 and to see many changes in American psychology. What he did first, however, was to associate himself with A. W. Moore and to get into the reaction-time problem, the topic that was then the center of acrimonious controversy between Titchener and Baldwin (pp. 413 f.). In 1896 Angell and Moore published their experimental study of reaction times, a paper which merits an important place in the history of experimental psychology because it performed the Hegelian synthesis between Titchener's thesis and Baldwin's antithesis. It showed that there are two types of reaction (sensorial and muscular: Titchener) and two types of reactors (sensory and motor: Baldwin). For unpractised subjects—and Baldwin noted that human nature is unpractised and that psychology should study human nature—the sensory subject reacts more rapidly with sensorial reaction and the motor subject with muscular reaction, but, when the subjects are practised the difference in attitude between sensorial and muscular expectation is the chief thing that matters and the muscular is always shorter. So Baldwin was right—about unpractised subjects' showing individual differences; and Titchener was right—about the reaction types' coming out in practised subjects. Angell and Moore published this paper in the same volume of the *Psychological Review* that carried Dewey's paper on the reflex arc, and they tried there to use Dewey's terminology. As a matter of fact, however, there never was much difference between the actual experiments of functional and structural psychologists; the difference came in the motive for the experiment and in the form of interpretation of the results.

It was Titchener who posed the systematic issue and who might, paradoxically, almost be said to have 'founded' functional psychology. In 1898 he adopted from James the phrase *structural psychology* as opposed to *functional*, reiterating the distinction in another pronouncement the following year. He was really replying to Dewey without mentioning him. He noted that biology is divided into three parts—taxonomy which is structural, physiology which is functional, and ontogeny which is genetic. He thought that psychological science presents a comparable picture, with structural, functional and genetic psychology all recognizable. Functional psychology, he argued not without some ground, had been the psychology which scholars had cultivated from time immemorial, whereas structural psychology was new. Functional psychology is the psychology of the *Is-for*, structural psychology the psychology of the *Is*. It was, he thought in the late 1890s, high time to cultivate the *Is* in order to know enough about it to deal properly with the *Is-for*. Titchener was not against functional psychology. He actually gave it status, but he thought that it had had too much attention and ought to wait.

As we have noted elsewhere, a movement can not move unless it has something to push against. Functional psychology needed the recognition of opposition and Titchener provided it.

The first consequences of the new movement were the furthering of animal psychology and educational psychology. Mead gave a course in animal psychology in 1899. John B. Watson obtained his doctorate from Angell in 1903 with a thesis called *Animal Education: the Psychical Development of the White Rat,* thus emphasizing both of the new fields at once, animals and education. Watson established an animal laboratory. It was his monograph of 1907 on "kinæsthetic and organic sensations" of the white rat in learning mazes that set him off, so it seemed, on behaviorism. The rule of functional animal psychology of that date was that, when you have finished your observations of behavior, you use the results to infer the nature of the animal's consciousness and then show how those processes function in the animal's behavior. Watson rebelled at lugging consciousness in, after he had adequately described the animal's functional behavior; but to pursue this historical development would take us into behavioristics which belongs to a later chapter. It is enough to see here that animal psychology was naturally functional, and that a functional psychology could get along without consciousness, even though Angell's brand of functionalism did not.

In 1900 Dewey made his presidential address before the American Psychological Association on *Psychology and Social Practice,* a plea and a program for educational psychology. In 1902 the University of Chicago celebrated its Decennial. Angell made an address on the nature of structural and functional psychology and Mead on the nature of the psychical. Both were published in 1903. Meanwhile Dewey's propaganda for the scientific study of education had borne fruit. He was made director of the new School of Education at Chicago in 1902. Then in 1904 Teachers College called him away to Columbia, where he remained until his retirement in 1930, becoming more and more influential as the practical philosopher of democracy and social change.

In 1904 Angell published the first edition of his text, which illustrates but does not explicate the functional point of view in psychology. This book was immediately a success in the colleges and the normal schools. It went at once into a second edition and into a fourth in 1908. It was what Americans wanted. The chapter on attention shows best what Angell was driving at. "Our purpose is . . . to adopt a biological point of view . . . and to attempt . . . to see just how the mind aids in the adjustment of the psychophysical human organism to its environment." "The fundamental function of consciousness is to better . . . adaptive activities." "The actual work of accommodation is going on at the point which we call the point of attention. Attention . . . represents the very heart of consciousness."

Angell was president of the American Psychological Association in 1906. He spoke on *The Province of Functional Psychology*. This paper is the best and clearest of his expositions. It is not rigorously systematic, for Angell presented three good views and left it open to the psychologist to accept any or all of them. They are these.

(1) Functional psychology may be regarded as the "psychology of mental operations in contrast to the psychology of mental elements." Elementism was still strong and Angell was putting functionalism in opposition to it. Structural psychology deals with psychology's *what*, but functional psychology, said Angell, adds the *how* and *why*. Perhaps Angell was wrong about the *how*, since Wundt and Titchener believed not only in analysis into elements, but also in understanding the principles of synthesis in accordance with which the compounds are formed; but he was quite right about the *why*. *Why* means either a purpose, which is item (2) below, or a cause, which would be neural and item (3) below.

(2) So Angell said that functional psychology may be thought of as the "psychology of the fundamental utilities of consciousness," in which mind is "primarily engaged in mediating between the environment and the needs of the organism." The function of the psychological act is "accommodatory service"; the function of consciousness is "accommodation to the novel," since consciousness wanes in the face of an habitual situation. This is essentially an emergency theory of consciousness. Habit rules for the familiar, but let the environment present a novel situation and "in steps consciousness" to take charge.

(3) The broadest view is that functional psychology is all of "psychophysics," that is to say, the psychology of the total mind-body organism. Such a view goes far beyond the conscious states, bringing in the well-habituated, half-unconscious acts as of service to the organism. Just as von Ehrenfels, fighting elementism, could not quite get away from it but conceived the form-quality as a new superordinate element, so Angell, fighting the taxonomy in consciousness, escaped from the taxonomy but not from the con-

sciousness. It was hard for him to think of psychology without consciousness. That was to come presently in the minds of others, of whom his pupil Watson was one.

Some of the strength of the Chicago school was due to the personality of Angell. Like James and Hall he stimulated loyal followers. Chicago turned out fifty doctorates in psychology during Angell's time there. Some of the more famous (if we have regard to Cattell's stars in *American Men of Science*) were, in order of the dates of their degrees: Helen Thompson Woolley (1900; d.1947), known for her work in child psychology; John B. Watson (1903), the founder of behaviorism; Harvey A. Carr (1905), Angell's successor at Chicago and the carrier of the torch of functionalism; June E. Downey (1907; d.1932), the author of many tests of personality and an authority on what handwriting can reveal; Joseph Peterson (1907; d.1935), well known for his work in acoustics, tests and learning; W. V. Bingham (1908), famous as an applied psychologist and lately as psychological advisor of the armed services of the United States; Walter S. Hunter (1912), at Clark and at Brown one of America's leading experimental psychologists with a broad range of interests. The First World War stopped this series of strong men out of Chicago. In 1919 Angell became chairman of the National Research Council, in 1920 president of the Carnegie Corporation, and from 1921 to 1937 president of Yale University. He died in 1949 after an extremely influential life, long after the issue of function vs. structure had ceased to be important in American psychology.

Harvey A. Carr (1873-   ), Angell's successor as Chicago's mouthpiece for functionalism, lacked the advantage of opposition to make his position clear by contrast, and the advantage of controversy to get attention for his argument. Almost anyone will take time to listen to a quarrel or even to assess its merits, but agreement has no news value. Carr, in his text of 1925, wrote about organic behavior and adaptive acts. He left dualism abandoned much more certainly than did Angell. He pointed out that the stimulus-reacted-to is so complex as to be a total situation, and that response occurs under the guidance of a motivating stimulus. Thus Carr introduced into functional psychology—as indeed he must have done at the time that he was writing—motivating factors in addition to stimulating and responding factors. So it is that functional psychology leads off into dynamic psychology, although not because it is functional. The rôle of motivation in both perception and action became less and less escapable as the twentieth century progressed.

Carr took, essentially, the point of view of this book—that functional psychology *is* American psychology. That had become true at the time he wrote and he might have included France and Britain too, as well as animal psychology and all applied psychology—the mental tests, educational psychology, child psychology, abnormal psychology and psychopathology. On the other hand, functional psychology as such was not dynamic, even though dynamic psychology is always functional. What has happened seems to be that the line between structure and function, between taxonomy and physiology, which Titchener found so clear in biology in 1858, does not persist when you are interested in only one species (*homo sapiens*) and its structure gets to be pretty well known. Even more important in the rise of functional psychology has been the disappearance of dualism. Modern psychology is nowadays chiefly interested in the reactions of organisms, mostly of the human organism. It studies, it is true, the functioning of structures; the structures which function are not, however, conscious states but the materials which the neurophysiologist and the neuroanatomist provide.

COLUMBIA'S FUNCTIONAL PSYCHOLOGY

It turns out that functional psychology is a name for what a psychologist does when freed of systematic compulsions. There are two such principal freedoms: (1) functional psychology need not be dualistic and (2) it need not be descriptive. These freedoms are, of course, only permissive. It is not in the nature of freedom to be mandatory. The functional psychologist may believe in mind and body as two kinds of data and also in the operations of the mind's functioning for the good of the body. He may believe in the description of the *what* coming first before the *why* of its functioning can be understood. The paradigm of this free psychology is to be found at Columbia in the contributions of three influential psychologists, Cattell, Thorndike and Woodworth; but before we turn to Columbia let us examine the total situation in respect of this functional freedom.

Psychology's functionalism spreads broad. In a sense all the American pioneers whom we considered in the preceding chapter—James, Hall, Ladd, Scripture, Baldwin, Cattell—were functionalists. In England, Galton was a functionalist, and so are the later experimentalists, Myers and Bartlett, though this thought may never have occurred to either of them. The French were functionalists—Ribot, Binet, Henri, and nowadays Piéron. The Swiss Claparède was a functionalist, and so is his successor Piaget. Michotte in Belgium is free of these tighter systematic constraints and, in general, western Europe is going functional in the modern age. Another way of saying this same thing is to note that all the new fields of psychology are functional, developed usually for their practical use. Almost inevitably, animal psychology, physiological psychology, abnormal psychology and social psychology are functional, seldom dualistic, not primarily descriptive. So too are the more specifically applied psychologies functional: child, educational, clinical, vocational and industrial psychology.

As to *dualism*, James' principle that psychology is "personal" has prevailed in the twentieth century. Psychology deals with persons, complete organisms whose conduct is the most obvious thing about them. A person is a whole, live organism who acts and is often conscious. You can bring his consciousness in when it is relevant, but you can also leave it out when you think it is unimportant, when you do not know what it is like, and when you are convinced that no consciousness is functioning in what you have under scrutiny. Functionalism is a home for the unconscious. The functionalist often makes use of his freedom to ignore consciousness and to bring in movement as an immediate datum of psychology. Then association of ideas gives way to association among data, to association of ideas with movement, of stimulation with movement. Then, too, behaviorism becomes one kind of functional psychology.

As to *description*, it is quite obvious that the more you know the better off you are, but that mere statements of capacities are useful and not to be scorned. To know that one organism runs faster than another, or passes intelligence tests better, is useful. To know that both capacities depend on the age of the organism and its degree of practice is to know more. Functional psychology looks for functional relations, for the dependency of this on that, and it thrives on correlations.

Now let us examine the Columbia tradition, if such it may be called. It is a tradition of freedom and serves as our example of free functionalism.

James McKeen Cattell we have already studied (pp. 532-540, 548 f.). He had gone to work with Wundt, Wundt had set him a thesis on cognitive reaction times, he had done what he was told to do, but he had also conceived the notion of studying individual differences in reaction. Some of these experiments he did in his own room, for Wundt did not approve of them for the Leipzig laboratory. In America he stood with Baldwin in the Baldwin-Titchener controversy, that is to say, he was for studying individual differences in reaction times, differences which could be observed without the control of introspection. In his research on time of perception he was also studying the capacities of individuals. Out of this work grew his studies on reading. In psychophysics we have seen how, with Fullerton, he turned functional, objected to the German introspective controls, and altered the problem of the size of the differential threshold into the problem of the amount of error in discrimination. He was the prime mover, back of American mental testing in the 1890s. He did not rule consciousness out of psychology, but he did not find much use for it. Even the determination of the range of simultaneous perception becomes as little dualistic as an animal experiment when all you want for your primary data is to know when the subject is right and when wrong.

Cattell established the atmosphere for graduate study at Columbia. Thorndike carried it on at Teachers College and Woodworth at Columbia proper. It is hard to describe the effects of freedom, because what you are found describing will be what was fixed and not what was free; nevertheless, Edna Heidbreder, a Columbia Ph.D. of Woodworth's in 1924, has caught the spirit fully as well as can be done. She has written:

> Psychology at Columbia is not easy to describe. It stands for no set body of doctrine, taught with the consistency and paternalism found in the more closely organized schools. Yet it shows definite recognizable characteristics. A graduate student in psychology cannot spend many weeks at Columbia without becoming aware of the immense importance in that atmosphere of curves of distribution, of individual differences, of the measurement of intelligence and other human capacities, of experimental procedures and statistical devices, of the undercurrent of physiological thought He discovers immediately that psychology does not lead a sheltered life; that it rubs elbows with biology, statistics, education, commerce, industry, and the world of affairs. He encounters many different trends of thought, and he frequently comes upon the same ones from different angles. But the separate strands of teaching are not knit together for him into a firm and patterned fabric. No one cares how he arranges the threads that are placed in his hands; certainly there is no model which he is urged to copy.

In psychology the land of the free included Columbia under Cattell, Thorndike and Woodworth. Wundt's *Verboten* were not for them.

Edward Lee Thorndike (1874-1949) was one of the many whose interest for psychology was first caught by James' *Principles*. Thorndike read certain chapters in these volumes while he was an undergraduate student at Wesleyan University, and then later, when he had got to Harvard for graduate work, he took James' course. The course was in 1895. Münsterberg was then back in Germany deciding whether to return permanently to Harvard. Delabarre was in charge of the laboratory. Thorndike first undertook an experiment on what might be called telepathy in young children, although his faith was placed on the perception of small unconscious movements as the means of communication. That undertaking led, however, to objection, and Thorndike then turned to the intelligence of chicks. When his landlady refused to let Thorndike incubate and hatch chicks in his bedroom, James tried to get him space for incubation and experimentation in the laboratory or in the museum building—tried and failed. So he took Thorndike and his whole outfit into the cellar of his own home, much to the glee of the James children. Thorndike had, however, to earn his living by tutoring, so, when Cattell offered him a fellowship at Columbia, he went to New York carrying his two most educated chicks along in a basket, found Cattell willing to have him continue his work with the animal intelligence—cats and dogs and no incubator this time—and went through to his doctorate in 1898.

Animal Intelligence: an Experimental Study of the Associative Processes in Animals was his thesis. It was published in 1898 and republished with other related studies in 1911. It is the famous, the much cited, research of the *puzzle-box*, the study in which the *law of effect* in learning, a principle already discussed by Lloyd Morgan, was firmly established and got ready for the use of educational psychology. Thorndike prepared fifteen puzzle-boxes for cats, boxes in which the cat was confined and from which it could escape by clawing down a rope, or pushing up a bobbin, or doing even as many as three different things. (He also had nine boxes for dogs, and three little labyrinth-pens, made of books on edge, for chicks.) He plotted learning curves, showing how long it took the animal to get out on the first trial, on the second, and so on. The animals learned "by trial and error, and accidental success." This kind of learning has been called *trial-and-error* learning ever since, but actually Thorndike was more concerned with the success. It was plain that the success of a correct movement, although it came after the movement, caused that movement to be impressed, to be learned. The success is the effect of the movement, and this effect "stamps in" the movements which were the cause of it. Sometimes it used to be said that this mechanism is "retroactive," since the effect, when it is a success, affects the cause; but that is nonsense. Thorndike never meant that the future determined the past, but merely that

the traces of the past were stamped in so that the past might thereafter more readily recur. Later Thorndike identified *success* with
pleasure, still later with *satisfaction*. He thought that this new principle operated in addition to frequency of repetition or, as he called
it, *exercise*. Since Ebbinghaus (1885) frequency had seemed to be
the only law. Now Thorndike had two: *exercise* and *effect*. These
principles were quite clear in 1898, although these terms were not
used until a little later.

The functionalistic nature of this research becomes apparent
when we see that it was movements that were entering into association, not ideas only. Lloyd Morgan had just issued (1894) his canon
of parsimony against Romanes' anthropomorphism (pp. 474 f.): always interpret behavior in the simplest possible psychological terms.
Now Thorndike, although he did not mention the canon as such,
turned it against Lloyd Morgan. Lloyd Morgan, while denying reason to the higher animals, had left them accredited with employing
associated ideas and "intelligent inferences of wonderful accuracy
and precision" in their solving of simple problems. Thorndike
thought that Lloyd Morgan was far too prodigal with these ideas
and inferences for animal learning. It seemed clear that the cats
started out with their original natures, used instinctive and already
habituated actions, stumbled on a success which then stamped in
the learning of the movement of which it was the effect. The animal may have no more conscious appreciation of the relationship
of cause to effect than has man in the habituated act of opening a
door by turning a knob. At any rate "entities should not be multiplied beyond necessity." Wundt had argued that, even though
habituated movements may become unconscious, all movement must
originally have been conscious. That was a mentalist's faith, but
functionalism slipped away from consciousness very easily.

Thorndike was made instructor in psychology at Teachers College, Columbia, in 1899. That was when Cattell asked him if he
would not like to try applying his animal techniques to children and
young people. Thorndike decided to try, and his interests shifted
toward human subjects. In 1901 he published with Woodworth
their famous paper on transfer of training. In 1903 the first edition
of his *Educational Psychology* appeared and he was made a full
professor. In 1904, the year that Dewey came from Chicago to
Teachers College, Thorndike published his *Introduction to the
Theory of Mental and Social Measurements*. He was very prolific. He
took up with the mental test movement and became a leader in it. He
retired in 1940 after four decades of service to Teachers College, but

he kept working. In 1942 he went back to Harvard as William James Lecturer, honoring the memory of the great man who had lent him his cellar for his chicks forty-four years before.

Robert Sessions Woodworth (1869-   ), when a senior at Amherst in 1890, got into the course in philosophy—the one which the students always called "psychology" and which was given by C. E. Garman, one of America's famously good teachers. Garman was shocked when he found that Woodworth was planning to take his course—or, for that matter, any course in philosophy—without having had extensive training in science; so he sent Woodworth to read up on science, a summer in advance, to get himself ready for philosophy. Just twenty-five years before, Brentano had given similar advice to Stumpf. Woodworth repaired his deficiency better than did Stumpf, for he left Amherst with his A.B. to teach science in a high school for two years and then mathematics in a small college for two years more. He wanted eventually to become a teacher, and it seemed best to get experience first and more education later.

In 1895, both Woodworth and Thorndike turned up at Harvard, both stayed two years, obtaining first an A.B. and then an A.M. Münsterberg was in Germany. Both were exposed to Royce and James. Woodworth had discovered both James and Stanley Hall through their writings while he was teaching. He liked James' psychology and Hall's conception of a university. The year that Thorndike was getting his Ph.D. with Cattell at Columbia, Woodworth was teaching physiology at the Harvard Medical School. Then Woodworth went to Columbia when Thorndike left in 1898 and got his Ph.D. with Cattell in 1899. After that Woodworth spent three years teaching physiology in New York hospitals and one year with Sherrington, the famous physiologist, at Liverpool. Then in 1903 he came back to Columbia as instructor, was made a full professor in 1909, succeeded Cattell when he retired in 1917, and finally retired himself in 1942.

Woodworth came as near to being the general experimental psychologist as any important man ever did. Consider his six most important books. There was *Le mouvement* in 1903, written during his year abroad. There was his revision of Ladd's *Physiological Psychology* in 1911, the "Ladd and Woodworth" which became the standard handbook for this field until 1934. There was his *Dynamic Psychology* in 1917, a plea for what we are calling functional psychology but with the psychology of motivation which he added to it. Then there was his astonishingly popular textbook, clear and very simple, with a first edition in 1921 and a fifth in 1947. For exactly twenty-five years it outsold all other texts so greatly as to be beyond competition. In 1931 he published *Contemporary Schools of Psychology*, a much used book which went into so radical a revision in 1948 that no reader of both could miss the fact that, in psychology, 1931 and 1948 are not contemporaneous. And then there was Woodworth's own handbook of experimental psychology, called simply *Experimental Psychology*, in 1938, the outcome of some previous mimeographed editions in which Poffenberger had collaborated.

Or consider Woodworth's papers. In 1939 his colleagues reprinted twenty-five of them in a commemorative volume. Ten of them were written on systematic issues. The other fifteen were distributed over abnormal psychology, differential psychology, motor phenomena and educational psychology, with not more than four papers in any one of these fields. It is hard to select among these. We have already mentioned the 1901 paper with Thorndike on transfer of training. There are several others, through the years, on the voluntary control of movement. He contributed one such paper to the Garman commemorative volume in 1906, and a paper on consciousness of relation to the James commemorative volume in 1908. His review of the problem of imageless thought made an impression. It was his presidential address before the American Psychological Association in 1915. He wrote articles on dynamic psychology in 1925 and 1930, following up his 1917 book.

These last two papers give as clear an exposition of Woodworth's systematic faith as any reader could ask. Woodworth called himself a dynamic psychologist, but actually he was a functional psychologist first and a dynamic second. Half of what he says about freedom from constraint, about using causal relations, about employing introspection and physiology and the study of movement as the occasion requires is good functionalism. Woodworth believed that psychologists were more in agreement than their quarrels indicated, and he sought a system to which all could subscribe. He very nearly succeeded. He could not, of course, succeed with his "bogey men," as he called them, the men from whose domination he "was most anxious to keep free." They were Münsterberg "with his assertion that a scientific psychology could never envisage real life," Titchener who insisted "that all the genuine findings of psychology must consist of sensations," and Watson who "announced that introspection must not be employed and that only motor (and glandular) activities must be discovered." Woodworth did not like psychologists who push their colleagues around.

In this free functionalism Woodworth planted a dynamic psychology. Back in 1897 at Harvard Woodworth had told Thorndike that he wanted to develop a "motivology." His *Dynamic Psychology*, motivated by his reaction against Titchener, Watson and McDougall, urged an understanding of the cause-and-effect mechanisms of human thought and action (that is the functional part of it) and of the motivating stimuli or situations which determine specificity of the drives. Woodworth noted how mechanisms, originally activated by motivating stimuli external to them, may presently, after continued activation, get along on their own without the added motivator. *The mechanism becomes a drive:* that phrase echoes within psychology always as the Woodworth leitmotif.

Some persons seem able to perceive who, at any time, is "the dean" of American psychology. Certainly James was the first 'dean' and rightly chosen as president of the first International Congress of Psychology planned in America in 1913. James, however, died in 1910, and the jealousy about the succession prevented the Congress' being held at all in 1913, and then, a year later, the First World War began and stopped it altogether. In 1929, when there was at last a first Congress in America, Cattell was certainly 'dean' and no one protested the choice of him as president. Münsterberg, Ladd, Hall and Titchener were all dead then. Later Thorndike rose to the deanship and to maximal prestige as determined by stars for *American Men of Science,* and many have felt, as Thorndike became less active, that Woodworth had succeeded him. In any case, the influence of Columbia was spread broad by its Ph.D.s.

Cattell's most distinguished students may be said to be Thorndike and Woodworth. After them we can accept Cattell's own statistics to name the more distinguished psychologists who recognized an intellectual debt from their graduate-student days to Cattell or Thorndike or Woodworth or some to two of them, or, in the case of Hollingworth, to all three of them. We have already listed (p. 540), as owing to Cattell a primary debt, Thorndike, Woodworth, Franz, Wissler, Dearborn, Wells, Warner Brown, Hollingworth, Strong, Poffenberger, Dashiell, Kelley and Gates. We may now add, as recognizing a debt primarily to Woodworth, both H. E. Jones (Ph.D., 1923), California's leader in the field of child development, and H. E. Garrett (Ph.D., 1923), who succeeded Poffenberger as chairman at Columbia. Then there are those who recognize debts to both Woodworth and Thorndike: M. A. May (Ph.D., 1917), for many years the director of Yale's Institute of Human Relations, and Florence L. Goodenough (Ph.D., Stanford, 1924), Minnesota's expert in developmental and child psychology.

EDUCATIONAL PSYCHOLOGY

Of the various applied psychologies which functional psychology may be said to have sponsored—or at least to have blessed and sent forth to seek a future—educational psychology is one of the best early instances. It is a development which began with the 1880s, and Stanley Hall had a great deal to do with what happened at first.

The history of theorizing about the educational process is, of course, very old and we can not undertake to discuss it here, even though the history of educational psychology is a part of it, a part not always clearly differentiated from the whole. There have been many great names. The reader will recognize Comenius (1592-1670), Pestalozzi (1746-1827), Froebel (1782-1852). We have seen that Herbart's psychology of 1824-1825, with its much cited doctrine of apperceptive mass, became proper educational doctrine for the later nineteenth century (pp. 256 f.). As recently as 1910 you could find in America professors of education who were known as Herbartians, and professors of educational psychology who emphatically were not. But none of this history belongs properly in this book.

Undoubtedly the *Zeitgeist* was working for functionalism, most effectively in America but also in Europe. The physiologist William Preyer at Jena became interested in the mind of the child in the late 1870s and published his *Die Seele des Kindes* in 1882, only the year after Stanley Hall had given his immensely successful Boston lectures to teachers. The National Education Association in America formed a section for child study in 1880, and the Germans got their Allgemeiner deutscher Verein für Schulreform in 1889. There was nothing comparable in France then. Binet's interest in the minds of school children did not appear until 1894.

When Stanley Hall came back from his two years in Germany in 1880, where he had been Wundt's first American student and had practically witnessed the 'founding' of the Leipzig laboratory, he had many ideas but no job. President Eliot of Harvard then for a second time intervened in his life by supplying him with a job. Hall was to give lectures in Boston on current educational problems. His Saturday morning lectures to teachers were enough of a success to lead to his being called to Hopkins the next year. In Boston, Hall introduced the questionnaire method to discover the contents of children's minds. Actually he had picked up the idea in Germany, where he heard about the results of a survey of Berlin primary schools in 1869, a survey of what knowledge children have about common things and places and objects in their neighborhoods. Hall got the Boston school teachers to question the children of the primary grades and they got for him a great deal of information. They found out, for instance, that 80 per cent of these six-year olds knew that milk comes from cows, but only 6 per cent that leather comes from animals. There were 94 per cent of them who knew where their stomachs are, 55 per cent where their hips are, but only 10 per cent where their ribs are. The moral was: show children objects, explain relationships to them, do not trust them to know meanings or referents of common words; they must be taught. Actually two Boston youngsters in ten had never seen a cow or a hen; five in ten had never seen a pig or a frog; eight in ten, a crow or a beehive.

Before the 1880s there had been no systematic investigation of child life. In 1879 H. P. Bowditch, the eclectic Harvard physiologist, had engineered a study of the physical measurements of Boston school-children from five to eighteen, and some of the anthropologists—Franz Boas, for instance—carried this work forward; but Hall was the pioneer in child psychology. His paper on children's lies was printed in 1882, and the results of his study of contents of children's minds in 1883. Other papers of this sort followed, but for the time being Hall was occupied in getting experimental psychology, America's "first" formal laboratory of psychology and the *American Journal of Psychology* all going at Hopkins. Meanwhile interest grew. Child-study groups were formed. The Worcester State Normal School, at Hall's suggestion, collected 35,000 records of observations on school-children, all taken under carefully prescribed conditions.

In 1889 Hall went to Clark as psychologist-president and in 1890 he attracted attention by creating there a department of pedagogy and putting W. H. Burnham, one of his Hopkins students, in charge, an arrangement which lasted for thirty-six years. In 1891 Hall started a new journal, the *Pedagogical Seminary*, thus pointing up the fact that there was already enough material concerned with the new scientific approach to education to fill up five hundred pages a year. Hall thought of a *seminary* as a workshop. That was the way he worked with students, colleagues and associates at data drawn from published observation and books. In the first volume of the *"Ped. Sem."* he editorialized: "Seminary and laboratory are now perhaps the noblest words in the vocabulary of higher education." In 1895, courses in the new pedagogy were being offered at Yale, Harvard, Princeton and the University of Pennsylvania. In 1896 Witmer founded the Psychological Clinic at Pennsylvania—a pioneer undertaking in child guidance. It was not until 1909 that William Healy began the Chicago Juvenile Psychopathic Institute (later called the Institute for Juvenile Research).

Hall was promoting the questionnaire method at Clark. The method was not new. It had been used in Bristol, England, in 1838 for collecting data about strikes, and later for other statistics in the old days when *statistics* meant getting data about the state. Galton had adopted it in his already famous study of imagery (1883), but Hall turned it to child study. From 1894 to 1903 Hall and his associates at Clark issued 102 questionnaires. The topics ranged widely: anger, dolls, crying and laughing, early sense of self, childhood fears, children's moral and religious experiences, children's prayers; and then, for adults, feelings about old age, disease and death, psychology of ownership vs. loss, pity, menstruation, education of women, religious conversion. Syllabi on the 102 topics were sent out by the thousands and returned to Clark where Hall's eager students might have a chance to convert them into publication, usually in the *Ped. Sem.* Hall had, however, gone too far. It is one thing to find out what Boston six-year olds know about cows and beehives; it is quite another to attempt to assess the experience of religious conversion through uncontrolled comments of the unknown members in an undetermined sample of an ill-defined population. Burnham carried on with more conservative techniques, while Hall turned to other things.

Meanwhile, in 1899, Columbia University had taken over the New York College for the Training of Teachers, had made it into what later became famous as Teachers College, and, at Cattell's suggestion, had taken on Thorndike. It was at this time that educational psychology became distinct from pedagogy and from child-study. Thorndike's first Educational Psychology was published in 1903, and in the next year his *Mental and Social Measurements*, the book that first made the Galton-Pearson biometrical statistical methods readily available for the run-of-the-mill mental tester. The test movement paralleled educational psychology, providing the latter with its most important tool. In the tests, the 1880s were Galton's decade, the 1890s Cattell's, the 1900s Binets; and by 1910 the movement was so far along that Whipple could publish a standard *Manual of Mental and Physical Tests* which included discussions of fifty-four tests and precise directions for their administration. By then educational psychology had become the general psychology of learning, motivation, emotion, heredity and environment, personality and individual difference—some of it derived from the use of tests and the rest of it taken over bodily from the experimental laboratories. Intelligence was its special discovery.

In the present century, educational psychology has taken up with all those schools which seem to further its special interests. It accepted Pavlov's reflexology because conditioning appeared to be the counterpart of learning. It accepted Watson's behaviorism for the same reason and because introspectionism was not useful to it. It looked with interest and concern to psychoanalysis because of what that new discipline had to say about motivation and personality, and because of the importance it put on the early years as determining later mental life. It took Gestalt psychology seriously because the Gestalt psychologists were themselves interested in interpreting the learning process in their own terms. It took also Thorndike's simpler connectionism, not merely because of Thorndike's prestige, but because it worked, while Thorndike kept changing his learning theory to meet new discovery. Of course, no one took all of these views, for some of them, awaiting the final synthesis, are incompatible. The point is that the educational psychologists were interested in the facts: they wanted to teach children better—and older students too. Applied scientists are pragmatists; they take what works and accept those systems which provide convenient terminology for new general principles.

And that is why functional psychology is the right background for educational psychology. It frees the psychologist to study both what is useful to society and what is useful to the individual organism. James and Dewey gave educational psychology its philosophical sanction, but Hall's compelling dynamism was what got it started. Later, Thorndike and then many others took over, and they looked more to Cattell and Galton for ancestry than to Hall. As for Darwin—he had more to do with the primary motivation of both Galton and Hall than did anyone else. Actually we must suppose that no one of these persons was essential. Given this trend of the *Zeitgeist*, it was inevitable that the methods and facts of psychology should presently be used to improve education. The achievements of these men are the means by which the end was accomplished.

MENTAL TESTS

Is a test an experiment? And does the history of mental testing belong in the history of experimental psychology? Not really, although there is no sharp logical line of demarcation. Tests usually are simple and quick and do not use elaborate apparatus, but a reaction time is a test and requires precise apparatus, and tests of color blindness could do with better optical apparatus for monochromatic lights than they usually have. A good experiment usually attempts to determine what function the variation of a dependent variable is of the variation of an independent variable. In the field of testing the primary variable is a difference of persons, which occurs at random and which is not an independent variable because these persons do not come labelled as amounts of anything nor arranged in a predetermined series. If the tests are to yield functional dependencies, then what is needed is two dependent variables, both dependent upon individual difference and thus becoming measures of individual difference. Between such dependent variables correlations can be determined. They are usually lower than they are in a good experiment, for with the tests there is nearly always more unspecified variability than in the experiment, and prediction in the single case is less accurate.

It is not hard to see how the schism between the testers and the experimentalists arose eventually, but there was no schism in the 1890s. There were quarrels, like the one between Baldwin and Titchener, but no systematic split. Let us see what was going on in this decade.

Galton's contribution had been made in the 1880s. He had opened his testing laboratory, the one for inventorying British abilities, in the South Kensington Museum in 1882. He had published *Inquiries into Human Faculty* in 1883. (See pp. 482-488.) Cattell, functionally minded even when he was with Wundt and reinforced presently by Galton, undertook at his new laboratory at the University of Pennsylvania to develop a set of tests. He had fifty which all his students took and a selected ten which he offered to those members of the public who wished to have their abilities appraised. He described all this in his paper of 1890, *Mental Tests and Measurements*, the paper which established the term *mental test* and which had a supporting appendix added to it by Galton. Cattell supplied American leadership to the new movement, but he was not needed to make it move. Here, if ever, is a case where the *Zeitgeist* is clear: with the new laboratories set up, the testing of individual differences in human abilities became inevitable.

Even in 1889 Kraepelin's student, Oehrn, at Heidelberg had worked out a set of tests, dividing capacities into four kinds: perception, memory, association and motor functions. In 1890 Jastrow at Wisconsin had a set of fifteen tests which he demonstrated at the Columbian Exposition at Chicago in 1893. Münsterberg had fourteen tests for school children in 1891, and in that same year

Boas, the anthropologist, then at Clark, came out with a program for anthropological measurements of school children. Gilbert at Yale reported on tests of 1200 school children in 1893 and 1896. In America two national committees were formed, one by the American Psychological Association in 1895 to further cooperation in testing among the various laboratories, the other by the American Association for the Advancement of Science in 1896 to sponsor a survey of the abilities of "the white race in the United States." Cattell and Farrand finished up their appraisal of Columbia freshmen and published the results in 1896. Meanwhile Binet in France, at that time in association with Victor Henri (1872-1940), had been interesting himself in individual differences. They published together seven papers from 1894 to 1898, the crucial one on tests in 1896. They proposed tests of memory, imagery, imagination, attention, comprehension, suggestibility, esthetic appreciation, moral sentiments, strength of will and motor skill. It was also at this time (1897) that Ebbinghaus in Breslau invented his completion test for the use of the school authorities. Certainly no one can say that testing was precipitated by the brilliant insight of any one man, not even Galton. It was the natural development of the period.

Now everyone in all this testing activity attacked the same proximate goal. Like Galton they all wished to assess human faculties. Some hoped they might find out what it is that makes genius run in families, some what makes freshmen succeed at Columbia, some what makes good scholars of school children. There turned out to be two ways of discovering test procedures. You could, for instance, since the laboratories were going concerns, turn to them for the human capacities which were usually measured there. That is what Cattell and the Americans tended to do. Cattell's 1890 set of fifty tests were actually all of them tests of sensory capacity, precision of discrimination and time of perception (reaction time). Galton and even Binet had argued that sensory discrimination, being discrimination, is one of the judgmental functions—as if a 'discriminating man' might have a low differential sensory threshold. On the other hand, Binet and Henri, as we have seen, invented tests of what are sometimes called the higher mental functions—tasks that involve the functions listed in the preceding paragraph. These tests touched more closely the faculties that everyone wished to assess, the abilities that make for success in life. Since educational psychology was supplying some of the motivation for the development of testing, success in school became for the time being the most desirable outcome to predict. As early as 1898 Stella Sharp at Cornell was able to show that Binet had won out over Cattell—if we may put this complex matter so simply. Sharp's conclusion was a decision of Titchener's laboratory that the Wundtian variables of experimental psychology are less adequate for a description of those human abilities which make for success than are Binet's devices, which he made up and which did not, in general, come directly out of the laboratories. Perhaps Titchener felt even then—as he did later—that applied psychology is scientifically unworthy and that failure of 'pure' experimental psychology to meet the requirements of functional use was not disparaging to the Wundtian school. Or perhaps he was glad to find Cattell in error.

From here on the history of mental testing needs a volume of its own, just as much as does the history of sensation and perception or of any other large field of psychological endeavor. We must pass the five decades of the present century in quick review, remembering that functional psychology is what freed this movement and some others from the constraints that might have hindered them and that the main course of the testing movement is parallel to the development of experimental psychology.

We have said that the 1880s were Galton's decade in this field, and the 1890s Cattell's, and the 1900s Binet's. *Alfred Binet* (1857-1911) was France's greatest psychologist of that generation, and he was an experimentalist after the French fashion of stressing individual differences more than apparatus and the techniques for dealing with the average faculties. With Henri Beaunis (1830-1921), Binet founded the first French psychological laboratory at the Sorbonne in 1889 and the first French journal of psychology, *L'année psychologique*, in 1895. Binet's first book, *La psychologie du raisonnement* (1886), prepared him for his life-long interest in the 'higher' mental processes. His *Les altérations de la personalité* came out in 1891, and in 1894, the year that he began his studies with Henri, he published studies of great calculators and chess-players and blindfold chess. He had other books and papers which were experimental in the traditional sense, but he was not laboratory-bound. Neither were Galton and Cattell, for that matter. Nevertheless it was reserved for Binet, not Galton or Cattell, to bring this interest in human intellectual capacities into the program for assessing human abilities by the use of tests. Binet died in 1911 at the age of fifty-four. It might have been useful to have had him live a little longer.

Binet published his *L'étude expérimentale de l'intelligence* in 1903. In 1905 with Simon he got out the first scale of intelligence for school-children, revising it in 1908 and 1911. Binet had long realized that intellectual capacity increases in children as they mature; so it became necessary for him to obtain norms for different ages. A scale of age norms, which were later called *mental ages,* resulted. Binet was not, however, proceeding alone. In Germany William Stern published his *Ueber Psychologie der individuellen Differenzen* in 1900, and was later to make the important contribution of the IQ. In America Thorndike took over from Cattell. Thorndike's study of fatigue in 1900 and his research with Woodworth on transfer of training in 1901 made use of many tests that have ever since been useful. So did the Chicago study of sex differences in 1903 by Helen B. Thompson (later Helen Thompson Woolley). Clark Wissler's review in 1901 of the earlier Columbia testing helped in a negative way by showing only low correlations. In that study the correlation of class standing with reaction time was only -0.02 and with the test of logical memory only +0.16, whereas the correlation of class standing with gymnasium score was +0.53, and of performance in Latin with performance in Greek +0.75. As we have already noted, Thorndike was in a position in his *Educational Psychology* of 1903 to show what kinds of tests were best for predicting educational success. At the end of this decade Goddard had gotten out his own revision of the Binet-Simon scale, and Whipple had published the first edition of his *Manual of Mental and Physical Tests* with his description of fifty-four tests and how to give them. By 1910 mental testing had clearly come to stay.

The 1910s were the decade of *intelligence testing.* The Binet principle of scaling was successful. Spearman's argument of 1904 for general ability, G, was accepted, although the argument about overlapping group factors began at once in Great Britain with Thomson and Garnett (pp. 480 f.). Stern in 1911 suggested that the mental age of a child can be divided by its chronological age to give a "mental quotient," which will remain more constant than the developing mental age. Terman and his associates renamed this ratio the *intelligence quotient* (IQ) when they issued the Stanford Revision of the Binet Scale in 1916, the form that remained standard for more than twenty years. For a while, Yerkes' Point Scale of 1915 was also used. Terman and his associates argued that the IQ remains fairly constant and that seemed to mean that the intelligence of an adult is predictable in early childhood, perhaps even at birth. Such a view fitted in pretty well with studies of feeble-mindedness, which was coming to be defined as very low IQ. Goddard published his account of *The Kallikak Family* in 1913 which seemed to show that feeble-mindedness is inherited and, once introduced into a strain, may run along through many generations. Strong believers in democracy, people who fear even an aristocracy of brains, argued against the immutability of intelligence, but the view was then pretty general that large changes in intelligence level, except of course those natural in the maturation of youth, do not occur.

The big event of the decade was the use of intelligence tests in the First World War. The tests were adopted in order to prevent getting feeble-minded incompetence into the ranks. They were successful for that purpose and also proved to be a quick way of getting the brighter recruits sorted out from the duller so that the more competent men could at once be given more responsible work. Although *group testing* had been suggested before and A. S. Otis was planning to adopt it with some of his tests, the Army procedures provided the first extensive use of this method. The recruits were got together in large rooms, as many as two or three hundred at a time. Every man had a pencil and test form. They all reacted and turned the pages together. In no other way would it have been possible to get the two million odd results on the Army Alpha Examination. The Armistice of 1918 came too soon to get much use out of the results, but the advertising that this testing gave psychology in America reached into the remotest corner of the laboratory and swelled college classes, creating a great demand for Ph.D. instructors.

The 1920s were a decade of diminished faith in the immutability of intelligence. The Army tests and the Stanford-Binet scale had proved to be culture-bound. You could not use the standard Army Alpha test with men who could not read and write English or with men who could not understand English. Because so many of the immigrant stock from southern Europe did poorly in the tests, including the pantomime Beta test for the non-English and the illiterate groups, it was desired to get a culture-free test that would compare samples of different nations, races and cultures. No such test was forthcoming. The usual intelligence tests were seen to be "bookish" or at least "verbal," having been made for school-children growing up in a normal educational environment, as indeed anyone studying the choice between Binet and Cattell in the 1890s might have anticipated. Common opinion was that general ability must be thought of as operating within the culture. It became clear also that Galton's dichotomy between nature and nurture can scarcely be realized in the assessment of specific abilities, because both factors are always operating. A child learns (nurture) to walk because he has inherited (nature) legs. Most structures are inherited; many human functions are learned; nevertheless, some functions, like spiders' web-making, are certainly inherited. All this change of view was supported by Thomson and Burt and even Spearman, who made it clear that, whatever may be the generality of "general ability," there are other basic abilities or factors which contribute in different degrees in different cases to a great variety of important human skills and activities (p. 481).

Meanwhile the variety of tests had been expanding. *Mental testing* and *intelligence testing* were no longer synonymous terms. In the U.S. Army during the First World War, intelligence tests had been supplemented by tests for personnel selection, trade tests and comparable devices. This led on to a growth of testing in applied psychology, a growth in which new tests were designed to sample the particular abilities to be assessed, and the common and specific factors were ignored.

The 1930s were the decade of *factorial analysis*. Thomson and Burt led in Britain (p. 481), L. L. Thurstone at Chicago. It was T. L. Kelley, once Thorndike's student, who successfully broke away in 1928 from Spearman's conceptions. Thurstone started multiple-factor analysis in 1931, and he published *Vectors of the Mind* in 1935 and a second book which works out the principles of the first, *Primary Mental Abilities*, in 1938. Thomson's *Factorial Analysis of Human Ability* followed quickly in 1939 and then Burt's *Factors of the Mind* in 1941. After the Second World War, Thurstone brought his work together again in *Multiple-Factor Analysis* (1947). By the end of the 1930s, this was the picture of human abilities: there are a great many factors which enter into all sorts of combinations in specific skills, but a few of these factors are more generally involved than others in successful human activity and these may be regarded as *primary mental abilities*.

Meanwhile, testing was multiplying in all sorts of practical endeavors, and intelligence was gradually going out of style—in spite of Terman and Merrill's newest revision of the Stanford-Binet Scale in 1937. There did not seem to be any one factor general enough to be called general ability, and intelligence began to be thought of as a sum of several important, all useful, but independently variable abilities. More was said about intelligence's being verbal, bookish and educational, and less about its being inherited. It was not thought that there is no inherited psychological capability, but there was doubt about our ability to make the analysis into nature and nurture. Galton's and Thorndike's method of twin control was used to show that nature is still important, and the custodians of the feeble-minded still found themselves unable to educate their wards beyond a certain ceiling of social and economic competence.

The 1940s were the culmination of the preceding decade. Psychology in America came into its own in the Second World War, and it was largely, at least at first, by way of the testing. Intelligence was no longer mentioned. For the Alpha Examination of 1917-1918 there was now the General Classification Test (GCT) which took the four of Thurstone's primary abilities which seemed most likely to measure military success, tested them separately and added up the total score. Later the Army and the Navy each had a GCT—an AGCT and a NGCT. Still later there was an attempt to consider the different items separately without adding them up and then to get up a battery of tests for eight different basic abilities. All the services wanted measures—quick ones—of abilities and of aptitudes. (An aptitude is an ability to acquire another ability.) After the War, industry wanted tests and got them from psychologists or trained their own testers. The clinical psychologists, multiplied under the need of veterans to what was for psychology enormous numbers, used tests too. Engineers, designing machines to fit their operators, had to test the operators to see what would fit them. Employers had to test the operators to see when they were trained to use the machines. Galton could never have imagined this sort of realization for his dream. He hoped for a set of values recorded on an inventory card, a card for every Briton. What had come about was an amazing activity of testing. If up-to-date authority wanted to select men for a given skillful performance, they might find a combination of tests of primary abilities that would do, or some test of a comparable skill; but, if they failed in their search (and they usually did), then they would invent a new test, perhaps a combination of acts which seemed to be included in the desired skill, and eventually, by validation and revision, they would come out with something better than anything else available but quite special. What history had given Galton was not a tested ration but a nation being perpetually tested.

Certainly the schism between experimental psychology and mental testing was partly healed in the 1940s. There was so much testing and it was working well. Besides, the War had produced an applied experimental psychology, and experimentalists could not longer look down their noses at applied psychology. All kinds of psychologists, moreover, needed to use the newer statistical methods as well as the Fisher techniques for assessing the significance of results. The two procedures, however, remained different. Experimental psychology had got more technical, and the experimentalist practically had to know something about electronics. The testers did not. The testers and the clinicists usually liked other people. The experimentalists often did not, preferring rats for subjects as being less embarrassing socially or at any rate more pliant, convenient and exploitable than human subjects. Psychology—but not experimental psychology—has in its professional personnel many more women than has any other science. Women take to testing more readily than to electronics. It is dangerous to generalize, but it may be that the schism between testing and experimenting is maintained by personalogical differences as well as by institutional ones.

NOTES

The concept of mind-in-use is so broad and the usefulness of mind is of such general interest that one can find functional psychology all through the past. In a sense British empiricism was functional because it showed how experience comes to afford knowledge of reality (pp. 168-203). The faculty psychology of the Scottish school was functional (pp. 205-208) and so was the psychology of the phrenologists (pp. 54-56). The French had essentially this point of view (pp. 211-216). On the other hand, Wundt and Brentano and their followers were not functionalists, and functional psychology was most definitely promoted when its opposites, the dualistic psychologies of content and of act, were vigorous.

On the use of the word *function* in *psychology*, see K. M. Dallenbach, The history and derivation of the word 'function' as a systematic term in psychology, *Amer. J. Psychol.*, 1915, 26, 473-484.

Chicago's Functionalism

In general, on American functionalism, see E. Heidbreder, *Seven Psychologies*, 1933, 201-233; R. S. Woodworth, *Contemporary Schools of Psychology*, 2 ed., 1948, 11-36. Woodworth makes the pervasiveness of functionalism quite clear in the 2 ed., whereas in the 1 ed. of 1931 he did not even have a chapter for functionalism. The American scene changed a great deal in those seventeen years. For one thing, the influence of Titchener (d. 1927) was fading, for he was no longer alive to maintain the vitality of his antithesis to functional psychology. For another thing, America was coming into its own. See C. R. Griffith, *Principles of Systematic Psychology*, 1943, 265-319.

For Dewey's early views, see his *Psychology*, 1886, 3 ed., 1891. At this time he wrote also The psychological standpoint, *Mind*, 1886, 11, 1-19; Psychology as philosophic method, *ibid.*, 153-173.

Dewey's classic paper is The reflex arc concept in psychology, *Psychol. Rev.*, 1896, 3, 357-370; reprinted by W. Dennis, *Readings in the History of Psychology*, 1948, 355-365. His important paper on educational psychology is Psychology and social practice, *ibid.*, 1900, 7, 105-124. For some of his later views, see his *Human Nature and Conduct*, 1922; Conduct and experience, in C. Murchison, *Psychologies of 1930*, 1930, 409-422. See also Heidbreder, *op. cit.*, 209-214.

Enough has been written by Dewey and about him to make his rôle in supporting functional psychology seem a very small part of his total influence. See, for instance, J. Ratner, *The Philosophy of John Dewey*, 1928; Intel-

ligence in the Modern World: John Dewey's Philosophy, 1939.

The fact that James R. Angell never earned a Ph.D. did not seem to matter very much. He was a leader of thought, a university professor, a university president, and eventually was found in possession of 21 LL.D.s, one Litt.D. and one honorary Ph.D. It is extremely unlikely that a Ph.D. received in course would have affected his capacities any more than did these later distinctions. The fact is that Angell almost got his Ph.D. from Benno Erdmann in Halle in 1893. Angell's thesis was accepted, subject to revision of its German style; but he would have had to remain at Halle without a stipend. He chose instead to return to America at Minnesota, where a position and a salary awaited him, a small salary but one large enough to enable him to marry.

Angell's paper on reaction times with A. W. Moore was Angell's first published research: Reaction-time: a study in attention and habit, *Psychol. Rev.*, 1896, 3, 245-258. The papers of Angell and Mead in the Chicago Decennial Celebration are Angell, The relations of structural and functional psychology to philosophy, *Univ. Chicago Decennial Publ.*, 1903, Ser. I, vol. 3, pt. 2, 55-73, also separate, also reprinted in *Philos. Rev.*, 1903, 12, 243-271; G. H. Mead, The definition of the psychical, *ibid.*, 77-112, also separate. Angell's presidential address before the American Psychological Association was The province of functional psychology, *Psychol. Rev.*, 1907, 14, 61-91, a clear and lucid exposition to which the reader should go for further information about functional psychology before the birth of behaviorism. It is reprinted in W. Dennis, *Readings in the History of Psychology*, 1948, 439-456.

Angell's *Psychology*, 1904, 4 ed., 1908, shows how the functional point of view works in the writing of a text. His *Introduction to Psychology*, 1918, replaced it later. His *Chapters from Modern Psychology*, 1912, exhibit his catholicity of mind but not his views on functionalism. See, however, his autobiography, in C. Murchison, *Psychology in Autobiography*, 1936, III, 1-38; also Heidbreder, *op. cit.*, 214-218; W. R. Miles, James Rowland Angell, 1869-1949, psychologist-educator, *Science*, 1949, 110, 1-4; W. S. Hunter, James Rowland Angell, 1869-1949, *Amer. J. Psychol.*, 1949, 62, 439-450.

The impetus toward making a self-conscious school of functional psychology was given from without by E. B. Titchener's criticism of it. See his Postulates of a structural psychology, *Philos. Rev.*, 1898, 7, 449-465, reprinted by Dennis, *op. cit.*, 366-376; Structural and functional psychology, *Philos. Rev.*, 1899, 8, 290-299.

Why was Titchener not found in the functionalists' camp? He grew up in England at a time when the theory of evolution reigned supreme in almost all advanced thought. He was saturated with English philosophy and English science. When he said *biology* he meant evolution, adaptation and adjustment, not physiology. His early publications were biological—in this sense of the word. If he appreciated Darwin, he could also have appreciated Galton and have followed him instead of Wundt. He might by early training have been a leader of functional psychology, whereas his only contribution to it was to emphasize it by opposing it. Perhaps, if Oxford had received him back from Wundt and the stuffy Oxonians had recognized the importance of the new experimental psychology, he would have come over into the British and American pattern. Instead he was forced into isolation in what he thought of as "the colonies." His loyalty to Wundt, sincere as it was, also seemed to have had in it an element of resentment against England and Oxford, all the stronger because of his stanch loyalty to Britain. Certainly he was ambivalent about England. A loyal British subject in the First World War, offering his services to the British ambassador, he remarked to an American, 'I can but wish your allies had a better psychology than our common enemy.' British and French functionalism was not up to the German psychology of content, he thought.

For the functional psychology of Harvey Carr (1873-), see his *Psychology*, 1925; his Functionalism, in C. Murchison, *Psychologies of 1930*, 1930, 59-78, which succeeds in making the case for functionalism only by contrasting it with Titchener's then-fading psychology; and his autobiography, in Murchison, *Psychology in Autobiography*, 1936, III, 69-82. See also Heidbreder, *op. cit.*, 219-226.

Carr, Angell's Ph.D. of 1905, went through the three levels of professorship at Chicago from 1908 to his retirement in 1938. He counts as Angell's successor, because Thurstone, at Chicago since 1924, distinguished in factor analysis, represents a quite different tradition.

On Angell's and Carr's important students, see M. D. Boring and E. G. Boring, Masters and pupils among the American psychologists, *Amer. J. Psychol.*, 1948, 61, 527-534.

Columbia's Functionalism

On the Columbia school, if school it be, see E. Heidbreder, *Seven Psychologies*, 1933, 287-327. Woodworth does not explicitly get his own group into his *Contemporary Schools of Psychology*, but he serves the group when he gives his own views on dynamic psychology, *opp. citt. infra*.

On Cattell, see pp. 532-540, 548 f. Many persons have tried to get Cattell to write autobiographically but he refused resolutely. He would reminisce about psychology but not in relation to his own affairs. He refused invitations to contribute to any of C. Murchison's three volumes of *Psychology in Autobiography*. He may have felt that description of achievement should come from without—as indeed it did, partly in his life-time and more after his death.

E. L. Thorndike wrote his autobiography briefly in Murchison, *op. cit.*, 1936, III, 263-270. His important books are: *Animal Intelligence* (the original Columbia thesis), *Psychol. Monog.*, 1898, no. 8; *Educational Psychology*

(a little 173-page first book on this topic), 1903; *An Introduction to the Theory of Mental and Social Measurements*, 1904, 2 ed., 1913; *Animal Intelligence* (reprints the first item *supra*, three other papers on chicks, fish and monkeys respectively, and adds three new chapters of general discussion), 1911; *Educational Psychology*, 3 vols., I, *The Original Nature of Man*, 1913; II, *The Psychology of Learning*, 1913; III, *Individual Differences and Their Causes*, 1914; *Fundamentals of Learning* (introduces the concept of "belongingness" in addition to "satisfyingness" as a principle of learning), 1932; *Your City* (measurement of sociological values), 1939; *Human Nature and the Social Order*, 1940; *Man and His Works* (William James Lectures), 1943.

Thorndike's bibliography is enormous. Over 250 items up to 1931 are printed in C. Murchison, *Psychological Register*, 1932, III, 484-490. The important paper on transfer of training, written with R. S. Woodworth, is The influence of improvement in one mental function upon the efficiency of other functions, *Psychol. Rev.*, 1901, 8, 247-261. W. Dennis, *Readings in the History of Psychology*, 1948, reprints this paper in part, 388-398; also Thorndike's 1898 *Animal Intelligence* in part, 377-387; also the 1905 paper on the measurement of twins, 399-406. See also Thorndike's *Selected Writings from a Connectionist's Psychology*, 1949, where his autobiography and twenty-two of his less accessible important papers, selected by himself, are reprinted.

R. S. Woodworth also wrote his autobiography in Murchison, *Psychology in Autobiography*, 1930, II, 359-380. It is written in Woodworth's most engaging style. His colleagues collected and reprinted twenty-five of his papers as *Psychological Issues*, 1939, a book which includes a bibliography of about 200 items at the end and reprints the autobiography.

Woodworth's more important books mentioned in the text are *Le mouvement*, 1903; with G. T. Ladd, *Elements of Physiological Psychology*, 2 ed.,

1911; *Dynamic Psychology*, 1917; *Psychology* (the popular textbook), 1921, 5 ed., with D. G. Marquis, 1947; *Contemporary Schools of Psychology*, 1931, 2 (very revised) ed., 1948; *Experimental Psychology* (descended from mimeographed ancestors which Columbia graduate students treasured), 1938, with rumors afloat about a revision.

For Woodworth's systematic views on dynamic psychology and what the text calls functional psychology, see his two very readable articles each called Dynamic psychology, in C. Murchison, *Psychologies of 1925*, 1926, 111-126 (a Powell Lecture at Clark); *Psychologies of 1930*, 1930, 327-336.

For the origin of the list of psychologists recognizing intellectual debts to Cattell, Thorndike and Woodworth, see Boring and Boring, *op. cit.*

On the numerousness of Columbia Ph.D.s in psychology, see R. S. Harper, Tables of American doctorates in psychology, *Amer. J. Psychol.*, 1949, 62, 579-587. In the 65 years from 1884 to 1948, Columbia gave 344 of these degrees, Iowa 269, Chicago 196, Ohio State 169, Harvard 155, Clark 149, Minnesota, 133, Yale 128, Cornell 112, and so on down through the list of 59 other institutions, each of which gave less than one hundred degrees in these three score years and five. Columbia ranked first in only two of the last six decades.

Educational Psychology

The text and these notes touch only upon the origin of educational psychology. The definitive history of the subject has, it would seem, yet to be written.

On the early history of child study by a close associate of Hall's, see Sara E. Wiltse, Preliminary sketch of the history of child study in America, *Ped. Sem. (J. genet. Psychol.)*, 1895, 3, 189-212. For a discussion of the early history in Germany, see W. H. Burnham, The new German school, *ibid.*, 1891, 1, 13-18. On Great Britain, see Kate Stevens, Child study in Great Britain,

ibid., 1906, 3, 245-249. She notes the importance of the child-study conference which Hall arranged for the Chicago World's Fair in 1893. That is apparently what first got the British interested.

For Hall's own summary for the early work at Clark and his list of the 102 questionnaires, see G. S. Hall, Child study at Clark University, *Amer. J. Psychol.*, 1903, 14, 96-106.

The early volumes of the *Pedagogical Seminary* make interesting reading. Many numbers begin with an editorial by Hall, explaining the state of the war on this kind of ignorance or the purpose to which the particular number was devoted. The *Ped. Sem.* was begun in 1891, but it gradually lost its special interest in child study as Hall turned to other matters and after his death became known as the *Journal of Genetic Psychology*. Lightner Witmer's *Psychological Clinic* ran from 1907 to 1925, and helps to show what was going on in those years. In 1910 the *Journal of Educational Psychology* was begun, and this date perhaps marks the coming of age of this subject-matter. In 1903 B. Rand, in J. M. Baldwin's *Dictionary of Philosophy and Psychology*, III, 964-974, found about 400 items to list under the topic Child Psychology. There was no topic Educational Psychology.

In Germany, Ernst Meumann, one of Wundt's students and the editor of the *Archiv für die gesamte Psychologie*, became the leader of the movement in experimental education and educational psychology. He started the *Zeitschrift für experimentelle Pädagogik* in 1905 which changed later with the times into the *Zeitschrift für pädagogische Psychologie und Jugendkunde*. Meumann is also author of the well-known *Ueber Oekonomie und Technik des Lernens*, 1903, and *Vorlesungen zur Einführung in die experimentelle Pädagogik und ihre psychologischen Grundlagen*, 2 vols., 1907.

Mental Tests

On the early history of mental testing (before the First World War), see the excellent account of J. Peterson, *Early Conceptions and Tests of Intelligence*, 1926. For the later history and an indication of the scope which testing eventually assumed, see F. N. Freeman, *Mental Tests: Their History, Principles and Applications*, 2 ed., 1939, and also incidental discussion in Garrett and Schneck and in Stoddard, *opp. citt. infra*. The reader must not forget that the text gives only a bird's-eye view of a broad field, a view centered upon America. It shows the relation of mental testing to functional psychology, but it does no more than introduce him to the history of mental testing.

The following chronological list of references follows the discussion of the text:

A. Oehrn, *Experimentelle Studien zur Individualpsychologie*, 1889; reprinted in *Psychol. Arbeiten*, 1895, 1, 92-152.

H. Münsterberg, Zur Individualpsychologie, *Centrbl. Nervenheilk. Psychiat.*, 1891, 14, 196-198.

F. Boas, Anthropological investigations in schools, *Ped. Sem.*, 1891, 1, 225-228.

T. L. Bolton, Growth of memory in school children, *Amer. J. Psychol.*, 1892, 4, 362-380.

J. Jastrow, Some anthropometric and psychologic tests on college students, *ibid.*, 420-427.

J. A. Gilbert, Researches on mental and physical development of school-children, *Studies from Yale Psychol. Lab.*, 1894, 2, 40-100.

E. Kraepelin, Der psychologische Versuch in der Psychiatrie, *Psychol. Arbeiten*, 1895, 1, 1-91.

J. McK. Cattell and L. Farrand, Physical and mental measurements of the students of Columbia University, *Psychol. Rev.*, 1896, 3, 618-648.

A. Binet and V. Henri, La psychologie individuelle, *L'année psychol.*, 1896, 2, 411-465. This is the crucial article. There are seven articles by Binet and Henri about this period and also half a hundred more by Binet from 1886 to 1911. See bibliography in Peterson, *op. cit.*

Gilbert, Researches upon school children and college students, *Univ. Iowa Studies Psychol.*, 1897, 1, 1-39.

H. Ebbinghaus, Ueber eine neue Methode zur Prüfung geistiger Fähigkeiten und ihre Anwendung bei Schulkindern, *Zsch. Psychol.*, 1897, 13, 401-459.

S. E. Sharp, Individual psychology: a study in psychological method, *Amer. J. Psychol.*, 1899, 10, 329-391.

W. Stern, *Ueber Psychologie der individuellen Differenzen*, 1900.

E. L. Thorndike, Mental fatigue, *Psychol. Rev.*, 1900, 7, 466-482, 547-579.

Thorndike and R. S. Woodworth, Influence of improvement in one mental function upon the efficiency of other mental functions, *ibid.*, 1901, 8, 247-261, 384-395, 553-564; excerpts reprinted in W. Dennis, *Readings in the History of Psychology*, 1948, 388-398.

C. Wissler, Correlation of mental and physical tests, *Psychol. Monog.*, 1901, no. 16.

H. B. Thompson (H. T. Woolley), *The Mental Traits of Sex*, 1903.

Thorndike, *Educational Psychology*, 1903, 2 ed., 3 vols., 1913-1914.

C. E. Spearman, "General Intelligence" objectively determined and measured, *Amer. J. Psychol.*, 1904, 15, 201-292.

Binet and Th. Simon, Méthodes nouvelles pour le diagnostic du niveau intellectuel des anormaux, *L'année psychol.*, 1905, 11, 191-336; excerpts in Eng. trans. reprinted in Dennis, *op. cit.*, 412-419.

Idem, Le développement de l'intelligence chez les enfants, *ibid.*, 1908, 14, 1-94; excerpts reprinted in Eng. trans. in Dennis, *op. cit.*, 419-424.

G. M. Whipple, *Manual of Mental and Physical Tests*, 1910; 2 ed., 2 vols., 1914-1915.

H. H. Goddard, A measuring scale for intelligence, *Training School*, 1910, 6, 146-154.

Binet, Nouvelles recherches sur la mesure du niveau intellectuel chez les enfants d'école, *L'année psychol.*, 1911, 17, 145-201.

W. Stern, *Die differentielle Psychologie*, 1911.

Idem, *Die psychologischen Meth-*

oden der Intelligenzprüfung, 1912, Eng. trans., 1914.

Goddard, *The Kallikak Family: a Study in the Heredity of Feeble-Mindedness*, 1913, Germ. trans., 1914.

R. M. Yerkes, J. W. Bridges and R. S. Hardwick, *A Point Scale for Measuring Ability*, 1915.

L. M. Terman, *The Measurement of Intelligence*, 1916; brief excerpts reprinted in Dennis, *op. cit.*, 485-496.

R. M. Yerkes, ed., Psychological examining in the United States Army, *Mem. Nat. Acad. Sci.*, 1921, vol. 15; brief excerpts reprinted in Dennis, *op. cit.*, 528-540.

Spearman, *The Nature of Intelligence and the Principles of Cognition*, 1923; 2 ed., 1927.

Idem., *The Abilities of Man*, 1927.

T. L. Kelley, *Crossroads in the Mind of Man: a Study of Differentiable Mental Abilities*, 1928.

L. L. Thurstone, *Vectors of the Mind*, 1935.

Terman and M. A. Merrill, *Measuring Intelligence*, 1937.

Thurstone, *Primary Mental Abilities*, 1938.

G. H. Thomson, *Factorial Analysis of Human Ability*, 1939.

D. Wolfle, Factor analysis to 1940, *Psychomet. Monog.*, 1940, no. 3.

C. L. Burt, *Factors of the Mind*, 1941.

Thurstone, *Multiple-Factor Analysis*, 1947.

The following books show the reader how broad and complicated the field of mental testing has become. In general, see Freeman, *op. cit.* On personality and intelligence tests, see H. E. Garrett and M. R. Schneck, *Psychological Tests, Methods and Results*, 1933. On intelligence and intelligence testing, with a slant toward the effect of nurture on tested intelligence, see G. D. Stoddard, *The Meaning of Intelligence*, 1943. On diagnosing personality by the Rorschach ink-blots, see H. Rorschach, *Psychodiagnostics*, 1942. On testing for vocational interests, see E. K. Strong, *Vocational Interests of Men and Women*, 1943. On tests for mechanical ability, see G. K. Bennett and R. M. Cruikshank, *Summary of Manual and Mechanical Ability Tests*, 1942. On total assessment of personality (tests, problem situations, interviews, etc.), see Office of Strategic Services, *Assessment of Men*, 1948. *The Third Mental Measurement Yearbook*, 1949, O. K Buros, ed., is an 'encyclopedia,' listing an enormous number of tests and books on tests and measurement together with comment on them. There are also a 1938 and a 1940 *Yearbook*.

On the question of whether women and men psychologists have different tastes or aptitudes in respect of testing and experimenting, see A. I. Bryan and E. G. Boring, Women in American psychology: statistics from the OPP questionnaire, *Amer. Psychologist*, 1946, 1, 71-79, esp. 73-76.

LATER TRENDS IN MODERN PSYCHOLOGY

CHAPTER 23

Gestalt Psychology

Functionalism, the subject of the preceding chapter and the fundamental American trend, leads directly on into behaviorism and the whole behavioristic development in America. In the next chapter we shall see how behavioristics ultimately absorbed functionalism, but first we must examine the nature and origin of Gestalt psychology. Often the two movements—Gestalt psychology and behaviorism—are said to be contemporaneous. That is because the starting point for modern Gestalt psychology is Wertheimer's paper on seen movement, published in June 1912, and the starting point for behaviorism is Watson's paper on "psychology as the behaviorist views it," published in March 1913. Both of the movements, however, have their roots in antiquity. Each is a symptom of a *Zeitgeist*, but they are different symptoms of different *Zeitgeister*. Each is a protest against the 'new' German psychology of the late nineteenth century, the psychology of Wundt, G. E. Müller and Titchener, but the two are different protests. Gestalt psychology primarily protested against the analysis of consciousness into elements and the exclusion of values from the data of consciousness, whereas behaviorism mostly protested against the inclusion of the data of consciousness in psychology.

As a protest behaviorism may be said to have been farther along in 1913 than was Gestalt psychology in 1912, for behaviorism was the second phase of the American protest against the Wundtian tradition. The first was functionalism. Gestalt psychology, however, was but the first phase of the German protest against the Wundtian tradition. That is why, when the Gestalt psychologists brought their protest to America in the 1920s, many American psychologists did not understand them, for they were protesting against something that was no longer important in America. America had already moved further away from conscious elementism than had Europe. The reasons are the reasons for American functionalism, the ones discussed in the preceding chapter (pp. 551 f., 579).

587

It seems best to consider the nature of Gestalt psychology first and then to go back to examine the trends of systematic thinking which led up to it and made its success a part of an historical continuity. After that we can consider what the school has accomplished and take a quick glance at what is happening to it now.

NATURE OF GESTALT PSYCHOLOGY

Gestalt psychology has suffered from its name which does not, like act psychology, functional psychology or behaviorism, indicate its nature. *Gestalt* means form or shape and, more broadly, manner or even essence. The English equivalents are also used broadly: *in top form, in good shape.* Form is often opposed to content, and in that sense *Gestaltpsychologie* might well be opposed to Wundt's *Inhaltpsychologie.* Spearman has spoken of *shape psychology* (1925), Titchener of *configurationism* (1925), but the former term is too likely to suggest spatial conformation and the latter implies an arrangement of parts. *Structural psychology* (*Strukturpsychologie*) might have served, since a structure is a whole in which the total organization is altered by the change of any part, but that term had already been pre-empted by James to indicate the Titchenerian antonym of *functional psychology.* Titchener's structural psychology is the descriptive anatomy of conscious elements—the exact opposite of Gestalt psychology. If the English word *whole* had had a generic adjective it could have been used, but *whole psychology* is strange and slightly humorous, and Jan Smuts' *holism* (1926), which has the right meaning but a Greek etymology, never caught on. The result is that *Gestalt* may now be considered to have come permanently over into English and on occasion even drops its initial capital.

The most concise way to characterize Gestalt psychology is to say that it deals with *wholes* and that its givens (data) are what have been called *phenomena.* The Gestalt psychologists believed that the word *Gestalt* carries both these implications, in part because they were convinced that it is really always wholes that are given in experience to conscious man. In perceiving a melody you get the melodic form, not a string of notes, a unitary whole that is something more than the total list of its parts or even the serial pattern of them. That is the way experience comes to man, put up in significant structured forms, Gestalten.

(1) *Wholes.* Many properties of wholes are, as the phrase is, *emergent.* They inhere in no single part but emerge when the parts constitute the whole. The whole, as the Gestalt psychologists

have said again and again, is more than the sum of its parts. Let us look to chemistry to see what happens when elements are compounded into wholes.

The chemist has elements and he has atoms. Nowadays he knows that the atom is divisible and that each element has several kinds of atoms (isotopes) with pretty much the same properties except for weight and atomic stability. You can combine the atoms of the elements into the molecules of compounds, and the compound has observable properties which were not predictable from the observed properties of the combining elements. In many complex molecules the same atoms may combine in more than one way (pattern of connection), and the properties of the compound are found to depend on the relationships formed in combination; that is to say, the properties of the compound depend in part on the relationships which are shown in the structural chemical formula, a formula which can vary while the empirical formula remains the same. Since the relationships between elements exist only in the compound, it is plain that at least the relationships emerge in the whole, in the compound, and that the whole is more than the sum of its parts because it is the parts in relation to each other. Some scientists would say that, if you knew all about the parts and their relations, you would necessarily know all about the whole. That may be plausible metaphysics, but it is not practical epistemology. Nearly always, adequate knowledge about a whole has to be obtained from observation of the compound itself and can not be inferred from the parts and their relationships. From knowing how oxygen and hydrogen combine to make water, you would still never guess the latent heat of fusion of ice.

There may be partial exceptions to this rule. Some of Ehrenfels' examples of form-quality seem pretty well determined by the knowledge of the elements and their relations (pp. 442-444). A square is more than four lines, but four lines, successively coterminous, at right angles, and forming a closed figure *are* a square. The picture in a mosaic—be it a pattern of small stones or of the tiny dots in colored reproduction—is similarly given by the elements and their relationships. What we call a sum of money is a whole almost independent of the relationships of its founding elements. You can have a hundred dollars' worth of wealth by getting hold of one hundred separate dollars, or ten thousand cents, or a proper set of checks or credits. That is a case of a true *Und-Verbindung*, which Wertheimer said Gestalten are not, and the whole sum of money seems actually to be somewhat less than the sum of its parts.

So the Gestalt psychologists set out to study wholes—wholes as given in experience. At first their stated program caused confusion, for the other experimental psychologists said that they too were studying wholes. What was there new, they wanted to know, about the aspirations of Gestalt psychologists? There was, however, something new about the avidity with which the Gestalt psychologists sought for new effective parameters that applied to old determinations—sought and in many cases found them. Their first concern, moreover, was to get rid of the conventional analysis of direct experience into sensations and other sensory elements. Let us make this matter clear by two examples, one from Külpe's anticipation of Gestalt theory and one from Wertheimer's inauguration of that theory.

Wundt had held that a sensation is a quality with a given intensity. Sensations, he thought, are organized in space and time, but space and time are not observed as such. Thus a sensation at a different place was for Wundt a different sensation, and a seen line had to be regarded as a row of sensations. Külpe (1893) realized, however, that space and time are as directly observable as are quality and intensity; so he added extent and duration to the list of observable sensory attributes. In this he followed Mach, another proper ancestor of Gestalt psychology, for Mach believed in sensations of space and sensations of time. For Külpe an extension—a line, perhaps—was what you observe as a whole and perhaps compare with another extension. It is not a row of sensations. Similarly an area can be observed and described as a whole and need not be considered as if it were a mosaic field of points or spots. In like manner a perceived duration is itself perceived; it is not a succession of instants. That systematic change of Külpe's was a great advance, although its significance was not fully recognized at the time.

Almost twenty years later (1912), Wertheimer was describing seen movement under the conditions of discrete displacement of the stimulus, as it occurs in the stroboscope or in the cinema. Wundtian elementism would have required him to say that a sensation of given quality changes its location in time. But seen movement does not have any quality, not in the sense of belonging at some place in the color solid, of being related to gray, black, white, red, yellow, green and blue. Movement looks different from quiescence. You can see movement as such, you can recognize it, you can distinguish it from stationariness, but you can not give it any further analytical definition. Such movement is not sensation as that word had been used by Wundt and Külpe. It could properly be called a *phenomenon*, as that word had been used by the phenomenologists, and thus Wertheimer called it *phenomenal movement* or simply the *phi-phenomenon*.

Suppose you have a stimulus which is discretely displaced from position A to position B, and then back to A again, and to B again, alternating ABABAB.... If the time-interval between the exposures at the two positions is long, you see simply discrete displacement, no movement. If the time-interval is shortened you begin to see some movement at A or at B or both. If it is still further shortened, you come to the optimal rate at which perfect movement back and forth is perceived between A and B and in which the phi-phenomenon marks the movement. If the interval gets still shorter, the phenomenal movement degenerates and presently, for rapid discrete displacement of the stimulus, you see continuously two simultaneous objects. Such *phi* is a visual perception, localized in space, with given extension, but it may have no color or else may partake of the color of the moving object. The point and value of the experiment would have been lost had it been necessary to analyze *phi* into conventional sensory attributes. *Phi* is, moreover, an emergent. It pertains to a whole psychophysical situation and not to any of the separate factors that enter into it. In that it is as much a 'founded' characteristic as is shape, melody or any other Gestalt.

Because Gestalt psychology tends to deal with wholes it frequently finds itself concerned with *fields* and *field theory*. A field is a dynamic whole, a system in which an alteration of any part affects all the other parts. An electrical network with a voltage impressed across it is a field. There are visual perceptual fields, in which a noteworthy change in any part can be seen to produce a change throughout the field. Some optical illusions are explained by the psychological field dynamics which treats the visual field as if it were the seat of interacting forces. Because perception seems often to follow laws of physical dynamics, Köhler has supposed that there are neural brain fields which underlie and account for the dynamics apparent in the phenomena of perception. Koffka has supposed that you must understand human action in terms of a behavioral field which includes, not the stimuli and the physical environment, but the outer world and its objects as perceived and conceived by the actor. Lewin has built up the conception of a life-space as the dynamic field within which a person lives and strives.

It should be added that the wholes of Gestalt psychology have practical limitations. The theory protests against formal analysis into the members of a predetermined list of elements, but recognizes that experience is nevertheless segregated, especially into objects. The universe must be regarded as divided into many systems, each of which is practically closed—at least each system is closed within the limits of tolerance applying to any particular consideration of it. Gestalt psychology never rejected all analysis. What it has demanded is freedom to use only the analysis which each particular problem requires.

(2) *Phenomena.* The Gestalt psychologists call their basic observational data, their givens, *phenomena.* What is given in experience is for them *phenomenal experience.* This is an arbitrary but useful and historically valid specification of the word *phenomenon.* The Gestalt psychologists have taken this word over from the phenomenologists as denoting neutral experience, unbiased and free, experience *per se.* They would have no truck with the fixed list of elements, with sensations, images and feeling, or with their attributes—quality, intensity, extensity and duration. Limitation to those terms was the sort of constraint that had made experimental psychology unproductive, so they thought. They argued, on the other hand, that you can see whole objects—a table, for instance, perceived without knowing of what conscious elements it is constituted. You can see movement—*phi*—without being able to specify its quality, except to give the ostensive definition that the quality of *phi* is "this." You can perceive anger—in a man, in an ape—and an ape can perceive anger in man; yet everyone knows that neither man nor ape can tell precisely what the perceived behavioral pattern for anger is. It was this freedom to identify experiences in psychological description without reference to psychology's antiquated Mendeleyev table that Gestalt psychologists sought and won—to psychology's great advantage, as it turned out.

Perhaps the most important thing about the Gestalt psychologists' phenomena is that they include objects and meanings. The straight and narrow path of orthodoxy for Wundt and Titchener, however, led only through pure description without interpretation. The givens were limited to what was conceived to be the most immediate datum of experience, and that turned out presently to be sensation. Images were held to be centrally excited sensations. Feelings were sensory in their basic nature. Relations were not observed except as sensations in relation. Objects were not observed as such; they were interpretations of the data. You could see a given spatial pattern. If you said it was a man, you were making an inference and transcending your data. If you said it was your brother, you were going still further beyond immediate observation. Since you really could not describe the pattern of sensations that make up a perceived man, you were forced in introspection at Leipzig or Cornell into such circumlocutions as: "I experience a pattern of sensations which is like what occur when I perceive a man." The Gestalt psychologists thought it much simpler to say, "I see a man"; but in so doing they were accepting objects as psychological givens.

The distinction here is not new and it is always difficult to draw. It lies in the difference between *knowledge of* and *knowledge about, cognitio rei* and *cognitio circa rem* (as Lotze said in 1852). Titchener, criticizing the Würzburg school (1912), called the first *description*, the latter *information*. In German the words were *Beschreibung* and *Kundgabe*. If you report what comes, you are describing. If you report what you infer from what comes, then you are giving information about the experience or are reporting, not what it is, but what it means. The Gestalt psychologists insisted that this line can not be drawn and that all meanings, all objects, all *Kundgaben* which are *immediate* and do not wait upon an inferential process are given and should take their places as phenomena. In so cutting that Gordian knot they really had little choice. Analysis of experience into sensory elements was in 1912 becoming more and more forced and artificial, and it might then have been argued that even sensory analysis itself is inferential and a knowledge-about. We shall see presently how Brentano and Ehrenfels and Stumpf and Külpe were all making the same decision before Wertheimer came to it. We are not disparaging Gestalt psychology if we say that it too, like all other movements, rode the *Zeitgeist*.

There is much more to be understood about Gestalt psychology than that it deals with wholes and phenomena. Usually it works in terms of field theory, as we have noted. The important Gestalt psychologists have accepted a special theory of relation between experienced phenomena and the underlying brain processes, the theory called *isomorphism*, and to that we shall return. First, however, we must note who the leading Gestalt psychologists have been, and then see how this movement actually grew out of all that went before it.

THE GESTALT PSYCHOLOGISTS

The principal Gestalt psychologists were Wertheimer, Köhler and Koffka. Seldom has a movement been so specifically attached to the names of a few men. There have been many movements associated with the leadership of a single man and many schools which have spread out broadly, embracing differences of view and internal controversy, but Gestalt psychology had three leaders, who doubtless differed in private but who agreed so thoroughly on fundamental principles that they could abstain from public controversy. There were others in Germany and later in America who attached themselves to the movement, fought for it or for their versions of it, but they were aides and not the cabinet.

Wertheimer, the oldest, was the originator and leader, and the other two promoted his pre-eminence. He published the least of the three men, but his influence was great though the total of his printed pages was small. The psychological world knew about him because Köhler and Koffka kept quoting him. Köhler, the youngest of the three, became the best known. He may be said to have taken on responsibility for the movement before the public. He has published less than Koffka, more than Wertheimer, but he has spoken with great care, precision and stylistic polish. Thus his books have become the authoritative word of Gestalt psychology on the topics with which the books are concerned, but Köhler's wisdom has led him to leave some issues without pronouncement. Koffka, the most productive, did indeed attempt to write a definitive system of Gestalt psychology. He produced a difficult and erudite book, but one which contains too many of Koffka's personal decisions to stand as Gestalt psychology's bible. It is interesting to observe that the originality of these three men varied inversely with their productivity.

Max Wertheimer (1880-1943) was born in Prague and went to the university there at the turn of the century to study law. After that he became interested in psychology, worked at Berlin under Stumpf and Schumann for a time (1901-1903) and then took his doctorate, *summa cum laude*, at Würzburg with Külpe in 1904. Although Wertheimer did not become one of the important figures in the Würzburg school, he was, nevertheless, there at the culmination of the demand that the imageless character of thought be recognized. His degree coincided with the papers of Watt and Ach (pp. 403-406). Külpe may, indeed, have had something to do with Wertheimer's progress away from sensationism toward phenomenology. During the five years following his degree, Wertheimer spent his time variously at Prague, Vienna and Berlin. It is not clear that any great man shaped his thinking in these days. Hering, the phenomenologist-physiologist whom the Gestalt psychologists revered, was no longer at Prague. Mach was at Vienna, but Brentano had left Vienna. Stumpf, just won over by Husserl and Brentano to phenomenology, was at Berlin, but the Gestalt psychologists have never admitted that Stumpf influenced their thinking. Wertheimer had known Schumann at Berlin earlier, but Schumann had left Berlin for Zürich in 1905.

The story is that Wertheimer in the summer of 1910 was on the way from Vienna to the Rhineland for a vacation and that on the train he conceived of a new way to treat the problem of seen movement. He got off of his train at Frankfurt, found a toy stroboscope in a store, and set to work in his hotel constructing various figures for the production of movement by discrete displacement of the stimulus-object and seeing what conditions were necessary to produce optimal movement. Schumann had just come as professor to Frankfurt that summer and Wertheimer made contact with him. He offered Wertheimer space and the use of his newly constructed tachistoscope. Wertheimer set to work. Köhler was already at Frankfurt, and, when a little later Koffka turned up, they both became Wertheimer's subjects. When the experiment was finished, Wertheimer called in first Köhler and later Koffka, to explain to them the significance, as he saw it, of what had been going on. Was that event, presumably early in 1912, the actual birth of the new Gestalt psychology, or was it Wertheimer's insight in 1910 on the train before it got to Frankfurt? At any rate, from this time on these three men found themselves linked together in a common evangelical effort to save psychology from elementism, sensationism and associationism, from *sinnlose Und-Verbindungen* (Wertheimer's phrase), and to bring it to the free study of phenomenal wholes.

Wolfgang Köhler (1887-   ) was born in Reval in the Baltic provinces. He studied at Tübingen, Bonn and finally Berlin, where he took his Ph.D. under Stumpf in 1909 on a thesis in psychoacoustics. Eventually—1909 to 1915—he published five installments of *Akustische Untersuchungen*, which are, however, pre-Gestalt psychology in their orientation. Köhler's work on the nature and number of tonal attributes and on vowel-character was at the time quite generally cited. After his degree Köhler went to Frankfurt, arriving just before Wertheimer appeared with his new insight ready for use. In 1913 Köhler left Frankfurt and Wertheimer to go to the ape station on the Spanish island of Teneriffe, there to study the psychology of anthropoid apes. At Teneriffe he, a German subject, was caught by the First World War, much to the ultimate advantage of psychology, as it turned out. Köhler experimented with the visual discrimination of chimpanzees and chickens and presently, in 1917, he published *Intelligenzprüfungen an Menschenaffen*, a book which became a classic and went into a second edition in 1924, into English in 1925, into French in 1928. The remarkable thing about these studies is that Köhler applied in them the new wisdom he had got from Wertheimer. It became clear to Köhler that it is relations which emerge in Gestalten. Apes and chickens perceive relations between stimuli, not the isolated stimuli, and may learn to choose the larger or the brighter of two stimuli, regardless of the actual sizes or brightnesses of the stimuli. This fact is what later in Gestalt psychology came to be called the law of *transposition* and is also what Ehrenfels had noted about melody. Köhler also observed that the perception of relations is a mark of intelligence, and he called the sudden perception of useful or proper relations *insight*. The ape who sees the relation of the box to the banana, sees that by dragging the box over he can stand upon it and reach the banana, has insight. The ape who sees that two poles fitted together make a long pole which is long enough to reach the distant banana that lies beyond the bars, sees this relation clearly enough to act upon it, has insight. The ape who sees he can get the banana, not by straining against the barrier bars of his cage, but by walking away from his goal, out the remote door and then around the cage to his reward, that ape has insight. Insight leads to quick learning. It seems at first to be a substitute for trial-and-error learning, and the Gestalt psychologists brought it forward as another principle derived from their new point of view toward experience.

Köhler stayed at Teneriffe until 1920, returned to Germany, served as acting director of the Berlin laboratory for a year, received the appointment to succeed G. E. Müller at Göttingen on Müller's retirement in 1921, and then actually did succeed Stumpf at Berlin on his retirement in 1922. Why did Köhler get the chief post at Germany's most important university? Such matters are never determined in a simple manner, but the outstanding event had been Köhler's publication of his *Die physischen Gestalten in Ruhe und im stationärem Zustand* in 1920, the most scholarly and scientific of the books published by Gestalt psychologists, difficult to read and never fully translated into English. It has in it a preface for philosophers and biologists, another for physicists and none for psychologists. Köhler was always a physicist in his thinking, indebted for stimulus in his student days at Berlin to Max Planck rather than to Stumpf. Was there no psychology in this basic charter addressed to biologists and physicists? Yes; but Köhler believed that physics holds the key to the biology that will eventually put psychology in order. In this book he discussed field systems and the possibility that their occurrence in the brain establishes the laws which underlie the formation of perceptions and other psychological Gestalten. It was right and appropriate that so scholarly a work should have received the recognition that it did.

Kurt Koffka (1886-1941) was born in Berlin and went to the university there for study in 1903-1908 except for a year which he spent at Edinburgh. He took his degree with Stumpf in 1909 with a thesis on rhythm, and turned up, as we have seen, at Frankfurt in 1910 to begin his long association with Wertheimer and Köhler. In 1911 he was habilitated as *Dozent* at Giessen, forty miles from Frankfurt, whence he could still easily make contact with Wertheimer. At Giessen he started a long series of experimental studies under the title *Beiträge zur Psychologie der Gestalt,* a series which ran to five issues from 1913 to 1921. Koffka was then as always the most vocal evangelist of these three men.

In 1921 Wertheimer, Köhler and Koffka, in association with the psychopathologists, Kurt Goldstein and Hans Gruhle, founded the *Psychologische Forschung* which, in spite of its announced aspiration for broad scientific service, was soon recognized as the organ of the Gestalt school. It had run through twenty-two volumes before it suspended in 1938, four years after Hitler had doomed German psychology and just before the Second World War. The *Forschung,* representing the most vigorous trend in German psychology, continued on while its chief editors—first Koffka, then Wertheimer, then Köhler—migrated to America to escape the Nazi blight on learning. The *Zeitschrift für Psychologie* deteriorated under Hitler's domination of the German intellectuals, but not the *Forschung.* At the end Köhler alone was editing it from Swarthmore in the United States.

Wertheimer had stayed at Frankfurt until 1916, when he went to Berlin. Thus, when Köhler came to Berlin after Teneriffe, they were together. Koffka stayed at Giessen until 1927. After the First World War rumors began to spread in America. It was said that a new school was being formed by a group of vigorous young German psychologists, that these men felt that they had at last the key to psychology's future, that they were even about to start a new journal to give outlet to their researches and ideas. In America the War had so increased the prestige of psychology that America was soon to take the leadership in psychology away from Germany, but the Americans did not know that then. They were, indeed, eager to get the latest news on the new movement from Germany, just as eager as was James in the 1870s, as were all the 'new' American psychologists in the 1890s. In 1922 Koffka was persuaded to write for the *Psychological Bulletin* a definitive article on the new movement, an article which he called *Perception: An Introduction to Gestalt-Theorie*. It gave the views of the three leaders and discussed the results and implications of many experiments. This article met with strong protest. Koffka wrote clearly and in excellent English, and America found itself talking about the new school. Köhler complained that the critics confounded themselves, that some said that Gestalt psychology was new but wrong, and others that it was right and obvious because not new.

In 1921 Koffka published his developmental child psychology, the book which was later translated under the title *The Growth of the Mind*. It was a success in both Germany and America. The revised German edition came out in 1925; the English of the two editions in 1924 and 1928. In 1921 and again in 1923, Wertheimer published in the *Forschung* his important characterizations of Gestalt psychology and his polemic against elementism and associationism. Perhaps he was not quite fair, for he was berating a crude atomism which had not been the enthusiastic belief of any important psychologist since James Mill in 1829; nevertheless, he made his point though his critics said he was annihilating straw men. Also in 1923 Köhler published his famous experiments on the time error, research which stimulated a great deal more research in both Germany and America. In 1920 Wertheimer had published a paper on productive thinking, and then in 1925 this paper and two others were printed as a book, with the title *Drei Abhandlungen zur Gestalttheorie*. In 1924 Koffka came to America, visiting at Cornell and Wisconsin and then in 1927 being appointed to a chair at Smith College, where he remained until his death in 1941. Köhler visited Clark and Harvard Universities in 1925-1926. In 1929 he wrote and published in English his *Gestalt Psychology*, the most thorough argument for the new point of view that had yet been made. It was the centennial year of James Mill's *Analysis of the Human Mind* and high time for an antidote, but it is doubtful if Köhler gave that great associationist a thought.

In 1933 Wertheimer escaped the Hitler menace and found asylum in New York in the New School for Social Research. In 1934 Köhler came to Harvard as William James Lecturer. In 1935 he accepted the appointment at Swarthmore. In the same year Koffka published his *Principles of Gestalt Psychology*, the difficult and erudite book already mentioned, the one which psychologists have studied and used for reference without accepting its systematic views. In 1938 Köhler published his William James Lectures as *The Place of Value in a World of Facts*, a book that made the case for the inclusion of meaning in psychology somewhat more effectively than Koffka's treatise had done. Köhler stressed the importance of psychologists' studying dynamic fields in his *Dynamics in Psychology* in 1940. Then Koffka died in 1941, and Wertheimer in 1943. Wertheimer's long promised volume on productive thinking was published posthumously in 1945. Köhler, with Hans Wallach, published *Figural After-Effects* in 1944, an experimental study which went far toward supporting Köhler's views of the relation between the field of perception and the concomitant brain field.

There have been, of course, other Gestalt psychologists than the principal three. In Germany there was Erich von Hornbostel (1877-1936), with a doctorate from Berlin in 1900. He cooperated with Wertheimer during the First World War on research on sonic submarine detection and they published together on sound localization in 1920. He was the chief proponent of the unity of the senses (1925), the belief that certain attributes like volume and brightness apply alike to all the senses. His special interest was the psychology of music and he took over responsibility for Stumpf's Phonogram Archiv, which collected phonographic records of primitive music. He died in England in 1936. There was also Wolfgang Metzger (1899-   ) with a Berlin Ph.D. of 1926. He was with Wertheimer at Frankfurt and succeeded him there in 1933. He is best known to many for his little book on visual perception (1936). There was Karl Duncker (1903-1940) who, after a year in America at Clark University, went back to Berlin for a Ph.D. in 1929, stayed on and then came to Swarthmore College in 1938, dying there in 1940. He wrote *Zur Psychologie des produktiven Denkens* in 1935 and it was translated into English in 1945. There are other persons, but lists of names without specification are the bane of historical texts. Kurt Lewin is often counted as a Gestalt psychologist, but he was primarily a dynamic psychologist although his system was founded upon the principles of Gestalt psychology (pp. 723-728).

In America R. M. Ogden, a Ph.D. of Külpe's at Würzburg in 1903 and for many years at Cornell, was one of the early men to welcome Gestalt psychology. It was he who got Koffka to write the *Perception* article in 1922. R. H. Wheeler, long at Kansas, followed Gestalt lines with vigorous argument, urging the organismic view of psychology upon his followers. He is perhaps known best by his *The Science of Psychology* of 1929. There was also for many years at Kansas J. F. Brown, a Yale Ph.D. but with two Berlin years in his history, known best to experimentalists for his work on the perceptions of velocity and movement.

Schools can fail, but they can also die of success. Sometimes success leads to later failure. The 'new' psychology of the 1890s was a rousing success, but it died in the 1910s because it could not get ahead and because there was something better with which to replace it. Functional psychology succeeded in America and died of that success by being absorbed into behaviorism. Gestalt psychology has been successful. Its old enemies of the Wundt-Titchener line are gone. Introspection in the sense of analysis of consciousness into sensory elements is no longer practised. The movement has produced much new important research, but it is no longer profitable to label it as Gestalt psychology. Had Gestalt psychology resisted the inclusion of behavioral data in psychology, there might have been a long war over the question of whether psychology is or is not principally the study of direct experience. As it was, Köhler's chimpanzees were admitted as data from the start. The result is that Gestalt psychology has already passed its peak and is now dying of its success by being absorbed into what is Psychology. If it seems already a little Americanized as compared with what it was in Berlin and Frankfurt, why that is only what should happen to the emigré who has to fit his basic values into a new culture.

ANTECEDENTS OF GESTALT PSYCHOLOGY

Gestalt psychology forms no exception to the general rule about scientific progress. It has its antecedents and it will in turn have proper consequences. Thus it has its place in the course of scientific development. From the broader perspective, scientific advance nearly always seems to be continuous, so Wertheimer's insight of 1910 appears merely as the sort of event which was required by the times. Had Wertheimer gone on in 1901 to practise law in Prague, presumably someone else would have been the person to push forward those conclusions about wholes and emergents and meanings which others—James, Ehrenfels, Külpe—had already made the objects of their separate propagandas.

Scientific activity must be thought of as occurring in a dynamic field. Science, in Wertheimer's phrase, is not an *Und-Verbindung.*

Analysis distorts the whole, yet some analysis is necessary for description. We may therefore conveniently distinguish three phases of the developing thought which led up within psychology to Gestalt psychology. Since each of these three trends developed most rapidly when it was being favored as a substitute for its opposite, we need to find and tabulate the phrases which characterize them. Here is the table of paired opposites. We put what led up to Gestalt psychology at the left and its antithesis at the right. The activities and conceptions at the right are the ones against which Gestalt psychology protested.

1. Phenomenological description *vs.* Analysis into elements
2. Emergence of form in wholes *vs.* Associative congeries
3. Meanings and objects   *vs.* Sensory contents

1. *Phenomenology.* In the preface to his William James Lectures Köhler remarked: "Never, I believe, shall we be able to solve any problems of ultimate principle until we go back to the sources of our concepts,—in other words, until we use the phenomenological method, the qualitative analysis of experience." He went on to note that the method had not received general acceptance and he spoke of its opponents as those who "prefer to deal with concepts which have acquired a certain polish in the history of scientific thought and . . . think little of the topics to which these concepts can not be directly applied." This was his plea for phenomenology as free description of immediate experience, without analysis into formal elements.

Certainly description comes first in science, and investigation, oriented by specific hypotheses, later. Certainly also freedom precedes constraint. So anatomy precedes physiology, and science starts with observation. When any phase of science is getting under way, good observation is indispensable, whereas good speculation can wait. Now, Aristotle was a good observer, and so was Archimedes, but the Scholastics were not; they speculated without accumulating facts. Leonardo was a splendid observer. Galileo was both a good observer and a good hypothesizer, as were Kepler and Newton. Linnaeus was chiefly a good observer and classifier, not an hypothesizer. He could be said to be a good phenomenologist. Phenomenology comes early in a science, as we have already noted (pp. 18-21).

Goethe was certainly a phenomenologist and in a way he stands at the head of the tradition in psychology (pp. 20, 99). His many observations of color phenomena were considered good at the time and his one large hypothesis about color was bad, being motivated mainly by his animus against Newton. Everyone accepts Purkinje as the example of the keen observer in the physiology of the 1820s (pp. 20 f., 98). As a matter of fact, the whole activity of the sense-physiologists before Helmholtz was principally phenomenological. Johannes Müller's first book of 1826 dealt with phenomenology of vision, even if it did also include the first statement of his theory of specific nerve energies (p. 98). Much of Fechner's *Psychophysik* (1860) was phenomenology (p. 281). His observations on memory colors (now called by Gestalt psychology *color constancy*) were phenomenological, as was his observation that receding objects do not shrink in size as rapidly as do their retinal images (now called *size constancy*). Hering took up the tradition of Goethe and Purkinje. He was the most influential phenomenologist of the period 1870-1900 (pp. 352-356). The Gestalt psychologists felt his influence and recognized its importance. Hering, like Fechner, described the phenomena of both 'color constancy' and 'size constancy.' There was much more freedom to describe fact then than those who remember only the Wundtian constraints realize.

In general the phenomenologist seeks to find an *experimentum crucis*, the convincing single demonstration of some observed generality. Purkinje's watching the colors change at dawn is such an instance. Since phenomenology deals with immediate experience, its conclusions are instantaneous. They emerge at once and need not wait upon the results of calculations derived from measurements. Nor does a phenomenologist use statistics, since a frequency does not occur at a given instant and can not be immediately observed. For these reasons many of Hering's elaborate pieces of apparatus for the study of color are more appropriately used for demonstration than for experimentation. Hering already knew the facts and he built the apparatus to convince others. In the same way one finds in the writings of the modern Gestalt psychologists many neat demonstrational diagrams printed on the page, *experimenta crucis* designed to make a phenomenologist of the reader, letting him have at once the immediate experience which constitutes the evidence.

It is tempting to suggest that phenomenology is more at home in Austria and Southern Germany than in Northern Germany and Prussia. We associate Vienna, Prague, Graz and even Munich with the freedom from scientific rigidity that is proper to phenomenology and act psychology and look to Berlin for the rigors of experimentalism. Unfortunately for this simple geo-epistemology the exceptions are serious. According to it, Wundt should have gone to Berlin with Helmholtz, Stumpf should have stayed at Munich or have gone to Prague instead of moving to Berlin, and Köhler should have been sent to Vienna to continue the Machian tradition—although there was certainly nothing soft and *gemütlich* about his *Physische Gestalten* of 1920.

Another question that arises is the relation of phenomenology to nativism. During the last forty years of the nineteenth century there raged a persistent controversy about space perception. The nativists said that perceived spatial relations are given immediately in experience. The empiricists said that the pattern of space has to be learned. Kant lent authority to the nativists. Lotze's theory of local signs and his beliefs about the organization of space in experience provided the basis of empiricism. Helmholtz and Wundt were empiricists. Hering and Stumpf were nativists. It seems to us quite clear that phenomenology is nativistic, that it is looking for givens and is not puzzling as to how perceptions are generated. Certainly the modern Gestalt psychologists have opposed Helmholtz's empiricism of space perception. They hold, for instance, that a line is an immediately perceived extension, not a perceived series of points. It thus seems fair to say that nativism was part of the preparation for Gestalt psychology, and it also seems fair to recall Lotze's comment that nativism, being the absence of a theory, explains nothing. That statement of Lotze's is, after all, consistent with the notion that psychology as a young science is not yet ready for many theories—which is, in a sense, the import of Köhler's comment quoted above.

The term phenomenology, as we have already seen, came into psychology because Husserl in 1901 drew attention to it (pp. 367 f., 408). When Stumpf in 1907 decided that psychology is a science of psychical functions and not of contents, he assigned the body of the psychology of content to phenomenology (p. 368). It was also true that Mach in regarding space as sensation in 1886 (p. 395) and Külpe in adding extensity to the list of sensory attributes in 1893 were taking the phenomenological position in accepting experiential givens—in spite of the contrary orthodoxy. That position has been called *positivism*, but the early positivism of Mach and Külpe was consistent with phenomenology and with Gestalt psychology as the later positivism of Schlick, Carnap and the logical positivists was not. One hears the Gestalt psychologists complaining about the modern positivism, but Mach was their ancestor, of whom they should be proud. If direct experience is the positive ultimate, then even Wertheimer is a positivist—like Mach.

That phenomenology was in the air and bound more and more to prescribe the mode for describing experience is shown by the publication from G. E. Müller's laboratory at Göttingen of certain monographs by Jaensch, Katz and Rubin in 1909-1915. Both Jaensch and Katz in these publications were anticipating Wertheimer's 'founding' of Gestalt psychology in 1912.

Erich R. Jaensch (1883-1940) took his doctorate with Müller in 1908 on a thesis published the next year under the title *Zur Analyse der Gesichtswahrnehmungen.* It dealt largely with complex problems of the way in which visual acuity varies for near and far vision, and as such it was both phenomenological and concerned with the total dynamic visual system. Helmholtz had supposed that visual acuity depends only on the separation of the receptor organs in the retina but Hering then and Jaensch now showed that larger interacting systems have to be taken into account. In 1911 Jaensch put out another monograph in which he dealt with the visual perception of depth. In it he discussed the phenomenology—he used that word—of empty space and the nature of its psychic representation, and he described situations in which perceived size varies independently of the size of the retinal image. He was laying the ground for what the Gestalt psychologists would presently be talking about. Jaensch is, of course, best known for his study of eidetic imagery, another topic which fits better with the phenomenological approach than did the more orthodox views of his teacher, G. E. Müller.

David Katz (1884-   ) took his degree with Müller in 1906. He published a paper on memory colors (*Gedächtnisfarben*) in 1907, but his important monograph on color, *Die Erscheinungsweisen der Farben,* came out in 1911. This is indeed a phenomenological study if ever there was one. Katz showed that the problems of color and space are interrelated and can not be separated. Orthodox psychology had assumed that the properties of monocular perception are limited by the properties of the retina, that all you can perceive with one eye is a bidimensional field, differentiated as finely as the separation of your retinal cones permits, with perceived shape and size remaining constant functions of your retinal pattern of excitation. But a phenomenologist, since he describes experience in its own right, can ignore the retina, and Katz did. He discovered that there are three kinds of colors: (a) surface colors, which are bidimensional, localized at a given distance and usually the colors of perceived objects; (b) volumic colors, which are the tridimensional colors of transparent media, like colored liquids, colored air or the appearance of lightless space; and (c) film colors, which are primary and without localization or precise spatial characteristics, like the color in a spectroscope. The surface colors are object colors and tend to maintain their color in changing illumination. A surface color is, however, reduced to a film color if it is viewed through a reduction screen, which is a screen with a small hole in it. The screen eliminates the clues to the third dimension and the color loses its objectivity, its distance and its tendency to remain constant under shifting illumination. Here we have the conception that the perception of color is extremely complex, but that you can reduce the complicated field of operating forces to the simpler situation of the film color if you eliminate certain factors that determine the total perception.

Katz stayed at Göttingen with Müller until 1919, when he went to Rostock and later to Stockholm. He published a phenomenological study of touch in 1925 and has always been counted as an ally of Gestalt psychology and an important contributor to its fund of facts, the facts that would not have been discovered if psychologists had stuck to the theory of sensory elements and their attributes. Müller himself was not friendly to Gestalt psychology and criticized it severely in 1923, but he seems to have shown great tolerance to the views of the younger men in his laboratory. Perhaps he had mellowed since his "peculiarly hideous" and "brutal" (James' words) trouncing of the youthful Münsterberg in 1891.

The third Göttingen phenomenologist was *Edgar Rubin* (1886-   ), who began his researches on the figure-ground phenomena of visual perception early in 1912, some months before Wertheimer's paper on movement appeared. Rubin found that a visual perception is normally divided into two parts, figure and ground. Usually the figure is at the focus of attention, is an object, is seen surrounded by a contour and has object character, which is to say that it looks like a thing or an object and is seen as a whole. The rest of the field is the ground, which lacks detail, is apt to be in the margin of attention, and is usually seen as further away than the figure. The ground does not appear to be an object.

All this phenomenological difference becomes of especial interest in the ambiguous figure-ground demonstrations, like the well-known goblet-profiles or the black claw and three white fingers of Figure 4. In that figure you see either the black claw in front of a white ground, or else you see the white fingers in front of a

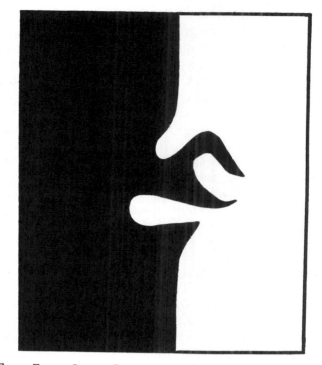

FIG. 4. FIGURE-GROUND PHENOMENON: RUBIN'S CLAW AND FINGERS

Ambiguous stimulus-object for figure-ground perception shows either the figure of the black claw on a white ground or the figure of the three white fingers on the black ground. From E. Rubin, 1915.

black ground. In shifting perception from one object to the other, you can see object character come and go and thus learn what it is. If, once shown this ambiguous pattern, you have seen the claw, then, when the picture is presented again, you are likely to see the claw again and to recognize it; but, if by chance you see the white fingers on the second presentation, then you will not recognize them, because fingers are not a claw and the perceived object is different even though the stimulus-object be the same. Here, indeed, we have a phenomenon that forces us into a consideration of dynamic totalities, a phenomenal change which is independent of retinal change and is induced by central factors. Rubin's work was good material for Gestalt psychology, and the men of that school quite properly hastened to appropriate it.

Rubin, a Dane, went back from Göttingen to Copenhagen, where he still is—Denmark's most distinguished psychologist. He published these Göttingen results in Danish in 1915, and in German in 1921.

By this time, however, the new Gestalt psychology had got itself well established and it was no longer possible for anyone to be an anticipator of it.

2. *Emergence.* In 1923 Wertheimer wrote: "I stand at the window and I see a house, trees, sky. I could now on theoretical grounds try to count them and could say: There are... 327 brightnesses (and hues). (Do I have '327'? No: sky, house, trees. The having of the '327' as such no man can realize.) And if there were in this odd reckoning perchance 120 for the house and 90 for the trees and 117 for the sky, nevertheless I would have *this* combination, this apportionment, and not, say, 127 and 100 and 100, or 150 and 177." Such an artificial enumeration of elements Wertheimer called a *sinnlose Und-Verbindung.* The constitution of a perception by the mere accumulation of elements in a congeries is what he named the *bundle hypothesis.* Gestalt psychology was, of course, a protest against such a mere addition of parts to parts. The whole is almost certain to be more than a collection of its parts. It is not a bundle, and its integration is more than an *Und.*

This fact of emergence of new properties in wholes is fairly obvious. Why, we may ask, did it have to be stressed and supported by so much controversial argument? There are perhaps two reasons. (a) In the first place, it is true that psychology's chemical analogy had turned out to be persuasive. All the things and substances in the universe had apparently been reduced to nothing more than the variety of combinations of less than a hundred elements. If the material world works in that way, Wundt and the others could ask, why not the psychical? At least the conception seemed worth a trial. The chemical analogy is, nevertheless, inadequate by itself, for the chemists never got rid of the fact of emergence. Their knowledge had not advanced to the stage where the properties of a compound could be predicted from the properties of its elements.

(b) The other and an essential reason was that association, the principle of psychological compounding, seemed actually to achieve the paradox of making a pair of elements unique without adding any *tertium quid.* Take recognition. There is (a) a sensory experience (of a face, perhaps) and that in itself is nothing but itself. When there is added to it by association (β) some additional conscious material (the imagery of a name, say), then ($a + \beta$) becomes a recognition which neither alone could be. At first this connection seems nothing more than an *Und-Verbindung.* That, surely, is what Bishop Berkeley thought (pp. 184-186). And that must be, too, what Titchener thought when, with his context theory of perception in mind, he said that it takes at least two sensations to make a meaning (pp. 415 f.). Deaf blind little Helen Keller in the garden, suddenly realizing that everything has a name, running around to touch an object and then to hold out her hand to have the verbal context spelled into it. Meaning by association can make some sense. Jacques Loeb said that associative memory could be taken as evidence of consciousness in animals, and that made a kind of sense too. The point is that two items in relation are already a whole that is more than the sum of the two, for they are in relation. So a conditioned response, as John Dewey said of the reflex in 1896, is more than an impinging change of energy followed by movement; it is a response *to* a stimulus. In other words, even Titchener's two sensations making a meaning showed emergence, the emergence of the meaning in the relation of the two. That emergence was, however, not easy to see. Association looked like mere addition without integration, and psychologists liked this simplicity. Nevertheless, it is doubtful if any great psychologist since James Mill (see pp. 225 f.) ever spoke as if a perception could be understood by listing 327 sensations. John Stuart Mill saw 'mental chemistry' for just what it is, the science of the emergence of new properties in compounds in which the parts actually have disappeared (pp. 229 f.). Wundt's discussion was contradictory. He talked about elements and their combination as if he were expounding a straight mental chemistry and then argued about creative synthesis, seeming to believe that it is by emergence that the *psychische Verbindungen* get their special characteristics (pp. 333-336). William James has been claimed by several writers as a chief anticipator of Gestalt psychology, and certainly James, with his vigorous rejection of mental elements and his description of the nature of the stream of consciousness, would have hailed the new Gestalt movement as a fresh breeze for driving out the stale atmosphere of Leipzig (pp. 512-515). James, of course, never knew Wertheimer. He died in the summer of 1910 at Chocorua, New Hampshire, not so very many days after Wertheimer had reached Frankfurt-am-Main in search of a toy stroboscope.

If more proof were needed that the associationism of the dominant German psychology of the late nineteenth century did not sufficiently recognize the importance of creative synthesis, that proof would lie in the formation of the school of form-quality (pp. 441-447). At first the Gestalt psychologists did not realize what a respectable and competent ancestor they had in von Ehrenfels, but presently they discovered him, and when he died in 1933 the *Psychologische Forschung* printed a brief but fitting recognition of his rôle. When we want illustrations of emergence, we now go back to Ehrenfels—to his geometrical figures and his melodies. Meinong, in general the more important philosopher, reinforced Ehrenfels and noted how relations, added to the 'founding contents,' become something new in the 'founded contents.' There is no need to rehearse here the contribution of this school: it made the protest and the argument about emergence that Gestalt psychology made again two decades later.

3. *Meanings and Objects*. What Gestalt psychology did was to set itself against what was the current trend for admitting only sensory contents as the proper psychological data of experience. It was in a way arguing for a return to Locke. The ideas which Locke thought could enter into association were such things as are expressed by the words "whiteness, motion, man, elephant, army." Even Berkeley was not much more limited in his conception of the mental unit, yet English empiricism had in it the germs of sensationism. The argument ran: in so far as experience, which makes up mind, is derived from the senses, the mind must be composed of sensations—associated sensations.

The further genetic course of empiricistic sensationism is plain. Hume's impressions and ideas (p. 188). Hartley's associated sensations and ideas, corresponding respectively to associated vibrations and vibratiuncles (pp. 196 f.). Condillac's paradigm of the statue which starts out in experience with but a single sense (p. 210). Reid and the problem of how sensations, which are immediately given, come to mean objects, which they are not (p. 206). Thomas Brown and his sensations of movement which, added to the other sensations, provide for the perception of space (p. 208). James Mill, writing when the physiology of sensation was advancing rapidly and listing first all the available kinds of sensation on which to build his associative structure (p. 222). Associationism reinforcing the notion that the basic elements are sensory (pp. 223 f.). Wundt taking over this view, listing the psychic elements and dealing with their combinations (p. 329). Wundt was sure of the sensations. Through the years he wavered about feelings: were they attributes or elements? And he ended in his tridimensional theory with a multitude of feelings that were so uncertainly specified as to raise the suspicion that they were functioning as meanings. Titchener was uncertain as to whether there were three kinds of elements—sensations, images and feelings—or whether all were sensory. In the end he came to the conclusion that introspection yields only sensory content, and that everything else which appears to be in consciousness is inferred, a meaning ((p. 417 f.). Titchener's view was essentially that sensations are immediately given and that the nature of objects is inferred from them. Hence, to report on the stimulus itself is to report on an inference and to be giving interpretations (*Kundgabe*) instead of sticking to straight scientific description (*Beschreibung*). To report on the stimulus itself is to make what he called the *stimulus-error*, but the Gestalt psychologists held that objects are given as such in experience, that they are the immediate observable data and that it is the sensory analysis of them which is inferred. (*Cf.* the quotation from Köhler, p. 601.)

In brief, then, it appears that orthodoxy had been led astray along the straight and narrow path of sensory analysis. It is the wide gate and the broad way of phenomenology that lead to life, yet the Gestalt psychologists were not the first to make this discovery. In a sense every phenomenologist knew that you had to describe experience by describing experienced objects and that you could not do justice to it by limiting description to an account of sensation. The act psychologists from Brentano (pp. 360 f.) to James Ward (pp. 463 f.) were against sensationalism, and Ward especially was for including the presentation of objects in psychology. William James, as we know, had no patience with Wundt's narrow definition of psychology and held that awarenesses of objects is what you find in consciousness (pp. 512-516). Titchener is said even to have ruled James out of psychology, on the ground that James was dealing with the knowledge of objects and therefore with epistemology. At any rate, Titchener ignored James when he was writing about functional psychology and presumably on this ground.

The outstanding anticipation of Gestalt psychology on this matter of the inclusion of experienced objects and meanings among the data of psychology occurred, of course, in the work of Külpe's Würzburg school, the school of imageless thought, as it was called, and thus also of sensationless contents (pp. 402-407). The *unanschauliche Bewusstheiten* of Ach, those impalpable awarenesses, were impalpable because they were not sensory. They were immediate enough, although Külpe did hold later that they had to be described in retrospection, whereas sensory content would stand up to immediate inspection. Nor is it impossible that Wertheimer, taking his doctorate with Külpe at Würzburg in 1904, the year of Watt's paper and the year before Ach's, got his faith in the power of free description formed or at least strengthened there, and that Gestalt psychology thus owes something to Külpe. In 1909 Titchener developed his context theory of meaning as a reply to Würzburg and an attempt to force a return from impalpable to palpable contents, for the context theory attempts to reduce a meaning to a relation between sensations (pp. 415 f.). Certainly the context theory was not wrong and it had, moreover, certain important consequences which are related to the unconscious nature of thinking and its dependence on attitude, but Titchener did not prevail in luring Külpe and his associates back to sensationism. Instead, Wertheimer and the Gestalt psychologists took over from Külpe and carried on.

It would be neither wise nor feasible to attempt in this book a précis of the enormous literature which has resulted from Gestalt psychology's four decades. Such essays belong in the handbooks and in the histories of special psychological topics. On the other hand, it seems unfair to leave Gestalt psychology here as the advocate of wholes, meanings and objectified phenomena and of but little more, for there is a great deal more. We may undertake, therefore, to mention some of the basic principles which Gestalt psychology had advocated or demonstrated, especially those principles that belong in experimental psychology. In this undertaking we see at once why it is that a history of experimental psychology can not avoid the history of psychological systems. The difference between what was done in the Leipzig laboratory in the 1880s and in the Berlin laboratory in the 1920s depended on the difference in the investigators' motivations, and each of those motivations was part of the enthusiasm of an in-group fighting for recognition of its new view of the truth.

1. *Laws of Form.* As long ago as 1933, one encyclopedist was able to find 114 laws of Gestalten. Most of them applied especially to visual form. They can all, however, be reduced to about a dozen basic principles. Let us see what they are like without attempting to make the list complete.

(a) A perceptual field tends to become organized, taking on form. Parts become connected and groups of parts unite to form *structures. Organization* is inevitable and natural where an *organism* is concerned. That organisms organize is psychology's great tautology. (b) One of the fundamental principles of this organization is the structuring of a perceptual field into *figure and ground.* The figure is set upon the ground and in visual perception it has *contour*. (c) A structure may be simple or complex, and the degree of complexity is the degree of *articulation*. (d) A *good form* is a well articulated one. It tends to impress itself on the observer, to persist, to recur. A circle is a good form. (e) A *strong form* coheres and resists disintegration by attentional analysis or by fusion with another form. When there is conflict, the stronger form absorbs the weaker. (f) A *closed form* is strong and good, whereas an *open form* tends to achieve *closure* by completing itself as a natural good form and thus gaining stability. (g) Organizations are naturally *stable*. Once formed they tend to persist or to recur when the original situation recurs, and the recurrence of a part tends to reinstate the whole. (h) In completing themselves, forms tend toward *symmetry*, balance and proportion. (i) *Adjacent* units and units of *similar* size, shape and color tend to combine into better articulated wholes. (j) Organization tends to form structured wholes that are *objects*. Organized forms are therefore *meaningful*. (k) An articulated form which is an object tends to preserve its proper shape, size and color in spite of change in the stimulus-situation. This stability is called *object constancy*. (l) Organization, form and therefore object character usually depend on the *relations* between parts and not on the particular characteristics of the parts. It follows that, if the parts change and the relations remain the same, the form or object remains the same, as in the transposed melody. This fact of persistence of form with *transposition* is a basic principle of *relativity* which underlies all perception and discrimination.

Now that is, all in all, a new chapter in psychology. Not all the items in it are new. Some of the principles have long been realized in common sense. Some are based on facts that were established in old experiments or were the bases of old experiments. But the whole chapter is a new structure which is more than the sum of its parts. It is a chapter which describes the organization of the items of experience into perceived objects and the structuring of those objects into larger systems with no reference whatsoever to 'sensations' or their 'attributes.'

2. *Relativity and Transposition*. The Wundtians could talk about observing sensations, but whenever they made any accurate observations, whenever they measured sensation, they were found to be observing relations and not the sensations related. The psychophysical experiment uses discrimination as its observational base. You compare a variable with a standard. Even in determining an

absolute threshold you are discriminating a bare something from a certain nothing. The absolute threshold for the light sensation is the illumination of the spot which is just as often as not distinguishable from the blackness of the ground as it is seen by the light-adapted eye. Thus psychophysics observes only relations, and Wundt, recognizing this fact, suggested that the principle of Weber's law might lie between the sensation itself and the judgment of it, with sensations proportional in magnitude to their stimuli but with judgment following a law of relativity. So it appears that everyone recognized that fact of relativity but did not recognize the consequence that, when relations are being observed, transposition is possible. They were surprised to have the Gestalt psychologists showing that an animal, having learned to choose the larger or brighter of two objects, would continue to choose the larger or the brighter even when the objects were changed in such a way that he now rejected what before he had preferred. To learn to prefer a six-inch circle to a four-inch one is to have learned to prefer a nine-inch to a six-inch, if what you have really learned is to take the bigger. Learning to accept an object in one relation is learning to reject it in another, because acceptance or rejection depends not on the object but on the relation.

There has been a similar failure to draw the most general conclusion from the special case of the transposability of melodies. Everyone knows about melody and accepts readily the fact of its transposability, but only a few realize that the same kind of relativity holds for brightnesses. The white-gray-black photograph looks the same in bright light as in shadow, although the change of illumination effects a transposition of brightness. As a matter of fact, the simpler cases of object constancy are nothing more than instances of this principle of relativity. The object stays the same because it is defined by its relations which do not change.

This principle, then, is old, but that is not to say that Gestalt psychology did not find a new importance for it and fit it into a key position in the new structure.

3. *Object Constancy*. Perceived objects tend to remain constant in size when their distance from the observer and thus the size of their retinal images varies. They tend to remain constant in shape when the angle from which they are regarded and thus the shape of their retinal images varies. They tend to remain constant in brightness when the intensity of illumination varies, and in hue when the color composition of illumination varies. Constancy holds up pretty well with changing conditions if the observer has in-

formation about the changing conditions, but, when his ability to judge the total situation is reduced (by a reduction screen or other devices), then the constancy is reduced. We may not enter here into the details of fact or the theories about them or the history of this kind of knowledge, which has all been set down elsewhere. The truth is that the constancy phenomena, like transposability, have been known for a long time, but the recognition of their full significance is new. Color constancy was known to Hering as *Gedächtnisfarbe*, and Katz, as we have just seen, experimented with brightness constancy.

That perceived size changes less rapidly than the size of the retinal image when the distance of the perceived object varies was known to the natural philosopher Bouguer before he died in 1758, to the chemist Priestley in 1772, to the physicist-physiologist H. Meyer in 1842, to the physiologist Ludwig in 1852, to Panum in 1859, to Fechner himself in 1860, to Hering himself in 1861, to Emmert who showed in 1881 that the apparent size of an after-image varies directly with the distance of the ground on which it is projected, to Wundt's student Martius who measured the phenomenon in 1889, to Hering's student Hillebrand who measured it in 1902, to Poppelreuter at Berlin in 1911, to Blumenfeld also at Berlin in 1913, and then to Köhler who demonstrated it with the apes in 1915. After that there were Götz's experiments with chickens in 1926, Beyrl's with children in 1926, Thouless' in England in 1932, Holaday's with Brunswik in Vienna in 1933, and many others. By studying these researches you see the continuity of science; yet, when you stand away to get the perspective, then you see that the new systematic setting of Gestalt psychology gave the facts a significance that they had not had before.

4. *Field Dynamics*. We have already seen that Gestalt psychology's concern with wholes leads its disciples to the use of *field theory* (p. 591). The organization of the items of experience into articulated forms can sometimes be understood if the materials are regarded as being shaped by interacting field forces or by a field of force which acts in a manner analogous to a magnetic or electrical field's action. Köhler and Wallach's study of figural after-effects (1944) details many such instances.

The constant use of the word *dynamics* by Köhler and his associates calls for special comment. Apparently for Köhler any field is dynamic, even a field of static forces which act to maintain an equilibrium. He is not thinking of mechanics as divided into statics and dynamics, nor of hydraulics as divided into hydrostatics and hydrodynamics. Rather he is opposing the free dynamics of fields with many degrees of freedom to the constrained kinematics of machines with few degrees of freedom. Köhler's *"physische Gestalten"* of 1920 were dynamic even though they were *"in Ruhe und im stationären Zustand."* The word dynamics does indeed have the advantage of not sounding mentalistic, of freeing the organizing principle of perception from such concepts as inference, unconscious inference, association, context, purpose, attitude. It also supports the theory of isomorphism, which holds that the dynamics of the perception matches the dynamics of the brain.

5. *Isomorphism.* There is nothing inherent in Gestalt psychology that requires any particular mind-body theory; yet the three principal Gestalt psychologists have all supported isomorphism—the theory that the perceptual field corresponds with the underlying excitatory brain field in its relations of order, although not necessarily in exact form. The correspondence is topological but not topographical. Adjacent spots in one system match adjacent spots in the other, but a shape in one may be greatly distorted in the other.

Wertheimer put forward this view in 1912 when he suggested that seen movement for the discrete displacement of stimulation may be due to a short-circuit in the brain between the two excited positions. Koffka supported the view in his systematic text (1935), and Köhler has organized his research about it. Thus the theory has become definitely associated with Gestalt psychology. In some ways it seems inconsistent with the Gestalt thesis and aspiration, because it implies, at least at the superficial epistemological level, a dualism of experience and neural excitation, two systems which can be correlated and be shown to correspond point for point, but which are, nevertheless, two different dynamic wholes, two Gestalten with no psychic or physical forces to integrate them into a single unity. It may, however, be unfair to classify Köhler as a dualist. There are other views of the mind-body relation which might fit his field dynamics better.

Since we must return to the consideration of isomorphism in connection with our examination of the history of brain function (pp. 678-680), we may leave it and Gestalt psychology here, turning to the contemporaneous American movement, behaviorism.

NOTES

Gestalt Psychologists

Reversing the of der of the text, we may note certain publications of the principal Gestalt psychologists first, turning later to what was written about Gestalt psychology. Here are the references cited directly or by implication in the text.

MAX WERTHEIMER:

Ueber das Denken des Naturvölker, *Zsch. Psychol.*, 1912, 60, 321-378, showing the author's early interest in the problem of thought. Excerpts in Eng. trans. are given by W. D. Ellis, *A Source Book of Gestalt Psychology*, 1938, 265-273.

Experimentelle Studien über das Sehen von Bewegungen, *ibid.*, 1912, 61, 161-265, the famous paper which started the movement.

Ueber Schlussprozesse im produktiven Denken, 1920, a little book. Ellis, *op. cit.*, 274-282, gives excerpts in Eng. trans.

Untersuchungen zur Lehre von der Gestalt, *Psychol. Forsch.*, 1921, 1, 47-58; 1923, 4, 301-350, the first draft of the constitution for Gestalt psychology. Koffka drew heavily upon the 1921 paper in his exposition for Americans in 1922. Ellis, *op. cit.*, 12-16, 71-88, gives excerpts from both articles in Eng. trans.

Drei Abhandlungen zur Gestalttheorie, 1925, a separately paged reprint of the first three items of this list.

Productive Thinking, 1945, a posthumously published book, going back to the author's original interest but presenting new and original ideas.

WOLFGANG KÖHLER:

Akustische Untersuchungen, *Zsch. Psychol.*, 1909, 54, 241-289; 1910, 58, 59-140; 1913, 64, 92-105; 1915, 72, 1-192; pre-Gestalt psychophysical studies of tones and their characteristics.

Ueber unbemerkte Empfindungen und Urteilstäuschungen, *ibid.*, 1913, 66, 51-80, an inquiry into the funda-mental principles of the physiological basis for perceptual experience, an argument against the assumption that stimulus configuration and perceived configuration correspond closely, a forerunner of the doctrine of isomorphism.

Die Farbe der Sehdinge beim Schimpansen und beim Haushuhn, *ibid.*, 1917, 77, 248-255, the law of transposition for color perception in animals. Excerpts from a similar article on the same subject are given in Eng. trans. by Ellis, *op. cit.*, 217-227.

Intelligenzprüfung an Menschenaffen, 1917; 2 ed., 1921; Eng. trans., 1925; the classic study of intelligence in apes and the establishment of the concept of insight. Excerpts from the 2 ed., Eng. trans., have been reprinted by W. Dennis, *Readings in the History of Psychology*, 1948, 497-505.

Die physischen Gestalten in Ruhe und im stationären Zustand, 1920, the application of physical systems to neural fields and thus to psychological events, the book that brought proper scholarly recognition to its author, but more often mentioned than read. Ellis, *op. cit.*, 17-55, has printed in Eng. trans. excerpts from this volume, and Dennis, *op. cit.*, 513-527, has excerpted Ellis' excerpts.

Zur Theorie des Sukzessivvergleichs und der Zeitfehler, *Psychol. Forsch.*, 1923, 4, 115-175, the paper that started all the work on the time-error.

Gestalt Psychology, 1929; 2 ed., 1947; the most important general exposition of the movement.

The Place of Value in a World of Facts, 1938, the William James Lectures of 1934 and the argument for the inclusion of meanings among the givens of experience.

Dynamics in Psychology, 1940, field theory in perception and memory.

Figural after-effects (with H. Wallach), *Proc. Amer. Philos. Soc.*, 1944, 88, 269-357, the researches that develop further the conception of physical fields as applicable in perception and thus the conception of isomorphism.

KURT KOFFKA:

Experimental - Untersuchungen zur Lehre vom Rhythmus, *Zsch. Psychol.*, 1909, 52, 1-109, his doctoral thesis with Stumpf.

Zur Analyse der Vorstellungen und ihrer Gesetze, 1912, a long experimental report which discusses how the course of ideas is dependent upon set and association. It is dedicated to Külpe.

Beiträge zur Psychologie der Gestalt, *Zsch. Psychol.,* 1913, 67, 353-449; 1915, 73, 11-90; 1919, 82, 257-292. These are the first of Koffka's experimental contributions to the new Gestalt psychology. He continued the series, sometimes under his own authorship, sometimes under the name of a student, usually in the *Psychol. Forsch.,* as far as No. 25 in 1932.

Die Grundlagen der psychischen Entwicklung: eine Einführung der Kinderpsychologie, 1921, 2 ed., 1925; Eng. trans., as *The Growth of the Mind,* 1924; 2 ed., 1928; the book which brought educational psychology and the learning process within the scope of Gestalt psychology.

Perception: an introduction to the Gestalt-theorie, *Psychol. Bull.,* 1922, 19, 531-585, the article which introduced Gestalt psychology to America.

Principles of Gestalt Psychology, 1935, the only attempt at a complete systematic Gestalt psychology.

No biographical sketch of Köhler is available. There are, however, accounts of Wertheimer and Koffka: W. Köhler, Max Wertheimer 1880-1943, *Psychol. Rev.,* 1944, 51, 143-146; E. B. Newman, Max Wertheimer 1880-1943, *Amer. J. Psychol.,* 1944, 57, 428-435; W. Köhler, Kurt Koffka 1886-1941, *Psychol. Rev.,* 1942, 49, 97-101; M. R. Harrower-Erickson, Kurt Koffka 1886-1941, *Amer. J. Psychol.,* 1942,

55, 278-281. For bibliographies of the three men up to 1932, see C. Murchison's *Psychological Register,* III, 1932. The bibliography in Koffka's *Principles (op. cit.)* is very full.

Gestalt Psychology

Reference now to the notes on Gestalt psychology in the 1929 edition of this book (pp. 591-593) shows how far the movement has advanced in the second twenty years of its existence (it is forty years since Wertheimer got off the train at Frankfurt in 1910). In 1929 there was confusion about the nature of the new undertaking, its purpose, its name, its novelty, its validity. Now the issue has become clear and the initial attempts of the 1920s to explain the movement or to translate the German for Americans all give place to a number of clear definitive expositions.

If the student wants to know what Gestalt psychology is, let him read in the lists of books given above, especially in Köhler's three books or, if he has patience and tolerance, in Koffka's *Principles.* One gets a broad view of the movement by reading the 34 excerpts by 18 authors in Eng. trans. in W. D. Ellis, *A Source Book of Gestalt Psychology,* 1938. The fullest secondary source and an excellent one is G. W. Hartmann, *Gestalt Psychology,* 1935. Very satisfactory but only in French is P. Guillaume, *La psychologie de la forme,* 1937. Older and limited to the scope of the present chapter is B. Petermann, *The Gestalt Theory and the Problem of Configuration,* 1932. Briefer but good is the account in E. Heidbreder, *Seven Psychologies,* 1933, 328-375. There is a brief recent account in R. S. Woodworth, *Contemporary Schools of Psychology,* 2 ed., 1948, 120-150. G. Murphy, *Historical Introduction to Modern Psychology,* 2 ed., 1949, discusses Gestalt psychology on pp. 284-296 and field theory on pp. 297-306. We have already noted that Dennis, *locc. citt.,* reprints parts of two of Köhler's articles. See also A. J. Levine, *Current Psychologies,* 1940, 77-105; C. R. Griffith, *Principles of Systematic Psychology*, 1943, 206-246.

Antecedents

Most of this section consists in bringing together into a single context various events which the text has already discussed. The text of this chapter includes the necessary cross-references.

The publications which are cited for the Göttingen phenomenologists are as follows:

E. R. Jaensch, *Zur Analyse der Gesichtswahrnehmung: experimentell-psychologische Untersuchungen nebst Anwendung auf die Pathologie des Sehens*, 1909 (*Zsch. Psychol.*, Ergbd. 4); *Ueber die Wahrnehmung des Raumes: eine experimentell-psychologische Untersuchung nebst Anwendung auf Aesthetik und Erkenntnislehre*, 1911 (*Zsch. Psychol.*, Ergbd. 6); *Die Eidetik*, 1925; 2 ed., 1927; Eng. trans., 1930. See also his *Ueber den Aufbau der Wahrnehmungswelt*, 1923, 2 ed., 1927. Jaensch has a huge bibliography which includes many long articles on perception. He was an intense writer, difficult to understand. H. Klüver cites 31 of Jaensch's articles in Studies on the eidetic type and on eidetic imagery, *Psychol. Bull.*, 1928, 25, 69-104.

David Katz, *Die Erscheinungsweisen der Farben und ihre Beeinflussung durch die individuelle Erfahrung*, 1911 (*Zsch. Psychol.*, Ergbd. 7); 2 ed., as *Der Aufbau der Farbwelt*, 1930; Eng. trans., 1935; *Der Aufbau der Tastwelt*, 1925 (*Zsch. Psychol.*, Ergbd. 11).

Edgar Rubin, *Synsoplevede Figurer*, 1915; German trans. as *Visuell wahrgenommene Figuren*, 1921.

For James' comment on G. E. Müller's "hideous" treatment of Münsterberg, see R. B. Perry, *The Thought and Character of William James*, 1935, II, 117 f.

In the 1910s Wundt in Germany was the chief obstacle across the path of the Gestalt psychologists. In the 1920s, with Wundt dead and the attention of the Gestalt psychologists turning to America, Titchener became the chief obstacle. It is well, then, to document here Titchener's position on the perception of objects and the report of meanings. E. B. Titchener first used the term *stimulus-error* in 1905 and cited a paper written by von Kries in 1882, a paper which held that the objectifying attitude is a source of error in observation. For all the references and full discussion, see E. G. Boring, The stimulus-error, *Amer. J. Psychol.*, 1921, 32, 449-471. For Titchener's lucid statement as to why he believed that you can not observe objects directly, see his *Text-Book of Psychology*, 1910, 202 f. For the context theory of meaning, see his *Lectures on the Experimental Psychology of the Thought - Processes*, 1909, 174-184; *Text-Book (op. cit.)*, 364-373. For his contention that psychology must limit itself to description (of sensory content) and not report meanings, see his Description vs. statement of meaning, *Amer. J. Psychol.*, 1912, 23, 165-182; Prolegomena to a study of introspection, *ibid.*, 427-448; The schema of introspection, *ibid.*, 485-508. In this connection it is interesting to examine E. Jacobson's attempt to take down introspective protocols in which all words reporting meanings are put in parentheses and all description of content is left outside of the parentheses: On meaning and understanding, *ibid.*, 1911, 22, 553-577. The material outside the parentheses is inadequate and barren; it is not at all clear that description of consciousness is possible without the use of meanings and objectification. For Titchener's final admission, summing up, as it were, his life experience, that the term *sensory*, after all is said and done, provides the best "material characterisation of psychological phenomena," see his posthumous *Systematic Psychology: Prolegomena*, 1929, 259-266, esp. 264-266, where the reader must be warned that a typographical error has interchanged the headings "Material" and "Formal" in the table.

Basic Principles

For the basic principles and laws, see Köhler's *Gestalt Psychology* and *Place of Value* and Koffka's *Principles of Gestalt Psychology,* cited in the first section of these notes (pp. 616 f.), and all the secondary sources about Gestalt psychology, cited in the second section (p. 617).

H. Helson's list of 114 Gestalt laws is The fundamental propositions of Gestalt psychology, *Psychol, Rev.,* 1933, 40, 13-32, which cites 24 basic references for 18 authors. On the laws of form, see also E. G. Boring, *Sensation and Perception in the History of Experimental Psychology,* 1942, 252-256, 261 f. On field dynamics for Gestalten, see *ibid.,* 246-252, 261, 299-303, 311. On the history of the variation of perceived size with perceived distance (size constancy) and the references to the researches indicated in the text, see *ibid.,* 288-299, 308-311. On isomorphism, see *ibid.,* 83-90, 95 f. On field theory, see also R. S. Woodworth, *Contemporary Schools of Psychology,* 2 ed., 1948, 131-135. Cf. also Lewin's views, p. 726.

CHAPTER 24

Behavioristics

Put in its simplest terms the basic problem about the data of psychology is this: Does psychology deal with the data of consciousness or the data of behavior or both?

The main line of tradition from Locke and Berkeley to Wundt and Titchener, or, for that matter, to Brentano and Külpe, was that psychology studies consciousness, even though you may decide to call it "physiological psychology" and attempt to specify what neural events underlie each conscious phenomenon. There are, however, other data about living organisms, data which nearly always interest the students of consciousness. They are the data of behavior. Descartes, for instance, thought that animal action is unconscious and many others have held to that view since Descartes. Nevertheless animal behavior continues to interest psychologists, for it seems to be intelligent and purposive and thus, even though unconscious, to share at least some of the characteristics of consciousness. There have been a few of these psychologists who, like Descartes, have denied consciousness to animals, and a few others who, like La Mettrie, have argued that the behavior of man is just as automatic as the behavior of animals. There have been many more who have argued that it is unprofitable to study consciousness directly and that better data for the same problems are obtained by limiting research to the study of behavior. This last position has been occupied by the Russian school of Sechenov, Bekhterev and Pavlov, and by the American behaviorists, Watson, Weiss, Holt and the others who came after them. There have been still more persons who have held that psychology must use both kinds of data—consciousness when behavior is inadequate, behavior when consciousness is inadequate, both when both can be used. It seems obvious that neither technic—neither the verbal reports that are introspection upon consciousness nor the observation of nonverbal behavior—is fully adequate alone. You can work out the laws of color vision easily with a human subject who is not color-blind, who uses your own language, who is intelligent and honest. He "describes his consciousness" to you, that is to say, he tells you what he sees. An animal can also tell you what he sees, but you have to build up with him a special language of conditioned responses before he can report to you. You could use that same technic with a man, and often you do use it with children, persons who are mentally ill, uneducated primitives and would-be liars; but in many cases the method is unnecessarily laborious. On the other hand, the motives are known to constitute a field where introspection often fails completely even with normal, educated, intelligent, honest men. Your subject simply can not report accurately on his own motives, and you have to remain ignorant of them or make inferences about them from his controlled behavior—as psychoanalysts and clinical psychologists do. As a practical matter in this age of functional psychology most psychologists use all available technics—introspective, verbal, behavioral—and forget about epistemology. Psychology has, however, only recently come to this stage.

The reason that this matter is less simple than it sounds is that there are relations between consciousness and behavior which make it possible at will, when information is sufficient, to transform the data of consciousness into the data of behavior. Introspection requires verbal report, but verbal report *is* behavior. The consciousness that the subject "has" is what he describes himself as having, and describing is behaving. Any experimenter who knows fully what went on in his introspective experiment can transform the data of consciousness into the data of behavior, a practice that has been called operational reduction, since it substitutes for the purported object of observation the observational operations themselves. Could that piece of logic have come into knowledge a century earlier, it would have saved a great deal of unnecessary talk.

There is no doubt that consciousness is going out of fashion in psychology at present, being replaced by these operational substitutes. The change is slow, however, because it is not inevitable. You can also make the reverse transformation, if you wish, transforming behavior into consciousness or its near equivalent, the unconscious, which is a name for that part of mind which acts like consciousness except that it is not immediately accessible to introspection. When an animal learns to avoid the shock, he is using his new-found language of conditioned response—not purposively, it is true, yet he is using it—to tell you that he does not like the shock, that he knows it is coming, that he knows how to avoid it. His movements are a one-way language. His discriminations are his words.

So much for our introduction. Now we can turn our attention to the history of this effort by psychologists to meet the problem of dualism. We shall begin with animal psychology, both because it is an important part of psychology's history and because the fact that psychologists actually did undertake to observe and describe animal behavior affected the development of human psychology. The observation of behavior became important in its own right and not merely as an indicator of consciousness. After animal psychology we shall consider objective psychology, the older schools who held that consciousness even in man is irrelevant, inaccessible, unimportant or non-existent. After that comes the naïve behaviorism of Watson, and after it the sophisticated behaviorisms of people like Holt and Tolman. Still later comes the *reductio ad actionem* of the operationists and the logical positivists, the men who invented the word *behavioristics* to mean the psychology of a physicalistic monism.

ANIMAL PSYCHOLOGY

As we have already seen (pp. 472-476), animal psychology, or comparative psychology as it has been more often called since Romanes coined the term, began in England. Darwin was the great originator, with his interest in the origin of the human mind; Romanes was his disciple and Lloyd Morgan founded the scientific movement. The self-conscious movement, however, belongs to America. It was there where animal psychology became a special division of psychology, where laboratories of animal psychology were begun, where a separate journal was ultimately founded. One reason for this ready growth of animal psychology in America was that American functional psychology could pick up animal psychology much more easily than could introspective psychology, because functional psychology, being interested in the capacities that help an organism to success, does not have to face the problem of introspection. If the capacities of animals to act successfully can be observed and measured, we can afford to ignore the questions of whether animals are conscious and whether they can introspect.

There is no need to rehearse here what we have already said about the beginning of animal psychology in Great Britain. Darwin, with his *Expression of the Emotions in Man and Animals* in 1872, had done his share toward establishing the continuity of mind between animals and man, although the problem of man's possession of a soul remained troublesome. Romanes reinforced the argument for continuity, bringing forth carefully selected anecdotal material which exhibited instances of animal intelligence and purposive action (1882). Lloyd Morgan counselled conservatism in discovering consciousness on the basis of behavior, laying down his canon of parsimony, his rule that, in reasoning from behavior to consciousness, the investigator must always choose the simplest kind of mind that is adequate as an explanation of the observed facts (1894). Loeb, then in Germany, brought out the tropism, a mechanistic interpretation of behavior without consciousness and applied the new concept most effectively to the behavior of the lower organisms (1890, 1899). Loeb is regarded as having started the mechanistic school and Lloyd Morgan the psychological school of experimental animal psychology. Presently Jennings reinforced Lloyd Morgan (1904).

There was a good deal of discussion about animal introspection. The argument usually ran that animal consciousness is revealed in the way that solipsism is avoided for human consciousness, that is to say, by the argument from analogy. The theory of introspection assumes that every man is his own observer and that the experimenter collects the observations of many observers and brings them together for generalization. Ordinarily no one raises the question of how the observer communicates with the experimenter, for language is held to be adequate. If, however, this problem is forced into consideration, then it can be said that words derive their community of meaning by analogy. If in a relatively simple situation, as when faced with a color, a subject uses the same words as the experimenter would use, the experimenter concludes that the subject's experience is the same as his own. From such a beginning—with many errors, such as happen with color names for the color-blind—community of meaning can be established, so that presently a subject may describe an experience which the experimenter does not or can not share. A congenitally blind psychologist could, for instance, investigate color sensation. The same principles apply to nonverbal behavior. The experimenter penetrates the subject's mind by way of analogy with his own. If one dislikes, as Titchener did, this emphasis on behavior in discussing introspection, he can substitute the conception of empathy for analogy. Then he notes that the experimenter feels himself empathically into the subject's mind while observing the subject's behavior, gross or verbal. In other words, intuition is substituted for inference. The two views come to the same thing in the end and make possible a kind of animal introspection.

So the rule is: if you want to appreciate the animal consciousness, put yourself in the same situation and see what it is like. That procedure, moreover, sometimes works. Human psychologists understood the performance of the rat in the maze much better after they had learned mazes themselves, but it is much harder for man successfully to play the rôle of the free-swimming protozoan that has no special organs of sense. Empathy works best across the smaller differences in biological form and structure.

For this reason a certain amount of difficulty arose about where to place consciousness in the animal scale. Not many persons were ready to deny consciousness to man. On the other hand, the ascription of consciousness to protozoa seemed gratuitous, especially after Loeb had made the mechanics of the tropism appear adequate. Biologists and psychologists tended, therefore, to establish criteria for consciousness, defining the point of its emergence in the ascending scale of organic complexity. The argument from analogy was used in settling upon this critical point: an animal has consciousness when it exhibits the kind of behavior that is characteristically conscious in human beings.

That conclusion, not being final, left room for both schools. The mechanists worked from below up, never reaching the apes and man. The psychologists worked from above down, seldom with confidence below the vertebrate when they were describing an animal's consciousness. Loeb proposed associative memory as the criterion of consciousness. If an animal can profit by experience, he suggested, it is conscious. (Just so Pflüger had argued in 1853 that the spinal cord is conscious because its actions are purposive.) Associative memory proved to be an unsatisfactory criterion when it was shown that the wood of a violin can acquire habits and that a paramecium can learn. (Actually, at the same time—in psychopathology and also in the Würzburg school—man was being discovered to be more and more unconscious than had almost anyone, except a few eccentrics like La Mettrie, ever supposed possible. That news, however, did not at once penetrate to the reaches of animal psychology.)

Jacques Loeb (1859-1924), the leader of the mechanistic movement, was a German zoologist and physiologist of exceptional brilliance, who spent most of his productive life in America and thus brought his influence geographically close to the American comparative psychologists. From 1891 until his death he was successively at Bryn Mawr College, the University of Chicago, the University of California and the Rockefeller Institute in New York. His application of tropistic theory to animals was first put forward in a German paper in 1890. The conception of the tropism as applied to the behavior of plants goes back, however, to de Candolle in 1835, and Max Verworn anticipated Loeb's extension of the mechanical explanation of behavior in animals.

Vergleichende Gehirnphysiologie und vergleichende Psychologie (1899) is the book, translated almost immediately into English, which brought Loeb's views before the scientific world and kept before investigators his contention that even unconscious behavior belongs in psychology. His later books—*The Mechanistic Conception of Life* (1912) and *Forced Movements, Tropisms and Animal Conduct* (1918)—provided a cumulative effect for the mechanistic argument. By 1918 behaviorism was in full swing and animals seemed to be getting along well enough in psychology with a minimal display of consciousness.

Quite early, other Germans came to Loeb's support, among whom the best known were Th. Beer, A. Bethe and J. von Uexküll. In 1899 these three men published a joint paper in which they proposed to discard all psychological terms, like sensation, memory and learning, and to substitute objective terms: *reception* for sensation, *reflex* for fixed movement, *antiklise* for modifiable movement, and *resonance* for memory or any dependence of behavior on past stimulation. Nor was it only the protozoa that seemed able to spare consciousness. The stereotyped behavior of the social insects, of the ants and bees, suggested that they might be robots. Bethe in 1898 had written on that topic. Should we, the title of his article asked, ascribe psychic qualities to ants and bees? No, he thought, we should not. The Cartesian view about animals, two centuries old, was finding support.

On the other hand, not even all the biologists accepted the mechanistic view. *Herbert Spencer Jennings* (1868-1947), at Hopkins from 1906 to 1938, undertook as early as 1899 to study the behavior of protozoa more psychologically. Jennings' thesis was that the behavior of even the simplest organisms is not to be explained by simple physicochemical reactions of the sort that were supposed by Loeb to underlie the tropisms. The reactions of protozoa are too variable and too readily modified. Modifiability of response immediately creates a suspicion of consciousness, not because modifiable behavior is free or indeterminate, but because its variety makes possible many kinds of adaptive responses. The functional psychologists thought of consciousness as an organ of man's adaptation, and Jennings was working at the peak period of functional psychology. He published his *Behavior of the Lower Organisms* in 1904, a volume summarizing a dozen published researches on the topic since 1897. The volume received immediate recognition and served to strengthen the hands of those who thought that animal life and consciousness are coextensive.

Experimental animal psychology belongs to the first decade of the twentieth century. It is usual to date it as beginning with the publication of Thorndike's report on animal intelligence, his work with cats and dogs in the puzzle boxes, published in 1898. Before that time there had been Spalding's very early experiments on the instinctive behavior of birds and animals, experiments which he performed before he had read Darwin's *Expression of the Emotions in Man and Animals*, which he published in 1872, and which fitted in so well with the new interest at the turn of the century that the paper was reprinted in 1902. There had been, as we have already noted (pp. 475 f.), a great deal of observation of the behavior of the social insects. The outstanding names in this field and for that time are J. Henri Fabre, whose studies began in 1879 and kept on for a quarter of a century, Sir John Lubbock's observations on ants, bees and wasps (1883-1888), the two Peckhams on spiders and wasps (1887-1905), and Auguste Forel's studies of ants (1888-1906). On the lower organisms, G. H. Parker's first study was published in 1896 and Jennings' in 1897.

Thorndike's work with the puzzle boxes is marked by a matter-of-fact common-sense ingenuity which characterized all his research for more than forty years (pp. 561-564). On the other hand, it is clear that we have here another instance of the man's fitting into the times and becoming the agent of the *Zeitgeist*. The application of the experimental method to psychological problems was in 1898 the great new interest. The discussion of animal intelligence was rife (pp. 473-476) and had not come to a satisfactory conclusion. The natural history of social insects had been extensively studied, and experiments on the reactions of the simpler organisms to stimulation were beginning. Thorndike did not start all that happened in experimental animal psychology after 1898, but he was, at the choice-point, the sign which pointed out the path of history.

No sooner had Thorndike left Harvard for Columbia in 1897 than Yerkes arrived, fresh from an A.B. at Ursinus. Deeply interested in biology, he had been forced to choose between studying medicine in Philadelphia and philosophy-psychology at Harvard, and had decided in favor of the latter, resolving to make philosophy as biological as possible. In 1899 Josiah Royce sent him to Münsterberg to discuss the possibility of his working in the psychology of animals —in comparative psychology. Yerkes' first research—the forerunner of a long distinguished series—appeared in 1899 from the

Laboratories of Comparative Zoology. In 1902 he was asked to take charge of comparative psychology at Harvard.

It was in 1899 that L. W. Kline published the outlines of a laboratory course in comparative psychology along the lines of instruction then being given at Clark. The next year W. S. Small at Clark published his study of "the mental processes of the rat," a report of experiments begun in 1898. The second part of this paper (1901) is noteworthy because it introduces the maze method into the study of animal intelligence. One can hardly say that the barriers of books, which Thorndike used in his study of chicks' learning, really initiated this method. Small used a reproduction of the Hampton Court maze for his rats, and so provided animal psychology with its maze technique. The maze is, of course, admirably adapted to the rat's habits. The white rat turned out to be an excellent laboratory animal. A rat-in-a-maze was bound sooner or later to become a standard means of studying learning. There were also two studies on the discrimination and intelligence of monkeys published at this time—Thorndike's from Columbia in 1901 and Kinnaman's from Clark in 1902. Kinnaman reported an instance of learning by imitation, but later studies did not fully confirm his observation.

At Chicago, John B. Watson, working under H. H. Donaldson and James R. Angell, completed a thesis in 1903 on the neurological and psychological maturation of the white rat. His study of somesthetic sensation in the white rat in the maze came in 1907, perhaps the last paper in which Watson consented to draw inferences about animal consciousness from research on animal behavior.

Laboratories of comparative psychology were established at Clark, Harvard and Chicago in the period 1899-1903. By 1910 there were at least eight such laboratories in the United States and almost a score of universities offering courses in comparative psychology. In 1911 the *Journal of Animal Behavior* was begun with an editorial board of psychologists and biologists. It lasted ten years to merge in 1921 with *Psychobiology*, forming the *Journal of Comparative Psychology*. In part this change meant that the coming of behaviorism had made the distinction between human and animal behavior less important, for in spite of its name the new journal accepted any physiological psychology, whether it was comparative or not.

Romanes had produced the term *comparative psychology* to encourage the study of mind in evolution—the observation and comparison of mental phenomena at different levels of the animal hierarchy. Lloyd Morgan had established the term. It is doubtful, however, if any American psychologist so fully accepted its implications as did *Robert M. Yerkes* (1876-   ). He certainly may be regarded as the leader in the American movement of comparative psychology, not merely because of his belief in comparative study, but also because of the volume of his work, his persistence, and the way in which he threw his influence toward the organization of investigation. He might almost be said to have climbed steadily up the evolutionary scale in his researches, for from 1900 on he worked successively on various lower animal forms, then on the crab, the turtle, the frog, the dancing mouse, the rat, the worm, the crow, the dove, the pig, the monkey and man (before and during the First World War). Finally, as he had always wanted to do, he brought his laboratories, first at Yale and then in Florida, to an extended systematic study of anthropoid apes. On his retirement in 1941 from this activity, his laboratories at Orange Park, Florida, were named in his honor, the Yerkes Laboratories of Primate Biology. In 1911 Yerkes supported Watson in his development of apparatus for using monochromatic light to study animals' color vision. Thitherto, investigators had used colored papers, assuming that papers which match for the human retina would match for the animal retina being studied—although that assumption depends, of course, on the way the laws of color mixture combine the different spectral compositions which pigments reflect. At the same time Yerkes first sponsored and then developed G. V. Hamilton's use of the multiple-choice method for testing abstraction in animals. Later he became interested in the pathology of mind, another comparison for comparative psychology, and in 1915 with others developed the Point Scale for measuring human ability. In the First World War he was chief of the psychological services which tested intelligence of the large drafted army (p. 575), and not long after he got his ape studies under way, for the most part with chimpanzees. The Yale Laboratories of Primate Biology operated under his directorship from 1919 to 1941.

The interest in animal intelligence continued unabated in animal psychology after the experimental period had begun. It is true that the majority of researches had to do with sensory discrimination or learning. The maze and the puzzle box had made animal subjects available for most of the problems of learning. The psychologists suspected, however—or at least many of them did—that they were not getting at the highest mental capacities of animals by testing only their discrimination and learning. The situation in comparative psychology was comparable to what had happened about human intelligence when Galton's simple tests were rejected for the more involved items of Binet's scale (pp. 572 f.). Thorndike found his cats in the puzzle boxes not very ingenious. They succeeded in getting out of the boxes by trial and error—Lloyd Morgan's phrase—by scratching, clawing and biting until they happened to work the combination that let them out of the box. When they had learned, they still kept a great many of these useless movements in their repertoire of successful conduct. Nor did they seem able to imitate each other. Didactic education from one cat to another seemed impossible; each taught himself in experience's hard school. It was suggested that animals—at least cats, dogs and animals lower in the scale—lack free imagery, a proposal which was consistent with Lloyd Morgan's canon of parsimony. The dog 'remembers' his master, not by 'thinking about him' when he is away, but by feeling uncomfortable in his absence and by recognizing him with joy when he reappears. That was a plausible view but in 1900 it was harder to accept for man's best friend than it would be now for man, who, in a Freudian age, is observed to be unhappy without knowing what it is he wants and to accept with gusto a goal-object without ever having known before what it was he wanted. In 1900, though, there seemed to be a missing link between man's mind and the dog's.

It is possible here only to indicate the way in which this question about animals' having 'ideas' about absent objects or situations was answered. There are five experimental situations to note.

(1) *Imitation.* Thorndike (1898) got no evidence of social imitation with his cats and dogs, nor did Small (1899) with his rats. Thorndike's monkeys (1901) were but little better, but Cole (1907) got some evidence of imitation in raccoons, and also of anticipatory images, as the raccoons would start toward the feeding place at a preparatory signal, and then pause and wait for the final signal before continuing. Later, when the apes came under psychological study, Köhler (1917) obtained definite evidence of chimpanzees' imitating other chimpanzees and man in those situations which they understood and in which they were interested. Yerkes later confirmed and elaborated these findings. The conclusion is that there is no discontinuity between animals and man, but that there is a steep gradient, with the apes quite near man, and cats and rats pretty far away.

(2) *Delayed response.* In 1913 W. S. Hunter hit on the scheme of letting an animal subject see, by means of a signal, in which of a set of boxes food was placed without allowing it to go immediately to the

box and get it. Could it 'remember' where the food was in order to go to it after an interval? Early results indicated that many animals could 'remember' the correct box only by maintaining a bodily orientation toward it, but later experiments showed that delayed responses in many species from rats to man are possible over periods which are fairly long—as long as four hours in one experiment with rats. Köhler (1917) told how chimpanzees, having seen food buried in the sand outside their cage and covered up with smooth sand, ran at once to the right spot on being liberated the next morning.

(3) *Multiple choice.* Hamilton (1911) used the multiple-choice method, placing a row of four boxes before the subject. Yerkes (1915 *et seq.*) developed this method, using any number of boxes up to nine. Some boxes were closed off, others, differing in number from time to time, had their doors open. The subject was to learn which of the open boxes had food in it when the number of open boxes was changed from time to time. The correct box could be "the one on the right," or "the second on the left," or "the middle one." More complicated rules could be devised for man, especially for man with pencil and paper, but the ones mentioned were hard enough for infrahuman subjects. It is much easier to choose "the one on the right" in a series that varies in number than "the second on the right," and "the middle one" is very hard even for apes.

(4) *Double and triple alternation.* Hunter invented what he called a temporal maze (1920), a maze in which partitions are shifted so as to cause a rat to run twice around a rectangle at one side and then reverse to run twice around a similar rectangular block on the other side, and so on, two right, two left, two right. It was a way of seeing whether the rat could count to *two*, or, with triple alternation, to *three*. The rats did badly with double alternation. Raccoons succeeded with double alternation, but failed with triple. Monkeys succeeded with triple. Rats can learn, however, to push a lever twice quickly to the left and then twice quickly to the right. In other words, rats have difficulty in learning to 'count' slowly to *two*, but can learn to count rapidly to *four*. The problem is one of 'memory' or, in less mentalistic terms, of temporal integration—like the problem of the range of attention and memory span in man.

(5) *Insight.* We have already seen (p. 596) how Köhler brought the concept of insight into the psychology of perception and learning, when he was working with the apes at Teneriffe (1917). Insight is perception of relation and, if the relation is simple and not the many relations of the parts or stages of a complicated puzzle, insight happens suddenly and not gradually. Thus learning by insight is apt

to be sudden and, if the insight is correct, immediately successful. The learning is often also permanent. When an animal has insight into a perceptual situation, it gives no more evidence of 'higher' mental processes than does the dog who recognizes his master when present and forgets him when gone, or the cow who licks affectionately the hay-stuffed skin of her calf until the hay, protruding, causes her to eat the hay. Köhler's apes, however, seemed able to include absent objects in their insights. The ape, who fits two short poles together to make a long one, then suddenly 'remembers' that there is across the cage beyond the bars a banana that can be reached with a long pole, and then goes and gets the banana with the long pole, he is adjusting to his present trace of a past perception. So too with the ape who takes the remote detour to get around to the prize when the direct path to it is barred. Many of Köhler's experiments with apes were anticipated by Hobhouse in 1901 who, along with his discussion of mind in evolution, wrote a chapter describing animal experiments. He was opposing trial and error as an explanation of all learning when that concept was still quite young. He described the detour solution of problems and the rapid learning in which the initial act is definite and successful. Nor is insight limited to the higher mammals. Rats show insight of a perceptual, but not of an imaginal, order when they look over an elevated maze and choose, without trial and error, the unblocked but longer path to the goal. Trial-and-error learning does not, of course, exclude insight, and sometimes insight is in error.

We may summarize these last paragraphs by saying that the continuity of mind was finally established in the evolutionary scale, but only after much more labor than had been anticipated in the time of Darwin and Romanes. There is no mental missing link. The chimpanzee brought up with a child begins by excelling the child, for the ape matures faster than the child. Presently development is shown to depend on the species and not on schooling alone. The ape drops behind the child in scholarly pursuits but remains ahead in certain athletic abilities and in feats of strength and agility.

OBJECTIVE PSYCHOLOGY

Comparative psychology led directly into behaviorism, which was also, of course, an objective psychology. To that development we shall come, presently. The purpose of the present section is to review the history of psychological objectivism prior to behaviorism —before 1913. Any psychology which purports to consider the mind and yet excludes consciousness from its consideration is objective. We shall thus make no mistake in this elementary exposition if we equate the *subjective* to the *conscious*.

This history does not properly begin until Descartes' dualism. The Greeks were quite thoroughly objective. Man is concerned first with the external world and discovers himself last. He can take his own ego for granted but not the objective world—not if he is to survive. Aristotle's dualism of matter and form was an objective dualism, since both matter and form were regarded as inherent in objects. The naïve alternative to Aristotle in those days was animism, which is an anthropomorphism of objects. The body was known to be solid substance, and the soul was thought to be vaporous substance, a pneuma, whence came the conception of animal spirits to account for the actions of the nerves and brain. Some of the neo-Platonists, attempting to define objects as God's ideas, were indeed subjectivists, and they thus prepared the way for Descartes' dualism.

1. *Descartes.* We have already discussed Descartes (pp. 162-165) and need only to refresh our memories here. Descartes was the first effective body-mind dualist, and his influence is still felt in modern common sense. In his effort to get to irrefutable truth he decided that only knowing is certain ("cogito ergo sum") and then, by a theological detour, he concluded that material objects also exist. Thus the universe was divided for him into *substantia cogitans*, which is the unextended rational soul, and *res extensa*, which is the human body and all other nature. An animal has no rational soul and is therefore an automaton. In a similar way the human body is mechanically controlled except that it interacts with the soul. On account of these views Descartes can be said to have begun an objective animal psychology, one that was supported by his conception of what came later to be called *reflex action*. It was natural for materialistic philosophers, like La Mettrie, to extend Descartes' doctrine for the animal so as to make it include man. Had Descartes himself been less devout he might have followed some such reasoning himself. His dualism was his way of resolving the conflict between religion and science. Thus he becomes the ancestor of both objectivism and subjectivism in modern psychology.

2. *Cartesian materialists.* La Mettrie, whose influence we have already examined (pp. 211-214), undertook in his *L'homme machine* (1748) to deny the immortality of the soul and the freedom of the mind and to uphold with fervor his conviction, at which he had arrived suddenly during an illness, that man is indeed a machine. He was extending Descartes' doctrine of the animals to man. He

had great influence but not so much as the more scientific Cabanis who came later.

Cabanis, who is also no stranger to us (pp. 214-216) and who is sometimes called the founder of physiological psychology, gave more scientific substance to La Mettrie's view of this problem of the body and the soul. The brain is the organ of consciousness. It 'secretes' thought. The operations of intelligence and the will are in their origins just like all other vital movements. *Les sciences morales*, like the natural sciences, belong to physics, he declared. They are nothing more than a branch of the natural history of man. The ways of verifying observations, of planning experiments, of extracting their results differ in no way from the means which are used confidently every day in the practical sciences. Of course, in 1802 even Cabanis with the best of intentions could not describe with certainty the way in which the brain generates thought, any more than the specifications can be given a century and a half later.

Other contemporaneous philosophers took this same attitude toward the mind. In France there was Destutt de Tracy (1754-1836). In Germany there was J. G. Herder (1744-1803), who sought to extend the work of the physiologist, Albrecht von Haller, to make it cover the phenomena of the mind.

3. *Positivism.* The term *positivism* comes from *Auguste Comte* (1798-1857) who wrote of *la philosophie positive, la politique positive, l'esprit positif* and similar matters. *Positive* for Comte carried the meaning of not speculative or inferential, of immediately observable, the immutable basis of fact which compels agreement because it is given prior to the inferences based upon it. Thus *positive* means *basic, observational, preinferential, undebatable.* Philosophers disagree, however, as to what data are positive in this sense. (a) Comte believed that the basic data are social, that introspection of the single private consciousness is impossible, that there can be no individual psychology but only social science, that we can investigate not the *me* but the *us,* since man can be understood only in his relation to his fellows. Comte disputed the validity of introspection. (b) On the other hand, Mach, as we have seen (p. 394), held that immediate experience provides all the basic data, and he too was called a positivist because he argued for getting back to the observational ultimate which is (he said) experience. Külpe and Titchener followed his view and for that reason are classified as positivists—Machian, not Comtean. (c) Nowadays there is a third positivism, the *logical positivism* of Schlick and Carnap, which holds that the preinferential basic data are the operations of scientific ob-

servation. This is the view that leads to what is sometimes called *operationism*. It has come into some acceptance in psychology because actually the introspective method of Külpe and Titchener did fail to produce preinferential undebatable results, and because it was seen that introspection is subject to errors of observation, that the givens of experience, being the takens of science, may include a bias of taking. Both the first and the third kinds of positivism tend to yield objective psychologies, but we need consider only the first here, since we return to operationism presently.

Comte, as we have said, was against introspection. He pointed out that "in order to observe, your intellect must pause from activity, and yet it is this very activity you want to observe. If you can not effect the pause you can not observe; if you do effect it there is nothing to observe"—except, of course, the pause. Comte thought that, although experience is unobservable, events in the brain are not. Thus his positivism brought him close to Cabanis' position, so far as psychology is concerned.

One of Comte's English followers was *G. H. Lewes* (1817-1878), whose positivistic logic reduced psychology to biology and sociology. He did not believe that introspection is impossible, but he did think that no science could be founded solely upon it. A younger English follower of Comte was *Henry Maudsley* (1835-1918), a psychiatrist (as we should call him nowadays). He stressed the fact that consciousness is less extensive than mind and that psychology must be concerned with unconscious phenomena. To that kind of objective psychology we shall, however, return presently in connection with our consideration of the concept of the unconscious.

4. *Functionalism.* Functional psychology is not in itself an objective psychology. As we have seen, James and Dewey and Angell all kept consciousness in psychology, thinking that it contributed to the weal of the organism (pp. 552-558). On the other hand, functional psychology can be objective and makes an objective psychology easy to accept. We have noted how Cattell was impatient of introspection and developed with Fullerton a psychophysics which measured, not the sensory experience of the individual, but his capacity as a behaving organism to discriminate among stimulus-objects (p. 534). Behaviorism is itself a kind of functional psychology, even though functional psychology is much broader than behaviorism. Mental testing, psychopathology, child psychology, all sorts of applied psychology are most usefully conceived as objective functional psychology with little or no attention paid to consciousness and introspection.

5. *The Russian school*. The most important self-conscious school of objectivism has been the Russian, which began with the work of Sechenov and was continued with the researches of Bekhterev and Pavlov. Bekhterev used the term *objective psychology* to designate his work at first, and then coined the name *reflexology*. Pavlov is known as the discoverer of the *conditioned reflex*.

I. M. Sechenov (1829-1905) took a degree in physiology at St. Petersburg in 1851. He continued there, doing research and making visits to the scientific centers and great physiologists of western Europe. Between 1856 and 1863 he visited Berlin, where he met Johannes Müller and Magnus; Vienna, where he met Carl Ludwig; Heidelberg, where he got to know Helmholtz, Bunsen and Mendeleyev; Paris, where he learned from Claude Bernard; Munich and Graz. He formed close friendships with Ludwig and Mendeleyev, and some of Ludwig's many letters to him have been published. From 1860 to 1870 he taught at the Military Medical Academy in St. Petersburg, resigned over a controversy about the appointment of Mechnikov (who was not appointed when Sechenov thought he should be), taught at Odessa for six years, returned to St. Petersburg in 1876 as professor of physiology, resigned after twelve years to go to Moscow (where he much preferred to be) as a mere lecturer but was given the chair of physiology at Moscow three years later (1891), where he remained until his retirement in 1901. He died in 1905.

One of Sechenov's early interests was the absorption of gases by liquids and in particular the blood's absorption of carbon dioxide. His other interest was the study of neural action. He soon became convinced that spinal reflexes are inhibited by action of the cerebral cortex and he developed this view in his published *Reflexes of the Brain* in 1863. He localized an inhibitory center in the brain, afterwards known as "Sechenov's center." He showed in "Sechenov's experiment" how salt on the cut end of the spinal cord will inhibit spinal reflexes. In his monograph he argued that all thinking and intelligence depend for their exercise on stimulation and that "all acts of conscious or unconscious life are reflexes." This view was popular with the intelligentsia of St. Petersburg, but the St. Petersburg Censorial Committee in 1866 condemned the book as materialistic, forbade its sale, and instituted court action against Sechenov for undermining public morals. This action was quashed the next year, as indeed it should have been, for Sechenov was a sympathetic, responsible, generous, public-spirited man. About 1870 he published a paper entitled *Who Must Investigate the Problems of Psychology and How?* The answer to *Who?* was: The physiologist. The answer to *How?* was: By studying reflexes.

Thus Sechenov became the Russian pioneer in reflexology. We must, moreover, remember that he was far ahead of western European thought on this matter. His papers of 1863 coincided with Wundt's *Vorlesungen über die Menschen- und Thierseele*, and 1870 was four years before Wundt's *Physiologische Psychologie*. In no other country did reflexes yet seem to provide a means for studying cognition. Later, Pavlov read Sechenov's work and was, as a young man, greatly influenced by his argument. Pavlov never received instruction in St. Petersburg from Sechenov, and he did not, of course, become interested in reflexes until the 1890s.

I. P. Pavlov (1849-1936) was twenty years Sechenov's junior. He was born in a peasant town in central Russia and went to a church school there, destined, it was thought, for the priesthood. In 1870 he changed his mind and went to St. Petersburg for an education at the university. He sat under many important men, including Mendeleyev, and in 1874 was asked by the physiologist Elie Tsyon to collaborate with him. Presently, however, Tsyon went to Paris leaving Pavlov behind. Pavlov seems to have worked discursively for some years. He received a fellowship in 1879, married in 1880, obtained a medical degree in 1883, went on a fellowship in 1884-1886 to work with Ludwig, who had gone to Leipzig, and with Heidenhain in Breslau, discovered the secretory nerves of the pancreas in 1888 (the beginning of the research for which he received the Nobel Prize in 1904), was elected professor of pharmacology in the Military Medical Academy of St. Petersburg in 1890, and was advanced to the professorship of physiology in 1895, although the appointment was delayed for two years more by the rector's resentment. Pavlov was professor of physiology from 1895 to 1924, the period of his greatest work. It was only his second most influential work, the research on the digestive secretions, that got him the Nobel Prize.

It was Pavlov's appointment in pharmacology which started him operating to bring the ducts for the digestive secretions to the surface of the body, so that secretion could be easily observed and measured. It was then he discovered how the digestive juices begin to flow when the animal subject anticipates food, and out of that observation grew the technique of the conditioned reflex, the measuring of anticipation by observing the flow of gastric and intestinal juices or saliva. Pavlov was quick to see that he had here a means for measuring many quantities that had thitherto been regarded as psychical. At first he spoke of "psychical secretion"; later he would write "the so-called psychical processes"; still later his phrase was "conditioned reflexes." At the start, it was his acquaintance with Sechenov's paper of 1863 and Thorndike's experiments of 1898 which encouraged him to continue in work of this kind.

Every student of psychology now knows the nature of "classical conditioning," in which a second stimulus, which occurs with or just before the stimulus of an unconditioned reflex, comes, with repetition, to elicit the reflex movement alone. Conditioning is an objective substitute for introspection, a form of language which enables an experimenter to know what discrimination an animal can make, what it does and does not perceive. Conditioning is, in fact, a kind of language, which the experimenter provides so as to enable an animal to communicate with him, but the phenomena of communication occur entirely on the objective level of stimuli, nerve-action and secretion, without any need for assuming consciousness as an entity. Nevertheless, because we are so accustomed to use the vocabulary of consciousness, the old psychical terms inevitably creep into common thought about these matters, as they did also in Pavlov's exposition.

The story of Pavlov's research is told excellently by himself in forty published lectures that are dated from 1903 to 1928. The facts that he discovered were many, but the data of conditioning constitute so large a field of research that the history of that work, being a part of the history of the experimental psychology of learning, belongs in a special volume. It is enough for us to see the nature of Pavlov's rôle in supporting objective psychology and why his work presently could furnish such apt support to Watson's behaviorism.

There remains *V. M. Bekhterev* (1857-1927), who was eight years younger than Pavlov but died nine years before him. Like Sechenov and Pavlov, he too worked at the Military Medical Academy in St. Petersburg and received his doctor's degree in 1881, two years ahead of Pavlov. Then he went 'abroad' to work with Flechsig and Wundt in Leipzig, with du Bois Reymond in Berlin, with Charcot in Paris. He was more of a psychiatrist than a physiologist, and he returned to the chair of mental diseases at the University of Kazan. In 1893 he went back to the Military Medical Academy at St. Petersburg and to the chair of mental and nervous diseases. He organized a mental hospital. He published many papers, was active in many public capacities. In 1907 he realized his long-formed wish, for he founded then the Psychoneurological Institute, with special departments for mental cases, alcoholics, epileptics and neuro-surgery.

From 1913 on he devoted all his time to the Institute because the unfriendly czarist government made his tenure at the Military Academy uncomfortable. At the Institute Bekhterev was responsible for a great deal of neurological research and a great deal of writing.

Bekhterev's neurological and psychiatric activities won him prestige and his pronouncements on general matters were listened to. He first published about 1910 an *Objective Psychology*, and then in 1917 a series of lectures which grew to fifty-four in the third edition. He called these *General Principles of Human Reflexology*. In them he argued for the objective approach to the problems of psychology and took a stand against the use of mentalistic terms. The word *reflexology* is his word. Of course Bekhterev came late. John Dewey's protest of 1896, against what he would have called *reflexology* had the word been in existence, was long past. Yet Bekhterev was not too late to support behaviorism and to help objective psychology along in its battle against introspectionism.

Russian psychology since the Revolution has remained largely unknown in the 'bourgeois' west because the westerners do not read Russian and the Russians repudiate the western ideology. There was first a determined effort to create a truly Marxian psychology. For instance, in the mid-1920s K. N. Kornilov was attempting to develop a system consistent with dialectical materialism. On the other hand, the Russians felt at this time some interest in Gestalt psychology and also in behaviorism, although they repudiated the American brand of behaviorism. After 1931 even behaviorism was denounced as not wholly free of dualistic philosophy, and the development of dialectical psychology was begun in an effort to obtain a truly sovietized psychology. There is not likely to be much interaction between Russian psychology and the western "bourgeois" kind until communication becomes freer than it is at the time of the writing of this book.

6. *The tropistic school.* We have just seen in the preceding section how, under the leadership of Jacques Loeb, the conception of the tropism grew up within animal psychology itself (pp. 624 f.). Loeb thought of a tropism as a physical-chemical action, as if a positively phototropic plant or simple animal were to expand on its dark side or contract on its light side, thus becoming bent toward the light. Later the conception became more general with less reference to physiological means: a tropism is the orientation of an organism in a field of force. Loeb thought that the organism is oriented by adjustive movements which equalize the innervation on its two sides—a cybernetic action if we may employ the modern phrase.

Tropistic action may, of course, be conscious, as Jennings thought was true of the protozoa, or as unconscious as the orientation of iron filings in a field of magnetic force. The point is that tropistic psychology is objective because the laws of tropisms are formulated without regard to consciousness, which may or may not be concurrent.

7. *The unconscious.* It is clear that psychology in coming to deal with unconsciousness as well as consciousness was moving toward an objective psychology. Since it is attitudes and motives which are most conspicuously unconscious and yet psychic, the history of the use and development of the conception of unconscious mind belongs in the history of dynamic psychology, to which we shall come in due course (pp. 706-714). It will, however, be useful to outline here the chief events in the history of the use of this paradoxical concept of unconscious mind.

Leibnitz (1714) had the concept of a threshold for apperception. The *petite perception* is unconscious. You may perceive but can not apperceive the drop of water falling on the beach, yet you do hear clearly the wave pounding the sand (p. 167). Herbart (1824) took over this conception in his limen of consciousness. Ideas are active and press always to rise above the threshold into consciousness, being kept below in "a state of tendency" by the limitation of accommodations in consciousness (pp. 255-260). Fechner (1860) took over the concept of the limen from Herbart. You can not hear one caterpillar eating a leaf on Unter den Linden, but you could hear enough thousands eating in unison. Below the threshold there are negative sensations, and the Weber function measures them by extrapolation (p. 290). Thought along these lines was brought together and given general status by the philosopher Eduard von Hartmann (1842-1906) in his much read *Philosophie des Unbewussten* (1869), which ran into many editions and translations.

Meanwhile the concept of the unconscious was being readied for psychopathology by the study of the phenomena of hypnosis (pp. 128-130). The names of Braid, Liébeault, Charcot, Bernheim and Heidenhain represent the transition from mystery to medicine, from hypnosis to hysteria. In England, Henry Maudsley was already saying in his *Psychology and Pathology of Mind* in 1868: "We cannot overestimate the importance of the fact that 'consciousness' is not coextensive with the mind." He was at pains to point out how many minds and how much of every mind are inaccessible to introspection. The center of this development in the late nineteenth century lay, however, in Paris with Charcot. Both Janet and Freud worked with him, and presently the concept of hysteria became the concept of neurosis or, in modern phrase, psychoneurosis. J. M. Charcot's work began about 1862 when he went to the Salpêtrière and his important publications began about 1873. He certainly may be regarded as the discoverer of psychoneurosis. Pierre Janet's influence begins with his *L'état mentale des hystériques* of 1892. Sigmund Freud was publishing papers on neurology in the 1880s. His famous paper with Breuer on unconscious hysterical mechanisms came out in 1893 and the *Traumdeutung* in 1899. One or the other of those papers must be taken as the start of the psychoanalytic movement. We need not at this place speak of the further development of this movement and the communalization of the concept of the unconscious. It was Stanley Hall's asking Freud, Jung, Ferenczi and Ernest Jones to Clark's vigentennial celebration in 1909 that made America fully conscious of the unconscious. In other words, just as Watson was losing his patience with introspection, a whole psychology which used the unconscious, even though it admitted also the existence of the conscious, came into scientific notice. In this way, via psychopathology, behaviorism was a sanction for psychology's doing something about people who act queerly without knowing it.

8. *The impalpable.* It seems strange to say that Külpe's Würzburg school of imageless thought, the school which argued so vigorously for "systematic experimental introspection" and which developed new technics for the control of introspection, played a rôle in the history of objective psychology; yet such was the case (pp. 451 f.). Külpe's final judgment about the work of that school was that contents of thought are conscious but impalpable (*unanschaulich*), that they do not stand up to introspection but can be described in retrospection. What is, however, of still more importance to us is the finding of Watt and Ach that the key to thought and action lies in the predetermination (in the set, *Aufgabe* or attitude) which carries on through the thought or action, determining its course without remaining conscious. Really the most important contribution of the Würzburg school was the discovery that the determining tendencies which control thought and action do not appear as such in consciousness and must be known by other means than introspection. Even Titchener was obliged to agree in his context theory of meaning that familiar perceptions or ideas carry their meanings without any conscious content at all (pp. 415 f.).

When this point about imageless thinking becomes clear, one can see at once where else in experimental psychology the unconscious data have lain. The organization of perception is unconscious, a fact

which led Helmholtz to support the doctrine of unconscious inference (pp. 308-311). There was also Ludwig Lange's discovery
in Wundt's laboratory in 1888 that reaction times are dependent
upon the initial attitude (p. 342), a finding that anticipated Watt
and Ach. It is not hard, even in the experimental psychology whose
main task is a description of consciousness, to find plenty of instances where mind, psychology's subject-matter, of necessity must
be regarded as including much more than consciousness.

BEHAVIORISM

Objective psychology became *behaviorism* (with the *ism*) in 1913
when John B. Watson initiated his vigorous propaganda against introspection and for an objective psychology. The event provides
an excellent example of the way in which movements start, for behaviorism had both positive and negative conscious reasons for being
brought forward and supported and there was also operative the
unconscious positive influence of the *Zeitgeist*. All three of these
factors seem to have been necessary causes of behaviorism, though no
one would have been sufficient in itself.

(a) On the conscious positive side there was Watson's firm belief
that behavior in itself is interesting and important. Watson was a
functionalist (with a small *f*) but he could not tolerate for long the
requirement of the Chicago school that even the animal psychologist
must take time out to translate positively observed behavior into
the vague terms of an inferred consciousness. It was more direct,
more positive (*cf. positivism*) and more interesting to study behavior for its own sake, describing it and noting its functional use
to the behaving organism. That was, of course, nothing new; yet
in cutting off consciousness completely from animal psychology he
was going beyond Lloyd Morgan, who had protested against Romanes' anthropomorphism in the interpretation of animal behavior.
Watson adopted an extreme parsimony of doing without any consciousness at all and used, as it might be put, William of Occam's
razor for the last drastic extirpation of Cartesian "unextended substance." Thus he almost joined Descartes in respect of the animals
and La Mettrie's expansion of Descartes in respect of man, except
that he did not deny the existence of consciousness. He merely
asked psychologists to ignore it and to deal with the more reliable
data of behavior. It is hard to state the positive except with regard
to its negative, but it is certain that behaviorism was more than a
protest for Watson. He believed in the power of studying behavior
in animals and man, especially since he could preserve the advan-

tages of functionalism while ridding it of consciousness, its impediment.

(b) On the conscious negative side there was the protest of behaviorism against introspectionism. Watson had just seen introspection fail at Würzburg—that is what most Americans in 1910 thought had happened there. In the 'new' psychology's first fifty years, the description of consciousness had resulted in no large interesting systematic body of knowledge. The facts of the 'new' psychology were mostly objective: abilities to reproduce correctly learned material, reaction times, bodily changes in emotion and capacities to discriminate differences in stimulation. Introspection had produced no agreement about feeling. Is feeling a sensation, an attribute of sensation or a new element? Does it really exist? Feelings do not always stand up to introspection, and even Titchener had had to say that feeling lacks the attribute of clearness and comes under introspective observation only indirectly. Borrowing the spirit of German polemical writing, the psychological journals were filled with protocols, long wordy arguments, disagreements and the inevitable invective. Psychology claimed to be science but it sounded like philosophy and a somewhat quarrelsome philosophy at that. No wonder Watson wanted to wield Occam's razor.

(c) The unconscious positive influence was, of course, the *Zeitgeist*. Psychology was all ready for behaviorism. America had reacted against its German parentage and gone functional, for reasons which we have already discussed (pp. 505-508). Behaviorism simply took from functionalism part but not all of the parental tradition. Meanwhile objectivism, as we have just been seeing, was growing to include, not only much of functional psychology, but most of psychopathology and all of the mental testing and applied psychology. Behaviorism could simply take over all these fields, and that is what it did more or less—or else it was they which took over behaviorism. At any rate, the times were ripe for more objectivity in psychology, and Watson was the agent of the times.

It is interesting to compare behaviorism as a protest with Gestalt psychology as a protest. The two movements were contemporaneous and each protested against the same orthodoxy. The fact that they were so different shows that new movements are something more than protests. In this case there were two somewhat different *Zeitgeister*—the German tradition of philosophical interest in consciousness and the American spirit of pragmatic functionalism. Orthodox psychology in 1910 was (i) experimental, (ii) introspective, (iii) elementistic and (iv) associationistic. Behaviorism and Gestalt psychology were agreed only on the first: both schools thought psychology should and could be experimental. Introspection behaviorism rejected in toto, whereas Gestalt psychology placed great store upon the phenomenal description of direct experience, although it rejected the sensationistic introspection of Wundt and Titchener. Behaviorism at first was elementistic because it made the reflex the unit of its system, whereas Gestalt psychology decried analysis and explained how you could deal with phenomenal wholes, directing its polemics in part against behaviorism. In taking over the conditioned reflex, behaviorism adopted an associationism, an *Und-Verbindung*, in which the conditioned stimulus gets stuck onto the response merely by its frequent contiguity with the unconditioned stimulus—a connectionism which leaves no place for such integrative principles as organization and insight. It is well to remember how important a difference in *Zeitgeister* can be in the dynamic psychology of scientific movements. America protested the Wundtian tradition and it got functionalism first and behaviorism next. Germany protested and got Gestalten. Given everything else in America as it was in 1910, the year of James' death, you could not have had a protest against Wundt developing as Gestalt psychology—not there and then.

1. *John B. Watson* (1878-   ) 'founded' behaviorism in the spring of 1913 with his paper entitled *Psychology as the Behaviorist Views It*. He had been at the University of Chicago, taken his Ph.D. there with a thesis under James Angell and Donaldson, the neurologist, in 1903, and had been then put in charge of animal psychology at Chicago. We have already noted that his monograph in 1907 was an investigation of the sensations [*sic!*] that the rat uses in solving the problem of the maze. That was Watson's temporary acceptance of orthodox functionalism with consciousness left in. In 1908 Baldwin, then at Hopkins, offered Watson a professorship, and Watson left Chicago and Angell reluctantly and went to Hopkins. He was already started on problems of the homing of birds and he continued with them and the measurement of visual sensitivity of animals to color.

Behaviorism was conceived and born at Hopkins. After the initial paper Watson published special discussions of imagery, feeling and association—that is to say, he translated these mentalist concepts into behavioristic terms. His behaviorism had room for verbal response and for vocal or subvocal thinking, so he translated imagery and thinking into vocimotor behavior—he thought they might consist of tiny laryngeal movements which could eventually be observed. He suggested that feeling might turn out to be glandular activity or tumescence and detumescence of genital tissues. Later he adopted the conditioned reflex of Pavlov as the behaviorist's substitute for association. Right after his crucial paper he published a comparative psychology, *Behavior: an Introduction to Comparative Psychology* (1914). The First World War interrupted these activities, but after that he was back at a task that was not unlike Wundt's in the 1870s—writing a complete text to demonstrate the adequacy of his point of view and definition of psychology to what was then the accepted range of psychological fact. *Psychology from the Standpoint of a Behaviorist* (1919) was the result. Meanwhile he was active in showing that behaviorism really can study the psychology of human beings: he was applying animal techniques to infants including experiments in conditioning. His work was interrupted by his divorce in 1920 and his resignation from Hopkins. He turned to the advertising business, keeping up his interest and writing in psychology, publishing more than one book on behaviorism and the application of its methods to the understanding and control of children and adults in the maze of life.

In a word, behaviorism became a psychology of *stimulus* and *response*. Watson came to think of imagery as dubious, and indeed it is hard to be sure of any imagery except the visual. Thinking can go on in verbal subvocal terms. Watson distinguished between *explicit* movements and *implicit* movements. He should perhaps have said *overt* and *covert*, for he believed that there were actually vocimotor movements in thinking and genital response in feeling, although the movements can not be observed. To call the covert *implicit*, is to suggest that these events are born of logic rather than of observation. He thought of them as covert and awaiting discovery.

Sensation, of course, Watson could handle as discrimination. Fullerton and Cattell had done it in psychophysics in 1892 (pp. 539 f.). It was ever so much safer than introspection for testing color blindness, as the researches of the 1890s showed. A dichromat is a man who can match every spectral color with some mixture of two spectral colors, and no one knew for sure what dichromats actually see until a subject turned up color-blind in one eye and normal in the other, able to compare the vision of his two eyes and thus to tell what he saw by making a further discrimination. So, too, Pavlov was able to work out—or at least to formulate—any sensory problem in terms of conditioned responses, because this technique measures discrimination. It is important to keep this point in mind, for it is the beginning of operationism: discrimination is the operation by which sensory facts are observed. It follows that all sensory facts can be reduced to the operations of their observation, which is discrimination.

Watson did not feel, however, that he could rule out of psychology all of the psychophysics which had purported to make use of introspection. He therefore admitted in the case of human subjects *verbal report* as a form of behavior. In this way all introspection could be reduced to the operation by which it is observed, verbal report, and come back into psychology after having been excluded. That is, of course, not at all what Watson wanted. He wished to let in discriminatory verbal report when it was accurate and verifiable, as it is, for instance, in the observation of difference tones, and to rule it out when it is unverifiable, as it is when it consists of statements about the nature of feeling or about the impalpable contents of imageless thinking. Nevertheless, the admission of verbal report was a damaging concession, for it made it appear that behaviorism was asking only for verbal changes and not for a reform in scientific procedures. The difficulty arose because Watson knew what he wanted in the concrete case (he always wanted the most positive and objective of available methods) but failed to provide his case with a rigorous epistemology. He was better as a dramatic polemicist and enthusiastic leader than as a logician. Later on, Watson's faith came to be spoken of as "naïve behaviorism," but, for all that, it was a positive faith and it fitted the American temper excellently.

For a while in the 1920s it seemed as if all America had gone behaviorist. Everyone (except the few associated with Titchener) was a behaviorist and no behaviorist agreed with any other. In the 1930s there were still behaviorists, but, with Titchener dead and introspection out of fashion, they were less anxious to display the label. The important names are Holt, Tolman, Lashley, Weiss, Hunter, Skinner and perhaps Hull, if we name them in the order of dates at which they would have readily accepted this title. Their behavioristic writings cover more than twenty-five years (1915-1940). Holt is the oldest, Skinner the youngest (Holt's junior by thirty-one years), Hull the most recent.

2. *Edwin B. Holt* (1873-1946), a man of brilliant and versatile if somewhat unpredictable intellect, a great admirer of James, was given a Harvard Ph.D. in 1901, stayed on at Harvard to teach until 1918, retired to write, taught at Princeton for ten years from 1926 on, and then retired again to write. Not many knew him well, but

those who did felt his stimulation and appreciated his erudition. He was half a philosopher, a realist, not a pragmatist, and half a good experimentalist. He finished *The Concept of Consciousness* in 1908 (and published it in 1914) and *The Freudian Wish and Its Place in Ethics* in 1915. It is the latter volume which gives him a place in the history of dynamic psychology (pp. 718 f.). The book reprints as a supplement Holt's important article called *Response and Cognition*. There was for many years the wishful rumor that Holt intended to revise James' *Principles*. He never did, but instead he published *Animal Drive and the Learning Process* in 1931. He was not militant enough to count formally as a behaviorist, but he believed intensely that psychology should study behavior, "the specific response relation," and that only in that way could it be said to have found "the key to the explanation of mind." For Watson's naïveté Holt substituted a philosophic sophistication, one which was scarcely recognized by the psychologists of the time but which eventually had an effect through its influence on Tolman.

Holt wanted psychologists to study specific response relations, but he himself did not slip into the atomistic reflexology of Pavlov and Watson which the Gestalt psychologists condemned. For Holt a response was a whole, what Tolman later called *molar*. This man who goes by the window, what is he doing? Is he walking forward? No, he is going to the grocer's. Such an act as going-to-the-grocer's has unity. It also has purpose and that was why Holt was applauding Freud and contributing to dynamic psychology with his behaviorism.

It was Holt who saw that the response relation is knowing, is, as he might have put it, meaning. The problem of knowledge and objective reference had baffled almost everyone—Berkeley, Reid, the Mills, Wundt, Külpe, Titchener. Titchener invented the context theory of meaning in order to deny that in familiar perceptions the context need be conscious. In old familiar perceptions (like words) meaning is unconscious and "is carried by brain habits," Titchener said. But how are you to know what you know when contexts are not added on and remain implicit only? You know—that is to say, you get the meaning—*because* you respond adequately. And that is really Holt's contribution—that response, when it is specific, specifies something or intends it. Behaviorism, as Holt conceived it, was really a psychology of meanings, and in that connection we may recall Titchener's thought that James was not truly a psychologist because he had written a psychology of knowledges. Knowledge is functional, for it is the capacity to respond adequately to the world's specificity.

3. *Edward C. Tolman* (1886-   ) came under the influence of Holt at Harvard and took his doctorate there in 1915. After three years at Northwestern University, he went to the University of California in Berkeley, where he has been ever since. His first experimental work was a study of the temporal relations of meaning and imagery, work inspired by some research from Külpe's laboratory and resulting in the conclusion that some meaning can precede some imagery. In California as early as 1922 he came out for what he called *purposive behaviorism,* a system which later seemed to show the Holtian influence. He spent a decade conducting experiments with rats—rats with a purpose, for they were in a maze and seeking food—and writing articles about maze learning, purpose, cognition, a behavioristic theory of ideas, a behavioristic definition of consciousness, insight in rats and degrees of hunger. His important and difficult book, *Purposive Behavior in Animals and Men,* came out in 1932. In it he had, for the sake of exact expression, developed an elaborate special terminology which we can not undertake to use here. Jennings had by his insight saved consciousness for protozoa. Tolman by a comparable insight had saved purposiveness for rats, but he had kept true to behaviorism and had not given them back consciousness. Perhaps the rats were conscious; that did not matter. They could act, and action itself can be purposive and remain objective.

Into his behaviorism Tolman welcomed all objective data. He has been criticized for making behaviorism so inclusive, but it is not clear that any distinction needs to be kept between behaviorism and objective psychology. The "raw feels" (data of consciousness) are ineffable and not public, and what is not public is not given for science. What you see with the eye of science is behavior and behavior is purposive if you look at the wholes, Tolman insisted. An analysis of action into elements gives you reflexology and what Tolman called *molecular behavior.* The wholes, on the other hand, are *molar behavior* and in it purposiveness emerges. Men and animals act in respect of ends.

Tolman's formula is $B = f(S, A)$, that is to say, Behavior is a function of the Situation and other Antecedent causes. The business of psychology is to determine these functional relations, by observing B when some A is varied for a given S, or some S for a given A. An A might be hunger, and you could measure it for use in the formula by the time the animal is deprived of food.

Between S and A, both of which are antecedents, and B, which is their consequent, there may be *Intervening Variables.* They, known now to every American psychologist, are constructs of Tolman's invention, which serve to fill in the empty correlations of behavior with the situation and other antecedents. In the past, psychologists have stuffed their stimulus-response relationships with hypothetical intervening physiology—a practice which Tolman believes to have been futile and which he has avoided. These intervening variables as constructs are quite as real as atoms and gravitation and the other things of science which are known only by their effects. Some of the intervening variables are *cognitive* and serve as knowledges or the wisdom which determines action. Others are *demand* variables and serve as motives, like the drives which determine action.

It is quite possible in this way to work out a whole psychology in objective terms. With much greater sophistication Tolman has been doing what Watson began: he has been using operational logic to transform subjective events into objective. In fact, at one time in the early 1930s he was talking about *operational behaviorism.* You can always translate the subjective into the objective if the subjective data are public, because you can refer them to the operations by which they have been publicized, *i.e.,* the operations of observation. To that matter we return, however, in the next section of this chapter.

4. *Karl S. Lashley* (1890-   ) is known chiefly for his work on the localization of brain functions and his discoveries of how little precise and persistent localization there is. Thus he belongs principally in the next chapter of this book. He was a student of Watson's at Hopkins where he obtained his Ph.D. in 1915. He went then to the University of Minnesota (1917-1926), the Behavior Research Fund (1926-1929), the University of Chicago (1929-1935), Harvard (1935-   ) and the Yerkes Laboratories of Primate Biology (still on Harvard appointment, 1942-   ). He has devoted himself to research and has usually abstained from the polemics of the schools because he thought that such argument does not promote scientific discovery. He has, however, at times crossed his self-imposed barrier, as he did notably in 1923 with his papers on the *Behavioristic Interpretation of Consciousness.* All his research illustrates how a physiological psychologist can get along without the concept of consciousness. Lashley uses mostly the functions of learning and discrimination and seeks to discover the neural bases for these capacities, both of which can be adequately measured by behavioral techniques.

5. *Albert P. Weiss* (1879-1931), born in Germany, migrated to America in early childhood. In 1909 he became assistant to Max

Meyer at the University of Missouri, where he took his A.B. in 1910 and his Ph.D. in 1916. He was appointed an instructor at Ohio State University in 1912, but he continued as Meyer's student at Missouri until he obtained his degree. Meyer—who says of himself that, at Berlin in the 1890s, he owed as much to the physicist, Max Planck, as to the psychologist, Stumpf—provided the inspiration which turned Weiss toward an exact behaviorism. From 1912 on, Weiss stayed at Ohio State University until his untimely death in 1931.

Weiss was a vigorous polemicist, and in 1925 he brought his many papers on the proper nature of psychology together into a *magnum opus*, *A Theoretical Basis of Human Behavior*, a book which went into an enlarged second edition in 1929. Its author insisted that all the phenomena of psychology can be reduced to physical-chemical terms or to social relations, a mixture, if you like, of La Mettrie (or Loeb) with Comte. Weiss was sure he was right. "Behaviorism claims to render a *more* complete and *more* scientific account of the totality of human achievement *without* the conception of consciousness, than traditional psychology is able to render *with* it. The factors which traditional psychology vaguely classifies as conscious or mental elements merely *vanish* without a remainder into the biological and social components of the behavioristic analysis." That statement of Weiss' expresses excellently the new behaviorism. Watson ignored consciousness without denying it, but the behavioristic sophisticates do neither. They keep consciousness, making it objective. They banish the mentalistic terminology and deal with objective data of social or physical entities, or (like Tolman) they introduce intervening variables which reduce to objective data when the operations of their observations are considered. One can eat his cake and have it too. Ingestion leads to absorption.

6. *Walter S. Hunter* (1889-   ) comes from the school of Chicago functionalism with a degree under Angell and Carr in 1912. He has held posts successively at Texas, Kansas, Clark and Brown universities, the last since 1936. We have already had occasion to note his contribution to the study of symbolic processes in the delayed reaction and in the temporal maze (pp. 629 f.). Like the other behaviorists, Hunter has rigorously avoided the use of mentalistic terms, even suggesting that *psychology* is too mentalistic a word and that *anthroponomy*, his synonym for *behaviorism*, would be a better term. While Hunter, like Lashley, has concerned himself more with research than with the polemics of the schools, he has written against introspection and for study of behavior; and, like

the others, he has formulae which will translate description of consciousness into the terms of stimulus and response.

7. *B. F. Skinner* (1904-   ), the youngest of the behaviorists to receive mention in this book, has a 1931 Ph.D. from Harvard, but he owes little to Harvard psychologists, although something to W. J. Crozier, Harvard's general physiologist, in whose laboratory he worked for three years. He went from Harvard to Minnesota, and then, after three years at Indiana, returned to Harvard in 1948 to promote there the study of behavior and its control. In 1938 he published *The Behavior of Organisms*, a book which summarizes his research and beliefs up to that date. Later he has turned to the problem of language regarded as behavior, and in 1947 he gave the William James Lectures at Harvard on the subject *Verbal Behavior*.

Skinner's doctoral dissertation was truly a thesis. He defended the proposition that the psychologist should regard the reflex as a correlation between stimulus and response. He ignored the possibility of intervening physiological links, which, for the psychologist, are often a queer make-believe physiology, a dummy physiology doing duty for truth when facts are missing. Skinner has held consistently and successfully to this view for twenty years, developing a stimulus-response psychology that is not in any sense a physiological psychology, and attracting many younger men to his banner. Such functional relations as $R = f(S)$ are established by observing the covariation of a stimulus S and a response R and lack the physical continuity between terms which most scientists prefer. Skinner's functions are mere Humian correlations of discrete variables, not causal continuities, and Skinner has sometimes been said— humorously by his friends—to deal with the empty organism. His view, as he himself has suggested, is similar to Tolman's, but he does not attempt to approximate continuity in his correlations by filling them in with intervening variables, nor does he view behavior as essentially purposive. There is, however, only a shade of difference between Skinner and Tolman in this respect. Skinner is concerned with drives which eventually do, indeed, push an organism to its goal. Tolman keeps his eye on the organism's goal. Skinner wants mathematical functions and Tolman biological Darwinian functions, for after all is said one finds that causes do have ends, and Tolman is not trying to do without descriptive observation.

The Skinner box, which is known to all experimental psychologists, is a simple box which originally was made to contain a rat, a lever, a device for delivering a pellet of food when the rat pressed the lever, and nothing else. Outside there were other devices to record on moving paper the rat's phageal behavior over long periods of time. You could go home at night and see in the morning what the rodent subject had been doing all night. Nowadays the pigeon has turned out to have certain advantages over the rat, but the principle is the same and there are Skinner boxes for pigeons. The organism—rat or pigeon—learns rapidly in such a box because there is so little else to do. When learning is established, extinction of the response by stopping the reinforcing food is slow. The experimenter can then study an extinction curve as a function of some additional parameter which is varied as the independent variable.

In this situation Skinner has pointed out that there are two kinds of reflexes: responses correlated with their stimuli, and responses that occur without observable external stimuli. The first he calls *respondent* behavior and the second *operant* behavior. Operant behavior might have tempted Skinner into assuming some hypothesized internal variables, if not imaginary physiology, some sort of psychologist's constructs which might resemble Tolman's intervening variables. That defection from his initial faith Skinner has, however, successfully resisted. It is quite easy to change other conditions when there is no stimulus and to note how behavior varies. For instance, you can observe the operant eating of a rat as a function of the time elapsed since it last had food. You can call the independent variable 'hunger,' if you like, but for Skinner hunger is defined by objective events and is not to be regarded as a physical state or as a conscious desire. When you know what function food-taking is of food deprivation, you can see how that function varies with other parameters, like the age of the organism. In this way Skinner has managed a reflexology that is much more satisfactory than that of the Russians. Sechenov and Bekhterev urged that all conscious processes be reduced to stimulus-response reflexes, but their arguments seemed unreal because it is not obvious what the stimuli are, even when you have consciousness formulated in terms of responses. Operant behavior avoids this difficulty.

8. *Clark L. Hull* (1884-   ), the fourth oldest man in this list of eight, comes last because he is a behaviorist only by acclamation and that not until the 1930s—just a little after Skinner. He never sought membership in the fraternity and for many years at Yale his ardent disciples—and he well knew how to induce enthusiasm and hard work in his followers—would have been sure they were Hullians but perhaps a little puzzled if called behaviorists. Yet for years it was Hull who put Yale's special mark on its newly trained psychologists.

Hull took his Ph.D. at Wisconsin in 1918 and stayed there until 1929, when he went to Yale for a long period of important and effective work. His early interests were in various matters: statistical devices, the effects of tobacco on mental efficiency, aptitude tests. At Yale he first became interested in hypnosis and suggestibility, publishing the classical experimental volume on that subject in 1933. He was also concerned with the question of the robot: can machines be built which will duplicate the capacities of the conscious human organism? Hull thought that they could, and that kind of interest grew with his behavioristic kind of thinking.

It was at Yale that his chief occupation with the problems of conditioned reflexes and learning began. He thought that the work of Pavlov could be formulated more rigorously and that Ebbinghaus' problems of memory could be restated in more precise terms. Presently we find him in the late 1930s, with the constant support of his industrious students, formulating a logically rigorous scientific system for those facts of learning with which he was dealing. He counselled adherence to the *hypothetico-deductive method* in scientific work. That method consists in the setting up of postulates, in deducing from them experimentally testable conclusions, in performing the tests, and then, if the tests fail, in revising the postulates, or, if they succeed, in adding the postulates, for the time-being at least, to the body of science. That program ultimately took him into the abstractions of mathematical logic, and with five other colleagues he published in 1940 *Mathematico-Deductive Theory of Rote Learning: a Study in Scientific Methodology*. For most psychologists it is a difficult and forbidding book, but it shows what can be done with rigorous logic in a scientific context and helps to make most of psychology's postulates, none too well established, seem even more insecure than ever. In 1943 Hull published a simpler book which ordinary psychologists can read, *Principles of Behavior*. This book shows the sure manner in which Hull sticks to objective terms and it provides the ground for classifying him as a behaviorist, or at least as an objective psychologist.

Unfortunately, Hull's system is too ponderous for us to examine an example of it here. We may note merely that a gain in rigor is necessarily accompanied by a loss of scope. You can believe more than you can be sure of. Hull's work is more valuable as a paradigm of method than as an addition to the body of psychological fact. Influenced by Thorndike, Hull has tended to think analytically and is regarded as one of the modern associationists. That puts him at once in opposition to Tolman, who has felt the influence of Gestalt psychology, always ignoring the molecules in order to see the moles.

This survey of the rôles of eight behaviorists in American psychology is much too superficial to do justice to any one, but as a whole (which is, of course, more than the sum of its parts) it shows the total pattern of what was going on, how America, already gone functional, also went objective. It is doubtful if any reader, pondering these paragraphs, will conceive of Watson, the founder, as the sufficient cause of all the behavioristic movement. Nor is it imaginable that a wicked witch could have snatched Watson from his crib and have substituted a mentalist baby who would then, thirty years later, have led American psychologists to such a variety of descriptive mentalisms as we now have of functional objectivisms.

OPERATIONISM

In psychology there is operationism, but there are hardly any operationists. Operationism is more of a principle than a school. It is a way of evaluating scientific activity after it has occurred, of increasing the precision of meaning for scientific concepts, of separating true scientific problems from the pseudoproblems, and of distinguishing between metaphysics and science. The movement assumed importance among the psychologists in the later 1930s because it stood as the conclusion of the three converging lines of thinking—from physics, from philosophy and from psychology itself.

(1) The pressure from physics was created by Harvard's physicist, P. W. Bridgman, who wrote in 1927 *The Logic of Modern Physics*, a book which turned out to be intelligible and interesting to psychologists. Bridgman was trying to clarify physical thinking in the face of confusion created by the theory of relativity. Concepts in science are to be defined in terms of the operations by which they are observed. "We mean," he wrote, "by any concept nothing more than a set of operations; *the concept is synonymous with the corresponding set of operations*. If the concept is physical, as of length, the operations are actual physical operations, namely, those by which length is measured." Bridgman said that length (of a table) and distance (to the sun) are different concepts because they are measured by different operations, but it has been generally admitted that there are operations for establishing the equivalence of different operations and that tape-measured length and triangulated length can be regarded as the same kind of length, when the magni-

tudes are terrestrial and small, provided only that you keep in mind the nature of the operation that defines *same*. Difficulties arise in determining simultaneity of events in places so remote from each other that it takes considerable time for any signal, like light, to pass from one place to the other, but those problems are not the psychologist's.

Bridgman helped the psychologists by his discussion of *pseudo-problems*, the "meaningless" questions which are perpetually being raised by scientists. They are the questions which can not be answered by any known observational test, like "May time have a beginning or an end?" (a Kantian antinomy), "May space have a fourth dimension, not directly detectible?" and "Is a universe possible in which $2 + 2 \neq 4$?" Among these examples Bridgman included, as a meaningless question, this: "Is the sensation which I call blue really the *same* as that which my neighbor calls blue? Is it possible that a blue object may arouse in him the same sensation that a red object does in me and *vice versa*?" That was Bridgman's way of saying that sensory quality can not be specified absolutely, but only relatively by discrimination. You can not compare Peter's sensations with Paul's. You can compare Peter's with Peter's and know that for him blue is not red and conversely, and the same for Paul. But that Peter's blue is not Paul's red must remain unknowable until the operation of cross-connecting the nervous systems of two persons is possible. Only then could an integrated Peterpaul compare his Peter vision with his Paul vision, as happened in 1880 when a man color-blind in one eye and normal in the other was discovered. Without direct comparison, psychologists can not learn that the color blind see only two of the four unique hues. So the rule of operationism is that propositions which can not be tested by observation are meaningless.

It is only a step from this view of Bridgman's to saying that private consciousness is a conception meaningless for science. If you have an operation, like introspection, for publicizing consciousness, well and good, but then the consciousness has become public and is no longer private. The ineffable, the unpublishable, makes no sense in science. That view, however, is what Max Meyer had said in 1921 and what Tolman was supporting more and more explicitly both before and after Bridgman's book came out. It was not new in psychology, but it gained support when physics, always scientific psychology's model, came out for it.

(2) The influence from philosophy arrived via the Vienna circle. Its better known members were Moritz Schlick, Otto Neurath,

Rudolph Carnap and Philipp Frank, and it formed in Vienna at just the time that Bridgman was publishing his book. The purpose of the group was the replacement of philosophy by a systematic investigation of the logic of science. In that manner there began a movement which Feigl later named *logical positivism*, which in science (including psychology) became *physicalism*, because it reduced all scientific language to the communal language of physics, and which in psychology became *behavioristics* because the psychological operations are all observation of behavior. Even the mentalistic entities, when they are reduced to the physical operations by which they are observed, reduce to behavior. This is the *reductio ad actionem* of behavioristics.

The Vienna circle was talking about the language of science, about the *formal propositions* which had to do with the relation of words and symbols to one another and which thus make up the subject-matter of *syntactics*, and about the *empirical propositions* which are assertions concerning the observable world and are capable of observational test as to their truth or falsity. The relations between the two systems, between objects and their signs or designating words, constitute the subject-matter of *semantics*. The concepts which can not participate in these meaningful relations are cast forth into outer darkness—into metaphysics which, they thought, claims to utter the unutterable.

The movement was positivistic. We have already seen that there are three kinds of positivism: (a) the *social positivism* of Comte; (b) the *experiential positivism* of Ernst Mach and Karl Pearson (in this respect Pearson was Mach's disciple); and (c) this *operational positivism*, which Feigl called *logical positivism* (pp. 533 f.). It was an attempt to get back to basic data and thus to increase agreement and diminish the misunderstandings that come about from unsuspected differences in meanings. Experience had proved unsuccessful as the scientific ultimate. Psychologists quarreled too much about what introspection reveals. The reason for substituting behaviorism for introspectionism in psychology was exactly the reason for substituting operational positivism for experiential positivism in the logic of science. Mach's intentions were good, but he failed to realize that the *given* in introspection gets warped in being *taken*. Introspection is a method of observation and as such is subject to error. Philosophers had thought of it as so primary as to be incapable of error.

(3) The background of operationism in animal psychology and behaviorism is the subject-matter of the preceding sections of this

book and needs no rehearsal beyond a *précis*. Darwin showed the probability of the continuity of mind between men and animals. Romanes exhibited the continuity. Lloyd Morgan urged parsimony of interpretation and brought out Occam's razor. Loeb suggested that there is no consciousness in the animal scale below the level where associative learning takes place, but Jennings indicated that the level may be, after all, at the very bottom. The psychologists noted that animal consciousness can be discovered by operations like those used for discovering the consciousness of any person other than the discoverer—the psychology of "the other one." Watson, impatient of hair splitting, dispensed with consciousness all around in one extreme act of parsimony. Many others flocked to his standard but not all of them were willing to recite his creed. Some—Holt and Tolman first—were clear that behaviorism does not exorcise consciousness but absorbs it, reducing it to the behavioral operations by which it is observed. One can not say that operationism began at any point. It was there all along, to be understood and used by the astute who were not blinded by their own impetuousness.

It was there all along; yet how did American psychologists become conscious of operational definitions as being an advance and how did they come to regard the new insight as a movement and call it *operationism?* The events, that fit into a trend of the times, turn out to be the events that make the trend.

Herbert Feigl (1902-   ), a Viennese, took his Ph.D. in philosophy at the University of Vienna in 1927, the year that the Vienna circle was getting formed, and he stayed in Vienna teaching until 1930. He knew what was going on in the new positivism, and he also knew Bridgman's book which had been published in 1927. In 1930 he came to Harvard on a fellowship to find out what Bridgman was thinking and to work in philosophy of science in general. It was he who introduced the Harvard psychologists to the ideas of their own colleague, Bridgman, to the work of the Vienna circle, to logical positivism and to operational procedures in general. Skinner, in his Harvard reflexological thesis of 1931, mentioned Bridgman along with Mach, and, indeed, he seemed ready to fit his concepts into this trend, for they did fit excellently, quite as well as Tolman's. In general, the Harvard psychologists in seminars and at the laboratory lunches talked about the 'new' approach and began to use the word *operationism.* It was S. S. Stevens who took the leadership at Harvard. He published general articles on the operational procedures in April and November 1935 and again in

1936. Meanwhile McGeoch at Wesleyan and Tolman at California had become involved. McGeoch read a paper on operational procedures in September 1935 and another in 1937, although he never published at length. Tolman, who has been thinking in this manner all along, published in 1936 on operational behaviorism and on operational analysis of demands. There was a paper by Waters and Pennington in 1938, and then Stevens published in April 1939 what became practically the handbook of the new 'psycho-logic,' *Psychology and the Science of Science*, a paper which reviewed the contributions of the physicists and the philosophers (not the animal and objective psychologists and the behaviorists, though), expounded, clarified and presented a bibliography of the discussion to that date. The interest at Harvard was increased because the Vth International Congress for the Unity of Science met there in 1939 and most of the important European logical positivists were there, although Schlick was dead. It is interesting to note that the Harvard experimental psychologists who took up with operationism were not behaviorists or animal psychologists, but men who were looking for rigor of definition in laboratory situations where introspection had once ruled. The same statement could be made of McGeoch, although not of Tolman, who did, of course, come to his operational behaviorism rat in hand. Skinner was at Harvard until 1936, in the Society of Fellows and working on animals in Crozier's laboratory of general physiology. He was certainly a practising operationist all along even when not a participant in a common concern.

This current of support for operationism by the tough-minded led quickly to a splatter of objections by the tender-minded, and to some extent the tough-minded were to blame. They had begun by demanding rigor, asking for operational definitions of some terms which were suspected of being wholly or partly meaningless. The tender-minded charged that operationism was a police measure directed against freedom of research and expression. The answer was—and it got clear in time—that operationism is not an ethic, that is has no authority to require anything of anyone. It is one of the tools which the scientist may use to clarify his own concepts or the concepts of others. If a fact is public, one can always ask how it became public, realizing that it still has upon it certain limitations that are inherent in the operations by which it was publicized.

Stevens listed seven characteristics of operationism, which may be stated here in greatly abbreviated form. (a) Operationism involves the reduction of all statements about phenomena (empirical propositions) to those simple terms which in general command agreement. This criterion is social. (b) Operationism deals only with public or publishable events. Private experience is excluded. (c) It deals only with the "other one," the person or organism who is not the experimenter. (d) An experimenter can consider events that occur in himself, but then he treats himself like "another one," accepting for science only what he publishes out of his privacy. (e) Operationism deals only with propositions whose truth or falsity can be tested on demand by the use of concrete operations. (f) The basic operation turns out to be discrimination. It plays the rôle that sensation (experience) played for Mach. All observation is at bottom discriminatory. (g) Finally, the operationist keeps formal and empirical propositions clearly differentiated in his own thinking, thus avoiding endless confusion.

Stevens also claimed to know nine things that operationism is *not*. Here they are. (a) It is not a new school of psychology. It is a technic. (b) It is not a set of rules for conducting experiments. (c) It is not an interdiction set up against theorizing and speculation. (d) It is no guarantee of agreement, though its purpose is to further agreement. (e) It is not the experiential positivism of Mach. (f) It is not the kind of behaviorism that excludes images or any other data from consideration. All the mentalistic entities come in as reduced to the operations by which they are observed. (g) It is not a monism, (h) nor a dualism, (i) nor a pluralism. It takes what comes by way of observation, and the unity of science which it promotes is a unity of a common language applied to common procedures.

It is not correct, as a conclusion to this chapter, to say that by 1950 all psychology had adopted operationism and that the schools had disappeared! The reduction of concepts to their operations turned out to be dull business. No one wants to trouble with it when there is no special need. The reduction takes thought and study, and they take time, and there may be little or no gain. A still more rigorous language is furnished by symbolic logic, but no one would want to reduce James' *Principles* to a set of postulates and conclusions after the manner of Hull in his most exact moments. The operational technic seems to have become something to use when the user thinks he can get somewhere with it. Meanwhile, the historical position of this whole argument is that the logic of science shows up the question of the existence or nonexistence of consciousness as a pseudoproblem. Quite contrary to expectation, it turns out that the behaviorist can eat the cake of consciousness and have it too. He may not always know it, but he can.

NOTES

Animal Psychology

There is no dearth of good handbooks on comparative psychology. N. R. F. Maier and T. C. Schneirla, *Principles of Animal Psychology*, 1935, is perhaps the best general work; it has a bibliography of over 600 titles. The classical text is M. F. Washburn, *The Animal Mind*, 4 ed., 1936, with a bibliography of about 1700 titles; it was first published in 1908 and was kept up-to-date as one of the chief responsibilities of its author. The most encyclopedic text is the three volumes of C. J. Warden, T. N. Jenkins and L. H. Warner, *Comparative Psychology*, I, *Principles and Methods*, 1935; II, *Plants and Invertebrates*, 1936; III, *Vertebrates*, 1940; with a bibliography of over 8450 references. An excellent, more recent text with chapters written by 11 authorities is F. A. Moss, *Comparative Psychology*, 2 ed., 1943, with bibliographies of over 500 items.

More specifically on the history of comparative psychology, see Warden *et al.*, *op. cit.*, I, 3-54; R. H. Waters in Moss, *op. cit.*, 7-31. Washburn, *op. cit.*, uses the historical form of exposition.

With such excellent bibliographies available, references here lose their importance. We may repeat only those which are specially mentioned in the text.

On tropistic behavior, see Jacques Loeb, *Der Heliotropismus der Tiere und seine Ueberstimmung mit den Heliotropismus der Pflanzen*, 1890; *Einleitung in die vergleichende Gehirnphysiologie und vergleichende Psychologie*, 1899, Eng. trans., 1900; *The Mechanistic Conception of Life*, 1912; *Forced Movements, Tropisms and Animal Conduct*, 1918; S. O. Mast, *Light and the Behavior of Organisms*, 1911 (history of tropisms, 1-58).

On the extreme mechanistic view, see A. Bethe. Dürfen wir den Ameisen und Bienen psychische Qualitäten zuschreiben?, *Arch. ges. Physiol.*, 1898, 70, 15-100; Th. Beer, A. Bethe and J. von Uexküll, Vorschläge zu einer objektivirender Nomenclatur in der Physiologie der Nervensystems, *Biol. Centbl.* 1899, 19, 517-521 or *Centbl. Physiol.*, 1899, 13, 137-141 (the two articles are identical); J. P. Nuel, La psychologie comparée est-elle légitime?, *Arch. psychol.*, 1906, 5, 326-343.

On the psychological approach to the behavior of the lower organisms, see H. S. Jennings, *Contributions to the Study of the Behavior of the Lower Organisms*, 1904 and 1906; S. J. Holmes, *The Evolution of Animal Intelligence*, 1911; *Studies in Animal Behavior*, 1916.

On the behavior of the social insects, see the references for Fabre, Lubbock and Forel, pp. 475 f.; W. M. Wheeler, *Ants, Their Structure, Development and Behavior*, 1910; *Social Life among the Insects*, 1923.

For the argument about animal introspection, see Washburn, *op. cit.*, 1-32.

For the early experiments in animal psychology which the text discusses, see D. A. Spalding, Instinct: with original observations on young animals, *Macmillan's Mag.*, 1873, 27, 282-293; reprinted in *Pop. Sci. Mo.*, 1902, 61, 126-142; E. L. Thorndike, *Animal Intelligence*, 1898 (*Psychol. Monog.*, no. 8), reprinted 1911, and portions reprinted in W. Dennis, *Readings in the History of Psychology*, 1948, 377-387; *The Mental Life of the Monkeys*, 1910 (*Psychol. Monog.*, no. 15); W. S. Small, An experimental study of the mental processes of the rat, *Amer. J. Psychol.*, 1899, 11, 133-165; 1901, 12, 206-239 (origination of the maze method); L. W. Kline, Suggestions toward a laboratory course in comparative psychology, *ibid.*, 1899, 10, 399-430; A. J. Kinnaman, Mental life of two *Macacus rhesus* monkeys in captivity, *ibid.*, 1902, 13, 98-148; J. B. Watson, *Animal Education: the Psychical Development of the White Rat*, 1903 (*Univ. Chicago Contr. Philos.*, 4, no. 2); *Kinæsthetic and Organic Sensations: Their Rôle in the Reactions of the White Rat to the Maze*, 1907 (*Psychol. Monog.*, no. 33).

On R. M. Yerkes, see his long bibliography in the general texts, *opp. citt.*; also his autobiography, in C. Murchison, *Psychology in Autobiography*, 1932, II, 381-407. For his own authoritative summary of his work on the apes, see his *Chimpanzees: a Laboratory Colony*, 1943. An autobiography, covering his varied activities, is said to be almost ready for publication as the proofs of the present volume return to the printer.

On the higher mental processes in animals, see in general Washburn, *op. cit.*, 328-381; Maier and Schneirla, *op. cit.*, 444-480; W. T. Heron in Moss, *op. cit.*, 248-279; L. T. Hobhouse, *Mind in Evolution*, 1901, 2 ed., 1915, esp. chap. 10 for the experiments which anticipated Köhler's; L. W. Cole, Concerning the intelligence of raccoons, *J. comp. Neurol. Psychol.*, 1907, 17, 211-261; G. V. Hamilton, A study of trial and error reactions in mammals, *J. animal Behav.*, 1911, 1, 33-66 (multiple choice method); W. S. Hunter, *The Delayed Reaction in Animals and Children*, 1913 (*Behavior Monog.*, no. 6); portions reprinted in Dennis, *op. cit.*, 472-481; The temporal maze and kinesthetic sensory processes in the white rat, *Psychobiol.*, 1920, 2, 1-18; The behavior of raccoons in a double alternation temporal maze, *J. genet. Psychol.*, 1927, 35, 374-388; W. Köhler, *Intelligenzprüfung an Menschenaffen*, 1917, 2 ed., 1921, Eng. trans., 1925; H. Schlosberg and A. Katz, Double alternation lever-pressing in the white rat, *Amer. J. Psychol.*, 1943, 56, 274-282 (integration of rapid successive movements).

On bringing up a chimpanzee with a child and the relative superiorities of each, see W. N. Kellogg and L. A. Kellogg, *The Ape and the Child*, 1933.

Objective Psychology

The text is indebted to an excellent resumé by C. M. Diserens, Psychological objectivism, *Psychol. Rev.*, 1925, 32, 121-152. The three Russians—Sechenov, Pavlov, Bekhterev—made propaganda for objective psychology (*vide infra*); so did the behaviorists (see next section) and the tropistic psychologists (see preceding section). Objective psychology is too pervasive to have an exclusive literature.

Most of the matter mentioned in the text are echoes of other discussions in this volume and need no additional notes. References for the men who are newly mentioned in this section follow.

Antoine Louis Claude Destutt de Tracy, the contemporary of Cabanis, published *Éléments d'idéologie*, 4 vols., 1818, but more immediate to the purpose of our discussion is his *Traité de la volonté et ses effets*, 1815.

The important paper of Johann Gottfried Herder's is *Vom Erkennen und Empfinden der menschlichen Seele*, 1778.

Auguste Comte wrote *Cours de philosophie positive*, 6 vols., 1830-42, which had many editions and translations. There are many other works of his which insist on the positivistic principle and which every bibliography of Comte lists. George Henry Lewes, the English disciple of Comte, wrote books that deal with psychology and positivism. The one that bears most directly on the present topic is his *The Study of Psychology*, 1879.

For Henry Maudsley on positivism in psychology and the unconscious, see his *Psychology and Pathology of Mind*, 1868.

For the work of Ivan Michailovich Sechenov there is his *Selected Works*, 1935, published in Moscow by the Russian government in honor of the XVth International Physiological Congress, which was meeting there. Unfortunately, this book, although meant as scientific propaganda in the English-speaking countries, is not generally available. It includes a biography of Sechenov by M. N. Shaternikov, some papers in German on the chemistry of the blood and three long papers, all translated into English, on the psychological importance of reflexes. The titles of these papers are: *The Reflexes of the Brain*, 1863, the monograph that was banned as immoral because materialistic (and then unbanned) and that influenced Pavlov; *Who Must Investigate the Problems of Psychology and How?*; and *The Elements of Thought*, an exposition, eight chapters long, which explicates Sechenov's mature mechanistic views about the nature of intellectual mental events.

Ivan Petrovich Pavlov's work is mostly in Russian with some articles in French and German. It is now available in Eng. trans. as *Conditioned Reflexes: an Investigation of the Physiological Activity of the Cerebral Cortex*, 1927, and *Lectures on Conditioned Reflexes*, 1928. The latter includes a biographical sketch by W. H. Gantt and contains forty-one lectures arranged chronologically from 1903 to 1928. For Pavlov's criticisms of psychological method as compared with physiological, see pp. 75, 113, 121, 169, 192, 219 and 329f. See also the reprint of the 1906 lecture (chap. 4, *op. cit.*, 1928) entitled Scientific study of the so-called psychical processes in the higher animals, reprinted in W. Dennis, *Readings in the History of Psychology*, 1948, 425-438. See also Y. P. Frolov, *Pavlov and His School*, Eng. trans. from Russian, 1937 (written after Pavlov's death in 1936); also the very recent biography by Pavlov's "senior surviving pupil," B. P. Babkin, *Pavlov: a Biography*, 1949.

Vladimir Michailovich Bekhterev is available to westerners in his *Objektive Psychologie oder Psychoreflexologie: die Lehre von den Assoziationsreflexen*, 1910 in Russian; German and French trans. in 1913; *General Principles of Human Reflexology: an Introduction to the Objective Study of Personality*, Russian eds., 1917, 1923, 1925; Eng. trans. of 3 ed., 1932. The latter volume in Eng. trans. includes a biographical sketch by A. Gerver.

An excellent summary of the development of Russian psychology from 1917 to 1936 has recently placed a slim bridge across the language barrier between Russia and the west: I. D. London, A historical survey of psychology in the Soviet Union, *Psychol. Bull.*, 1949, 241-277 (bibliography of 137 titles).

Behaviorism

On behaviorism in general, see R. S. Woodworth, *Contemporary Schools of Psychology*, 2 ed., 1948, 68-119; G. Murphy, *Historical Introduction to Modern Psychology*, 2 ed., 1949, 251-268; A. A. Roback, *Behaviorism and Psychology*, 1923; *Behaviorism at Twenty-Five*, 1937; E. Heidbreder, *Seven Psychologies*, 1933, 234-286; C. R. Griffith, *Principles of Systematic Psychology*, 247-265, 320-356.

Most of the secondary sources, *opp. citt.*, deal more extensively with Watson's behaviorism than with others', so for Watson see them. The birth of behaviorism took place in J. B. Watson, Psychology as the behaviorist views it, *Psychol. Rev.*, 1913, 20, 158-177, reprinted in W. Dennis, *Readings in the History of Psychology*, 1948, 457-471. This paper was followed immediately by Watson's Image and affection in behavior, *J. Philos.*, 1913, 10, 421-428. Then came *Behavior: an Introduction to Comparative Psychology*, 1914, in which the first chapter reprints, with minor changes and omissions and considerable additions, the two articles just cited. Next among the crucial papers was The place of the conditioned reflex in psychology, *Psychol. Rev.*, 1916, 23, 89-116; it was his presidential address before the American Psychological Association. Then came the systematic text, *Psychology from the Standpoint of a Behaviorist*, 1919, 2 ed., 1924. For his later writings, see his *Behaviorism*, 1924, and his three lectures in C. Murchison, *Psychologies of 1925*, 1926, 1-81. Watson's autobiography is in C. Murchison, *Psychology in Autobiography*, 1936, III, 271-281.

E. B. Holt's important book is *The Freudian Wish and Its Place in Ethics*, 1915, which reprints as a supplement Response and cognition, *J. Philos.*, 1915, 12, 365-373, 393-409. His other important book is *Animal Drive and the Learning Process*, 1931. Earlier there were *The Concept of Consciousness*, 1914, but completed in 1908; The place of illusory experience in a realistic world, in *The New Realism*, 1912, 303-373. There are two biographical sketches: H. S. Langfeld, Edwin Bissell Holt 1873-1946, *Psychol. Rev.*, 1946, 53, 251-258; L. Carmichael, same title, *Amer. J. Psychol.*, 1946, 59, 478-480.

E. C. Tolman's early paper on meaning and imagery was More concerning the temporal relations of meaning and imagery, *Psychol. Rev.*, 1917, 24, 114-138. Tolman published so many important theoretical papers in the period 1920 to 1932 that it is hard to select a few for citation here. We may note A new formula for behaviorism, *ibid.*, 1922, 29, 44-53; A behavioristic account of the emotions, *ibid.*, 1923, 30, 217-227; Purpose and cognition: the determiners of animal learning, *ibid.*, 1925, 32, 285-297; A behavioristic theory of ideas, *ibid.*, 1926, 33, 352-369; A behaviorist's definition of consciousness, *ibid.*, 1927, 34, 433-439. All this is brought together in what for a time was Tolman's *magnum opus*, *Purposive Behavior in Animals and Men*, 1932. Later there was Psychology versus immediate experience, *Philos. Sci.*, 1935, 2, 356-380, and his presidential address before the American Psychological Association, The determiners of behavior at a choice point, *Psychol. Rev.*, 1938, 45, 1-41. On Tolman and operational behaviorism, see the next section of these notes. For the study and criticism of Tolman's psychology, see A. Tilquin, Un "behaviorisme téléologique": la psychologie de Tolman, *J. psychol. norm. pathol.*, 1935, 32, 731-775; Woodworth, *op. cit.*, 103-108; and, for his sign-gestalt theory of learning, E. R. Hilgard, *Theories of Learning*, 1948, 261-293.

For K. S. Lashley's chief excursion into the defense of behaviorism, see his The behavioristic interpretation of consciousness, *Psychol. Rev.*, 1923, 30, 237-272, 329-353.

A. P. Weiss' important book is *A Theoretical Basis of Human Behav-ior*, 1925, 2 ed., 1929. See also his The biosocial standpoint in psychology, in C. Murchison, *Psychologies of 1930*, 1930, 301-306. Two biographical sketches are R. M. Elliott, Albert Paul Weiss 1879-1931, *Amer. J. Psychol.*, 1931, 43, 707-709; S. Renshaw, same title, *J. general Psychol.*, 1932, 6, 3-7.

W. S. Hunter, whose studies of symbolic processes have been discussed in the preceding section of this chapter, may be cited here for his behavioristic polemics: The problem of consciousness, *Psychol. Rev.*, 1924, 31, 1-31; The symbolic process, *ibid.*, 478-497; The subject's report, *ibid.*, 1925, 32, 153-170; General anthroponomy and its systematic problems, *Amer. J. Psychol.*, 1925, 36, 286-302; Psychology and anthroponomy, in C. Murchison, *Psychologies of 1925*, 1926, 83-107; same title and editor, *Psychologies of 1930*, 1930, 281-300; and his presidential address before the American Psychological Association, The psychological study of behavior, *Psychol. Rev.*, 1932, 39, 1-24.

B. F. Skinner's more important writings, selected with the purpose of this chapter in mind, are The concept of the reflex in the description of behavior, *J. general Psychol.*, 1931, 5, 427-458 (the original thesis); Drive and reflex strength, *ibid.*, 1932, 6, 22-48; The measurement of spontaneous activity, *ibid.*, 1933, 9, 3-24; The generic nature of the concepts of stimulus and response, *ibid.*, 1935, 12, 40-65; and finally the book, the *vade mecum* of his disciples, *The Behavior of Organisms: an Experimental Analysis*, 1938. On Skinner's psychology, see Woodworth, *op. cit.*, 112-116; on his "descriptive behaviorism," see Hilgard, *op. cit.*, 116-145.

C. L. Hull's presidential address before the American Psychological Association gives his basic principles and examples of his procedure: Mind, mechanism and adaptive behavior, *Psychol. Rev.*, 1937, 44, 1-32. The elaborate exercise in logic is by Hull in association with C. I. Hovland, R. T. Ross, M. Hall, D. T. Perkins and F. B. Fitch, *Mathematico-Deductive Theory of Rote Learning: a Study in*

Scientific Methodology, 1940. The general text by Hull alone is *Principles of Behavior: an Introduction to Behavior Theory*, 1943. On Hull's psychology, see Woodworth, *op. cit.*, 108-112; Hilgard, *op. cit.*, 76-115.

The text omits mention of Max Meyer (1873-   ), who is sometimes regarded as a pre-Watsonian behaviorist. His position is stated in his *The Fundamental Laws of Human Behavior*, 1911. He is an objectively oriented psychologist, trained with Stumpf and the physicist, Max Planck, at Berlin, where he received his Ph.D. in 1896. He also wrote *The Psychology of the Other One*, 1921, a textbook which makes the point that psychology must study public data and not private consciousness. Unless the private consciousness can be made public, it is not material for science. This point of view is good behavioristics and operational positivism. See the next section.

Operationism

The best place to go for orientation in this subject is S. S. Stevens, Psychology and the science of science, *Psychol. Bull.*, 1939, 36, 221-263. His annotated bibliography of 66 items gives all the important references to that date. More recently the history and meaning of the positivistic movement has been clearly and attractively expounded by Philipp Frank, *Modern Science and its Philosophy*, 1949.

The *casus belli* of operationism is P. W. Bridgman, *The Logic of Modern Physics*, 1927. For Bridgman's other books and for the many contributions and criticisms of philosophers and physicists, see Stevens, *loc. cit.* We may cite here some of the early publications by psychologists:

S. S. Stevens, The operational basis of psychology, *Amer. J. Psychol.*, 1935, 47, 323-330; The operational definition of psychological concepts, *Psychol. Rev.*, 1935, 42, 517-527; Psychology: the propædeutic science, *Philos. Sci.*, 1936, 3, 90-103.

J. A. McGeoch, Learning as an operationally defined concept, *Psychol. Bull.*, 1935, 32, 688; A critique of operational definition, *ibid.*, 1937, 34, 703 f.

Both of these are single-page abstracts and of interest only as establishing the date of McGeoch's concern with operationism.

E. C. Tolman, An operational analysis of 'demands,' *Erkenntnis*, 1936, 6, 383-390; Operational behaviorism and current trends in psychology, *Proc. 25th Anniv. Celebr. Univ. So. Calif.*, 1936, 89-103.

E. G. Boring. Temporal perception and operationism, *Amer. J. Psychol.*, 1936, 48, 519-522; An operational restatement of G. E. Müller's psychophysical axioms, *Psychol. Rev.*, 1941, 48, 457-464.

R. H. Seashore and B. Katz, An operational definition and classification of mental mechanisms, *Psychol. Rev.*, 1, 1937, 3-24.

R. H. Waters and L. A. Pennington, Operationism in psychology, *Psychol. Rev.*, 1938, 45, 414-423, an unenthusiastic and critical paper.

A book of this same date, which is sympathetic to operationism but calls itself "critical positivism" is C. C. Pratt, *The Logic of Modern Psychology*, 1939.

In 1944 H. E. Israel and B. Goldstein published Operationism in psychology, *Psychol. Rev.*, 1944, 51, 177-188, an article so critical of operationism that the present author suggested that the *Psychol. Rev.* conduct a symposium on operationism in order to clear up some of the disputed points. The next year the plan was realized: Symposium on operationism, *ibid.*, 1945, 52, 241-294. The separate papers and rejoinders are: E. G. Boring, The use of operational definitions in science, 243-245, 278-281; P. W. Bridgman, Some general principles of operational analysis, 246-249, 281-284; H. Feigl, Operationism and scientific method, 250-259, 284-288; H. E. Israel, Two difficulties in operational thinking, 260 f.; C. C. Pratt, Operationism in psychology, 262-269, 288-291; B. F. Skinner, The operational analysis of psychological terms, 270-277, 291-294. The psychologists were fortunate in being joined by the physicist Bridgman and the philosopher Feigl, but unfortunate in the fact that war activities prevented the participation of Stevens and Tolman.

CHAPTER 25

Brain Function

In the early chapters of this book we considered the history of some of the problems that arose about the localization of mental functions in the nervous system: Gall, phrenology and the mind-body problem of the 1810s; Flourens, *action propre, action commune* and localization of brain function in the 1820s; Bell, Johannes Müller and Helmholtz on specific nerve energies and specific fiber energies, the localization of functions in nerves and fibers; Broca, Fritsch and Hitzig and others on the discovery of centers in the brain. We took the account up to the 1870s. Now it is time to pick up these threads, to say something about what happened later, to show how this line of history shows the effects of cultural lag and the inertia of the *Zeitgeist*.

We can not undertake here to review the history of the last eighty years of physiological psychology and the related brain-and-nerve physiology. That history needs a book for itself as much as does the history of perception or the history of learning. What we can do is to sketch in broad outline general advance, stressing the manner in which the development of thinking about the psychophysiology of perception and brain function reflected not only the progress of research but also those other factors of social dynamics which are perpetually influencing scientific opinion.

MIND AND BRAIN

The chief function of the brain is—thought, perhaps, or consciousness. Cabanis said that the brain secretes thought and he was asked to say whether a body left twitching by the guillotine was conscious. He said it was not, since the brain is in the head. The view that the brain is the seat of mind is old. Pythagoras and Plato held it, though not Aristotle. Galen fixed the idea on the medical world. (See pp. 50 f. for the early theories.) Descartes did more than add the great weight of his authority to this view; he made mind seem real and separate from matter, for he substantialized consciousness as unextended substance, something that can exist in the body without occupying space (pp. 162 f.). Descartes' realistic dualism, with his specifications of how the soul (mind) interacts with the animal spirits in the brain, how it directs them and is altered by them, this theory fixed both the notion that there exists some such thing as conscious mind and the belief that the brain is its special organ. That mind depends on brain is what every philosopher—natural, mental or moral—has thought, in one form or another, since the seventeenth century. Recall Hartley (pp. 193-199), Gall (pp. 53-56), Flourens (pp. 63-67) and then all the physiologists and psychologists of the nineteenth century. Even a crass materialist like La Mettrie believed in the existence of thought as something which the brain creates (pp. 212-214).

The soul, mind, unextended substance (in Descartes' phrase of the seventeenth century), impalpable consciousness (in Külpe's phrase of the twentieth) is, however, pretty flimsy stuff for scientific control and manipulation. With consciousness being *unanschaulich* in the sense that it will not stand still and deliver itself to observation and the brain being literally *unanschaulich* in the sense that you can not directly observe its secretion of thought, it is no wonder that theories of the relation of mind to brain—the "mind-body" theories—were speculative and not observed correlations. There have been four of these theories.

(1) *Interactionism* is Descartes' form of *dualism* (pp. 162-165). Brain and mind are distinct substances, one extended and the other unextended, and they interact at a specified place. There have been other interactionists since Descartes. William James was one. The theory can not be disproved so long as there are mental phenomena whose neural correlates, if any, remain unknown.

(2) *Psychophysical parallelism* assumes that the brain is part of the physical world and that the physical world is a closed system. Mental phenomena form a second universe in a *dualism*, and these mental phenomena coincide with brain phenomena or are parallel with them. This was Hartley's view in 1749 (pp. 195-197). The conception of pre-established non-interacting correlation was, of course, Leibnitz's (p. 168). Nearly all the nineteenth-century physiological psychologists held it—Wundt, for instance. *No psychosis without neurosis* was the phrase of the 1870s when these words were usually applied to normal mental and neural states. "The ground of every state of consciousness is a material process, a psychophysical process, as it were, to whose occurrence the presence of the conscious state is joined," said G. E. Müller in 1896 in the first of his famous psychophysical axioms. The principle is, of course, irrevers-

ible: there are thought to be plenty of brain events that lack conscious accompaniments, even though the physiologist Pflüger did
in 1853 suppose that consciousness accompanies adaptive action of
the spinal cord.

In all this discussion of the relation of mind to body we must
remember that thoughtful men ever since Descartes had been so
sure of the existence of mind (consciousness) that they accepted
the concept without rigorous definition. The fact of consciousness
was so obvious to all that a denial or doubt of consciousness seemed
absurd and impossible. It was only later, when unconsciousness had
come in as a concept, that the line between it and the conscious
turned out to be difficult to draw. If you respond adequately to
stimulation and then forget it but ten minutes later, were you conscious? Presumably, yes. You could have written your introspection
down in ten minutes. What if your memory is not there one second
or half a second later? Can you be conscious of what is unreportable,
unreportable because report takes time and your memory will not
last? Can a pain hurt if any instant of it has gone from memory half
a second later? These are twentieth-century questions, the sort that
the operationists ask when they are wondering whether the distinction between consciousness and unconsciousness may not be a
pseudoproblem; but the fact that the questions can be asked and
were not answered in the nineteenth century shows how there could
be no clear decision between Pflüger, who said that the reflexes of
the cord should be conscious, and Lotze, who said they were not,
or between Loeb and Jennings on the criterion for appearance of
consciousness in the evolutionary scale. The psychophysical parallelists were sure of the existence of unconscious neural events but
not sure of the criteria for consciousness. There were only a few
panpsychists, men like Fechner, who would have said *No neurosis
without psychosis*, including, of course, the negative sensations
among the psychoses (pp. 278 f., 290).

As we have already noted, the establishment of the principle of
the conservation of energy in the 1840s favored the principle of
psychophysical parallelism (pp. 236 f., 245). The discovery of the
mechanical equivalent of heat by Joule in 1849 and the realization
that work done on a body may be stored as "potential energy" and
given out as work done by the body tended to fix attention on the
serial nature of cause and effect and their equivalence in terms of
energy. Very able thinkers came to believe in 'chains' of causes and
effects, series in which any event is the effect of the preceding one
and the cause of the succeeding one and in which all events are equal

in energy. That is, of course, nonsense. Multiple causation is the rule in nature; hence there are *release mechanisms*, where a weak finger presses the button that explodes a ton of dynamite, and there are *summations*, where the little straw actually does break the camel's back. Bain, however, in the 1870s did not see that point when he argued against interactionism and for parallelism. He did not see how a neural event could cause a psychic one without transferring energy to it, nor a psychic event, with no physical energy to give up, cause a neural one. Being a dualist and believing in the conservation of physical energy within the closed system of the physical world, he could not believe that physical energy could be lost into the psychical world or acquired from it. That was the argument which gave the victory to parallelism in the late nineteenth century. If the new theory of the conservation of energy had not loomed so large then, there might have been more rigorous thinking.

(A Cartesian interactionism consistent with the conservation of energy is possible, just as there can be interaction between two systems, each of which is self-contained except as energy in it is released or directed by signals which the other system provides. In such a case, it is the transfer of communication which is important, not the transfer of energy. The systems may be regarded as self-contained yet intercommunicating.)

(3) The *double-aspect theory* of mind and brain assumes that there is but one underlying reality and that physiology sees one aspect and psychology another. Research on the brain's functions is slow and there are not many good instances yet, but hemianopia is a good case. The subject declares that he can see nothing in what would normally be the right half of his field of vision. That is a psychological fact, the "psychosis" which should have its "neurosis." In postmortem examination it is found that the left occipital lobe of the subject's brain has been destroyed. That is the "neurosis." May we not now say that these observations represent different aspects of the same fact, that the subject could in a sense 'see' that his left occipital lobe was not working? This kind of theory represents the trend toward operationism. It is a *metaphysical monism* and an *epistemological dualism*.

(4) One step further along toward monism is the *identity theory*. It is like the double-aspect theory except that it overlooks the difference in methods of observation and concentrates on the underlying reality (construct) as what is observed. It makes introspection into a method for observing the functioning of the brain.

These theories have become less important with the advance of operational thinking. It is now taken for granted that the same generality is found by many different observational techniques which supplement and confirm each other. Even when twentieth-century psychologists refuse to accept physicalism, still they are apt to find dualism less important than did their teachers and their teachers' teachers.

The list of the brain's functions varies with opinion, with the times and with schemes of classification. The faculty psychologists and the phrenologists had many functions for the brain. Here we may mention six.

(1) *Perception.* For empiricists perception is the brain's primary function. Information comes from outside and the mind (soul, sensorium) 'notes' the inbound traffic. The chief tradition of experimental psychology through Locke, Johannes Müller and the early experimentalists makes perception the first problem of psychology. Especially is that true of physiological psychology within which the study of the senses formed the chief occasion for the founding of the new science. We shall review this history in the next section of this chapter.

(2) *Reaction.* As we have already seen (pp. 147-149), the problem of reaction came into psychology from the astronomers and their discovery of the personal equation in the observation of stellar transits. In itself the personal equation began as a matter of times of perception, but the invention of the chronoscope (1842) and the chronograph (1869) made it possible to study the absolute personal equation by the reaction method. Donders invented compound reactions in 1868, and Wundt took over the method as one of the chief undertakings in the new Leipzig laboratory. The first paper published from that laboratory was Friedrich's study of the apperception time of simple and compound mental processes, experiments which he started in 1879, the year of the founding of the laboratory. From the same laboratory nine years later (1888) Ludwig Lange published his discovery of the effect of attitude on reaction time, the paper that is in a way the pioneer paper in the experimental psychology of attitude. The extensive use of the subtractive procedure in compound reactions ended with Külpe's criticism of it in 1893, a criticism based on Lange's experiments; but the reaction experiment itself had a further history, and with Ach, who was working under Külpe's aegis at Würzburg in 1905, it became the paradigm for the

effect of instruction or attitude upon the course of conscious content. In the 1880s the Wundtians had thought they were measuring the times of neural functions, that the times for perception, apperception and will were actually the times of cerebral additions to the times of simple reflexes (see pp. 148 f.).

The reflex may be said to have been discovered and named by Astruc in 1736. Robert Whytt and some others in the eighteenth century, Marshall Hall and many others in the nineteenth century concerned themselves with it (pp. 35-38). By 1896 Dewey was founding a functional psychology on his protest against a too analytical reflexology, but functional psychology tended nevertheless to be reflexological (p. 554). Meanwhile objective psychology, including both animal psychology (pp. 622-631) and the reflexology of the Russians (pp. 635-638), was developing and becoming ready for transformation into behaviorism (pp. 641-653). Is a stimulus-response reaction a function of the brain?

Well, yes; but there was not too much to say about reaction and the brain. There were, of course, the motor areas, and the simple connectionism that looks to the synapses as the seats of learning assumes that response gets tied to stimulus by *association* or *conditioning*. The term used depends upon date and semantic preference. There was, however, no good neurology or association or conditioning. The Russians called the fact of conditioning a physiological fact, but they did not specify what happens in the brain. The 'silent areas' of the frontal lobes were for a time called 'association areas,' largely because there was no other function known for them. The unvalidated phrenology of common sense held that a high forehead indicates potential genius. In the next section but one we shall consider just how much association does go on or can go on without the use of these areas. For the most part, however, experimental psychology has studied reaction in an 'empty organism' because there is as yet no certain knowledge of how the brain gets a particular response out of a particular stimulation.

(3) *Learning.* The formation of new connections, associations or conditioned responses, is not understood at present in terms of brain physiology—as we have just observed. Some special problems as to what is learned arise, but they show less how the brain works than they tell what capacities it has. For instance, it is known that a discriminative reaction to a *relation* can be learned independently of the absolute values of the items related (the animal chooses the brighter no matter how bright the pair to choose from). How does the brain perceive relations and put them on to final common paths?

Perception of a novel relation is *insight*, and the capacity to have many correct insights quickly must be part of genius. How does the brain handle insight, and why is learning so easy with insightful relations? We shall touch on these matters presently in connection with Lashley's work.

(4) *Memory*. Where or how does the brain store its memories? That is the great mystery. How can learning persist unreproduced, being affected by other learning while it waits? On the proper occasion what was learned reappears somewhat modified. Where was it in the meantime? The Gestalt psychologists speak of traces which may be altered before they are reproduced. The psychoanalysts speak of the unconscious or the foreconscious where the ideas await call in what Herbart described as a "state of tendency." The physiology of memory has been so baffling a problem that most psychologists in facing it have gone positivistic, being content with hypothesized intervening variables or with empty correlations.

(5) *Symbolic processes*. It now seems quite clear that thinking can go on without detectable muscular response. For instance, you can ponder a chess situation and decide on a move. That is to say, your thinking becomes observable to another person only after a notable time, in fact, not until you make overt responses which constitute the scientific evidence for your having thought. There are, however, prepublication brain events, which are called symbolic processes because they represent the real objects and events with which the thinking is concerned. A word, thought or uttered, or an image is a symbolic process because it has some concrete referent. The question now arises as to the precise neural nature of symbolic processes.

It is known that neural processes can take time. Nerve conduction is not instantaneous, and there are reverberatory phenomena where the process, being unable to 'park,' stays put by 'running around the block'—since the neural traffic can not stand still. The rat which can push the lever quickly twice to right and then twice to the left (p. 630) is presumably exhibiting a temporal integration of this sort. The dog who remembers a location by pointing to a bird or a food box carries some of his memory in his posture. Does he perhaps need some other trace in order that he should know what he was pointing at or for? In other words, the problem of the neurology of the symbolic process is not distinguishable from the problem of the memory trace.

With the definition of consciousness becoming more vague and less scientifically useful, the distinction between conscious and unconscious thinking evaporates, leaving us, however, without any good neurology of thinking.

(6) *Attitude.* A similar difficulty arises with the directive principle of neural action, with the nervous substrate of such dynamic entities as *set, Einstellung, determining tendency, Aufgabe* and *attitude.* It is hard to define an attitude. An associationist thinks of it as a set or instruction which renders what is normally a weaker association prepotent over what is normally a stronger association and which reinforces the weak against the strong without further learning. The normal associate for *black* is *white*, but, if you have been asked to give only rhymes, you may say *tack* or, if you have been talking about railroads before you were asked to find rhymes, you may say *track*. What are these switching mechanisms in the brain? The behavioral facts are known and the way thought works is understood in its gross outlines, but the neurology of the determining tendency still remains a puzzle to the physiological psychologists.

PERCEPTION

The reason for the problem of perception being historically the basic problem of experimental psychology is merely that experimentalism emerged directly from empiricism, was indeed a kind of controlled empiricism, and that perception was thus basic in empiricistic psychology. How does the mind learn about the external world? That question made good empiristic sense after Descartes had fixed the mind—or at least its gateway—inside the head. It was a question about the way in which empiricism works, a question especially important in the nineteenth century, yet one which goes back to antiquity. There was a second question which came up later, a question about the nature of perception: Of what does perception consist? We shall consider both of these questions in this section. The first is especially interesting because it illustrates certain facts about the dynamics of scientific thinking, showing the inertia of thought and how the refutation of a wrong theory does not destroy the theory but leaves the same victory to be won again and again as time goes on. It has been said that only a new theory can obliterate an old wrong one, and to a certain extent this bit of history illustrates that point (p. 23).

Since Descartes the answer to the first question has usually involved the hypothesization of an homunculus, a little man within the head who has the perceptive capacities which the 'big man' (total organism) was supposed to have. Such a theory can not be final. It states that the body can not perceive the external world directly because the percipient principle—the Sensorium, the Soul, the homunculus—is imprisoned in the head and requires some means of communication with the outside. A theory that tells merely how to get word about external objects into the skull leaves open, however, the question as to how the homunculus itself does its perceiving when information arrives. Does the little man have a still smaller man within his little head? The spiritualists answered that question by saying that it was of the nature of the Soul to perceive. The materialists eventually became the reflexologists, believing in the twentieth century that perception is discriminatory response. The parallelists were, for the most part, in between, holding to some kind of associationism. They attempted to describe perception as a synthesis of *Empfindungen* into such a *Vorstellung* as has meaning by virtue of its composition. In any case there was, however, the problem of how the information gets inside.

Now let us look at this matter of communication from Johannes Müller's point of view (pp. 81-88). He had no doubt that the Sensorium can perceive anything with which it can make contact. There were thus three possibilities.

(a) Conceivably there might be *direct presentation* of the object to the Sensorium. That is what common sense is apt to believe, but it is plainly wrong. The object itself can not be brought inside to the Sensorium nor can the Sensorium be taken outside to the object. The nerves are necessary intermediaries, and communication must take place by way of them. The Sensorium can get at only those representatives of the objects which come to it along the nerves.

(b) There could be *simulative representation*, in which the representatives of the objects that get through to the Sensorium are enabled to deliver significant messages because each is similar to its object. In primitive picture language the signs indicate their referents immediately just by being similar to them. This relation formed the Greeks' theory of perception, the theory of Empedocles, Democritos and Epicuros, who held that the objects give off faint images of themselves, simulacra or eidola, which, on being conducted to the mind, acquaint the mind with the nature of the objects which they simulate. That, in fact, is the too simple view which Johannes Müller fought. Such simulative representation has been often rejected and has then recurred to be rejected again. It seems to be a natural assumption which is usually made when there are no facts contradictory to it in plain sight.

(c) The remaining possibility is *symbolic representation*, in which the representatives of the objects carry information about their referents to those who know the semantic code. In a sophisticated language, words are symbols but not simulacra. They do not resemble their referents but stand for them to those who know what they mean. For instance, the word *red* can mean its color without being printed in red ink. Johannes Müller believed that the Sensorium knows directly only the state of the nerves, but that these nerves, having specific irritabilities, thus provide the necessary information for the Sensorium's assessment of the external world of stimulation. That meant, of course, either that the Sensorium is born to take these specific irritabilities into account (nativism) or that it has to learn how to use them in assessing the external world (empiricism). He was not concerned, however, with how the Sensorium knows or learns the code, but with the fact that it is dependent on a code and can, therefore, be deceived. Press hard enough on your eyeball and you perceive light in the dark when there is no light, because the Sensorium gets the optic signal.

Let us now go back into the history of this choice of simulative *vs.* symbolic representation and see what happened. In general, simulative representation tended to be preferred *a priori* as more obvious and simpler and also as permitting the Soul more contact with reality. (The accepted characteristics of the Soul, like the capacity for free, spontaneous action, were not being wholly ignored by psychologists even as late as the twentieth century. McDougall's argument for free will in 1923 is an example.) In general, however, research showed that representative simulation is inexact (as in perceived shape) or does not occur at all (as in perceived quality). When research is lacking, the battle for substituting complicated fact for simple opinion usually goes in favor of representative symbolism. Later, research conquers. We may take four examples: the perceptions of quality, orientation, attributes and shape.

1. *Perception of quality.* How does the Sensorium, or for that matter the brain, know whether an object is green, shrill, cold, redolent or bitter? An eidolon of the object would presumably simulate all its qualities and carry them to the brain along the nerves. But there are no eidola.

John Locke knew in 1690 that not all inner representation is simulative. The ideas simulate the primary qualities, like intensity, shape and size, but the secondary qualities, like greenness and shrillness, have only symbolic representation. In the external object greenness and shrillness are vibrations; in the mind they are sense qualities (pp. 174 f.). One might think that Locke had settled Johannes Müller's problem for him, but, although the eidolon theory was too crude for an age which believed in animal spirits or *vis viva* in the nerves, the notion that perception is correct because it matches its object persisted.

Hartley in 1749 was perfectly clear that the representation of an object of the brain can not be by simulation, for he held that the neural action in the nerves is vibration and that underlying the ideas in the brain there are miniature vibrations (pp. 195 f.). There ought not to have been any doubt after Hartley that the nerves intervene between the object and the mind and therefore impose on the mind their own nature; yet there was.

In 1801 Thomas Young suggested that color vision and color mixture might be explained by the existence of the different kinds of nerve fibers in the optic nerve—thus anticipating not only Müller's specific nerve energies but also Helmholtz's specific fiber energies (pp. 91 f.). In 1811 Charles Bell in his lectures and in the hundred-copy pamphlet which he printed privately for his friends anticipated Müller on every important point (pp. 81-88). Had he sought more publicity he might have advanced the *Zeitgeist* a little in this respect, but not much. The *Zeitgeist* has inertia.

As we have seen, Müller himself came out with his theory of specific nerve energies in 1826 and made it up into his elaborate doctrine in 1838. That he felt the necessity of insisting upon the fact that the Sensorium perceives only the state of the nerves and not the properties of objects shows that the notion of central representation by simulation had not died. To Müller *energy* meant quality. Instead of animal spirits, *vires vivae, vires nervosae*, he was speaking of specific energies. The nerve of each of the five senses has its own peculiar neural quality. As so often happens, Müller, in reforming thought, was unable completely to overcome the common inertia in his own thinking. While insisting that the nerve qualities are different from the qualities of the objects which specifically stimulate the nerves, he was still thinking of the Sensorium's perceiving qualities directly, the neural qualities ("energies") of the excited nerves with which it had contact. That in itself is a remnant of the old eidolon theory, a belief in an *homunculus ex machina* which can do the perceiving if only you can get it in contact with the proper objects of perception—in this case with the specific nerve energies, each of which has its meaning fixed by its specific irritability. Yet Müller had advanced thought, and he also suggested one tiny new point which became of the greatest importance presently. He noted that the specificity may lie not in the nerve itself but in its central termination. In that suggestion you get the beginning of a theory of sensory centers.

The extension of specific nerve energies to specific fiber energies by Helmholtz and others (pp. 91 f.) was an obvious step, but the establishment of the notion that there are sensory centers was much more complexly determined. The conception originated, of course, in the notion that various psychical functions have bodily seats. By 1810 Gall had 'found' localizations in the brain for all the mental functions (pp. 53-56). Even Flourens, who opposed him, admitted *actions propres* for specific regions of the brain (pp. 64-67). Broca described the speech center in 1861 (pp. 70-72), Fritsch and Hitzig discovered the motor area of the cortex in 1870 (pp. 73-75), and the arguments for sensory centers followed with the researches of Ferrier, Munk and Goltz (pp. 683 f.). Even a function seems better established if it occurs in some particular place.

Perhaps nothing influenced the belief in sensory centers more than the knowledge of the partial decussation of the optic fibers at the optic chiasma considered in relation to the fact that binocular vision is single. The first mystery of vision is that two-eyed persons do not see every object doubled. Galen in the second century A. D. had connected this seeming contradiction with the semi-decussation of the optic fibers, assuming correctly that vision is single because fibers from both eyes lead to the same part of the brain. In 1611 Kepler suggested that all points of the retina are projected on the brain, and in 1613 Aguilonius described the horopter, the line in the field of vision for which all points are seen as single. Various writers in the eighteenth century—including Newton—supported this conception, and in 1824 Wollaston, a friend of Thomas Young's, described his own hemianopia which occurred after great fatigue. He concluded that the fibers from the right halves of both retinas pass to the right hemisphere of the brain, so that dysfunction of the right hemisphere would cause blindness for the left half of the field of vision (since the lens of the eye reverses the field of vision in the retinal image). In the 1870s Ferrier fixed the visual center for monkeys in the occipital lobe by experiments in which the lobe was removed, and Munk with similar experiments proved that each lobe functions for the contralateral half of the field of vision. Later research has shown that the auditory center lies in the temporal lobe and the somesthetic center in the postcentral parietal region. The right and left auditory centers seem to be duplicative; neither is essential so long as the other is intact. Such discoveries would seem pretty well to settle the center theory positively.

Although the center theory constitutes a success for Johannes Müller because it establishes the fact of symbolic representation as against simulative, still it does nothing to show how a particular spot in the brain perceives color. Köhler once ventured a guess (1929) that there might be different kinds of excitation for the different qualities, but that view would be a return toward Müller and the qualitatively different specific energies. For the most part, psychologists have remained practising parallelists, content with empty correlations, and have made no attempt to answer the question: *why* does excitation of this region give rise to this experience?

The fault here lies in parallelism. Leibnitz never meant that theory to explain anything. You were asked by him to be content with the descriptive fact of observed coincidence. The modern connectionists and reflexologists know that neural excitation is not ordinarily captured in centers but passes on through tracts. You are equally blind wherever the optic tract is interrupted. If all the tract is essential, why is one part more of a center than another? There is a hint that modern behaviorists and operationists see that the psychophysiology of sensory quality must eventually include a consideration of the consequences of excitation of the essential 'centers.' Introspection must be the efferent events which follow on the excitation of the center and which result in making public what used to be described as private sensory experience. If you tell me you are seeing lights, then you are telling me about the excitation of your visual areas, provided I know the code of relationships so that you can communicate to me intelligibly.

On the other hand, the empty correlation of the parallelist seems not wholly to avoid Johannes Müller's difficulty. In parallelism you assume that you have an adequate symbolic representation of the perceived objective world, and that these symbols are differentiated enough to imply the perceived differentiations of the world even though they do not resemble it. Who or what now makes use of all these clues or cues for perception? Almost inevitably there appears an *homunculus ex machina* to take them into account, to make the inferences which will reconstitute the external world which is being perceived. It is all very well to say that experience parallels the neural pattern without inference, but the constant use of the words *clue* and *cue* in speaking of the psychology of perception seems to the author of this book to mean that we still have not thought ourselves clear of the conception of an initiating intelligence, one which uses sensory data to reconstruct an external world by unconscious inference (pp. 308-311).

2. *Perception of orientation.* When the astronomer Kepler in 1604 decided that the crystalline body in the eye is not the percipient organ but a lens which focuses an image of the external world upon the retina, which is the percipient organ, he raised the question as to why we see right side up when the retinal image, inverted by the lens, is upside down. For three centuries this pseudoproblem has plagued psychology, not because thoughtful men have failed to see it as a pseudoproblem, but because the less thoughtful are still, influenced no doubt by Descartes, unconsciously thinking in terms of the *homunculus ex machina.*

For the most part the history of sensory research in psychophysiology has consisted in following stimulation in from the outside, of specifying the effective stimulus more and more proximally. In the early nineteenth century a huge amount of research was undertaken to show exactly how the retinal image is formed in the eyes of various animals (pp. 99-102). In the late nineteenth century the same process was going on to get the auditory stimulus specified in terms of the action of the inner ear. In the twentieth century electronic amplification has provided a great deal of information, not only about the cochlear response of the inner ear but also about the activation of afferent nerves and of sensory tracts in the brain. Yet there still persists the belief that, if you could get properly differentiated patterns of excitation to appropriate cortical centers, perception would occur. Almost inevitably at this point in the argument a dualist slips into the brain an *homunculus ex machina* to perceive what it is that the nerves have brought in.

That is what Kepler was doing when he asked why the inverted image was seen in its correct orientation. Molyneux in 1691 was clear that Kepler has raised no real problem, that visual orientation is relative. He wrote: "*Erect and Inverted* are only Terms of *Relation* to *Up* or *Down*, or *Farther from* or *Nigher to* the Center of the Earth. . . . But the Eye or Visive Faculty takes no Notice of the Internal Posture of its own Parts, but uses them as an Instrument only." Bishop Berkeley in 1709 argued that the retinal image is not inverted in itself but only in relation to other parts of the body. Johannes Müller was clear about the matter in 1838. So was A. W. Volkmann (1836) whom Müller quoted on the subject. The interesting point for us here is not the opinions (all the men agreed), but the fact that they felt they needed in 1691 and 1709 and 1838 so much space to say it. That they did protest so much must mean that they knew they had against them the homunculus theory which persisted with enough effectiveness to have to be dismissed again and again, century by century.

In 1896 Stratton put the matter to test, having his subjects wear a system of lenses which reversed the retinal image and made it right side up. The expected happened. The perceived world looked upside down for a time and then became reversed. Taking the glasses off resulted once again in reversal which was soon corrected. Stratton was not, however, confused by the homunculus. He described how *up* was nothing in the visual sensory pattern other than the opposite of *down*, and that orientation is achieved by the relation of the visual pattern to somesthesis and behavior. When you reach up to get an object imaged at the top of the retina, then you have indeed got the visual field reversed and will not find the object unless you have on Stratton's lenses. Ewert repeated this experiment in 1930, with similar results. For the layman there is still something odd about being able to see correctly by means of a reversed retinal image. There has been clearly a cultural lag in the assimilation of this scientific concept. Had the view of a freely perceiving agent in the brain not been so strongly entrenched, this problem could not have continued to seem so important in 1604, 1691, 1709, 1838, 1896 and 1930.

3. *Attributes.* The doctrine of sensory attributes hardly dates later than Külpe's definitions of 1893, although discussion of some of the problems goes back to Lotze in 1852. The attributes of sensation, said Külpe, are *quality, intensity, duration* and *extension*. These attributes were supposed to show some simple simulative relations to the attributes of the stimulus. Intensity of sensation depended on intensity of stimulation, duration upon duration, extension upon extension. Quality, which Locke called *secondary* because there was for it no simple simulative relation, had to have a dimension of the stimulus discovered for it. Newton (1672) had done that for color: its stimulus attribute is the refrangibility of light which later turned out to be wave length. Galileo (1638) had done that for tone: the stimulus correlate of pitch is frequency. We may ignore the other senses about which there is less positive information.

The important point for us to realize here is that the notion of simple correspondence, which is a form of simple simulation, prevailed in theorizing until it was rooted out by a considerable mass of factual evidence.

It has turned out that the attributes of sensation depend each on several or all of the stimulus attributes. Take tone. For three centuries it has been said that pitch corresponds to stimulus frequency and loudness to stimulus energy or amplitude—it was never clear which. Only since 1930 have we known that pitch is a function of both frequency and energy, and that loudness is a different function of both frequency and energy. There is a story about tonal volume which is relevant. Tones have an attribute of volume; they can be large or small, and the judgments made of their size are reliable and precise. Low tones tend to be large; high tones small. Loud tones tend to be large; faint tones small. Actually, as Stevens showed in 1934, a faint low tone may be the same size as a loud high tone. So here you have three sensory attributes of tone—pitch, loudness and volume—each of them depending on both the stimulus attributes—frequency and energy. The case for color is comparable: hue, brightness and saturation all vary for spectral lights, that is to say, as joint functions of wave length and energy. There are many other joint functional relations known, of which one of the oldest is that the magnitude of the stars depends upon energy and not upon the extension of the star's image, and that for small objects brightness depends upon stimulus duration and extension as well as energy. It is difficult even now to get psychologists and physicists to think in these terms. For centuries pitch has been equated to frequency, and wave length to hue. How can the items of each pair be different? But they are and the difference is proven by their independent variability.

It was in 1896 that G. E. Müller put forward his psychophysical axioms, which posited a similarity between the perception and its cortical excitation in the brain. He presented these rules as axioms, appealing not to observation but to their inherent obviousness, to the habits of thought which are rooted in the culture. "To an equality, similarity or difference in the constitution of sensations . . . there corresponds an equality, similarity or difference in the constitution of the psychophysical [brain] process, and conversely." For greater or lesser similarity of sensation there is always greater or lesser similarity of brain process. If the sensation can vary in n dimensions, then the brain processes can vary in n dimensions. G. E. Müller found support for this view from Lotze (1852), Fechner (1860), Mach (1865) and Hering (1878), and yet there is no logic that compels its acceptance. Recently it has been proposed that low pitches may vary with the frequency of impulses in the acoustic nerve, that high pitches may depend on the particular nerve fiber stimulated most, and that the series of pitches may nevertheless appear continuous to introspection. That would be a discontinuity yielding a continuity and would contradict Müller's axioms; yet there is no reason why a discontinuity should not be symbolized by a continuity. We do the opposite with the integers and in the decimal system when we add a new digit in passing from 99 to 100.

Another place where the predilection for simple correlations turns up in the nineteenth century is in the theories of Weber's Law. If $S = k \log R$, where, the psychologists asked, does the logarithmic relation get itself introduced in the chain of events? Let us consider the causal chain of stimulus-excitation-sensation-judgment and use, respectively, the symbols R, E, S and J. Fechner said that the log relation enters in inner psychophysics, between E and S. For him, if we omit constants of proportionality, $J = S$, $S = \log E$, $E = R$. G. E. Müller said that the crucial change is physiological: $J = S = E$, but $E = \log R$. Wundt said that the logarithm was a consequence of the law of relativity in respect of which judgment operates: $J = \log S$, but $S = E = R$ (pp. 286-292). The interesting matter here is these simple equalities. Why did Fechner, Wundt and Müller suppose that the appearance of the log relation needs special explanation as something exceptional, and that ordinarily simple proportionality should be the rule? One relation is as good as another until you have evidence of the facts.

4. *Perception of shape.* The problem of shape resolves itself into the problem of projection. If there were evidence that the pattern of excitation on the retina is projected upon the visual areas of the cortex with anything like the fidelity that the pattern of the external world is projected by light upon the retina, then we should indeed for the visual perception of shape have an excellent example of simulative representation.

We have just seen how Kepler suggested that the retinas are projected upon the brain and how the facts of singleness of binocular vision and the semi-decussation of the optic nerve at the chiasma were taken to mean that corresponding points on the two retinas have common projection in the brain. By the end of the nineteenth century it was clear that the right halves of both retinas are projected upon the visual area of the right hemisphere, and conversely (p. 684).

It was E. H. Weber who, in developing his researches on the *Ortsinn* of the skin in 1852, suggested that the skin be regarded as divided into "sensory circles," tiny regions of common innervation which are projected upon the brain in the order of their arrangement on the skin. He drew his "circles" as hexagons so that they would fit together without overlapping, and proposed that on the forearm, for instance, the "circles" are greatly elongated in the direction of the major axis. He made that proposal because the threshold for the discrimination of two points on the arm is greater in the longitudinal than in the transverse direction, and Weber thought it probable that two stimulated circles must be separated by a third unstimulated circle if the dual stimulation is to be perceived as two points. Weber's projection theory fits in well with other research on the cutaneous two-point limen and on the error of localization.

In 1871 Julius Bernstein made this projection theory explicit and drew the often reprinted diagram that shows how projection of stimulation at the skin upon the cortex, when there is a certain amount of dispersion at the cortex, would produce many of the observed facts of cutaneous space perception.

In the twentieth century the Gestalt psychologists have argued for *isomorphism*. Wertheimer suggested this relation for seen movement in 1912, but Köhler has been its most effective supporter since 1920. Isomorphism is not projection but it implies it. The Gestalt theory is that a spatial pattern of perception is isomorphic with the spatial pattern of the underlying excitation in the brain. *Isomorphic* means corresponding topologically, but not topographically. Shapes are not preserved, but orders are. In-betweenness is preserved. A point between two points in one system will, in an isomorphic system, have its correspondent between the correspondents of the other points. It seems pretty clear that Wertheimer and Köhler got this view, not from the results of research, but from the atmosphere of the times, perhaps from G. E. Müller's axioms, which, like all axioms, ask for acceptance without proof. On the other hand, the belief in both visual and somesthetic cortical projection was growing and the two theories, projection and isomorphism, support each other. The stimulus-object and the peripheral excitation are isomorphic. The perception and the stimulus-object are isomorphic. If perception and the cortical excitation are isomorphic, then the cortical and peripheral excitation must also be isomorphic, since patterns isomorphic with the same pattern would be isomorphic with each other.

It is true that Wertheimer went out of his way to object to isomorphism between peripheral excitation and perception because he had in mind the many instances, like the perceptual 'constancies,' where the correspondence is not exact topographically; but these arguments deal with gross approximations. There is no doubt that the reason that Köhler's contention seemed so plausible was due in part to the growth of the belief in projection. For the same reason some of Köhler's more recent experimental demonstrations of the isomorphic relation between perception and brain excitation are consistent with the theory of central projection or at least with central isomorphic reduplication if projection is not the physiological means which the organism employs.

There has been in recent years some research that indicates a point-to-point correspondence between the retinal fields and the cortical visual areas and between the body soma and the cortical somesthetic areas. The facts remain uncertain because of the difficulties of research. It is hard to be sure of blindness or anesthesia in animals, because their means of communication are so limited. Nor can one reason safely from animals to man when the encephalization of function in the ascending evolutionary scale endangers the analogy. Lower forms may not need cortices to see; man surely does. Fortunately, the chimpanzee is very like man. Yet, even in man, it is hard to tell whether a blindness due to a brain injury is absolute, as absolute as it would be if the optic nerve had been sectioned, or whether it is partly functional as it is in hysteria and other disorders where the insensitivity is due to strongly reinforced inattention. The evidence for point-to-point correspondence between the retinas and the visual cortical areas is weakened by counterevidence that the spatial order is not preserved in the intervening tracts and that the numbers of neurons is less in the intervening parts of the visual tract than in the optic nerve or at the cortex. It begins to look as if isomorphism between retina and cortex depends not upon projection, but upon the capacity of the brain to reconstitute an adequate symbolic basis for the perception. That is what happens in tridimensional visual perception derived from bidimensional retinal images. There the perception does not simulate the retinal images but reduplicates the solid stimulus object.

There is a general belief that projection is topological, that shapes are lost but continuities preserved or, if not preserved, reconstituted in the cortex. That is, however, a hard thesis to prove at the present time. There are too many ways in which adjacent retinal excitations interact with each other or substitute for each other for the projection pattern to be purely random. On the other hand, we must remember that a figure which extends beyond the macula both up-and-down and left-and-right would have its cortical representation divided—half in one hemisphere and half in the other—and probably show some very strange distortions or even discontinuities between the macular and extramacular parts. In respect of somesthetic projection we are constrained to remember that large errors of cutaneous localization are less frequent than small—a simple and well known fact. Why should they be if projection is random? If adjacent points on the skin correspond to adjacent points in the cortex, would you not then expect the near ones to be confused oftener than the remote ones in setting off the localizing reactions?

It is hard to say whether the underlying faith in simulative representation has helped or hindered progress in this field. There is as yet no evidence that the simulation is very good. If correspondence is to be established, it should be found right here in respect of spatial pattern, for spatial differentiation is almost the only kind of differentiation the brain has to give in its activation. There are no qualitative differences in neural excitation, no specific nerve energies, for qualitative difference seems always to turn into spatial difference. The centers are at least spatially distinct. We might, however, expect some simulation of extensive patterns simply from knowing what kind of an organ the brain is. In these days there is not much left of the Cartesian Soul or of the freely percipient *homunculus ex machina;* yet you may be sure they are not entirely banished when you hear the question: "Why do I see right side up when my retinal image is upside down?"

LOCALIZATION OF FUNCTION

We have already examined the story of the localization of brain function up to 1870 (pp. 61-75). In the nineteenth century first there was Gall and phrenology from 1810 on (pp. 51-58). Then from 1822 on there was Flourens with his specific functions for the principal segments of the brain and his communal functioning for each segment—different functions for the cerebrum and the cerebellum, but no specific localization within the cerebrum (pp. 64-67). Broca's localization of a speech center in 1861 forced opinion to move away from Flourens toward more exact localization (pp. 70-72). Then Fritsch and Hitzig in 1870, by electrical stimulation of the brain, discovered the motor area in the precentral cortex and specific localization of functions within it (pp. 73-75). After that the search for centers was on.

The important investigators of the 1870s and 1880s were *David Ferrier* (1843-1928), a Scot in London, who published *The Functions of the Brain* in 1876 (Fig. 2, p. 74), *Hermann Munk* (1839-1912) at Göttingen, who tended to support Ferrier in finding fairly exact localizations, and *Friedrich Leopold Goltz* (1834-1902), at Strassburg after 1872, who held more closely to Flourens' notion that function is communal and its localization only gross.

We have just seen how the visual center was localized in the occipital lobes (pp. 682 f.). Ferrier removed one lobe in some monkeys and found that they seemed to be blind, as he thought, in the eye opposite to the side of ablation. Munk corrected him, showing that the removal of an occipital lobe does not entirely blind either eye, but produces hemianopia, a blindness of each eye for the half of the field of vision contralateral to the side of the ablation. Goltz doubted these facts, but Munk was right. There are half a dozen technical reasons why research by the method of ablation may fail to produce clear-cut results. The operation itself may have temporary effects. Specific localizations change with conditions. There are alternative ways of impairing the same function and, given time for recovery, alternative ways of functioning. By the end of the 1890s opinion favored exact localization but there were many contradictory facts.

With the turn of the century new methods became available. Before 1900 you could excise or destroy brain tissue in animal subjects, checking up on the exact area affected in a post-mortem, but you could not get from the animals good reports of their experiences. They lacked the language for introspective communication. Human subjects could describe their sensitivities and insensitivities, but you can not remove brain tissue from human beings at will. You have to wait for accidental lesions of the brain. Experimental animal psychology, which is regarded as having been begun by Thorndike at Columbia in 1898, provided methods for testing animal learning, intelligence (defined as ability to learn quickly) and sensory discrimination. Pavlov's methods of conditioning were not yet available, but they were added very soon.

It was *Shepherd Ivory Franz* (1874-1933) who began the new animal experimental psychophysiology with the new technics for testing learning and discrimination. He had his Ph.D. from Cattell at Columbia in 1899, held posts in physiology at the Harvard Medical School, the Dartmouth Medical School and McLean Hospital from 1899 to 1906, then went to the Government Hospital for the Insane in Washington, D. C., for eighteen years (1907-1924) and then to the University of California at Los Angeles (1924-1933). In 1902 Franz published his first paper on the topic that was to make him famous: *On the Functions of the Cerebrum: the Frontal Lobes in Relation to the Production and Retention of Simple*

Sensory Habits. In the establishment of the centers, the frontal lobes had been left out. Some called them the *silent areas* because they had no demonstrable function. Others assigned association to them, for it was the only important function left without a locus. There were clinical cases which showed that the simple functions were not disturbed by a frontal lesion but that the complex functions were. There had long been the famous case of Phineas P. Gage through whose skull and left frontal lobe a crowbar was projected by an explosion in 1848. He lived on for thirteen years, changed from an "active, steady alert workman" to a "restless, adventurous, unreliable" person, who spent his time travelling around the country exhibiting his head and crowbar for an admission fee. (The skull and crowbar are still on view in the Warren Museum of the Harvard Medical School.)

So Franz used the new technics of animal behavior to tackle the association areas. What he found in this and later experiments was that lobectomy of the frontal lobes of cats and monkeys might cause the loss of recent habits when the tissues of both lobes are destroyed but not the loss of old habits, that the lost habits can be relearned although the tissue is never restored, that destruction of only one lobe diminishes efficiency without destroying the habit. There followed many researches which went to show that localization of function tends not to be exact and is easily disturbed by changed conditions, that loss of function is often subsequently restored. By 1912 Franz was poking fun at the belief in exact localization, calling it "the new phrenology." "We have," he said, "no facts which will enable us to locate the mental processes in the brain any better than they were located fifty years ago." He was exaggerating. "Fifty years ago" was the year after Broca's discovery and eight years before Fritsch and Hitzig.

Karl S. Lashley (1890-   ), while he was taking his doctorate with John B. Watson at Hopkins, went over to work with Franz at Washington, and they published together in 1917 on the effects of cerebral destruction on habit-formation and retention in the white rat. (On Lashley as a behaviorist, see p. 648.) Presently Lashley took over these brain problems from Franz and continued with a distinguished series of researches, using the rat as a subject and noting the effect of the destruction of brain tissue upon 'intelligence' (speed and errors in learning a maze) and sensory discrimination. He invented the jumping technique for rats: the rat learns a visual discrimination by being obliged to jump from a platform across a chasm to the correct one of two visual stimulus-objects. The correct rat jumps against a door which opens and lets him into food. The rat in error bumps his nose and falls—presumably without pleasure—into a net.

Lashley brought his general conclusions together in a monograph in 1929: *Brain Mechanisms and Intelligence.* Here he plotted errors in learning a maze against the amount of destruction of cortical tissue and against the difficulty of the maze. For an easy maze the errors increased as the amount of available cortical tissue decreased, but all rats learned the maze. For a harder maze, the errors increased more rapidly with the amount of destruction. For a very hard maze and 50 percent destruction, the rats eventually learned, but only after very many errors. From these results Lashley laid down his law of *mass action:* the more cortical tissue available, the more rapid and accurate the learning. It would be unwise to extend this principle to include the layman's cliché: intelligence depends on the amount of brains.

Learning depends on the amount of cortical tissue available but it does not depend on what particular tissue is available. That is Lashley's principle of *equipotentiality,* the modern substitute for Flourens' *action commune* and for *vicarious function.* The rule holds for the entire cortex, but there is also in the cortex specific localization. For instance, in the rat, the visual areas are necessary for the discrimination of visual patterns, although not at all for the discrimination of brightnesses. (It is not possible to extend these conclusions directly to men, for there is encephalization of function from rat to man. Man probably needs his cortex to discriminate brightnesses.)

The principle of equipotentiality is not necessarily different from what has been called vicarious functioning. A man who loses his right hand can learn to work with his left and can, as a matter of fact, learn more readily to use the left on those operations which he could already perform with his right. A rat which has learned to run through a maze on its feet can swim the same maze filled with water. The average discrimination is finer when there are five clues to the difference than when there is only one. In 1930 Hunter suggested that some such explanation might be proper for equipotentiality, and there seems no reason to believe that he is wrong. If the total organism can employ different means to the same end, so can the brain. Equipotentiality serves to stress the complexity of habit-formation, whereas the exceptions—as in pattern vision where there is no vicarious functioning—show that a simple response may after all have only one means available for it. In general it looks as if vision were so highly developed in man as to be crowding the brain's capacity. Hearing seems still to have left a spare; you can hear satisfactorily with either half of your brain, whereas in vision a crucial injury in the visual area of a man's cortex seems to leave a scotoma, a permanent blind spot.

To leave this matter standing still where it was in 1930 seems to argue that the vast amount of research on cerebral functions during the last twenty years has come to naught. That is not true. The details of the history of determining the brain's functions would make a volume in themselves, not a chapter in this book. Much more is known now about tracts, projection and projection areas. Nevertheless, the main issue between Flourens and Gall, between Goltz and Ferrier, between the modern equipotentialists and the connectionists, is not settled.

It is plain that connectionism—explanation in terms of synaptic connections of fibers—works, in the peripheral nervous system, largely in the spinal cord and probably at the lower brain levels. In the cortex we do not know. Gestalt psychology believes in applying field theory to the brain and in expecting an isomorphic cortex to follow whatever physical field principles perception follows. The cortex is tremendously complex and an excitation, as we have said, could 'park' itself, like an electrostatic field, simply by running around a synaptic circuit. Lashley, sensitive to the claims of the Gestalt psychologists, raised, however, as early as 1929 the question of reaction to a gradient—that is to say, reaction to a relation that is independent of the particular values of the terms related, the problem of transposition of form without change of the form (pp. 612 f.). How do you put a relation between two excitations on a final common path which carries the report of what is discriminated? when the related terms are simultaneous? when successive? And how, Lashley has asked recently—as Hunter asked when he invented the temporal maze—do you get temporal integrations which take account of order? Both those questions are related to the problem of the cortical nature of attitude, of the set or switching mechanism which in an instant turns off one system of responses and turns on another—as when the bilingual person shifts languages. These questions remain unanswered, and the historian who tries to select the important research from the decade preceding his writing would be brash to try to predict the decade of the immediate future.

Meanwhile, new methods are hoped for. Köhler employs electroencephalography to see whether he can not get some direct evidence of the isomorphic relation in spatial perception, and he has success. Ward C. Halstead has recently brought factor analysis into the neurosurgical hospital. He made up twenty-seven likely tests, gave them to each of more than two hundred patients with brain injuries, lobectomies or lobotomies, extracted C, A, P and D factors (Central integrative, Abstractive, Power and Directive) from the statistical intercorrelations, figured for "biological intelligence" an impairment index as a function of these factors, and then undertook to show how these factors depend on the functioning of the frontal lobes. Such brain correlations are, however, only preliminary and they are also doubly 'empty.' The factors—the statistical resultants of a multidimensional orthogonal system—are so novel and operationally complex that they do not seem psychologically real. On this account there is even less chance than usual to answer the psychophysiologist's second question which parallelism (correlationism) avoids, the question as to *how* or *why* the particular region of the brain has this or that function.

In general it seems safe to say that progress in this field is held back, not by lack of interest, ability or industry, but by the absence of some one of the other essentials for scientific progress. Knowledge of the nature of the nerve impulse waited upon the discovery of electric currents and galvanometers of several kinds. Knowledge in psychoacoustics seemed to get nowhere until electronics developed. The truth about how the brain functions may eventually yield to a technique that comes from some new field remote from either physiology or psychology. Genius waits on insight, but insight may wait on the discovery of new concrete factual knowledge.

NOTES

The present chapter takes up the topic of chapters 2-5 of this book. On the early physiology of the nervous system, see pp. 27-49; on the mind-body problem and phrenology, see pp. 50-60; on the physiology of the brain up to 1870, see pp. 61-79; on specific nerve energies, see pp. 80-95. The notes of these chapters give many references relevant here.

An alternative discussion of closely related topics is chapter 2, Physiology of sensation, in E. G. Boring, *Sensation and Perception in the History of Experimental Psychology*, 1942, 53-96,

including notes. The reader is referred to this chapter as a fuller discussion of some of the topics of the present chapter. It does not seem wise to repeat all this comment in each of two books.

Mind and Brain

On the mind-body problem, Bain's relation to it and references to Bain on the subject, see pp. 236 f., 245 *supra* See also Boring, *op. cit.*, 83-90, 95 f The best book on the mind-body problem is C. A. Strong, *Why the Mind Has a Body*, 1903.

The phrase *no psychosis without neurosis*, quite common in the later nineteenth century, may have been derived from T. H. Huxley's phrase, "the relation of consciousness with molecular changes in the brain—of *psychoses with neuroses*," in his On the hypothesis that animals are automata, and its history, *Fortnightly Review*, 1874, 22 (N.S. 16), 555-580, esp. 575.

On E. Pflüger's belief that the spinal cord ought to be conscious, see the discussion of the Pflüger-Lotze controversy, F. Fearing, *Reflex Action*, 1930, 161-186. On Loeb, Jennings and the criterion of consciousness, see pp. 622-626, *supra*.

The Brain's Functions

For current views of the brain's functions, see C. T. Morgan, *Physiological Psychology*, 1943, esp. 330-352, 457-567. Somewhat less psychological are the chapters by J. F. Fulton, T. C. Ruch *et al.*, in J. F. Fulton, *Howell's Textbook of Physiology*, 15 ed., 1946, 178-547, esp. 255-304, 525-547; or Fulton, *Physiology of the Nervous System*, 2 ed., 1943, esp. 274-444.

On the history of this problem up to 1870, see J. Soury, *Système nerveux central*, 1899, or the same author's article, Cerveau, in C. Richet's *Dictionnaire de physiologie*, 1897, II, 547-670. On recent history, see the excellent historical notes at the beginnings of the chapters in Fulton, *op. cit.*, 1943.

Perception

Most of the topics of this section have been discussed more fully with more complete notes in E. G. Boring, *Sensation and Perception in the History of Experimental Psychology*, 1942, to which the reader is specifically referred below. The present section differs from the discussion in that book by stressing the historical dynamics of cultural lag and scientific inertia.

In general, on the problem of communication and on the implications of specific nerve energies, see Boring, *op. cit.*, 68-74, 93 f.

With respect to the perception of quality, see *ibid.*, 110-112, 123, on Thomas Young and specific energies; *ibid.*, 226-230, 257 f., on single vision and the semi-decussation of the optic fibers at the chiasma; *ibid.*, 74-78, 94 f., on sensory centers. On this last matter, see also the notes to the preceding section.

On the perception of orientation, the inversion of the retinal image and Stratton's experiment, see Boring, *op. cit.*, 222-230, 237 f., 257-260. The references are all given there, but we may repeat six of them: Johann Kepler, *Ad vitellionem paralipomena*, 1604, 158-221 (chap. 5); William Molyneux, *A Treatise of Dioptricks*, 1692, 105 f.; George Berkeley, *An Essay towards a New Theory of Vision*, 1709, sects. 88-121; Johannes Müller, *Handbuch der Physiologie des Menschen*, 1838, ¶, bk. v, sect. i, chap. 3, pt. 1; G. M. Stratton, Vision without inversion of the retinal image, *Psychol. Rev.*, 1897, 4, 341-360, 463-481; P. H. Ewert, A study of the effect of inverted retinal stimulation upon spatially coordinated behavior, *Genet. Psychol. Monog.*, 1930, 7, 177-363.

On sensory attributes see, in general, Boring, *op. cit.*, 19-27, 48 f., and on tonal attributes, *ibid.*, 375-381, 396 f. See also S. S. Stevens, The volume and intensity of tones, *Amer. J. Psychol.*, 1934, 46, 397-408; Tonal density, *J. exper. Psychol.*, 1934, 17, 585-592; The relation of pitch to intensity, *J. acoust. Soc. Amer.*, 1935, 6, 150-154; Stevens and H. Davis, *Hearing*, 1938, 69-166; E. G. Boring, The psychophysics of color tolerance (three color attributes as functions of two stimulus variables), *Amer. J. Psychol.*, 1939, 52, 384-394, esp. 391-394. On Newton, hue and wave length, see Boring, *Sensation and Perception (op. cit.)*, 101-107, 122. On Galileo, pitch and frequency, see *ibid.*, 322-324, 346, and the Eng. trans. of Galileo's discovery, in W. Dennis, *Readings in the History of Psychology*, 1948, 17-24. On G. E. Müller's psychophysical axioms, see Boring, An operational restatement of G. E. Müller's psychophysical axioms, *Psychol. Rev.*, 1941, 48, 457-464, and references there cited. On Fechner's, Wundt's and G. E. Müller's theories of Weber's law, see E. B. Titchener, *Experimental Psychology*, 1905, II, pt. ii, pp. xci-xciv, 62-65. On why the sensory attributes need not correspond one-for-one with the dimensions of the stimulus and on how many attributes a two-dimensioned stimulus could have, see Boring, The relation of the attributes of sensation to the dimensions of the stimulus, *Philos. Sci.*, 1935, 2, 236-245.

On projection, see, in general, Boring, *Sensation and Perception* (*op. cit.*), 78-83, 95; and for Weber on projection and sensory circles, *ibid.*, 475-485, 515-517. Although E. H. Weber's important work on the *Ortsinn* was published in 1834 and 1846, his chief paper about projection and the sensory circles is his Ueber den Raumsinn und die Empfindungskreise in der Haut und im Auge, *Ber. sächs. Gesell. Wiss.*, math. phys. Cl., 1852, 85-164. J. Bernstein's theory of projection is in his *Untersuchungen über den Erregungsvorgang im Nerven- und Muskelsystem*, 1871, 165-202. For modern physiological fact on projection, see T. C. Ruch, in J. F. Fulton, *Howell's Textbook of Physiology*, 15 ed., 1946, 354-368, 379-382, 434-439, 511-523; also p. 331 for a modern diagram of Bernstein's theory. See also J. F. Fulton, *Physiology of the Nervous System*, 2 ed., 1943, 274-417.

On proximal auditory stimulation, see Boring, *op. cit.*, 400-436 and references there cited.

On isomorphism, see Boring, *op. cit.*, 83-90, 95 f. For the implications of phenomena of seen movement for isomorphism, see *ibid.*, 588-600, 604-606. For a discussion of the perception of form and the Gestalt psychologists' reasons for being more interested in the way the perception differs from the stimulus object than in the way it simulates it, see *ibid.*, 246-256, 260-262. For references to Lotze, Grassmann, Mach, Hering, Donders, G. E. Müller, Wertheimer, Köhler and Koffka on the development of the psychophysical axioms into the principle of isomorphism, see *ibid.*, 96. The chief references to W. Köhler in this regard are his *Die physische Gestalten in Ruhe und im stationären Zustand*, 1920, 173-195, esp. 193; *The Place of Value in a World of Facts*, 1938, 185-232; *Gestalt Psychology*, 2 ed., 1947, 55-66.

Localization of Function

A brief discussion of localization of function is in Boring, *Sensation and Perception* (*op. cit.*), 74-77, 94 f. Fulton's historical notes which introduce his chapters are remarkably good and ought to be expanded into a book. On this topic see J. F. Fulton, *Physiology of the Nervous System*, 2 ed., 1943, 314, 320 f., 337, 348 f., 368-370, where half a hundred references are cited.

On the work cited for 1870-1890, see D. Ferrier, *The Functions of the Brain*, 1876, 2 ed., 1886; H. Munk, *Ueber die Funktionen der Grosshirnrinde*, 1890 (17 papers, 1877-1889); F. L. Goltz, *Ueber die Verrichtungen des Grosshirns*, 1881 (4 papers, 1876-1881). For a contemporaneous account, citing the literature up to 1900, see E. A. Schäfer's chapter, The cerebral cortex, in his own *Text-Book of Physiology*, 1900, II, 697-782.

On S. I. Franz, see his autobiography in C. Murchison, *Psychology in Autobiography*, 1932, II, 89-113; R. S. Woodworth, Shepherd Ivory Franz 1874-1933, *Amer. J. Psychol.*, 1934, 46, 151 f. About 80 of Franz's scientific publications are given by C. Murchison, *Psychological Register*, 1932, 171-173, which includes 12 important research papers, On the functions of the cerebrum, in 1902 to 1917. The last is a joint paper with Lashley. We may cite here only On the functions of the cerebrum: the frontal lobes in relation to the production and retention of simple sensory-motor habits, *Amer. J. Physiol.*, 1902, 8, 1-22; On the functions of the cerebrum: the frontal lobes, *Arch. Psychol.*, 1907, no. 2; New phrenology, *Science*, 1912, 35, 321-328; with K. S. Lashley, The effects of cerebral destructions upon habit-formation and retention in the albino rat, *Psychobiol.*, 1917, 1, 71-139. Two excerpts from the last item have been reprinted by W. Dennis, *Readings in the History of Psychology*, 1948, 506-512.

K. S. Lashley's work is more recent and continues. C. Murchison, *Psychological Register* (*op. cit.*), 295-297, gives about 50 references up to 1932 only. The list includes seven Studies of cerebral function in learning, from 1921 to 1926. The important book is *Brain Mechanisms and Intelligence*, 1929, in which see esp. 23-26, 86-89, 157-174. For three reprinted excerpts from this book, see Dennis, *op. cit.*, 557-570. C. J. Herrick, *Brains of Rats and Men*, 1926, summarized much of Lashley's work to that date. W. S. Hunter's criticism is A consideration of Lashley's theory of equipotentiality of cerebral action, *J. general Psychol.*, 1930, 3, 455-488.

For Köhler's more recent views on how the brain works and how to find out how it works, see W. Köhler and H. Wallach, Figural after-effects: an investigation of visual processes, *Proc. Amer. Philos. Soc.*, 1944, 88, 269-357, esp. 327-357; Köhler and R. Held, The cortical correlate of pattern vision, *Science*, 1949, 110, 414-419. These authors remark in an earlier note: "Psychological experience and cortical events are likely to be much more sensibly connected if brain action is mainly a matter of field physics than they would be if brain action consisted only of nerve impulses."

On Halstead's use of factor analysis to determine the nature of the functions of the cortex, especially in the frontal lobes see W. C. Halstead, *Brain and Intelligence: a Quantitative Study of the Frontal Lobes*, 1947.

The most recent important study of brain functioning, one which criticizes both Lashley's and Köhler's views, is D. G. Hebb, *The Organization of Behavior: a Neuropsychological Study*, 1949.

CHAPTER 26

Dynamic Psychology

Dynamic psychology is a field, the psychology of motivation. It is an interest and a concern. It is also a movement for those psychologists who, disappointed in the description of consciousness and behavior, seek a more satisfying psychology of what they sometimes call "human nature." The psychology of human nature is a motivational psychology, because the prediction and control of behavior is the most important practical thing to know about man as a living, choosing, adapting organism. Thus dynamic psychology is not a school. It has no leader, no founder. The dynamic psychologists do not like to wear a party label, as the behaviorists did. Most of the psychologists who make propaganda for dynamic psychology are not interested solely in the topic of motivation but are exerting themselves to enlarge psychology so that it will cover what they believe is a neglected field.

On the other hand, dynamic psychology, while not a school, includes a number of schools. The psychology of the psychoanalysts is a dynamic psychology if ever there was one—a school with a founder, leaders, party labels, a special language, ideational intensity and the boundary that integrates a new in-group by setting it off against an intrenched orthodoxy. Dynamic psychology also includes purposive psychology—McDougall's hormic psychology and Tolman's purposive behaviorism. McDougall would have liked a school. Tolman has one. And then, of course, it includes the dynamic psychologies proper—Woodworth's early dynamic psychology, Lewin's later one, the system of ideas that grew up at Yale in the 1930s, the contributions of H. A. Murray from the Harvard Psychological Clinic, of the Catholic psychologist, T. V. Moore, of J. T. MacCurdy who discussed psychoanalysis under that term, and of many other psychologists who are concerned with the problems of personality and motivation. Woodworth did not want a school. Lewin had many enthusiastic disciples and a group of older men who sought out his stimulation. For a while there was enough agreement among the Yale group to make it seem like a school. Murray. a restless spirit, untrammeled by orthodoxy, keen for the understanding of human nature, held his "Clinic" together long enough for twenty-eight of its members to produce *Explorations in Personality*. Dynamic psychology seems to fit more readily than other psychologies into the milieu of the Catholic Church, which, being concerned with human responsibility, is especially interested in the nature of human motives. Altogether dynamic psychology is a broad field, though it is only within the last three decades that it has appeared as a subject-matter with a title attached and has made such use of the experimental method as properly to require its mention in this book.

The principal source of dynamic psychology is, of course, Freud. Those who deny that Freud is psychology's greatest figure are usually those who read Freud out of psychology without overthrowing his claim to the attributes of greatness. The reason that Freud seemed for so many years outside of psychology was that he dealt with motives, used a special terminology and ignored the orthodox psychology which in turn gave scant attention to the topic of motivation. Freud's antecedents lie in psychopathology—mostly in the French tradition of Mesmer, Liébeault, Charcot, Bernheim, and also of Janet, who was Freud's contemporary and in a sense Charcot's successor. We shall consider this line of development first.

Less important but not to be ignored are the lines from activity psychology—from Leibnitz, Herbart, Brentano, James Ward. Some of Freud's early conceptions resemble Herbart's. It is possible that Brentano influenced him directly. Ward drew from Brentano and McDougall drew from Ward and, of course, from Freud. The notion of active ideas or motives is basic to the conception of conflict and so to the psychological mechanisms of motivation which constitute a principal subject-matter of dynamic psychology.

Another antecedent of dynamic psychology is hedonism, a motivational doctrine closely related to associationism. There is a line of development that passes from Hobbes through Locke and Hartley to Jeremy Bentham, who founded utilitarianism and influenced both James Mill and John Stuart Mill—the latter at first positively but later by negation. Freud's pleasure principle is derived from the utilitarians' hedonism, which came to be nineteenth-century common sense. The twentieth century has also seen an emphasis on what is called psychological hedonism, a conception which in its simplest form is Thorndike's law of effect—the notion that pleasure assures its own recurrence by reinforcing the learning of the actions which have led to it.

PSYCHONEUROSIS

It is fair to define psychoneurosis as a motivational disorder, and the history of the discovery and gradual understanding of the nature of the psychoneurotic state becomes the early phase of the history of the psychology of motivation. Write in order the words *magnetism, mesmerism, hypnotism, hysteria, suggestion,* translate them into proper names, writing Van Helmont, Mesmer, Braid, Charcot, Bernheim, and you have an outline of the psychology of motivation before Freud.

The plight of the psychoneurotic in the Middle Ages need not concern us here. He met with little sympathy and with almost no understanding. The concept of mental disease did not exist in any clear form because the mind was supposed to be free and responsible for its own states and acts. The only medicines that the ancients knew for derangements of the will were blame, admonition and punishment, and the causes of these derangements were supposed to be perversity, wickedness, magic and demoniacal possession. Freedom of will was God's gift to man. and, if the will were controlled, that were most likely the work of the devil. In general, it was not until the nineteenth century that science and materialism had advanced far enough to include the mind in their determinism and thus to make possible humanitarian treatments of the neurotic and the insane.

The first change in the state of the mentally ill was for the worse. The great changes in the social structure at the time of the Renaissance created a general feeling of uncertainty and insecurity (pp. 7-9). Insecure men, uncertain of the future, frustrated by change, stand ready to exorcise the threat of evil by an uncritical distribution of blame and punishment. Then, as now, they were ready to go witch hunting because they were afraid, and in the fifteenth century the Church did it for them. In 1489 *Jacob Sprenger* and *Heinrich Kraemer*, two Dominican brothers, taking advantage of the recent invention of the printing press, published the *Malleus maleficarum*, a title which perhaps can be best translated as the *Witch Hammer*, since the book was designed to be a tool for hammering at the witches. The *Malleus maleficarum* is a cruel encyclopedia on witchcraft, the detection of witches and the procedures for examining them by torture and for sentencing them. The treatise had the approval of the Pope, of the King of Rome and, after some reluctant resistance, of the Faculty of Theology at the University of Cologne. It identified witchcraft with heresy and for us it identifies witchcraft with the mental disorders, many of whose symptoms it describes with care. For three hundred years in nineteen editions this malevolent compendium remained the authority and guide of the Inquisition as it sought out heresy and demoniacal possession among the people.

The picture is, however, not entirely unrelieved. Among the ancients before the doctrine of demonology prevailed, there was some scientific interest in these phenomena. Zilboorg has suggested that the first psychiatric revolution against the doctrine of demonology began in a minor fashion contemporaneously with the intensification of witch hunting by the Inquisition. In this context the names of *Juan Luis Vives* (1492-1540) and *Johann Weyer* (1515-1588) stand out. Notable progress in the amelioration of the treatment of the insane waited, however, upon the growth of humanitarianism in an age that was headed toward democracy. The Inquisition lingered on through the eighteenth century and died out. The American and French revolutions were striking events and the birth of feminism less so (Mary Wollstonecraft wrote *Vindication of the Rights of Women* in 1792), but the ferment of the Renaissance was working everywhere slowly. So *Philippe Pinel* (1745-1826), who wrote in 1791 *Traité medico-philosophique de l'aliénation mentale* and was appointed in 1794 chief at the Salpêtrière (the Parisian hospital for insane women), was the agent of the *Zeitgeist* when he succeeded in establishing new attitudes toward the treatment of mental illness. One sees here how complicated are the dynamics of history. Pinel was a man of charitable temper, who had witnessed Louis XVI's execution in 1793 with repugnance and in the same year took advantage of the spirit of the new times to strike the chains and fetters from the insane at the Bicêtre (the Parisian hospital for insane men). In America in the nineteenth century the greatest reforms in the treatment of the mentally ill are associated with the name of *Dorothea Lynde Dix* (1802-1887), who, from 1841 on, conducted a campaign to remedy the condition of the indigent mentally ill in the jails and almshouses. Into this interesting topic we may not, however, penetrate further. The present chapter is about motivation, and we see now why it was that the causes of motivation could at last come under calm scientific consideration at the end of the eighteenth century, whereas they could not in the earlier centuries of the new age when the weight of religion and superstition, the carry-over from the Middle Ages, was still so great.

Thus we get back to Mesmer and hypnotism, the topic of an earlier chapter in this book (pp. 116-119). When Paracelsus (1493-

1541) established the doctrine that magnets, like the stars, influence human bodies, and Van Helmont (1577-1644) inaugurated the doctrine of animal magnetism, there was no promise that such events would lead eventually either to the discovery of psychoneurosis or to an understanding of human motivation. Mesmer (1734-1815) came on the scene just when the belief in magic was weakening and faith in the power of natural phenomena was getting stronger. In Paris he played the rôle of the magician to the crowds who flocked to his *baquet,* but he was a sincere, if egotistical, believer in his own powers, and modern opinion is that he did indeed cure some psychoneurotics without, of course, having any true insight into what was the matter with them or how he cured them. What Mesmer had done was to stumble upon a powerful motivational determinant with but little understanding of what was essential and what irrelevant in the new phenomenon (pp. 117-119). That was Mesmer's secret, a secret kept from himself, though not from us.

Esdaile seized upon the anesthetic properties of mesmerism. Certainly he did not think that the long elaborate operations which he performed on elephantiasis under hypnotic anesthesia were motivational, that the patient suffered no pain because he willed not to feel it. Such a conclusion would have applied as well to Ward's amputation case in which the man was accused of connivance with the surgeon (pp. 120 f.). Elliotson had the therapeutic possibilities of mesmerism in mind but he was hampered by opposition. Both he and Esdaile were handicapped by their use of the word *mesmerism,* a term in disrepute in scientific circles, and Elliotson's aggressive reaction to criticism increased his difficulties (pp. 120-122). The temper of the 1840s was, however, different from the temper of the 1790s Scientific medicine had acquired status, and when Braid, convinced that a mesmeric subject showed physiological symptoms which could not have been voluntarily induced, attested the genuineness of the phenomena, cried down "mesmerism," named the new state *neurypnology,* and put the whole matter in 1843 into a book, under the title *Neurypnology, or the Rationale of Nervous Sleep,* then many of the critics relaxed, believing that what is nervous is not magical and that sleep, even when nervous, is not the business of charlatans (pp. 125-128). In his notion that hypnosis is a *monoideism,* a concentration on a particular idea and one of such intensity that memories will often not carry over from the sleeping to the waking state, Braid found himself on the right track. Later he favored the belief that suggestion is basic to the hypnotic state, and thus he anticipated the finally accepted view. Braidism was not, however, fully accepted by the medical profession. That step in progress did not come until 1882 with Charcot.

In 1860 *A. A. Liébeault* (1823-1904) a French country doctor, began the study and practice of mesmerism. He settled at Nancy in 1864 and two years later published a book: *Du sommeil et des états analogues, considérés surtout au point de vue de l'action de la morale sur le physique.* (Eighty years later that was *le point de vue* of psychosomatic medicine.) Liébeault loved his patients and they called him *le bon père Liébeault.* He treated them with drugs for the usual fee, but free by mesmerism; and he got into no trouble because he was not an egotist and had no general theory. He wanted to cure people and he actually did. *La morale* really did act on *le physique.* In addition to these kindly successes, Liébeault had the distinction of converting Bernheim to his art in 1882. Thence arose the Nancy school of hypnotism, which was opposed to Charcot's school of the Salpêtrière.

Jean Martin Charcot (1825-1893), having received his M.D. at Paris in 1853, was appointed at the same university as professor of pathological anatomy in 1860. His appointment at the Salpêtrière was in 1862, and there he established the famous neurological clinic which remained unsurpassed in Europe or elsewhere in the nineteenth century. Janet and Freud were both his pupils and many physiologists, who made the rounds of the universities in their student days or immediately after they had received their doctorates, arranged to spend a year at Charcot's clinic.

What Charcot did was to study the hysterical patients—the psychoneurotics—who came to the clinic. He classified their symptoms. He noted their paralyses, anesthesias and amnesias, and also the fact that their paralyses and anesthesias were more apt to fit their ideas of what constitutes an anatomical member than nature's own arrangements of the nerves of the body. Charcot was also concerned with the convulsive seizures and often spoke of *hystero-epilepsy*, as if it were a single entity. Originally, hysteria had been supposed to be predominantly a female sexual disease: the Greek *hystera* means uterus. Charcot more or less adhered to this view of hysteria, and thus he succeeded in being both very modern and very ancient at the same time—modern because he was anticipating Freud in the view that sex is an important factor in producing the psychoneuroses—ancient in that he was being consistent with the demonological belief that the possessed are more often female than male. (Sprenger and Kraemer had written a *Malleus maleficarum,* not a *maleficorum.*)

Charcot undertook to treat his hysterical patients hypnotically, and he had, of course, some success since both hysteria and hypnosis are distortions or exaggerations of normal motivation. He believed that hypnosis always passes through three stages—from lethargy to catalepsy to somnambulism. He found that the symptoms of these stages closely resemble the symptoms of hysteria. He felt sure that the symptoms can not be simulated: what patient could manage consistently to fake these signs? he asked. He described the symptoms of both states—hysteria and hypnosis—in standard medical terms as modifications in muscular states, reflex movements and sensory responses. It was in such form that he reported to the Académie des Sciences on February 13, 1882, the Académie which had thrice rejected mesmerism, and Charcot won a complete acceptance for these medical findings. When the sheep growled magic the medicos beat it down, but when it bleated physiology they welcomed it in.

The similarity between the symptoms of hypnosis and hysteria led Charcot to think that hypnotizability is characteristic of hysteria and in a sense a symptom of it. That was a mistake, for, as the Nancy school showed presently, hypnosis depends on suggestibility and suggestibility is not a psychoneurotic symptom. The mistake was, however, fortunate because, in giving a medical slant to the whole substance of hypnosis at a time when approval by the Académie was crucial, it won approval and started a whole generation of young practising neurologists off in the right general direction—even though the aim did need slight correction later. Science is full of instances where wrong theories have promoted true progress.

Hippolyte Bernheim (1837-1919), a physician practising in Nancy, was converted by Liébeault to the use of hypnotism when Liébeault cured a case of sciatica with which Bernheim had failed. That was in 1882, the year in which Charcot convinced the Académie, but Bernheim did not accept Charcot's thesis that hypnosis is an hysterical symptom. Liébeault and he were certain they could use the hypnotic therapy on patients who were not neurotic. Thus Bernheim developed Braid's thesis that hypnosis is suggestion. He published several important papers on that theme: *De la suggestion dans l'état hypnotique et dans l'état de veille* in 1884, an argument for similar suggestibility in the hypnotic and waking states; *De la suggestion et ses applications à la thérapeutique* in 1886; *L'hypnotisme et la suggestion dans leurs rapports avec la médecine légale et les maladies mentales,* a paper on the legal responsibilities of criminals which he read before a congress of medicine at Moscow in 1897.

That last was, in a way, a letting the cat out of the bag, for Bernheim argued that the will of man is not always free.

Bernheim was a better expositor and generalizer than Liébeault but he was not a propagandist nor the founder of a school, as was Charcot. The 'school' of Nancy, as it has been called. was influential and eventually it became famous because it was right. Charcot, we have noted, was successfully wrong. Bernheim was right and eventually successful. He lived to be eighty-two, but long before his death (1919) Janet first and then Freud had taken over the field. Charcot himself had died in 1893.

Pierre Janet (1859-1947) was Charcot's pupil and successor. Janet's early interests lay in natural and moral philosophy, including psychology, and at the age of twenty-two he found himself appointed to teach philosophy at a lycée in Le Havre. He wanted while there to prepare a thesis on hallucinations to present to the University of Paris, but a friendly physician put him in the way of investigating a case, Léonie, a girl who had been an hypnotic for Dupotet (p. 120) and who exhibited unusual phenomena of clairvoyance and of hypnosis at a distance. In 1882 he reported on Léonie, a report which was often to be cited later by enthusiasts for what is called psychic research but which Janet in his mature years —so he said—would have been glad to suppress. This report brought him into contact with some of the psychologists at Paris and with Charcot in particular. Janet began to study up on the ideas of Charcot and Bernheim and to bring their work into relation with the history of hysteria and of mesmerism. He published on these topics in 1886 and immediately thereafter, and then, shifting his activity to the description of automatic action, he found that Charcot was becoming more and more interested in his work. In 1889 Janet received his doctorate at Paris on a thesis entitled *L'autoisme psychologique*, a work which went into six editions by 1913 and which formed the basis of Janet's later claim that he thought of the concept of the unconscious sooner than did Freud. Freud, as well as some more impartial critics, disallowed this claim, holding that Janet's use of the term at that time was but a *façon de parler* and not a serious attempt to establish a new conception.

In 1890 Charcot invited Janet to the Salpêtrière as the director of its psychological laboratory. Janet, in this new post, undertook at once to bring the body of clinical facts about hysteria into systematic order and also into relation with some of the more generally understood concepts of psychology. There resulted in 1892 the volume for which Janet is best known, *L'état mental des hys-*

tériques, to which Charcot wrote a preface saying that the work had been completed at the Salpêtrière and that he, Charcot, sympathized with Janet's attempt to unite clinical with academic psychology. For this work Janet was granted the M.D. degree in 1893. Charcot died that same year.

Janet was elected to a chair at the Sorbonne in 1895 and it was in his lectures there that he was shocked to discover how great indeed was the chasm between clinical and academic psychology, that is to say of Paris then, between Charcot and Descartes. Janet set about remedying this situation by introducing clinical conceptions and terms into his lectures on general psychology and by insisting on limiting all discussion of phenomena to observed fact. It may be presumed that the image of Descartes soon faded out from Janet's lectures and exposition of cases.

Janet succeeded to Ribot's chair in the Collège de France in 1902 and continued, until his retirement in 1936, to write and lecture on systematized anesthesia, abulia, fixed ideas, hysteria, obsessions, psychasthenia, fugues, personality, hypnotic surgery, neurosis, amnesia, *déjà vu*—to repeat most of the items in one biographer's list. His lectures at Harvard in 1906, published the next year as *The Major Symptoms of Hysteria,* were well known and went into a second edition in 1920. Some of his later views appeared in the three volumes of his *Les médications psychologiques* in 1919. With Charcot dead in 1893, Binet in 1911 and Ribot in 1916, Janet clearly became the dean of French psychology. Dumas was a little his junior and Piéron much younger. So Janet was made honorary president of the XIth International Congress of Psychology which met in Paris in 1937, and Piéron was president. Janet in 1947, the year he died, was almost the last Frenchman who had published important psychological research in the nineteenth century.

As a systematic psychopathologist, Janet wins a place between Charcot and Freud. He never quite got over regarding hysteria as degenerative, and he still called the major symptoms of hysteria *stigmata,* a term originally borrowed from the symptomatology of witchcraft. The stigmata were the anesthesias, amnesias, abulias and motor disturbances, to which Janet added the accidents, the symptoms which occur irregularly—subconscious acts, fixed ideas, attacks, somnambulisms and deliriums. In 1892 Janet's main argument about hysteria was that it is a splitting of the personality, caused by a concentration of the field of consciousness on one system of ideas and its retraction from others. As these conceptions developed in Janet's thinking, he moved more and more away from the position of Charcot toward the position that had been held by Braid and Bernheim. Janet's notion about the concentration of the field of consciousness reminds us of Braid's conception of hypnosis as a state of monoideism. Janet appealed to suggestion as the means whereby these changes occur, and he described them in terms of attention and absent-mindedness. In short, he was advancing the motivational theory of hysteria, using the vocabulary of attention—as did every other psychologist in the 1890s—where later the words *set*, *Einstellung, attitude* and *Aufgabe* were to supervene. There has always been a shortage of acceptable words for the dynamic principles.

In subsequent years, Janet adopted a more hormic system, speaking of *tensions* and of *forces mentales*, but this phase of his systematization, overwhelmed by the advance of psychoanalysis, has had little appreciation or influence.

In general, the world owes Janet credit for starting the movement to bring clinical and academic psychology together toward a single intelligible set of concepts. Freud and his followers, denounced by the academics, never tried to compromise nor would the Freudians have been welcome in academic halls in those early days when concepts were getting formed. The man who more than any other took over from Janet was *Morton Prince* (1854-1929) in America, Janet's contemporary, a student of multiple and coconscious personalities, and in 1927 the founder of the Harvard Psychological Clinic. That Clinic was founded for the express purpose of bringing clinical and academic psychology together. The deed of gift specified that the Clinic should promote instruction and research "in abnormal and dynamic psychology"—thus imbedding the term *dynamic psychology* into an official record—and that the Clinic should operate under the Faculty of Arts and Sciences and not in the Medical School. His intent was realized as well as are the intents of most donors. Whether he achieved his end by this specification or whether his desire was only an indicator for the direction of the *Zeitgeist's* current is one of the unanswerable questions of historical dynamics.

ACTIVE IDEAS

The word *dynamic* carries with it the conceptions of both force and activity. Even in physics the two are related, for *force* is defined in terms of the rate of change of movement which it will induce. Pressure is tension, and tension released is action. That much physics is involved in common-sense experience, and it is from common sense that science gets its primitive rubrics, like *heat* and *light* as separate entities in early physics.

Man experiences *effort*. Life for all animals and plants is built around the *struggle* for existence. The function of consciousness is to *preserve* the organism, and it succeeds because it is an organ of *attention* and *intention*. Nor is it an etymological accident that both these words are related to *tension*. The conscious organism *tends* toward apprehension of the external world in *attention* and of the future world in *intention*. So it becomes obvious that psychology has to consider the activity of an organism which acts in accordance with tensions which are its potentialities for action.

We have just noted that Janet came over to such a view in his dynamic psychology, and we shall presently assess the concepts of tension and activity in the systems of Freud, McDougall, Lewin and other dynamicists. These men were trying to bring psychology back from straight description of conscious content or behavior to an account of how thought and conduct change and how struggle and frustration are the essence of living in the perpetually goal-directed organism. Dynamic psychology thus includes *purposive psychology*.

The present section of this book is inserted for the purpose of reminding the reader where we have already considered the conception of active ideas and of tension and intent, for there can be found part of the background for dynamic psychology.

Leibnitz begins the tradition with his monadology. Each monad is *active*, striving independently for its own realization. *Activity* and *consciousness* are two words for the same thing. The active development of an idea consists in its clarification, and thus you have *degrees of consciousness* because the ideas grow from *petites perceptions* up to their conscious actualization in *apperception*. To speak of degrees of consciousness is to imply the existence of a *threshold of consciousness* at each degree. The lower degrees are *less conscious*—not unconscious but less. (See pp. 166-168.) All this conceptualization passes over into Herbart's, Freud's and McDougall's views with less change than one might expect.

Herbart dealt with a *dynamics of the soul*. Its ideas are all struggling for realization in consciousness, kept down in a *state of tendency* below the *limen of consciousness* because there is not enough room for all in consciousness. The ideas thus come into *conflict* and *inhibit* one another. Their realization in *apperception* above the threshold is determined by the mechanics of their *interaction*. (See pp. 255-260.) Here we have activity (induced by tension), the threshold of consciousness, and, in addition, something new—the conception of conflict among the ideas, mutual inhibition and resolution. The relation to the modern psychological mechanisms is clear.

Fechner scarcely belongs in this list, yet we ought not to forget how he took from Herbart the concept of the limen and how he reinforced the doctrine of the unconscious by his own doctrine of the negative intensities of those sensations which lie below the limen. (See pp. 290, 293.)

Nor does Wundt, the apostle of the psychology of content and Brentano's opponent, belong properly in this list; yet we must remind ourselves that Wundt accepted the notion of *degrees of consciousness*, the fact of the *limen*, and the concepts of active *apperception* and of *creative synthesis*. His theory of actuality prevents him from being a static psychologist. He made, moreover, the grand gesture toward dynamics by giving his elements the name *process*, thereby admitting the Leibnitzian contention that activity is basic to consciousness. (See pp. 334-336.) These items are, of course, Wundt's exceptions, which show him compromising with necessity. His most definite relation to dynamic psychology was that he moved psychology far enough away from it to build up the tensions that brought its return.

Brentano is, of course, the symbol of act psychology and the leader of the school. He substituted *acts* for contents and described the acts by their *intentionality* (pp. 359-361). His influence was very great, and, besides, he had the rightness of the obvious on his side: anyone could see by the scantiest introspection that mind is intentional and directed upon objects. Brentano won Stumpf to his side (pp. 367 f., 452) and eventually, if one speaks generally, Külpe (pp. 408 f., 451 f.). He had numerous followers who patterned their views on his—for example, Witasek and Messer (pp. 449 f.). It is known that Freud, at Brentano's recommendation, translated into German the twelfth volume of Theodor Gomperz's edition of John Stuart Mill's *Gesammelte Werke*, thus coming into contact with both Brentano and Mill at the same time. Freud was Brentano's student and took six courses in philosophy with him during four semesters in 1874-1876. Did Freud find it easier to believe in active ideas because he had sat under Brentano? It seems probable that he did.

HEDONISM

The great motivational theory of the eighteenth century was hedonism, and it lasted well over into the nineteenth. Hedonism is the theory that human action arises out of the desire of men to gain pleasure and to avoid pain. It is associated with utilitarianism and the name of Jeremy Bentham. It has also gained support from some of the British associationists—Hobbes, Locke, Hume, Hartley, the Mills, Spencer—because the principle of association seemed necessary to explain why men would suffer present pain in order to win future pleasure. Actually, hedonism goes back to the Greeks, to the writings of Socrates' pupil, Aristippos (*ca.* 435-356 B.C.) and to Epicuros (341-270 B.C.).

Troland has distinguished three kinds of hedonism—hedonism of the present, of the future and of the past. *Hedonism of the present* was the doctrine of Aristippos and the Cyrenaics that immediate pleasure is the *summmum bonum* of human action. That in itself is an ethical canon, since it lays down what man ought to do. It would be a psychological theory if it stated that man always or usually acts to gain immediate pleasure or to avoid immediate pain, and in that form it would be more nearly tenable of animals which lack the symbolic processes necessary for the anticipation of the future than of man who is always looking forward. As ethics the simple theory quickly becomes involved in contradictions and the Epicureans modified it greatly in the direction of taking account of future pleasure and pain.

The hedonism of the eighteenth and nineteenth centuries was basically a *hedonism of the future* as well as a hedonism of the community. Hobbes, Locke, Hume, Bentham and the two Mills were concerned with the state and society. If the individual seeks only his immediate pleasure, he finds that pain is often the delayed consequence. Given time, profligacy results badly. Hence the individual must learn prudence, a fact which the Epicureans recognized. There are, moreover, the cases of human conflict, which come about when one man's pleasure is another's pain. How then, the philosopher asks, can the pleasure of the future be assured? It can not be when human desires conflict, as they inevitably do. For this reason the utilitarians, of whom Bentham was the premier and exemplar, argued that you must apply the hedonistic principle to the community, integrating pleasures and pains, and taking "the greatest good to the greatest number" as the social goal.

It is here that association comes in. Each individual accepts the communal goal because the alternative is conflict, which provides pain and no pleasure for all parties. Presently the individual comes to associate pleasure instead of pain with those actions which lead to the communal goal, to the greatest pleasure for the greatest number. In this way the altruistic impulses are built up. Prudence is established in the same manner by association; the individual associates the pain of future calamity with the action which would otherwise have yielded present joy.

Jeremy Bentham (1748-1832) got his hedonism directly from Hume and his associationism from Hartley. He was also influenced by Adam Smith, whose *Inquiry into the Nature and Causes of the Wealth of Nations* appeared in 1776. Smith had argued that the greatest wealth and happiness of nations come from the exercise of self-interest in free trade. Smith was not a reformer, but Bentham, young enough to be escaping from the complacency of the eighteenth century into the radical nineteenth, saw the utilitarian principle as a cause to champion. He published *An Introduction to the Principles of Morals and Legislation* in 1779. "Nothing can act of itself as a motive but the ideas of pleasure or pain." Human action occurs "under the governance of two sovereign masters, pain and pleasure." All action is self-interested, but free self-interest results in "the greatest good to the greatest number," which is measured by the "sum total of human happiness." The familiarity of those phrases shows how the utilitarian philosophy has penetrated present-day common sense.

Bentham was not a liberal in the modern sense. He believed firmly in established authority. He said that talk about liberty and the rights of man was nonsense, that the greatest good to the greatest number depended on security, not on liberty, and that punishment is a means by which self-interest is persuaded to support authority.

Bentham impressed *James Mill* (1773-1836), who was his junior by twenty-five years and who took over his doctrine, presenting it, as he did that other doctrine, associationism, in such rigid and uncompromising terms as to alienate the more flexible minds. Then, about 1822, the young *John Stuart Mill* (1806-1873), aged sixteen, dominated by his father, took up with the doctrine enthusiastically. Four years later, however, he reacted against the principle as being oversimplified and opposed to humanitarian ethics. He maintained that benevolence is not based solely on self-interest. After Bentham died in 1832, John Mill attacked the Benthamites, remaining, however, a sophisticated utilitarian. His essay on *Utilitarianism*, published in 1863, was a much cited classic, effective in maintaining the political, but not the psychological, hedonistic doctrine.

Herbert Spencer (1820-1903) brought utilitarianism into relation with evolutionism. He argued that the hedonism of the present belongs to the evolutionary stage where sensations are more important than ideas, and that the development of ideas in man makes possible anticipation of and the preference for greater future pleasure at the sacrifice of lesser present pleasure. In this instance, there was no conflict between theology and the doctrine of evolution, for the Christian church relied on pleasure in heaven as against pain in hell to guide men to righteousness. Spencer, however, did not admit that present righteousness is painful for the wise man. Given enough wisdom, the hedonistic principle suffices, he thought, and there would be no need for the threat of hell.

It was the hedonism of the future that Freud took over as the pleasure principle in his earlier thinking about human motivation. The experimental psychologists, however, rejected the future and looked to the past for the determinants of action. Purpose, they thought, must push, not pull. Intentions must be referred to their causes. Thus they looked for a *hedonism of the past*, which is, of course, essentially the *law of effect* as it was emerging in Thorndike's experiments with the puzzle boxes in 1898 (pp. 561-563). This is the principle that action which leads immediately to pleasure is impressed and remembered and so repeats itself as habit, whereas action which leads immediately to pain is not impressed and is perhaps even suppressed from later reproduction.

It would not be proper in this place to enter into the history of the law of effect during the twentieth century. There is no doubt that successes in goal-seeking by trial and error tend to perpetuate themselves, and that failures tend to disappear. It is usual to say that *satisfaction* (which means success when there is a goal) reinforces the actions that lead to it. The terms *pleasure* and *pain* have given way to *pleasantness* (P) and *unpleasantness* (U), but there is some doubt that the existence of P and U in either animal or human subjects can be established for any given instant. The animals can not be trained to use a language which describes their own feelings, and in man the masochistic (intrapunitive) paradox of him who likes to be hurt makes the definition of P and U exceedingly difficult. *Acceptance* and *rejection, success* and *failure*, are terms that will work. That they are not at all the sole determiners of action was discovered by Lange in 1888 and later by the Würzburg school, which found that particular action depends upon set and attitude—a matter to which we return shortly (p. 716).

PSYCHOANALYSIS

In *Sigmund Freud* (1856-1939) we meet a man with the attributes of greatness. He was a pioneer in a field of thought, in a new technique for the understanding of human nature. He was also an originator, even though he picked his conceptions out of the stream of the culture—an originator who remained true to his fundamental intent for fifty years of hard work, while he altered and brought to maturity the system of ideas that was his contribution to knowledge. He was a leader who gathered about him an effective group of competent supporters, some of whom remained loyal to him throughout their lives and others of whom rejected the father image, criticized Freud's doctrine and started competitive schools of their own. His work passed first from obscurity into the notoriety of contumely, and then gradually, bit by bit, supported by an ever widening group of disciples and by an always reluctant acceptance of particular items by his critics, his ideas spread until they pervaded all thinking about human motivation both among the psychologists and among the lay public, for whom the adjective *Freudian* is almost as familiar as *Darwinian*. He gave the concept of the unconscious mind to common sense. At the very last, Nazi barbarism detained him in Vienna until his stock of unsold books could be brought back from Switzerland for public burning, but after that he escaped to honor in London where he died a year later. It was Freud who put the dynamic conception of psychology where psychologists could see it and take it. They took it, slowly and with hesitation, accepting some basic principles while rejecting many of the trimmings. It is not likely that the history of psychology can be written in the next three centuries without mention of Freud's name and still claim to be a general history of psychology. And there you have the best criterion of greatness: posthumous fame. The great man is he whom the historian can not ignore. Perhaps, had Freud been smothered in his cradle, the times would have produced a substitute. It is hard to say. The dynamics of history lack control experiments.

The psychoanalytic movement was, therefore, a personal school centered upon Freud and the group of his loyal disciples. As the movement spread beyond his control with the defection of Adler, Jung and finally even Rank, it became an in-between field, a science and a means of therapy which was accepted by neither the academic psychologists nor the medical profession. It grew eventually by infiltration into both these groups. After the work of the Würzburg school, the psychologists practically had to accept the conception of unconscious motivation and they had available little which seemed as positive as the Freudian concepts. In the medical profession, the psychiatrists, faced with a dearth of understanding of the psychoneuroses, took over various fundamental items of Freud's system, even while still making formal protest against what they took to be

Freud's pansexualism. It was only with the emergence of dynamic psychology in the 1920s that the chasm between the two fields—between normal and abnormal psychology—began to get filled in.

We ask, naturally enough, whence Freud got his ideas? They were there, ready for him, in the culture. He had only to take them over. One important one, oddly enough, was the theory of the conservation of energy.

In 1845, eleven years before Freud's birth, four young, enthusiastic and idealistic physiologists, all pupils of the great Johannes Müller, all later to be very famous, met together and formed a pact (*cf.* pp. 34, 299 f.). They were, in order of age, Carl Ludwig, who was then twenty-nine, Emil du Bois-Reymond, Ernst Brücke and Hermann von Helmholtz, then twenty-four. They were joining forces to fight vitalism, the view that life involves forces other than those found in the interaction of inorganic bodies. The great Johannes Müller was a vitalist, but these men were of the next generation. Du Bois and Brücke even pledged between them a solemn oath that they would establish and compel the acceptance of this truth: "No other forces than common physical chemical ones are active within the organism." It was in support of this thesis that Helmholtz, two years later, read and published his famous paper on the conservation of energy, a paper which, along with some by other men, places the origin of this theory in the 1840s. Thirty-five years later, Helmholtz and du Bois at Berlin, Ludwig at Leipzig and Brücke at Vienna saw their aspiration well on its way to complete acceptance. Meanwhile Brücke had acquired a new student named Freud.

Sigmund Freud was born in Moravia in 1856 and lived in Vienna from 1860 on. His parents were in modest circumstances, and eventually that made a difference because it forced Freud into private practice to support himself when he might have waited around the university for a position to become vacant. It was in his practice that he did his research, tested his hypotheses. Interested in Darwin's theory and putting aside some daydreams of a political career, in 1873 he entered the university at Vienna under the medical faculty, thinking to make natural science his speciality. By 1876 he was a member of Brücke's physiological institute, working hard and well under Brücke's direction, studying with the microscope and making the discovery of the analgesic power of the leaves of the coca plant. He took his doctor's degree in 1881 and the following year began the private practice of neurological therapy in association with Breuer, an older physiologist who had also worked under

Brücke, who had become a *Dozent,* and who then in 1871 had turned to private practice, while continuing a few lectures at the university. Both Breuer and Freud, then, had been drilled in physicalistic physiology under Brücke. They were taught that psychology is the study of the central nervous system and that psychical energy is physical energy which is supplied by the brain cells.

Joseph Breuer (1842-1925)—also known as the person who, independently of Ernst Mach, discovered the function of the semicircular canals just before 1875—had some definite views of cerebral action which were founded on Brücke's tenets for nervous energy. Breuer held that a certain amount of the organism's energy goes into intracerebral excitation and that there is a tendency in the organism to hold this excitation at a constant level. Psychic activity increases the excitation, discharging the energy. Rest and sleep allow it again to be built up. This theory resembles Avenarius' of 1888-1890 (pp. 395 f.) enough to make us wonder whether this kind of thinking was not then in the air. What Breuer and Freud had from it, however, was the conception of psychic events' depending upon energy which is provided by the organism and which requires discharge when the level is too high. Because Brücke had trained them into being uncompromising physicalists, they slipped easily over from the brain to the mind without raising any of the questions which at that time were bothering the dualists.

Breuer, when Freud joined him, had already tried treating hysterical cases with hypnosis and had discovered what he and Freud came to call *catharsis,* the "talking cure." A girl with a great many symptoms, including an inability to drink water, found her difficulties relieved and her ability to drink restored after she had been induced under hypnosis to describe the emotional event which brought on her trouble and after she had given full expression to her feelings about it. Here, then, was a new therapy. and Freud gave the credit to Breuer for the cathartic method.

Freud went to study with Charcot in 1885-1886, and it was then that Charcot made, in Freud's hearing, the often-quoted exclamation: "But, in this kind of case, it is always something genital—alway, always, always!" Freud thought: "Yes, but if he knows this, why does he not say so?" Later Freud went to Nancy where he saw the hypnotic work of Liébeault and Bernheim. He learned that their methods worked better with charity patients than with those who paid fees. That gave him some insight into the limitations of hypnosis. Back in Vienna he had to ponder both the sexual etiology of hysteria and the fact that hysteria is not limited to women. His

Viennese colleagues laughed at the idea of male hysteria; it is contradiction of terms, for everyone knows that a man has no uterus.

Breuer and Freud kept on with their work. They published on aphasia in 1891 and then in 1895 on hysteria. Freud was responsible for adding many new concepts, and they were all more psychological than physiological in their connotation. The early concepts were *defense, resistance, repression* and *abreaction*. The psychic functions were seen to occur in the realm of *the unconscious,* and thus there grew up, consistent with an earlier conception of the unconscious, the notion of a universe in which unconscious ideas interact after the manner of conscious ideas and strive, under certain conditions, to become conscious—an unconscious consciousness, as it were. Meanwhile the hypnotic technique was getting into difficulties. The patients did not stay cured; their symptoms returned. *Transference* was discovered; the patients tended to fall in love with the therapists. It was these two difficulties that drove Breuer presently to other kinds of work, leaving the field after 1895 to Freud.

The next development was Freud's stumbling upon the method of *free association* as a substitute for hypnosis. Freud found that patients encouraged to talk freely, to babble of everything that comes into mind, often, once they realize that the therapist will never condemn them for a mean or immoral thought, reveal the same repressed memories that had been brought out by hypnosis. Gradually Freud abandoned hypnosis.

At the same time, Freud was beginning to discover the significance of the dream as the partially concealed expression of repressed wishes. He used free association to analyze dreams. He discovered the importance of childhood experience in the emotional life of the adult. All of that resulted in his publication of *Die Traumdeutung* in 1900, a volume which is considered to be his greatest work and which advances psychoanalysis far. It showed many of the *psychological mechanisms* at work in the concealment of the true meaning of dreams. It introduced the concept of the *endopsychic censor,* which acted as the agent in repression and did duty for conscience until the superego was invented.

It is impossible here to outline the history of the development of psychoanalysis. That belongs in a special volume on the history of the psychological investigation of motivation. We may, however, trace through the movement to see what happened in it.

Freud's sixty years of active work can be roughly divided into decades.

(1) The 1880s were, as we have seen, his period of training and preparation. Breuer's chief contribution belongs then.

(2) The 1890s were the decade of trial and error and of first maturation. They ended with the great achievement of the publication of *Die Traumdeutung*.

(3) The 1900s were the period of further maturity and the beginning of fame—and also of notoriety, for at first the fame was opprobrious because of the rôle which Freud gave the sexual impulse in human life. Freud now gathered around him a group of disciples. Alfred Adler was his vicar. The association with Otto Rank (1884-1939) was early. Hanns Sachs (1881-1947) heard him lecture in 1904 and became at once a convert. Carl G. Jung had already started analysis and the use of free association in Zürich, for he knew about Freud's work. Then Freud met him in 1907. Sándor Ferenczi (1873-1933) of Budapest and Ernest Jones (1879-   ), then of London and later at Toronto for a while, belonged in the inner circle. The decade ended with G. Stanley Hall's inviting Freud, Jung, Ferenczi and Jones to Clark University's celebration of its vigentennium in 1909. A score of distinguished psychologists were the other guests— James, Titchener, Cattell and Boas among them. It was the first recognition of the importance of his work that Freud had had from scholars and scientists, and he came to Clark much heartened, although he found that he did not like America.

(4) The 1910s began with trouble. The second local congress on psychoanalysis was held at Nuremberg. It was decided there to establish three groups of analysts which would cooperate in communal affairs—a group at Berlin under Abraham, another at Zürich under Jung, and a third at Vienna, which Freud insisted should be placed under Adler. An international congress was planned for 1913 and Jung was to be president. Adler's views on inferiority and compensation were, however, already forming and soon there was serious conflict between Freud and those loyal to Freud's views, on the one side, and Adler, on the other. The result was that Adler left the Vienna group in 1911, Rank was promoted to Adler's place, and Sachs to Rank's. The International Congress was held in 1913, Jung was elected president, but his antagonism to Freud and Freud's beliefs was so great and so ungraciously expressed that a break ensued here. The difficulty with Jung was partly the vagueness of his theories. Sachs, defending Freud against Jung and quoting a Swiss poet, remarked that a Swiss, within a room with but two open doors, one leading to paradise and the other to a lecture on paradise would choose the second. (Zürich is in Switzerland.) At any rate,

by the time of the First World War there were three camps established, and Freud sought successfully to preserve the name *psychoanalysis* for his own. Not much intellectual advance was possible during the war.

(5) The 1920s were a period of final maturation and of spreading fame. Freud kept busy every day, from nine to one, analyzing patients, but with three months' vacation in the summer. The system began, under Freud's leadership but with discussion by the group, to lose the simple hyperboles of its youth. Some of the older concepts, like that of the censor, disappeared. The *unconscious, resistance, repression, regression, infantile sexuality*, the *libido*, the *Oedipus complex* were still valid, but *narcissism*, the *life and death instincts*, and the analysis of the personality into *superego, ego* and *id* were new. Psychoanalysis was now far away from psychoneurosis and fast becoming the means for understanding all human motivation and personality—a conceptual system in terms of which the human pattern of world events could be understood. To secure this progress Freud had organized in 1920 a secret inner circle of loyal analysts: himself, Otto Rank and Hanns Sachs in Vienna, Karl Abraham and Max Eitingon in Berlin, Sándor Ferenczi in Budapest and Ernest Jones in London. He had given the six others rings similar to one he had, an old Egyptian stone with a face of an old man cut on it. They were to correspond, meet biennially, oftener if necessary. Then, without warning, Rank, loyal for almost twenty-five years, published his work on the birth trauma. The others disagreed with it vigorously; Freud tried in vain to mediate; and presently Rank withdrew from the circle. Freud should never have created a 'crown prince' if he wished to continue to reign unchallenged. Abraham died the same year, and Freud discovered that he had cancer of the mouth.

(6) The 1930s, the sixth decade of Freud's active professional work, were the period of culmination. Freud kept at work. He suffered a great deal of pain, underwent several operations. He withdrew more and more from personal contacts, remaining available to his analysands and those disciples who still sought his counsel and wisdom. His fame spread around the world. There was a great celebration at his eightieth birthday in 1936, but Freud, with his house filled with gifts, did not attend. Finally in 1938 the Nazi terror burst upon Viennese Jews. Freud was saved from personal injury and the extreme humiliations that many others suffered, and he died peacefully in London a year later. In 1944, when Sachs

wrote his book about Freud, only Sachs and Jones of the seven with the rings were still alive. Then Sachs died in 1947.

Alfred Adler (1870-1937), when he broke with Freud in 1911, founded the school of *individual psychology*. At that time the sexual libido was regarded by the Freudians as the primary driving force of the personality. Adler substituted the need for superiority and power. Admitted inferiority he called the *inferiority complex*, a term now rife in common speech, and the effort to overcome it is *compensation*. Thus aggression may be the result, not of felt superiority but a felt inferiority, and it often becomes *overcompensation*.

Carl G. Jung (1875-   ), after his break with Freud in 1913, founded the school of *analytical psychology*. He broadened the term *libido* so that it lost almost entirely its specifically sexual connotation. He dealt with the differences in personality, and the best known of his parameters is the one between *introversion* and *extraversion*. It is impossible to pursue the complexities of Jung's system further.

Nor would there be any merit in listing the names of the other prominent psychoanalysts who have come into influence since Freud died and who write books of which titles can be given in a list. If the reader wants to know more about psychoanalysis, he will not lack for willing guides, and, if the man from Mars who has never heard of the movement chances to begin his study with this book, he can soon get elsewhere by reading the notes of this chapter.

What psychoanalysis will have done for experimental psychology, when the doing has got into history, is another matter. We can say, without any lack of appreciation for what has been accomplished, that psychoanalysis has been prescientific. It has lacked experiments, having developed no technique for control. In the refinement of description without control, it is impossible to distinguish semantic specification from empirical fact. Nevertheless, it is true that psychology was suffering from repression of its love of human nature, and this last half century of free association has been a talking cure, freeing psychology of its inhibitions so that it can go its normal way. Psychoanalysis had provided hypotheses galore, and, since operational definitions of its terms are possible, many of its hypotheses can have their consequences tested out by the hypothetico-deductive method. Long ago experimental psychology took the will out of its texts, leaving the space for conation blank. Now, thanks to Freud, it has got motivation back in. In 1943 R. R. Sears undertook to assess this very situation. He surveyed over a hundred and fifty studies, many of them experimental, dealing with infantile sexuality, the child-parent relation, especially the heterosexual one, child development, regression at all ages, the operation of the so-called mental mechanisms, and similar topics. He concluded as we have—the problems are there, they are being attacked, psychoanalysis has opened up the field, but you can not hurry insight. As a matter of fact, other important moves have been made to meet the need for a scientific understanding of motivation. Tolman's experimental program is in a sense an attack on the problem. Lewin's psychology is a quasi-experimental applied psychology of motivation, with a new system of description that seems less subjective than Freud's. To both these we come presently.

As against his past, we may note that Freud picked up and carried forward the activity notion of Leibnitz, Herbart and Brentano (pp. 701-703), the concept of the unconscious which these men had developed and which von Hartmann had carried on, and also the hedonism of the utilitarians (pp. 703-706). This last was embodied by Freud in his *pleasure principle*, which he abandoned in the more mature stages of psychoanalysis to substitute a less simple dynamism of the complex structure of the personality. Freud's whole life is a lesson that one lives not for pleasure, for he held rigidly to his main ambition to contribute the total endeavor of one human being to furthering the understanding of human nature. He even refused after the First World War to try for the fame that might have come with an attempt to present psychoanalysis as the remedy for the ills of civilization, for he doubted the potency of the remedy and believed that understanding must precede use.

One other thing has held dynamic psychology back. After the First World War, when psychoanalysis was gathering strength for its renewed progress, leadership in psychology was already beginning to pass from Germany to America. In Germany and Austria the culture favored subjective psychology, and psychoanalysis advanced there. In America, psychology, having gone functional, was about to go behavioristic. Behavioristics does not readily assimilate psychoanalysis, which is so subjective as to be suspect of harboring *homunculi ex machina* (pp. 674-678) in its superego, ego and id. Brücke would have been puzzled had he been told that the pact of 1845 with Helmholtz and the others to keep physiology physicalistic would result eventually, a hundred years later, in the belief that there are three little warring men in every head.

PURPOSIVE PSYCHOLOGY

Under this title we may conveniently discuss (1) set and attitude, those situations in which a specific *Aufgabe* carries the purpose, (2) McDougall's purposive or hormic psychology, (3) Holt's cognitive behaviorism and his concern with the Freudian wish, and (4) Tolman's purposive behaviorism. The first sets the stage for the others, and the third is preparation for the fourth.

1. *Attitude and Set.* When the history of the experimental psychology of motivation is written, it will show how difficult it has been all along to arrive at psychological generalizations which do not involve a purposive determinant—for purpose enters psychology more often as an independent variable than as a dependent variable, more often as a determinant than as a subject of investigation.

The dynamic principle—the specific determinant of the psychological event—has of necessity been recognized all along in scientific psychology, although it has been obscured under the camouflage of a diversified vocabulary. Here follow seventeen words which have been used at different times or in different contexts to imply this same concept. It would be an interesting exercise to write a dozen little textbooks of dynamic psychology, using a different one of these words for the dynamic principle in each book.

Throughout the nineteenth century, psychologists talked about (1) *attention* when the effective predisposing factor was fully conscious and (2) *expectation* when consciousness was less characteristic. You looked, for instance, into an anaglyptoscope (1855) and you saw a cameo or an intaglio depending, not upon the actual direction of the light but upon what you thought was the direction of the light. That was *expectation*. *Attention* determined which phase of the reversible perspective was seen, and the fluctuation of the perspective was supposed to measure the fluctuation of attention. *Expectation* was one factor which determined how unconscious inference makes use of clues to form perceptions (pp. 308-311). *Expectation* was the effective determinant for prior entry (pp. 142-147) and later of reaction times. It was even suggested that you might cut reaction times down to zero if you made expectation optimal by always having a warning signal precede the stimulus by a fixed interval. Schumann (1900) used *attention* to explain the displacements which occur in optical illusions. There was some truth in Titchener's remark that you could understand a psychologist's system if you but knew what he meant by *attention*.

In 1888 Ludwig Lange in Wundt's laboratory discovered that the differences between the sensorial and muscular reactions depend on the observer's *attention* before he reacts (p. 149). Külpe was quite clear then: the word to use is (3) *preparation* or (4) *predisposition*. Later, when the Würzburg school had brought out the contributions of Watt and Ach (pp. 403-406), we had a new dynamic vocabulary. (5) *Einstellung* was either used in English or translated as (6) *set*. (7) *Aufgabe*, the factor which sets up the *Einstellung*, was used in English or translated as (8) *instruction*. Because both the action consciousness and the thought consciousness turned out to be (9) *predetermined*, Ach invented the term (10) *determining tendency*, analogous to the associative, impressional and perseverative tendencies of G. E. Müller. When an *instruction predetermines* a subject so that a weaker association is realized instead of one that normally is stronger, then a *determining tendency* is operating. If I tell you to think of rhymes, then you will think of *tack* for *black* instead of *white*. It is possible to write a whole dynamic psychology in terms of *determining tendency*, *determination* and *predetermination*.

The word (11) *attitude* came in about this time. The older German word was (12) *Anlage*. Then with the Würzburg school we began to hear about *Bewusstseinslagen* and conscious attitudes. Later in social psychology *attitude* became the substitute for *Einstellung* and *set*.

(13) *Instinct* appeared in animal psychology under the Darwinian stimulus, but, since instinct is supposed to be fixed by inheritance, it is not a substitute for these other dynamic words. After that the word (14) *drive* began to be used, along with the word (15) *incentive* as applied to goal-directed behavior.

It was McDougall, influenced by Ward and Brentano but writing of behavior, who applied the word (16) *purpose* to behavior and Tolman who reinforced him.

The latest term is (17) *need*. The *primary needs* are the instincts and the *derived needs* are the habits. In general, the *needs* are more biological than the *attitudes*. To want air, food and love are *needs*. *Attitudes* determine preferences, especially in matters of taste and judgment.

This list is not complete nor accurately documented as to times of first uses. It shows, however, that the psychologist, and the experimental psychologist at that, has never been free of the dynamic principle. In the study of perception, action, attention, emotion, learning and thought, the dynamic principle always demands attention. The acceptance of the principle of association removed some of this pressure from the topic of learning, but not all. Even emotion does not escape. Does running from a bear constitute fear, as James seemed once to say? Yet I do run if I have no gun; or I do run if I am a poor shot. Guns and skills affect attitudes and determine running.

2. *McDougall.* The essentials about William McDougall we have already learned in a previous chapter (pp. 465-467, 491 f., 496 f.). McDougall's purposive psychology was based on his conviction that the organism is always striving toward a goal. His is a psychology of activity, which draws from Ward from Brentano via Ward, and from the Scottish school. It deals with both experience and behavior, but quite early McDougall was claiming behavior as the chief subject-matter of psychology. He was thus a pre-Watsonian behaviorist, but he renounced any such title when later he battled with Watson. The earlier reference also gives McDougall's "seven marks of behavior," the characteristics which attest the purposiveness of behavior, distinguishing it from reflex movement (pp. 466 f.). or McDougall, purposiveness included some degree of freedom in action, of indeterminateness—a view which got him into the bad graces of the physicalists among the psychologists. These were his views as of 1923 when he wrote his *Outline of Psychology.*

McDougall's most important contribution to dynamic psychology was, however, the publication of his *Social Psychology* in 1908 and his constant revision of it afterward to meet the huge demand which it created. The book deals with the description and nature of human action, and the picture is built up in terms of instincts. Left over from the nineteenth century, there was a great literature about animal instincts (pp. 625 f.), and McDougall undertook to show that you can regard all human action—and therefore social interaction—as the result of basic inherited instinctive action and its modifications in experience. He also related the instincts to the emotions. For each primary instinct there corresponds, he thought, a primary emotion—for the instinct of flight, the emotion of fear; for the instinct of repulsion, the emotion of disgust; for curiosity, wonder; for pugnacity, anger; for the parental instinct, the tender emotion. There are other instincts, McDougall averred: self-abasement, self-assertion, reproduction, gregariousness, acquisition, and so on. There is never an end to such a list, and McDougall wrote his entire book about the development of instincts in the individual and their interaction among individuals. This kind of dynamic psychology was popular because it was so simple and direct. It fell later into scientific disrepute, when psychologists discovered that anyone can make up his own list of instincts and that there is no way to prove that one list is more certainly correct than another. McDougall seemed to have borrowed too much from the faculty psychology of his Scottish ancestors (pp. 205 f.), who confused description with explanation. If you write well, they would have said, you have a faculty for writing. If you fight much, McDougall implied, you have an instinct for fighting.

In 1930 McDougall renamed his system *hormic psychology*, arguing that instincts, being goal-directed, consist of the liberation of energy that guides the organism toward a goal. The guidance, he said, is effected through cognitive awareness; the activity toward the goal tends to continue until the goal is reached; then the activity is terminated by success. Progress toward a goal is always pleasant; the thwarting or blocking of the progress is always unpleasant. That theory is by no means new. The Yale determinists also hold that action by trial and error continues until success puts an end to it, but the atmosphere of their thinking is utterly different from McDougall's. He used teleological concepts when possible, believed that energy can be directed into channels of action and that the cognitive realization of the goal's nature can keep the not-yet-successful organism on the right path—or at least on what the organism, not yet successful, takes to be the right path. Present action depends on knowing whither it is directed.

McDougall's thinking shows here the effect of the older beliefs about energy (*cf.* Brücke's and Breuer's conceptions of brain energy waiting to be discharged, p. 709, *supra*), and also the influence of Freud and psychoanalysis. McDougall wrote extensively with great sincerity and he had considerable influence, although more effect upon social psychology than upon general systematic psychology. He did not influence Holt, but presumably he did influence Tolman a little. At any rate both McDougall and Tolman were purposive behaviorists, although it was Tolman who introduced that term.

3. *Holt.* We have already seen who Edwin B. Holt was and how he made behaviorism over into a cognitive psychology *par excellence* by showing that the *specific response relation* is the essence of the event which is called "having a meaning" or simply "knowing" (pp. 645 f., 661 f.). We have here to note further that Holt believed that this specific response relation is not only the

basic cognitive principle, but also, *ipso facto*, the basic dynamic principle.

Holt's term for the dynamic principle is *wish*, an item which we could have added to our list of seventeen dynamic terms if it had been used more generally. Holt wrote *The Freudian Wish and its Place in Ethics* in 1915. Freud has given psychology back its will, Holt said. The wish, as the specific response relation. provides scientific psychology for the first time with a causal category; Freud, "to put it less academically, has given us a key to the explanation of mind." Furthermore, the wish may be regarded as *purpose*, Holt said, and a negative wish is a negative purpose. A way to define a wish is to say that it is "*a course of action* which some mechanism of the body is *set* to carry out, whether it actually does so or not." Those italics are Holt's. The organism is always going somewhere. To go somewhere is to act with a purpose, but to go somewhere is also to act as the result of predetermination, to act as the effect of cause. Holt is no teleologist like McDougall, who seemed to think that the future pulls the present toward it. He is a straight determinist and sees the 'pull of the future on the present' as nothing more than a pushing of the past upon the present, viewed *a posteriori*. To understand behavior in causal terms is to know both how and why the organism gets on from where it is to its future. When an organism responds to a stimulus. it is discriminating the stimulus and that in itself is an act of cognition, but the organism is also behaving in respect of the stimulus and in accordance with its own needs and that is an act of will. Behavior is purposive *because* it is caused, and it could have been Holt who used Tolman's title *purposive behaviorism*.

Holt, an erudite if somewhat eccentric genius, was a stimulating teacher and friend to those few students who won his approbation. Although Tolman came mainly under Münsterberg's influence, it is clear that Holt's influence upon him was crucial.

4. *Tolman.* We have already seen how Edward Chace Tolman, after touching on the problem of whether meanings can exist in advance of their imaginal carriers (the problem that Titchener posed about imageless Würzburgian thoughts), turned to the development of his *purposive behaviorism* which is also an *operational behaviorism*. Tolman's *magnum opus—Purposive Behavior in Animals and Men*—with its strange vocabulary of purposive terms appeared in 1932 and that volume remains the key to Tolman until he synthetizes the later development of his system which at present lies in many scattered articles (pp. 647 f., 662).

It is clear that Tolman was carrying on from Holt. He was also influenced by Gestalt psychology, for he was writing about *molar* behavior, the total action of the whole organism, and not about the "molecular behavior" of reflexology. He left out of psychology the unpublishable "raw feels" that introspection used to be supposed to yield, and studied behavior as a function of antecedent situations and causes. Between the antecedent terms and the response terms Tolman introduced *intervening variables*, which are not born of the physiologistic "word magic" against which Holt warned, for they all have clear operational definitions. As a matter of fact, Tolman's system has the great advantage that it is based upon many specific experiments and leads to other definite experiments. That sort of positivism is always a safeguard against word magic.

It is interesting to see how this deterministic purposivism comes about. You can observe purpose. For instance, you can see a rat respond to a stimulus (Watson's behavior), but you can also see that the rat is doing something when it responds (Holt's behavior) and eventually, if you are familiar with rodent conduct, that its behavior is goal-directed or purposive (Tolman's behavior). You may, indeed, need to be as good a phenomenologist as Goethe, who looked at the sheep's skull on the Lido and saw it as an instance of homologous parts (p. 20). Observation is not necessarily invalidated by inference, else how could Helmholtz have argued that all perception involves unconscious inference? So the phenomenologists at Würzburg described thoughts when imagery seemed not to be present, and Tolman in 1917 could believe that meaning can be observed without imagery. Now—the development is consistent—Tolman tells you that you can observe purpose and the arguments for that view are the same as those for phenomenology.

This matter becomes clearer if we note a few of the terms with which Tolman works. *Demands* are needs, primary or derived, including instincts. *Goal-objects* are the "to-be-got-to" objects toward which behavior is directed. Arrival at a goal-object terminates behavior. *Means-objects* and *means-situations* are secondary goals, the means for reaching the ultimate goal-objects. They derive their power from association with the goal-objects. *Expectation* is the intentional forward-looking determinant which makes behavior goal-directed. It is really one of the *intervening variables*, but that term was invented later. *Means-end-readiness* is the set or preparation which causes the subject to seize upon the means-objects which enable him to proceed toward the goal. The *dis-*

criminanda are the characters of objects which can act as signs indicating how to reach the goal-objects. They are the effectively differentiated stimuli which provide clues at a choice point. The *manipulanda* are the characters of those objects which can be used to reach the goal—an alley to run along or a string to pull. Both discriminanda and manipulanda are *behavior supports* since they support goal-directed behavior, that is to say, they make goal-directed behavior possible. *Means-end-relations* are perceptions that relate means-objects to one another or to goal-objects. A *sign-gestalt* is a behavior-support which consists of a means-object, a goal-object and a means-end-relation—all of which is to say that it is a total external situation in respect of which the goal-directed behavior occurs.

There are many more of these concepts in Tolman's system. He put, including synonyms, one hundred twenty-three such items into his glossary and defined them rigorously in terms of one another—not, as we have done, by reference to a conventional terminology. The purpose of the preceding paragraph is, however, not to teach the reader a new language but to show him the kinds of concepts that enter into Tolman's purposive behaviorism and how necessarily indeterminate is the line between the direct observation of datum, on the one hand, and the not-fully-conscious inference of function, on the other.

Undoubtedly Tolman's neologisms have prevented many psychologists from following his leadership. Nevertheless, his special language has called attention to many characteristics of behavioral concepts which would otherwise have been overlooked, or else noted and then forgotten. The language also serves, as in any secret society, to motivate to greater activity the members of the in-group who know what all the words mean.

OTHER DYNAMIC PSYCHOLOGIES

The last need not be the least. We have still something to say about Woodworth, Lewin, Henry Murray, and what we may call the Yale schema of motivation. Köhler does not appear again, for he means by *dynamics* the applicability of field theory to phenomena, not something to do with motivation.

1. *Woodworth.* We have already met Woodworth, a student of James', Cattell's lieutenant at Columbia and then his successor (pp. 564-566, 580 f.). Along about 1896 Woodworth had remarked to Thorndike, when they were both graduate students at Harvard, that what psychology needed was a "motivology." It was some-

time near the beginning of this century that Woodworth got from C. L. Herrick the idea that psychology ought to be dynamic. About 1910 Woodworth began to use the expression *dynamic psychology*. In 1918 he published a set of lectures under the title *Dynamic Psychology*. In 1925 and again in 1930 he described the nature of dynamic psychology. It seems likely that this term might have come into use without Woodworth's introduction, but, as matters stand, he was certainly its father, or at least its god-father.

This book has presented Woodworth as a functional psychologist, perhaps the best representative of the broad functionalism that is characteristic of American psychology. Most of Woodworth's dynamics consists in his faith in the adequacy of cause-and-effect for the understanding of psychology's problems and in his other belief that the organism's activity, being what psychology considers, may be seen either in its conscious processes or in its behavior. We have already noted that Münsterberg, Titchener and Watson were his bogey men who showed what to avoid in psychology (p. 565), but we might also add McDougall, for whose teleological interpretation of instincts Woodworth had no use. In respect of his beliefs in cause and effect and in conscious and behavioral activity, Woodworth did not differ widely from Angell and the Chicago functionalists who supported both of these views earlier. Woodworth's notion that the acceptance of such principles brings motivation into psychology was, moreover, just what Holt was saying at the same time and what Tolman had to say later.

It is interesting to note here that Woodworth, deploring Titchener's attempt to analyze all consciousness into·sensory elements, was also, like Tolman, on Külpe's side of the argument about imageless thought. His presidential address before the American Psychological Association in 1914 was on this topic. You have, more or less, to take the Würzburg position or at least the phenomenologists' attitude—this is what we have just been noting for Tolman—if you are to see that cause-and-effect relations *are* motivations. Otherwise you find yourself seeing only the analytic terms and then inferring to the relation.

Woodworth in 1918 was emphasizing the importance of *mechanism* and *drive*, trying to show that these two concepts can together account for all of human activity. The mechanism of an act is the linkage. To describe the mechanism is to answer the question *how* about the phenomenon. Cause-and-effect relations, stimulus-and-response relations (S-R) are mechanisms which can be described. Outside the mechanism, however, lie sources of energy ready to activate this or that mechanism. To discover them is to answer the question *why* about the mechanism. They are the drives. If an animal is thirsty, the go-to-water mechanism is activated by the thirst drive; if hungry, the hunger drive activates the get-food mechanism. The drive acts like a determining tendency which produces rhymes instead of opposites for stimulus words.

It is plain that the mechanism, being a cause-and-effect relation, contains an antecedent or causal term. If the mechanism is a simple compulsory reflex, like the knee-jerk, then its stimulus is its drive. More often, however, there is some state, internal to the organism but external to the mechanism, which, when activated, activates the mechanism. Taking food depends on seeing food (stimulus) and being hungry (drive). You can regard the drive as reinforcing the mechanism, but you can also view the entire system as an instance of multiple causation. Woodworth's notion that habits develop interests, that mechanisms become drives, fits into this conception.

2. *Lewin.* Kurt Lewin (1890-1947) was studying psychology at Berlin in 1909-1914, just after Koffka and Köhler had taken their doctors' degrees there. He stayed on, publishing presently some important papers. His study of association in 1917 was one of those which show that the strength of association does not depend alone on the frequency of contiguity of the associated terms but also upon the motive which associates them. At that time Lewin was already prepared to make a Gestalt psychology of motivation his primary concern, and that meant then a scientific adaptation of the only thorough-going psychology of motivation extant—the Freudian system. In 1922 Lewin became a *Dozent* at Berlin, and in 1927 an *ausserordentlicher Professor*. He published again on association and motivation in the first volumes of the new *Psychologische Forschung* and then began a series of researches conducted by a score of his students, a series which carried forward this program on the dynamics of human action. He was already known in America when, in 1932, he migrated thither to spend first three years at Stanford and Cornell and then ten years at the University of Iowa, making a series of studies of action in children. The Second World War eagerly employed his services in several researches on human action and motivation, and then at the close of the War in 1945 the Massachusetts Institute of Technology brought him to Cambridge as chief of a new Research Center for Group Dynamics. Unfortunately, this plan to use Lewin's able insights, his remarkable originality and zeal and his almost peerless capacity for demo-

cratic leadership to build up a new 'realistic' experimental social psychology was terminated by his unexpected death in 1947.

Tolman has classed Lewin with Freud. "Freud, the clinician, and Lewin, the experimentalist, these are the two men who will always be remembered because of the fact that their contrasting but complementary insights first made of psychology a science which was applicable both to real individuals and to real society." A different writer might have linked Lewin with James to say that they two, more than any others, had opened new fields in psychology by the reasonableness of their unaggressive insistence, reinforced by their unusual capacity for friendship. All three of these men attracted disciples—James more often through his writings, Freud and Lewin by gathering loyal groups in conference about them. Freud's inner circle was encamped behind firm barriers, and the disloyal, who could no longer remain true, left. Lewin seems not to have required loyalty, yet to have received it. There used to be annual meetings, in which Lewin, with a blackboard to talk upon, was always the central figure and to which psychologists from far and near, those who believed in Lewin, came to be stimulated by the discussion and went away eager to return another year. We shall not understand Lewin's place in American psychology in 1933-1947 except in relation to the enthusiasm which his generous, friendly, insistent zealotry created. Whether Tolman is right in comparing him with Freud history will decide. Those who were closest to him felt very sure of his genius.

Some who were not close to him criticized him severely. The out-group never enjoys the cheer of the in-group. In general, the outsiders complained that *Lewinpsychologie* was pretentious, that it called itself *topology* when it had but slight relation to that highly developed field of mathematics, that it was concerned mostly with common-sense solutions of social problems in experimental or quasi-experimental situations, solutions which described phenomena in the terms of the new dynamism and with chalked or printed diagrams which made description resemble discovery. History will decide about this matter too. Persistent posthumous importance is the test of greatness. Helmholtz and James were great.

Many of Lewin's papers were brought together in English translation in 1935 under the title *A Dynamic Theory of Personality*, to which was added a chapter surveying the experiments which supported this new approach to psychology. His *Principles of Topological Psychology* came out the next year, and then in 1938 he published a monograph on the mathematical logic of his conceptual system of psychological forces. He was, however, not like James. The persuasive charm of his personality did not quicken his books.

Lewin began with the intention of describing human action in the terms of a field theory. You picture a person in his *life-space*. That term means his immediate environment as perceived or conceived by him—his 'live space,' as it were, since the phrase does not at all mean the person's geographical environment or his environment throughout his entire life. Lewin was, indeed, against genetic accounts, for he believed that a full understanding of the total field in which the subject exists at the moment constitutes not only a description of his action but also an explanation of it. Such a description would answer the questions both of *how* and of *why*. When *how* and *why* have been satisfactorily answered, there is no point in asking *whence*.

The person is a locomotor organism. He lives by moving around. He wishes to get to places or away from them, to get hold of things or to get rid of them. You can represent his desires (what Holt called *Freudian wishes*) as *valences*. An object that a person wants has for him a *positive valence*, and you may represent that by a *vector* which indicates a force pushing the organism toward the desired object. An object with a *negative valence* pushes the person away. If you have a man in a field with a lot of objects, the amounts and directions of whose vector-valences are known, can you not compute a resultant of the forces in order to tell what the man will do?

The difficulty here is this: the man is not acting in a physical world but in a psychological environment where the reality is what he perceives or believes. The longest (physical) way around is often the shortest (psychological) way there—in life-space. You can put a *barrier* between a child and a desired object. It may be a fence or it may be a parental prohibition. The distance to the object is increased by the barrier and may decrease again when the child sees the way around the fence or the prohibition. Lewin met these difficulties by introducing the basic conception of *topology*—the conception of a space which has in it only order, neither direction nor distance. (Order is what remains constant in a pattern on rubber membrane when by distortion the distances and directions are radically altered.) In topological life-space the distance from here to there is only the number of intervening events. In turning to topology, however, Lewin lost his vectors and the possibility of their being combined by simple laws of resolution. He tried later to regain some of this advantage by suggesting that life-space is "hodological," that is to say, a topological space in which paths are differentiated.

It is no wonder that Tolman felt at home in this system. Holt might have too. All three men—Holt, Tolman and Lewin—believed that, if you can describe motive and purpose in deterministic terms, you will have explained them and have obtained the predictive psychology of human nature that so many have sought. Holt spoke of cause and effect, but Lewin, not liking that analysis, spoke of field forces. Field theory, Lewin thought, is the newer scientific conceptual system. He called it Galilean. The older views depend on Aristotelian class theory, he said. In class theory you 'explain' an object or event by referring it to the class in which it belongs, ignoring all the particular ways in which the special object or event differs from the representative average of the class. In field theory you note, on the other hand, all the particulars in their interrelations. Ideally you have no variability to discard, since the individual case is what you want to understand. In this respect Lewin's views accord well with the basic values of American psychology, which, aiming at being functional, has always welcomed the concern with individual differences.

There is a great deal more to Lewin's psychology. He used the concept of *tension* for motivation or need, and held that the tension is discharged when the goal is reached or when some other means of relief, like the achievement of a substitute goal, is realized. Perhaps the use of this concept is the true mark of a dynamic psychology. Such a statement is not inconsistent with the other assertion that dynamic psychologies all use field theory, for it is another way of saying that, when the forces in a field are in disequilibrium, action continues until equilibrium is reached. Equilibrium is success; failure and frustration create tension.

Those who are enthusiastic about Lewin's contribution to psychology point to what they call the rich harvest of research and experimentally established fact. Lewin himself in 1935 listed about forty topics to which twenty of his students had contributed importantly during the preceding decade. We may pick a few examples.

Zeigarnik (1927), in the first and one of the best known of these important researches under Lewin's direction, found that uncompleted tasks are better remembered than completed tasks. The theory is that the tension of motivation is discharged by completion of the task, but that, when the activity is interrupted, the tension persists and keeps alive the memory. Ovsiankina (1928) showed that adults who fail to complete an activity tend to wish to resume it when there is opportunity later, whereas those who have completed the activity will most often choose something new. The explanation in terms of tensions is the same as in Zeigarnik's case. Lissner (1933) found that the tension for one uncompleted activity can be partially discharged by completion of a similar substituted activity. Here we have a dynamic resembling Freudian sublimation.

There are several studies which show that success and failure depend psychologically upon the level at which the subject has set his aspiration. To fail in what is known to be impossible is no failure at all, nor does success in what is very easy seem like success. The tension created and the degree of success at which it is relieved depend on the level of aspiration which the subject established for himself. Hoppe (1931) began this study and Frank (1935) worked out many more details.

There is a well-known research by Barker, Dembo and Lewin (1941) on the way in which young children react to frustration. The frustration consisted in letting a child play first with ordinary toys, then giving him extraordinarily desirable toys, then shutting him off from the splendid toys by a wire partition and giving him back only the common toys to play with again while he can still see the others. In the face of frustration, his use of the common toys deteriorates, becoming "dedifferentiated" to simpler and less maturely structured kinds of play. In that way we obtain a description of an experimentally induced Freudian regression.

When the Second World War needed leaders, the psychologists turned to Lewin because of his research with Lippitt and White (1939), in which types of leadership for groups of boys had been studied. Leaders had been trained to the production of different "social climates" through different kinds of leadership: the authoritarian, the *laissez-faire* and the democratic types. The democratically led groups had the greatest success.

We can not say whether it was Lewin's system that made possible the formulation of these problems and their solution, or whether the common factor here was Lewin's infectious personality. Certainly those who found themselves within the boundaries of his enthusiastic group accepted from him both his modes of thought and his mission for research. There was, of course, no hard and fast orthodoxy which disciples had to accept as there was with Freud and Titchener, for Lewin was a truly democratic leader and his gospel matured with group discussion. The movement was, however, energized by Lewin and the motivation which he supplied did more than provide a convenient language of word and diagram for the description of these facts. It could be that a handbook on the psychology of motivation might present all of these facts and many others without even mentioning Lewin's system, his concepts and his schemata. That is possible. On the other hand, it may have been that Lewin was the *Zeitgeist's* agent in freeing the psychology of motivation from conventional inhibitions, in winning again Galileo's victory over Aristotle and the victory of Gestalt psychology over Wundtian analysis. History will eventually have made this judgment for us.

3. *Murray*. If we are discussing the chief systems of dynamic psychologies, we have no right to omit *Henry A. Murray's* views which were developed at the Harvard Psychological Clinic and put forward in the *Explorations in Personality* which that group of investigators published in 1938 under Murray's leadership.

The system, with its long lists of needs and its many neologisms, is, however, too complex and too specialized in vocabulary to be properly described here. Basically it is like the others—Holt's, Tolman's, Lewin's. An initial total situation is changed by the action of an organism until a new situation results, one which has the property of terminating the action. Such an event establishes the existence of a *need*, and a need, which causes the action, is to be characterized by its effect, not by the particular movements which lead to it. Murray calls these irrelevant movements *actones*, dividing them into *verbones* (verbal activity) and *motones* (other muscular movements). A particular need is what brings about the particular effects, no matter what actones have been employed. You use your lighter or you borrow a match; the need is for a light. That was the distinction Holt was making. The boy, he said, is not going by the house; he is going to the grocery. Going-by-the-house was the irrelevant actone. Needs—and Murray, as we have already noted, has his long list of them—are directional (Lewin's vectors) simply because they aim at effects. Operationally the word *directed* means primarily that the achievement of the effect (goal) terminates the need and so also the activity. The effect (goal) is whatever change is necessary to dispel the need. A *positive viscerogenic need*, like "n Food" (need for food) is obviously directed toward an end state—getting nutriment into the stomach—which abolishes the need for the time being. A *negative viscerogenic need*, like "n Noxavoidance," is the need to get rid of noxious objects by spitting them up or by looking away so as not to see them. A *psychogenic need*, like "n Acquisition," the acquisitive attitude, is harder to define operationally, since the end-situation may be mere credits in bank, not a pile of gold on a strong-room floor.

As with Lewin, so with Murray: it is hard to tell whether the special language so clarifies problems as to suggest important research that would not otherwise be undertaken or whether the language is merely the symptom of in-group enthusiasm which is what produces the research. Certainly Murray's group has been effective; and certainly his capacity for leadership is part of the explanation of what his followers have done. It was Murray, with his belief in understanding personality by an intensive inventory of the whole person in all his capacities, who started the work on assessment of men in the U. S. Army during the Second World War.

4. *The Yale Schema*. Still another effective group of psychologists interested in the problems of motivation was formed in the Institute of Human Relations at Yale. There Hull (pp. 651-653) was the stimulus, although he confined his own activity to the problems of learning. The conceptual schema was brought out in the monograph called *Frustration and Aggression* (1939). It consisted of essays by John Dollard, L. W. Doob, Neal E. Miller, O. H. Mowrer and R. R. Sears. This work shows that a group of experts can engage in prolonged and enthusiastic discussion of the problems of motivation without finding it necessary to create a special language to further their communication. In this fact there is a hint that the neologisms of Tolman, Lewin and Murray may be playing a motivational rather than an intellectual rôle in scientific process. It seems probable that psychology already has enough language—the Yale language—to make a "motivology" clear. The special vocabularies may belong to the pragmatics of science, not to its semantics, for they seem to be related to group loyalties which stimulate research. Perhaps these languages prevent lethargy in thinking. Certainly they are symptoms of intellectual alertness.

Yale's dynamic schema is straight-forward and direct. Here it is in outline. There is *goal-directed behavior*, as defined by whither it leads. Something starts it off and that can be called an *instigator*. Such instigated action is the *goal-response*, which is terminated by success in reaching the goal. In a wholly novel situation success must come by trial and error. Every success, however, *reinforces* the goal-response so that it occurs more surely or quickly when the situation has become familiar. That is the core of the system, which depends—in good Hullian fashion—on the concept of reinforcement. The particular theory goes on to explain aggression. Interference with an instigated goal-response is *frustration*, and frustration leads either to a *substitute response* or to *aggression,* which is in itself a kind of substitute. When aggression is blocked, it may discharge itself upon a substitute or turn inward and become *self-aggression.* If these terms sound vague, one can say only that the operational definitions for them were known at Yale in 1939 and that these definitions are less elaborate than Tolman's, Lewin's and Murray's.

NOTES

Most of the allusions in the introductory paragraphs are made specific in their proper places elsewhere in this chapter or this book. We may note here two dynamic psychologies which are not mentioned again in this book: J. T. MacCurdy, *Problems in Dynamic Psychology: a Critique of Psychoanalysis and Suggested Formulations,* 1922; T. V. Moore, *Dynamic Psychology,* 1924, 2 ed., 1926; *Cognitive Psychology,* 1939. It seems to have been R. S. Woodworth in 1918 who first used the term *dynamic* to characterize a special kind of psychology.

Psychoneurosis

See first and foremost Gregory Zilboorg's *A History of Medical Psychology,* 1941, which makes this historical information easily available for the first time. On the early attitudes toward mental illness, see 27-92; on the subsequent decline in psychiatric sophistication, 93-117; on the rise of demonology, 118-143; on the *Malleus maleficarum* and three centuries of witch-hunting by the Inquisition, 144-174; on first revolt against superstition, 175-244; on the discovery and understanding of the psychoneuroses, 245-378. More specific reference to Zilboorg is made below. A very brief comment on the history of psychoneurosis occurs in G. Murphy, *Historical Introduction to Modern Psychology,* 2 ed., 1949, 131-136. Jacob Sprenger's and Heinrich Kraemer's *Malleus maleficarum* was published first in 1489. There is a German trans., *Der Hexenhammer,* 1906; and an Eng. trans., with the Latin title, 1928, reprinted, photographically re-duced in size, with a new introduction, 1940. Sprenger's first name seems to be Jacob, translated James, though Zilboorg calls him Johann. Zilboorg translates the book's title as *The Witches' Hammer,* but that title leaves it uncertain as to who pounds and who is pounded. *The Witch Hammer* is better. They wanted the book to hammer witches with. See Zilboorg, *op. cit.,* 144-174.

On Vives, see Zilboorg, *op. cit.,* 180-195 *et passim.* On Weyer, *ibid.,* 207-235 *et passim.* On Pinel, *ibid.,* 319-341 *et passim;* also Murphy, *op. cit.,* 39-43 On Dorothea Dix, see Zilboorg *et al., One Hundred Years of American Psychiatry,* 1944, 78 f.

On Mesmer, Esdaile, Elliotson and Braid, see the text of Chapter 7 and also the notes on pp. 116-128. See also the notes there on Liébeault and Charcot, pp. 129 f. The references to the significance of these men, in Zilboorg's *History of Medical Psychology (op. cit.),* are: Mesmer, 342-355; Elliotson, 351-354; Braid, 356 f.; Liébeault, 357-359; Charcot, 361-378. For a brief personalized sketch of Charcot, see William Osler, Jean-Martin Charcot, *Johns Hopkins Hospital Bull.,* 1893, 4, 87 f.

On Janet, see W. S. Taylor, Pierre Janet 1859-1947, *Amer. J. Psychol.,* 1947, 60, 637-645; E. R. Guthrie, Pierre Janet 1859-1947, *Psychol. Rev.,* 1948, 55, 65 f.; also his not very enlightening autobiography in C. Murchison, *Psychology in Autobiography,* 1930, I, 123-133; also his long bibliography in Murchison's *Psychological Register,* 1932, 723-725. The important books are his *L'état mental des hystériques,* 1892; 2 ed., 1911; Eng. trans., 1901; *The*

Major Symptoms of Hysteria, 1907; 2 ed., 1920; *Les médications psychologiques*, 3 vols., 1919. *Dédoubler* means to double, divide or split (a personality into two). Why the translator of *L'état mental des hystériques* has reversed the meaning of the word and hopelessly involved the text in contradiction by writing *undouble* for *dédoubler* may never be known. She died before she could read her proofs; her husband read them, but Titchener helped him.

Morton Prince's two best known books are *The Dissociation of a Personality* (the case of Miss Beauchamp), 1906; *The Unconscious*, 1914. W. S. Taylor has tried to interpret him to the world in *Morton Prince and Abnormal Psychology*, 1928. Both Prince and Janet, as well as Münsterberg and Ribot, contributed to the famous symposium on *Subconscious Phenomena*, 1910. Prince founded the Harvard Psychological Clinic in 1927 with money given him by an anonymous donor who believed in Prince's wisdom. Prince furnished the ideas. One of them—Titchener was still alive and introspection had not yet gone out of style—was to get coconscious introspection. A primary consciousness might look with the eyes and introspect with the mouth on what it saw, while a coconsciousness, having taken over the ears for perceiving, could publish its introspection with paper and pencil. Prince's thought was that the two consciousnesses might run on together, each reporting on itself. Conceivably they might interfere, or each might be found speculating on what the other was at the moment up to.

Active Ideas

Since this section is a review of earlier parts of this book, no notes are necessary beyond the cross-references in the text, and the reminder that the relation of Freud to Brentano was indicated by P. Merlan, Brentano and Freud, *J. Hist. Idea*, 1945, 6, 375-377; Brentano and Freud—a sequel, *ibid.*, 1949, 10, 451.

Hedonism

Many of the British empiricists and associationists referred to in this chapter have already been more fully considered in this book: Locke, pp. 169-176; Hume and Hartley, pp. 186-199; James Mill, John Stuart Mill and Spencer, pp. 219-233, 240-243. On the relation of all these men and of Aristippos, Epicuros, and Bentham to hedonism, see John Watson, *Hedonistic Theories from Aristippus to Spencer*, 1895; Leslie Stephen, *The English Utilitarians*, 1900, 3 vols. (on Bentham, Jas. Mill and J. S. Mill respectively); Ernest Albee, *A History of English Utilitarianism*, 1902. These books deal with all the men mentioned and with some others in addition (Albee spreads broadest), and they give the references to the particular writings of the different authors. Jeremy Bentham's *An Introduction to the Principles of Morals and Legislation*, 1779, has been reprinted with an introduction in 1948.

There are discussions of this matter in relation to experimental psychology in L. T. Troland, *Fundamentals of Human Motivation*, 1928, 273-306; P. T. Young, *Motivation of Behavior*, 1936, 327-337. A brief orientation is given by G. Murphy, *Historical Introduction to Modern Psychology*, 2 ed., 1949, 4-43.

Psychoanalysis

On the history of psychoanalysis, see Sigmund Freud's earlier account at the Clark vigentennium, The origin and development of psychoanalysis, *Amer. J. Psychol.*, 1910, 21, 181-218; and a little later, *Zur Geschichte der psychoanalytischen Bewegung*, 1914, Eng. trans., 1917, variously reprinted in both German and English, including *The Basic Writings* (*op. cit. infra*). Then there is Freud's *Selbstdarstellung*, 1925, Eng. trans., 1927, reprinted in Eng. trans., 1946. The best book about Freud is the little volume by Hanns Sachs, *Freud, Master and Friend*, 1944. Excellent for the earlier part of Freud's life is F. Wittels, *Sigmund Freud: der*

Mann, die Lehre, die Schule, 1924, Eng. trans., 1924. Less satisfactory is Theodor Reik, *From Thirty Years with Freud,* 1940. Sachs, devoted disciple for thirty-five years (1904-1939), loyal when others deserted, loyal yet writing with the ring of objectivity, skilled in the assessment of personality and in writing about it, has rendered Freud's memory a great service by his intimate portrait. Some day someone will compare the personalities of Freud and Titchener; they are remarkably alike, even in many small details, though Freud was, of course, the much greater man. Sachs thought that Freud, even though he disclaimed being a *Menschenkenner,* should have known that loyalty is least likely in the crown prince and have spared himself some pain when Adler and Rank deserted. On Freud's early relations with Brücke and Breuer, and Brücke's pact of 1845 with Ludwig, du Bois and Helmholtz, see S. Bernfeld, Freud's earliest theories and the school of Helmholtz, *Psychoanal. Quart.,* 1944, 13, 341-362. On how Freud heard Brentano lecture and translated J. S. Mill into German, *vide supra* and Merlan *locc. citt.* See also H. W. Puner, *Freud: His Life and Mind, a Biography,* 1947.

Freud's writings were very numerous indeed. They have been brought together in his *Gesammelte Werke,* vols. I-XVII, 1940-1948. Some of the books by Freud mentioned in the text are: *Studien über Hysterie* (with J. Breuer), 1895, Eng. trans., 1909; *Die Traumdeutung,* 1900, Eng. trans., *The Interpretation of Dreams,* 1913; *Zur Psychopathologie des Alltagslebens,* 1901, Eng trans., *Psychopathology of Everyday Life,* 1914; *Der Witz und seine Beziehung zum Unbewussten,* 1905, Eng. trans., *Wit and Its Relation to the Unconscious,* 1916; *Vorlesungen zur Einführung in die Psychoanalyse,* 1917, Eng. trans., *Introductory Lectures on Psycho-Analysis,* 1922; *Jenseits des Lustprinzips,* 1920, Eng. trans., *Beyond the Pleasure Principle,* 1922; *Das Ich and das Es,* 1923, Eng. trans., *The Ego and the Id,* 1927. *The Basic Writings of Sigmund Freud,* 1938, contains A. A. Brill's Eng. trans. of *Psychopathology of Everyday Life, Interpretation of Dreams, Three Contributions to Sexual Theory, Wit and Its Relation to the Unconscious, Totem and Taboo,* and *History of the Psychoanalytic Movement.* American psychologists, turning behavioristic, might take up with Freud's views but slowly. On the other hand, these many Eng. trans. show that the American public, always functionally minded and recognizing functional psychology in Freud (and sex, of course), was not slow to recognize him.

C. Murchison, *Psychological Register,* 1932, gives long bibliographies for Alfred Adler, Sándor Ferenczi, Freud, Ernest Jones and Carl Gustav Jung. Out of this wealth, specific citation here is futile, but we may mention for the three dissidents the three books which were in a way the three *casus bellorum:* Adler (who broke with Freud in 1911), *Ueber den nervösen Charakter: Grundzüge einer vergleichenden Individualpsychologie und Psychotherapie,* 1912, Eng. trans., 1917; Jung (who broke in 1913), *Die Psychologie der unbewussten Prozesse: ein Ueberblick über die moderne Theorie und Methode der analytischen Psychologie,* 1917, Eng. trans., 1917; Otto Rank (who broke in 1925), *Das Trauma der Geburt und seine Bedeutung für die Psychoanalyse,* 1924, Eng. trans., 1929. Very influential in the early days were Ernest Jones' *Papers on Psycho-Analysis,* 1913. Jones was at Toronto for a while, but after 1913 in London. Ferenczi stayed in Budapest until his death in 1933. Sachs took on the Psychoanalytisches Institut at Berlin, and then in 1932 he came to Boston. He analyzed the author of this book, or at least began an analysis in 168 sessions. Perhaps there was not enough transfer. See E. G. Boring and H. Sachs, Was this analysis a success?, *J. abnorm. soc. Psychol.,* 1940, 35, 3-16.

There are a number of accounts of psychoanalysis written by psychologists for didactic purposes. Two very excellent ones are: G. Murphy, *Historical Introduction to Modern Psychology,* 2 ed., 1949, 307-348; R. S. Woodworth, *Contemporary Schools* of *Psychology*, 2 ed., 1948, 156-212. Less satisfactory (two of them are out of date) are: E. Heidbreder, *Seven Psychologies*, 1933, 376-412; J. C. Flugel, *A Hundred Years of Psychology 1833-1933*, 1933, 279-303; A. J. Levine, *Current Psychologies*, 1940, 148-228. John Rickman, *Index Psychoanalyticus 1893-1926*, 1928, gives a bibliography of 4739 articles and books on psychoanalysis for the period noted in his title, as well as all the data about the names of prominent analysts and important analytic journals. Probably the best guide for a newcomer to this field, in addition to the works already cited in this paragraph, is Ives Hendrick, *Facts and Theories of Psychoanalysis*, 1934, 2 ed., 1939, in which the suggestions for further reading should not be overlooked. A book that is good in exposition but not as a guide to the literature is W. Healy, A. F. Bronner and A. M. Bowers, *The Structure and Meaning of Psychoanalysis*, 1930.

The text notes that psychoanalysis is interpenetrating general psychology wherever the problems of motivation are under consideration. Thus see R. R. Sears' *Survey of Objective Studies of Psychoanalytic Concepts*, 1943, (*Soc. Sci. Res. Counc. Bull.*, no. 51). Note also how psychoanalytic concepts and problems have entered into at least six tenths of the chapters in S. S. Tomkins, *Contemporary Psychopathology*, 1943.

Purposive Psychology

The paragraphs on set and attitude indicate a field which has yet to be worked out in detail. It is not possible to document it at the present time. If the reader does not know what an anaglyptoscope is, let him see E. G. Boring, *Sensation and Perception in the History of Experimental Psychology*, 1942, 266, 304. On attention and reaction, see W. James, *Principles of Psychology*, 1890, I, 427-434. Wundt simply calls the dynamic principle *psychic*, and there is no doubt that the purposive factor was often hidden under this more general term: W. Wundt, Veränderungen der einfachen

Reaktion durch psychische Einflüsse, *Grundzüge der physiologischen Psychologie*, 6 ed., 1911, III, 409-421.

On William McDougall, see pp. 465-467, 491 f., and for references to biographies and to some of his books, pp. 496 f. To those references we may add here the paper on hormic psychology in C. Murchison, *Psychologies of 1930*, 1930, 3-36. For a modern list of needs that far outreaches McDougall's modest list of instincts, see Henry A. Murray, *Explorations in Personality*, 1938, esp. 54-242.

On Holt and Tolman, see pp. 645-648. The notes, pp. 661 f., indicate the chief books of each, the biographies of Holt and the comment on Tolman's system.

Other Dynamic Psychologies

On Woodworth, see pp. 564-566 and the notes on pp. 580 f. The important items in this context are the 1918 book and the 1925 and 1930 articles.

Out of a large bibliography of Kurt Lewin's writings, we may note these items to which the text refers: Die psychische Tätigkeit bei der Hemmung von Willensvorgängen und der Grundgesetz der Assoziation, *Zsch. Psychol.*, 1917, 77, 212-247; Das Problem der Willensmessung und das Grundgesetz der Assoziation, *Psychol. Forsch.*, 1922, 1, 191-302; 2, 65-140; *A Dynamic Theory of Personality*, 1935 (Eng. trans. or Eng. originals of seven articles or chapters which appeared elsewhere in 1926-33, and a new survey chapter at the end); *Principles of Topological Psychology*, 1936 (the standard presentation of what to do about life-space); The conceptual representation and the measurement of psychological forces, *Contributions to Psychological Theory*, 1938 (the mathematical logical development of the topological or 'hodological' system).

The researches mentioned in the text as representative of Lewin's influence are: B. Zeigarnik, Ueber das Behalten von erledigten und unerledigten Handlungen, *Psychol. Forsch.*, 1927, 9, 1-85; M. Ovsiankina, Die Wiederaufnahme unterbrochener Handlungen, *ibid.*, 1928, 6, 302-379; K. Lissner, Die Entspannen von Bedürfnissen durch Ersatzhandlungen, *ibid.*, 1933, 18, 218-250; F. Hoppe, Erfolg und Misserfolg, *ibid.*, 1931, 14, 1-62; J. D. Frank, Individual differences in certain aspects of the level of aspiration, *Amer. J. Psychol.*, 1935, 47, 119-128; Some psychological determinants of the level of aspiration, *ibid.*, 285-293; The influence of the level of performance in one task on the level of aspiration in another, *J. exper. Psychol.*, 1935, 18, 159-171; R. G. Barker, T. Dembo and K. Lewin, *Frustration and Regression: an Experiment with Young Children*, 1941 (*Univ. Iowa Stud. Child Welfare*, 18, no. 1); K. Lewin, R. Lippitt and R. K. White, Patterns of aggressive behavior in experimentally created 'social climates,' *J. soc. Psychol.*, 1939, 10, 271-299. There is a story related to Zeigarnik's experiment. Lewin and his friends were in a restaurant in Berlin, in the sort of prolonged conversation which always surrounded Lewin. It was a long time since they had ordered and the waiter hovered in the distance. Lewin called him over, asked what he owed, was told instantly and paid, but the conversation went on. Presently Lewin had an insight. He called the waiter back and asked him how much he had been paid. The waiter no longer knew. When his tension was relieved by having the bill paid, the memory was no longer kept alive. In vols. 9 to 19 (1927-1934) of the *Psychol. Forsch.* there appeared 17 studies in Lewin's Untersuchungen zur Handlungs- und Affektpsychologie. Most of the researches cited in this paragraph were in that series.

There is no good biography of Lewin. Most of the necrologies are eulogies with few facts in them. Three by G. W. Allport, E. C. Tolman and A. J. Marrow are reprinted from other sources in *J. soc. Issues*, 1948, Suppl. Ser. no. 1. For the original of Tolman's account, quoted in the text, see his Kurt Lewin 1890-1947, *Psychol. Rev.*, 1948, 55, 1-4.

There are brief accounts of Lewin's psychology in R. S. Woodworth, *Contemporary Schools of Psychology*, 2 ed., 1948, 151-155; G. Murphy, *Historical Introduction to Modern Psychology*, 2 ed., 1949, 296-306; A. J. Levine, *Current Psychologies*, 1940, 106-126. The last does not claim to be about Lewin, yet it really is. The most thorough and extensive exposition of Lewin's thought is by R. W. Leeper, *Lewin's Topological and Vector Psychology: a Digest and Critique*, 1943 (*Univ. Ore. Publ. Stud. Psychol.*, no. 1). The most stormy denunciation of Lewin's use of concepts is I. D. London, Psychologists' misuse of the auxiliary concepts of physics and mathematics, *Psychol. Rev.*, 1944, 51, 266-291.

Light is thrown on both Tolman and Lewin by R. K. White, The case for the Tolman-Lewin interpretation of learning, *Psychol. Rev.*, 1943, 50, 157-186. The question here is whether learning requires repetition for reinforcement. Tolman and Lewin think that a single unrepeated perception can be learned if motivation is sufficient.

For H. A. Murray's dynamic psychology, see *Explorations in Personality*, 1938, by Murray et al., 36-141, esp. on needs, 54-115. The work on the assessment of personality in the U. S. Army was started by Murray but carried on by some of his erstwhile students and presently by many psychologists. The final result resembled the work of the Harvard Psychological Clinic, not in vocabulary and conceptual system, but in the way in which many measures of personality were synthetized under group discussion into the final assessment. See *Assessment of Men*, 1948, by the Staff of the Office of Strategic Services.

For the Yale schema, see J. Dollard, L. W. Doob, N. E. Miller, O. H. Mowrer and R. R. Sears, *Frustration and Aggression*, 1939; also Sears' article on this topic in P. L. Harriman, *Encyclopedia of Psychology*, 1946, 215-218. Sears uses this schema to outline a systematic child psychology in W. Dennis et al., *Current Trends in Psychology*, 1947, 50-74.

ASSESSMENT

CHAPTER 27

Retrospect

C an we say over now in two thousand words how experimental psychology—scientific psychology—came into being and what it is like?

First there was the Renaissance and then the emergence of science, with the names of Copernicus (1543), Kepler (1609), Galileo (1638) and finally Newton (1687) standing out. The new era meant a shift away from the authoritarianism of the church and the autocracy of the state, a shift toward democracy and a recognition of the rights of the individual. Power, which had remained with those of noble birth, shifted then toward those who could and did acquire wealth, and the opening up of the new lands in both the west and the east provided new opportunities of sudden great success for those not born to authority. Science, whose ultimate sanction is practical, however pure and esoteric it may often seem to be, prospered with democracy. The resulting changes, which occurred slowly in western Europe, were, moreover, accelerated in the new world, so that America became a practical nation and a democracy quite early. Therein lies the reason why America, still a pioneer country, accepted so easily the Darwinian theory and the belief in the survival of the fittest, and then, taking over the descriptive psychology of the Germans, made it at once into the functional psychology which has become the American characteristic.

The philosophical lineage of modern psychology can be taken back to Descartes (1650), who, in giving us dualism, gave psychology both the free human soul and the wholly determined human body. French materialism comes from Descartes, but so today does all subjectivism and mentalism. Descartes gave us both. Leibnitz (1714) contributed the parallelism which made it possible for the nineteenth-century psychologists to stick to mentalism in spite of the theory of the conservation of energy, and he also gave the conception mental activity, which persisted, not only in the act school of Brentano (1874), but also in more recent conceptualizations of motivation, like Freud's. Locke (1690) started empiricism, which,

737

coming on down to the present through Berkeley (1710), Hume (1740), Thomas Brown (1820), the Mills (1829, 1843), Helmholtz (1867) and Wundt (1874), helped to make psychology so sensationistic in the nineteenth century. Associationism grew out of empiricism and flourished, not only in England but also in France. Condillac (1754) was an associationist. French materialism (La Mettrie, 1748; Cabanis, 1802) helped to found physiological psychology and prepared the way for later reflexology. Kant (1781) contributed nativism and a belief in describing what is given *a priori;* he thus stands at the head of a tradition that passes from Johannes Müller (1838) to Hering (1864) to Stumpf (1873) to Gestalt psychology (1912). The Scottish school (1764 *et seq.*) furnished faculties, which came to public notice and scientific disapproval under the phrenologists (1810), and now have reappeared in functional America as abilities, aptitudes and the traits which factor analysis yields. Bentham (1789) provided hedonism which, via Freud (1920) and the pleasure principle, played a rôle in starting the psychology of motivation.

The developments in physiology which carried over into experimental psychology or affected it occurred in four fields of research: sensation, reflexes, nerve excitation and brain function. We can mention only a few names for each. Sensation: Bell and the Bell-Magendie law (1811), Purkinje (1825), E. H. Weber (1834), Johannes Müller and specific nerve energies (1838), Fechner (1860), Helmholtz (1867). Reflexology: Robert Whytt (1751), Marshall Hall (1833), Johannes Müller (1833), and then later the Russians— Sechenov (1863), Bekhterev (1907) and Pavlov (1902 *et seq.*). Nerve excitation: Galvani (1791), Volta (1800), du Bois-Reymond (1849), Bernstein (1866), Lucas (1909), Adrian (1912). Brain function: Flourens (1824), Broca (1861), Fritsch and Hitzig (1870), Ferrier (1876), Goltz (1881), Munk (1890), Franz (1902 *et seq.*), Lashley (1929).

From astronomy psychology got the personal equation (Bessel, 1826), reaction times (Donders, 1868), the beginnings of the experimental psychology of attitude and motivation (Lange, 1888).

From the occult, psychology got animal magnetism with Mesmer (1781), mesmerism with Elliotson (1843), and Esdaile (1846), hypnosis with Braid (1843) and Liébeault (1866), hysteria with Charcot (1878), Bernheim (1884) and Janet (1890), neurosis and psychoanalysis with Freud (1900), and thence a whole psychology of motivation with men like Holt (1915) and Lewin (1935).

The "new" experimental psychology began in Germany. Fechner

(1860) contributed mental measurement, having got some of his concepts from Herbart (1825). Helmholtz contributed a great wealth of research and fact about vision (1867) and hearing (1863). Wundt was the founder and promoter (1874, 1879, *etc.*). He was not so great a man as Helmholtz but he did, with indefatigable zeal and huge erudition, all the things necessary to get a movement going. Lotze (1852) provided a setting for this new venture. Brentano's act psychology (1874) furnished the contrast for analytical psychology of content which Wundt (1874) derived from the associationists. Hering (1864) and Stumpf (1873) provided a nativistic opposition to Wundt. G. E. Müller (1896) was on the empiricistic side with Helmholtz (1855 *et seq.*) and Wundt (1874). Mach (1886) influenced Külpe (1893) and Titchener (1910) toward greater systematic specificity, though somewhat differently, as both were starting out in the Wundtian tradition. Titchener kept to the faith in elementistic contents until his death (1927), but Külpe, tackling the problem of thought at Würzburg (1901-1908), was won away from his faith in sensational elements to a position more nearly resembling Brentano's. Later, Gestalt psychology (1912), with its phenomenology, took over the problems that the Würzburg school had left. The German contribution to psychology ceased with the rise of the Nazi state (1934).

France was at all times primarily the country of abnormal psychology. The tradition of Descartes (1650), La Mettrie (1748) and Cabanis (1802), runs over later into the line of Liébeault (1866), Charcot (1878), Bernheim (1884) and Janet (1890). Even Ribot (1881 *et seq.*) concerned himself mostly with psychopathology. Binet (1903) was an experimentalist but his great contribution turned out to be in mental testing.

England's great scientific contribution was Darwin (1859) and his theory. Galton (1869) was the avenue by which Darwin first affected psychology. The problems of mental inheritance and mental evolution loomed large. The beginnings of animal psychology came via Darwin (1872), Romanes (1882) and Lloyd Morgan (1894). From Germany, Loeb (1890) contributed the theory of tropisms. Then animal psychology passed over to America, where Thorndike's experiments (1898) joined it with the new psychology. Galton (1883) contributed the basic notions about mental testing and the statistical measurement of human capacities, and then the movement went to America where Cattell (1890) promoted it.

American psychology starts off with James (1890), who, after discovering what the Germans were doing, reported to the

Americans on the new movement in his *Principles*. It was he who began that metamorphosis of German psychology which was to alter the Teutonic worm of sensory content into the American butterfly of functional reality. Stanley Hall (1883, 1887, *etc.*) was its entrepreneur. Ladd (1887) was its expositor. Baldwin (1895) was the purveyor of evolutionary theory. Dewey (1896) was a second voice after James', crying in the wilderness. Cattell (1890, *etc.*) was the practical man of sense and thus the promoter of tests. Titchener (1898) remained Moses on the mountain, ten commandments in hand, while the "dollar-grubbing" Americans danced around their golden functionalism. A little later there were Angell (1907) with Chicago's special functionalism, Woodworth (1918) with Columbia's general functionalism, Thorndike (1914) with educational psychology and tests.

The movement in America was away from mentalism. That was, it seems, inevitable—at least as inevitable as were America's democracy and functionalism. Angell's functionalism was a step away from dualism and toward the validation of behavior as a psychological datum. Watson's move to behaviorism (1913) was explicit and clear. Briefly this trend was retarded by the arrival of all the Gestalt psychologists in America. They were not prepared to give up consciousness. Köhler, however, had been working with apes and soon there had been enough adjustments with the newcomers to prevent quarreling. Lewin (1935) was more like an American than a German. Finally the talk about positivism and operationism seemed to settle the matter of consciousness, since it made optional the translation of mentalistic concepts into behavioral ones.

Another way to look at this history is to examine the central core of general psychology, the core that lies behind the applications of psychology in education, in therapy and in industrial use. General experimental psychology has had three successive phases. (1) At first it was devoted almost entirely to the problems of *sensation and perception*. Those were the problems that had just been taken over by Fechner, Helmholtz and Wundt in the mid-nineteenth century from the experimental physiologists. (2) Then came the experimental psychology of *learning*, which began with Ebbinghaus in 1885. Külpe picked this event as starting the psychology of the higher mental processes, but the work of his own school on thought belongs properly in the third category. (3) Finally, there is the psychology of *motivation*, and that includes, of course, the psychology of the *unconscious* which is where the motives lie. Külpe's Würzburg school was demonstrating this fact, showing that thought is motivated and that its motivation is unconscious. The real start on the unconsciousness of motivation lay, however, not in psychology proper but outside of it with Freud. The student of the history of psychology would not be promoting an absurdity if he placed on the horizon of his imagination these three landmarks: Fechner's *Elemente der Psychophysik* of 1860, Ebbinghaus' *Ueber das Gedächtnis* of 1885, and Freud's *Die Traumdeutung* of 1900.

* * * * *

In 1929, twenty-one years ago, in the first edition of this book, the author wrote in this last chapter as follows:

"It is now proper to ask ourselves the question: To what extent has the new psychology justified itself? There is a criticism of modern psychology, often spoken and sometimes written, that the new science has not quite succeeded, that it has been, as compared with its ambitions, relatively sterile, that it set out to study mind by the experimental method, and that it has gained a mass of knowledge about sensation (which the physiologists might have gained), a little else, and nothing of great moment about the rational mind, the personality and human nature. This criticism, when expressed by philosophers, may be suspected of reflecting the disappointment of philosophers at the turn which the new psychology took, or even their reaction to the negativism of the psychologists toward philosophy. However, it is not at all impossible that psychologists themselves might express some dissatisfaction with the advance of psychology, were they relieved of the necessity of defending themselves. Has psychology been relatively ineffective in attacking its problems?— we may ask, now that the perspective of seventy years is before us."

Seventy years! And now the perspective has been extended to ninety years. What does the author say after ninety years?

In 1950 no apology is necessary. Psychology has prospered and expanded. It has, for the most part, crossed the Atlantic to America. There is an ebullition of activity, some in Europe as it struggles for rehabilitation after the War, much more in America. In twenty years the American Psychological Association has grown from a thousand to six thousand members. In 1910 it had but 228 members. Now the fields of applied psychology, especially clinical psychology, are flourishing, and experimental psychology is also demanded in the public service and in the universities. Within America there is the internal criticism and complaint that is normal to healthy institutional growth and the men of each field believe that their own *Fach* is weakened by the competition of the others, but the old inferiorities are gone. That is progress. There are temporary frustrations when scientific aspiration outstrips material support, but, in general, society has not been slow to put new scientific insight to work.

In 1929 the author complained that the progress of psychology had been slowed by "the internal conflict within psychology itself, a conflict that is the natural outgrowth of its history. Psychology has never succeeded in taking philosophy to itself or in leaving it alone . . . . A division of the mind within psychology is not healthy . . . . Psychology ought to fare better when it can completely surrender its philosophical heritage, in fact as well as in voiced principle, and proceed, unimpeded by a divided soul, about its business." In both Great Britain and America psychology's battle had been to become independent of philosophy—its parent—not only in obtaining separate living arrangements in laboratories, but also in its thinking. There were—in 1910, say—too many theoretical papers written in proportion to the empirical base upon which they were founded, and there was not enough research outside of the field of sensation and perception to make it certain that experimental psychology had grown to be anything more than a mixture of physiology with philosophy. That conflict between parent fixation and the need for independence was still felt in 1929, but now it has all gone. America, which has multiplied its psychologists sixfold since 1930, thirtyfold since 1910, has now relatively few psychologists among its great numbers who knew at first hand this complex about philosophy. Psychology as an institution, recapitulating the life of an individual, has now passed beyond adolescence to an independent maturity of both living and thinking. Actually the change has been secured more by proliferation than by individual growth. Institutional maturation is gained, not by changing the habits and thinking of the old members of the group but by letting in the members of new generations whose values and patterns of thought have been formed at a later stage of the *Zeitgeist*.

In gaining this new confidence in its own maturity, psychology has been able to appraise itself with some satisfaction. The mass of research on sensation and perception, while it continues to grow effectively, has been supplemented by fully as much research activity in the field of learning, and now we see the third field, the research on motivation opening up. With this development the complaint that psychology fails to study human nature is evaporating. At the same time psychology is gaining self-confidence from the successful application of its facts and principles. There is a demand for an applied psychology of sensation and perception—psychoacoustics, visual psychophysics; educational psychology still applies the psychology of learning; and clinical psychology is the applied psychology of motivation, while personnel psychology also depends in part upon the assessment of human motives. The academics now know that psychology is not a mean and narrow subject which they themselves have dreamed up in order to be able to criticize one another. It is something the world can use and is using, as it asks for more. Psychology has thus escaped from the neurosis of adolescence by getting itself wanted, for, by becoming married to reality, it has gained its maturity. The dire warning of its doubtful parent that it would come to no good end now seems very long ago.

The author's other regret in 1929 was that "there have been no great psychologists. Psychology," he said, "has never had a great man to itself. Wundt was not a great man of the order of Helmholtz or Darwin . . . . There are signs that psychologists are ready for a great man or a great event, for they seize eagerly upon every new movement that aspires to greatness; but the great event has not yet occurred." That judgment now needs considerable revision.

In the first place, let it be said that the history of psychology is its past. The great men who were in it stand by whatever their influence was eventually to be. Helmholtz may never have belonged to a *deutsche psychologische Gesellschaft* or Darwin to a British psychological society, yet they stand great figures in psychology's past—Darwin as the greater. So Freud. Psychologists long refused him admission to their numbers, yet now he is seen as the greatest originator of all, the agent of the *Zeitgeist* who accomplished the invasion of psychology by the principle of the unconscious process. If the author were to pick out psychology's great, in order to satisfy the reader's curiosity, then he would say that, judged by the criterion of their persistent posthumous importance, there are at least four very great men in psychology's history: Darwin, Helmholtz, James and Freud. Measured by the same criterion, Darwin and Freud have produced a greater revolution in thinking than have Helmholtz and James. Freud's effect is, however, still too recent to compare with Darwin's. For that we must wait fifty years.

No other criterion of greatness is safe. Judgments of the living change when their personal relations cease. James' relations with his friends, Titchener's with his students, Freud's with his disciples, Lewin's with his followers—all these, though interesting, eventually become unessential when we ask how the main current was being shifted. Nor will erudition do as a measure of greatness. Wundt was erudite, so full of information that the range of his knowledge is almost proverbial among the older psychologists. Titchener was erudite, and so was Freud. There were, indeed, many personal ways in which Titchener resembled Freud, but the great difference is that Titchener was swimming against the current of the *Zeitgeist* and Freud with it.

And that brings us to the *great-man theory* of scientific progress. The author has in twenty years changed his view of that matter. What is the function of the great man in science or, for that matter, in history? Are these great men the *causes* of progress or are they merely its *symptoms*? The answer is: they are neither; they are the *agents* of progress. The tiniest element of scientific progress —the all-or-nothing step-phenomenon that takes science further on toward whither it is going—is a human event in a man's thought and brain, the insight that creates something new by relating two old items that had never before been put together in just that way. That man is counted great whose insights are crucial and lead to long continued important progress in new directions. With proper advertising, the new development becomes identified with the name of the man in whose brain the crucial initiating insight occurred. For this reason the *a posteriori* great—men like Mendel whose research of 1865 de Vries unearthed and publicized in 1900—have their names given to any important new development which they initiated. Such a simple assignment of credit occurs in spite of the fact that collateral scientists and successors have been necessary to give the new movement the importance which justifies considering it great, and in spite of the fact that a change in scientific direction occurs readily only when it moves with the *Zeitgeist* and is perhaps stifled too early for notice when the times are against it. History is a part of nature where multiple causation rules and where single effective causes are the over-simplifications, devised to bring the incomprehensible complexity of reality within the narrow compass of man's understanding.

So the great man is seen to be only one of many causes of any piece of progress and he stands also as a symptom of the times, since causes have their causes. The times must be working with him if he is to have success. He can not, in fact, be successful without an audience, and he has to speak his wisdom in the right century or even the right decade to be heard. There are also the inevitable historical anticipations (Charles Bell and Johannes Müller) and the many almost simultaneous independent discoveries (Bell and Magendie) which show that it is the times and not magics which produce the great man. If Bell had not had these two insights, Magendie would have had one of them presently and Müller the other. nor was either of the 'flashes of genius' utterly new with Bell. To think of the man whose brilliant novel thought heads an important development as the *originator* is to abandon scientific psychology and suppose that among all orderly lawful mental phenomena the insights of genius constitute an exception in that they occur without causes. That view of nature makes the great man, if not a *deus*, at least an *homunculus ex machina*.

Genius can, of course, stand alone, be unique or almost unique. Seemingly no one anticipated Newton's theory of color, and the fact that it was ridiculed after Newton had propounded it, at first by his eminent contemporaries and a century later by the great Goethe, makes the discovery seem all the more surely unique. A man of even greater uniqueness of thought was the mathematician Fermat, who undoubtedly had the proof that no integers will fit the equation $x^n + y^n = a^n$ when n is greater than 2—had it but did not leave it where it could be found. After three centuries mathematicians are still trying to have the insight which Fermat had but could not write in the margin of his book because there was too little space. Yet even Fermat depended on what had gone before and stimulated what came after. A crucial thought by a great man is neither cause nor symptom, but an event in the space-time field of history. The complexity of the human brain is a wholly suitable place for the historical forces in the field of thought to meet and be resolved, with the novel resultant issuing forth in a new direction. If the emerging thought is important, if it works its way well into human thinking for the next one hundred years, then the name of the man who owned the brain which had the insight becomes great.

Index of Names

The important items are keyed by subject and given first. Less important items and incidental mentions of a name are labelled "inc." and given next. Citations of the literature are labelled "ref." and given last. No "inc." item is included when there is an important subject item or a "ref." item for the same page.

Abraham, K., inc., 711f.
Abraham, O., inc., 382
Ach, N., action and thought, 404-6; reaction set, 149
  inc., 233, 377, 382, 418, 514, 594, 610, 640, 668, 716
  ref., 435
Adams, D. K., ref., 496
Adams, J., ref., 271
Adler, A., individual psychology, 713
  inc., 707, 711
  ref., 732
Adrian, E. D., refractory period, 43
  inc., 49, 738
A., E. C., ref., 382
Agassiz, L., inc., 510
Aguilonius, F., horopter, 75, 105
  inc., 675
Airy, G. B., inc., 150
Albee, E., ref., 731
Albertus Magnus, inc., 50
Alembert, J. Le R. d', inc., 19
Alison, A., associationism, 203
  inc., 216
Allesch, G. J. v., inc., 382
Allport, G. W., ref., 438, 544, 734
Angell, F., inc., 324, 341, 411f., 548
  ref., 383, 438
Angell, J. R., biography, 554-7, 579; doctorate, 579; functional psychology, 554-8, 579; influence, 558
  inc., 548, 553, 627, 634, 643, 722, 740
  ref., 436, 579
Angier, R. P., ref., 544
Anschütz, G., ref., 437
Arago, D. F., personal equation, 139f.
  ref., 151
Archimedes, inc., 6, 14, 601
Argelander, F. W. A., personal equation, 136f.
Aristippos, inc., 704

Aristotle, influence, 158f., sense-qualities, 84
  inc., 6, 12, 15, 17, 50, 81, 157, 182, 221f., 238, 356, 359, 372, 601, 632, 664
  ref., 94, 177
Armstrong, A. C., ref., 546
Arrer, M., inc., 341
Asher, L., ref., 383
Aster, E. v., inc., 406
  ref., 435, 437, 455
Astruc, J., reflex, 35
  inc., 190
Aubert, H., adaptation, 103; color, 103; peripheral vision, 104; vision, 422
  inc., 281, 384, 421
  ref., 115
Avenarius, R., epistemology, 395f., 433
  inc., 332, 385, 393, 399f., 416, 419, 527, 709
  ref., 433
Azam, E., inc., 127, 129

Babkin, B. P., ref., 661
Bache, A. D., chronograph, 140
Bacon, F., induction, 13
  inc., 17, 20
Bader, P., inc., 341
Bain, A., biography, 233-6; psychology, 236-40
  inc., 211, 219, 221, 228, 241, 246, 275, 316, 324, 357, 389, 462f., 468, 524, 547, 667
  ref., 177, 244f.
Baird, J. W., inc., 405, 410, 523
  ref., 383, 435, 438
Baldwin, J. M., biography, 529-32, 547; evolutionary psychology, 530f.; individual psychology, 532; Titchener, 413f.

747

Index of Subjects

Mechanistic psychology, Cabanis, 214-6; La Mettrie, 212-4
See also *Behavioristics*
Memory, brain traces, 670; Ebbinghaus, 387., 432; G. E. Müller, 375, 377f.; Hering, 354
Mental chemistry, 607-9; Berkeley, 184-6; Hartley, 199; Herbart, 258; Hume, 190f.; Jas. Mill, 221-6; J. S. Mill, 229-31; T. Brown, 208; Wundt, 329f., 333
Mental chronometry, Leipzig, 341f.
Mental disease, amelioration of patients, 695, 730; Middle Ages, 694; persecution, 694
Mental inheritance, Galton, 476-8, 482f., 501
Mental measurement, Ebbinghaus, 387f., 432
Mental process, Wundt, 334
Mental tests, Binet, 573f.; Cattell, 533, 539; Columbia, 574; early instances, 571f.; Ebbinghaus, 390, 432; education, 569f.; factor analysis, 576f.; Galton, 484-7, 501, 571; group testing, 575; intelligence, 572-6, 581-3; primary abilities, 576; World Wars, 575-7
Mesmerism, psychoneurosis, 695f., 730
See also *Hypnosis*
Mind, seat, 50f., 58, 78, 664f.
Mind-body theories, Descartes, 162f.; double aspect, 667; Fechner, 286; identity, 667; interactionism, 665; Leibnitz, 168; Lotze, 272; psychophysical parallelism, 665-7, 688f.
Molar behavior, Tolman, 647
Monads, Leibnitz, 166f.
Monism, mind and body, 667
Morphology, 17
Motivation, Woodworth, 565f.
See also *Dynamic psychology*
Movement, Wertheimer, 590-2
Multiple choice method, Hamilton and Yerkes, 628, 630
Muscle sense, 112
Music, Stumpf, 364, 367

Nancy school, Bernheim, 699
National Institute for Industrial Psychology, 493
Nativism, Descartes, 165; Helmholtz, 304-8; Hering, 353; Kant, 247f.; Lotze, 267f.; phenomenology, 603; Stumpf, 363

Natural philosophy, Agassiz and James, 510
Need, dynamic term, 716; Murray, 728
Negative sensation, Fechner, 290, 293
Neologism, in-groups, 728f.
Nerve physiology, adequate stimulation, 87f.; all-or-none, 43; Bell, 81-9, 94f.; Bell-Magendie law, 27, 31-3, 45f.; Bernstein, 42; connections, 68-70; du Bois, 40-2, 47f.; early nineteenth century, 27-49, 78f.; electrical, 30, 39-41, 47-9; fiber specificity, 91-5; Galvani, 39f., 47; handbooks, 97f., 114f.; Hartley's vibrations, 195-7; Head, 491; Helmholtz, 41f., 48f.; histology, 67-70, 78f.; impulse, 30. 39-45, 47-9; Joh. Müller, 33-5, 41, 46f., 80-9, 94f.; membrane theory, 43; motor, 27, 31-3; neuron theory, 79; reflex action, 29f., 35-9, 46f.; refractory phase, 43; secondary degeneration, 78f.; sensorium commune, 36; sensory, 27f., 31-3; Sherrington, 490, 492; specific energies, 27f., 80-95; specific irritability, 87f.; spinal roots, 27, 31-3, 45f.; wave of negativity, 42; vis insita, 17, 36f.; vis nervosa, 17, 36; Volta, 40, 47
See also *Brain physiology, Hearing, Reflex action, Sensation, Touch, Vision*
New learning, science, 7-9, 23f.
Nonsense syllables, Ebbinghaus, 388
Normal law, Cattell, 538; Fechner, 285; Galton, 477, 499; Quetelet, 285, 476f., 499
Null hypothesis, 481

Object perception, Helmholtz, 312f.
Objective psychology, Bekhterev, 637f., 661; Cabanis, 633; Comte, 633f., 660; Descartes, 632; dynamic psychology, 639f.; functionalism, 634; Greeks, 632; Helmholtz, 640f.; Külpe, 640; La Mettrie, 632f.; materialists, 633, 660; Pavlov, 636f., 661; positivism, 633f.; positivists, 634, 660; Russian, 635-8, 660f.; Sechenov, 635f., 660f.; tropism, 638f.; unconsciousness, 639f.; Würzburg school, 640
Objects, Berkeley's theory, 184-6, 201; Gestalt psychology, 592, 609-11, 618
Observation, Helmholtz, 313f.